WESTMAR COLLEGE

W9-CDC-134

THE MODERN LIBRARY

OF THE WORLD'S BEST BOOKS

THE PHILOSOPHY

OF SANTAYANA

*The publishers will be pleased to send, upon request, an
illustrated folder setting forth the purpose and scope of
THE MODERN LIBRARY, and listing each volume
in the series. Every reader of books will find titles he has
been looking for, handsomely printed, in unabridged
editions, and at an unusually low price.*

THE
PHILOSOPHY
OF
SANTAYANA

EDITED, WITH

AN INTRODUCTORY ESSAY, BY

IRWIN EDMAN

Professor of Philosophy at Columbia University

THE
MODERN
LIBRARY

89449

191.9
S233ph

B
945
.S21
1936

COPYRIGHT, 1896, 1901, 1905, 1922, 1923, 1935, 1936,

BY CHARLES SCRIBNER'S SONS

COPYRIGHT, 1905, 1906, 1921, 1923, 1933, *by George Santayana*

COPYRIGHT, 1910, *by Harvard University Press*

COPYRIGHT, 1930, *by The Macmillan Company*

COPYRIGHT, 1935, *by The Oxford University Press*

COPYRIGHT, 1894, 1896, *by Stone & Kimball*

All rights reserved. No part of this book may be reproduced in any form without the permission of Charles Scribner's Sons.

Random House IS THE PUBLISHER OF

THE MODERN LIBRARY

BENNETT A. CERF · DONALD S. KLOPFER · ROBERT K. HAAS

Manufactured in the United States of America

Printed by Parkway Printing Company   Bound by H. Wolff

89448

PREFACE

THE project of this volume of Selections was suggested to Mr. George Santayana by the publishers some two years ago. His consent was obtained, and the present writer was selected by him to be the editor.

For the selections chosen and the interpretation given in the introductory essay, the editor is solely responsible. Mr. Santayana generously gave him a free hand, and the consequences of that freedom must be taken by him alone. In Mr. Santayana's own idiom, the substance of his philosophy may be quite different from the essence present to the intuition of the editor.

It is hoped that the present volume will give to the reader the conspectus and characteristic illustrations of the philosophy it aims summarily to represent. The principle of selection has been philosophical rather than literary. Some passages of special eloquence have been sacrificed in the interest of selections that, in the context of the whole volume, would better represent the total movement of the author's general philosophy. But it is believed the reader will find all the characteristics facets of the author's mind, and nearly all the aspects of experience over which his mind has played. As far as possible, essays or chapters from books have been taken in their entirety; where it seemed wise for the sake of displaying a developing argument, parts of chapters have been taken. Where for reasons of special beauty or significance a fragment of an essay or a chapter has been used, a connecting word or two has sometimes been added or removed.

Acknowledgments are hereby made, to the Oxford University Press for permission to reprint the Foreword to *Leopardi* by Iris Origo; to the Macmillan Company for "Brief History of My Opinions" from *Contemporary American Philosophy;* and to the Harvard University Press for the Introduction from *Three Philosophical Poets*. I wish also to make acknowledgment to Miss Shirley M. Carson for her patient, understanding, and careful assistance in the preparation of the manuscript.

I. E.

Columbia University, July, 1936.

CONTENTS

INTRODUCTORY ESSAY

THE SELECTIONS from the works of George Santayana here included speak for themselves. The author himself, in the opening essay, "Brief History of My Opinions," gives with authority the facts of his biography, and, with a persuasiveness that even the most sympathetic outsider could not possibly match, the cardinal themes of his thought. No one could speak more circumspectly, and there are none living who could speak more eloquently, of this philosopher's views of life and nature, of truth and spirit, than he himself does. The autobiographical sketch and the selections which follow in chronological order, read with care and imagination (two traits highly characteristic of their author), will give both the conspectus and the genesis of Santayana's thought. No introduction could do more, or as much.

An introduction may not be without its uses, however, especially in the case of a philosopher who, though he has dealt at one time or another with the most technical and delicate, as well as the most profound and ultimate of philosophical problems, retains throughout the elliptical ironies of the man of the world, and the rich, reverberant ambiguities of the poet. This is writing strewn with aphorisms which, the more they are pondered, the more variant stores of meaning and allusion they seem to contain. There are epithets which distract by the beauty of their own quality and the manner in which they at once fix a point and transfix an opponent, while translating an argument into a picture or a musical motif. Santayana's reputation has suffered in some respects from this very gift. It requires a studious reader to discover that in this author one is dealing not simply with a gifted man of letters, but with a philosopher, one of whose great but incidental gifts is a rhetoric adequate, in its finesse and elevation, to the height and subtlety of his themes: the life of reason, the phases of human progress, the origins and the potentialities of the spirit of man, the animal presumption of knowledge, and the rapt, disillusioned intuition of pure Being.

One can perhaps indicate to the reader something of what he will find—or what one reader has found—something of the manner in which he will find it, what are the constant lights that play across the shimmer of a discourse that for sheer wit and grace is unequalled in contemporary philosophy, or, one is tempted to add, in contemporary literature. What in sum is the character of this wisdom, what conclusions has their author reached after what analysis, and what, in passing, are the issues which his conclusions raise? Again, though this philosopher is singularly free from the jargon of the schools, his own vocabulary (despite, or perhaps because of, its genial poetry) might well be defined to the newcomer, or its context and connotations broached.

The manner and the substance of this philosophy are so inextricably interfused that they can scarcely be discussed apart. This is not simply because of the fact that the manner is, from a purely literary point of view, so distinctive, so jewelled with surface felicities, with adjectives that carry on the argument while they halt the reader by their flagrant charm, with epigrams that condense a system of philosophy and allusions that telescope a history, a theory, or a civilisation. The whole approach to philosophy here is itself imaginative, and, despite the involvement in professional issues, essentially that of a poet.

In philosophy itself investigation and reasoning are only preparatory and servile parts, means to an end. They terminate in insight, or what in the noblest sense of the word may be called *theory*, θεωρία,—a steady contemplation of all things in their order and worth. Such contemplation is imaginative. No one can reach it who has not enlarged his mind and tamed his heart. A philosopher who attains it is, for the moment, a poet; and a poet who turns his practised and passionate imagination on the order of all things, or on anything in the light of the whole, is for that moment a philosopher.*

It is no accident that Santayana began his writing career in verse—though he claims not to be a poet, in the magic sense of the word—nor that his first complete published prose work was devoted to an analysis of *The Sense of Beauty*. But while the atmosphere of this writing is in the domain of the imagination (myth, as in Plato, breaks into the most learned argument and poetry invades the most exact dialectic), the interest and the substance are for the most part moral, and the wisdom to be gleaned is a moral wisdom. John Dewey could write in 1907, in reviewing *The Life of Reason*, whose five volumes constituting a single work had by that time been published, "We are grateful to Mr. Santayana for what he has given us; the most adequate contribution America has yet made, always excepting Emerson, to moral philosophy." Santayana himself could write, some fifteen years later: "In moral philosophy (which is my chosen subject) . . ."† *The Last Puritan,* a memoir in the form of a novel, is an estimate and a condemnation of Puritanism in the light of a candid acceptance of the conditions of existence as action and the circumstances of life reveal them. It is true, as there have not been wanting those to point out, that in the last decade and in later works Santayana has seemed to be concerned with other issues than moral ones and to be immersed in a theory of knowledge half sceptical, half pragmatic, whose oblique corollary is an ideal of detachment profoundly different from his earlier concern with the harmonising of impulse and the adaptation of nature to those ideals which nature itself generated. He has seemed to move beyond good and evil, and to have spoken in his later works as if the true good for a completely

Three Philosophical Poets, Introduction, p. 11; *Selections,* pp. 339, 340.

†"On My Friendly Critics," *Soliloquies in England,* p. 257.

purified spirit lay in an ascetic detachment from all human loves and ideals. But that detachment, as he himself admits, though unattainable, is after all a human ideal, like others a reflective modification of a human impulse. Though he may have shifted the terms of his morality and substituted contemplative detachment for progress or realisation as an ideal, the interest is still a moral one. It is the ethos of the intellectual saint and the philosophical ascetic. But as long ago as one of his youthful sonnets, Santayana could speak of it being his "to mock the runner's heat."* His concern, though always touched with irony and reservation, was moral at the beginning and remains moral to the end. It is the accent, not the interest that has changed. Rather, the accent itself has returned to his early absorption in those forms which might become themes of entertainment to the dreaming and the contemplative mind, to the poet surveying all essences in their intrinsic qualities. These essences, all animal anxieties discounted, "have lost their urgency and their venom," have ceased to be signals of action, and have become for him objects of contemplation and, in some cases, objects of love, "all things crystallised into the image of themselves."† In the early days the images were those of a poet's intense intuition; in the later books they have been translated into themes of the metaphysician's meditation, and in that meditation become citizens of a timeless realm of being.

It will remain for us later to examine the ingenious and complicated argument by which essences are first broached and then developed as a primary and ultimate category of being, and to examine "some uses of this discovery" which Santayana makes both morally and otherwise. It remains first to consider the earlier version, by no means superseded completely in his later writings, of that moral philosophy which is, by his own announcement, his chosen subject. It

*Poems, p. 15; Selections, p. 24.
†Scepticism and Animal Faith, p. 76; Selections, p. 397.

must be noted at once that moral philosophy, as he conceives it, is a conception much wider and much more humane than that which commonly goes by the name. It is the survey of all excellences as those are defined by a reflective spirit, a life understanding its own conditions; an estimate of all human enterprises, including that of philosophy itself, in terms of the extent to which they are realisations of those goods which nature both suggests and potentially sustains. The suggestions arise in human imagination, itself a generation of nature, in the form of ideals which are recognised and pursued. Such a critique is the substance of Santayana's comprehensive five-volume work (held by not a few to be his masterpiece) entitled *The Life of Reason*. Despite changes in the character of the questions discussed and of some of the solutions offered, the fundamental tendencies of *The Life of Reason* are in large measure confirmed by the later works.* In both, to whatever exalted remoteness of mysticism or Platonism Santayana may occasionally seem to have removed, he remains throughout essentially a naturalist in philosophy, believing, like Aristotle before him, that all ideals are natural in their basis, and all nature ideal in its possibilities. To understand *The Life of Reason* is, despite some incidental recantations in a Preface twenty years later, to understand Santayana's moral philosophy and, save for some refinements of doctrine, largely concerned with the theory of knowledge, and a shift in the author's personal preoccupations, his philosophy *überhaupt*.

THE LIFE OF REASON

The Life of Reason, though published in five volumes, in theme and intention constitutes a single work. It is the consideration by a highly cultivated mind, by a sympathetic

*However, the author points out in the Preface to the second edition of *The Life of Reason* that nature has come into the foreground, the Life of Reason having for him receded into the background.

(though sometimes amused) observer, of "the phases of human progress," of the attempts of mankind as revealed in society, art, religion and science, to live a rational life. By a rational life, Santayana does not mean a life lived according to some logic laid down in advance, but a life lived as a harmonious realisation of ideals, themselves reflective modifications of the impulses of an animal born into a world whose conditions must be taken into account if those ideals are to be, within limits, fulfilled. The work is in one sense philosophical history, an account of the various ways in which humanity has attempted to rationalise itself, together with a critical estimate of the worth of those attempts. But such criticism implies a standard and thus the work constitutes a philosophy of civilisation or a moral review of it. That moral review is taken frankly from the standpoint of a philosophy which on the whole accepts the biological basis of life and the ideals (and *only* those ideals) which life generates. It is a philosophy which recognises in physics, broadly considered, the efficacious instrument for the realisation of human goods. Santayana himself describes his work as a sort of "retrospective politics"; "an estimate of events in reference to the moral ideal which they embodied and betrayed, might supervene upon positive history. . . . The present work is an essay in that direction."* But there *is* a standard; for all the author's insistence that the enlightened philosophical historian must be sensitive to all the goods which life in its various manifestations has evolved and sustained, he has a criterion: "a variegated omnipresent human happiness." That standard again is formally but significantly expressed: "Reason as such represents or rather constitutes a single formal interest, the interest in harmony."†

The five volumes are variations on this theme. They are studies of the characteristic experiments by which are

---

Reason in Science, p. 58.
†*Reason in Common Sense*, p. 267; *Selections*, p. 86.

achieved those excellences and that harmony which constitute happiness. This achievement is furthered by a wide and studious recognition of the natural basis from which they are generated. They trace, too, the deviations and blindnesses, the pathetic, well-intentioned truancies from rational practice, which have led men astray. The Life of Reason is, in a broad sense, another name for art, for life in which "ideas . . . have ceased to be visionary and actions . . . have ceased to be vain."* The five books are reflections in various contexts, of a single conception, the passage, often circuitous and oftener frustrated, from nature to the ideals which it suggests, and which, if efficaciously understood, it may come to incarnate. The Life of Reason is led on the one hand in affairs and in social passions, and on the other in religion, art and science.

The Life of Reason may be studied, therefore, from two different interests. It constitutes one of the most serious contributions of our time to an interpretation of the achievements and the failures of human action in the family, in government, industry, and war, and of human imagination as revealed in the symbols of religion and science and in the monuments and the images of art. It may be studied further, incidentally or even primarily, as a wonderfully sympathetic account of the typical adventures of human enterprise, and the characteristic dramatic perspectives of the human spirit. For though Santayana's own preferences and attitudes are clearly enough revealed—his love, for instance, of the naturalistic Greeks and his impatience with the arbitrary willfulness, the "egotism" of the German philosophers—he has the poet's and the dramatist's eye and ear. He can see points of view in their own terms and gives, for the most part, both just and communicative versions of all the characteristic flowerings of the mind of man as embodied in history. Though he seldom condescends to a footnote, the reader acquainted with the history of one or another of the high

*Reason in Common Sense, p. 6; Selections, p. 52.

matters reviewed will recognise the telling summaries, the incisive and apt metaphors, the neat thrusts with regard to one or another of them. The ironies flow oftener from detachment than from scorn, and Santayana reveals a singular capacity for delineating convictions he has never had and emotions he has never felt save as a poet, through "a habit of poetic sympathy with the dreaming mind whatever it might dream."* From the standpoint of his naturalistic standards his work is entitled *The Life of Reason* but the work constitutes also a "presumptive biography of the human intellect," which, instead of *The Life of Reason*, might have been called *The Romance of Wisdom*.

To the suasion of each of the various episodes of that romance, so "polyglot, interrupted, [and] insecure," he yields himself in turn, and to each, save for the smiling malice of some phrase or paragraph, he almost converts the reader. The irony is usually half affectionate, for even in systems of thought or religion or society that seem to him erroneous or even perverse, he sees evidence of some human ideal struggling to expression, or even sober sense partially and gaudily expressed. Thus his own patrician instincts, while leading him to question the actual operation of democracy, enable him to see the ideal toward which it implicitly moves: a society in which excellence has grown general and virtue collective, where the common man is become something of a hero and a saint. Though through background and temperament he vibrates most sensitively to the images of the Catholic tradition, he can give a striking and intimate sense of primitive tribal religion or of the religions of the East, or Mohammedanism, or the Buddhist doctrine of Karma; in which latter "a pathetic feminine quality was imparted to moral feeling, we were to be good for pity's sake, for the sake of a great distant deliverance from profound sorrows."† "If there is something in a purely

*The Life of Reason, second edition, p. vii; Selections, p. 43.
†Reason in Science, p. 293.

remedial system of morality which seems one-sided and extreme, we must call to mind the far less excusable one-sidedness of those moralities of prejudice to which we are accustomed in the Occident—the ethics of irrational acquisitiveness, irrational faith, and irrational honour. Buddhistic morality, so reasonable and beautifully persuasive, rising so willingly to the ideal of sanctity, merits in comparison the profoundest respect. It is lifted as far above the crudities of intuitionism as the whisperings of an angel are above a schoolboy's code."*

One may thus be tempted to browse in *The Life of Reason* for its shrewd estimates and dramatic insights into the accomplishments of the past, to treat it as a discerning and aphoristic history. But it is clearly and importantly something more. "The story might be romantic but the moral of it was classical . . ." The intention was not the study of history or psychology for their own sake, but to be "frankly selective and critical, guided by a desire to discriminate the better from the worse."†

Thus the whole work, in addition to being a dramatic evocation of the characteristic tempers of religions, philosophies and systems of society, each seen from its own transcendental point of vantage, is the work of a moralist who trusts, for the conditions of action with which intelligence must reckon, to physics and dialectics for their reports, to physics for the facts and their discoverable relations, to dialectics for the explication of intent and for the development and refinement of meanings. "Dialectic," as Santayana says elsewhere, "is the conscience of discourse."‡ Physics and dialectics enlighten the moralist about the conditions and possible forms of human happiness. The conditions of happiness are the functional synonym for Nature, whose lineaments as met with in action and in its functional and

*Reason in Science, p. 294.

†Reason in Common Sense, second edition, p. x; Selections, pp. 45, 46.

‡The Realm of Essence, p. 100; Selections, p. 514.

pictorial aspects nameable in human discourse, and the gradual discernments of these, are described in *Reason in Common Sense* and *Reason in Science*. The author's own interest in the origin and development of efficacious human discourse about existence leads by his own admission* to a certain equivocation. It is sometimes hard in the first volume of *The Life of Reason* (*Reason in Common Sense*) to be sure whether the author is talking about Nature, or about those moral and dramatic syntheses, those fictions, both constructive and efficacious, which constitute our "idea of Nature." For the most part he is discussing the latter, the gradual discernment by human intelligence ("Life understanding its own conditions") of things, of the unity of things in a common system, and (by dramatic sympathy with outward physical manifestations) of other minds. In the case of the "discovery of fellow minds" we are indulging in a pathetic fallacy which happens in this instance not to be fallacious, as it is when primitive science or religion peoples neutral mechanism with living intentions and identifies steady and indifferent causes and effects as friendly or alien powers. The world of nature, as commonly intended, is the name for those existences independent of our caprice or our wishes (of which, indeed, our caprice and our wishes are a part and a product) which move in a network of calculable relations to each other. That network of calculable relations is the one disclosed in mechanism, clarified by dialectic. "What we mean, indeed, by the natural world in which the conditions of consciousness are found and in reference to which mind and its purposes can attain practical efficacy, is simply the world constructed by categories found to yield a constant, sufficient and consistent object."†

*"One consequence was that I was often betrayed into expressions which, if not taken dramatically, would contradict my naturalism; that vulgar belief in material things about us which not only underlay the whole life of reason as I conceived it, but was also its explicit final deliverance." (*Reason in Common Sense*, second edition, p. vii; *Selections*, p. 43.)

†*Reason in Religion*, p. 20.

Reason in Common Sense is the natural history of this gradual disciplining of the imagination to such efficacious categories. It is a dream tamed, an apparition made responsible and reliable. Mechanism does not exist; it is not things lifted to an eternal hypostasis of forms or ideas. It is a consistent and comprehensive system of operation, contemplation and understanding. What exists is the irrational flux, later to be called (in the works on *The Realms of Being*) Matter or Substance. Mechanism is the system of categories whereby origins and transmutations can be calculated and, within limits, controlled. But Matter itself is a brute surd, an irrational actuality which can neither be explained nor explained away. It is that which is met with in action, and that upon which action depends. Matter is the flux within which all events are distinguished as events, in which, and indeed by which, forms and essences are discerned, and in or out of which consciousness comes to flame in feeling and to light in thought. Some special description of matter, even one highly dependable and fruitful, like that of Democritus, or of modern physics—indeed all human notions of matter, may be inadequate or mistaken. Indeed, as they are human and relative they are bound to be so. In *The Life of Reason* one notion of matter, the realm of art and calculation, is insisted on in terms sometimes reminiscent of the billiard-ball physics of the nineteenth century, and the description of our human discernment of it recalls the nineteenth-century British atomic psychology of sensations. But the structure of mechanism is a structure of operations. "Mechanism," writes our author in *Reason in Science*, "might be called the dialectic of the irrational. It is such a measure of intelligibility as is compatible with flux and with existence."* Matter itself *is* the irrational. Matter is intimated in *The Life of Reason*, as it is deliberately declared in a later work, *The Realm of Matter*, to be something deeper than calculation or dialectic, and in its own characteristic, native exist-

Reason in Science, pp. 77, 78; *Selections*, p. 289.

ence, opaque to the latter, though it is itself "the medium of calculable art." Matter is the "reality" confronted in action; it is the substance which generates all the more or less adequate myths, definitions or images by which men try to describe or express it. But these murmurs of nature, "wayward and narcotic," may be less wayward and narcotic in some instances than in others, may come to be more or less adequately representative of the conditions men must face in action, or the potentialities which matter suggests to them as ideals. Their actions generate and necessitate institutions, as do their animal impulses of gregariousness and love. Rationality finds in the collective activities of mankind fitful and fumbling realisation. In society men pass from animal hordes to ordered governments, they learn to use the instruments of industry and polity, and, in their dis-locations with each other, the artifices of war. Humanity, in its rarer moments, or in its rarer exemplars, passes into friendship, which is Free Society, and the civilised soliloquist moves on to the society of his and other men's dreams and symbols, the ideal society of religion, art and science.

The chapter on "Love" and the closing chapter on "Ideal Society" in this second volume of *The Life of Reason* serve at once to define and illustrate the central pre-occupation of the whole work. The first-mentioned illustrates as well the revealing dual awareness which gives Santayana his ground in common sense and the empyrean of his flights. Love is animal in its basis, but ideal in its aspiration, and is ad-dressed to an ideal object. To speak the whole truth about it one must be at once a physiologist and a Platonist. "Love, to the lover, is a noble and immense inspiration; to the naturalist a thin veil and prelude to the self-assertion of lust."* Both are dealing with half truths. The truth is that love, like every other ideal, expresses some natural function. "Love is a brilliant illustration of a principle everywhere discoverable; namely, that human reason lives by turning

Reason in Society, p. 8; *Selections*, p. 92.

the friction of material forces into the light of ideal goods."*

This example in love of the spiritual flowering or sublimation of the animal basis of life is treated with a special
eloquence in this remarkable chapter. The passion itself is,
in its honest fleshliness, celebrated with something of the
ardour with which Lucretius treats the theme at the beginning of his *De Rerum Natura.* It is recognised as the brightest page in many a thin human biography, the joy in which
the blood of the universe flows through the animal heart.
But equal justice is done to the transcendental heights
toward which the momentum of this physical ecstasy may
carry the lover, the ideal objects which that passion rationalised comes to involve. "The lover knows much more about
absolute good and universal beauty than any logician or
theologian, unless the latter, too, be lovers in disguise."†
"Love is a truly natural religion; . . . it sanctifies a natural mystery; and finally, when understood, it recognises
that what it worshipped under a figure was truly the principle of all good."‡ "The machinery which serves reproduction thus finds kindred but higher uses, as every organ
does in a liberal life; and what Plato called a desire for
birth in beauty may be sublimated even more, until it yearns
for an ideal immortality in a transfigured world, a world
made worthy of that love which its children have so often
lavished upon it in its dreams."§

What those dreams are becomes evident in the treatment
of art, religion and science, the forms of ideal society; or
more strictly, the society of ideals. This is a community in
which companionship is with "the symbols it [the mind]
breeds and possesses for excellence, beauty and truth."‖
But animal love is a beginning toward that end; there are
two intermediate stages. There is natural society, whose

Reason in Society, p. 9; *Selections*, p. 93.
†*Reason in Society*, p. 30; *Selections*, p. 108.
‡*Reason in Society*, p. 32; *Selections*, p. 109.
§*Reason in Society*, p. 34; *Selections*, pp. 110, 111.
‖*Reason in Society*, p. 205; *Selections*, p. 143.

function is to produce the individual and equip him with the prerequisites of moral freedom. Offspring are the consequence of animal love, and the immaturity of offspring is the condition which necessitates the family. The family assumes functions other than the absolutely necessary ones of rearing children. It comes to involve a common dwelling, friends, religion, and property. The family may come to be an enemy of more adequate political arrangements, a limitation, even, upon the spontaneous and natural affections of its members, a frustration of rational nature and a provincial and habitual obstacle to moral freedom. Industry is a device for rendering materials fit for human purposes, and government a way of enabling men to live together. "Government neither subsists nor arises because it is good or useful, but solely because it is inevitable. It becomes good in so far as the inevitable adjustment of political forces which it embodies is also a just provision for all the human interests which it creates or effects."*

The ideal state would be a family, we are assured, where all would not be equal, but all would be happy; in a successful democracy, about which Santayana seems to have his doubts, there would be a co-operation in excellence, a soviet of virtue.

In general, Santayana as a social philosopher seems to pay obeisance to the necessities of government and industry, rather than to regard them as in themselves liberal ends. "The formidable judgment industrialism has to face is that of reason, which demands that the increase and specification of labour be justified by benefits somewhere actually realised and integrated in individuals."† Politics and machinery are imposed upon us by the fact that materials must be turned to ideal uses, and that men forced by gregariousness and mutual need to live together devise and need to devise arrangements for doing so. Natural society is the instance in

*Reason in Society, p. 71.
†Reason in Society, p. 65.

the sphere of social relations of the primacy of nature over spirit. It is the basis and condition of companionship that is based on unanimity of feeling and intent. A commonwealth might be measured by the extent to which it might render friendship possible. Friendship is the illustration, warm and perfect, of liberal society. Its warmth derives from animal contagion, from a shared comradeship in a common environment and, most generally, from origins in a common youth. Good fellowship and personal affinity may be present, to yield vividness and intimate accent to the relationship of friendship, but its essence is spiritual communion. "Friendship might thus be called ideal sympathy refracted by a human medium, or comradeship and sensuous affinity colouring a spiritual light."* Patriotism, like friendship accidental and somewhat ambiguous in its origins and its obstinacies (what *is* the France a Frenchman loves?), is, in its ideal import, an imaginative passion. "It belongs to the free forms of society and ennobles a man not so much because it nerves him to work or to die, which the basest passions may also do, but because it associates him, in working or dying, with an immortal and friendly companion, the spirit of his race."†

But no actual and operative society, not aristocracy at its most courteous and generous, not democracy even were it co-operative virtue, would be ideal. This is not to say that it would miss the ideal in the sense of missing its own goal or being realised in its own terms. Ideal society (which requires natural society as its basis) is, for Santayana, society in a special, in almost a Pickwickian sense, for it is realised only in imagination, in soliloquy, or in dialectic. Ideal society belongs entirely to the realm of kindly illusion, for it is the society of symbols. It may be shared by us with those who live in the same imaginative atmosphere; "Whatever spirit in the past or future, or in the remotest regions

*Reason in Society, p. 154; Selections, p. 124.
†Reason in Society, p. 183.

of the sky, shares our love or pursuit, say of mathematics or of music, or of any ideal object, becomes, if we can somehow divine his existence, a partner in our joys and sorrows, and a welcome friend."*

But "ideal society" is not the companionship of those who share the same spiritual objects and interests; it is rather the companionship in the mind of those objects themselves. The dreaming imagination is peopled with its dreams; its symbols are its intimates, and its themes its friends. There is no loneliness in that soliloquy but a vivid companionship with congenial presences, æsthetically delightful, morally enlightening and practically significant. In the fine arts, symbols are intrinsically delightful; in music the sounds themselves may absorb the enraptured spirit, the instruments that support the sounds may be forgotten, as also the martial or mournful suggestions the sounds may have. So, too, even in religion and science, whose overt purpose is to represent truth or existence, the symbols may become entertainment and society for the mind, like an equation to a mathematician or a myth to an enchanted poet. But those symbols which delight the mind and warm it, may also enlighten it. Symbols both foreshorten and focus complex experiences. Symbols become theories, presumptions, hypotheses. They are not only friends to free contemplation; they are guides to the harassed human, eloquent testimony of things absent and latent as well as vivid and pleasurable sensations of the mind.† Science and religion are both imaginative discourse, the one a hypothesis about our conditions, the other a myth, often taken with false literalness, about our pertinent aspiration. The symbols of art at once express our impulses and adapt our conditions to their more exquisite and harmonious

---

Reason in Society, p. 189; *Selections*, p. 132.

†It is perhaps worth remarking at this point, that though the terms "essence" and "animal faith" are not here used, the two aspects of "symbols" here presented, correspond quite closely with essences as the objects of intuition, and essences as *terms* or symbols in the later works on *The Realms of Being*.

fulfillment. Impulse speaks in the arts, and it at the same time makes the world, or portions of it, more adequate to our impulse. The world in the arts speaks to us in sound or form, in the language we would fain speak, in the language we would have things speak, too; things become the sympathetic echoes of our own intent.

Reason in Religion is a study of one set of kindly illusions somewhat less kindly than the frank illusions of art, because, taken literally, as representations of another world elsewhere, a supernatural extension of this one, the illusions of religion are simply bad physics. When taken as representations of a supernatural and celestial geography, they are misleading hypotheses for action. They are the language of superstition, where *felt* causes are taken to be necessary ones, instead of being taken as expressions of aspiration, anagrams of some desired or intended good. They are falsely taken to be the efficacious categories of action. Magic is alleged to be science, and prayer is addressed to mythical beings, friendly and alien powers, by a pathetic projection believed to be administrators of nature and of destiny. Traditional theologies are untrue science, misleading analyses of the structure of the intelligible order of action; traditional mythologies are false as descriptions of cosmic history, or as cosmic prophecy. But they have their uses, which uses are those of moral ideals. Religion becomes thoroughly moral when it ceases "to represent or to misrepresent material conditions, and has learned to embody spiritual goods."* The way in which religions may embody spiritual goods, although these embodiments are open to misinterpretation, is to be studied in mythology. Myths are poetry, they are eloquence, they are expression; they are observations of things in dramatic and human perspective. Mythology is unconscious poetry and misleading science. It is the use of "psychic and passionate categories in reading nature."†

Reason in Religion, p. 38; *Selections*, p. 157.
†*Reason in Religion*, p. 50; *Selections*, p. 166.

But myths only half deceive, for all language, all science, even, is in a sense mythological; discourse can never *be* what it expresses. But the symbols of science lead to "real facts and define their experimental relations."† Myths are misinformation about conditions; they are "poetically true"; they are expressions of spiritual penetration, articulations of the soul's impulses and its needs. So Dante gives "bad cosmography and worse history";‡ he exhibits true wisdom in a false setting. The great mythologies exhibit, and their power has depended on, a sense for moral values. They are poetically vivid and humanly pertinent. They are moralisers of imagination. Myth, too, gives in the form of a metaphysical mystery or a dramatic history, a justification and a rational assimilation of magic to recognisable principles of human action. The development of myth illustrates once again the general principle of the Life of Reason. The god, first believed in as a physical thing, or a dramatic picture of an existent power, by turns malign or beneficent, becomes an ideal standard of excellence to be contemplated and loved; a companion to the hopes and generosities of the spirit of man. The jealous god becomes the God of righteousness; the historical Jesus becomes the symbol of perfect charity; Apollo ceases to be the material sun and becomes the symbol of prophecy and healing and poetry and song, all the longing of mankind toward vitality and poise compacted into that clear single image of divinity.

The whole panorama of religions is briefly but aptly studied with reference to the moral truths they have by a kind of periphrasis embodied. The Christian epic, summarised in a noble sketch,§ is a dream, but a dream that has shaped, haunted, perturbed and exalted the imagination of Europe for two thousand years. It must not, Santayana tells us, be treated as a dangerous error in science or philos-

---

†*Reason in Religion*, p. 55; *Selections*, p. 169.
‡*Reason in Religion*, p. 56; *Selections*, p. 170.
§*Reason in Religion*, pp. 92-97; *Selections*, pp. 174-178.

ophy. "We seek rather to honour the piety and to understand the poetry embodied in those fables."* For, like all
fables, Christianity has a moral, but one implicit in the
fiction itself rather than appended as an afterthought at the
close. There is in these fictions persuasion by enchantment,
not conviction by argument. Yet though Santayana stresses
this, he himself exhibits in analytic summary what the chief
moral lessons are which religions have incarnated. These he
finds to be three: the inculcation of piety, spirituality, and
charity. He remarks that in turning to piety and spirituality,
he is turning from religious ideas to religious emotions, from
imaginative history and science to imaginative morals. The
myths, he might well admit, were the conventional sustenance to religious morals, but the literal grounds of piety
are less significant or worthy of respect than the ideal of
piety inculcated, which latter may survive its mythical supports. Piety is "man's reverent attachment to the sources of
his being,"† whether that be the family, his parents, his
nation, or his race. Piety, broadened and deepened, may become piety to the gods, who are usually the names for current ideals, or to humanity. "There is, finally, a philosophic
piety which has the universe for its object. This feeling,
common to ancient and modern Stoics, has an obvious justification in man's dependence upon the natural world, and
its service to many sides of the mind."‡ "Why should we
not look on the universe with piety? Is it not our substance?
Are we made of other clay? All our possibilities lie from
eternity hidden in its bosom."§ Piety is, for Santayana, the
instinctive and normal obeisance the best in us pays to Nature, the source of that best. It is the domestic impulse of
the soul; man's acknowledgment of citizenship in the universe and kinship to universal substance. Piety looks toward

---

*Reason in Religion, p. 97; Selections, p. 178.
†Reason in Religion, p. 179; Selections, p. 180.
‡Reason in Religion, p. 190; Selections, p. 189.
§Reason in Religion, p. 191; Selections, p. 189.

Nature; it is retrospective; spirituality looks to the ideal. "A man is spiritual when he lives in the presence of the ideal, and whether he eat or drink does so for the sake of a true and ultimate good."*

The whole principle of the Life of Reason might be said to be brought to focus and to climax in the theme of spirituality. Life is justified by its fruits, and the spiritual man lives as much as may be in practise, and always in imagination, among ultimate things. By an ultimate is meant a good, and by a good, an intrinsic delight to the senses, to the affections and to the mind. The sensualist, the refined connoisseur, the lover and the friend, all episodically confront ultimate and intrinsic, though precarious and vanishing, things. "The spiritual man needs, therefore, something more than a cultivated sympathy with the brighter scintillation of things."† He needs some steadying synthesis, some principle of goodness which the scattered excellence and self-justifying episodes of life may be said variously to exemplify. Such a principle of goodness, such a standard of excellence or canon of ideality has been, according to Santayana, the essential principle, the high insight of all religions worthy of the name. Heaven is a vision of ideal happiness, God a synonym for perfection; and whatever materialisation these may undergo in the literalisms of the learned or the anxious credulities of the vulgar, the ideal of our true happiness, the vision of perfection, has been what the spiritual man has worshipped in religion. Religion has clarified our ideals, as the language of prayer often illustrates, and made those ideals authoritative. And by a radical extension, charity comes to be a religious ideal, an imaginative sympathy with the spirituality, or a living in the light of the ultimates of other creatures, not ourselves but not wholly alien to us, because their psychic life and fundamental circumstances are similar. Because religions cannot easily discard myth and

*Reason in Religion, p. 193; Selections, pp. 190, 191.
†Reason in Religion, p. 211; Selections, p. 204.

magic and literalness, they have, of course, continued to report, and often were believed to be, descriptions of another world. Indeed, a characteristic promise of traditional religions has been an endless life in another world, a "future life" with the stains and inequalities and insecurities of this one removed. Idealised, immortality, too, becomes ideal, a living in the light of the eternal. "The better a man evokes and realises the ideal . . . his presence in the society of immortals . . . becomes . . . more pervasive. He not only vanquishes time by his own rationality, . . . but he continually lives again in all rational beings."*

It will be observed from the preceding summary that uses of religion for Santayana are the persuasions poetry to the troubled and aspiring heart. Taken as religion is false; taken as poetry it is both expressiv compelling. Its supernatural machinery is either symbo natural conditions (which, in a tangled and roundabo it frequently is) or of moral aims. Taken in any ot supernaturalism is for Santayana worthless, or, wh more serious, perverse and misleading, false as physi leading, therefore, as a guide in action.

There has probably been no better treatment in m philosophy of religion as an imaginative embodiment most serious concerns of man with his destiny. It m argued, as it is argued by many, both anti-religious an vout, that the very values of which Santayana speaks wo vanish when the mythical and magical supports of the ceased to win credence. God would not continue to be synthesis of all good for those who do not even believe in his existence. When religion was seen to be simply eloquent morality, or the poetry of aspiration, the eloquence would come to seem mere rhetoric, and the poetry simply inaccurate prose. Our author himself insists, however, that only the pedantic metaphysicians ever took religion literally, and that both the genuine prophets and the faithful populace took

*Reason in Religion, p. 272; Selections, pp. 215, 216.

religion in a more liberal and imaginative way. Religions are, in this work, surveyed from the point of view of what contribution they have made to the Life of Reason. That they have been literalised and materialised goes without saying. But they are in essence better or worse, never true or false. In *Reason in Religion*, Santayana has tried to draw from each the secret of its inspiration, the enlarging vistas upon life which each formulated. But it is the special poetic accent and moral revelation of each, its embodiment of ultimates, of which the Life of Reason is the seat, with which this book is concerned. Not religion in all its phases, but religion as it ⸀ into the Life of Reason is that with which Santayana ⸀cerned. It enters as the poetic expression of ultimate ⸀sts, and a perspective, oblique and humanised, on the ⸀ contours of existence.

⸀h volume is the progress toward rationality exhibited ⸀her aspect. But in one enterprise, art, reason is per⸀t efficacious in its operation and most signal in its ⸀ne Life of Reason rationalises experience, and art ⸀ost explicit form of that rationalisation. Art is the ⸀ which gives propitious forms to matter. It has in⸀e sources, as in the dance and poetry and song. It has ⸀l embodiments as in architecture and painting and ⸀re. It is "action which transcending the body makes ⸀ld a more congenial stimulus to the soul."*

⸀etween sensation and abstract discourse lies a region of de⸀yed sensibility or synthetic representation. . . . This region, ⸀lled imagination, has pleasures more airy and luminous than those of sense, more massive and rapturous than those of intelligence. The values inherent in imagination, in instant intuition, in sense endowed with form, are called æsthetic values; they are found mainly in nature and living things, but also in man's artificial works, in images evoked by language, and in the realm of sound.†

Reason in Art, p. 15; *Selections*, p. 226.
†*Reason in Art*, p. 15; *Selections*, p. 226.

In one sense, *Reason in Art* is a work in the moral philosophy of art rather than what is more strictly called a work in æsthetics. For the latter, one would have to turn to Santayana's early work, *The Sense of Beauty*, in which the "materials of beauty" are surveyed, the elements in the constitution of objects and in human consciousness studied, the interaction of which produces "pleasure objectified" which is for him another name for beauty or the experience of it.*

There is one chapter ("The Criterion of Taste") in the book here under consideration which comes nearest being æsthetics in the narrower sense of an analysis of standards of taste and judgment.† For the most part the volume is a consideration of the psychological and social sources, the moral and ideal functions of that implicitly or deliberately rational activity, action fulfilling an end, which is art, and which might be said to be a synonym for the Life of Reason. The specifically æsthetic values perspicaciously dealt with are, in *Reason in Art*, considered to be simply the felt quality of rational action. "Neither in the history of art nor in a rational estimate of its value can the æsthetic function of things be divorced from the practical and moral. . . . The rose's grace could more easily be plucked from its petals than the beauty of art from its subject, occasion and use."‡ The fine and practical arts are not in fact or in theory completely divorced, but broadly speaking in the context of the

*It should be pointed out however that in this early work Santayana attributes a moral status to beauty at the end of his psychological and structurally objective analysis of it. "Beauty therefore seems to be the clearest manifestation of perfection, and the best evidence of its possibility. If perfection is, as it should be, the ultimate justification of being, we may understand the ground of the moral dignity of beauty. Beauty is a pledge of the possible conformity between the soul and nature, and consequently a ground of faith in the supremacy of the good." (*The Sense of Beauty*, pp. 269-270.)

†But taste itself, widely based, has a moral context. Cf. *Reason in Art*, pp. 212-215 (*Selections*, pp. 243-245), where it is said that the "sad values of appearance . . . need to be made prophetic of practical goods."

‡*Reason in Art*, p. 16; *Selections*, pp. 226, 227.

Life of Reason, a distinction may be made. "Industry merely gives nature that form which, if more thoroughly humane, she might have originally possessed for our benefit; liberal arts bring to spiritual fruition the matter which either nature or industry has prepared and rendered propitious."*

In the course of his examination of how the arts rise now out of automatic impulse and now out of necessity, the arts of expression on the one hand and of manipulation of things on the other, Santayana has many subtle and evocative things to say about those arts themselves. Thus there are noted the differing functions of poetry and prose, the former moving toward algebra, the latter toward pure music, language in general oscillating between the two. Music itself is treated briefly but tellingly, its world considered as a rationalisation of sound, a mathematics become audible and a dialectic that moves and sensuously thrills, "as impassioned as any animal triumph or any moral drama,"† of which in its poignant generality it may become the celebration, more poignant than words. Plastic construction affords an opportunity to study the moral functions of constructed things and the varying elements of effect due to structure and to decoration. In plastic representation, represention itself is seen to be something more than that. A Tintoretto "is not a design in spots, meant merely to outdo a sunset; it is a richer dream of experience meant to outshine the reality."‡

But the major concern of this study is the "justification of art" and the contribution it makes to happiness. The activity and the enjoyment of art are instances of that with which a rational moralist would be concerned; "a morality organised about the human heart . . . would involve every fine art and would render the world pervasively beautiful."§ "Happiness is the ultimate sanction of art, [and] art in turn is the

---

*Reason in Art, pp. 32-33.
†Reason in Art, p. 45.
‡Reason in Art, p. 159.
§Reason in Art, p. 223; Selections, p. 251.

best instrument of happiness."* The combined competence and freedom, in a word, the creativeness of art, would, if incarnate in all the enterprises of men, be the principle of their morality.

The elegiac note with which Santayana talks of much religion and art ("religion and art have had their day")† forsakes him when he turns to the part that science plays in the Life of Reason. For not only is science a new thing and far from final; it is the very technique of following a subject matter in its own terms, the device that enables man to modify nature toward the good. It is as well in its intellectual essence a landscape for contemplation and a formulation of what it most behooves a man to know. The whole group of sciences which elaborates ideas Santayana calls dialectics; the whole group which describes existence, physics.‡ But the two imply each other: "living dialectic comes to clarify existence."§ It is the ideal of physics to gain such an insight into causes that effects may be deduced. "But a little logic is all that can be read into the cataract of events."‖ Science is common knowledge refined and extended; scepticism may be playfully or logically indulged in as a transcendental exercise, but science is the instrument of our arts and the technique of our candid contemplation of existence. History is "the least artificial extension of common knowledge"; it is "associated and recorded memory."¶ But science becomes demonstrable as it becomes abstract, and mechanism is a system (as pointed out earlier, in the discussion of *Reason in Common Sense*), of relevant and efficacious abstraction. The validity of science "is established merely by establishing the truth of its particular propositions, in dialectic on the author-

---

Reason in Art, p. 229; *Selections*, p. 255.
†*Reason in Science*, p. 3; *Selections*, p. 258.
‡*Reason in Science*, p. 29; *Selections*, p. 276.
§*Reason in Science*, p. 32; *Selections*, p. 278.
‖*Reason in Science*, p. 33; *Selections*, p. 279.
¶*Reason in Science*, p. 39.

ity of intent and in physics on that of experiment."* We must consult the sciences to discover what sort of universe we live in, though the sciences have not yet joined hands and its principles have not been clearly extended as yet to the confused realm of morals. Science is at once a use and a delight, like relevant art, but—in contrast with Santayana's later doctrine of contemplation—"there is nothing stable or useful to contemplate except objects relevant to action."† Science clarified and completed would be a vista sympathetic to the mind and would be the adequate technique for living. "There is a pathetic capacity in men to live nobly if only they would give one another the chance."‡ Political perfection as an ideal would involve all relevant truth, knowledge at once expressing and guiding a perfect life.

THE REALMS OF BEING

The reader of Santayana will discover what at first and perhaps at last seems a very different atmosphere in that group of works entitled *The Realms of Being* to which *Scepticism and Animal Faith* constitutes a critical introduction. First published in 1923, sixteen years after *The Life of Reason* was completed, this later series, as we shall see, rests upon that Greek naturalism to which Mr. Santayana says he cleaves rather than upon that Indian mysticism which he distantly admires and emulates. But it has a different apparatus, a different intent, and a whole set of refinements of doctrine unknown to *The Life of Reason*. The style itself is less aphoristic, as it is also, despite some dazzling passages and for all its persistent poetry, more austere. But the ostensible and obvious concern of this later series is in marked contrast with that humane survey of human progress, that sketch of the human tentatives toward rationality with which *The Life of Reason* was preoccupied. *Scepticism and Ani-*

Reason in Science, p. 318; *Selections*, p. 331.
†*Reason in Science*, p. 319; *Selections*, p. 332.
‡*Reason in Science*, p. 320; *Selections*, p. 332.

mal Faith is an attempt to examine the evidence for our belief in nature, experience, memory, demonstration, the self, animation in nature—after a sceptical dissolution of our conventional knowledge. It is also an attempt to distinguish with some care the various categories of being. Santayana has become in these later works a theorist of knowledge and of the nature of Being itself, of which Nature, commonly so-called, is only one form. Yet, since he is in the traditional sense a humanist, he cannot discuss even these questions without canvassing of the moral incidence of the conclusions concerning these matters at which he arrives; and, it must be added, the moral perversities of the conclusions arrived at by others. There is, as will be seen, no fundamental relinquishment of, rather an insistence upon, the obduracy (as well as the potentiality) of matter, and the reliable deliverances of common sense, extended and rendered exact in science. But the specific intellectual enterprise here undertaken is different, both more professional and more personal. Though there is an allusiveness, both veiled and learned, to other doctrines, this is not a survey of civilisation or of philosophy, however much reference there is to historical doctrine. "Here," says Santayana bluntly in the first line of the very first page, "is one more system of philosophy."* He adds at once and in italics, *"My system is not mine nor new."* He remarks that the system is one whose principles the smiling reader appeals to when he smiles. But it is for all that a system, and one with a quite personal accent. It is *"no system of the universe."* It is, rather, after a thoroughgoing and ultimate sceptical analysis of all conventions and "sophistries of thought," an attempt to distinguish the various kinds and categories, or Realms of Being. *Scepticism and Animal Faith* constitutes a critical introduction to these realms. *The Realm of Essence* and *The Realm of Matter*, the first of which is logically, the second biologically, primary, are the analytic traversing of the several kinds of being

Scepticism and Animal Faith, p. v; *Selections*, p. 376.

themselves, with the intent scrupulously to survey their fields and their limits. They are to be followed by two volumes: *The Realm of Truth* and *The Realm of Spirit*, though the characteristics of these latter are already explicitly made evident in the three works already published.

It might be well at the outset to indicate the critical dissolution and the rehabilitation of knowledge attempted in *Scepticism and Animal Faith*, and to delineate summarily the character of each of the "realms" there and in the succeeding volumes distinguished. *Scepticism and Animal Faith* has two phases, indicated in the title itself. The first and, as it were, downward movement is that of scepticism. It is Santayana's conviction that most alleged sceptical enterprises in philosophy have concealed half-hearted and implicit dogmatisms, great and small, in their critical disintegrations. It is his insistence that there *is no first principle of criticism*, a principle itself being already an assumption. "The more drastic this criticism is, the more revolutionary the view to which it reduces me, the clearer will be the contrast between what I find I know and what I thought I knew."*

The position of the ultimate sceptic, or the ultimate position of the sceptic, then, is the very remarkable, and, to Santayana, indubitable one that "nothing given exists"; nothing that is a datum to attention or to consciousness, nothing that appears as an image, a sensation or an idea, *exists*. Ingeniously, though not altogether originally (since the student of philosophy will recognise elements of this scepticism among the Greeks, and in Hume, Kant, and Schopenhauer, for all Santayana's criticism of these latter as not quite honest sceptics), belief in the self, in time, and in external change are rendered logically suspect. Data as given are, for Santayana, nothing but what they are as they appear in intuition. Nor can one securely call them appearances. By intuition he means all "instances of conscious-

Scepticism and Animal Faith, p. 4.

ness." The consciousness of data does not carry with it a guarantee that the datum is an existence. By *existence* he means facts or events believed to occur in nature, of which the data of intuition may be signs. "Existences, then, from the point of view of knowledge, are facts or events affirmed, not images seen or topics merely entertained."* But the loss of faith in the existence of the data of intuition does not abolish their presence to intuition. "In the critic, as in the painter, suspension of belief and of practical understanding is favourable to vision; the arrested eye renders every image limpid and unequivocal."† "The sceptic, then, as a consequence of carrying his scepticism to the greatest lengths, finds himself in the presence of more luminous and less equivocal objects than does the working and believing mind; only these objects are without meaning, they are only what they are obviously, all surface."‡ Remove the pressure of animal haste and animal interest, and illusions and the objects of illusion cease to be illusions; they are become simply, impeccably what, as objects of intuition, they are. Each "will appear dwelling in its own world, and shining by its own light, however brief may be my glimpse of it: for no date will be written on it, no frame of full or of empty time will shut it in. . . . The quality of it will have ceased to exist: it will be merely the quality which it inherently, logically and inalienably is. It will be an ESSENCE."§ Scepticism has here, for Santayana, "touched bottom" and found "honourable rest in the absolutely indubitable."‖

But to intuit an essence "is not even to broach knowledge of fact"; an essence is an ideal object, with "no natural significance, though it has æsthetic immediacy and logical definition."¶ One discounts all dogmas, all beliefs and all claims

---

*Scepticism and Animal Faith, pp. 47-48.
†Scepticism and Animal Faith, p. 67.
‡Scepticism and Animal Faith, p. 70; Selections, p. 391.
§Scepticism and Animal Faith, pp. 73, 74; Selections, p. 394.
‖Scepticism and Animal Faith, p. 74; Selections, p. 394.
¶Scepticism and Animal Faith, p. 75; Selections, p. 395.

and rests in the security that an essence is in its own character, logically, æsthetically and inalienably what it is. To the mind is thus opened "a sweet and marvellous solitude, . . . as if through the gorges of death it had passed into a paradise where all things are crystallised into the images of themselves."† Essences possess intrinsically in their own ontological plane only æsthetic or logical being. They are the realm of the possible or imaginable in sense, or action, or discourse; they include, as well, that infinity of forms which will never swim into anybody's ken, tortures undreamed of in hell, and delights unthought of in heaven. They are eternal objects, out of time, in the strict sense non-existent,— but eternal. They constitute the *Realm of Essence.*

But essences play, quite accidentally to their own being, and innocent, as it were, of their own intention, a part in the life of men and in the context of existence. Some of them, those relevant to the interests of a given self, in given circumstances in the tangle and context of events, constitute *terms.* They are the terms in which things startle and awaken the human animal; they are signals. "They may accordingly become terms in knowledge if interpreted judiciously, and if interpreted injudiciously, they may become illusions."‡

Essences serve as signs, portents for the precarious animal life which has to find its way and increase or guard its fortunes in the *Realm of Matter,* of which it is itself a part and a product. "There is . . . a circle of material events called nature, to which all minds belonging to the same society are responsive in common."§ "Assuming such a common world, it is easy to see how animals may acquire knowledge of it and may communicate it."* Material events arouse intuitions, and the interests and necessities of animal psyches will

---

†*Scepticism and Animal Faith,* p. 76; *Selections,* p. 397.
‡*The Realm of Essence,* p. viii; *Selections,* p. 473.
§*The Realm of Essence,* p. vi; *Selections,* p. 471.
The Realm of Essence, p. vii; *Selections,* pp. 471, 472.

compel them to regard those of the essences given to them as intuitions, as signs for the environment in which they act and undergo, do and suffer. The system men may make of these signs, in proportion to their adjustment to and mastery of things, constitutes the presumptive and practically (though not logically) justified Realm of Matter. The system of signs will be representative pictures; the pictures, since men's perspectives differ, will be different too, though variant representation, like various languages, may be equally efficacious for different purposes. "The same battle in the clouds will be known to the deaf only as lightening and to the blind only as thunder."†

The terms selected by animal care and necessity are such as fit into action, and "which nature can accept and weave into her own material economy."‡ But these essences which occur as intuitions to the dreaming psyche are expressive of that psyche's energies as well as of the routine of nature, of which psyches are indeed themselves complications. "This world of free expression, this drift of sensations, passions, and ideas, perpetually kindled and fading in the light of consciousness, I call the *Realm of Spirit*."§ (Those essences which constitute a standard comprehensive description of all existence, constitute the *Realm of Truth*.) Literature and philosophy, ideal love and imaginative patriotism and religion are compacted of these. Spirit is the actuality of sensation, feeling and thought, and where expression is controlled so as to be representative of conditions of existence, it is what, in the dialogue by that name, Santayana calls "Normal Madness."‖ Uncontrolled, it may be the madness of the lunatic—or of the free and inspired poet.

There are distinguished, then, four realms: matter, essence, truth, and spirit. These represent not simply four

†*The Realm of Essence*, p. vii; *Selections*, p. 472.
‡*The Realm of Essence*, p. ix; *Selections*, p. 474.
§*The Realm of Essence*, pp. x, xi; *Selections*, p. 475.
‖*Dialogues in Limbo*, pp. 36-58; *Selections*, pp. 451-466.

ontological distinctions, but in terms of each of them and in their relation to each other, they constitute in themselves, and in their context with each other, a system of philosophy. Each of them reflects also a characteristic facet of Santayana's philosophical temperament and approach to experience. Matter is his steadfast recognition of the unknowable but omnipresent basis of action, as well as the source and matrix of ideals. Essence testifies to his equally steadfast recognition of the timeless elements which any considered experience involves. Spirit is the realm of fruitions and ultimates, of purities and immediacies, among which the free mind would like to play, and to which the philosopher and poet are by choice addressed. The Realm of Truth is a "tragic segment of the realm of essence," (tragic is a characteristic note of disillusion) of those complementary and more or less correct views which refer to the same system of nature, to the irrevocable and brutally irrational network of facts, past and future.

Two of these realms, in two different senses, may be said to be primary. Actually—one might almost say in the order of actuality—matter is primary. In the order of logic (where essences express the defined interest of a living psyche) and in the order of morals, essences are primary. Santayana never for a moment, however, forgets that essences would never be discerned were there not a realm of matter, a flux of events, and a living psyche generated by matter itself. Readers who have kept their attention on his recent refinements of doctrine with respect to essence and the problems (and they are not a few) which these raise, have forgotten Santayana's own constant adherence to the basic character of matter in all action, and as the vehicle and source of all expression, however free and poetical and however directed upon essences as expressive of moral ultimates or of imaginative liberation. Matter is primary in life, in action and as the source and sustainer of feeling and thought. It can never be known, but it is that which must be reckoned with in all knowledge, that which is encountered in all action. Knowledge, which is the faith involved in all action, is the positing of substance, another name for matter, whose characteristics are thus summarised:

When, . . . in perception, action, memory, or hope, experience is treated as significant, a substance is posited which must be external to thought, with its parts external to one another and each a focus of existence; a substance which passes through various phases is unequally distributed in the field of action, and forms a relative cosmos surrounding each agent.*

Matter must not be conceived as dead and static, rather as dynamic, fertile and alive.

We may fancy that a sort of sub-soul or potential life sleeps, and will always sleep, in the universe of matter, ready to shape it, when opportunity occurs, into the likeness of all essence.†

There is a movement of living substance, on which animal faith *means* to be directed, on which the animal depends, and on which he can act. Wisdom discovers that all systems fall together into one system called nature, all models of the familiar substance called matter. Matter falls into habits or tropes, which make prediction always possible and possibilities always genuine—and always tentative and hypothetical. Animation or intentional discourse is attributed to some of these habits, the habits of animals with minds which an apt "literary psychology" or dramatic inspiration may divine. Further, on the hypothesis that anything exists, truth is implied. *Truth* is a dateless description of existence. "It is a picture of change. It is frozen history."‡ It is the standard comprehensive description of existence. All truths constitute the *Realm of Truth*. "All truths—not a few grand ones—are equally eternal." §

*The Realm of Matter, p. 42; Selections, p. 570.
†The Realm of Matter, p. 149.
‡Scepticism and Animal Faith, p. 271.
§Scepticism and Animal Faith, p. 268; Selections, p. 445.

The realm of matter remains the source of action, though the assumption that action makes and involves is always an audacious leap, a recklessness and (though practically justi-fied) a precarious adventure of the psyche involved in cir-cumstances where it must make guesses, choices and de-cisions. Essences themselves would not appear if all animal predicaments were resolved; in such a case there would be no organ and no occasion for intuition. But essences would remain, since their character, in Santayana's analysis, does not depend on their being intuited.

Now, that matter exists can never be logically proved. That question must be and is begged in and by action. The shocks of experience and the interruptions in it first bring presumptive testimony to the existence of a self; the shock comes to signify something pertinent to the alarm or sur-prise with which the self is filled. But the self is deeper than discourse—itself an experience in which the self first comes to be assumed; it is "a fountain of joy, folly, and sorrow, a waxing and waning, stupid and dreaming creature, in the midst of a vast natural world, of which it catches but a few transient and odd perspectives."†

The self remembers, and the claims of memory are a typi-cal instance of knowledge, for "in remembering I believe that I am taking cognisance not of a given essence but of a remote existence, so that, being myself here and now, I can consider and describe something going on at another place and time."‡ The centre of the doctrine of knowledge in Santayana, is faith in the absent, symbolised by essences which, quite adventitiously to their own character, serve as symbols. Knowledge is an animal creed whose articles can-not be guaranteed. Logical analysis may dissolve the credi-bility of the existence of any or all things, but while life lasts animal faith endures, and believes in a world. Knowl-edge "arises by a movement of the self sympathetic or re-

†*Scepticism and Animal Faith*, p. 149.
‡*Scepticism and Animal Faith*, p. 164; *Selections*, p. 412.

sponsive to surrounding beings, so that these beings become its intended objects."* "It is involved in any pang of hunger, of fear, or of love."† The effort of knowledge is to explore effectively matter or substance, which is ancient, vast and recalcitrant. But "it yields wonderful treasures to courage, when courage is guided by art and respects the limits set to it by nature."‡ The ideal of knowledge is then to become natural science. Knowledge that seeks to devour its objects, or to assume it *knows* what is present to it, rather than what that presence signifies, is not knowledge but intuition. Intuition is concerned with essences. And essences, though their recognition is dependent on the animal fortunes of the bodily psyche, itself a complication of material life, are not dependent for their being on being intuited, nor is their character determined by intuition, nor is their usefulness as signs and portents in the adventure of knowledge or the arts of man identical with their proper being, or, even to man, their characteristic good. Their being is their qualitative uniqueness; they are good only when they express *our* good. Intuition itself is the recognition or simply the awakening of consciousness to an essence in its own proper being, not to that essence as a signal of something other than itself.

The consideration of the nature of one essence as revealed to intuition is an introduction to the nature of all essences and their proper being: "We may say that for the mind there is a single avenue to essence, namely attention."§ But there are various kinds of attention: the urgent attention of interest or necessity, the contemplative perusal of a term or a meaning, or the loving absorption in a consummation such as a simple beauty which a complex physical machinery may be necessary to produce or to render recognisable. A harmony heard as a unity may involve a whole orchestra for

*Scepticism and Animal Faith, p. 180; Selections, p. 427.
†Scepticism and Animal Faith, p. 181; Selections, p. 427.
‡Scepticism and Animal Faith, p. 191; Selections, p. 434.
§The Realm of Essence, p. 15.

the playing, as it involves a complicated human ear for the hearing. But the being intuited in each case is the same; as recognised, it is specific, however complex the elements included. It is a character, an identity; it is "individuated internally by its character, not externally by its position in the flux of nature."*

After things lose their existence, as before they attain it, although it is true of them that they have existed or will exist, they have no internal being except their essences, quite as if they had never broached Existence at all; yet the identity of each essence with itself and difference from every other essence suffices to distinguish and define them all in eternity, where they form the *Realm of Essence.*†

This realm of the individuated, self-identified, eternal forms of being does not, for Santayana, constitute in its own character possible beings, existences, problematical facts, abstractions, sensations, thoughts or natural elements. These all exhibit some essence, though they involve contingent existence. The realm is infinite; it includes all that may ever be enacted or imagined, much that may never be envisaged or incarnate. Essences, for Santayana, are morally neutral; he distinguishes his Realm of Essence from that Platonic realm which it resembles by pointing out that the Realm of Essence is not the home merely of the Good, the True, and the Beautiful; essences are called true, good, beautiful only when they express the fulfillments of some human impulse or interest or some natural fact or condition. Essences, furthermore, are not causes or powers, nor are they goals of any natural process. The Realm of Essence is plural, anarchic, inert, neutral and eternal.

The student of the history of philosophy cannot help noticing that though essences are distinguished from sensations and thoughts, they sometimes appear to be just those psycho-

The Realm of Essence, p. 36.
†*The Realm of Essence*, p. 24; *Selections*, p. 490.

logical atoms of consciousness given eternal status in or as a realm of being. Santayana insists, however, that what seems to be psychological about them is their context, their use or their discernment by an animal psyche. The conditions under which they are intuited does not, for him, determine their character. Again, though he repeatedly insists that there is a great liberation in the discovery of the Realm of Essence, there is for him, he insists, no æsthetic function or moral glamour about them. Essence gives the spirit at once ultimacy and immediacy in the actuality of which, indeed, spirit is constituted. Existence itself is a momentary victory of essence, form in some mode become manifest in things. "I myself," he writes, "have no passionate attachment to existence, and value this world for the intuitions it can suggest rather than for the wilderness of facts that composes it. To turn away from it may be the deepest wisdom in the end."*
A hundred passages could be cited that support the suspicion that our author, though he says essences are morally indifferent, is not indifferent to the moral incidence of the Realm of Essence. Spiritual discipline, not altogether distinguishable from moral purification, is indeed cited as one approach to essence.

Essences provide for the contemplative spirit objects of æsthetic delight, or of rapt contemplation. They afford release from the pressure and contingency and absurdity of existence. They are all pervaded by pure Being,† contemplation of which constitutes "the last secret of a religious life."‡ Consideration of pure Being and of the Realm of Essence shows that "both are absolutely infinite, the one implicitly, the other explicitly; they therefore release the mind from any exclusive allegiance to this or that good."§ Santayana dis-

---

*Scepticism and Animal Faith, p. 171; Selections, p. 418.
†Pure Being varies in Santayana's discussion of it from the logical character of identity to the plenitude of Being envisaged by mystics of East and West.
‡The Realm of Essence, p. 63; Selections, p. 506.
§The Realm of Essence, p. 65; Selections, p. 507.

claims his desire to go into the Indian wilderness and contemplate pure Being. But though revealing an admiration for
Eastern saints, he prefers to be "a rational animal rather
than a pure spirit,"† to recognise nature scrupulously rather
than to contemplate Being in spiritual freedom.

But it is not on moral grounds nor on those of spiritual aspiration that he claims to have established essence. Scepticism, throwing its dissolvents upon existence, leaves the
data or *given* of intuition, data that "are what they are."
Every disillusion about the existential implications of a
datum thus for him establishes an essence. Every term defined in dialectic is a testimony to its being. "Distinguishable essences such as the terms of dialectic are the most real
of beings."‡ Sensuous images are evidence for essence, for,
as in the case of beautiful things, it is not the natural complication of the facts or the manner of our perceiving it, but
the essence by which we are arrested. Even activity, where
it is masterful, is accompanied by relevant images. In every
focus of synthesis or reflection or fruition, intuition may fall
on some essence beyond which it need not look. Whenever a
form or a relation transcending time is intuited by an animal
psyche living in time, there is, in this presence to awareness,
testimony again to the timeless being of essence. All denial
of essence seems to involve it, for the *what* denied is precisely
what the essence is.

Santayana's doctrine of essence raises, as a studious inventory of his analysis will show, very considerable questions, both moral and noetic. The data, which are such essences as come to intuition, may be sensations, or feelings or
thoughts. A toothache or pure Being, cabbages and kings,
green dragons and square circles, all are indifferently suitable
instances of essences. Essences have no *meaning*; they are
all surface, Santayana tells us. Such meaning as any pragmatic, functional account might give to meaning is excluded.

†*The Realm of Essence*, p. 65; *Selections*, p. 508.
‡*The Realm of Essence*, p. 4.

Essences are what they are, not what they signify in action. They are objects of awareness, as direct as an ache or an ecstasy. Yet at times they *seem* to be all meaning, eternal logical axioms. As forms of, characters of, Being in the infinite catalogue of the Realm of Essence, they have the eternity of Platonic forms, though not their moral primacy. Good essences are such as express a good life. True essences are such as are used in correct descriptions of facts past or future. Beauty is found where harmony is felt and perceived. Essences themselves are innocent of such human perspectives. Essences are apprehended directly, are present to consciousness like ideas in Locke or in Berkeley. But it is not, we are told, their apprehension that constitutes their being.

In action, essences are names, almost nicknames, which make the world familiar to us. But they are more than names. They are eternal beings, logically, if not cosmologically prior to the things they may be used to designate or signify. They are, as one critic has called them, dream-images; the real world of substances is always dressed up in the garments with which intuition endows it. Yet sometimes the Realm of Essence sounds in these pages more substantial than substance or matter. "So much more profound is the eternal being of the essences traversed in change than that of the matter or attention or discourse which plays with those essences at touch and go."* Though logically, if not practically indubitable, substance itself is unknowable. "The existence of this world—unless we lapse for a moment into an untenable scepticism—is certain, or at least it is unquestionably to be assumed . . . but after you have wandered up and down in it for many years, and have gathered all you could of its ways by report, this same world, because it exists substantially and is not invented, remains a foreign thing and a marvel to the spirit: unknowable as a drop of water is unknowable, or unknowable like a person loved."†

*The Realm of Essence, p. 24; Selections, p. 490.
†Essences also are never known, but their being does not even

Yet this unknowable is unknowable only in its inmost intrinsic character. It is known "by report" of its portents and its possibilities, for these come to us as significant essences. Substance is the matter to which, in the language of *Reason in Religion*, we could and should pay retrospective piety, the obeisance of life recognising its sources and circumstances. In *The Life of Reason*, spirituality was regarded as the fixing of the eyes on the ideals which nature generated, the living in the presence of ultimate purposes and ideal issues. In the light of the critical examination of the nature and grounds of belief undertaken in these later works, spirituality is differently conceived, or at least conceived with a different emphasis. Spirituality is still a concern with ultimates, but not primarily with those ultimates which are fulfillments of relevant ideals of action. Spirituality is the actuality of the Realm of Spirit. It is, as far as may be, a freeing of contemplation from the accidental origins of contemplation, and an absorption, living and liberated, in whatever objects of contemplation a casual animal destiny has set before consciousness.

Spirit, the expression of animal life, is "a living light ready to fall upon things."† Spirit is exemplified in attention, synthesis, perception.‡ Spirit, wakefulness of attention, arises in the interests of animal impulse and conditions, but as pure spirit, it is "an impartial readiness to know."§ Spirit is "the actual light of consciousness falling upon anything—the ultimate invisible emotional fruition of life in feeling and thought."* What it will feel and think depends on the animal psyche and its fortunes. But spirit is occasionally, and in rare spirits often, free. Spirituality is the name for this freedom of actuality of feeling or contemplation. It is the liberty

have to be assumed; even doubt establishes them. ("The Unknowable," *Obiter Scripta*, p. 188).

†*Scepticism and Animal Faith*, p. 273; *Selections*, p. 446.
‡Cf. *Scepticism and Animal Faith*, p. 281.
§*Scepticism and Animal Faith*, p. 284.
The Realm of Matter, p. 139.

of insight. The spirit may lose self-consciousness, the sense of its own or of any separable existence; it forgets its origins, its pieties and its obligations; it finds union and ecstasy in selfless intuition of pure Being. All perspectives are transcended, all interests forgotten, essences themselves are beheld, and the beholding itself is unselfconscious. The pure Being present in all essences is that in which spirit is completely lost and saved, or, since loss and salvation are terms of animal prudence, it were better perhaps to say by which it is absorbed. Neither man nor any transitory form of being has prerogative for the free spirit. "Piecemeal amid the accidents of existence, ultimate good is attained whenever the senses and the heart are suddenly flooded by the intuition of those essences to which they were secretly addressed."† But bathing in the light of any essence which floods awareness is an act of spirit. The saint and the philosopher are free sometimes; a pure actuality, pure spirit, a godhead, would be free for such untrammelled and disinterested contemplation. Pure Being in such a pure spirit would be the whole object of its intuition, the whole of its own actuality, for nothing would importune it to make distinctions.

Santayana protests that this is an almost impossible ideal for the rational animal. It is none the less the intimation of an ideal of detachment that recurs repeatedly in his later pages. Matter is an inexplicable absurdity; the Life of Reason, as seen from the standpoint of uncommitted contemplation, is romantic, troubled and insecure. Pure spirit shines freely only occasionally in the lives of harassed and troubled animals. But to live absorbed in eternal forms, in endless themes of an unillusioned and unanxious intuition of forms of intellectual entertainment is what the philosopher might most clearly desire. And *all* of pure Being, rather than any form of Being accidentally lighted upon, might come to absorb him in the end. He would have attained Nirvana and perfect peace.

†*The Realm of Essence*, p. 61; *Selections*, p. 504.

The student of Santayana will find thus two, though not, I think, contradictory, tempers in this philosopher. Even in the midst of his celebration of the mystical aspiration to pure Being, he can say:

As for me, I frankly cleave to the Greeks and not to the Indians, and I aspire to be a rational animal rather than a pure spirit. Preferences are matters of morals, and morals are a part of politics. It is for the statesman or the humanist to compare the functions of various classes in the state and the importance or timeliness of the various arts. He must honour the poets as poets and the saints as saints, but on occasion he is not forbidden to banish them.*

To the contemplative mind, all existence is an essence dreamed or remembered. To the reflective moralist matter is the substance to be explored and studied in the interest of the realisation of discerned or imagined goods. Santayana remains fundamentally a naturalist through these later books, a naturalist whose own gaze is directed to those forms to which he himself is by temperament, as a poet and a speculative mind, addressed. He worships not existence but such fruitions or discernments as it makes possible. He recognises universal power and respects it. But he worships other things, the goals of life, insofar as any of them can be defined or attained anywhere, for so defined or attained, they become glory and beauty, "not the troubled glories and brief perfections of this world only, but rather that desired perfection, that eternal beauty which lies sealed in the heart of each living thing."†

The net impression left by the total body of Santayana's work is that of a philosopher who realises that all religions and philosophies are murmurs, at once lyric and dramatic, in which the spirit of man has been talking to itself. But he is a thinker who most cherishes talk that is either wise or de-

*The Realm of Essence, p. 65; Selections, p. 508.
†"Ultimate Religion," Obiter Scripta, p. 297; Selections, p. 593.

lightful or both. Sometimes man's discourse is wonderfully expressive of private fancies or fantastic dreams; sometimes the human babble becomes representative. Democritus, the ancient atomist who, along with native common sense, is the classic source of Santayana's own naturalism, is made to say in *Dialogues in Limbo* of that "Normal Madness" by which men manage to live: "Two protecting deities, indeed, like two sober friends, supporting a drunkard, flank human folly and keep it within bounds. One of these deities is Punishment and the other Agreement."† Follies are healed and harmonised. Man lives and learns. Wisdom itself is a dreaming soliloquy, but one that no longer deceives. "The more foolish images of sense may be disallowed in favor of those others more faithful to the true rhythms and divisions of nature."‡

It is clear which of man's dreams Santayana thinks wisest. It is that dream in which the stories man tells himself and the images he uses both guide his action and liberate his fancy. He emphasises normal madness, which is not really madness. It is another name for animal faith, and would be mad only if it took its presumptive knowledge for literal insight. But while he stresses normal madness, conventional sanity, the deliverances of enlightened common sense, of physics and of a dialectic vital and tethered to fact, the whole of Santayana's writings reveals an extraordinary sympathy with another sort of madness, that which Plato called divine. The "divine Autologos, patron of madness" is invoked in the dialogue succeeding "Normal Madness" quoted above. Autologos is "the speaking Spirit in all of us, whenever it speaks."* Expression reveals to us our own thoughts. Santayana has been unwilling to accept passionate and exclusive attachment to one form of madness, though he has his own shrewd instinct and articulate statement as to which is least erratic. He has rather had a delicate divination, a

† *Dialogues in Limbo*, p. 47; *Selections*, p. 459.
‡ *Dialogues in Limbo*, p. 46; *Selections*, p. 458.
* *Dialogues in Limbo*, p. 59.

remarkably exact gift of appreciation of the import of all the illusions, the poetries which the human imagination, itself a fruit of nature, has generated and loved. He has drunk each draught pure and without the illusion that in drinking each he was drinking from the fountain of absolute truth. This sympathy, conniving but unconvinced, with all forms of poetic imagination (and in this sense philosophies and religions are all poetry) has confused some of his readers. They have sometimes mistaken his dramatic understandings for successive idolatries, as if he were a spectator at a theatre who believed each play in succession to be "real," and remained inconsolable for the death of each hero. His own philosophy is singularly distinguished as poetry, but it is poetry that happens to have as its cardinal syntax those parts of human speech which express at once the human condition and its pertinent ideals. His various essays in literary criticism, such as the one on Hamlet† or on Browning or on Shelley are studies of the way in which certain poetic expressions have been more or less adequate images for fact or inspiration. His comments on social life as in *Character and Opinion in the United States* or *Soliloquies in England*, have been instances of the same fundamental enterprise. And since, to this sympathetic-minded realist the human condition is touched with fatality and illusion in fact, though exalted by its own dreams, he has treated the world of existence with detachment and irony, mostly affectionate, and sometimes turned away from it altogether to meditate on the changeless forms of those illusions themselves. There is thus no inconsistency or surprise in the fact that late in a life of philosophical imagination he should have written a novel, for philosophies and religions have always seemed to him more or less convincing or revealing fictions men have told themselves about the world and their place in it. The very last words of *The Last Puritan* are an appropriate comment on his own temper.

†*Obiter Scripta*, pp. 41-67.

"In this novel," [remarks one of the characters to the author] ". . . the argument is dramatised, the views become human persuasions, and the presentation is all the truer for not professing to be true. You have said it somewhere yourself, though I may misquote the words: After life is over and the world has gone up in smoke, what realities might the spirit in us still call its own without illusion save the form of those very illusions which have made up our story?"*

Santayana himself distinguishes between the conditions under which intuitions of forms or images arise in the mind and those images or essences themselves. He makes clear both explicitly and by repeated internal evidences in his work on what thematic pictures he has loved particularly to dwell. Intellectually he might be called the last Greek. Certainly it is the clear outlines of Greek thinking that he prefers, along with the cogent honesty of Spinoza among the moderns. Socially, his image of a decent quiet happiness comes from his love of well-bred English life, and among the English he finds as nowhere else an echo of Hellenic order and vitality. The tenderness enshrined in Catholic imagery, the world conceived "in terms of the human heart" are the familiars of his own imaginative pieties. He recognises the energy and the good-will, as well as the blindness, and the Puritanism of American life (*The Last Puritan* is an indirect memoir of his life here). But he is "The Spirit of a Stranger" to the contemporary world, in which he can find no prophet or leader to follow, and no religion to believe. Like a philosopher, he lives as much as may be in the eternal, among essences beautiful or tragic which existence may briefly incarnate and render luminous to a detached inspection. As a poet, he delights in their immediacy, and as an honest moralist, he indicates what forms or system of forms may be expressive of possible human good. In him the poet, the Platonistic logician, the materialist in nature and morals, conspire to make a body of writing that is a systematic natu-

*The Last Puritan, p. 602; Selections, p. 596

mantic and prosperous days. My father had studied the country and the natives, and had written a little book about the Island of Mindanao; he had been three times round the world in the sailing-ships of the period, and had incidentally visited England and the United States, and been immensely impressed by the energy and order prevalent in those nations. His respect for material greatness was profound, yet not unmixed with a secret irony or even repulsion. He had a seasoned and incredulous mind, trained to see other sorts of excellence also: in his boyhood he had worked in the studio of a professional painter of the school of Goya, and had translated the tragedies of Seneca into Spanish verse. His transmarine experiences, therefore, did not rattle, as so often happens, in an empty head. The sea itself, in those days, was still vast and blue, and the lands beyond it full of lessons and wonders. From childhood I have lived in the imaginative presence of interminable ocean spaces, coconut islands, blameless Malays, and immense continents swarming with Chinamen, polished and industrious, obscene and philosophical. It was habitual with me to think of scenes and customs pleasanter than those about me. My own travels have never carried me far from the frontiers of Christendom or of respectability, and chiefly back and forth across the North Atlantic—thirty-eight fussy voyages; but in mind I have always seen these things on an ironical background enormously empty, or breaking out in spots, like Polynesia, into nests of innocent particoloured humanity.

My mother's figure belonged to the same broad and somewhat exotic landscape; she had spent her youth in the same places; but the moral note resounding in her was somewhat different. Her father, José Borrás, of Reus in Catalonia, had been a disciple of Rousseau, an enthusiast and a wanderer: he taught her to revere pure reason and republican virtue and to abhor the vices of a corrupt world. But her own temper was cool and stoical, rather than ardent, and her disdain of corruption had in it a touch of elegance. At Manila, during the time of her first marriage, she had been rather the grand lady, in a style half Creole, half early Victorian. Virtue, beside those tropical seas, might stoop to be indolent. She had given a silver dollar every morning to her native major-domo, with which to provide for the family and the twelve servants, and keep the change for his wages. Meantime she bathed, arranged the flowers, received visits, and did embroidery. It had been a spacious life; and in our narrower circumstances in later years the sense of it never forsook her.

Her first husband, an American merchant established in Manila, had been the sixth son of Nathaniel Russell Sturgis, of Boston (1779-1856). In Boston, accordingly, her three Sturgis children had numerous relations and a little property, and there she had promised their father to bring them up in case of his death. When this occurred, in 1857, she therefore established herself in Boston; and this fact, by a sort of pre-natal or pre-established destiny, was the cause of my connection with the Sturgis family, with Boston, and with America.

It was in Madrid in 1862, where my mother had gone on a visit intended to be temporary, that my father and she were married. He had been an old friend of hers and of her first husband's, and was well aware of her settled plan to educate her children in America, and recognised the propriety of that arrangement. Various projects and combinations were mooted: but the matter eventually ended in a separation, friendly, if not altogether pleasant to either party. My mother returned with her Sturgis children to live in the United States and my father and I remained in Spain. Soon, however, this compromise proved unsatisfactory. The education and prospects which my father, in his modest retirement, could offer me in Spain were far from brilliant; and in 1872 he decided to take me to Boston, where, after remaining for one cold winter, he left me in my mother's care and went back to Spain.

I was then in my ninth year, having been born on December 16, 1863, and I did not know one word of English. Nor was I likely to learn the language at home, where the family always continued to speak a Spanish more or less pure. But by a happy thought I was sent during my first winter in Boston to a kindergarten, among much younger children, where there were no books, so that I picked up English by ear before knowing how it was written: a circumstance to which I probably owe speaking the language without a marked foreign accent. The Brimmer School, the Boston Latin School, and Harvard College then followed in order: but apart from the taste for English poetry which I first imbibed from our excellent English master, Mr. Byron Groce, the most decisive influences over my mind in boyhood continued to come from my family, where, with my grown-up brother and sisters, I was the only child. I played no games, but sat at home all the afternoon and evening reading or drawing; especially devouring anything I could find that regarded religion, architecture, or geography.

In the summer of 1883, after my Freshman year, I returned for the first time to Spain to see my father. Then, and during many subsequent holidays which I spent in his company, we naturally discussed the various careers that might be open to me. We should both of us have liked the Spanish army or diplomatic service: but for the first I was already too old, and our means and our social relations hardly sufficed for the second. Moreover, by that time I felt like a foreigner in Spain, more acutely so than in America, although for more trivial reasons: my Yankee manners seemed outlandish there, and I could not do myself justice in the language. Nor was I inclined to overcome this handicap, as perhaps I might have done with a little effort: nothing in Spanish life or literature at that time particularly attracted me. English had become my only possible instrument, and I deliberately put away everything that might confuse me in that medium. English, and the whole Anglo-Saxon tradition in literature and philosophy, have always been a medium to me rather than a source. My natural affinities were elsewhere. Moreover, scholarship and learning of any sort seemed to me a means, not an end. I always hated to be a professor. Latin and Greek, French, Italian, and German, although I can read them, were languages which I never learned well. It seemed an accident to me if the matters which interested me came clothed in the rhetoric of one or another of these nations: I was not without a certain temperamental rhetoric of my own in which to recast what I adopted. Thus in renouncing everything else for the sake of English letters I might be said to have been guilty, quite unintentionally, of a little stratagem, as if I had set out to say plausibly in English as many un-English things as possible.

This brings me to religion, which is the head and front of everything. Like my parents, I have always set myself down officially as a Catholic: but this is a matter of sympathy and traditional allegiance, not of philosophy. In my adolescence, religion on its doctrinal and emotional side occupied me much more than it does now. I was more unhappy and unsettled; but I have never had any unquestioning faith in any dogma, and have never been what is called a practising Catholic. Indeed, it would hardly have been possible. My mother, like her father before her, was a Deist: she was sure there was a God, for who else could have made the world? But God was too great to take special thought for man: sacrifices, prayers, churches, and tales of immortality were invented by rascally priests in order to dominate the foolish. My father, except for the Deism, was emphatically of the same opinion. Thus, although I learned my prayers and catechism by rote, as was then inevitable in Spain, I knew that my parents regarded all religion as a work of human imagination: and I agreed, and still agree, with them there. But this carried an implication in their minds against which every instinct in me rebelled, namely that the works of human imagination are bad. No, said I to myself even as a boy: they are good, they alone are good; and the rest—the whole real world—is ashes in the mouth. My sympathies were entirely with those other members of my family who were devout believers. I loved the Christian epic, and all those doctrines and observances which bring it down into daily life: I thought how glorious it would have been to be a Dominican friar, preaching that epic eloquently, and solving afresh all the knottiest and sublimest mysteries of theology. I was delighted with anything, like Mallock's *Is Life Worth Living?*, which seemed to rebuke the fatuity of that age. For my own part, I was quite sure that life was not worth living; for if religion was false everything was worthless, and almost everything, if religion was true. In this youthful pessimism I was hardly more foolish than so many amateur mediævalists and religious æsthetes of my generation. I saw the same alternative between Catholicism and complete disillusion: but I was never afraid of disillusion, and I have chosen it.

Since those early years my feelings on this subject have become less strident. Does not modern philosophy teach that our idea of the so-called real world is also a work of imagination? A religion—for there are other religions than the Christian—simply offers a system of faith different from the vulgar one, or extending beyond it. The question is which imaginative system you will trust. My matured conclusion has been that no system is to be trusted, not even that of science in any literal or pictorial sense; but all systems may be used and, up to a certain point, trusted as symbols. Science expresses in human terms our dynamic relation to surrounding reality. Philosophies and religions, where they do not misrepresent these same dynamic relations and do not contradict science, express destiny in moral dimensions, in obviously mythical and poetical images: but how else should these moral truths be expressed at all in a traditional or popular fashion? Religions are the great fairy-tales of the conscience.

When I began the formal study of philosophy as an undergraduate at Harvard, I was already alive to the fundamental questions, and even had a certain dialectical nimbleness, due to familiarity with the fine points of theology: the arguments for and against free will and the proofs of the existence of God were warm and clear in my mind. I accordingly heard James and Royce with more wonder than serious agreement: my scholastic logic would have wished to reduce James at once to a materialist and Royce to a solipsist, and it seemed strangely irrational in them to resist such simplification. I had heard many Unitarian sermons (being taken to hear them lest I should become too Catholic), and had been interested in them so far as they were rationalistic and informative, or even amusingly irreligious, as I often thought them to be: but neither in those discourses nor in Harvard philosophy was it easy for me to understand the Protestant combination of earnestness with waywardness. I was used to see water flowing from fountains, architectural and above ground: it puzzled me to see it drawn painfully in bucketfuls from the subjective well, muddied, and half spilt over.

There was one lesson, however, which I was readier to learn, not only at Harvard from Professor Palmer and afterwards at Berlin from Paulsen, but from the general temper of that age well represented for me by the *Revue des Deux Mondes* (which I habitually read from cover to cover) and by the works of Taine and of Matthew Arnold—I refer to the historical spirit of the nineteenth century, and to that splendid panorama of nations and religions, literatures and arts, which it unrolled before the imagination. These picturesque vistas into the past came to fill in circumstantially that geographical and moral vastness to which my imagination was already accustomed. Professor Palmer was especially skilful in bending the mind to a suave and sympathetic participation in the views of all philosophers in turn: were they not all great men, and must not the aspects of things which seemed persuasive to them be really persuasive? Yet even this form of romanticism, amiable as it is, could not altogether put to sleep my scholastic dogmatism. The historian of philosophy may be as sympathetic and as self-effacing as he likes: the philosopher in him must still ask whether any of those successive views were true, or whether the later ones were necessarily truer than the earlier: he cannot, unless he is a shameless sophist, rest content with a truth *pro tem*. In reality the sympathetic reconstruction of history is a literary art, and it depends for its plausibility as well as for its materials on a conventional belief in the natural world. Without this belief no history and no science would be anything but a poetic fiction, like a classification of the angelic choirs. The necessity of naturalism as a foundation for all further serious opinions was clear to me from the beginning. Naturalism might indeed be criticised—and I was myself intellectually and emotionally predisposed to criticise it, and to oscillate between supernaturalism and solipsism—but if naturalism was condemned, supernaturalism itself could have no point of application in the world of fact; and the whole edifice of human knowledge would crumble, since no perception would then be a report and no judgment would have a transcendent object. Hence historical reconstruction seemed to me more honestly and solidly practised by Taine, who was a professed naturalist, than by Hegel and his school, whose naturalism, though presupposed at every stage, was disguised and distorted by a dialectic imposed on it by the historian and useful at best only in simplifying his dramatic perspectives and lending them a false absoluteness and moralistic veneer.

The influence of Royce over me, though less important in the end than that of James, was at first much more active. Royce was the better dialectician, and traversed subjects in which I was naturally more interested. The point that particularly exercised me was Royce's Theodicy or justification for the existence of evil. It would be hard to exaggerate the ire which his arguments on this subject aroused in my youthful breast. Why that emotion? Romantic sentiment that could find happiness only in tears and virtue only in heroic agonies was something familiar to me and not unsympathetic: a poetic play of mine, called *Lucifer*, conceived in those days, is a clear proof of it. I knew Leopardi and Musset largely by heart; Schopenhauer was soon to become, for a brief period, one of my favourite authors. I carried Lucretius in my pocket: and although the spirit of the poet in that case was not romantic, the picture of human existence which he drew glorified the same vanity. Spinoza, too, whom I was reading under Royce himself, filled me with joy and enthusiasm: I gathered at once from him a doctrine which has remained axiomatic with me ever since, namely that good and evil are relative to the natures of animals, irreversible in that relation, but indifferent to the march of cosmic events, since the force of the universe infinitely exceeds the force of any one of its parts. Had I found, then, in Royce only a romantic view of life, or only pessimism, or only stoical courage and pantheistic piety, I should have taken no offence, but readily recognised the poetic truth or the moral legitimacy of those positions. Conformity with fate, as I afterwards came to see, belongs to post-rational morality, which is a normal though optional development of human sentiment: Spinoza's "intellectual love of God" was a shining instance of it.

But in Royce these attitudes, in themselves so honest and noble, seemed to be somehow embroiled and rendered sophistical: nor was he alone in this, for the same moral equivocation seemed to pervade Hegel, Browning, and Nietzsche. That which repelled me in all these men was the survival of a sort of forced optimism and pulpit unction, by which a cruel and nasty world, painted by them in the most lurid colours, was nevertheless set up as the model and standard of what ought to be. The duty of an honest moralist would have been rather to distinguish, in this bad or mixed reality, the part, however small, that could be loved and chosen from the remainder, however large, which was to be rejected and renounced. Certainly the universe was in flux and dynamically single: but this fatal flux could very well take care of itself; and it was not so fluid that no islands of a relative permanence and beauty might not be formed in it. Ascetic conformity was itself one of these islands: a scarcely inhabitable peak from which almost all human passions and activities were excluded. And the Greeks, whose deliberate ethics was rational, never denied the vague early Gods and the environing chaos, which perhaps would return in the end: but meantime they built their cities bravely on the hill-tops, as we all carry on pleasantly our temporal affairs, although we know that to-morrow we die. Life itself exists only by a modicum of organisation, achieved and transmitted through a world of change: the momentum of such organisation first creates a difference between good and evil, or gives them a meaning at all. Thus the core of life is always hereditary, steadfast, and classical; the margin of barbarism and blind adventure round it may be as wide as you will, and in some wild hearts the love of this fluid margin may be keen, as might be any other loose passion. But to *preach* barbarism as the only good, in ignorance or hatred of the possible perfection of every natural thing, was a scandal: a belated Calvinism that remained fanatical after ceasing to be Christian. And there was a further circumstance which made this attitude particularly odious to me. This romantic love of evil was not thoroughgoing: wilfulness and disorder were to reign only in spiritual matters; in government and industry, even in natural science, all was to be order and mechanical progress. Thus the absence of a positive religion and of a legislation, like that of the ancients, intended to be rational and final, was very far from liberating the spirit for higher flights: on the contrary, it opened the door to the pervasive tyranny of the world over the soul. And no wonder: a soul rebellious to its moral heritage is too weak to reach any firm definition of its inner life. It will feel lost and empty unless it summons the random labours of the contemporary world to fill and to enslave it. It must let mechanical and civic achievements reconcile it to its own moral confusion and triviality.

It was in this state of mind that I went to Germany to continue the study of philosophy—interested in all religious or metaphysical systems, but sceptical about them and scornful of any romantic worship or idealisation of the real world. The life of a wandering student, like those of the Middle Ages, had an immense natural attraction for me—so great that I have never willingly led any other. When I had to choose a profession, the prospect of a quiet academic existence seemed the least of evils. I was fond of reading and observation, and I liked young men; but I have never been a diligent student either of science or art, nor at all ambitious to be learned. I have been willing to let cosmological problems and technical questions solve themselves as they would or as the authorities agreed for the moment that they should be solved. My pleasure was rather in expression, in reflection, in irony: my spirit was content to intervene, in whatever world it might seem to find itself, in order to disentangle the intimate moral and intellectual echoes audible to it in that world. My naturalism or materialism is no academic opinion: it is not a survival of the alleged materialism of the nineteenth century, when all the professors of philosophy were idealists: it is an everyday conviction which came to me, as it came to my father, from experience and observation of the world at large, and especially of my own feelings and passions. It seems to me that those who are not materialists cannot be good observers of themselves: they may hear themselves thinking, but they cannot have watched themselves acting and feeling; for feeling and action are evidently accidents of matter. If a Democritus or Lucretius or Spinoza or Darwin works within the lines of nature, and clarifies some part of that familiar object, that fact is the ground of my attachment to them: they have the savour of truth; but what the savour of truth is, I know very well without their help. Consequently there is no opposition in my mind between materialism and a Platonic or even Indian discipline of the spirit. The recognition of the material world and of the conditions of existence in it merely enlightens the spirit concerning the source of its troubles and the means to its happiness or deliverance: and it was happiness or deliverance, the supervening supreme expression of human will and imagination, that alone really concerned me. This alone was genuine philosophy; this alone was the life of reason.

Had the life of reason ever been cultivated in the world by people with a sane imagination? Yes, once, by the Greeks. Of the Greeks, however, I knew very little: the philosophical and political departments at Harvard had not yet discovered Plato and Aristotle. It was with the greater pleasure that I heard Paulsen in Berlin expounding Greek ethics with a sweet reasonableness altogether worthy of the subject: here at last was a vindication of order and beauty in the institutions of men and in their ideas. Here, through the pleasant medium of transparent myths or of summary scientific images, like the water of Thales, nature was essentially understood and honestly described; and here, for that very reason, the free mind could disentangle its true good, and could express it in art, in manners, and even in the most refined or the most austere spiritual discipline. Yet, although I knew henceforth that in the Greeks I should find the natural support and point of attachment for my own philosophy, I was not then collected or mature enough to pursue the matter; not until ten years later, in 1896–1897, did I take the opportunity of a year's leave of absence to go to England and begin a systematic reading of Plato and Aristotle under Doctor Henry Jackson of Trinity College, Cambridge. I am not conscious of any change of opinion supervening, nor of any having occurred earlier; but by that study and change of scene my mind was greatly enriched; and the composition of *The Life of Reason* was the consequence.

This book was intended to be a summary history of the human imagination, expressly distinguishing those phases of it which showed what Herbert Spencer called an adjustment of inner to outer relations; in other words, an adaptation of fancy and habit to material facts and opportunities. On the one hand, then, my subject being the imagination, I was never called on to step beyond the subjective sphere. I set out to describe, not nature or God, but the ideas of God or nature bred in the human mind. On the other hand, I was not concerned with these ideas for their own sake, as in a work of pure poetry or erudition, but I meant to consider them in their natural genesis and significance; for I assumed throughout that the whole life of reason was generated and controlled by the animal life of man in the bosom of nature. Human ideas had, accordingly, a symptomatic, expressive, and symbolic value: they were the inner notes sounded by man's passions and by his arts: and they became rational partly by their vital and inward harmony—for reason is a harmony of the passions—and partly by their adjustment to external facts and possibilities—for reason is a harmony of the inner life with truth and with fate. I was accordingly concerned to discover what wisdom is possible to an animal whose mind, from beginning to end, is poetical: and I found that this could not lie in discarding poetry in favour of a science supposed to be clairvoyant and literally true. Wisdom lay rather in taking everything good-humouredly, with a grain of salt. In science there was an element of poetry, pervasive, inevitable, and variable: it was strictly scientific and true only in so far as it involved a close and prosperous adjustment to the surrounding world, at first by its origin in observation and at last by its application in action. Science was the mental accompaniment of art.

Here was a sort of pragmatism: the same which I have again expressed, I hope more clearly, in one of the *Dialogues in Limbo* entitled "Normal Madness." The human mind is a faculty of dreaming awake, and its dreams are kept relevant to its environment and to its fate only by the external control exercised over them by Punishment, when the accompanying

conduct brings ruin, or by Agreement, when it brings prosperity. In the latter case it is possible to establish correspond-
ences between one part of a dream and another, or between
the dreams of separate minds, and so create the world of literature, or the life of reason. I am not sure whether this notion, that thought is a controlled and consistent madness, appears among the thirteen pragmatisms which have been distinguished, but I have reason to think that I came to it under
the influence of William James; nevertheless, when his book
on *Pragmatism* appeared about the same time as my *Life of
Reason*, it gave me a rude shock. I could not stomach that
way of speaking about truth; and the continual substitution
of human psychology—normal madness, in my view—for the
universe, in which man is but one distracted and befuddled
animal, seemed to me a confused remnant of idealism, and
not serious.

The William James who had been my master was not this
William James of the later years, whose pragmatism and
pure empiricism and romantic metaphysics have made such a
stir in the world. It was rather the puzzled but brilliant
doctor, impatient of metaphysics, whom I had known in my
undergraduate days, one of whose maxims was that to study
the abnormal was the best way of understanding the normal;
or it was the genial author of *The Principles of Psychology*,
chapters of which he read from the manuscript and discussed
with a small class of us in 1889. Even then what I learned
from him was perhaps chiefly things which explicitly he
never taught, but which I imbibed from the spirit and background of his teaching. Chief of these, I should say, was a
sense of the immediate: for the unadulterated, unexplained,
instant fact of experience. Actual experience, for William
James, however varied or rich its assault might be, was always and altogether of the nature of a sensation: it possessed a vital, leaping, globular unity which made the only
fact, the flying fact, of our being. Whatever continuities of
quality might be traced in it, its existence was always mo-

mentary and self-warranted. A man's life or soul borrowed its reality and imputed wholeness from the intrinsic actuality of its successive parts; existence was a perpetual re-birth, a travelling light to which the past was lost and the future uncertain. The element of indetermination which James felt so strongly in this flood of existence was precisely the pulse of fresh unpredictable sensation, summoning attention hither and thither to unexpected facts. Apprehension in him being impressionistic—that was the age of impressionism in paint-ing too—and marvellously free from intellectual assumptions or presumptions, he felt intensely the fact of contingency, or the contingency of fact. This seemed to me not merely a pe-culiarity of temperament in him, but a profound insight into existence, in its inmost irrational essence. Existence, I learned to see, is intrinsically dispersed, seated in its distributed mo-ments, and arbitrary not only as a whole, but in the charac-ter and place of each of its parts. Change the bits, and you change the mosaic: nor can we count nor limit the elements, as in a little closed kaleidoscope, which may be shaken together into the next picture. Many of them, such as pleas-ure and pain, or the total picture itself, cannot possibly have pre-existed.

But, said I to myself, were these novelties for that reason unconditioned? Was not sensation, by continually surprising us, a continual warning to us of fatal conjunctions occurring outside? And would not the same conjunctions, but for mem-ory and habit, always produce the same surprises? Experi-ence of indetermination was no proof of indeterminism; and when James proceeded to turn immediate experience into ultimate physics, his thought seemed to me to lose itself in words or in confused superstitions. Free will, a deep moral power contrary to a romantic indetermination in being, he endeavoured to pack into the bias of attention—the most temperamental of accidents. He insisted passionately on the efficacy of consciousness, and invoked Darwinian arguments for its utility—arguments which assumed that consciousness was a material engine absorbing and transmitting energy: so that it was no wonder that presently he doubted whether consciousness existed at all. He suggested a new physics or metaphysics in which the essences given in immediate experience should be deployed and hypostatised into the constituents of nature: but this pictorial cosmology had the disadvantage of abolishing the human imagination, with all the pathos and poetry of its animal status. James thus renounced that gift for literary psychology, that romantic insight, in which alone he excelled; and indeed his followers are without it. I pride myself on remaining a disciple of his earlier unsophisticated self, when he was an agnostic about the universe, but in his diagnosis of the heart an impulsive poet: a master in the art of recording or divining the lyric quality of experience as it actually came to him or to me.

Lyric experience and literary psychology, as I have learned to conceive them, are chapters in the life of one race of animals, in one corner of the natural world. But before relegating them to that modest station (which takes nothing away from their spiritual prerogatives) I was compelled to face the terrible problem which arises when, as in modern philosophy, literary psychology and lyric experience are made the fulcrum or the stuff of the universe. Has this experience any external conditions? If it has, are they knowable? And if it has not, on what principle are its qualities generated or its episodes distributed? Nay, how can literary psychology or universal experience have any seat save the present fancy of the psychologist or the historian? Although James had been bothered and confused by these questions, and Royce had enthroned his philosophy upon them, neither of these my principal teachers seemed to have come to clearness on the subject: it was only afterwards, when I read Fichte and Schopenhauer, that I began to see my way to a solution. We must oscillate between a radical transcendentalism, frankly reduced to a solipsism of the living moment, and a materialism posited as a presupposition of conventional sanity. There was no contradiction in joining together a scepticism which was not a dogmatic negation of anything and an animal faith which avowedly was a mere assumption in action and description. Yet such oscillation, if it was to be justified and rendered coherent, still demanded some understanding of two further points: what, starting from immediate experience, was the *causa cognoscendi* of the natural world; and what, starting from the natural world, was the *causa fiendi* of immediate experience?

On this second point (in spite of the speculations of my friend Strong) I have not seen much new light. I am constrained merely to register as a brute fact the emergence of consciousness in animal bodies. A psyche, or nucleus of hereditary organisation, gathers and governs these bodies, and at the same time breeds within them a dreaming, suffering, and watching mind. Such investigations as those of Fraser and of Freud have shown how rich and how mad a thing the mind is fundamentally, how pervasively it plays about animal life, and how remote its first and deepest intuitions are from any understanding of their true occasions. An interesting and consistent complement to these discoveries is furnished by behaviourism, which I heartily accept on its positive biological side: the hereditary life of the body, modified by accident or training, forms a closed cycle of habits and actions. Of this the mind is a concomitant spiritual expression, invisible, imponderable, and epiphenomenal, or, as I prefer to say, hypostatic: for in it the moving unities and tensions of animal life are synthesised on quite another plane of being, into actual intuitions and feelings. This spiritual fertility in living bodies is the most natural of things. It is unintelligible only as all existence, change, or genesis is unintelligible; but it might be better understood, that is, better assimilated to other natural miracles, if we understood better the life of matter everywhere, and that of its different aggregates.

On the other point raised by my naturalism, namely on

the grounds of faith in the natural world, I have reached more positive conclusions. Criticism, I think, must first be invited to do its worst: nothing is more dangerous here than timidity or convention. A pure and radical transcendentalism will disclaim all knowledge of fact. Nature, history, the self become ghostly presences, mere notions of such things; and the being of these images becomes purely internal to them; they exist in no environing space or time; they possess no substance or hidden parts, but are all surface, all appearance. Such a being, or quality of being, I call an essence; and to the consideration of essences, composing of themselves an eternal and infinite realm, I have lately devoted much attention. To that sphere I transpose the familiar pictures painted by the senses, or by traditional science and religion. Taken as essences, all ideas are compatible and supplementary to one another, like the various arts of expression; it is possible to perceive, up to a certain point, the symbolic burden of each of them, and to profit by the spiritual criticism of experience which it may embody. In particular, I recognise this spiritual truth in the Neo-Platonic and Indian systems, without admitting their fabulous side: after all, it is an old maxim with me that many ideas may be convergent as poetry which would be divergent as dogmas. This applies, in quite another quarter, to that revolution in physics which is now loudly announced, sometimes as the bankruptcy of science, sometimes as the breakdown of materialism. This revolution becomes, in my view, simply a change in notation. Matter may be called gravity or an electric charge or a tension in an ether; mathematics may readjust its equations to more accurate observations; any fresh description of nature which may result will still be a product of human wit, like the Ptolemaic and the Newtonian systems, and nothing but an intellectual symbol for man's contacts with matter, in so far as they have gone or as he has become distinctly sensitive to them. The real matter, within him and without, will meantime continue to rejoice in its ancient ways, or to adopt new ones, and incidentally to create these successive notions of it in his head.

When all the data of immediate experience and all the constructions of thought have thus been purified and reduced to what they are intrinsically, that is, to eternal essences, by a sort of counterblast the sense of existence, of action, of ambushed reality everywhere about us, becomes all the clearer and more imperious. This assurance of the not-given is involved in action, in expectation, in fear, hope, or want: I call it animal faith. The object of this faith is the substantial energetic thing encountered in action, whatever this thing may be in itself; by moving, devouring, or transforming this thing I assure myself of its existence; and at the same time my respect for it becomes enlightened and proportionate to its definite powers. But throughout, for the description of it in fancy, I have only the essences which my senses or thought may evoke in its presence; these are my inevitable signs and names for that object. Thus the whole sensuous and intellectual furniture of the mind becomes a store whence I may fetch terms for the description of nature, and may compose the silly home-poetry in which I talk to myself about everything. All is a tale told, if not by an idiot, at least by a dreamer; but it is far from signifying nothing. Sensations are rapid dreams: perceptions are dreams sustained and developed at will; sciences are dreams abstracted, controlled, measured, and rendered scrupulously proportional to their occasions. Knowledge accordingly always remains a part of imagination in its terms and in its seat; yet by virtue of its origin and intent it becomes a memorial and a guide to the fortunes of man in nature.

In the foregoing I have said nothing about my sentiments concerning æsthetics or the fine arts; yet I have devoted two volumes to those subjects, and I believe that to some people my whole philosophy seems to be little but rhetoric or prose poetry. I must frankly confess that I have written some verses; and at one time I had thoughts of becoming an archi-

tect or even a painter. The decorative and poetic aspects of
art and nature have always fascinated me and held my attention above everything else. But in philosophy I recognise
no separable thing called æsthetics; and what has gone by
the name of the philosophy of art, like the so-called philosophy of history, seems to me sheer verbiage. There is in art
nothing but manual knack and professional tradition on the
practical side, and on the contemplative side pure intuition
of essence, with the inevitable intellectual or luxurious pleasure which pure intuition involves. I can draw no distinction—
save for academic programmes—between moral and æsthetic
values: beauty, being a good, is a moral good; and the practice and enjoyment of art, like all practice and all enjoyment,
fall within the sphere of morals—at least if by morals we
understand moral economy and not moral superstition. On
the other hand, the good, when actually realised and not
merely pursued from afar, is a joy in the immediate; it is
possessed with wonder and is in that sense æsthetic. Such
pure joy when blind is called pleasure, when centred in some
sensible image is called beauty, and when diffused over the
thought of ulterior propitious things is called happiness, love,
or religious rapture. But where all is manifest, as it is in intuition, classifications are pedantic. Harmony, which might
be called an æsthetic principle, is also the principle of health,
of justice, and of happiness. Every impulse, not the æsthetic
mood alone, is innocent and irresponsible in its origin and
precious in its own eyes; but every impulse or indulgence,
including the æsthetic, is evil in its effect, when it renders
harmony impossible in the general tenor of life, or produces
in the soul division and ruin. There is no lack of folly in the
arts; they are full of inertia and affectation and of what
must seem ugliness to a cultivated taste; yet there is no need
of bringing the catapult of criticism against it: indifference
is enough. A society will breed the art which it is capable of,
and which it deserves; but even in its own eyes this art will
hardly be important or beautiful unless it engages deeply the

resources of the soul. The arts may die of triviality, as they were born of enthusiasm. On the other hand, there will always be beauty, or a transport akin to the sense of beauty, in any high contemplative moment. And it is only in contemplative moments that life is truly vital, when routine gives place to intuition, and experience is synthesised and brought before the spirit in its sweep and truth. The intention of my philosophy has certainly been to attain, if possible, such wide intuitions, and to celebrate the emotions with which they fill the mind. If this object be æsthetic and merely poetical, well and good: but it is a poetry or æstheticism which shines by disillusion and is simply intent on the unvarnished truth.

POEMS

III

O WORLD, thou choosest not the better part!
It is not wisdom to be only wise,
And on the inward vision close the eyes,
But it is wisdom to believe the heart.
Columbus found a world, and had no chart,
Save one that faith deciphered in the skies;
To trust the soul's invincible surmise
Was all his science and his only art.
Our knowledge is a torch of smoky pine
That lights the pathway but one step ahead
Across a void of mystery and dread.
Bid, then, the tender light of faith to shine
By which alone the mortal heart is led
Unto the thinking of the thought divine.

IV

I WOULD I had been born in nature's day,
When man was in the world a wide-eyed boy,
And clouds of sorrow crossed his sky of joy
To scatter dewdrops on the buds of May.
Then could he work and love and fight and pray,
Nor heartsick grow in fortune's long employ.
Mighty to build and ruthless to destroy
He lived, while maskèd death unquestioned lay.
Now ponder we the ruins of the years,
And groan beneath the weight of boasted gain;
No unsung bacchanal can charm our ears

And lead our dances to the woodland fane,
No hope of heaven sweeten our few tears
And hush the importunity of pain.

VI

LOVE not as do the flesh-imprisoned men
Whose dreams are of a bitter bought caress,
Or even of a maiden's tenderness
Whom they love only that she loves again.
For it is but thyself thou lovest then,
Or what thy thoughts would glory to possess;
But love thou nothing thou wouldst love the less
If henceforth ever hidden from thy ken.
Love but the formless and eternal Whole
From whose effulgence one unheeded ray
Breaks on this prism of dissolving clay
Into the flickering colours of thy soul.
These flash and vanish; bid them not to stay,
For wisdom brightens as they fade away.

VII

I WOULD I might forget that I am I,
And break the heavy chain that binds me fast,
Whose links about myself my deeds have cast.
What in the body's tomb doth buried lie
Is boundless; 'tis the spirit of the sky,
Lord of the future, guardian of the past,
And soon must forth, to know his own at last.
In his large life to live, I fain would die.
Happy the dumb beast, hungering for food,
But calling not his suffering his own;
Blessèd the angel, gazing on all good,
But knowing not he sits upon a throne;
Wretched the mortal, pondering his mood,
And doomed to know his aching heart alone.

XI

DEEM not, because you see me in the press
Of this world's children run my fated race,
That I blaspheme against a proffered grace,
Or leave unlearned the love of holiness.
I honour not that sanctity the less
Whose aureole illumines not my face,
But dare not tread the secret, holy place
To which the priest and prophet have access.
For some are born to be beatified
By anguish, and by grievous penance done;
And some, to furnish forth the age's pride,
And to be praised of men beneath the sun;
And some are born to stand perplexed aside
From so much sorrow—of whom I am one.

XIII

SWEET are the days we wander with no hope
Along life's labyrinthine trodden way,
With no impatience at the steep's delay,
Nor sorrow at the swift-descended slope.
Why this inane curiosity to grope
In the dim dust for gems' unmeaning ray?
Why this proud piety, that dares to pray
For a world wider than the heaven's cope?
Farewell, my burden! No more will I bear
The foolish load of my fond faith's despair,
But trip the idle race with careless feet.
The crown of olive let another wear;
It is my crown to mock the runner's heat
With gentle wonder and with laughter sweet.

XXII

'TIS love that moveth the celestial spheres
In endless yearning for the Changeless One,

And the stars sing together, as they run
To number the innumerable years.
'Tis love that lifteth through their dewy tears
The roses' beauty to the heedless sun,
And with no hope, nor any guerdon won,
Love leads me on, nor end of love appears.
For the same breath that did awake the flowers,
Making them happy with a joy unknown,
Kindled my light and fixed my spirit's goal;
And the same hand that reined the flying hours
And chained the whirling earth to Phœbus' throne,
In love's eternal orbit keeps the soul.

XXV

As in the midst of battle there is room
For thoughts of love, and in foul sin for mirth;
As gossips whisper of a trinket's worth
Spied by the death-bed's flickering candle-gloom;
As in the crevices of Cæsar's tomb
The sweet herbs flourish on a little earth:
So in this great disaster of our birth
We can be happy, and forget our doom.
For morning, with a ray of tenderest joy
Gliding the iron heaven, hides the truth,
And evening gently woos us to employ
Our grief in idle catches. Such is youth;
Till from that summer's trance we wake, to find
Despair before us, vanity behind.

XLIX

After grey vigils, sunshine in the heart;
After long fasting on the journey, food;
After sharp thirst, a draught of perfect good
To flood the soul, and heal her ancient smart.
Joy of my sorrow, never can we part;

Thou broodest o'er me in the haunted wood,
And with new music fill'st the solitude
By but so sweetly being what thou art.
He who hath made thee perfect, makes me blest.
O fiery minister, on mighty wings
Bear me, great love, to mine eternal rest.
Heaven it is to be at peace with things;
Come chaos now, and in a whirlwind's rings
Engulf the planets. I have seen the best.

ON A VOLUME OF SCHOLASTIC PHILOSOPHY

WHAT chilly cloister or what lattice dim
Cast painted light upon this careful page?
What thought compulsive held the patient sage
Till sound of matin bell or evening hymn?
Did visions of the Heavenly Lover swim
Before his eyes in youth, or did stern rage
Against rash heresy keep green his age?
Had he seen God, to write so much of Him?
Gone is that irrecoverable mind
With all its phantoms, senseless to mankind
As a dream's trouble or the speech of birds.
The breath that stirred his lips he soon resigned
To windy chaos, and we only find
The garnered husks of his disusèd words.

ON THE DEATH OF A METAPHYSICIAN

UNHAPPY dreamer, who outwinged in flight
The pleasant region of the things I love,
And soared beyond the sunshine, and above
The golden cornfields and the dear and bright
Warmth of the hearth,—blasphemer of delight,

Was your proud bosom not at peace with Jove,
That you sought, thankless for his guarded grove,
The empty horror of abysmal night?
Ah, the thin air is cold above the moon!
I stood and saw you fall, befooled in death,
As, in your numbèd spirit's fatal swoon,
You cried you were a god, or were to be;
I heard with feeble moan your boastful breath
Bubble from depths of the Icarian sea.

TO W. P.

II

WITH you a part of me hath passed away;
For in the peopled forest of my mind
A tree made leafless by this wintry wind
Shall never don again its green array.
Chapel and fireside, country road and bay
Have something of their friendliness resigned;
Another, if I would, I could not find,
And I am grown much older in a day.
But yet I treasure in my memory
Your gift of charity, and young heart's ease,
And the dear honour of your amity;
For these once mine, my life is rich with these.
And I scarce know which part may greater be,—
What I keep of you, or you rob from me.

THE SENSE OF BEAUTY

INTRODUCTION

The Materials of Beauty

THE sense of beauty has a more important place in life than æsthetic theory has ever taken in philosophy. The plastic arts, with poetry and music, are the most conspicuous monuments of this human interest, because they appeal only to contemplation, and yet have attracted to their service, in all civilised ages, an amount of effort, genius, and honour, little inferior to that given to industry, war, or religion. The fine arts, however, where æsthetic feeling appears almost pure, are by no means the only sphere in which men show their susceptibility to beauty. In all products of human industry we notice the keenness with which the eye is attracted to the mere appearance of things: great sacrifices of time and labour are made to it in the most vulgar manufactures; nor does man select his dwelling, his clothes, or his companions without reference to their effect on his æsthetic senses. Of late we have even learned that the forms of many animals are due to the survival by sexual selection to the colours and forms most attractive to the eye. There must therefore be in our nature a very radical and wide-spread tendency to observe beauty, and to value it. No account of the principles of the mind can be at all adequate that passes over so conspicuous a faculty.

That æsthetic theory has received so little attention from the world is not due to the unimportance of the subject of

28

which it treats, but rather to lack of an adequate motive for speculating upon it, and to the small success of the occasional efforts to deal with it. Absolute curiosity, and love of comprehension for its own sake, are not passions we have much leisure to indulge: they require not only freedom from affairs but, what is more rare, freedom from prepossessions and from the hatred of all ideas that do not make for the habitual goal of our thought.

Now, what has chiefly maintained such speculation as the world has seen has been either theological passion or practical use. All we find, for example, written about beauty may be divided into two groups: that group of writings in which philosophers have interpreted æsthetic facts in the light of their metaphysical principles, and made of their theory of taste a corollary or footnote to their systems; and that group in which artists and critics have ventured into philosophic ground, by generalising somewhat the maxims of the craft or the comments of the sensitive observer. A treatment of the subject at once direct and theoretic has been very rare: the problems of nature and morals have attracted the reasoners, and the description and creation of beauty have absorbed the artists; between the two reflection upon æsthetic experience has remained abortive or incoherent.

A circumstance that has also contributed to the absence or to the failure of æsthetic speculation is the subjectivity of the phenomenon with which it deals. Man has a prejudice against himself: anything which is a product of his mind seems to him to be unreal or comparatively insignificant. We are satisfied only when we fancy ourselves surrounded by objects and laws independent of our nature. The ancients long speculated about the constitution of the universe before they became aware of that mind which is the instrument of all speculation. The moderns, also, even within the field of psychology, have studied first the functions of perception and the theory of knowledge, by which we seem to be informed about external things; they have in comparison neglected the exclusively subjective and human department of imagination and emotion. We have still to recognise in practice the truth that from these despised feelings of ours the great world of perception derives all its value, if not also its existence. Things are interesting because we care about them, and important because we need them. Had our perceptions no connection with our pleasures, we should soon close our eyes on this world; if our intelligence were of no service to our passions, we should come to doubt, in the lazy freedom of reverie, whether two and two make four.

Yet so strong is the popular sense of the unworthiness and insignificance of things purely emotional, that those who have taken moral problems to heart and felt their dignity have often been led into attempts to discover some external right and beauty of which our moral and æsthetic feelings should be perceptions or discoveries, just as our intellectual activity is, in men's opinion, a perception or discovery of external fact. These philosophers seem to feel that unless moral and æsthetic judgments are expressions of objective truth, and not merely expressions of human nature, they stand condemned of hopeless triviality. A judgment is not trivial, however, because it rests on human feelings; on the contrary, triviality consists in abstraction from human interests; only those judgments and opinions are truly insignificant which wander beyond the reach of verification, and have no function in the ordering and enriching of life.

Both ethics and æsthetics have suffered much from the prejudice against the subjective. They have not suffered more because both have a subject-matter which is partly objective. Ethics deals with conduct as much as with emotion, and therefore considers the causes of events and their consequences as well as our judgments of their value. Æsthetics also is apt to include the history and philosophy of art, and to add much descriptive and critical matter to the theory of our susceptibility to beauty. A certain confusion is thereby introduced into these inquiries, but at the same time the discussion is enlivened by excursions into neighbouring provinces, perhaps more interesting to the general reader.

We may, however, distinguish three distinct elements of ethics and æsthetics, and three different ways of approaching the subject. The first is the exercise of the moral or æsthetic faculty itself, the actual pronouncing of judgment and giving of praise, blame, and precept. This is not a matter of science but of character, enthusiasm, niceness of perception, and fineness of emotion. It is æsthetic or moral activity, while ethics and æsthetics, as sciences, are intellectual activities, having that æsthetic or moral activity for their subject-matter.

The second method consists in the historical explanation of conduct or of art as a part of anthropology, and seeks to discover the conditions of various types of character, forms of polity, conceptions of justice, and schools of criticism and of art. Of this nature is a great deal of what has been written on æsthetics. The philosophy of art has often proved a more tempting subject than the psychology of taste, especially to minds which were not so much fascinated by beauty itself as by the curious problem of the artistic instinct in man and of the diversity of its manifestations in history.

The third method in ethics and æsthetics is psychological, as the other two are respectively didactic and historical. It deals with moral and æsthetic judgments as phenomena of mind and products of mental evolution. The problem here is to understand the origin and conditions of these feelings and their relation to the rest of our economy. Such an inquiry, if pursued successfully, would yield an understanding of the reason why we think anything right or beautiful, wrong or ugly; it would thus reveal the roots of conscience and taste in human nature and enable us to distinguish transitory preferences and ideals, which rest on peculiar conditions, from those which, springing from those elements of mind which all men share, are comparatively permanent and universal.

To this inquiry, as far as it concerns æsthetics, the following pages are devoted. No attempt will be made either to impose particular appreciations or to trace the history of art and criticism. The discussion will be limited to the nature and elements of our æsthetic judgments. It is a theoretical inquiry and has no directly hortatory quality. Yet insight into the basis of our preferences, if it could be gained, would not fail to have a good and purifying influence upon them. It would show us the futility of a dogmatism that would impose upon another man judgments and emotions for which the needed soil is lacking in his constitution and experience; and at the same time it would relieve us of any undue diffidence or excessive tolerance towards aberrations of taste, when we know what are the broader grounds of preference and the habits that make for greater and more diversified æsthetic enjoyment.

Therefore, although nothing has commonly been less attractive than treatises on beauty or less a guide to taste than disquisitions upon it, we may yet hope for some not merely theoretical gain from these studies. They have remained so often without practical influence because they have been pursued under unfavourable conditions. The writers have generally been audacious metaphysicians and somewhat incompetent critics; they have represented general and obscure principles, suggested by other parts of their philosophy, as the conditions of artistic excellence and the essence of beauty. But if the inquiry is kept close to the facts of feeling, we may hope that the resulting theory may have a clarifying effect on the experience on which it is based. That is, after all, the use of theory. If when a theory is bad it narrows our capacity for observation and makes all appreciation vicarious and formal, when it is good it reacts favourably upon our powers, guides the attention to what is really capable of affording entertainment, and increases, by force of new analogies, the range of our interests. Speculation is an evil if it imposes a foreign organisation on our mental life; it is a good if it only brings to light, and makes more perfect by training, the organisation already inherent in it.

We shall therefore study human sensibility itself and our actual feelings about beauty, and we shall look for no deeper, unconscious causes of our æsthetic consciousness. Such value as belongs to metaphysical derivations of the nature of the beautiful comes to them not because they explain our primary feelings, which they cannot do, but because they express, and in fact constitute, some of our later appreciations. There is no explanation, for instance, in calling beauty an adumbration of divine attributes. Such a relation, if it were actual, would not help us at all to understand why the symbols of divinity pleased. But in certain moments of contemplation, when much emotional experience lies behind us, and we have reached very general ideas both of nature and of life, our delight in any particular object may consist in nothing but the thought that this object is a manifestation of universal principles. The blue sky may come to please chiefly because it seems the image of a serene conscience, or of the eternal youth and purity of nature after a thousand partial corruptions. But this expressiveness of the sky is due to certain qualities of the sensation, which bind it to all things happy and pure, and, in a mind in which the essence of purity and happiness is embodied in an idea of God, bind it also to that idea.

So it may happen that the most arbitrary and unreal theories, which must be rejected as general explanations of æsthetic life, may be reinstated as particular moments of it. Those intuitions which we call Platonic are seldom scientific, they seldom explain the phenomena or hit upon the actual law of things, but they are often the highest expression of that activity which they fail to make comprehensible. The adoring lover cannot understand the natural history of love; for he is all in all at the last and supreme stage of its development. Hence the world has always been puzzled in its judgment of the Platonists; their theories are so extravagant, yet their wisdom seems so great. Platonism is a very refined and beautiful expression of our natural instincts; it embodies conscience and utters our inmost hopes. Platonic philosophers have therefore a natural authority, as standing on heights to which the vulgar cannot attain, but to which they naturally and half-consciously aspire.

When a man tells you that beauty is the manifestation of God to the senses, you wish you might understand him, you grope for a deep truth in his obscurity, you honour him for his elevation of mind, and your respect may even induce you to assent to what he says as to an intelligible proposition. Your thought may in consequence be dominated ever after by a verbal dogma, around which all your sympathies and antipathies will quickly gather, and the less you have penetrated the original sense of your creed, the more absolutely will you believe it. You will have followed Mephistopheles' advice:—

> Im ganzen haltet euch an Worte,
> So geht ihr durch die sichere Pforte
> Zum Tempel der Gewissheit ein.

Yet reflection might have shown you that the word of the master held no objective account of the nature and origin of beauty, but was the vague expression of his highly complex emotions.

It is one of the attributes of God, one of the perfections which we contemplate in our idea of him, that there is no duality or opposition between his will and his vision, between the impulses of his nature and the events of his life. This is what we commonly designate as omnipotence and creation. Now, in the contemplation of beauty, our faculties of perception have the same perfection: it is indeed from the experience of beauty and happiness, from the occasional harmony between our nature and our environment, that we draw our conception of the divine life. There is, then, a real propriety in calling beauty a manifestation of God to the senses, since, in the region of sense, the perception of beauty exemplifies that adequacy and perfection which in general we objectify in an idea of God.

But the minds that dwell in the atmosphere of these analogies are hardly those that will care to ask what are the conditions and the varieties of this perfection of function, in other words, how it comes about that we perceive beauty at all, or have any inkling of divinity. Only the other philosophers, those that wallow in Epicurus' sty, know anything about the latter question. But it is easier to be impressed than to be instructed, and the public is very ready to believe that where there is noble language not without obscurity there must be profound knowledge. We should distinguish, however, the two distinct demands in the case. One is for comprehension; we look for the theory of a human function which must cover all possible cases of its exercise, whether noble or base. This the Platonists utterly fail to give us. The other demand is for inspiration; we wish to be nourished by the maxims and confessions of an exalted mind, in whom the æsthetic function is pre-eminent. By responding to this demand the same thinkers may win our admiration.

To feel beauty is a better thing than to understand how we come to feel it. To have imagination and taste, to love the best, to be carried by the contemplation of nature to a vivid faith in the ideal, all this is more, a great deal more, than any science can hope to be. The poets and philosophers who express this æsthetic experience and stimulate the same function in us by their example, do a greater service to mankind and deserve higher honour than the discoverers of historical truth. Reflection is indeed a part of life, but the last part. Its specific value consists in the satisfaction of curiosity, in the smoothing out and explanation of things: but the greatest pleasure which we actually get from reflection is borrowed from the experience on which we reflect. We do not often indulge in retrospect for the sake of a scientific knowledge of human life, but rather to revive the memories of what once was dear. And I should have little hope of interesting the reader in the present analysis, did I not rely on the attractions of a subject associated with so many of his pleasures.

But the recognition of the superiority of æsthetics in experience to æsthetics in theory ought not to make us accept as an explanation of æsthetic feeling what is in truth only an expression of it. When Plato tells us of the eternal ideas in conformity to which all excellence consists, he is making himself the spokesman of the moral consciousness. Our conscience and taste established these ideals; to make a judgment is virtually to establish an ideal, and all ideals are absolute and eternal for the judgment that involves them, because in finding and declaring a thing good or beautiful, our sentence is categorical, and the standard evoked by our judgment is for that case intrinsic and ultimate. But at the next moment, when the mind is on another footing, a new ideal is evoked, no less absolute for the present judgment than the old ideal was for the previous one. If we are then expressing our feeling and confessing what happens to us when we judge, we shall be quite right in saying that we have always an absolute ideal before us, and that value lies in conformity with that ideal. So, also, if we try to define that ideal, we shall hardly be able to say of it anything less noble and more definite than that it is the embodiment of an infinite good. For it is that incommunicable and illusive excellence that haunts every beautiful thing, and

like a star
Beacons from the abode where the eternal are.

For the expression of this experience we should go to the poets, to the more inspired critics, and best of all to the immortal parables of Plato. But if what we desire is to increase our knowledge rather than to cultivate our sensibility, we should do well to close all those delightful books; for we shall not find any instruction there upon the questions which most press upon us; namely, how an ideal is formed in the mind, how a given object is compared with it, what is the common element in all beautiful things, and what the substance of the absolute ideal in which all ideals tend to be lost; and, finally, how we come to be sensitive to beauty at all, or to value it. These questions must be capable of answers, if any science of human nature is really possible.—So far, then, are we from ignoring the insight of the Platonists, that we hope to explain it, and in a sense to justify it, by showing that it is the natural and sometimes the supreme expression of the common principles of our nature.

PART II

The Materials of Beauty

WE have now gone over those organs of perception that give us the materials out of which we construct objects, and mentioned the most conspicuous pleasures which, as they arise from those organs, are easily merged in the ideas furnished by the same. We have also noticed that these ideas, conspicuous as they are in our developed and operating consciousness, are not so much factors in our thought, independent contributors to it, as they are discriminations and excisions in its content, which, after they are all made, leave still a background of vital feeling. For the outer senses are but a portion of our sensorium, and the ideas of each, or of all together, but a portion of our consciousness.

The pleasures which accompany ideation we have also found to be unitary and vital; only just as for practical purposes it is necessary to abstract and discriminate the contribution of one sense from that of another, and thus to become aware of particular and definable impressions, so it is natural that the diffused emotional tone of the body should also be divided, and a certain modicum of pleasure or pain should be attributed to each idea. Our pleasures are thus described as the pleasures of touch, taste, smell, hearing, and sight, and may become elements of beauty at the same time as the ideas to which they are attached become elements of objects. There is, however, a remainder of emotion as there is a remainder of sensation; and the importance of this remainder—of the continuum in which lie all particular pleasures and pains— was insisted upon in the beginning.

The beauty of the world, indeed, cannot be attributed wholly or mainly to pleasures thus attached to abstracted sensations. It is only the beauty of the materials of things which is drawn from the pleasures of sensation. By far the most important effects are not attributable to these materials, but to their arrangement and their ideal relations. We have yet to study those processes of our mind by which this arrangement and these relations are conceived; and the pleasures which we can attach to these processes may then be added to the pleasures attached to sense as further and more subtle elements of beauty.

But before passing to the consideration of this more intricate subject, we may note that however subordinate the beauty may be which a garment, a building, or a poem derives from its sensuous material, yet the presence of this sensuous material is indispensable. Form cannot be the form of nothing. If, then, in finding or creating beauty, we ignore the materials of things, and attend only to their form, we miss an ever-present opportunity to heighten our effects. For whatever delight the form may bring, the material might have given delight already, and so much would have been gained towards the value of the total result.

Sensuous beauty is not the greatest or most important element of effect, but it is the most primitive and fundamental, and the most universal. There is no effect of form which an

effect of material could not enhance, and this effect of material, underlying that of form, raises the latter to a higher
power and gives the beauty of the object a certain poignancy,
thoroughness, and infinity which it otherwise would have
lacked. The Parthenon not in marble, the king's crown not
of gold, and the stars not of fire, would be feeble and prosaic
things. The greater hold which material beauty has upon the
senses stimulates us here, where the form is also sublime,
and lifts and intensifies our emotions. We need this stimulus
if our perceptions are to reach the highest pitch of strength
and acuteness. Nothing can be ravishing that is not beautiful
pervasively.

And another point. The wider diffusion of sensuous beauty
makes it as it were the poor man's good. Fewer factors are
needed to produce it and less training to appreciate it. The
senses are indispensable instruments of labour, developed by
the necessities of life; but their perfect development produces
a harmony between the inward structure and instinct of the
organ and the outward opportunities for its use; and this harmony is the source of continual pleasures. In the sphere of
sense, therefore, a certain cultivation is inevitable in man;
often greater, indeed, among rude peoples, perhaps among
animals, than among those whose attention takes a wider
sweep and whose ideas are more abstract. Without requiring,
therefore, that a man should rise above his station, or develop capacities which his opportunities will seldom employ,
we may yet endow his life with æsthetic interest, if we allow
him the enjoyment of sensuous beauty. This enriches him
without adding to his labour, and flatters him without alienating him from his world.

Taste, when it is spontaneous, always begins with the
senses. Children and savages, as we are so often told, delight
in bright and variegated colours; the simplest people appreciate the neatness of muslin curtains, shining varnish, and
burnished pots. A rustic garden is a shallow patchwork of the
liveliest flowers, without that reserve and repose which is

given by spaces and masses. Noise and vivacity is all that childish music contains, and primitive songs add little more of form than what is required to compose a few monotonous cadences. These limitations are not to be regretted; they are a proof of sincerity. Such simplicity is not the absence of taste, but the beginning of it.

A people with genuine æsthetic perceptions creates traditional forms and expresses the simple pathos of its life, in unchanging but significant themes, repeated by generation after generation. When sincerity is lost, and a snobbish ambition is substituted, bad taste comes in. The essence of it is a substitution of non-æsthetic for æsthetic values. To love glass beads because they are beautiful is barbarous, perhaps, but not vulgar; to love jewels only because they are dear is vulgar, and to betray the motive by placing them ineffectively is an offence against taste. The test is always the same: Does the thing itself actually please? If it does, your taste is real; it may be different from that of others, but is equally justified and grounded in human nature. If it does not, your whole judgment is spurious, and you are guilty, not of heresy, which in æsthetics is orthodoxy itself, but of hypocrisy, which is a self-excommunication from its sphere.

Now, a great sign of this hypocrisy is insensibility to sensuous beauty. When people show themselves indifferent to primary and fundamental effects, when they are incapable of finding pictures except in frames or beauties except in the great masters, we may justly suspect that they are parrots, and that their verbal and historical knowledge covers a natural lack of æsthetic sense. Where, on the contrary, insensibility to higher forms of beauty does not exclude a natural love of the lower, we have every reason to be encouraged; there is a true and healthy taste, which only needs experience to refine it. If a man demands light, sound, and splendour, he proves that he has the æsthetic equilibrium; that appearances as such interest him, and that he can pause in perception to enjoy. We have but to vary his observation, to enlarge his thought, to multiply his discriminations—all of which education can do—and the same æsthetic habit will reveal to him every shade of the fit and fair. Or if it should not, and the man, although sensuously gifted, proved to be imaginatively dull, at least he would not have failed to catch an intimate and wide-spread element of effect. The beauty of material is thus the groundwork of all higher beauty, both in the object, whose form and meaning have to be lodged in something sensible, and in the mind, where sensuous ideas, being the first to emerge, are the first that can arouse delight.

REASON IN COMMON SENSE

PREFACE TO THE SECOND EDITION OF THE LIFE OF REASON

TWENTY years separate me from the man I was when I wrote this book—years enlivened for me by many changes of scene and branded by a great war. There is hardly a page that would not need to be rewritten, if it was perfectly to express my present feelings.

> *Mais quand l'homme change sans cesse,*
> *au passé pourquoi rien changer?*

Some readers would perhaps prefer the original to my revised version, and if I lived another twenty years I might myself prefer it. The written letter, then, may as well stand; especially as nothing hinders me from setting forth my matured views in fresh works, leaving it for others to decide whether I have changed for the better. After all, there has been no change in my deliberate doctrine; only some changes of mental habit. I now dwell by preference on other perspectives, in which the same objects appear with their relative bulks reversed, and inversely hiding one another; what lay before in the background—nature—has come forward, and the life of reason, which then held the centre of the stage, has receded. The vicissitudes of human belief absorb me less; the life of reason has become in my eyes a decidedly episodical thing, polyglot, interrupted, insecure. I cannot take every phase of art or religion or philosophy seriously, simply because it takes itself so. These things seem to me less tragic than they did, and more comic; and I am less eager to choose and to judge among them, as if only one form could be right. When our architecture is too pretentious, before we have set the cross on the spire, the foundations are apt to give way.

I am consequently far less inclined to take a transcendental point of view, as if the spirit at every point were absolute, and its objects its creations. Spirit is absolute enough, so to speak, relatively, and in its own eyes, since willy-nilly it must soliloquise; but any puppet in the hands of a ventriloquist seems to soliloquise, if we have no notion whence its voice comes. The self that speaks in us is deeper than we suppose, and less ours; but that is nothing against it. Spirit is always worth listening to, and worth understanding sympathetically; the ventriloquist, if not the manikin, deserves admiration. It is spirit, too, that listens and understands, and grows thereby riper and more secure. Yet the oracles of spirit all have to be discounted; they are uttered in a cave.

It was this murmur of nature, wayward and narcotic as it is, that I called reason in this book, and tried to catch and interpret nobly. I could hardly have undertaken or carried out such a task if I had not been accustomed to slip into the subjective, recovering at each step as far as I might the innocence of intellectual illusion, and painting things as they would seem from that angle, not as they are. From childhood up I had lived in imagination, being fond of religion and poetry, and driven by circumstances to lead my inner life alone; and the philosophy that prevailed about me, though not one which I ever personally trusted, could not help encouraging me in this subjective habit, representing it as deeper, more critical, and more philosophical than any dogmatism. Nevertheless, subjectivity in me was never more than a method, a habit of poetic sympathy with the dreaming mind, whatever it might dream. It was a method appropriate to a book like this, a presumptive biography of the human intellect, which instead of the Life of Reason might have been called the Romance of Wisdom. Moreover, the thoughts I was endeavouring to evoke and to analyse were not all dead thoughts. Many of them survived in my own perplexities or in the various idealisms of those about me. One consequence was that I was often betrayed into expressions which, if not taken dramatically, would contradict my naturalism; that vulgar belief in material things about us which not only underlay the whole life of reason as I conceived it, but was also its explicit final deliverance. Another consequence was that, when I knew or feared that my reader might harbour the very illusion I was rehearsing, I was tempted to analyse it destructively, or argue against it: something really alien to the essential character of my task. It was only when the thoughts considered were unmistakably dead—as was Greek mythology or (to my probable reader) Catholic piety—that I could warm freely to my work, without fear of confusing myself or other people. On the other hand, when the idea considered was a living and indispensable one (no better description of the envisaged reality being as yet at hand) it was hard to relegate this idea to its native subjective sphere, where all ideas, of course, belong, without seeming to assert that its object also was a figment of human thought—a simply bottomless fallacy.

Let a single instance suffice as a hint to the critic, and as an apology for all the equivocations of this kind of which I may have been guilty. I find myself saying (Vol. I, page 125) that "nature is drawn like a sponge, heavy and dripping from the waters of sentience." Obviously the "nature" in question is the *idea* of nature, vague at first and overloaded with myth, then growing distinct, constant, articulate. Existing nature could not be drawn either soaking or dry from the waters of sentience: for existing nature is a system of bodies long antedating sentience and making sentience appropriate and significant: or else (on the hypothesis of idealism) existing nature is the flood of sentience itself, from which nothing can ever emerge. That which on its first appearance comes drenched out of its watery element is the dramatic notion of nature created by mythology. And matching this primitive notion of nature, and growing slowly distinguishable over against it, is another primitive notion which I mention in the same passage, the ghostly notion of mind. This, I say, is composed of the "parings of experience, when the material world has been cut out of the whole cloth." "Mind," too, is here a personage in the play of reason; it is the *category* of mind. Evidently the origin of existing mind could not lie in a discrimination which mind itself is making; but the discovery of mind may well come in that way. Shall I be blamed for giving the same name to the idea of nature and to existing nature, to the category of mind and to existing mind? I admit that, if the words are pressed, they become confusing; and yet at the play I might innocently say to a friend: "There is Hamlet coming on the stage. What a get-up! He looks more like Bunthorne." Clearly the phenomenon I should then be calling Hamlet would not be the real Hamlet, neither the Danish prince nor the presumable ideal in the mind of Shakespeare. This Hamlet is only the absurd actor playing Hamlet for the time being. Why should the verbal ambiguity be more annoying if in reviewing the life of reason I confidentially turn to the friendly reader, whom I suppose to be watching the same drama, and say: "See mind and nature coming on the scene. What a travesty the green-room of fancy has made of them! Here is nature tricked out in will and purpose like a moral being, and mind tumbling about in motley and gibbering!"

This drama, as I conceived it, was far from being a mere comedy of errors, to be treated satirically; it was a chequered experience from which wisdom might be gleaned. The story might be romantic, but the moral of it was classical. Error, under the influence of the existing object which it attempts to describe, suffers correction: and those first mythical notions of nature and of mind may be gradually clarified, until nature is seen to be a mechanism, and mind to be pure intelligence. The life of reason will mark a real progress whenever it gives fuller expression to the interests that prompt its gropings, and reaches the truth about such facts as, for its own purposes, it is concerned to discover. I was not studying history or psychology for their own sake: my retrospect was to be frankly selective and critical, guided by a desire to discriminate the better from the worse.

But by what standard could I distinguish them? The first suggestion for such a work had come to me in my student days, on reading Hegel's *Phaenomenologie des Geistes*. It had seemed to me that myth and sophistry there spoiled a very fine subject. The subject was the history of human ideas: the sophistry was imposed on Hegel by his ambition to show that the episodes he happened to review formed a dialectical chain, and the myth sprang from the constant suggestion that this history of human ideas made up the whole of cosmic evolution, and that those episodes were the scattered syllables of a single eternal oracle. It occurred to me that a more honest criticism of progress might be based on tracing the distracted efforts of man to satisfy his natural impulses in his natural environment. Yet if these impulses were infinitely wayward and variable, and if the environment itself was inconstant or undiscoverable, what criterion of progress could it be possible to set up? As for me, I was utterly without the learning and the romantic imagination that might have enabled some emancipated rival of Hegel, some systematic Nietzsche or some dialectical Walt Whitman, to write a history of the Will to Be Everything and Anything. An omnivorous spirit was no spirit for me, and I could not write the Life of Reason without distinguishing it from madness.

The suggestion of such a work accordingly lay dormant in my mind for years, until maturity, aided by Platonic studies, supplied me with a fresh point of departure, and enabled me to conceive the whole subject in a way that seemed to rescue it at once from pretension and from futility. All that was needed was to know oneself. No unnatural constancy need be imposed on human nature at large: it sufficed that the critic himself should have a determinate character and a sane capacity for happiness. He was not likely to be so original that, if he was sincere, nobody else would be found to share and approve his judgments. No conceited postulates need be made about the universe, commanding it to be exceptionally friendly, or to preserve us or those like us forever, or to "conserve values," as if the duration or the multiplication of instances had anything to do with excellence. The wisdom of Socrates was enough for living and judging rightly in any world, the most magical or the most mechanical, the best or the worst. I had no need to adopt the cosmology of Plato—a mythical and metaphysical creation, more or less playful and desperate, designed to buttress his moral philosophy. I was old enough, when I came under his influence, to discount this sort of priestcraft in thought, so familiar in Christian apologists. Experience, knowledge of my own heart, attachment to Spinoza, even the science of the day, protected me against those voluntary illusions. Indeed, to undermine them gently, by showing how unnecessary and treacherous they are in the healthy life of the spirit, was a chief part of my undertaking. In order to discern this healthy life, for the soul no less than for the body, not much learning is required; only a little experience, a little reflection, and a little candour.

Moral philosophy is not a science. It moves exclusively in the realm of familiar discourse. The units it distinguishes are dramatic units, like those of literary psychology and historical fiction: ideas, persons, passions, destinies such as imagination presents to me when I survey my own past, or conceive the adventures of another. This limitation is far from involving the assumption that nothing but human discourse can exist, or that nature must be composed of rhetorical unities of that description. On the contrary, it is important for sanity and for art that human discourse should acknowledge the far deeper embosoming realms of matter and of essence, to which physics and dialectic are respectively addressed; otherwise moral philosophy would threaten to become myth and discourse mere ravings. Nevertheless, the uses of science remain human, in that it employs the mind nobly, chastens the feelings, or increases the safety and comfort of life. To investigate nature or refine dialectic beyond those uses, out of mere curiosity, may be an innocent automatic impulse in men of science, but it is vain. Physics and dialectic accordingly enter the life of reason only as developments of human discourse, coloured by human passions and serving them: the moralist accepts their reports, as he does those of memory and history, that they may enlighten him about the conditions and the possible forms of happiness. His own art, to which this book is essentially dedicated, is to express his reasoned preferences amongst all the forms of experience which his imagination can propose. To imagination the reader must appeal in turn if he would understand the argument; and if he would correct the conclusion, he must make sure that he is speaking for his heart, for his most secret dream of happiness.

INTRODUCTION

The Subject of This Work, Its Methods and Antecedents

Progress Is Relative to an Ideal Which Reflection Creates.

WHATEVER forces may govern human life, if they are to be recognised by man, must betray themselves in human experience. Progress in science or religion, no less than in morals and art, is a dramatic episode in man's career, a welcome variation in his habit and state of mind; although this variation may often regard or propitiate things external, adjustment to which may be important for his welfare. The importance of these external things, as well as their existence, he can establish only by the function and utility which a recognition of them may have in his life. The entire history of progress is a moral drama, a tale man might unfold in a great autobiography, could his myriad heads and countless scintillas of consciousness conspire, like the seventy Alexandrian sages, in a single version of the truth committed to each for interpretation. What themes would prevail in such an examination of heart? In what order and with what emphasis would they be recounted? In which of its adventures would the human race, reviewing its whole experience, acknowledge a progress and a gain? To answer these questions, as they may be answered speculatively and provisionally by an individual, is the purpose of the following work.

Efficacious Reflection Is Reason.

A philosopher could hardly have a higher ambition than to make himself a mouth-piece for the memory and judgment of his race. Yet the most casual consideration of affairs already involves an attempt to do the same thing. Reflection is pregnant from the beginning with all the principles of synthesis and valuation needed in the most comprehensive criticism. So soon as man ceases to be wholly immersed in sense, he looks before and after, he regrets and desires; and the moments in which prospect or retrospect takes place constitute the reflective or representative part of his life, in contrast to the unmitigated flux of sensations in which nothing ulterior is regarded. Representation, however, can hardly remain idle and merely speculative. To the ideal function of envisaging the absent, memory and reflection will add (since they exist and constitute a new complication in being) the practical function of modifying the future. Vital impulse, however, when it is modified by reflection and veers in sympathy with judgment pronounced on the past, is properly called reason. Man's rational life consists in those moments in which reflection not only occurs but proves efficacious. What is absent then works in the present, and values are imputed where they cannot be felt. Such representation is so far from being merely speculative that its presence alone can raise bodily change to the dignity of action. Reflection gathers experiences together and perceives their relative worth; which is as much as to say that it expresses a new attitude of will in the presence of a world better understood and turned to some purpose. The limits of reflection mark those of concerted and rational action; they circumscribe the field of cumulative experience, or, what is the same thing, of profitable living.

The Life of Reason a Name for All Practical Thought and All Action Justified by Its Fruits in Consciousness.

Thus if we use the word life in a eulogistic sense to designate the happy maintenance against the world of some definite ideal interest, we may say with Aristotle that life is reason in operation. The *Life of Reason* will then be a name for that part of experience which perceives and pursues ideals—all conduct so controlled and all sense so interpreted as to perfect natural happiness.

Without reason, as without memory, there might still be pleasures and pains in existence. To increase those pleasures and reduce those pains would be to introduce an improvement into the sentient world, as if a devil suddenly died in hell or in heaven a new angel were created. Since the beings, however, in which these values would reside, would, by hypothesis, know nothing of one another, and since the betterment would take place unprayed-for and unnoticed, it could hardly be called a progress; and certainly not a progress in man, since man, without the ideal continuity given by memory and reason, would have no moral being. In human progress, therefore, reason is not a casual instrument, having its sole value in its service to sense; such a betterment in sentience would not be progress unless it were a progress in reason, and the increasing pleasure revealed some object that could please; for without a picture of the situation from which a heightened vitality might flow, the improvement could be neither remembered nor measured nor desired. The Life of Reason is accordingly neither a mere means nor a mere incident in human progress; it is the total and embodied progress itself, in which the pleasures of sense are included in so far as they can be intelligently enjoyed and pursued. To recount man's rational moments would be to take an inventory of all his goods; for he is not himself (as we say with unconscious accuracy) in the others. If he ever appropriates them in recollection or prophecy, it is only on the ground of some physical relation which they may have to his being.

Reason is as old as man and as prevalent as human nature; for we should not recognise an animal to be human unless his instincts were to some degree conscious of their ends and rendered his ideas in that measure relevant to conduct. Many sensations, or even a whole world of dreams, do not amount to intelligence until the images in the mind begin to represent in some way, however symbolic, the forces and realities confronted in action. There may well be intense consciousness in the total absence of rationality. Such consciousness is suggested in dreams, in madness, and may be found, for all we know, in the depths of universal nature. Minds peopled only by desultory visions and lusts would not have the dignity of human souls even if they seemed to pursue certain objects unerringly; for that pursuit would not be illumined by any vision of its goal. Reason and humanity begin with the union of instinct and ideation, when instinct becomes enlightened, establishes values in its objects, and is turned from a process into an art, while at the same time consciousness becomes practical and cognitive, beginning to contain some symbol or record of the co-ordinate realities among which it arises.

Reason accordingly requires the fusion of two types of life, commonly led in the world in well-nigh total separation, one a life of impulse expressed in affairs and social passions, the other a life of reflection expressed in religion, science, and the imitative arts. In the Life of Reason, if it were brought to perfection, intelligence would be at once the universal method of practice and its continual reward. All reflection would then be applicable in action and all action fruitful in happiness. Though this be an ideal, yet everyone gives it from time to time a partial embodiment when he practises useful arts, when his passions happily lead him to enlightenment, or when his fancy breeds visions pertinent to his ultimate good. Everyone leads the Life of Reason in so far as he finds a steady light behind the world's glitter and a clear residuum of joy beneath pleasure or success. No experience not to be repented of falls without its sphere. Every solution to a doubt, in so far as it is not a new error, every practical achievement not neutralised by a second maladjustment consequent upon it, every consolation not the seed of another greater sorrow, may be gathered together and built into this edifice. The Life of Reason is the happy marriage of two elements—impulse and ideation—which if wholly divorced would reduce man to a brute or to a maniac. The rational animal is generated by the union of these two monsters. He is constituted by ideas which have ceased to be visionary and actions which have ceased to be vain.

It Is the Sum of Art.

Thus the Life of Reason is another name for what, in the widest sense of the word, might be called Art. Operations become arts when their purpose is conscious and their method teachable. In perfect art the whole idea is creative and exists only to be embodied, while every part of the product is rational and gives delightful expression to that idea. Like art, again, the Life of Reason is not a power but a result, the spontaneous expression of liberal genius in a favouring environment. Both art and reason have natural sources and meet with natural checks; but when a process is turned successfully into an art, so that its issues have value and the ideas that accompany it become practical and cognitive, reflection, finding little that it cannot in some way justify and understand, begins to boast that it directs and has created the world in which it finds itself so much at home. Thus if art could extend its sphere to include every activity in nature, reason, being everywhere exemplified, might easily think itself omnipotent. This ideal, far as it is from actual realisation, has so dazzled men, that in their religion and mythical philosophy they have often spoken as if it were already actual and efficient. This anticipation amounts, when taken seriously, to a confusion of purposes with facts and of functions with causes, a confusion which in the interests of wisdom and progress it is important to avoid; but these speculative fables, when we take them for what they are— poetic expressions of the ideal—help us to see how deeply rooted this ideal is in man's mind, and afford us a standard by which to measure his approaches to the rational perfection of which he dreams. For the Life of Reason, being the sphere of all human art, is man's imitation of divinity.

It Has a Natural Basis Which Makes It Definable.

To study such an ideal, dimly expressed though it be in human existence, is no prophetic or visionary undertaking. Every genuine ideal has a natural basis; anyone may understand and safely interpret it who is attentive to the life from which it springs. To decipher the Life of Reason nothing is needed but an analytic spirit and a judicious love of man, a love quick to distinguish success from failure in his great and confused experiment of living. The historian of reason should not be a romantic poet, vibrating impotently to every impulse he finds afoot, without a criterion of excellence or a vision of perfection. Ideals are free, but they are neither more numerous nor more variable than the living natures that generate them. Ideals are legitimate, and each initially envisages a genuine and innocent good; but they are not realisable together, nor even singly when they have no deep roots in the world. Neither is the philosopher compelled by his somewhat judicial office to be a satirist or censor, without sympathy for those tentative and ingenuous passions out of which, after all, his own standards must arise. He is the chronicler of human progress, and to measure that progress he should be equally attentive to the impulses that give it direction and to the circumstances amid which it stumbles toward its natural goal.

Modern Philosophy Not Helpful.

There is unfortunately no school of modern philosophy to which a critique of human progress can well be attached. Almost every school, indeed, can furnish something useful to the critic, sometimes a physical theory, sometimes a piece of logical analysis. We shall need to borrow from current science and speculation the picture they draw of man's conditions and environments, his history and mental habits. These may furnish a theatre and properties for our drama; but they offer no hint of its plot and meaning. A great imaginative apathy has fallen on the mind. One half the learned world is amused in tinkering obsolete armour, as Don Quixote did his helmet; deputing it, after a series of catastrophes, to be at last sound and invulnerable. The other half, the naturalists who have studied psychology and evolution, look at life from the outside, and the processes of Nature make them forget her uses.

Positivism No Positive Ideal.

Bacon indeed had prized science for adding to the comforts of life, a function still commemorated by positivists in their eloquent moments. Habitually, however, when they utter the word progress it is, in their mouths, a synonym for inevitable change, or at best for change in that direction which they conceive to be on the whole predominant. If they combine with physical speculation some elements of morals, these are usually purely formal, to the effect that happiness is to be pursued (probably, alas! because to do so is a psychological law); but what happiness consists in we gather only from casual observations or by putting together their national prejudices and party saws.

The truth is that even this radical school, emancipated as it thinks itself, is suffering from the after-effects of supernaturalism. Like children escaped from school, they find their whole happiness in freedom. They are proud of what they have rejected, as if a great wit were required to do so; but they do not know what they want. If you astonish them by demanding what is their positive ideal, further than that there should be a great many people and that they should be all alike, they will say at first that what ought to be is obvious, and later they will submit the matter to a majority vote. They have discarded the machinery in which their ancestors embodied the ideal; they have not perceived that those symbols stood for the Life of Reason and gave fantastic and embarrassed expression to what, in itself, is pure humanity; and they have thus remained entangled in the colossal error that ideals are something adventitious and unmeaning, not having a soil in mortal life nor a possible fulfilment there.

Christian Philosophy Mythical: It Misrepresents Facts and Conditions.

The profound and pathetic ideas which inspired Christianity were attached in the beginning to ancient myths and soon crystallised into many new ones. The mythical manner pervades Christian philosophy; but myth succeeds in expressing ideal life only by misrepresenting its history and conditions. This method was indeed not original with the Fathers; they borrowed it from Plato, who appealed to parables himself in an open and harmless fashion, yet with disastrous consequences to his school. Nor was he the first; for the instinct to regard poetic fictions as revelations of supernatural facts is as old as the soul's primitive incapacity to distinguish dreams from waking perceptions, sign from thing signified, and inner emotions from external powers.

Such confusions, though in a way they obey moral forces, make a rational estimate of things impossible. To misrepresent the conditions and consequences of action is no merely speculative error; it involves a false emphasis in character and an artificial balance and co-ordination among human pursuits. When ideals are hypostasised into powers alleged to provide for their own expression, the Life of Reason cannot be conceived; in theory its field of operation is preempted and its function gone, while in practice its inner impulses are turned awry by artificial stimulation and repression.

The Patristic systems, though weak in their foundations, were extraordinarily wise and comprehensive in their working out; and while they inverted life they preserved it. Dogma added to the universe fabulous perspectives; it interpolated also innumerable incidents and powers which gave a new dimension to experience. Yet the old world remained standing in its strange setting, like the Pantheon in modern Rome; and, what is more important, the natural springs of human action were still acknowledged, and if a supernatural discipline was imposed, it was only because experience and faith had disclosed a situation in which the pursuit of earthly happiness seemed hopeless. Nature was not destroyed by its novel appendages, nor did reason die in the cloister: it hibernated there, and could come back to its own in due season, only a little dazed and weakened by its long confinement. Such, at least, is the situation in Catholic regions, where the Patristic philosophy has not appreciably varied. Among Protestants Christian dogma has taken a new and ambiguous direction, which has at once minimised its disturbing effect in practice and isolated its primary illusion. The symptoms have been cured and the disease driven in.

Liberal Theology a Superstitious Attitude Toward a Natural World.

The tenets of Protestant bodies are notoriously varied and on principle subject to change. There is hardly a combination of tradition and spontaneity which has not been tried in some quarter. If we think, however, of broad tendencies and ultimate issues, it appears that in Protestantism myth, without disappearing, has changed its relation to reality: instead of being an extension to the natural world myth has become its substratum. Religion no longer reveals divine personalities, future rewards, and tenderer Elysian consolations; nor does it seriously propose a heaven to be reached by a ladder nor a purgatory to be shortened by prescribed devotions. It merely gives the real world an ideal status and teaches men to accept a natural life on supernatural grounds. The consequence is that the most pious can give an unvarnished description of things. Even immortality and the idea of God are submitted, in liberal circles, to scientific treatment. On the other hand, it would be hard to conceive a more inveterate obsession than that which keeps the attitude of these same minds inappropriate to the objects they envisage. They have accepted natural conditions; they will not accept natural ideals. The Life of Reason has no existence for them, because, although its field is clear, they will not tolerate any human or finite standard of value, and will not suffer extant interests, which can alone guide them in action or judgment, to define the worth of life.

The after-effects of Hebraism are here contrary to its foundations; for the Jews loved the world so much that they brought themselves, in order to win and enjoy it, to an intense concentration of purpose; but this effort and discipline, which had of course been mythically sanctioned, not only failed of its object, but grew far too absolute and sublime to think its object could ever have been earthly; and the supernatural machinery which was to have secured prosperity, while that still enticed, now had to furnish some worthier object for the passion it had artificially fostered. Fanaticism consists in redoubling your effort when you have forgotten your aim.

An earnestness which is out of proportion to any knowledge or love of real things, which is therefore dark and in

ward and thinks itself deeper than the earth's foundations—
such an earnestness, until culture turns it into intelligent
interests, will naturally breed a new mythology. It will try
to place some world of Afrites and shadowy giants behind
the constellations, which it finds too distinct and constant
to be its companions or supporters; and it will assign to itself
vague and infinite tasks, for which it is doubtless better
equipped than for those which the earth now sets before it.
Even these, however, since they are parts of an infinite
whole, the mystic may (histrionically, perhaps, yet zealously) undertake; but as his eye will be perpetually fixed on
something invisible beyond, and nothing will be done for
its own sake or enjoyed in its own fugitive presence, there
will be little art and little joy in existence. All will be a toss-
ing servitude and illiberal mist, where the parts will have
no final values and the whole no pertinent direction.

The Greeks Thought Straight in Both Physics and Morals.

In Greek philosophy the situation is far more auspicious.
The ancients led a rational life and envisaged the various
spheres of speculation as men might whose central interests
were rational. In physics they leaped at once to the conception of a dynamic unity and general evolution, thus giving
that background to human life which shrewd observation
would always have descried, and which modern science has
laboriously rediscovered. Two great systems offered, in two
legitimate directions, what are doubtless the final and radical accounts of physical being. Heraclitus, describing the
immediate, found it to be in constant and pervasive change:
no substances, no forms, no identities could be arrested
there, but as in the human soul, so in nature, all was instability, contradition, reconstruction, and oblivion. This remains the empirical fact; and we need but to rescind the
artificial division which Descartes has taught us to make
between nature and life, to feel again the absolute aptness
of Heraclitus' expressions.

Heraclitus and the Immediate.

These were thought obscure only because they were so disconcertingly penetrating and direct. The immediate is what nobody sees, because convention and reflection turn existence, as soon as they can, into ideas; a man who discloses the immediate seems profound, yet his depth is nothing but innocence recovered and a sort of intellectual abstention. Mysticism, scepticism, and transcendentalism have all in their various ways tried to fall back on the immediate; but none of them has been ingenuous enough. Each has added some myth, or sophistry, or delusive artifice to its direct observation. Heraclitus remains the honest prophet of immediacy: a mystic without raptures or bad rhetoric, a sceptic who does not rely for his results on conventions unwittingly adopted, a transcendentalist without false pretensions or incongruous dogmas.

The immediate is not, however, a good subject for discourse, and the expounders of Heraclitus were not unnaturally blamed for monotony. All they could do was to iterate their master's maxim, and declare everything to be in flux. In suggesting laws of recurrence and a reason in which what is common to many might be expressed, Heraclitus had opened the door into another region: had he passed through, his philosophy would have been greatly modified, for permanent forms would have forced themselves on his attention no less than shifting materials. Such a Heraclitus would have anticipated Plato; but the time for such a synthesis had not yet arrived.

Democritus and the Naturally Intelligible.

At the opposite pole from immediacy lies intelligibility. To reduce phenomena to constant elements, as similar and simple as possible, and to conceive their union and separation to obey constant laws, is what a natural philosopher will inevitably do so soon as his interest is not merely to utter experience but to understand it. Democritus brought this scientific ideal to its ultimate expression. By including psychic existence in his atomic system, he indicated a problem which natural science has since practically abandoned but which it may some day be compelled to take up. The atoms of Democritus seem to us gross, even for chemistry, and their quality would have to undergo great transformation if they were to support intelligibly psychic being as well; but that very grossness and false simplicity had its merits, and science must be for ever grateful to the man who at its inception could so clearly formulate its mechanical ideal. That the world is not so intelligible as we could wish is not to be wondered at. In other respects also it fails to respond to our ideals; yet our hope must be to find it more propitious to the intellect as well as to all the arts in proportion as we learn better how to live in it.

The atoms of what we call hydrogen or oxygen may well turn out to be worlds, as the stars are which make atoms for astronomy. Their inner organisation might be negligible on our rude plane of being; did it disclose itself, however, it would be intelligible in its turn only if constant parts and constant laws were discernible within each system. So that while atomism at a given level may not be a final or metaphysical truth, it will describe, on every level, the practical and efficacious structure of the world. We owe to Democritus this ideal of practical intelligibility; and he is accordingly an eternal spokesman of reason. His system, long buried with other glories of the world, has been partly revived; and although it cannot be verified in haste, for it represents an ultimate ideal, every advance in science reconstitutes it in some particular. Mechanism is not one principle of explanation among others. In natural philosophy, where to explain means to discover origins, transmutations, and laws, mechanism is explanation itself.

Heraclitus had the good fortune of having his physics absorbed by Plato. It is a pity that Democritus' physics was

not absorbed by Aristotle. For with the flux observed, and
mechanism conceived to explain it, the theory of existence is
complete; and had a complete physical theory been incorporated into the Socratic philosophy, wisdom would have
lacked none of its parts. Democritus, however, appeared too
late, when ideal science had overrun the whole field and
initiated a verbal and dialectical physics; so that Aristotle,
for all his scientific temper and studies, built his natural
philosophy on a lamentable misunderstanding, and condemned thought to confusion for two thousand years.

Socrates and the Autonomy of Mind.

If the happy freedom of the Greeks from religious dogma
made them the first natural philosophers, their happy political freedom made them the first moralists. It was no accident
that Socrates walked the Athenian agora; it was no petty
patriotism that made him shrink from any other scene. His
science had its roots there, in the personal independence,
intellectual vivacity, and clever dialectic of his countrymen.
Ideal science lives in discourse; it consists in the active exercise of reason, in signification, appreciation, intent, and self-
expression. Its sum total is to know oneself, not as psychology or anthropology might describe a man, but to know, as
the saying is, one's own mind. Nor is he who knows his own
mind forbidden to change it; the dialectician has nothing to
do with future possibilities or with the opinion of anyone but
the man addressed. This kind of truth is but adequate veracity; its only object is its own intent. Having developed
in the spirit the consciousness of its meanings and purposes,
Socrates rescued logic and ethics for ever from authority.
With his friends the Sophists, he made man the measure of
all things, after bidding him measure himself, as they neglected to do, by his own ideal. That brave humanity which
had first raised its head in Hellas and had endowed so many
things in heaven and earth, where everything was hitherto
monstrous, with proportion and use, so that man's works

might justify themselves to his mind, now found in Socrates its precise definition; and it was naturally where the Life of Reason had been long cultivated that it came finally to be conceived.

Plato Gave the Ideal Its Full Expression.

Socrates had, however, a plebeian strain in his humanity, and his utilitarianism, at least in its expression, hardly did justice to what gives utility to life. His condemnation for atheism—if we choose to take it symbolically—was not altogether unjust: the gods of Greece were not honoured explicitly enough in his philosophy. Human good appeared there in its principle; you would not set a pilot to mend shoes, because you knew your own purpose; but what purposes a civilised soul might harbour, and in what highest shapes the good might appear, was a problem that seems not to have attracted his genius. It was reserved to Plato to bring the Socratic ethics to its sublimest expression and to elicit from the depths of the Greek conscience those ancestral ideals which had inspired its legislators and been embodied in its sacred civic traditions. The owl of Minerva flew, as Hegel says, in the dusk of evening; and it was horror at the abandonment of all creative virtues that brought Plato to conceive them so sharply and to preach them in so sad a tone. It was after all but the love of beauty that made him censure the poets; for like a true Greek and a true lover he wished to see beauty flourish in the real world. It was love of freedom that made him harsh to his ideal citizens, that they might be strong enough to preserve the liberal life. And when he broke away from political preoccupations and turned to the inner life, his interpretations proved the absolute sufficiency of the Socratic method; and he left nothing pertinent unsaid on ideal love and ideal immortality.

Aristotle Supplied Its Natural Basis.

Beyond this point no rendering of the Life of Reason has ever been carried. Aristotle improved the detail, and gave breadth and precision to many a part. If Plato possessed greater imaginative splendour and more enthusiasm in austerity, Aristotle had perfect sobriety and adequacy, with greater fidelity to the common sentiments of his race. Plato, by virtue of his scope and plasticity, together with a certain prophetic zeal, outran at times the limits of the Hellenic and the rational; he saw human virtue so surrounded and oppressed by physical dangers that he wished to give it mythical sanctions, and his fondness for transmigration and nether punishments was somewhat more than playful. If as a work of imagination his philosophy holds the first place, Aristotle's has the decisive advantage of being the unalloyed expression of reason. In Aristotle the conception of human nature is perfectly sound; everything ideal has a natural basis and everything natural an ideal development. His ethics, when thoroughly digested and weighed, especially when the meagre outlines are filled in with Plato's more discursive expositions, will seem therefore entirely final. The Life of Reason finds there its classic explication.

Philosophy Thus Complete, Yet in Need of Restatement.

As it is improbable that there will soon be another people so free from preoccupations, so gifted, and so fortunate as the Greeks, or capable in consequence of so well exemplifying humanity, so also it is improbable that a philosopher will soon arise with Aristotle's scope, judgment, or authority, one knowing so well how to be both reasonable and exalted. It might seem vain, therefore, to try to do afresh what has been done before with unapproachable success; and instead of writing inferior things at great length about the Life of Reason, it might be simpler to read and to propagate what Aristotle wrote with such immortal justness and masterly brevity. But times change; and though the principles of reason remain the same the facts of human life and of human conscience alter. A new background, a new basis of application, appears for logic, and it may be useful to restate old truths in new words, the better to prove their eter-

nal validity. Aristotle is, in his morals, Greek, concise, and
elementary. As a Greek, he mixes with the ideal argument
illustrations, appreciations, and conceptions which are not
inseparable from its essence. In themselves, no doubt, these
accessories are better than what in modern times would be
substituted for them, being less sophisticated and of a nobler
stamp; but to our eyes they disguise what is profound and
universal in natural morality by embodying it in images
which do not belong to our life. Our direst struggles and the
last sanctions of our morality do not appear in them. The
pagan world, because its maturity was simpler than our
crudeness, seems childish to us. We do not find there our
sins and holiness, our love, charity, and honour.

The Greek too would not find in our world the things he
valued most, things to which he surrendered himself, perhaps, with a more constant self-sacrifice—piety, country,
friendship, and beauty; and he might add that his ideals
were rational and he could attain them, while ours are extravagant and have been missed. Yet even if we acknowledge
his greater good fortune, it would be impossible for us to
go back and become like him. To make the attempt would
show no sense of reality and little sense of humour. We must
dress in our own clothes, if we do not wish to substitute a
masquerade for practical existence. What we can adopt from
Greek morals is only the abstract principle of their development, their foundation in all the extant forces of human
nature and their effort toward establishing a perfect harmony
among them. These forces themselves have perceptibly
changed, at least in their relative power. Thus we are more
conscious of wounds to stanch and wrongs to fight against,
and less of goods to attain. The movement of conscience has
veered; the centre of gravity lies in another part of the
character.

Another circumstance that invites a restatement of rational ethics is the impressive illustration of their principle
which subsequent history has afforded. Mankind has been

making extraordinary experiments of which Aristotle could not dream; and their result is calculated to clarify even his philosophy. For in some respects it needed experiments and clarification. He had been led into a systematic fusion of dialectic with physics, and of this fusion all pretentious modern philosophy is the aggravated extension. Socrates' pupils could not abandon his ideal principles, yet they could not bear to abstain from physics altogether; they therefore made a mock physics in moral terms, out of which theology was afterward developed. Plato, standing nearer to Socrates and being no naturalist by disposition, never carried the fatal experiment beyond the mythical stage. He accordingly remained the purer moralist, much as Aristotle's judgment may be preferred in many particulars. Their relative position may be roughly indicated by saying that Plato had no physics and that Aristotle's physics was false; so that ideal science in the one suffered from want of environment and control, while in the other it suffered from misuse in a sphere where it had no application.

Plato's Myths in Lieu of Physics.

What had happened was briefly this: Plato, having studied many sorts of philosophy and being a bold and universal genius, was not satisfied to leave all physical questions pending, as his master had done. He adopted, accordingly, Heraclitus' doctrine of the immediate, which he now called the realm of phenomena; for what exists at any instant, if you arrest and name it, turns out to have been an embodiment of some logical essence, such as discourse might define; in every fact some idea makes its appearance, and such an apparition of the ideal is a phenomenon. Moreover, another philosophy had made a deep impression on Plato's mind and had helped to develop Socratic definitions: Parmenides had called the concept of pure Being the only reality; and to satisfy the strong dialectic by which this doctrine was supported and at the same time to bridge the infinite chasm between one formless substance and many appearances irrelevant to it, Plato substituted the many Socratic ideas, all of which were relevant to appearance, for the one concept of Parmenides. The ideas thus acquired what is called metaphysical subsistence; for they stood in the place of the Eleatic Absolute, and at the same time were the realities that phenomena manifested.

The technique of this combination is much to be admired; but the feat is technical and adds nothing to the significance of what Plato has to say on any concrete subject. This barren triumph was, however, fruitful in misunderstandings. The characters and values a thing possessed were now conceived to subsist apart from it, and might even have preceded it and caused its existence; a mechanism composed of values and definitions could thus be placed behind phenomena to constitute a substantial physical world. Such a dream could not be taken seriously, until good sense was wholly lost and a bevy of magic spirits could be imagined peopling the infinite and yet carrying on the business of earth. Aristotle rejected the metaphysical subsistence of ideas, but thought they might still be essences operative in nature, if only they were identified with the life or form of particular things. The dream thus lost its frank wildness, but none of its inherent incongruity: for the sense in which characters and values make a thing what it is, is purely dialectical. They give it its status in the ideal world; but the appearance of these characters and values here and now is what needs explanation in physics, an explanation which can be furnished, of course, only by the physical concatenation and distribution of causes.

Aristotle's Final Causes. Modern Science Can Avoid Such Expedients.

Aristotle himself did not fail to make this necessary distinction between efficient cause and formal essence; but as his science was only natural history, and mechanism had no plausibility in his eyes, the efficiency of the cause was always due, in his view, to its ideal quality; as in heredity the father's human character, not his physical structure, might seem to warrant the son's humanity. Every ideal, before it could be embodied, had to pre-exist in some other embodiment; but as when the ultimate purpose of the cosmos is considered it seems to lie beyond any given embodiment, the highest ideal must somehow exist disembodied. It must pre-exist, thought Aristotle, in order to supply, by way of magic attraction, a physical cause for perpetual movement in the world.

It must be confessed, in justice to this consummate philosopher, who is not less masterly in the use of knowledge than unhappy in divination, that the transformation of the highest good into a physical power is merely incidental with him, and due to a want of faith (at that time excusable) in mechanism and evolution. Aristotle's deity is always a moral ideal and every detail in its definition is based on discrimination between the better and the worse. No accommodation to the ways of nature is here allowed to cloud the kingdom of heaven; this deity is not condemned to do whatever happens nor to absorb whatever exists. It is mythical only in its physical application; in moral philosophy it remains a legitimate conception.

Truth certainly exists, if existence be not too mean an attribute for that eternal realm which is tenanted by ideals; but truth is repugnant to physical or psychical being. Moreover, truth may very well be identified with an impassible intellect, which should do nothing but possess all truth, with no point of view, no animal warmth, and no transitive process. Such an intellect and truth are expressions having a different metaphorical background and connotation, but, when thought out, an identical import. They both attempt to evoke that ideal standard which human thought proposes to itself. This function is their effective essence. It insures their eternal fixity, and this property surely endows them with a very genuine and sublime reality. What is fantastic is only the dynamic function attributed to them by Aristotle, which obliges them to inhabit some fabulous extension to the physical world. Even this physical efficacy, however, is spiritualised as much as possible, since deity is said to move the cosmos only as an object of love or an object of knowledge may move the mind. Such efficacy is imputed to a hypostasised end, but evidently resides in fact in the functioning and impulsive spirit that conceives and pursues an ideal, endowing it with whatever attraction it may seem to have. The absolute intellect described by Aristotle remains, therefore, as pertinent to the Life of Reason as Plato's idea of the good. Though less comprehensive (for it abstracts from all animal interests, from all passion and mortality), it is more adequate and distinct in the region it dominates. It expresses sublimely the goal of speculative thinking; which is none other than to live as much as may be in the eternal and to absorb and be absorbed in the truth.

The rest of ancient philosophy belongs to the decadence and rests in physics on eclecticism and in morals on despair. That creative breath which had stirred the founders and legislators of Greece no longer inspired their descendants. Helpless to control the course of events, they took refuge in abstention or in conformity, and their ethics became a matter of private economy and sentiment, no longer aspiring to mould the state or give any positive aim to existence. The time was approaching when both speculation and morals were to regard the other world; reason had abdicated the throne, and religion, after that brief interregnum, resumed it for long ages.

Such are the threads which tradition puts into the hands of an observer who at the present time might attempt to knit the Life of Reason ideally together. The problem is to unite a trustworthy conception of the conditions under which man lives with an adequate conception of his interests. Both

conceptions, fortunately, lie before us. Heraclitus and Democritus, in systems easily seen to be complementary, gave
long ago a picture of nature such as all later observation,
down to our own day, has done nothing but fill out and
confirm. Psychology and physics still repeat their ideas,
often with richer detail, but never with a more radical or
prophetic glance. Nor does the transcendental philosophy,
in spite of its self-esteem, add anything essential. It was a
thing taken for granted in ancient and scholastic philosophy
that a being dwelling, like man, in the immediate, whose
moments are in flux, needed constructive reason to interpret
his experience and paint in his unstable consciousness some
symbolic picture of the world.

Transcendentalism True but Inconsequential.

To have reverted to this constructive process and studied
its stages is an interesting achievement; but the construction
is already made by common-sense and science, and it was
visionary insolence in the Germans to propose to make that
construction otherwise. Retrospective self-consciousness is
dearly bought if it inhibits the intellect and embarrasses the
inferences which, in its spontaneous operation, it has known
perfectly how to make. In the heat of scientific theorising or
dialectical argument it is sometimes salutary to be reminded
that we are men thinking; but, after all, it is no news. We
know that life is a dream, and how should thinking be more?
Yet the thinking must go on, and the only vital question is
to what practical or poetic conceptions it is able to lead us.

Verbal Ethics.

Similarly the Socratic philosophy affords a noble and
genuine account of what goods may be realised by living.
Modern theory has not done so much to help us here, however, as it has in physics. It seldom occurs to modern moralists that theirs is the science of all good and the art of its
attainment; they think only of some set of categorical pre-

cepts or some theory of moral sentiments, abstracting altogether from the ideals reigning in society, in science, and in art. They deal with the secondary question, What ought I to do? without having answered the primary question, What ought to be? They attach morals to religion rather than to politics, and this religion unhappily long ago ceased to be wisdom expressed in fancy in order to become superstition overlaid with reasoning. They divide man into compartments and the less they leave in the one labelled "morality" the more sublime they think their morality is; and sometimes pedantry and scholasticism are carried so far that nothing but an abstract sense of duty remains in the broad region which should contain all human goods.

Spinoza and the Life of Reason.

Such trivial sanctimony in morals is doubtless due to artificial views about the conditions of welfare; the basis is laid in authority rather than in human nature, and the goal in salvation rather than in happiness. One great modern philosopher, however, was free from these preconceptions, and might have reconstituted the Life of Reason had he had a sufficient interest in culture. Spinoza brought man back into nature, and made him the nucleus of all moral values, showing how he may recognise his environment and how he may master it. But Spinoza's sympathy with mankind fell short of imagination; any noble political or poetical ideal eluded him. Everything impassioned seemed to him insane, everything human necessarily petty. Man was to be a pious tame animal, with the stars shining above his head. Instead of imagination Spinoza cultivated mysticism, which is indeed an alternative. A prophet in speculation, he remained a levite in sentiment. Little or nothing would need to be changed in his system if the Life of Reason, in its higher ranges, were to be grafted upon it; but such affiliation is not necessary, and it is rendered unnatural by the lack of sweep and generosity in Spinoza's practical ideals.

Modern and Classic Sources of Inspiration.

For moral philosophy we are driven back, then, upon the ancients; but not, of course, for moral inspiration. Industrialism and democracy, the French Revolution, the Renaissance, and even the Catholic system, which in the midst of ancient illusions enshrines so much tenderness and wisdom, still live in the world, though forgotten by philosophers, and point unmistakably toward their several goals. Our task is not to construct but only to interpret ideals, confronting them with one another and with the conditions which, for the most part, they alike ignore. There is no need of refuting anything, for the will which is behind all ideals and behind most dogmas cannot itself be refuted; but it may be enlightened and led to reconsider its intent, when its satisfaction is seen to be either naturally impossible or inconsistent with better things. The age of controversy is past; that of interpretation has succeeded.

Here, then, is the programme of the following work: Starting with the immediate flux, in which all objects and impulses are given, to describe the Life of Reason; that is, to note what facts and purposes seem to be primary, to show how the conception of nature and life gathers around them, and to point to the ideals of thought and action which are approached by this gradual mastering of experience by reason. A great task, which it would be beyond the powers of a writer in this age either to execute or to conceive, had not the Greeks drawn for us the outlines of an ideal culture at a time when life was simpler than at present and individual intelligence more resolute and free.

IX

How Thought Is Practical

Its Worthlessness as a Cause and Value as an Expression.

THOUGHT is essentially practical in the sense that but for thought no motion would be an action, no change a progress; but thought is in no way instrumental or servile; it is an experience realised, not a force to be used. That same spontaneity in nature which has suggested a good must be trusted to fulfil it. If we look fairly at the actual resources of our minds we perceive that we are as little informed concerning the means and processes of action as concerning the reason why our motives move us. To execute the simplest intention we must rely on fate: our own acts are mysteries to us. Do I know how I open my eyes or how I walk down stairs? Is it the supervising wisdom of consciousness that guides me in these acts? Is it the mind that controls the bewildered body and points out the way to physical habits uncertain of their affinities? Or is it not much rather automatic inward machinery that executes the marvellous work, while the mind catches here and there some glimpse of the operation, now with delight and adhesion, now with impotent rebellion? When impulses work themselves out unimpeded we say we act; when they are thwarted we say we are acted upon; but in neither case do we in the least understand the natural history of what is occurring. The mind at best vaguely forecasts the result of action: a schematic verbal sense of the end to be accomplished possibly hovers in consciousness while the act is being performed; but this premonition is itself the sense of a process already present and betrays the tendency at work; it can obviously give no aid or direction to the unknown mechanical process that produced it and that must realise its own prophecy, if that prophecy is to be realised at all.

That such an unknown mechanism exists, and is adequate to explain every so-called decision, is indeed a hypothesis far outrunning detailed verification, although conceived by legitimate analogy with whatever is known about natural processes; but that the mind is not the source of itself or its own transformations is a matter of present experience; for the world is an unaccountable datum, in its existence, in its laws, and in its incidents. The highest hopes of science and morality look only to discovering those laws and bringing one set of incidents—facts of perception—into harmony with another set—facts of preference. This hoped-for issue, if it comes, must come about in the mind; but the mind cannot be its cause since, by hypothesis, it does not possess the ideas it seeks nor has power to realise the harmonies it desiderates. These have to be waited for and begged of destiny; human will, not controlling its basis, cannot possibly control its effects. Its existence and its efforts have at best the value of a good omen. They show in what direction natural forces are moving in so far as they are embodied in given men.

Thought's March Automatic and Thereby Implicated in Events.

Men, like all things else in the world, are products and vehicles of natural energy, and their operation counts. But their conscious will, in its moral assertiveness, is merely a sign of that energy and of that will's eventual fortunes. Dramatic terror and dramatic humour both depend on contrasting the natural pregnancy of a passion with its conscious intent. Everything in human life is ominous, even the voluntary acts. We cannot, by taking thought, add a cubit to our stature, but we may build up a world without meaning it. Man is as full of potentiality as he is of impotence.

A will that represents many active forces, and is skilful in divination and augury, may long boast to be almighty without being contradicted by the event.

That thought is not self-directive appears best in the most immaterial processes. In strife against external forces men, being ignorant of their deeper selves, attribute the obvious effects of their action to their chance ideas; but when the process is wholly internal the real factors are more evenly represented in consciousness and the magical, involuntary nature of life is better perceived. My hand, guided by I know not what machinery, is at this moment adding syllable to syllable upon this paper, to the general fulfilment, perhaps, of my felt intent, yet giving that intent an articulation wholly unforeseen, and often disappointing. The thoughts to be expressed simmer half-consciously in my brain. I feel their burden and tendency without seeing their form, until the mechanical train of impulsive association, started by the perusal of what precedes or by the accidental emergence of some new idea, lights the fuse and precipitates the phrases. If this happens in the most reflective and deliberate of activities, like this of composition, how much more does it happen in positive action. "The die is cast," said Cæsar, feeling a decision in himself of which he could neither count nor weigh the multitudinous causes; and so says every strong and clear intellect, every well-formed character, seizing at the same moment with comprehensive instinct both its purposes and the means by which they shall be attained. Only the fool, whose will signifies nothing, boasts to have created it himself.

Contemplative Essence of Action.

We must not seek the function of thought, then, in any supposed power to discover either ends not suggested by natural impulse or means to the accomplishment of those irrational ends. Attention is utterly powerless to change or create its objects in either respect; it rather registers without surprise—for it expects nothing in particular—and watches eagerly the images bubbling up in the living mind and the processes evolving there. These processes are themselves full of potency and promise; will and reflection are no more inconsequential than any other processes bound by natural links to the rest of the world. Even if an atomic mechanism suffices to mark the concatenation of everything in nature, including the mind, it cannot rob what it abstracts from of its natural weight and reality: a thread that may suffice to hold the pearls together is not the whole cause of the necklace. But this pregnancy and implication of thought in relation to its natural environment is purely empirical. Since natural connection is merely a principle of arrangement by which the contiguities of things may be described and inferred, there is no difficulty in admitting consciousness and all its works into the web and woof of nature. Each psychic episode would be heralded by its material antecedents; its transformations would be subject to mechanical laws, which would also preside over the further transition from thought into its material expression.

Mechanical Efficacy Alien to Thought's Essence.

This inclusion of mind in nature, however, is as far as possible from constituting the mind's function and value, or its efficacy in a moral and rational sense. To have prepared changes in matter would give no rationality to mind unless those changes in turn paved the way to some better mental existence. The worth of natural efficacy is therefore always derivative; the utility of mind would be no more precious than the utility of matter; both borrow all their worth from the part they may play empirically in introducing those moral values which are intrinsic and self-sufficing. In so far as thought is instrumental it is not worth having, any more than matter, except for its promise; it must terminate in something truly profitable and ultimate which, being good in itself, may lend value to all that led up to it. But this ultimate good is itself consciousness, thought, rational activity;

so that what instrumental mentality may have preceded might be abolished without loss, if matter suffices to sustain reason in being; or if that instrumental mentality is worth retaining, it is so only because it already contains some premonition and image of its own fulfilment. In a word, the value of thought is ideal. The material efficacy which may be attributed to it is the proper efficacy of matter—an efficacy which matter would doubtless claim if we knew enough of its secret mechanism. And when that imputed and incongruous utility was subtracted from ideas they would appear in their proper form of expressions, realisations, ultimate fruits.

Thought the Entelechy of Being.

What, indeed, could be more fitting than that consciousness, which is self-revealing and transcendentally primary, should be its own excuse for being and should contain its own total value, together with the total value of everything else? What could be more proper than that the whole worth of ideas should be ideal? To make an idea instrumental would be to prostitute what, being self-existent, should be self-justifying. That continual absoluteness which consciousness possesses, since in it alone all heaven and earth are at any moment revealed, ought to convince any radical and heart-searching philosopher that all values should be continually integrated and realised there, where all energies are being momently focussed. Thought is a fulfilment; its function is to lend utility to its causes and to make actual those conceived and subterranean processes which find in it their ultimate expression. Thought is nature represented; it is potential energy producing life and becoming an actual appearance.

Its Exuberance.

The conditions of consciousness, however, are far from being its only theme. As consciousness bears a transcendent relation to the dynamic world (for it is actual and spiritual, while the dynamic is potential and material) so it may be exuberant and irresponsibly rich. Although its elements, in point of distribution and derivation, are grounded in matter, as music is in vibrations, yet in point of character the result may be infinitely redundant. The complete musician would devote but a small part of his attention to the basis of music, its mechanism, psychology, or history. Long before he had represented to his mind the causes of his art, he would have proceeded to practise and enjoy it. So sense and imagination, passion and reason, may enrich the soil that breeds them and cover it with a maze of flowers.

The theme of consciousness is accordingly far more than the material world which constitutes its basis, though this also is one of its themes; thought is no less at home in various expressions and embroideries with which the material world can be overlaid in imagination. The material world is conceived by digging beneath experience to find its cause; it is the efficacious structure and skeleton of things. This is the subject of scientific retrospect and calculation. The forces disclosed by physical studies are of course not directed to producing a mind that might merely describe them. A force is expressed in many other ways than by being defined; it may be felt, resisted, embodied, transformed, or symbolised. Forces work; they are not, like mathematical concepts, exhausted in description. From that matter which might be describable in mechanical formulæ there issue notwithstanding all manner of forms and harmonies, visible, audible, imaginable, and passionately prized. Every phase of the ideal world emanates from the natural and loudly proclaims its origin by the interest it takes in natural existences, of which it gives a rational interpretation. Sense, art, religion, society, express nature exuberantly and in symbols long before science is added to represent, by a different abstraction, the mechanism which nature contains.

XI

Some Abstract Conditions of the Ideal

The Ultimate End a Resultant.

REASON'S function is to embody the good, but the test of excellence is itself ideal; therefore before we can assure ourselves that reason has been manifested in any given case we must make out the reasonableness of the ideal that inspires us. And in general, before we can convince ourselves that a Life of Reason, or practice guided by science and directed toward spiritual goods, is at all worth having, we must make out the possibility and character of its ultimate end. Yet each ideal is its own justification; so that the only sense in which an ultimate end can be established and become a test of general progress is this: that a harmony and co-operation of impulses should be conceived, leading to the maximum satisfaction possible in the whole community of spirits affected by our action. Now, without considering for the present any concrete Utopia, such, for instance, as Plato's Republic or the heavenly beatitude described by theologians, we may inquire what formal qualities are imposed on the ideal by its nature and function and by the relation it bears to experience and to desire.

Demands the Substance of Ideals.

The ideal has the same relation to given demands that the reality has to given perceptions. In the face of the ideal, particular demands forfeit their authority and the goods to which a particular being may aspire cease to be absolute; nay, the satisfaction of desire comes to appear an indifferent or unholy thing when compared or opposed to the ideal to be realised. So, precisely, in perception, flying impressions come to be regarded as illusory when contrasted with a stable conception of reality. Yet of course flying impressions are the only material out of which that conception can be formed. Life itself is a flying impression, and had we no personal and instant experience, importuning us at each successive moment, we should have no occasion to ask for a reality at all, and no materials out of which to construct so gratuitous an idea. In the same way present demands are the only materials and occasions for any ideal: without demands the ideal would have no *locus standi* or foothold in the world, no power, no charm, and no prerogative. If the ideal can confront particular desires and put them to shame, that happens only because the ideal is the object of a more profound and voluminous desire and embodies the good which they blindly and perhaps deviously pursue. Demands could not be misdirected, goods sought could not be false, if the standard by which they are to be corrected were not constructed out of them. Otherwise each demand would render its object a detached, absolute, and unimpeachable good. But when each desire in turn has singed its wings and retired before some disillusion, reflection may set in to suggest residual satisfactions that may still be possible, or some shifting of the ground by which much of what was hoped for may yet be attained.

Discipline of the Will.

The force for this new trial is but the old impulse renewed; this new hope is a justified remnant of the old optimism. Each passion, in this second campaign, takes the field conscious that it has indomitable enemies and ready to sign a reasonable peace, and even to capitulate before superior forces. Such tameness may be at first merely a consequence of exhaustion and prudence; but a mortal will, though absolute in its deliverances, is very far from constant, and its sacrifices soon constitute a habit, its exile a new home. The old ambition, now proved to be unrealisable, begins to seem capricious and extravagant; the circle of possible satisfactions becomes the field of conventional happiness. Experience, which brings about this humbler and more prosaic state of mind, has its own imaginative fruits. Among those forces which compelled each particular impulse to abate its pretensions, the most conspicuous were other impulses, other interests active in oneself and in one's neighbours. When the power of these alien demands is recognised they begin, in a physical way, to be respected; when an adjustment to them is sought they begin to be understood, for it is only by studying their expression and tendency that the degree of their hostility can be measured.

Demands Made Practical and Consistent.

But to understand is more than to forgive, it is to adopt; and the passion that thought merely to withdraw into a sullen and maimed self-indulgence can feel itself expanded by sympathies which in its primal vehemence it would have excluded altogether. Experience, in bringing humility, brings intelligence also. Personal interests begin to seem relative, factors only in a general voluminous welfare expressed in many common institutions and arts, moulds for whatever is communicable or rational in every passion. Each original impulse, when trimmed down more or less according to its degree of savageness, can then inhabit the state, and every good, when sufficiently transfigured, can be found again in the general ideal. The factors may indeed often be unrecognisable in the result, so much does the process of domestication transform them; but the interests that animated them survive this discipline and the new purpose is really esteemed; else the ideal would have no moral force. An ideal representing no living interest would be irrelevant to practice, just as a conception of reality would be irrelevant to perception which should not be composed of the materials that sense supplies, or should not re-embody actual sensations in an intelligible system.

The Ideal Natural.

Here we have, then, one condition which the ideal must fulfil: it must be a resultant or synthesis of impulses already afoot. An ideal out of relation to the actual demands of living beings is so far from being an ideal that it is not even a good. The pursuit of it would be not the acme but the atrophy of moral endeavour. Mysticism and asceticism run into this danger, when the intent to be faithful to a supreme good too symbolically presented breeds a superstitious repugnance toward everything naturally prized. So also an artificial scepticism can regard all experience as deceptive, by contrasting it with the chimera of an absolute reality. As an absolute reality would be indescribable and without a function in the elucidation of phenomena, so a supreme good which was good for nobody would be without conceivable value. Respect for such an idol is a dialectical superstition; and if zeal for that shibboleth should actually begin to inhibit the exercise of intelligent choice or the development of appreciation for natural pleasures, it would constitute a reversal of the Life of Reason which, if persistently indulged in, could only issue in madness or revert to imbecility.

Need of Unity and Finality.

No less important, however, than this basis which the ideal must have in extant demands, is the harmony with which reason must endow it. If without the one the ideal loses its value, without the other it loses its finality. Human nature is fluid and imperfect; its demands are expressed in incidental desires, elicited by a variety of objects which perhaps cannot coexist in the world. If we merely transcribe these miscellaneous demands or allow these floating desires to dictate to us the elements of the ideal, we shall never come to a Whole or to an End. One new fancy after another will seem an embodiment of perfection, and we shall contradict each expression of our ideal by every other. A certain school of philosophy—if we may give that name to the systematic neglect of reason—has so immersed itself in the contemplation of this sort of inconstancy, which is indeed prevalent enough in the world, that it has mistaken it for a normal and necessary process. The greatness of the ideal has been put in its vagueness and in an elasticity which makes it wholly indeterminate and inconsistent. The goal of progress, beside being thus made to lie at every point of the compass in succession, is removed to an infinite distance, whereby the possibility of attaining it is denied and progress itself is made illusory. For a progress must be directed to attaining some definite type of life, the counterpart of a given natural endowment, and nothing can be called an improvement which does not contain an appreciable benefit. A victory would be a mockery that left us, for some new reason, as much impeded as before and as far removed from peace.

Ideals of Nothing.

The picture of life as an eternal war for illusory ends was drawn at first by satirists, unhappily with too much justification in the facts. Some grosser minds, too undisciplined to have ever pursued a good either truly attainable or truly satisfactory, then proceeded to mistake that satire on human folly for a sober account of the whole universe; and finally others were not ashamed to represent it as the ideal itself— so soon is the dyer's hand subdued to what it works in. A barbarous mind cannot conceive life, like health, as a harmony continually preserved or restored, and containing those natural and ideal activities which disease merely interrupts. Such a mind, never having tasted order, cannot conceive it, and identifies progress with new conflicts and life with continual death. Its deification of unreason, instability, and strife comes partly from piety and partly from inexperience. There is piety in saluting nature in her perpetual flux and in thinking that since no equilibrium is maintained for ever none, perhaps, deserves to be. There is inexperience in not considering that wherever interests and judgments exist, the natural flux has fallen, so to speak, into a vortex, and created a natural good, a cumulative life, and an ideal purpose. Art, science, government, human nature itself, are self-defining and self-preserving: by partly fixing a structure they fix an ideal. But the barbarian can hardly regard such things, for to have distinguished and fostered them would be to have founded a civilisation.

Darwin on Moral Sense.

Reason's function in defining the ideal is in principle extremely simple, although all time and all existence would have to be gathered in before the applications of that principle could be exhausted. A better example of its essential working could hardly be found than one which Darwin gives to illustrate the natural origin of moral sense. A swallow, impelled by migratory instincts to leave a nest full of unfledged young, would endure a moral conflict. The more lasting impulse, memory being assumed, would prompt a moral judgment when it emerged again after being momentarily obscured by an intermittent passion. "While the mother bird is feeding or brooding over her nestlings, the maternal instinct is probably stronger than the migratory; but the instinct which is more persistent gains the victory, and at last, at a moment when her young ones are not in sight, she takes flight and deserts them When arrived at the end of her long journey, and the migratory instinct ceases to act, what an agony of remorse each bird would feel if, from being endowed with great mental activity, she could not prevent the image continually passing before her mind of her young ones perishing in the bleak north from cold and hunger."* She would doubt-

* *Descent of Man,* chapter iii.

less upbraid herself, like any sinner, for a senseless perfidy to her own dearest good. The perfidy, however, was not wholly senseless, because the forgotten instinct was not less natural and necessary than the remembered one, and its satisfaction no less true. Temptation has the same basis as duty. The difference is one of volume and permanence in the rival satisfactions, and the attitude conscience will assume toward these depends more on the representability of the demands compared than on their original vehemence or ultimate results.

Conscience and Reason Compared.

A passionate conscience may thus arise in the play of impulses differing in permanence, without involving a judicial exercise of reason. Nor does such a conscience involve a synthetic ideal, but only the ideal presence of particular demands. Conflicts in the conscience are thus quite natural and would continually occur but for the narrowness that commonly characterises a mind inspired by passion. A life of sin and repentance is as remote as possible from a Life of Reason. Yet the same situation which produces conscience and the sense of duty is an occasion for applying reason to action and for forming an ideal, so soon as the demands and satisfactions concerned are synthesised and balanced imaginatively. The stork might do more than feel the conflict of his two impulses, he might do more than embody in alternation the eloquence of two hostile thoughts. He might pass judgment upon them impartially and, in the felt presence of both, conceive what might be a union or compromise between them.

This resultant object of pursuit, conceived in reflection and in itself the initial goal of neither impulse, is the ideal of a mind occupied by the two: it is the aim prescribed by reason under the circumstances. It differs from the prescription of conscience, in that conscience is often the spokesman of one interest or of a group of interests in opposition to other pri-

mary impulses which it would annul altogether; while reason
and the ideal are not active forces nor embodiments of passion at all, but merely a method by which objects of desire
are compared in reflection. The goodness of an end is felt inwardly by conscience; by reason it can be only taken upon
trust and registered as a fact. For conscience the object of
an opposed will is an evil, for reason it is a good on the same
ground as any other good, because it is pursued by a natural
impulse and can bring a real satisfaction. Conscience, in fine,
is a party to moral strife, reason an observer of it who, however, plays the most important and beneficent part in the
outcome by suggesting the terms of peace. This suggested
peace, inspired by sympathy and by knowledge of the world,
is the ideal, which borrows its value and practical force from
the irrational impulses which it embodies, and borrows its
final authority from the truth with which it recognises them
all and the necessity by which it imposes on each such sacrifices as are requisite to a general harmony.

Reason Imposes No New Sacrifice.

Could each impulse, apart from reason, gain perfect satisfaction, it would doubtless laugh at justice. The divine, to
exercise suasion, must use an *argumentum ad hominem*;
reason must justify itself to the heart. But perfect satisfaction is what an irresponsible impulse can never hope for: all
other impulses, though absent perhaps from the mind, are
none the less present in nature and have possession of the
field through their physical basis. They offer effectual resist-
ance to a reckless intruder. To disregard them is therefore to
gain nothing: reason, far from creating the partial renunciation and proportionate sacrifices which it imposes, really
minimises them by making them voluntary and fruitful. The
ideal, which may seem to wear so severe a frown, really fosters all possible pleasures; what it retrenches is nothing to
what blind forces and natural catastrophes would otherwise

cut off; while it sweetens what it sanctions, adding to spontaneous enjoyments a sense of moral security and an intellectual light.

Natural Goods Attainable and Compatible in Principle.

Those who are guided only by an irrational conscience can hardly understand what a good life would be. Their Utopias have to be supernatural in order that the irresponsible rules which they call morality may lead by miracle to happy results. But such a magical and undeserved happiness, if it were possible, would be unsavoury: only one phase of human nature would be satisfied by it, and so impoverished an ideal cannot really attract the will. For human nature has been moulded by the same natural forces among which its ideal has to be fulfilled, and, apart from a certain margin of wild hopes and extravagances, the things man's heart desires are attainable under his natural conditions and would not be attainable elsewhere. The conflict of desires and interests in the world is not radical any more than man's dissatisfaction with his own nature can be; for every particular ideal, being an expression of human nature in operation, must in the end involve the primary human faculties and cannot be essentially incompatible with any other ideal which involves them too.

To adjust all demands to one ideal and adjust that ideal to its natural conditions—in other words, to live the Life of Reason—is something perfectly possible; for those demands, being akin to one another in spite of themselves, can be better furthered by co-operation than by blind conflict, while the ideal, far from demanding any profound revolution in nature, merely expresses her actual tendency and forecasts what her perfect functioning would be.

Harmony the Formal and Intrinsic Demand of Reason.

Reason as such represents or rather constitutes a single formal interest, the interest in harmony. When two interests are simultaneous and fall within one act of apprehension the desirability of harmonising them is involved in the very effort to realise them together. If attention and imagination are steady enough to face this implication and not to allow impulse to oscillate between irreconcilable tendencies, reason comes into being. Henceforth things actual and things desired are confronted by an ideal which has both pertinence and authority.

V

REASON IN SOCIETY

I

Love

Fluid Existences Have None but Ideal Goals.

IF man were a static or intelligible being, such as angels are thought to be, his life would have a single guiding interest, under which all other interests would be subsumed. His acts would explain themselves without looking beyond his given essence, and his soul would be like a musical composition, which once written out cannot grow different and once rendered can ask for nothing but, at most, to be rendered over again. In truth, however, man is an animal, a portion of the natural flux; and the consequence is that his nature has a moving centre, his functions an external reference, and his ideal a true ideality. What he strives to preserve, in preserving himself, is something which he never has been at any particular moment. He maintains his equilibrium by motion. His goal is in a sense beyond him, since it is not his experience, but a form which all experience ought to receive. The inmost texture of his being is propulsive, and there is nothing more intimately bound up with his success than mobility and devotion to transcendent aims. If there is a transitive function in knowledge and an unselfish purpose in love, that is only because, at bottom, there is a self-reproductive, flying essence in all existence.

If the equilibrium of man's being were stable he would need neither nutrition, reproduction, nor sense. As it is, sense must renew his ideas and guide his instincts otherwise than as their inner evolution would demand; and regenerative processes must strive to repair beneath the constant irreparable lapse of his substance. His business is to create and remodel those organisms in which ideals are bred. In order to have a soul to save he must perpetually form it anew; he must, so to speak, *earn his own living*. In this vital labour, we may ask, is nutrition or reproduction the deeper function? Or, to put the corresponding moral question, is the body or the state the primary good?

Nutrition and Reproduction.

If we view the situation from the individual's side, as self-consciousness might view it, we may reply that nutrition is fundamental, for if the body were not nourished every faculty would decay. Could nutrition only succeed and keep the body young, reproduction would be unnecessary, with its poor pretence at maintaining the mobile human form in a series of examples. On the other hand, if we view the matter from above, as science and philosophy should, we may say that nutrition is but germination of a pervasive sort, that the body is a tabernacle in which the transmissible human spirit is carried for a while, a shell for the immortal seed that dwells in it and has created it. This seed, however, for rational estimation, is merely a means to the existence and happiness of individuals. Transpersonal and continuous in its own fluid being, the potential grows personal in its ideal fulfilments. In other words, this potentiality is material (though called sometimes an idea) and has its only value in the particular creatures it may produce.

Priority of the Latter.

Reproduction is accordingly primary and more completely instrumental than nutrition is, since it serves a soul as yet

non-existent, while nutrition is useful to a soul that already
has some actuality. Reproduction initiates life and remains
at life's core, a function without which no other, in the end,
would be possible. It is more central, crucial, and representative than nutrition, which is in a way peripheral only; it is a
more typical and rudimentary act, marking the ideal's first
victory over the universal flux, before any higher function
than reproduction itself has accrued to the animal. To nourish an existing being is to presuppose a pause in generation;
the nucleus, before it dissolves into other individuals, gathers
about itself, for its own glory, certain temporal and personal
faculties. It lives for itself; while in procreation it signs its
own death-warrant, makes its will, and institutes its heir.

*Love Celebrates the Initial Triumph of Form and Is Deeply
Ideal.*

This situation has its counterpart in feeling. Replenish-
ment is a sort of delayed breathing, as if the animal had to
hunt for air: it necessitates more activity than it contains; it
engages external senses in its service and promotes intelligence. After securing a dumb satisfaction, or even in preparing it, it leaves the habits it employed free for observation
and ideal exercise. Reproduction, on the contrary, depletes;
it is an expense of spirit, a drag on physical and mental life;
it entangles rather than liberates; it fuses the soul again into
the impersonal, blind flux. Yet, since it constitutes the primary and central triumph of life, it is in itself more ideal
and generous than nutrition; it fascinates the will in an absolute fashion, and the pleasures it brings are largely spiritual. For though the instrumentalities of reproduction may
seem gross and trivial from a conventional point of view, its
essence is really ideal, the perfect type, indeed, of ideality,
since form and an identical life are therein sustained successfully by a more rhythmical flux of matter.

It may seem fanciful, even if not unmeaning, to say that a
man's soul more truly survives in his son's youth than in his

own decrepitude; but this principle grows more obvious as we descend to simpler beings, in which individual life is less elaborated and has not intrenched itself in so many adventitious and somewhat permanent organs. In vegetables soul and seed go forth together and leave nothing but a husk behind. In the human individual love may seem a mere incident of youth and a sentimental madness; but that episode, if we consider the race, is indispensable to the whole drama; and if we look to the order in which ideal interests have grown up and to their superposition in moral experience, love will seem the truly primitive and initiatory passion. Consciousness, amused ordinarily by the most superficial processes, itself bears witness to the underlying claims of reproduction and is drawn by it for a moment into life's central vortex; and love, while it betrays its deep roots by the imperative force it exerts and the silence it imposes on all current passions, betrays also its ideal mission by casting an altogether novel and poetic spell over the mind.

Difficulty in Describing Love.

The conscious quality of this passion differs so much in various races and individuals, and at various points in the same life, that no account of it will ever satisfy everybody.* Poets and novelists never tire of depicting it anew; but although the experience they tell of is fresh and unparalleled in every individual, their rendering suffers, on the whole, from a great monotony. Love's gesture and symptoms are noted

*The wide uses of the English word love add to the difficulty. I shall take the liberty of limiting the term here to imaginative passion, to being in love, excluding all other ways of loving. It follows that love—like its shadow, jealousy—will often be merely an ingredient in an actual state of feeling; friendship and confidence, with satisfaction at being liked in return, will often be mingled with it. We shall have to separate physiologically things which in consciousness exist undivided, since a philosophic description is bound to be analytic and cannot render everything at once. Where a poet might conceive a new composite, making it live, a moralist must dissect the experience and rest in its eternal elements.

and unvarying; its vocabulary is poor and worn. Even a poet, therefore, can give of love but a meagre expression, while the philosopher, who renounces dramatic representation, is condemned to be avowedly inadequate. Love, to the lover, is a noble and immense inspiration; to the naturalist it is a thin veil and prelude to the self-assertion of lust. This opposition has prevented philosophers from doing justice to the subject. Two things need to be admitted by anyone who would not go wholly astray in such speculation: one, that love has an animal basis; the other, that it has an ideal object. Since these two propositions have usually been thought contradictory, no writer has ventured to present more than half the truth, and that half out of its true relations.

One-sided or Inverted Theories About It.

Plato, who gave eloquent expression to the ideal burden of the passion, and divined its political and cosmic message, passed over its natural history with a few mythical fancies; and Schopenhauer, into whose system a naturalistic treatment would have fitted so easily, allowed his metaphysics to carry him at this point into verbal inanities; while, of course, like all profane writers on the subject, he failed to appreciate the oracles which Plato had delivered. In popular feeling, where sentiment and observation must both make themselves felt somehow or other, the tendency is to imagine that love is an absolute, non-natural energy which, for some unkonwn reason, or for none at all, lights upon particular persons, and rests there eternally, as on its ultimate goal. In other words, it makes the origin of love divine and its object natural: which is the exact opposite of the truth. If it were once seen, however, that every ideal expresses some natural function, and that no natural function is incapable, in its free exercise, of evolving some ideal and finding justification, not in some collateral animal, but in an inherent operation like life or thought, which being transmissible in its form is also eternal, then the philosophy of love should not prove permanently barren. For love is a brilliant illustration of a principle everywhere discoverable: namely, that human reason lives by turning the friction of material forces into the light of ideal goods. There can be no philosophic interest in disguising the animal basis of love, or in denying its spiritual sublimations, since all life is animal in its origin and all spiritual in its possible fruits.

Sexual Functions Its Basis.

Plastic matter, in transmitting its organisation, takes various courses which it is the part of natural history to describe. Even after reproduction has become sexual, it will offer no basis for love if it does not require a union of the two parent bodies. Did germinal substances, unconsciously diffused, meet by chance in the external medium and unite there, it is obvious that whatever obsessions or pleasures maturity might bring they would not have the quality which men call love. But when an individual of the opposite sex must be met with, recognised, and pursued, and must prove responsive, then each is haunted by the possible other. Each feels in a generic way the presence and attraction of his fellows; he vibrates to their touch, he dreams of their image, he is restless and wistful if alone. When the vague need that solicits him is met by the presence of a possible mate it is extraordinarily kindled. Then, if it reaches fruition, it subsides immediately, and after an interval, perhaps, of stupor and vital recuperation, the animal regains his independence, his peace, and his impartial curiosity. You might think him on the way to becoming intelligent; but the renewed nutrition and cravings of the sexual machinery soon engross his attention again; all his sprightly indifference vanishes before nature's categorical imperative. That fierce and turbid pleasure, by which his obedience is rewarded, hastens his dissolution; every day the ensuing lassitude and emptiness give him a clearer premonition of death. It is not figuratively only that his soul has passed into his offspring. The vocation to produce them was a chief part of his being, and when that function is sufficiently fulfilled he is superfluous in the world and becomes partly superfluous even to himself. The confines of his dream are narrowed. He moves apathetically and dies forlorn.

Some echo of the vital rhythm which pervades not merely the generations of animals, but the seasons and the stars, emerges sometimes in consciousness; on reaching the tropics in the mortal ecliptic, which the human individual may touch many times without much change in his outer fortunes, the soul may occasionally divine that it is passing through a supreme crisis. Passion, when vehement, may bring atavistic sentiments. When love is absolute it feels a profound impulse to welcome death, and even, by a transcendental confusion, to invoke the end of the universe.* The human soul reverts at such a moment to what an ephemeral insect might feel, buzzing till it finds its mate in the noon. Its whole destiny was wooing, and, that mission accomplished, it sings its *Nunc dimittis*, renouncing heartily all irrelevant things, now that the one fated and all-satisfying good has been achieved. Where parental instincts exist also, nature soon shifts her loom: a milder impulse succeeds, and a satisfaction of a gentler sort follows in the birth of children. The transcendental illusion is here corrected, and it is seen that the extinction the lovers had accepted needed not to be complete. The death they welcomed was not without its little resurrection. The feeble worm they had generated bore their immortality within it.

The varieties of sexual economy are many and to each may

*One example, among a thousand, is the cry of Siegfried and Brünhilde in Wagner:

Lachend lass' uns verderben,
Lachend zu Grunde geh'n.
Fahr hin, Walhall's
Leuchtende Welt! . . .
Leb' wohl, pragende
Götter Pracht!
Ende in Wonne,
Du ewig Geschlecht!

correspond, for all we know, a special sentiment. Sometimes the union established is intermittent; sometimes it crowns the end of life and dissolves it altogether; sometimes it remains, while it lasts, monogamous; sometimes the sexual and social alertness is constant in the male, only periodic in the female. Sometimes the group established for procreation endures throughout the seasons, and from year to year; sometimes the males herd together, as if normally they preferred their own society, until the time of rut comes, when war arises between them for the possession of what they have just discovered to be the fair.

Structure the Ground of Faculty and Faculty of Duty.

A naturalist not ashamed to indulge his poetic imagination might easily paint for us the drama of these diverse loves. It suffices for our purpose to observe that the varying passions and duties which life can contain depend upon the organic functions of the animal. A fish incapable of coition, absolved from all care for its young, which it never sees or never distinguishes from the casual swimmers darting across its path, such a fish, being without social faculties or calls to co-operation, cannot have the instincts, perceptions, or emotions which belong to social beings. A male of some higher species that feels only once a year the sudden solicitations of love cannot be sentimental in all the four seasons: his headlong passion, exhausted upon its present object and dismissed at once without remainder, leaves his senses perfectly free and colourless to scrutinise his residual world. Whatever further fears or desires may haunt him will have nothing mystical or sentimental about them. He will be a man of business all the year round, and a lover only on May-day. A female that does not suffice for the rearing of her young will expect and normally receive her mate's aid long after the pleasures of love are forgotten by him. Disinterested fidelity on his part will then be her right and his duty. But a female that, once pregnant, needs, like the hen, no further co-operation on the

male's part will turn from him at once with absolute indifference to brood perpetually on her eggs, undisturbed by the
least sense of solitude or jealousy. And the chicks that at first
follow her and find shelter under her wings will soon be forgotten also and relegated to the mechanical landscape. There
is no pain in the timely snapping of the dearest bonds where
society has not become a permanent organism, and perpetual
friendship is not one of its possible modes.

Transcendent and ideal passions may well judge themselves to have an incomparable dignity. Yet that dignity is
hardly more than what every passion, were it articulate, would
assign to itself and to its objects. The dumbness of a passion
may accordingly, from one point of view, be called the index
of its baseness; for if it cannot ally itself with ideas its affinities can hardly lie in the rational mind nor its advocates be
among the poets. But if we listen to the master-passion itself
rather than to the loquacious arts it may have enlisted in its
service, we shall understand that it is not self-condemned because it is silent, nor an anomaly in nature because inhar-
monious with human life. The fish's heartlessness is his
virtue; the male bee's lasciviousness is his vocation; and if
these functions were retrenched or encumbered in order to
assimilate them to human excellence they would be merely
dislocated. We should not produce virtue where there was
vice, but defeat a possible arrangement which would have had
its own vitality and order.

Glory of Animal Love.

Animal love is a marvellous force; and while it issues in
acts that may be followed by a revulsion of feeling, it yet deserves a more sympathetic treatment than art and morals
have known how to accord it. Erotic poets, to hide their
want of ability to make the dumb passion speak, have played
feebly with veiled insinuations and comic effects; while more
serious sonneteers have harped exclusively on secondary and
somewhat literary emotions, abstractly conjugating the verb

to love. Lucretius, in spite of his didactic turns, has been on this subject, too, the most ingenuous and magnificent of poets, although he chose to confine his description to the external history of sexual desire. It is a pity that he did not turn, with his sublime sincerity, to the inner side of it also, and write the drama of the awakened senses, the poignant suasion of beauty, when it clouds the brain, and makes the conventional earth, seen through that bright haze, seem a sorry fable. Western poets should not have despised what the Orientals, in their fugitive stanzas, seem often to have sung most exquisitely: the joy of gazing on the beloved, of following or being followed, of tacit understandings and avowals, of flight together into some solitude to people it with those ineffable confidences which so naturally follow the outward proofs of love. All this makes the brightest page of many a life, the only bright page in the thin biography of many a human animal; while if the beasts could speak they would give us, no doubt, endless versions of the only joy in which, as we may fancy, the blood of the universe flows consciously through their hearts.

The darkness which conventionally covers this passion is one of the saddest consequences of Adam's fall. It was a terrible misfortune in man's development that he should not have been able to acquire the higher functions without deranging the lower. Why should the depths of his being be thus polluted and the most delightful of nature's mysteries be an occasion not for communion with her, as it should have remained, but for depravity and sorrow?

Its Degradation when Instincts Become Numerous and Competitive.

This question, asked in moral perplexity, admits of a scientific answer. Man, in becoming more complex, becomes less stably organised. His sexual instinct, instead of being intermittent, but violent and boldly declared, becomes practically constant, but is entangled in many cross-currents of desire, in many other equally imperfect adaptations of structure to various ends. Indulgence in any impulse can then easily become excessive and thwart the rest; for it may be aroused artificially and maintained from without, so that in turn it disturbs its neighbours. Sometimes the sexual instinct may be stimulated out of season by example, by a too wakeful fancy, by language, by pride—for all these forces are now working in the same field and intermingling their suggestions. At the same time the same instinct may derange others, and make them fail at their proper and pressing occasions.

Moral Censure Provoked.

In consequence of such derangements, reflection and public opinion will come to condemn what in itself was perfectly innocent. The corruption of a given instinct by others and of others by it, becomes the ground for long attempts to suppress or enslave it. With the haste and formalism natural to language and to law, external and arbitrary limits are set to its operation. As no inward adjustment can possibly correspond to these conventional barriers and compartments of life, a war between nature and morality breaks out both in society and in each particular bosom—a war in which every victory is a sorrow and every defeat a dishonour. As one instinct after another becomes furious or disorganised, cowardly or criminal, under these artificial restrictions, the public and private conscience turns against it all its forces, necessarily without much nice discrimination; the frank passions of youth are met with a grimace of horror on all sides, with *rumores senum severiorum*, with an insistence on reticence and hypocrisy. Such suppression is favourable to corruption: the fancy with a sort of idiotic ingenuity comes to supply the place of experience; and nature is rendered vicious and overlaid with pruriency, artifice, and the love of novelty. Hereupon the authorities that rule in such matters naturally redouble their vigilance and exaggerate their reasonable censure: chastity begins to seem essentially holy and perpetual virginity ends by becoming an absolute ideal. Thus the disorder in man's life and disposition, when grown intolerable, leads him to condemn the very elements out of which order might have been constituted, and to mistake his total confusion for his total depravity.

The Heart Alienated from the World.

Banished from the open day, covered with mockery, and publicly ignored, this necessary pleasure flourishes none the less in dark places and in the secret soul. Its familiar presence there, its intimate habitation in what is most oneself, helps to cut the world in two and to separate the inner from the outer life. In that mysticism which cannot disguise its erotic affinities this disruption reaches an absolute and theoretic form; but in many a youth little suspected of mysticism it produces estrangement from the conventional moralising world, which he instinctively regards as artificial and alien. It prepares him for excursions into the private fairy-land in which unthought-of joys will blossom amid friendlier magic forces. The truly good then seems to be the fantastic, the sensuous, the prodigally unreal. He gladly forgets the dreary world he lives in to listen for a thousand and one nights to his dreams.

Childish Ideals.

This is the region where those who have no conception of the Life of Reason place the ideal; and an ideal is indeed there but the ideal of a single and inordinate impulse. A rational mind, on the contrary, moves by preference in the real world, cultivating all human interests in due proportion. The love-sick and luxurious dream-land dear to irrational poets is a distorted image of the ideal world; but this distortion has still an ideal motive, since it is made to satisfy the cravings of a forgotten part of the soul and to make a home for those elements in human nature which have been denied overt

89448

existence. If the ideal is meantime so sadly caricatured, the fault lies with the circumstances of life that have not allowed the sane will adequate exercise. Lack of strength and of opportunity makes it impossible for man to preserve all his interests in a just harmony; and his conscious ideal, springing up as it too often does in protest against suffering and tyranny, has not scope and range enough to include the actual opportunities for action. Nature herself, by making a slave of the body, has thus made a tyrant of the soul.

Their Light All Focussed on the Object of Love.

Fairy-land and a mystical heaven contain many other factors besides that furnished by unsatisfied and objectless love. All sensuous and verbal images may breed after their own kind in an empty brain; but these fantasies are often supported and directed by sexual longings and vaguely luxurious thoughts. An Oriental Paradise, with its delicate but mindless æstheticism, is above everything a garden for love. To brood on such an Elysium is a likely prelude and fertile preparation for romantic passion. When the passion takes form it calls fancy back from its loose reveries and fixes it upon a single object. Then the ideal seems at last to have been brought down to earth. Its embodiment has been discovered amongst the children of men. Imagination narrows her range. Instead of all sorts of flatteries to sense and improbable delicious adventures, the lover imagines but a single joy: to be master of his love in body and soul. Jealousy pursues him. Even if he dreads no physical betrayal, he suffers from terror and morbid sensitiveness at every hint of mental estrangement.

This attachment is often the more absorbing the more unaccountable it seems; and as in hypnotism the subject is dead to all influences but that of the operator, so in love the heart surrenders itself entirely to the one being that has known how to touch it. That being is not selected; it is recognised and obeyed. Prearranged reactions in the system respond to whatever stimulus, at a propitious moment, happens to break through and arouse them pervasively.

Three Environments for Love.

Nature has opened various avenues to that passion in whose successful operation she has so much at stake. Sometimes the magic influence asserts itself suddenly, sometimes gently and unawares. One approach, which in poetry has usurped more than its share of attention, is through beauty; another, less glorious, but often more efficacious, through surprised sense and premonitions of pleasure; a third through social sympathy and moral affinities. Contemplation, sense, and association are none of them the essence nor even the seed of love; but any of them may be its soil and supply it with a propitious background. It would be mere sophistry to pretend, for instance, that love is or should be nothing but a moral bond, the sympathy of two kindred spirits or the union of two lives. For such an effect no passion would be needed, as none is needed to perceive beauty or to feel pleasure.

What Aristotle calls friendships of utility, pleasure, or virtue, all resting on common interests of some impersonal sort, are far from possessing the quality of love, its thrill, flutter, and absolute sway over happiness and misery. But it may well fall to such influences to awaken or feed the passion where it actually arises. Whatever circumstances pave the way, love does not itself appear until a sexual affinity is declared. When a woman, for instance, contemplating marriage, asks herself whether she really loves her suitor or merely accepts him, the test is the possibility of awakening a sexual affinity. For this reason women of the world often love their husbands more truly than they did their lovers, because marriage has evoked an elementary feeling which before lay smothered under a heap of coquetries, vanities, and conventions.

Subjectivity of the Passion.

Man, on the contrary, is polygamous by instinct, although often kept faithful by habit no less than by duty. If his fancy is left free, it is apt to wander. We observe this in romantic passion no less than in a life of mere gallantry and pleasure. Sentimental illusions may become a habit, and the shorter the dream is the more often it is repeated, so that any susceptible poet may find that he, like Alfred de Musset, "must love incessantly, who once has loved." Love is indeed much less exacting than it thinks itself. Nine-tenths of its cause are in the lover, for one-tenth that may be in the object. Were the latter not accidentally at hand, an almost identical passion would probably have been felt for someone else; for although with acquaintance the quality of an attachment naturally adapts itself to the person loved, and makes that person its standard and ideal, the first assault and mysterious glow of the passion is much the same for every object. What really affects the character of love is the lover's temperament, age, and experience. The objects that appeal to each man reveal his nature; but those unparalleled virtues and that unique divinity which the lover discovers there are reflections of his own adoration, things that ecstasy is very cunning in. He loves what he imagines and worships what he creates.

Machinery Regulating Choice.

Those who do not consider these matters so curiously may feel that to refer love in this way chiefly to inner processes is at once ignominious and fantastic. But nothing could be more natural; the soul accurately renders, in this experience, what is going on in the body and in the race. Nature had a problem to solve in sexual reproduction which would have daunted a less ruthless experimenter. She had to bring together automatically, and at the dictation, as they felt, of their irresponsible wills, just the creatures that by uniting might reproduce the species. The complete sexual reaction had to be woven together out of many incomplete reactions to various stimuli, reactions not specifically sexual. The outer senses had to be engaged, and many secondary characters found in bodies had to be used to attract attention, until the deeper instinctive response should have time to gather itself together and assert itself openly. Many mechanical preformations and reflexes must conspire to constitute a determinate instinct. We name this instinct after its ultimate function, looking forward to the uses we observe it to have; and it seems to us in consequence an inexplicable anomaly that many a time the instinct is set in motion when its alleged purpose cannot be fulfilled; as when love appears prematurely or too late, or fixes upon a creature of the wrong age or sex. These anomalies show us how nature is built up and, far from being inexplicable, are hints that tend to make everything clear, when once a verbal and mythical philosophy has been abandoned.

Responses which we may call sexual in view of results to which they may ultimately lead are thus often quite independent, and exist before they are drawn into the vortex of a complete and actually generative act. External stimulus and present idea will consequently be altogether inadequate to explain the profound upheaval which may ensue, if, as we say, we actually fall in love. That the senses should be played upon is nothing, if no deeper reaction is aroused. All depends on the juncture at which, so to speak, the sexual circuit is completed and the emotional currents begin to circulate. Whatever object, at such a critical moment, fills the field of consciousness becomes a signal and associate for the whole sexual mood. It is breathlessly devoured in that pause and concentration of attention, that rearrangement of the soul, which love is conceived in; and the whole new life which that image is engulfed in is foolishly supposed to be its effect. For the image is in consciousness, but not the profound predispositions which give it place and power.

The Choice Unstable.

This association between passion and its signals may be merely momentary, or it may be perpetual: a Don Juan and a Dante are both genuine lovers. In a gay society the gallant addresses every woman as if she charmed him, and perhaps actually finds any kind of beauty, or mere femininity anywhere, a sufficient spur to his desire. These momentary fascinations are not necessarily false: they may for an instant be quite absorbing and irresistible; they may genuinely suffuse the whole mind. Such mercurial fire will indeed require a certain imaginative temperament; and there are many persons who, short of a lifelong domestic attachment, can conceive of nothing but sordid vice. But even an inconstant flame may burn brightly, if the soul is naturally combustible. Indeed these sparks and glints of passion, just because they come and vary so quickly, offer admirable illustrations of it, in which it may be viewed, so to speak, under the microscope and in its formative stage.

Thus Plato did not hesitate to make the love of all wines, under whatever guise, excuse, or occasion, the test of a true taste for wine and an unfeigned adoration of Bacchus; and, like Lucretius after him, he wittily compiled a list of names, by which the lover will flatter the most opposite qualities, if they only succeed in arousing his inclination. To be omnivorous is one pole of true love: to be exclusive is the other. A man whose heart, if I may say so, lies deeper, hidden under a thicker coat of mail, will have less play of fancy, and will be far from finding every charm charming, or every sort of beauty a stimulus to love. Yet he may not be less prone to the tender passion, and when once smitten may be so penetrated by an unimagined tenderness and joy, that he will declare himself incapable of ever loving again, and may actually be so. Having no rivals and a deeper soil, love can ripen better in such a constant spirit; it will not waste itself in a continual patter of little pleasures and illusions. But unless the passion of it is to die down, it must somehow assert its universality: what it loses in diversity it must gain in applicability. It must become a principle of action and an influence colouring everything that is dreamt of; otherwise it would have lost its dignity and sunk into a dead memory or a domestic bond.

Instinctive Essence of Love.

True love, it used to be said, is love at first sight. Manners have much to do with such incidents, and the race which happens to set, at a given time, the fashion in literature makes its temperament public and exercises a sort of contagion over all men's fancies. If women are rarely seen and ordinarily not to be spoken to; if all imagination has to build upon is a furtive glance or casual motion, people fall in love at first sight. For they must fall in love somehow, and any stimulus is enough if none more powerful is forthcoming. When society, on the contrary, allows constant and easy intercourse between the sexes, a first impression, if not reinforced, will soon be hidden and obliterated by others. Acquaintance becomes necessary for love when it is necessary for memory. But what makes true love is not the information conveyed by acquaintance, not any circumstantial charms that may be therein discovered: it is still a deep and dumb instinctive affinity, an inexplicable emotion seizing the heart, an influence organising the world, like a luminous crystal, about one magic point. So that although love seldom springs up suddenly in these days into anything like a full-blown passion, it is sight, it is presence, that makes in time a conquest over the heart; for all virtues, sympathies, confidences will fail to move a man to tenderness and to worship, unless a poignant effluence from the object envelop him, so that he begins to walk, as it were, in a dream.

Not to believe in love is a great sign of dulness. There are some people so indirect and lumbering that they think all real affection must rest on circumstantial evidence. But a finely constituted being is sensitive to its deepest affinities. This is precisely what refinement consists in, that we may feel in things immediate and infinitesimal a sure premonition of things ultimate and important. Fine senses vibrate at once to harmonies which it may take long to verify; so sight is finer than touch, and thought than sensation. Well-bred instinct meets reason half-way, and is prepared for the consonances that may follow. Beautiful things, when taste is formed, are obviously and unaccountably beautiful. The grounds we may bring ourselves to assign for our preferences are discovered by analysing those preferences, and articulate judgments follow upon emotions which they ought to express, but which they sometimes sophisticate. So, too, the reasons we give for love either express what it feels or else are insincere, attempting to justify at the bar of reason and convention something which is far more primitive than they and underlies them both. True instinct can dispense with such excuses. It appeals to the event and is justified by the response which nature makes to it. It is, of course, far from infallible; it cannot dominate circumstances, and has no discursive knowledge; but it is presumably true, and what it foreknows is always essentially possible. Unrealisable it may indeed be in the jumbled context of this world, where the Fates, like an absent-minded printer, seldom allow a single line to stand perfect and unmarred.

The profoundest affinities are those most readily felt, and though a thousand later considerations may overlay and override them, they remain a background and standard for all happiness. If we trace them out we succeed. If we put them by, although in other respects we may call ourselves happy, we inwardly know that we have dismissed the ideal, and all that was essentially possible has not been realised. Love in that case still owns a hidden and potential object, and we sanctify, perhaps, whatever kindnesses or partialities we indulge in by a secret loyalty to something impersonal and unseen. Such reserve, such religion, would not have been necessary had things responded to our first expectations. We might then have identified the ideal with the object that happened to call it forth. The Life of Reason might have been led instinctively, and we might have been guided by nature herself into the ways of peace.

Its Ideality.

As it is, circumstances, false steps, or the mere lapse of time, force us to shuffle our affections and take them as they come, or as we are suffered to indulge them. A mother is followed by a boyish friend, a friend by a girl, a girl by a wife, a wife by a child, a child by an idea. A divinity passes through these various temples; they may all remain standing, and we may continue our cult in them without outward change, long after the god has fled from the last into his native heaven. We may try to convince ourselves that we have lost nothing when we have lost all. We may take comfort in praising the mixed and perfunctory attachments which cling to us by force of habit and duty, repeating the empty names of creatures that have long ceased to be what we once could love, and assuring ourselves that we have remained constant, without admitting that the world, which is in irreparable flux, has from the first been betraying us.

Ashamed of being so deeply deceived, we may try to smile cynically at the glory that once shone upon us, and call it a dream. But cynicism is wasted on the ideal. There is indeed no idol ever identified with the ideal which honest experience, even without cynicism, will not some day unmask and discredit. Every real object must cease to be what it seemed, and none could ever be what the whole soul desired. Yet what the soul desires is nothing arbitrary. Life is no objectless dream, but continually embodies, with varying success, the potentialities it contains and that prompt desire. Everything that satisfies at all, even if partially and for an instant, justifies aspiration and rewards it. Existence, however, cannot be arrested; and only the transmissible forms of things can endure, to match the transmissible faculties which living beings hand down to one another. The ideal is accordingly significant, perpetual, and as constant as the nature it expresses; but it can never itself exist, nor can its particular embodiments endure.

Its Universal Scope.

Love is accordingly only half an illusion; the lover, but not his love, is deceived. His madness, as Plato taught, is divine; for though it be folly to identify the idol with the god, faith in the god is inwardly justified. That egregious idolatry may therefore be interpreted ideally and given a symbolic scope worthy of its natural causes and of the mystery it comes to celebrate. The lover knows much more about absolute good and universal beauty than any logician or theologian, unless the latter, too, be lovers in disguise. Logical universals are terms in discourse, without vital ideality, while traditional gods are at best natural existences, more or less indifferent facts. What the lover comes upon, on the contrary, is truly persuasive, and witnesses to itself, so that he worships from the heart and beholds what he worships. That the true object is no natural being, but an ideal form essentially eternal and capable of endless embodiments, is far from abolishing its worth; on the contrary, this fact makes love ideally relevant to generation, by which the human soul and body may be for ever renewed, and at the same time makes it a thing for large thoughts to be focussed upon, a thing representing all rational aims.

Whenever this ideality is absent and a lover sees nothing in his mistress but what everyone else may find in her, loving her honestly in her unvarnished and accidental person, there is a friendly and humorous affection, admirable in itself, but no passion or bewitchment of love; she is a member of his group, not a spirit in his pantheon. Such an affection may be altogether what it should be; it may bring a happiness all the more stable because the heart is quite whole, and no

divine shaft has pierced it. It is hard to stanch wounds in-
flicted by a god. The glance of an ideal love is terrible and
glorious, foreboding death and immortality together. Love
could not be called divine without platitude if it regarded
nothing but its nominal object; to be divine it must not envisage an accidental good but the principle of goodness, that
which gives other goods their ultimate meaning and makes
all functions useful. Love is a true natural religion; it has
a visible cult, it is kindled by natural beauties and bows to
the best symbol it may find for its hope; it sanctifies a natural mystery; and, finally, when understood, it recognises
that what it worshipped under a figure was truly the principle of all good.

The loftiest edifices need the deepest foundations. Love
would never take so high a flight unless it sprung from
something profound and elementary. It is accordingly most
truly love when it is irresistible and fatal. The substance of
all passion, if we could gather it together, would be the basis
of all ideals, to which all goods would have to refer. Love
actually accomplishes something of the sort; being primordial
it underlies other demands, and can be wholly satisfied only
by a happiness which is ultimate and comprehensive. Lovers
are vividly aware of this fact: their ideal, apparently so inarticulate, seems to them to include everything. It shares the
mystical quality of all primitive life. Sophisticated people
can hardly understand how vague experience is at bottom,
and how truly that vagueness supports whatever clearness is
afterward attained. They cling to the notion that nothing can
have a spiritual scope that does not spring from reflection.
But in that case life itself, which brings reflection about,
would never support spiritual interests, and all that is moral
would be unnatural and consequently self-destructive. In
truth, all spiritual interests are supported by animal life; in
this the generative function is fundamental; and it is therefore no paradox, but something altogether fitting, that if
that function realised all it comprises, nothing human would

remain outside. Such an ultimate fulfilment would differ, of course, from a first satisfaction, just as all that reproduction reproduces differs from the reproductive function itself, and vastly exceeds it. All organs and activities which are inherited, in a sense, grow out of the reproductive process and serve to clothe it; so that when the generative energy is awakened all that can ever be is virtually called up and, so to speak, made consciously potential; and love yearns for the universe of values.

Its Euthanasia.

This secret is gradually revealed to those who are inwardly attentive and allow love to teach them something. A man who has truly loved, though he may come to recognise the thousand incidental illusions into which love may have led him, will not recant its essential faith. He will keep his sense for the ideal and his power to worship. The further objects by which these gifts will be entertained will vary with the situation. A philosopher, a soldier, and a courtesan will express the same religion in different ways. In fortunate cases love may glide imperceptibly into settled domestic affections, giving them henceforth a touch of ideality; for when love dies in the odour of sanctity people venerate his relics. In other cases allegiance to the ideal may appear more sullenly, breaking out in whims, or in little sentimental practices which might seem half-conventional. Again it may inspire a religious conversion, charitable works, or even artistic labours. In all these ways people attempt more or less seriously to lead the Life of Reason, expressing outwardly allegiance to whatever in their minds has come to stand for the ideal. If to create was love's impulse originally, to create is its effort still, after it has been chastened and has received some rational extension. The machinery which serves reproduction thus finds kindred but higher uses, as every organ does in a liberal life; and what Plato called a desire for birth in beauty may be sublimated even more, until it yearns for an ideal immortality in a transfigured world, a world made worthy of that love which its children have so often lavished on it in their dreams.

VI

Free Society

Primacy of Nature over Spirit.

NATURAL society unites beings in time and space; it fixes affection on those creatures on which we depend and to which our action must be adapted. Natural society begins at home and radiates over the world, as more and more things become tributary to our personal being. In marriage and the family, in industry, government, and war, attention is riveted on temporal existences, on the fortunes of particular bodies, natural or corporate. There is then a primacy of nature over spirit in social life; and this primacy, in a certain sense, endures to the end, since all spirit must be the spirit of something, and reason could not exist or be conceived at all unless a material organism, personal or social, lay beneath to give thought an occasion and a point of view, and to give preference a direction. Things could not be near or far, worse or better, unless a definite life were taken as a standard, a life lodged somewhere in space and time. Reason is a principle of order appearing in a subject-matter which in its subsistence and quantity must be an irrational datum. Reason expresses purpose, purpose expresses impulse, and impulse expresses a natural body with self-equilibrating powers.

At the same time, natural growths may be called achievements only because when formed, they support a joyful and liberal experience. Nature's works first acquire a meaning in the commentaries they provoke; mechanical processes have interesting climaxes only from the point of view of the life that expresses them, in which their ebb and flow grows impassioned and vehement. Nature's values are imputed to her retroactively by spirit, which in its material dependence has a logical and moral primacy of its own. In themselves events are perfectly mechanical, steady, and fluid, not stopping where we see a goal nor avoiding what we call failures. And so they would always have remained in crude experience, if no cumulative reflection, no art, and no science had come to dominate and foreshorten that equable flow of substance, arresting it ideally in behalf of some rational interest.

Thus it comes to pass that rational interests have a certain ascendancy in the world, as well as an absolute authority over it; for they arise where an organic equilibrium has naturally established itself. Such an equilibrium maintains itself by virtue of the same necessity that produced it; without arresting the flux or introducing any miracle, it sustains in being an ideal form. This form is what consciousness corresponds to and raises to actual existence; so that significant thoughts are something which nature necessarily lingers upon and seems to serve. The being to whom they come is the most widely based and synthetic of her creatures. The mind spreads and soars in proportion as the body feeds on the surrounding world. Noble ideas, although rare and difficult to attain, are not naturally fugitive.

All Experience at Bottom Liberal.

Consciousness is not ideal merely in its highest phases; it is ideal through and through. On one level as much as on another, it celebrates an attained balance in nature, or grieves at its collapse; it prophesies and remembers, it loves and dreams. It sees even nature from the point of view of ideal interests, and measures the flux of things by ideal standards. It registers its own movement, like that of its objects, entirely in ideal terms, looking to fixed goals of its own imagining, and using nothing in the operation but concretions in discourse. Primary mathematical notions, for instance, are evidences of a successful reactive method attained in the organism and translated in consciousness into a stable grammar which has wide applicability and great persistence, so that it has come to be elaborated ideally into prodigious abstract systems of thought. Every experience of victory, eloquence, or beauty is a momentary success of the same kind, and if repeated and sustained becomes a spiritual possession.

Social Experience Has Its Ideality Too.

Society also breeds its ideal harmonies. At first it establishes affections between beings naturally conjoined in the world; later it grows sensitive to free and spiritual affinities, to oneness of mind and sympathetic purposes. These ideal affinities, although grounded like the others on material relations (for sympathy presupposes communication), do not have those relations for their theme but rest on them merely as on a pedestal from which they look away to their own realm, as music, while sustained by vibrating instruments, looks away from them to its own universe of sound.

The Self an Ideal.

Ideal society is a drama enacted exclusively in the imagination. Its personages are all mythical, beginning with that brave protagonist who calls himself I and speaks all the soliloquies. When most nearly material these personages are human souls—the ideal life of particular bodies—or floating mortal reputations—echoes of those ideal lives in one another. From this relative substantiality they fade into notions of country, posterity, humanity, and the gods. These figures all represent some circle of events or forces in the real world; but such representation, besides being mythical, is usually most inadequate. The boundaries of that province which each spirit presides over are vaguely drawn, the spirit itself being correspondingly indefinite. This ambiguity is most conspicuous, perhaps, in the most absorbing of the personages which a man constructs in this imaginative fashion —his idea of himself. "There is society where none intrudes"; and for most men sympathy with their imaginary selves is a powerful and dominant emotion. True memory offers but a meagre and interrupted vista of past experience, yet even that picture is far too rich a term for mental discourse to bandy about; a name with a few physical and social connotations is what must represent the man to his own thinkings. Or rather it is no memory, however eviscerated, that fulfils that office. A man's notion of himself is a concretion in discourse for which his more constant somatic feelings, his ruling interests, and his social relations furnish most of the substance.

Romantic Egotism.

The more reflective and self-conscious a man is the more completely will his experience be subsumed and absorbed in his perennial "I." If philosophy has come to reinforce this reflective egotism, he may even regard all nature as nothing but his half-voluntary dream and encourage himself thereby to give even to the physical world a dramatic and sentimental colour. But the more successful he is in stuffing everything into his self-consciousness, the more desolate will the void become which surrounds him. For self is, after all, but one term in a primitive dichotomy and would lose its specific and intimate character were it no longer contrasted with anything else. The egotist must therefore people the desert he has spread about him, and he naturally peoples it with mythical counterparts of himself. Sometimes, if his imagination is sensuous, his alter-egos are incarnate in the landscape, and he creates a poetic mythology; sometimes, when the inner life predominates, they are projected into his own forgotten past or infinite future. He will then say that all experience is really his own and that some inexplicable illusion has momentarily raised opaque partitions in his omniscient mind.

Vanity.

Philosophers less pretentious and more worldly than these have sometimes felt, in their way, the absorbing force of self-consciousness. La Rochefoucauld could describe *amour propre* as the spring of all human sentiments. *Amour propre* involves preoccupation not merely with the idea of self, but with that idea reproduced in other men's minds; the soliloquy has become a dialogue, or rather a solo with an echoing chorus. Interest in one's own social figure is to some extent a material interest, for other men's love or aversion is a principle read into their acts; and a social animal like man is dependent on other men's acts for his happiness. An individual's concern for the attitude society takes toward him is therefore in the first instance concern for his own practical welfare. But imagination here refines upon worldly interest. What others think of us would be of little moment did it not, when known, so deeply tinge what we think of ourselves. Nothing could better prove the mythical character of self-consciousness than this extreme sensitiveness to alien opinions; for if a man really knew himself he would utterly despise the ignorant notions others might form on a subject in which he had such matchless opportunities for observation. Indeed, those opinions would hardly seem to him directed upon the reality at all, and he would laugh at them as he might at the stock fortune-telling of some itinerant gypsy.

As it is, however, the last breath of irresponsible and anonymous censure lashes our self-esteem and sometimes quite transforms our plans and affections. The passions grafted on wounded pride are the most inveterate; they are green and vigorous in old age. We crave support in vanity, as we do in religion, and never forgive contradictions in that sphere; for however persistent and passionate such prejudices may be, we know too well that they are woven of thin air. A hostile word, by starting a contrary imaginative current, buffets them rudely and threatens to dissolve their being.

Ambiguities of Fame.

The highest form of vanity is love of fame. It is a passion easy to deride but hard to understand, and in men who live at all by imagination almost impossible to eradicate. The good opinion of posterity can have no possible effect on our fortunes, and the practical value which reputation may temporarily have is quite absent in posthumous fame. The direct object of this passion—that a name should survive in men's mouths to which no adequate idea of its original can be attached—seems a thin and fantastic satisfaction, especially when we consider how little we should probably sympathise with the creatures that are to remember us. What comfort would it be to Virgil that boys still read him at school, or to Pindar that he is sometimes mentioned in a world from which everything he loved has departed? Yet, beneath this desire for nominal longevity, apparently so inane, there may lurk an ideal ambition of which the ancients cannot have been unconscious when they set so high a value on fame. They often identified fame with immortality, a subject on which they had far more rational sentiments than have since prevailed.

Fame, as a noble mind conceives and desires it, is not embodied in a monument, a biography, or the repetition of a strange name by strangers; it consists in the immortality of a man's work, his spirit, his efficacy, in the perpetual rejuvenation of his soul in the world.

Its Possible Ideality.

When Horace—no model of magnanimity—wrote his *exegi monumentum,* he was not thinking that the pleasure he would continue to give would remind people of his trivial personality, which indeed he never particularly celebrated and which had much better lie buried with his bones. He was thinking, of course, of that pleasure itself; thinking that the delight, half lyric, half sarcastic, which those delicate cameos had given him to carve would be perennially renewed in all who retraced them. Nay, perhaps we may not go too far in saying that even that impersonal satisfaction was not the deepest he felt; the deepest, very likely, flowed from the immortality, not of his monument, but of the subject and passion it commemorated; that tenderness, I mean, and that disillusion with mortal life which rendered his verse immortal. He had expressed, and in expressing appropriated, some recurring human moods, some mocking renunciations; and he knew that his spirit was immortal, being linked and identified with that portion of the truth. He had become a little spokesman of humanity, uttering what all experience repeats more or less articulately; and even if he should cease to be honoured in men's memories, he would continue to be unwittingly honoured and justified in their lives.

What we may conceive to have come in this way even within a Horace's apprehension is undoubtedly what has attached many nobler souls to fame. With an inversion of moral derivations which all mythical expression involves we speak of fame as the reward of genius, whereas in truth genius, the imaginative dominion of experience, is its own reward and fame is but a foolish image by which its worth is symbolised. When the Virgin in the Magnificat says, "Behold, from henceforth all generations shall call me blessed," the psalmist surely means to express a spiritual exaltation exempt from vanity; he merely translates into a rhetorical figure the fact that what had been first revealed to Mary would also bless all generations. That the Church should in consequence deem and pronounce her blessed is an incident describing, but not creating, the unanimity in their religious joys. Fame is thus the outward sign or recognition of an inward representative authority residing in genius or good fortune, an authority in which lies the whole worth of fame. Those will substantially remember and honour us who keep our ideals, and we shall live on in those ages whose experience we have anticipated.

Free society differs from that which is natural and legal precisely in this, that it does not cultivate relations which in the last analysis are experienced and material, but turns exclusively to unanimities in meanings, to collaborations in an ideal world. The basis of free society is of course natural, as we said, but free society has ideal goals. Spirits cannot touch save by becoming unanimous. At the same time public opinion, reputation, and impersonal sympathy reinforce only very general feelings, and reinforce them vaguely; and as the inner play of sentiment becomes precise, it craves more specific points of support or comparison. It is in creatures of our own species that we chiefly scent the aroma of inward sympathy, because it is they that are visibly moved on the same occasions as ourselves; and it is to those among our fellow-men who share our special haunts and habits that we feel more precise affinities. Though the ground for such feeling is animal contact and contagion, its deliverance does not revert to those natural accidents, but concerns a represented sympathy in represented souls. Friendship, springing from accidental association, terminates in a consciousness of ideal and essential agreement.

Comradeship.

Comradeship is a form of friendship still akin to general sociability and gregariousness. When men are "in the same boat together," when a common anxiety, occupation, or sport unites them, they feel their human kinship in an intensified form without any greater personal affinity subsisting between them. The same effect is produced by a common estrangement from the rest of society. For this reason comradeship lasts no longer than the circumstances that bring it about. Its constancy is proportionate to the monotony of people's lives and minds. There is a lasting bond among schoolfellows because no one can become a boy again and have a new set of playmates. There is a persistent comradeship with one's countrymen, especially abroad, because sel-

dom is a man pliable and polyglot enough to be at home
among foreigners, or really to understand them. There is an
inevitable comradeship with men of the same breeding or
profession, however bad these may be, because habits soon
monopolise the man. Nevertheless a greater buoyancy, a
longer youth, a richer experience, would break down all these
limits of fellowship. Such clingings to the familiar are three
parts dread of the unfamiliar and want of resource in its
presence, for one part in them of genuine loyalty. Plasticity
loves new moulds because it can fill them, but for a man of
sluggish mind and bad manners there is decidedly no place
like home.

External Conditions of Friendship.

Though comradeship is an accidental bond, it is the condition of ideal friendship, for the ideal, in all spheres, is nothing but the accidental confirming itself and generating its
own standard. Men must meet to love, and many other accidents besides conjunction must conspire to make a true
friendship possible. In order that friendship may fulfil the
conditions even of comradeship, it is requisite that the friends
have the same social status, so that they may live at ease together and have congenial tastes. They must further have
enough community of occupation and gifts to give each an
appreciation of the other's faculty; for qualities are not
complementary unless they are qualities of the same substance. Nothing must be actual in either friend that is not
potential in the other.

Identity in Sex Required.

For this reason, among others, friends are generally of the
same sex, for when men and women agree, it is only in their
conclusions; their reasons are always different. So that
while intellectual harmony between men and women is easily
possible, its delightful and magic quality lies precisely in the
fact that it does not arise from mutual understanding, but

is a conspiracy of alien essences and a kissing, as it were, in the dark. As man's body differs from woman's in sex and strength, so his mind differs from hers in quality and function: they can co-operate but can never fuse. The human race, in its intellectual life, is organised like the bees: the masculine soul is a worker, sexually atrophied, and essentially dedicated to impersonal and universal arts; the feminine is a queen, infinitely fertile, omnipresent in its brooding industry, but passive and abounding in intuitions without method and passions without justice. Friendship with a woman is therefore apt to be more or less than friendship: less, because there is no intellectual parity; more, because (even when the relation remains wholly dispassionate, as in respect to old ladies) there is something mysterious and oracular about a woman's mind which inspires a certain instinctive deference and puts it out of the question to judge what she says by masculine standards. She has a kind of sibylline intuition and the right to be irrationally *à propos*. There is a gallantry of the mind which pervades all conversation with a lady, as there is a natural courtesy toward children and mystics; but such a habit of respectful concession, marking as it does an intellectual alienation as profound as that which separates us from the dumb animals, is radically incompatible with friendship.

And in Age.

Friends, moreover, should have been young together. Much difference in age defeats equality and forbids frankness on many a fundamental subject; it confronts two minds of unlike focus: one near-sighted and without perspective, the other seeing only the background of present things. While comparisons in these respects may be interesting and borrowings sometimes possible, lending the older mind life and the younger mind wisdom, such intercourse has hardly the value of spontaneous sympathy, in which the spark of mutual intelligence flies, as it should, almost without words.

Contagion is the only source of valid mind-reading: you must imitate to understand, and where the plasticity of two minds is not similar their mutual interpretations are necessarily false. They idealise in their friends whatever they do not invent or ignore, and the friendship which should have lived on energies conspiring spontaneously together dies into conscious appreciation.

Constituents of Friendship.

All these are merely permissive conditions for friendship; its positive essence is yet to find. How, we may ask, does the vision of the general *socius*, humanity, become specific in the vision of a particular friend without losing its ideality or reverting to practical values? Of course, individuals might be singled out for the special benefits they may have conferred; but a friend's only gift is himself, and friendship is not friendship, it is not a form of free or liberal society, if it does not terminate in an ideal possession, in an object loved for its own sake. Such objects can be ideas only, not forces, for forces are subterranean and instrumental things, having only such value as they borrow from their ulterior effects and manifestations. To praise the utility of friendship, as the ancients so often did, and to regard it as a political institution justified, like victory or government, by its material results, is to lose one's moral bearings. The value of victory or good government is rather to be found in the fact that, among other things, it might render friendship possible. We are not to look now for what makes friendship useful, but for whatever may be found in friendship that may lend utility to life.

Personal Liking.

The first note that gives sociability a personal quality and raises the comrade into an incipient friend is doubtless sensuous affinity. Whatever reaction we may eventually make on an impression, after it has had time to soak in and to merge in some practical or intellectual habit, its first assault is always on the senses, and no sense is an indifferent organ. Each has, so to speak, its congenial rate of vibration and gives its stimuli a varying welcome. Little as we may attend to these instinctive hospitalities of sense, they betray themselves in unjustified likes and dislikes felt for casual persons and things, in the *je ne sais quoi* that makes instinctive sympathy. Voice, manner, aspect, hints of congenial tastes and judgments, a jest in the right key, a gesture marking the right aversions, all these trifles leave behind a pervasive impression. We reject a vision we find indigestible and without congruity to our inner dream; we accept and incorporate another into our private pantheon, where it becomes a legitimate figure, however dumb and subsidiary it may remain.

In a refined nature these sensuous premonitions of sympathy are seldom misleading. Liking cannot, of course, grow into friendship overnight as it might into love; the pleasing impression, even if retained, will lie perfectly passive and harmless in the mind, until new and different impressions follow to deepen the interest at first evoked and to remove its centre of gravity altogether from the senses. In love, if the field is clear, a single glimpse may, like Tristan's potion, produce a violent and irresistible passion; but in friendship the result remains more proportionate to the incidental causes, discrimination is preserved, jealousy and exclusiveness are avoided. That vigilant, besetting, insatiable affection, so full of doubts and torments, with which the lover follows his object, is out of place here; for the friend has no property in his friend's body or leisure or residual ties; he accepts what is offered and what is acceptable, and the rest he leaves in peace. He is distinctly not his brother's keeper, for the society of friends is free.

The Refracting Human Medium for Ideas.

Friendship may indeed come to exist without sensuous liking or comradeship to pave the way; but unless intellectual sympathy and moral appreciation are powerful enough to react on natural instinct and to produce in the end the personal affection which at first was wanting, friendship does not arise. Recognition given to a man's talent or virtue is not properly friendship. Friends must desire to live as much as possible together and to share their work, thoughts, and pleasures. Good-fellowship and sensuous affinity are indispensable to give spiritual communion a personal accent; otherwise men would be indifferent vehicles for such thoughts and powers as emanated from them, and attention would not be in any way arrested or refracted by the human medium through which it beheld the good.

Affection Based on the Refraction.

No natural vehicle, however, is indifferent; no natural organ is or should be transparent. Transparency is a virtue only in artificial instruments, organs in which no blood flows and whose intrinsic operation is not itself a portion of human life. In looking through a field-glass I do not wish to perceive the lenses nor to see rainbows about their rim; yet I should not wish the eye itself to lose its pigments and add no dyes to the bulks it discerns. The sense for colour is a vital endowment and an ingredient in human happiness; but no vitality is added by the intervention of further media which are not themselves living organs.

A man is sometimes a coloured and sometimes a clear medium for the energies he exerts. When a thought conveyed or a work done enters alone into the observer's experience, no friendship is possible. This is always the case when the master is dead; for if his reconstructed personality retains any charm, it is only as an explanation or conceived nexus for the work he performed. In a philosopher or artist, too, personality is merely instrumental, for, although in a sense pervasive, a creative personality evaporates into its expression, and whatever part of it may not have been translated into ideas is completely negligible from the public point of view. That portion of a man's soul which he has not alienated and objectified is open only to those who know him otherwise than by his works and do not estimate him by his public attributions. Such persons are his friends. Into their lives he has entered not merely through an idea with which his name may be associated, nor through the fame of some feat he may have performed, but by awakening an inexpressible animal sympathy, by the contagion of emotions felt before the same objects. Estimation has been partly arrested at its medium and personal relations have added their homely accent to universal discourse. Friendship might thus be called ideal sympathy refracted by a human medium, or comradeship and sensuous affinity colouring a spiritual light.

The Medium Must Also Be Transparent.

If we approach friendship from above and compare it with more ideal loyalties, its characteristic is its animal warmth and its basis in chance conjunctions; if we approach it from below and contrast it with mere comradeship or liking, its essence seems to be the presence of common ideal interests. That is a silly and effeminate friendship in which the parties are always thinking of the friendship itself and of how each stands in the other's eyes; a sentimental fancy of that sort, in which nothing tangible or ulterior brings people together, is rather a feeble form of love than properly a friendship. In extreme youth such a weakness may perhaps indicate capacity for friendship of a nobler type, because when taste and knowledge have not yet taken shape, the only way, often, in which ideal interests can herald themselves is in the guise of some imagined union from which it is vaguely felt they might be developed, just as in love sexual and social instincts mask themselves in an unreasoning obsession, or as for mystic devotion every ideal masks itself in God. All these sentimental feelings are at any rate mere preludes, but preludes in fortunate cases to more discriminating and solid interests, which such a tremulous overture may possibly pitch on a higher key.

Common Interests Indispensable.

The necessity of backing personal attachment with ideal interests is what makes true friendship so rare. It is found chiefly in youth, for youth best unites the two requisite conditions—affectionate comradeship and ardour in pursuing such liberal aims as may be pursued in common. Life in camp or college is favourable to friendship, for there generous activities are carried on in unison and yet leave leisure for playful expansion and opportunity for a choice in friends. The ancients, so long as they were free, spent their whole life in forum and palæstra, camp, theatre, and temple, and in consequence could live by friendship even in their maturer years; but modern life is unfavourable to its continuance. What with business cares, with political bonds remote and invisible, with the prior claims of family, and with individualities both of mind and habit growing daily more erratic, early friends find themselves very soon parted by unbridgeable chasms. For friendship to flourish personal life would have to become more public and social life more simple and humane.

Friendship between Man and Wife.

The tie that in contemporary society most nearly resembles the ancient ideal of friendship is a well-assorted marriage. In spite of intellectual disparity and of divergence in occupation, man and wife are bound together by a common dwelling, common friends, common affection for children, and, what is of great importance, common financial interests. These bonds often suffice for substantial and lasting unanimity, even when no ideal passion preceded; so that what is called a marriage of reason, if it is truly reasonable, may give a fair promise of happiness, since a normal married life can produce the sympathies it requires.

Between Master and Disciple.

When the common ideal interests needed to give friendship a noble strain become altogether predominant, so that comradeship and personal liking may be dispensed with, friendship passes into more and more political fellowships. Discipleship is a union of this kind. Without claiming any share in the master's private life, perhaps without having ever seen him, we may enjoy communion with his mind and feel his support and guidance in following the ideal which links us together. Hero-worship is an imaginative passion in which latent ideals assume picturesque shapes and take actual persons for their symbols. Such companionship, perhaps wholly imaginary, is a very clear and simple example of ideal society. The unconscious hero, to be sure, happens to exist, but his existence is irrelevant to his function, provided only he be present to the idealising mind. There is or need be no comradeship, no actual force or influence transmitted from him. Certain capacities and tendencies in the worshipper are brought to a focus by the hero's image, who is thereby first discovered and deputed to be a hero. He is an unmoved mover, like Aristotle's God and like every ideal to which thought or action is directed.

The symbol, however, is ambiguous in hero-worship, being in one sense ideal, the representation of an inner demand, and in another sense a sensible experience, the representative of an external reality. Accordingly the symbol, when highly prized and long contemplated, may easily become an idol; that in it which is not ideal nor representative of the worshipper's demand may be imported confusedly into the total adored, and may thus receive a senseless worship. The devotion which was, in its origin, an ideal tendency grown conscious and expressed in fancy may thus become a mechanical force vitiating that ideal. For this reason it is very important that the first objects to fix the soul's admiration should be really admirable, for otherwise their accidental blemishes will corrupt the mind to which they appear *sub specie boni.*

Conflict between Ideal and Natural Allegiance.

Discipleship and hero-worship are not stable relations. Since the meaning they embody is ideal and radiates from within outward, and since the image to which that meaning is attributed is controlled by a real external object, meaning and image, as time goes on, will necessarily fall apart. The idol will be discredited. An ideal, ideally conceived and known to be an ideal, a spirit worshipped in spirit and in truth, will take the place of the pleasing phenomenon; and in regard to every actual being, however noble, discipleship will yield to emulation, and worship to an admiration more or less selective and critical.

Automatic Idealisation of Heroes.

A disembodied ideal, however, is unmanageable and vague; it cannot exercise the natural and material suasion proper to a model we are expected to imitate. The more fruitful procedure is accordingly to idealise some historical figure or natural forcee, to ignore or minimise in it what does not seem acceptable, and to retain at the same time all the unobjectionable personal colour and all the graphic traits that can help to give that model a persuasive vitality. This poetic process is all the more successful for being automatic. It is in this way that heroes and gods have been created. A legend or fable lying in the mind and continually repeated gained insensibly at each recurrence some new eloquence, some fresh congruity with the emotion it had already awakened, and was destined to awake again. To measure the importance of this truth the reader need only conceive the distance traversed from the Achilles that may have existed to the hero in Homer, or from Jesus as he might have been in real life, or even as he is in the gospels, to Christ in the Church.

VIII

Ideal Society

The Gregarious Instinct All Social Instincts in Suspense.

To many beings—to almost all that people the earth and sky—each soul is not attached by any practical interest. Some are too distant to be perceived; the proximity of others passes unnoticed. It is far from requisite, in pursuing safety, that every strange animal be regarded as either a friend or an enemy. Wanton hostilities would waste ammunition and idle attachments would waste time. Yet it often happens that some of these beings, having something in common with creatures we are wont to notice, since we stand to them in sexual, parental, or hostile relations, cannot well go unobserved. Their presence fills us with a vague general emotion, the arrested possibility at once of sexual, of parental, and of hostile actions. This emotion is gregarious or impersonally social. The flock it commonly regards may be described as an aggregate in which parents and children have been submerged, in which mates are not yet selected, and enemies not yet descried.

Gregarious sentiment is passive, watchful, expectant, at once powerful and indistinct, troubled and fascinated by things merely possible. It renders solitude terrible without making society particularly delightful. A dull feeling of familiarity and comfort is all we can reasonably attribute to uninterrupted trooping together. Yet banishment from an accustomed society is often unbearable. A creature separated from his group finds all his social instincts bereft of objects and of possible exercise; the sexual, if by chance the sexual be at the time active; the parental, with all its extensions; and the combative, with all its supports. He is helpless and idle, deprived of all resource and employment.

Yet when restored to his tribe, he merely resumes a normal existence. All particular feats and opportunities are still to seek. Company is not occupation. Society is like the air, necessary to breathe but insufficient to live on.

Similar beings herding together in the same places are naturally subject to simultaneous reactions, and the sense of this common reaction makes possible the conception of many minds having a common experience. The elements of this experience they express to one another by signs. For when spontaneous reactions occur together in many animals, each, knowing well his own emotion, will inevitably take the perceived attitude and gesture of his fellows for its expression —for his own attitude and gesture he knows nothing of; and he will thus possess, without further instruction, the outward sign for his inner experience.

It Gives Rise to Conscience or Sympathy with the Public Voice.

It is easy to see how a moral world can grow out of these primary intuitions. Knowing, for instance, the expression of anger, a man may come to find anger directed against himself; together with physical fear in the presence of attack, he will feel the contagion of his enemy's passion, especially if his enemy be the whole group whose reactions he is wont to share, and something in him will strive to be angry together with the rest of the world. He will perfectly understand that indignation against himself which in fact he instinctively shares. This self-condemning emotion will be his sense of shame and his conscience. Words soon come to give definition to such a feeling, which without expression in language would have but little stability. For when a man is attracted to an act, even if it be condemned by others, he views it as delightful and eligible in itself; but when he is forced, by the conventional use of words, to attach to that act an opprobrious epithet, an epithet which he himself has always applied with scorn, he finds himself unable to suppress the emotion connoted by the word; he cannot defend his rebellious intuition against the tyranny of language; he is inwardly confused and divided against himself, and out of his own mouth convicted of wickedness.

A proof of the notable influence that language has on these emotions may be found in their transformations. The connivance of a very few persons is sufficient to establish among them a new application of eulogistic terms; it will suffice to suppress all qualms in the pursuance of their common impulse and to consecrate a new ideal of character. It is accordingly no paradox that there should be honour among thieves, kindness among harlots, and probity among fanatics. They have not lost their conscience; they have merely introduced a flattering heresy into the conventional code, to make room for the particular passion indulged in their little world.

Guises of Public Opinion.

Sympathy with the general mind may also take other forms. Public opinion, in a vivacious and clear-headed community, may be felt to be the casual and irresponsible thing which in truth it is. Homer, for instance, has no more solemn vehicle for it than the indefinite and unaccentable τις. "So," he tells us, "somebody or anybody said." In the Greek tragedians this unauthoritative entity was replaced by the chorus, an assemblage of conventional persons, incapable of any original perception, but possessing a fund of traditional lore, a just if somewhat encumbered conscience, and the gift of song. This chorus was therefore much like the Christian Church and like that celestial choir of which the church wishes to be the earthly echo. Like the church, the tragic chorus had authority, because it represented a wide, if ill-digested, experience; and it had solemnity, because it spoke in archaic tropes, emotional and obscure symbols of prehistoric conflicts. These sacramental forms retained their power to move in spite of their little pertinence to living issues, partly on account of the mystery which enshrouded their forgotten passion and partly on account of the fantastic interpretations which that pregnant obscurity allowed.

Oracles and Revelations.

Far more powerful, however, are those embodiments of the general conscience which religion furnishes in its first and spontaneous phase, as when the Hebrew prophets dared to cry, "So saith the Lord." Such faith in one's own inspiration is a more pliable oracle than tradition or a tragic chorus, and more responsive to the needs and changes of the hour. Occidental philosophers, in their less simple and less eloquent manner, have often repeated that arrogant Hebraic cry: they have told us in their systems what God thinks about the world. Such pretensions would be surprising did we not remind ourselves of the obvious truth that what men attribute to God is nothing but the ideal they value and grope for in themselves, and that the commandments, mythically said to come from the Most High, flow in fact from common reason and local experience.

If history did not enable us to trace this derivation, the ever-present practical standard for faith would sufficiently indicate it; for no one would accept as divine a revelation which he felt to be immoral or found to be pernicious. And yet such a deviation into the maleficent is always possible when a code is uprooted from its rational soil and transplanted into a realm of imagination, where it is subject to all sorts of arbitrary distortions. If the sexual instinct should attach us (as in its extensions and dislocations it sometimes does) to beings incapable of satisfying it or of uniting with us in propagating the race, we should, of course, study to correct that aberration so that our joys and desires might march in step with the possible progress of the world. In the same way, if the gregarious instinct should bring us into the imagined presence of companions that really did not exist, or on whose attitude and co-operation our successes in no way depended, we should try to lead back our sense of fellowship to its natural foundations and possible sanctions.

Society exists so far as does analogous existence and community of ends. We may, in refining the social instinct, find some fellowship in the clouds and in the stars, for these, though remote, are companions of our career. By poetic analogy we may include in the social world whatever helps or thwarts our development, and is auxiliary to the energies of the soul, even if that object be inanimate. Whatever spirit in the past or future, or in the remotest regions of the sky, shares our love and pursuit, say of mathematics or of music, or of any ideal object, becomes, if we can somehow divine his existence, a partner in our joys and sorrows, and a welcome friend.

The Ideal a Measure for All Existences and No Existence Itself.

Those ideal objects, however, for whose sake all revolutions in space and time may be followed with interest, are not themselves members of our society. The ideal to which all forces should minister is itself no force or factor in its own realisation. Such a possible disposition of things is a mere idea, eternal and inert, a form life might possibly take on and the one our endeavours, if they were consistent, would wish to impose on it. This ideal itself, however, has often been expressed in some mythical figure or Utopia. So to express it is simply to indulge an innocent instinct for prophecy and metaphor; but unfortunately the very innocence of fancy may engage it all the more hopelessly in a tangle of bad dreams. If we once identify our Utopia or other ideal with the real forces that surround us, or with any one of them, we have fallen into an illusion from which we shall emerge only after bitter disappointments; and even when we have come out again into the open, we shall long carry with us the desolating sense of wasted opportunities and vitiated characters. For to have taken our purposes for our helpers is to have defeated the first and ignored the second; it is to have neglected rational labour and at the same time debauched social sense.

The religious extensions of society should therefore be carefully watched; for while sometimes, as with the Hebrew prophets, religion gives dramatic expression to actual social forces and helps to intensify moral feeling, it often, as in mystics of all creeds and ages, deadens the consciousness of real ties by feigning ties which are purely imaginary. This self-deception is the more frequent because there float before men who live in the spirit ideals which they look to with the respect naturally rendered to whatever is true, beautiful, or good; and the symbolic rendering of these ideals, which is the rational function of religion, may be confused with its superstitious or utilitarian part—with exploiting occult forces to aid us in the work of life.

Occult forces may indeed exist, and they may even be so disposed that the ideal is served by their agency; but the most notable embodiment of a principle is not itself a principle, being only an instance, and the most exact fulfilment of a law is not a law, being simply an event. To discover a law may meantime be the most interesting of events, and the image or formula that expresses a principle may be the most welcome of intellectual presences. These symbols, weighted with their wide significance, may hold the mind and attract its energies into their vortex; and human genius is certainly not at its worst when employed in framing a good myth or a good argument. The lover of representation, be he thinker or dramatist, moves by preference in an ideal society. His communion with the world is half a soliloquy, for the personages in his dialogue are private symbols, and being symbols they stand for what is not themselves; the language he imputes to them is his own, though it is their ways that prompt him to impute that language to them. Plastic images of his own making and shifting are his sole means of envisaging eternal principles and ultimate substances, things ideal and potential, which can never become phenomenal in their own persons.

Contrast between Natural and Intellectual Bonds.

It is an inspiring thought, and a true one, that in proportion as a man's interests become humane and his efforts rational, he appropriates and expands a common life, which reappears in all individuals who reach the same impersonal level of ideas—a level which his own influence may help them to maintain. Patriotism envisages this ideal life in so far as it is locally coloured and grounded in certain racial aptitudes and traditions; but the community recognised in patriotism is imbedded in a larger one embracing all living creatures. While in some respects we find sympathy more complete the nearer home we remain, in another sense there is no true companionship except with the universe. Instinctive society, with its compulsory affections, is of course deeper and more elementary than any free or intellectual union. Love is at once more animal than friendship and more divine; and the same thing may be said of family affection when compared with patriotism. What lies nearer the roots of our being must needs enjoy a wider prevalence and engage the soul more completely, being able to touch its depths and hush its primordial murmurs.

On the other hand, the free spirit, the political and speculative genius in man, chafes under those blind involutions and material bonds. Natural, beneficent, sacred, as in a sense they may be, they somehow oppress the intellect and, like a brooding mother, half stifle what they feed. Something drives the youth afield, into solitude, into alien friendships; only in the face of nature and an indifferent world can he become himself. Such a flight from home and all its pieties grows more urgent when there is some real conflict of temper or conscience between the young man and what is established in his family; and this happens often because, after all, the most beneficent conventions are but mechanisms which must ignore the nicer sensibilities and divergences of living souls.

Appeal from Man to God, from Real to Ideal Society.

Common men accept these spiritual tyrannies, weak men repine at them, and great men break them down. But to defy the world is a serious business, and requires the greatest courage, even if the defiance touch in the first place only the world's ideals. Most men's conscience, habits, and opinions are borrowed from convention and gather continual comforting assurances from the same social consensus that originally suggested them. To reverse this process, to consult one's own experience and elicit one's own judgment, challenging those in vogue, seems too often audacious and futile; but there are impetuous minds born to disregard the chances against them, even to the extent of denying that they are taking chances at all. For in the first instance it never occurs to the inventor that he is the source of his new insight; he thinks he has merely opened his eyes and seen what, by an inconceivable folly, the whole world had grown blind to. Wise men in antiquity, he imagines, saw the facts as he sees them, as the gods see them now, and as all sane men shall see them henceforward.

Thus, if the innovator be a religious soul, grown conscious of some new spiritual principle, he will try to find support for his inspiration in some lost book of the law or in some early divine revelation corrupted, as he will assert, by wicked men, or even in some direct voice from heaven; no delusion will be too obvious, no reinterpretation too forced, if it can help him to find external support somewhere for his spontaneous conviction. To denounce one authority he needs to invoke another, and if no other be found, he will invent or, as they say, he will postulate one. His courage in facing the actual world is thus supported by his ability to expand the world in imagination. In separating himself from his fellow-men he has made a new companion out of his ideal. An impetuous spirit when betrayed by the world will cry, "I know that my redeemer liveth"; and the antiphonal response will come more wistfully after reflection:

> It fortifies my soul to know
> That thought I wander, Truth is so.

Significant Symbols Revert to the Concrete.

The deceptions which nature practises on men are not always cruel. There are also kindly deceptions which prompt him to pursue or expect his own good when, though not destined to come in the form he looks for, this good is really destined to come in some shape or other. Such, for instance, are the illusions of romantic love, which may really terminate in a family life practically better than the absolute and chimerical unions which that love had dreamed of. Such, again, are those illusions of conscience which attach unspeakable vague penalties and repugnances to acts which commonly have bad results, though these are impossible to forecast with precision. When disillusion comes, while it may bring a momentary shock, it ends by producing a settled satisfaction unknown before, a satisfaction which the coveted prize, could it have been attained, would hardly have secured. When on the day of judgment, or earlier, a man perceives that what he thought he was doing for the Lord's sake he was really doing for the benefit of the least, perhaps, of the Lord's creatures, his satisfaction, after a moment's surprise, will certainly be very genuine.

Nature a Symbol for Destiny.

Such kindly illusions are involved in the symbolic method by which general relations and the inconceivably diffuse reality of things have to be apprehended. The stars are in human thought a symbol for the silent forces of destiny, really embodied in forms beyond our apprehension; for who shall say what actual being may or may not correspond to that potentiality of life or sensation which is all that the external world can be to our science? When astrology invented the horoscope it made an absurdly premature translation of celestial hieroglyphics into that language of universal destiny which in the end they may be made to speak. The perfect astronomer, when he understood at last exactly what pragmatic value the universe has, and what fortunes the stars actually forebode, would be pleasantly surprised to discover that he was nothing but an astrologer grown competent and honest.

Representative Notions Have Also Inherent Values.

Ideal society belongs entirely to this realm of kindly illusion, for it is the society of symbols. Whenever religion, art, or science presents us with an image or a formula, involving no matter how momentous a truth, there is something delusive in the representation. It needs translation into the detailed experience which it sums up in our own past or prophecies elsewhere. This eventual change in form, far from nullifying our knowledge, can alone legitimise it. A conception not reducible to the small change of daily experience is like a currency not exchangeable for articles of consumption; it is not a symbol, but a fraud. And yet there is another aspect to the matter. Symbols are presences, and they are those particularly congenial presences which we have inwardly evoked and cast in a form intelligible and familiar to human thinking. Their function is to give flat experience a rational perspective, translating the general flux into stable objects and making it representable in human discourse. They are therefore precious, not only for their representative or practical value, implying useful adjustments to the environing world, but even more, sometimes, for their immediate or æsthetic power, for their kinship to the spirit they enlighten and exercise.

This is prevailingly true in the fine arts which seem to

express man even more than they express nature; although in art also the symbol would lose all its significance and much of its inward articulation if natural objects and eventual experience could be disregarded in constructing it. In music, indeed, this ulterior significance is reduced to a minimum; yet it persists, since music brings an ideal object before the mind which needs, to some extent, translation into terms no longer musical—terms, for instance, of skill, dramatic passion, or moral sentiment. But in music pre-eminently, and very largely in all the arts, external propriety is adventitious; so much can the mere presence and weight of a symbol fill the mind and constitute an absolute possession.

Religion and Science Indirectly Cognitive and Directly Ideal.

In religion and science the overt purpose of symbols is to represent external truths. The inventors of these symbols think they are merely uncovering a self-existent reality, having in itself the very form seen in their idea. They do not perceive that the society of God or Nature is an ideal society, nor that these phantoms, looming in their imagination, are but significant figments whose existent basis is a minute and indefinite series of ordinary perceptions. They consequently attribute whatever value their genial syntheses may have to the object as they picture it. The gods have, they fancy, the aspect and passions, the history and influence which their myth unfolds; nature in its turn contains hypostatically just those laws and forces which are described by theory. Consequently the presence of God or Nature seems to the mythologist not an ideal, but a real and mutual society, as if collateral beings, endowed with the conceived characters, actually existed as men exist. But this opinion is untenable. As Hobbes said, in a phrase which ought to be inscribed in golden letters over the head of every talking philosopher: *No discourse whatsoever can end in absolute knowledge of fact.* Absolute knowledge of fact is immediate, it is experiential. We should have to *become* God or Nature in order to know for a fact that they existed. Intellectual knowledge, on the other hand, where it relates to existence, is faith only, a faith which in these matters means trust. For the forces of Nature or the gods, if they had crude existence, so that we might conceivably become what they are, would lose that causal and that religious function which are their essence respectively. They would be merely collateral existences, loaded with all sorts of irrelevant properties, parts of the universal flux, members of a natural society; and while as such they would have their relative importance, they would be embraced in turn within an intelligible system of relations, while their rights and dignities would need to be determined by some supervening ideal. A nature existing in act would require metaphysics—the account of a deeper nature—to express its relation to the mind that knew and judged it. Any actual god would need to possess a religion of his own, in order to fix his ideal of conduct and his rights in respect to his creatures or rather, as we should then be, to his neighbours. This situation may have no terrors for the thoughtless; but it evidently introduces something deeper than Nature and something higher than God, depriving these words of the best sense in which a philosopher might care to use them.

Their Opposite Outlook.

The divine and the material are contrasted points of reference required by the actual. Reason, working on the immediate flux of appearances, reaches these ideal realms and, resting in them, perforce calls them realities. One—the realm of causes—supplies appearances with a basis and calculable order; the other—the realm of truth and felicity—supplies them with a standard and justification. Natural society may accordingly be contrasted with ideal society, not because Nature is not, logically speaking, ideal too, but because in natural society we ally ourselves consciously with our origins and surroundings, in ideal society with our purposes. There is an immense difference in spirituality, in ideality of the moral sort, between gathering or conciliating forces for action and fixing the ends which action should pursue. Both fields are ideal in the sense that intelligence alone could discover or exploit them; yet to call nature ideal is undoubtedly equivocal, since its ideal function is precisely to be the substance and cause of the given flux, a groundwork for experience which, while merely inferred and potential, is none the less mechanical and material. The ideality of nature is indeed of such a sort as to be forfeited if the trusty instrument and true antecedent of human life were not found there. We should be frivolous and inconstant, taking our philosophy for a game and not for method in living, if having set out to look for the causes and practical order of things and having found them, we should declare that they were not *really* causal or efficient, on the strange ground that our discovery of them had been a feat of intelligence and had proved a priceless boon. The absurdity could not be greater if in moral science, after the goal of all effort had been determined and happiness defined, we declared that this was not *really* the good.

Those who are shocked at the assertion that God and Nature are ideal, and that their contrasted prerogatives depend on that fact, may, of course, use the same words in a different way, making them synonymous, and may readily "prove" that God or Nature exists materially and has absolute being. We need but agree to designate by those terms the sum of existences, whatever they (or it) may be to their own feeling. Then the ontological proof asserts its rights unmistakably. Science and religion, however, are superfluous if what we wish to learn is that there is Something, and that All-there-is must assuredly be All-there-is. Ecstasies may doubtless ensue upon considering that Being is and Non-Being is not, as they are said to ensue upon long enough considering one's navel; but the Life of Reason is made of more variegated stuff. Science, when it is not dialectical, describes an ideal order of existences in space and time, such that all incidental facts, as they come, may fill it in and lend it body. Religion, when pure, contemplates some pertinent ideal of intelligence and goodness. Both religion and science live in imaginative discourse, one being an aspiration and the other a hypothesis. Both introduce into the mind an ideal society.

The Life of Reason is no fair reproduction of the universe, but the expression of man alone. A theory of nature is nothing but a mass of observations, made with a hunter's and an artist's eye. A mortal has no time for sympathy with his victim or his model; and, beyond a certain range, he has no capacity for such sympathy. As in order to live he must devour one-half the world and disregard the other, so in order to think and practically to know he must deal summarily and selfishly with his materials; otherwise his intellect would melt again into endless and irrevocable dreams. The law of gravity, because it so notably unifies the motions of matter, is something which these motions themselves know nothing of; it is a description of them in terms of human discourse. Such discourse can never assure us absolutely that the motions it forecasts will occur; the sensible proof must ensue spontaneously in its own good time. In the interval our theory remains pure presumption and hypothesis. Reliable as it may be in that capacity, it is no replica of anything on its own level existing beyond. It creates, like all intelligence, a secondary and merely symbolic world.

In Translating Existence into Human Terms They Give Human Nature Its Highest Exercise.

When this diversity between the truest theory and the simplest fact, between potential generalities and actual particulars, has been thoroughly appreciated, it becomes clear that much of what is valued in science and religion is not lodged in the miscellany underlying these creations of reason, but is lodged rather in the rational activity itself, and in the intrinsic beauty of all symbols bred in a genial mind. Of course, if these symbols had no real points of reference, if they were symbols of nothing, they could have no great claim to consideration and no rational character; at most they would be agreeable sensations. They are, however, at their best good symbols for a diffused experience having a certain order and tendency; they render that reality with a difference, reducing it to a formula or a myth, in which its tortuous length and trivial detail can be surveyed to advantage without undue waste or fatigue. Symbols may thus become eloquent, vivid, important, being endowed with both poetic grandeur and practical truth.

The facts from which this truth is borrowed, if they were rehearsed unimaginatively, in their own flat infinity, would be far from arousing the same emotions. The human eye sees in perspective; its glory would vanish were it reduced to a crawling, exploring antenna. Not that it loves to falsify anything. That to the worm the landscape might possess no light and shade, that the mountain's atomic structure should be unpicturable, cannot distress the landscape gardener nor the poet; what concerns them is the effect such things may produce in the human fancy, so that the soul may live in a congenial world.

Naturalist and prophet are landscape painters on canvases of their own; each is interested in his own perception and perspective, which, if he takes the trouble to reflect, need not deceive him about what the world would be if not foreshortened in that particular manner. This special interpretation is nevertheless precious and shows up the world in that light in which it interests naturalists or prophets to see it. Their figments make their chosen world, as the painter's apperceptions are the breath of his nostrils.

Science Should Be Mathematical and Religion Anthropomorphic.

While the symbol's applicability is essential to its worth —since otherwise science would be useless and religion demoralising—its power and fascination lie in its acquiring a more and more profound affinity to the human mind, so long as it can do so without surrendering its relevance to practice. Thus natural science is at its best when it is most thoroughly mathematical, since what can be expressed mathematically can speak a human language. In such science only the ultimate material elements remain surds; all their further movement and complication can be represented in that kind of thought which is most intimately satisfactory and perspicuous. And in like manner, religion is at its best when it is most anthropomorphic; indeed, the two most spiritual religions, Buddhism and Christianity, have actually raised a man, overflowing with utterly human tenderness and pathos, to the place usually occupied only by cosmic and thundering deities. The human heart is lifted above misfortune and encouraged to pursue unswervingly its inmost ideal when no compromise is any longer attempted with what is not moral or human, and Prometheus is honestly proclaimed to be holier than Zeus. At that moment religion ceases to be superstitious and becomes a rational discipline, an effort to perfect the spirit rather than to intimidate it.

Summary of This Book.

We have seen that society has three stages—the natural, the free, and the ideal. In the natural stage its function is to produce the individual and equip him with the prerequisites of moral freedom. When this end is attained society can rise to friendship, to unanimity and disinterested sympathy, where the ground of association is some ideal interest, while this association constitutes at the same time a personal and emotional bond. Ideal society, on the contrary, transcends accidental conjunctions altogether. Here the ideal interests themselves take possession of the mind; its companions are the symbols it breeds and possesses for excellence, beauty, and truth. Religion, art, and science are the chief spheres in which ideal companionship is found. It remains for us to traverse these provinces in turn and see to what extent the Life of Reason may flourish there.

REASON IN RELIGION

I

How Religion May Be an Embodiment of Reason

Religion Certainly Significant.

EXPERIENCE has repeatedly confirmed that well-known maxim of Bacon's, that "a little philosophy inclineth man's mind to atheism, but depth in philosophy bringeth men's minds about to religion." In every age the most comprehensive thinkers have found in the religion of their time and country something they could accept, interpreting and illustrating that religion so as to give it depth and universal application. Even the heretics and atheists, if they have had profundity, turn out after a while to be forerunners of some new orthodoxy. What they rebel against is a religion alien to their nature; they are atheists only by accident, and relatively to a convention which inwardly offends them, but they yearn mightily in their own souls after the religious acceptance of a world interpreted in their own fashion. So it appears in the end that their atheism and loud protestation were in fact the hastier part of their thought, since what emboldened them to deny the poor world's faith was that they were too impatient to understand it. Indeed, the enlightenment common to young wits and worm-eaten old satirists, who plume themselves on detecting the scientific ineptitude of religion—something which the blindest half see —is not nearly enlightened enough: it points to notorious facts incompatible with religious tenets literally taken, but it leaves unexplored the habits of thought from which those tenets sprang, their original meaning, and their true function. Such studies would bring the sceptic face to face with the mystery and pathos of mortal existence. They would make him understand why religion is so profoundly moving and in a sense so profoundly just. There must needs be something humane and necessary in an influence that has become the most general sanction of virtue, the chief occasion for art and philosophy, and the source, perhaps, of the best human happiness. If nothing, as Hooker said, is "so malapert as a splenetic religion," a sour irreligion is almost as perverse.

But Not Literally True.

At the same time, when Bacon penned the sage epigram we have quoted he forgot to add that the God to whom depth in philosophy brings back men's minds is far from being the same from whom a little philosophy estranges them. It would be pitiful indeed if mature reflection bred no better conceptions than those which have drifted down the muddy stream of time, where tradition and passion have jumbled everything together. Traditional conceptions, when they are felicitous, may be adopted by the poet, but they must be purified by the moralist and disintegrated by the philosopher. Each religion, so dear to those whose life it sanctifies, and fulfilling so necessary a function in the society that has adopted it, necessarily contradicts every other religion, and probably contradicts itself. What religion a man shall have is a historical accident, quite as much as what language he shall speak. In the rare circumstances where a choice is possible, he may, with some difficulty, make an exchange; but even then he is only adopting a new convention which may be more agreeable to his personal temper but which is essentially as arbitrary as the old.

All Religion Is Positive and Particular.

The attempt to speak without speaking any particular language is not more hopeless than the attempt to have a religion that shall be no religion in particular. A courier's or a dragoman's speech may indeed be often unusual and drawn from disparate sources, not without some mixture of personal originality; but that private jargon will have a meaning only because of its analogy to one or more conventional languages and its obvious derivation from them. So travellers from one religion to another, people who have lost their spiritual nationality, may often retain a neutral and confused residuum of belief, which they may egregiously regard as the essence of all religion, so little may they remember the graciousness and naturalness of that ancestral accent which a perfect religion should have. Yet a moment's probing of the conceptions surviving in such minds will show them to be nothing but vestiges of old beliefs, creases which thought, even if emptied of all dogmatic tenets, has not been able to smooth away at its first unfolding. Later generations, if they have any religion at all, will be found either to revert to ancient authority, or to attach themselves spontaneously to something wholly novel and immensely positive, to some faith promulgated by a fresh genius and passionately embraced by a converted people. Thus every living and healthy religion has a marked idiosyncrasy. Its power consists in its special and surprising message and in the bias which that revelation gives to life. The vistas it opens and the mysteries it propounds are another world to live in; and another world to live in—whether we expect ever to pass wholly into it or no —is what we mean by having a religion.

It Aims at the Life of Reason.

What relation, then, does this great business of the soul, which we call religion, bear to the Life of Reason? That the relation between the two is close seems clear from several circumstances. The Life of Reason is the seat of all ultimate values. Now the history of mankind will show us that whenever spirits at once lofty and intense have seemed to attain the highest joys, they have envisaged and attained them in religion. Religion would therefore seem to be a vehicle or a factor in rational life, since the ends of rational life are attained by it. Moreover, the Life of Reason is an ideal to which everything in the world should be subordinated; it establishes lines of moral cleavage everywhere and makes right eternally different from wrong. Religion does the same thing. It makes absolute moral decisions. It sanctions, unifies, and transforms ethics. Religion thus exercises a function of the Life of Reason. And a further function which is common to both is that of emancipating man from his personal limitations. In different ways religions promise to transfer the soul to better conditions. A supernaturally favoured kingdom is to be established for posterity upon earth, or for all the faithful in heaven, or the soul is to be freed by repeated purgations from all taint and sorrow, or it is to be lost in the absolute, or it is to become an influence and an object of adoration in the places it once haunted or wherever the activities it once loved may be carried on by future generations of its kindred. Now reason in its way lays before us all these possibilities: it points to common objects, political and intellectual, in which an individual may lose what is mortal and accidental in himself and immortalise what is rational and human; it teaches us how sweet and fortunate death may be to those whose spirit can still live in their country and in their ideas; it reveals the radiating effects of action and the eternal objects of thought.

Yet the difference in tone and language must strike us, so soon as it is philosophy that speaks. That change should remind us that even if the function of religion and that of reason coincide, this function is performed in the two cases by very different organs. Religions are many, reason one. Religion consists of conscious ideas, hopes, enthusiasms, and objects of worship; it operates by grace and flourishes by prayer. Reason, on the other hand, is a mere principle or potential order, on which, indeed, we may come to reflect, but which exists in us ideally only, without variation or stress of any kind. We conform or do not conform to it; it does not urge or chide us, nor call for any emotions on our part other than those naturally aroused by the various objects which it unfolds in their true nature and proportion. Religion brings some order into life by weighting it with new materials. Reason adds to the natural materials only the perfect order which it introduces into them. Rationality is nothing but a form, an ideal constitution which experience may more or less embody. Religion is a part of experience itself, a mass of sentiments and ideas. The one is an inviolate principle, the other a changing and struggling force. And yet this struggling and changing force of religion seems to direct man toward something eternal. It seems to make for an ultimate harmony within the soul and for an ultimate harmony between the soul and all the soul depends upon. So that religion, in its intent, is a more conscious and direct pursuit of the Life of Reason than is society, science, or art. For these approach and fill out the ideal life tentatively and piecemeal, hardly regarding the goal or caring for the ultimate justification of their instinctive aims. Religion also has an instinctive and blind side, and bubbles up in all manner of chance practices and intuitions; soon, however, it feels its way toward the heart of things, and, from whatever quarter it may come, veers in the direction of the ultimate.

But Largely Fails to Attain It.

Nevertheless, we must confess that this religious pursuit of the Life of Reason has been singularly abortive. Those within the pale of each religion may prevail upon themselves to express satisfaction with its results, thanks to a fond partiality in reading the past and generous draughts of hope for the future; but any one regarding the various religions at once and comparing their achievements with what reason requires, must feel how terrible is the disappointment which they have one and all prepared for mankind. Their chief anxiety has been to offer imaginary remedies for mortal ills, some of which are incurable essentially, while others might have been really cured by well-directed effort. The Greek oracles, for instance, pretended to heal our natural ignorance, which has its appropriate though difficult cure, while the Christian vision of heaven pretended to be an antidote to our natural death, the inevitable correlate of birth and of a changing and conditioned existence. By methods of this sort little can be done for the real betterment of life. To confuse intelligence and dislocate sentiment by gratuitous fictions is a short-sighted way of pursuing happiness. Nature is soon avenged. An unhealthy exaltation and a one-sided morality have to be followed by regrettable reactions. When these come, the real rewards of life may seem vain to a relaxed vitality, and the very name of virtue may irritate young spirits untrained in any natural excellence. Thus religion too often debauches the morality it comes to sanction, and impedes the science it ought to fulfil.

Its Approach Imaginative.

What is the secret of this ineptitude? Why does religion, so near to rationality in its purpose, fall so far short of it in its texture and in its results? The answer is easy: Religion pursues rationality through the imagination. When it explains events or assigns causes, it is an imaginative substitute for science. When it gives precepts, insinuates ideals, or remoulds aspiration, it is an imaginative substitute for wisdom—I mean for the deliberate and impartial pursuit of all good. The conditions and the aims of life are both represented in religion poetically, but this poetry tends to arrogate to itself literal truth and moral authority, neither of which it possesses. Hence the depth and importance of religion become intelligible no less than its contradictions and practical disasters. Its object is the same as that of reason, but its method is to proceed by intuition and by unchecked poetical conceits. These are repeated and vulgarised in proportion to their original fineness and significance, till they pass for reports of objective truth and come to constitute a world of faith, superposed upon the world of experience and regarded as materially enveloping it, if not in space at least in time and in existence. The only truth of religion comes from its interpretation of life, from its symbolic rendering of that moral experience which it springs out of and which it seeks to elucidate. Its falsehood comes from the insidious misunderstanding which clings to it, to the effect that these poetic conceptions are not merely representations of experience as it is or should be, but are rather information about experience or reality elsewhere—an experience and reality which, strangely enough, supply just the defects betrayed by reality and experience here.

When Its Poetic Method Is Denied Its Value Is Jeopardised.

Thus religion has the same original relation to life that poetry has; only poetry, which never pretends to literal validity, adds a pure value to existence, the value of a liberal imaginative exercise. The poetic value of religion would initially be greater than that of poetry itself, because religion deals with higher and more practical themes, with sides of life which are in greater need of some imaginative touch and ideal interpretation than are those pleasant or pompous things which ordinary poetry dwells upon. But this initial advantage is neutralised in part by the abuse to which religion is subject, whenever its symbolic rightness is taken for scientific truth. Like poetry, it improves the world only by imagining it improved, but not content with making this addition to the mind's furniture—an addition which might be useful and ennobling—it thinks to confer a more radical benefit by persuading mankind that, in spite of appearances, the world is really such as that rather arbitrary idealisation has painted it. This spurious satisfaction is naturally the prelude to many a disappointment, and the soul has infinite trouble to emerge again from the artificial problems and sentiments into which it is thus plunged. The value of religion becomes equivocal. Religion remains an imaginative achievement, a symbolic representation of moral reality which may have a most important function in vitalising the mind and in transmitting, by way of parables, the lessons of experience. But it becomes at the same time a continuous incidental deception; and this deception, in proportion as it is strenuously denied to be such, can work indefinite harm in the world and in the conscience.

It Precedes Science Rather than Hinders It.

On the whole, however, religion should not be conceived as having taken the place of anything better, but rather as having come to relieve situations which, but for its presence, would have been infinitely worse. In the thick of active life, or in the monotony of practical slavery, there is more need to stimulate fancy than to control it. Natural instinct is not much disturbed in the human brain by what may happen in that thin superstratum of ideas which commonly overlays it. We must not blame religion for preventing the development of a moral and natural science which at any rate would seldom have appeared; we must rather thank it for the sensibility, the reverence, the speculative insight which it has introduced into the world.

It Is Merely Symbolic and Thoroughly Human.

We may therefore proceed to analyse the significance and the function which religion has had at its different stages, and, without disguising or in the least condoning its confusion with literal truth, we may allow ourselves to enter as sympathetically as possible into its various conceptions and emotions. They have made up the inner life of many sages, and of all those who without great genius or learning have lived steadfastly in the spirit. The feeling of reverence should itself be treated with reverence, although not at a sacrifice of truth, with which alone, in the end, reverence is compatible. Nor have we any reason to be intolerant of the partialities and contradictions which religions display. Were we dealing with a science, such contradictions would have to be instantly solved and removed; but when we are concerned with the poetic interpretation of experience, contradiction means only variety, and variety means spontaneity, wealth of resource, and a nearer approach to total adequacy.

If we hope to gain any understanding of these matters we must begin by taking them out of that heated and fanatical atmosphere in which the Hebrew tradition has enveloped them. The Jews had no philosophy, and when their national traditions came to be theoretically explicated and justified, they were made to issue in a puerile scholasticism and a rabid intolerance. The question of monotheism, for instance, was a terrible question to the Jews. Idolatry did not consist in worshipping a god who, not being ideal, might be unworthy of worship, but rather in recognising other gods than the one worshipped in Jerusalem. To the Greeks, on the contrary, whose philosophy was enlightened and ingenuous, monotheism and polytheism seemed perfectly innocent and compatible. To say God or the gods was only to use different expressions for the same influence, now viewed in its abstract unity and correlation with all existence, now viewed in its various manifestations in moral life, in nature, or in history. So that what in Plato, Aristotle, and the Stoics meets us at every step—the combination of monotheism with polytheism—is no contradiction, but merely an intelligent variation of phrase to indicate various aspects or functions in physical and moral things. When religion appears to us in this light its contradictions and controversies lose all their bitterness. Each doctrine will simply represent the moral plane on which they live who have devised or adopted it. Religions will thus be better or worse, never true or false. We shall be able to lend ourselves to each in turn, and seek to draw from it the secret of its inspiration.

III

Magic, Sacrifice, and Prayer

RELIGION is a form of rational living more empirical, looser, more primitive than art. Man's consciousness in it is more immersed in nature, nearer to a vegetative union with the general life; it bemoans division and celebrates harmony with a more passive and lyrical wonder. The element of action proper to religion is extremely arbitrary, and we are often at a loss to see in what way the acts recommended conduce at all to the result foretold.

As theoretical superstition stops at any cause, so practical superstition seizes on any means. Religion arises under high pressure: in the last extremity, every one appeals to God. But in the last extremity all known methods of action have proved futile; when resources are exhausted and ideas fail, if there is still vitality in the will it sends a supreme appeal to the supernatural. This appeal is necessarily made in the dark: it is the appeal of a conscious impotence, of an avowed perplexity. What a man in such a case may come to do to propitiate the deity, or to produce by magic a result he cannot produce by art, will obviously be some random action. He will be driven back to the place where instinct and reason begin. His movement will be absolutely experimental, altogether spontaneous. He will have no reason for what he does, save that he must do something.

Meanness and Envy in the Gods Suggesting Sacrifice.

What he will do, however, will not be very original; a die must fall on some one of its six faces, shake it as much as you please. When Don Quixote, seeking to do good absolutely at a venture, let the reins drop on Rocinante's neck, the poor beast very naturally followed the highway; and a man wondering what will please heaven can ultimately light on nothing but what might please himself. It is pathetic to observe how lowly the motives are that religion, even the highest, attributes to the deity, and from what a hard-pressed and bitter existence they have been drawn. To be given the best morsel, to be remembered, to be praisd, to be obeyed blindly and punctiliously—these have been thought points of honour with the gods, for which they would dispense favours and punishments on the most exorbitant scale. Indeed, the widespread practice of sacrifice, like all mutilations and penances, suggests an even meaner jealousy and malice in the gods; for the disciplinary functions which these things may have were not aimed at in the beginning, and would not have associated them particularly with religion. In setting aside the fat for the gods' pleasure, in sacrificing the first-born, in a thousand other cruel ceremonies, the idea apparently was that an envious onlooker, lurking unseen, might poison the whole, or revenge himself for not having enjoyed it, unless a part—possibly sufficient for his hunger—were surrendered to him voluntarily. This onlooker was a veritable demon, treated as a man treats a robber to whom he yields his purse that his life may be spared.

To call the gods envious has a certain symbolic truth, in that earthly fortunes are actually precarious; and such an observation might inspire detachment from material things and a kind of philosophy. But what at first inspires sacrifice is a literal envy imputed to the gods, a spirit of vengeance and petty ill-will; so that they grudge a man even the good things which they cannot enjoy themselves. If the god is a tyrant, the votary will be a taxpayer surrendering his tithes to secure immunity from further levies or from attack by other potentates. God and man will be natural enemies, living in a sort of politic peace.

Ritualistic Arts.

Sacrifices are far from having merely this sinister meaning. Once inaugurated they suggest further ideas, and from the beginning they had happier associations. The sacrifice was incidental to a feast, and the plenty it was to render safe existed already. What was a bribe, offered in the spirit of barter, to see if the envious power could not be mollified by something less than the total ruin of his victims, could easily become a genial distribution of what custom assigned to each: so much to the chief, so much to the god, so much to the husbandman. There is a certain openness, and as it were the form of justice, in giving each what is convention-ally his due, however little he may really deserve it. In reli-gious observances this sentiment plays an important part, and men find satisfaction in fulfilling in a seemly manner what is prescribed; and since they know little about the ground or meaning of what they do, they feel content and safe if at least they have done it properly. Sacrifices are often performed in this spirit; and when a beautiful order and religious calm have come to dignify the performance, the mind, having meantime very little to occupy it, may em-broider on the given theme. It is then that fable, and new religious sentiments suggested by fable, appear prominently on the scene.

Thank-offerings.

In agricultural rites, for instance, sacrifice will naturally be offered to the deity presiding over germination; that is the deity that might, perhaps, withdraw his favour with disas-trous results. He commonly proves, however, a kindly and responsive being, and in offering to him a few sheaves of corn, some barley-cakes, or a libation from the vintage, the public is grateful rather than calculating; the sacrifice has become an act of thanksgiving. So in Christian devotion (which often follows primitive impulses and repeats the dialectic of paganism in a more speculative region) the redemption did not remain merely expiatory. It was not merely a debt to be paid off and a certain quantum of suffering to be endured which had induced the Son of God to become man and to take up his cross. It was, so the subtler theologians declared, an act of affection as much as of pity; and the spell of the doctrine over the human heart lay in feeling that God wished to assimilate himself to man, rather than simply from above to declare him forgiven; so that the incarnation was in effect a rehabilitation of man, a redemption in itself, and a forgiveness. Men like to think that God has sat at their table and walked among them in disguise. The idea is flattering; it suggests that the courtesy may some day be returned, and for those who can look so deep it expresses pointedly the philosophic truth of the matter. For are not the gods, too, in eternal travail after their ideal, and is not man a part of the world, and his art a portion of the divine wisdom? If the incarnation was a virtual redemption, the truest incarnation was the laborious creation itself.

The Sacrifice of a Contrite Heart.

If sacrifice, in its more amiable aspect, can become thanksgiving and an expression of profitable dependence, it can suffer an even nobler transformation while retaining all its austerity. Renunciation is the cornerstone of wisdom, the condition of all genuine achievement. The gods, in asking for a sacrifice, may invite us to give up not a part of our food or of our liberty but the foolish and inordinate part of our wills. The sacrifice may be dictated to us not by a jealous enemy needing to be pacified but by a far-seeing friend, wishing we may not be deceived. If what we are commanded to surrender is only what is doing us harm, the god demanding the sacrifice is our own ideal. He has no interests in the case other than our own; he is no part of the environment; he is the goal that determines for us how we should proceed in order to realise as far as possible our inmost aspirations. When religion reaches this phase it has become thoroughly moral. It has ceased to represent or misrepresent material conditions, and has learned to embody spiritual goods.

Sacrifice is a rite, and rites can seldom be made to embody ideas exclusively moral. Something dramatic or mystical will cling to the performance, and, even when the effect of it is to purify, it will bring about an emotional catharsis rather than a moral improvement. The mass is a ritual sacrifice, and the communion is a part of it, having the closest resemblance to what sacrifices have always been. Among the devout these ceremonies, and the lyric emotions they awaken, have a quite visible influence; but the spell is mystic, the god soon recedes, and it would be purely fanciful to maintain that any permanent moral effect comes from such an exercise. The Church has felt as much and introduced the confession, where a man may really be asked to consider what sacrifices he should make for his part, and in what practical direction he should imagine himself to be drawn by the vague Dionysiac influences to which the ritual subjects him.

Prayer Is Not Utilitarian in Essence.

As sacrifice expresses fear, prayer expresses need. Common-sense thinks of language as something meant to be understood by another and to produce changes in his disposition and behaviour, but language has pre-rational uses, of which poetry and prayer are perhaps the chief. A man overcome by passion assumes dramatic attitudes surely not intended to be watched and interpreted; like tears, gestures may touch an observer's heart, but they do not come for that purpose. So the fund of words and phrases latent in the mind flow out under stress of emotion; they flow because they belong to the situation, because they fill out and complete a perception absorbing the mind; they do not flow primarily to be listened to. The instinct to pray is one of the chief avenues to the deity, and the form prayer takes helps immensely to define the power it is addressed to; indeed, it is in the act of praying that men formulate to themselves what God must be, and tell him at great length what they believe and what they expect of him. The initial forms of prayer are not so absurd as the somewhat rationalised forms of it. Unlike sacrifice, prayer seems to be justified by its essence and to be degraded by the transformations it suffers in reflection, when men try to find a place for it in their cosmic economy; for its essence is poetical, expressive, contemplative, and it grows more and more nonsensical the more people insist on making it a prosaic, commercial exchange of views between two interlocutors.

Prayer is a soliloquy; but being a soliloquy expressing need, and being furthermore, like sacrifice, a desperate expedient which men fly to in their impotence, it looks for an effect: to cry aloud, to make vows, to contrast eloquently the given with the ideal situation, is certainly as likely a way of bringing about a change for the better as it would be to chastise one's self severely, or to destroy what one loves best, or to perform acts altogether trivial and arbitrary. Prayer also is magic, and as such it is expected to do work. The answer looked for, or one which may be accepted instead, very often ensues; and it is then that mythology begins to enter in and seeks to explain by what machinery of divine passions and purposes that answering effect was produced.

Its Supposed Efficacy Magical.

Magic is in a certain sense the mother of art, art being the magic that succeeds and can establish itself. For this very reason mere magic is never appealed to when art has been found, and no unsophisticated man prays to have that done for him which he knows how to do for himself. When his art fails, if his necessity still presses, he appeals to magic, and he prays when he no longer can control the event, provided this event is momentous to him. Prayer is not a substitute for work; it is a desperate effort to work further and to be efficient beyond the range of one's powers. It is not the lazy who are most inclined to prayer; those pray most who care most, and who, having worked hard, find it intolerable to be defeated.

Theological Puzzles.

No chapter in theology is more unhappy than that in which a material efficacy is assigned to prayer. In the first place the facts contradict the notion that curses can bring evil or blessings can cure; and it is not observed that the most orthodox and hard-praying army wins the most battles. The facts, however, are often against theology, which has to rely on dialectical refinements to explain them away; but unfortunately in this instance dialectic is no less hostile than experience. God must know our necessities before we ask and, if he is good, must already have decided what he would do for us. Prayer, like every other act, becomes in a providential world altogether perfunctory and histrionic; we are compelled to go through it, it is set down for us in the play, but it lacks altogether that moral value which we assign to it. When our prayers fail, it must be better than if they had succeeded, so that prayer, with all free preference whatsoever, becomes an absurdity. The trouble is much deeper than that which so many people find in determinism. A physical predetermination, in making all things necessary, leaves all values entire, and my preferences, though they cannot be efficacious unless they express preformed natural forces, are not invalidated ideally. It is still true that the world would have been better to all eternity if my will also could have been fulfilled. A providential optimism, on the contrary, not merely predetermines events but discounts values; and it reduces every mortal aspiration, every pang of conscience, every wish that things should be better than they are, to a blind impertinence, nay, to a sacrilege. Thus, you may not pray that God's kingdom may come, but only—what is not a prayer but a dogma—that it has come already. The mythology that pretends to justify prayer by giving it a material efficacy misunderstands prayer completely and makes it ridiculous, for it turns away from the heart, which prayer expresses pathetically, to a fabulous cosmos where aspirations have been turned into things and have thereby stifled their own voices.

A Real Efficacy Would Be Mechanical.

The situation would not be improved if we surrendered that mystical optimism, and maintained that prayer might really attract superhuman forces to our aid by giving them a signal without which they would not have been able to reach us. If experience lent itself to such a theory there would be nothing in it more impossible than in ordinary telepathy; prayer would then be an art like conversation, and the exact personages and interests would be discoverable to which we might appeal. A celestial diplomacy might then be established not very unlike primitive religions. Religion would have reverted to industry and science, to which the grosser spirits that take refuge under it have always wished to assimilate it. But is it really the office of religion to work upon external powers and extract from them certain calculable effects? Is it an art, like empiric medicine, and merely a dubious and mystic industry? If so, it exists only by imperfection; were it better developed it would coincide with those material and social arts with which it is identical in essence. Successful religion, like successful magic, would have passed into the art of exploiting the world.

True Uses of Prayer.

What successful religion really should pass into is contemplation, ideality, poetry, in the sense in which poetry includes all imaginative moral life. That this is what religion looks to is very clear in prayer and in the efficacy which prayer consistently can have. In rational prayer the soul may be said to accomplish three things important to its welfare: it withdraws within itself and defines its good, it accommodates itself to destiny, and it grows like the ideal which it conceives.

It Clarifies the Ideal.

If prayer springs from need it will naturally dwell on what would satisfy that necessity; sometimes, indeed, it does nothing else but articulate and eulogise what is most wanted and prized. This object will often be particular, and so it should be, since Socrates' prayer "for the best" would be perfunctory and vapid indeed in a man whose life had not been spent, like Socrates', in defining what the best was. Yet any particular good lies in a field of relations; it has associates and implications, so that the mind dwelling on it and invoking its presence will naturally be enticed also into its background, and will wander there, perhaps to come upon greater goods, or upon evils which the coveted good would make inevitable. An earnest consideration, therefore, of anything desired is apt to enlarge and generalise aspiration till it embraces an ideal life; for from almost any starting-point the limits and contours of mortal happiness are soon descried. Prayer, inspired by a pressing need, already relieves its importunity by merging it in the general need of the spirit and of mankind. It therefore calms the passions in expressing them, like all idealisation, and tends to make the will conformable with reason and justice.

It Reconciles to the Inevitable.

A comprehensive ideal, however, is harder to realise than a particular one: the rain wished for may fall, the death feared may be averted, but the kingdom of heaven does not come. It is in the very essence of prayer to regard a denial as possible. There would be no sense in defining and begging for the better thing if that better thing had at any rate to be. The possibility of defeat is one of the circumstances with which meditation must square the ideal; seeing that my prayer may not be granted, what in that case should I pray for next? Now the order of nature is in many respects well known, and it is clear that all realisable ideals must not transgress certain bounds. The practical ideal, that which under the circumstances it is best to aim at and pray for, will not rebel against destiny. Conformity is an element in all religion and submission in all prayer; not because what must be is best, but because the best that may be pursued rationally lies within the possible, and can be hatched only in the general womb of being. The prayer, "Thy will be done," if it is to remain a prayer, must not be degraded from its original meaning, which was that an unfulfilled ideal should be fulfilled; it expressed aspiration after the best, not willingness to be satisfied with anything. Yet the inevitable must be accepted, and it is easier to change the human will than the laws of nature. To wean the mind from extravagant desires and teach it to find excellence in what life affords, when life is made as worthy as possible, is a part of wisdom and religion. Prayer, by confronting the ideal with experience and fate, tends to render that ideal humble, practical, and efficacious.

It Fosters Spiritual Life by Conceiving It in Its Perfection.

A sense for human limitations, however, has its foil in the ideal of deity, which is nothing but the ideal of man freed from those limitations which a humble and wise man accepts for himself, but which a spiritual man never ceases to feel as limitations. Man, for instance, is mortal, and his whole animal and social economy is built on that fact, so that his practical ideal must start on that basis, and make the best of it; but immortality is essentially better, and the eternal is in many ways constantly present to a noble mind; the gods therefore are immortal, and to speak their language in prayer is to learn to see all things as they do and as reason must, under the form of eternity. The gods are furthermore no respecters of persons; they are just, for it is man's ideal to be so. Prayer, since it addresses deity, will in the end blush to be selfish and partial; the majesty of the divine mind envisaged and consulted will tend to pass into the human mind.

This use of prayer has not been conspicuous in Christian times, because, instead of assimilating the temporal to the eternal, men have assimilated the eternal to the temporal, being perturbed fanatics in religion rather than poets and idealists. Pagan devotion, on the other hand, was full of this calmer spirit. The gods, being frankly natural, could be truly ideal. They embodied what was fairest in life and loved men who resembled them, so that it was delightful and ennobling to see their images everywhere, and to keep their names and story perpetually in mind. They did not by their influence alienate man from his appropriate happiness, but they perfected it by their presence. Peopling all places, changing their forms as all living things must according to place and circumstance, they showed how all kinds of being, if perfect in their kind, might be perfectly good. They asked for a reverence consistent with reason, and exercised prerogatives that left man free. Their worship was a perpetual lesson in humanity, moderation, and beauty. Something prerational and monstrous often peeped out behind their serenity, as it does beneath the human soul, and there was certainly no lack of wildness and mystic horror in their apparitions. The ideal must needs betray those elemental forces on which, after all, it rests; but reason exists to exorcise their madness and win them over to a steady expression of themselves and of the good.

Discipline and Contemplation Are Their Own Reward.

Prayer, in fine, though it accomplishes nothing material, constitutes something spiritual. It will not bring rain, but until rain comes it may cultivate hope and resignation and may prepare the heart for any issue, opening up a vista in which human prosperity will appear in its conditioned existence and conditional value. A candle wasting itself before an image will prevent no misfortune, but it may bear witness to some silent hope or relieve some sorrow by expressing it; it may soften a little the bitter sense of impotence which would consume a mind aware of physical dependence but not of spiritual dominion. Worship, supplication, reliance on the gods, express both these things in an appropriate parable. Physical impotence is expressed by man's appeal for help; moral dominion by belief in God's omnipotence. This belief may afterwards seem to be contradicted by events. It would be so in truth if God's omnipotence stood for a material magical control of events by the values they were to generate. But the believer knows in his heart, in spite of the confused explanations he may give of his feelings, that a material efficacy is not the test of his faith. His faith will survive any outward disappointment. In fact, it will grow by that discipline and not become truly religious until it ceases to be a foolish expectation of improbable things and rises on stepping-stones of its material disappointments into a spiritual peace. What would sacrifice be but a risky investment if it did not redeem us from the love of those things which it asks us to surrender? What would be the miserable fruit of an appeal to God which, after bringing us face to face with him, left us still immersed in what we could have enjoyed without him? The real use and excuse for magic is this, that by enticing us, in the service of natural lusts, into a region above natural instrumentalities, it accustoms us to that rarer atmosphere, so that we may learn to breathe it for its own sake. By the time we discover the mechanical futility of religion we may have begun to blush at the thought of using religion mechanically; for what should be the end of life if friendship with the gods is a means only? When thaumaturgy is discredited, the childish desire to work miracles may itself have passed away. Before we weary of the attempt to hide and piece out our mortality, our concomitant immortality may have dawned upon us. While we are waiting for the command to take up our bed and walk we may hear a voice saying: Thy sins are forgiven thee.

IV

Mythology

Status of Fable in the Mind.

PRIMITIVE thought has the form of poetry and the function of prose. Being thought, it distinguishes objects from the experience that reveals them and it aspires to know things as they are; but being poetical, it attributes to those objects all the qualities which the experience of them contains, and builds them out imaginatively in all directions, without distinguishing what is constant and efficacious in them. This primitive habit of thought survives in mythology, which is an observation of things encumbered with all they can suggest to a dramatic fancy. It is neither conscious poetry nor valid science, but the common root and raw material of both. Free poetry is a thing which early man is too poor to indulge in; his wide-open eyes are too intently watching this ominous and treacherous world. For pure science he has not enough experience, no adequate power to analyse, remember, and abstract; his soul is too hurried and confused, too thick with phantoms, to follow abstemiously the practical threads through the labyrinth. His view of things is immensely overloaded; what he gives out for description is more than half soliloquy; but his expression of experience is for that very reason adequate and quite sincere. Belief, which we have come to associate with religion, belongs really to science; myths are not believed in, they are conceived and understood. To demand belief for an idea is already to contrast interpretation with knowledge; it is to assert that that idea has scientific truth. Mythology cannot flourish in that dialectical air; it belongs to a deeper and more ingenuous level of thought, when men pored on the world with intense indiscriminate interest, accepting and recording the mind's vegetation no less than that observable in things, and mixing the two developments together in one wayward drama.

It Requires Genius.

A good mythology cannot be produced without much culture and intelligence. Stupidity is not poetical. Nor is mythology essentially a half-way house between animal vagueness in the soul and scientific knowledge. It is conceivable that some race, not so dreamful as ours, should never have been tempted to use psychic and passionate categories in reading nature, but from the first should have kept its observations sensuous and pure, elaborating them only on their own plane, mathematically and dialectically. Such a race, however, could hardly have had lyric or dramatic genius, and even in natural science, which requires imagination, they might never have accomplished anything. The Hebrews, denying themselves a rich mythology, remained without science and plastic art; the Chinese, who seem to have attained legality and domestic arts and a tutored sentiment without passing through such imaginative tempests as have harassed us, remain at the same time without a serious science or philosophy. The Greeks, on the contrary, precisely the people with the richest and most irresponsible myths, first conceived the cosmos scientifically, and first wrote rational history and philosophy. So true it is that vitality in any mental function is favourable to vitality in the whole mind. Illusions incident to mythology are not dangerous in the end, because illusion finds in experience a natural though painful cure. Extravagant error is unstable, unless it be harmless and confined to a limbo remote from all applications; if it touches experience it is stimulating and brief, while the equipoise of dulness may easily render dulness eternal. A developed mythology shows that man has taken a deep and active interest both in the world and in himself, and has tried to link the two, and interpret the one by the other. Myth is therefore a natural prologue to philosophy, since the love of ideas is the root of both. Both are made up of things admirable to consider.

It Only Half Deceives.

Nor is the illusion involved in fabulous thinking always so complete and opaque as convention would represent it. In taking fable for fact, good sense and practice seldom keep pace with dogma. There is always a race of pedants whose function it is to materialise everything ideal, but the great world, half shrewdly, half doggedly, manages to escape their contagion. Language may be entirely permeated with myth, since the affinities of language have much to do with men gliding into such thoughts; yet the difference between language itself and what it expresses is not so easily obliterated. In spite of verbal traditions, people seldom take a myth in the same sense in which they would take an empirical truth. All the doctrines that have flourished in the world about immortality have hardly affected men's natural sentiment in the face of death, a sentiment which those doctrines, if taken seriously, ought wholly to reverse. Men almost universally have acknowledged a Providence, but that fact has had no force to destroy natural aversions and fears in the presence of events; and yet, if Providence had ever been really trusted, those preferences would all have lapsed, being seen to be blind, rebellious, and blasphemous. Prayer, among sane people, has never superseded practical efforts to secure the desired end; a proof that the sphere of expression was never really confused with that of reality. Indeed, such a confusion, if it had passed from theory to practice, would have changed mythology into madness. With rare exceptions this declension has not occurred and myths have been taken with a grain of salt which not only made them digestible, but heightened their savour.

It is always by its applicability to things known, not by its revelation of things unknown and irrelevant, that a myth at its birth appeals to mankind. When it has lost its symbolic value and sunk to the level of merely false information, only an inert and stupid tradition can keep it above water. Parables justify themselves but dogmas call for an apologist. The genial offspring of prophets and poets then has to be kept alive artificially by professional doctors. A thing born of fancy, moulded to express universal experience and its veritable issues, has to be hedged about by misrepresentation, sophistry, and party spirit. The very apologies and unintelligent proofs offered in its defence in a way confess its unreality, since they all strain to paint in more plausible colours what is felt to be in itself extravagant and incredible.

Its Interpretative Essence.

Yet if the myth was originally accepted it could not be for this falsity plainly written on its face; it was accepted because it was understood, because it was seen to express reality in an eloquent metaphor. Its function was to show up some phase of experience in its totality and moral issue, as in a map we reduce everything geographically in order to overlook it better in its true relations. Had those symbols for a moment descended to the plane of reality they would have lost their meaning and dignity; they would tell us merely that they themselves existed bodily, which would be false, while about the real configuration of life they would no longer tell us anything. Such an error, if carried through to the end, would nullify all experience and arrest all life. Men would be reacting on expressions and meeting with nothing to express. They would all be like word-eating philosophers or children learning the catechism.

The true function of mythical ideas is to present and interpret events in terms relative to spirit. Things have uses in respect to the will which are direct and obvious, while the inner machinery of these same things is intricate and obscure. We therefore conceive things roughly and superficially by their eventual practical functions and assign to them, in our game, some counterpart of the interest they affect in us. This counterpart, to our thinking, constitutes their inward character and soul. So conceived, soul and character are purely mythical, being arrived at by dramatising events according to our own fancy and interest. Such ideas may be adequate in their way if they cover all the uses we may eventually find in the objects they transcribe for us dramatically. But the most adequate mythology is mythology still; it does not, like science, set things before us in the very terms they will wear when they are gradually revealed to experience. Myth is expression, it is not prophecy. For this reason myth is something on which the mind rests; it is an ideal interpretation in which the phenomena are digested and transmuted into human energy, into imaginative tissue.

Contrast with Science.

Scientific formulas, on the contrary, cry aloud for retranslation into perceptual terms; they are like tight-ropes, on which a man may walk but on which he cannot stand still. These unstable symbols lead, however, to real facts and define their experimental relations; while the mind reposing contentedly in a myth needs to have all observation and experience behind it, for it will not be driven to gather more. The perfect and stable myth would rest on a complete survey and steady focussing of all interests really affecting the one from whose point of view the myth was framed. Then each physical or political unit would be endowed with a character really corresponding to all its influence on the thinker. This symbol would render the diffuse natural existences which it represented in an eloquent figure; and since this figure would not mislead practically it might be called true. But truth, in a myth, means a sterling quality and standard excellence, not a literal or logical truth. It will not, save by a singular accident, represent their proper internal being, as a forthright unselfish intellect would wish to know it. It will translate into the language of a private passion the smiles and frowns which that passion meets with in the world.

Importance of the Moral Factor.

There are accordingly two factors in mythology, a moral consciousness and a corresponding poetic conception of things. Both factors are variable, and variations in the first, if more hidden, are no less important than variations in the second. Had fable started with a clear perception of human values, it would have gained immensely in significance, because its pictures, however wrong the external notions they built upon, would have shown what, in the world so conceived, would have been the ideals and prizes of life. Thus Dante's bad cosmography and worse history do not detract from the spiritual penetration of his thought, though they detract from its direct applicability. Had nature and destiny been what Dante imagined, his conception of the values involved would have been perfect, for the moral philosophy he brought into play was Aristotelian and rational. So his poem contains a false instance or imaginary rehearsal of true wisdom. It describes the Life of Reason in a fantastic world. We need only change man's situation to that in which he actually finds himself, and let the soul, fathomed and chastened as Dante left it, ask questions and draw answers from this steadier dream.

Its Submergence.

Myth travels among the people, and in their hands its poetic factor tends to predominate. It is easier to carry on the dialectic or drama proper to a fable than to confront it again with the facts and give them a fresh and more genial interpretation. The poet makes the fable; the sophist carries it on. Therefore historians and theologians discuss chiefly the various forms which mythical beings have received, and the internal logical or moral implications of those hypostases. They would do better to attend instead to the moral factor. However interesting a fable may be in itself, its religious value lies wholly in its revealing some function which nature has in human life. Not the beauty of the god makes him adorable, but his dispensing benefits and graces. Side by side with Apollo (a god having moral functions and consequently inspiring a fervent cult and tending himself to assume a moral character) there may be a Helios or a Phaëthon, poetic figures expressing just as well the sun's physical operation, and no less capable, if the theologian took hold of them, of suggesting psychological problems. The moral factor, however, was not found in these minor deities. Only a verbal and sensuous poetry had been employed in defining them; the needs and hopes of mankind had been ignored. Apollo, on the contrary, in personifying the sun, had embodied also the sun's relations to human welfare. The vitality, the healing, the enlightenment, the lyric joy flowing into man's heart from that highest source of his physical being are all beautifully represented in the god's figure and fable. The religion of Apollo is therefore a true religion, as religions may be true: the mythology which created the god rested on a deep, observant sense for moral values, and drew a vivid, if partial, picture of the ideal, attaching it significantly to its natural ground.

The first function of mythology is to justify magic. The weak hope on which superstition hangs, the gambler's instinct which divines in phenomena a magic solicitude for human fortunes, can scarcely be articulated without seeking to cover and justify itself by some fable.

Myth Justifies Magic.

A magic function is most readily conceived and defined by attributing to the object intentions hostile or favourable to men, together with human habits of passion and discourse. For lack of resources and observations, reason is seldom able to discredit magic altogether. Reasonable men are forced, therefore, in order to find some satisfaction, to make magic as intelligible as possible by assimilating it to such laws of human action as may be already mastered and familiar. Magic is thus reduced to a sort of system, regulated by principles of its own and naturalised, as it were, in the commonwealth of science.

Myths Might Be Metaphysical.

Such an avowed and defended magic usually takes one of two forms. When the miracle is interpreted dramatically, by analogy to human life, we have mythology; when it is interpreted rationalistically, by analogy to current logic or natural science, we have metaphysics or theosophy. The metaphysical sort of superstition has never taken deep root in the western world. Pythagorean mysteries and hypnotisations, although periodically fashionable, have soon shrivelled in our too salubrious and biting air. Even such charming exotics as Plato's myths have not been able to flourish without changing their nature and passing into ordinary dramatic mythology—into a magic system in which all the forces, once terms in moral experience, became personal angels and demons. Similarity with the Christian sacraments: these magic rites, had they been established in India among a people theosophically minded, might have furnished cues to high transcendental mysteries. Baptism might have been interpreted as a symbol for the purged and abolished will, and Communion as a symbol for the escape from personality. But European races, though credulous enough, are naturally positivistic, so that, when they were called upon to elucidate their ceremonial mysteries, what they lit upon was no metaphysical symbolism but a material and historical drama. Communion became a sentimental interview between the devout soul and the person of Christ; baptism became the legal execution of a mythical contract once entered into between the first and second persons of the Trinity. Thus, instead of a metaphysical interpretation, the extant magic received its needful justification through myths.

They Appear Ready Made, Like Parts of the Social Fabric.

When mythology first appears in western literature it already possesses a highly articulate form. The gods are distinct personalities, with attributes and histories which it is hard to divine the source of and which suggest no obvious rational interpretation. The historian is therefore in the same position as a child who inherits a great religion. The gods and their doings are *prima facie* facts in his world like any other facts, objective beings that convention puts him in the presence of and with which he begins by having social relations. He envisages them with respect and obedience, or with careless defiance, long before he thinks of questioning or proving their existence. The attitude he assumes towards them makes them in the first instance factors in his moral world. Much subsequent scepticism and rationalising philosophy will not avail to efface the vestiges of that early communion with familiar gods. It is hard to reduce to objects of science what are essentially factors in moral intercourse. All thoughts on religion remain accordingly coloured with passion, and are felt to be, above all, a test of loyalty and an index to virtue. The more derivative, unfathomable, and opaque is the prevalent idea of the gods, the harder it is for a rational feeling to establish itself in their regard. Sometimes the most complete historical enlightenment will not

copies of himself in various degrees. These, of which man was the chief, began their career in the year 4004 B. C., and they would live on an indefinite time, possibly, that chronological symmetry might not be violated, until A. D. 4004. The opening and close of this drama were marked by two magnificent tableaux. In the first, in obedience to the word of God, sun, moon, and stars, and earth with all her plants and animals, assumed their appropriate places, and nature sprang into being with all her laws. The first man was made out of clay, by a special act of God, and the first woman was fashioned from one of his ribs, extracted while he lay in a deep sleep. They were placed in an orchard where they often could see God, its owner, walking in the cool of the evening. He suffered them to range at will and eat of all the fruits he had planted save that of one tree only. But they, incited by a devil, transgressed this single prohibition, and were banished from that paradise with a curse upon their head, the man to live by the sweat of his brow and the woman to bear children in labour. These children possessed from the moment of conception the inordinate natures which their parents had acquired. They were born to sin and to find disorder and death everywhere within and without them.

At the same time God, lest the work of his hands should wholly perish, promised to redeem in his good season some of Adam's children and restore them to a natural life. This redemption was to come ultimately through a descendant of Eve, whose foot should bruise the head of the serpent. But it was to be prefigured by many partial and special redemptions. Thus, Noah was to be saved from the deluge, Lot from Sodom, Isaac from the sacrifice, Moses from Egypt, the captive Jews from Babylon, and all faithful souls from heathen forgetfulness and idolatry. For a certain tribe had been set apart from the beginning to keep alive the memory of God's judgments and promises, while the rest of mankind, abandoned to its natural depravity, sank deeper and deeper into crimes and vanities. The deluge that came to punish

these evils did not avail to cure them. "The world was renewed* and the earth rose again above the bosom of the
waters, but in this renovation there remained eternally some
trace of divine vengeance. Until the deluge all nature had
been exceedingly hardy and vigorous, but by that vast flood
of water which God had spread out over the earth, and by
its long abiding there, all saps were diluted; the air, charged
with too dense and heavy a moisture, bred ranker principles
of corruption. The early constitution of the universe was
weakened, and human life, from stretching as it had formerly
done to near a thousand years, grew gradually briefer. Herbs
and roots lost their primitive potency and stronger food had
to be furnished to man by the flesh of other animals. . . .
Death gained upon life and men felt themselves overtaken
by a speedier chastisement. As day by day they sank deeper
in their wickedness, it was but right they should daily, as it
were, stick faster in their woe. The very change in nourish-
ment made manifest their decline and degradation, since as
they became feebler they became also more voracious and
blood-thirsty."

Henceforth there were two spirits, two parties, or, as Saint
Augustine called them, two cities in the world. The City of
Satan, whatever its artifices in art, war, or philosophy, was
essentially corrupt and impious. Its joy was but a comic
mask and its beauty the whitening of a sepulchre. It stood
condemned before God and before man's better conscience
by its vanity, cruelty, and secret misery, by its ignorance of
all that it truly behoved a man to know who was destined
to immortality. Lost, as it seemed, within this Babylon, or
visible only in its obscure and forgotten purlieus, lived on at
the same time the City of God, the society of all the souls
God predestined to salvation; a city which, however humble
and inconspicuous it might seem on earth, counted its
myriad transfigured citizens in heaven, and had its destinies,
like its foundations, in eternity. To this City of God be-

* Bossuet: Discours sur l'histoire universelle, Part II, Chap. I.

longed, in the first place, the patriarchs and the prophets
who, throughout their plaintive and ardent lives, were faithful to what echoes still remained of a primeval revelation,
and waited patiently for the greater revelation to come. To
the same city belonged the magi who followed a star till it
halted over the stable in Bethlehem; Simeon, who divined
the present salvation of Israel; John the Baptist, who bore
witness to the same and made straight its path; and Peter,
to whom not flesh and blood, but the spirit of the Father in
heaven, revealed the Lord's divinity. For salvation had indeed come with the fulness of time, not, as the carnal Jews
had imagined it, in the form of an earthly restoration, but
through the incarnation of the Son of God in the Virgin
Mary, his death upon a cross, his descent into hell, and his
resurrection at the third day according to the Scriptures. To
the same city belonged finally all those who, believing in
the reality and efficacy of Christ's mission, relied on his
merits and followed his commandment of unearthly love.

All history was henceforth essentially nothing but the
conflict between these two cities; two moralities, one natural, the other supernatural; two philosophies, one rational,
the other revealed; two beauties, one corporeal, the other
spiritual; two glories, one temporal, the other eternal; two
institutions, one the world, the other the Church. These,
whatever their momentary alliances or compromises, were
radically opposed and fundamentally alien to one another.
Their conflict was to fill the ages until, when wheat and
tares had long flourished together and exhausted between
them the earth for whose substance they struggled, the harvest should come; the terrible day of reckoning when those
who had believed the things of religion to be imaginary
would behold with dismay the Lord visibly coming down
through the clouds of heaven, the angels blowing their
alarming trumpets, all generations of the dead rising from
their graves, and judgment without appeal passed on every
man, to the edification of the universal company and his

own unspeakable joy or confusion. Whereupon the blessed would enter eternal bliss with God their master and the wicked everlasting torments with the devil whom they served.

The drama of history was thus to close upon a second tableau: long-robed and beatified cohorts passing above, amid various psalmodies, into an infinite luminous space, while below the damned, howling, writhing, and half transformed into loathsome beasts, should be engulfed in a fiery furnace. The two cities, always opposite in essence, should thus be finally divided in existence, each bearing its natural fruits and manifesting its true nature.

Let the reader fill out this outline for himself with its thousand details; let him remember the endless mysteries, arguments, martyrdoms, consecrations that carried out the sense and made vital the beauty of the whole. Let him pause before the phenomenon; he can ill afford, if he wishes to understand history or the human mind, to let the apparition float by unchallenged without delivering up its secret. What shall we say of this Christian dream?

Mythology Is a Language and Must Be Understood to Convey Something by Symbols.

Those who are still troubled by the fact that this dream is by many taken for a reality, and who are consequently obliged to defend themselves against it, as against some dangerous error in science or in philosophy, may be allowed to marshal arguments in its disproof. Such, however, is not my intention. Do we marshal arguments against the miraculous birth of Buddha, or the story of Cronos devouring his children? We seek rather to honour the piety and to understand the poetry embodied in those fables. If it be said that those fables are believed by no one, I reply that those fables are or have been believed just as unhesitatingly as the Christian theology, and by men no less reasonable or learned than the unhappy apologists of our own ancestral creeds. Matters of religion should never be matters of controversy. We neither argue with a lover about his taste, nor condemn him, if we are just, for knowing so human a passion. That he harbours it is no indication of a want of sanity on his part in other matters. But while we acquiesce in his experience, and are glad he has it, we need no arguments to dissuade us from sharing it. Each man may have his own loves, but the object in each case is different. And so it is, or should be, in religion. Before the rise of those strange and fraudulent Hebraic pretensions there was no question among men about the national, personal, and poetic character of religious allegiance. It could never have been a duty to adopt a religion not one's own any more than a language, a coinage, or a costume not current in one's own country. The idea that religion contains a literal, not a symbolic, representation of truth and life is simply an impossible idea. Whoever entertains it has not come within the region of profitable philosophising on that subject. His science is not wide enough to cover all existence. He has not discovered that there can be no moral allegiance except to the ideal. His certitude and his arguments are no more pertinent to the religious question than would be the insults, blows, and murders to which, if he could, he would appeal in the next instance. Philosophy may describe unreason, as it may describe force; it cannot hope to refute them.

x

Piety

The Core of Religion Not Theoretical.

HEBRAISM is a striking example of a religion tending to discard mythology and magic. It was a Hebraising apostle who said that true religion and undefiled was to visit the fatherless and the widow, and do other works of mercy. Although a complete religion can hardly remain without theoretic and ritual expression, we must remember that after all religion has other aspects less conspicuous, perhaps, than its mythology, but often more worthy of respect. If religion be, as we have assumed, an imaginative symbol for the Life of Reason, it should contain not only symbolic ideas and rites, but also symbolic sentiments and duties. And so it everywhere does in a notable fashion. Piety and spirituality are phases of religion no less important than mythology, or than those metaphysical spectres with which mythology terminates. It is therefore time we should quite explicitly turn from religious ideas to religious emotions, from imaginative history and science to imaginative morals.

Piety, in its nobler and Roman sense, may be said to mean man's reverent attachment to the sources of his being and the steadying of his life by that attachment. A soul is but the last bubble of a long fermentation in the world. If we wish to live associated with permanent racial interests we must plant ourselves on a broad historic and human foundation, we must absorb and interpret the past which has made us, so that we may hand down its heritage reinforced, if possible, and in no way undermined or denaturalised. This consciousness that the human spirit is derived and responsible, that all its functions are heritages and trusts, involves a sentiment of gratitude and duty which we may call piety.

Loyalty to the Sources of Our Being.

The true objects of piety are, of course, those on which life and its interests really depend: parents first, then family, ancestors, and country; finally, humanity at large and the whole natural cosmos. But had a lay sentiment toward these forces been fostered by clear knowledge of their nature and relation to ourselves, the dutifulness or cosmic emotion thereby aroused would have remained purely moral and historical. As science would not in the end admit any myth which was not avowed poetry, so it would not admit any piety which was not plain reason and duty. But man, in his perplexities and pressing needs, has plunged, once for all, into imaginative courses through which it is our business to follow him, to see if he may not eventually reach his goal even by those bypaths and dark circumlocutions.

The Pious Æneas.

What makes piety an integral part of traditional religions is the fact that moral realities are represented in the popular mind by poetic symbols. The awe inspired by principles so abstract and consequences so remote and general is arrested at their conventional name. We have all read in boyhood, perhaps with derision, about the pious Æneas. His piety may have seemed to us nothing but a feminine sensibility, a faculty of shedding tears on slight provocation. But in truth Æneas's piety, as Virgil or any Roman would have conceived it, lay less in his feelings than in his function and vocation. He was bearing the Palladium of his country to a new land, to found another Troy, so that the blood and traditions of his ancestors might not perish. His emotions were only the appropriate expression of his priestly office. The hero might have been stern and stolid enough on his own martial ground, but since he bore the old Anchises from the ruins of Ilium he had assumed a sacred mission. Henceforth a sacerdotal unction and lyric pathos belonged rightfully to his person. If those embers, so religiously guarded, should by chance have been extinguished, there could never have been a Vestal fire nor any Rome. So that all that Virgil and his readers, if they had any piety, revered in the world had been hazarded in those legendary adventures. It was not Æneas's own life or private ambition that was at stake to justify his emotion. His tenderness, like Virgil's own, was ennobled and made heroic by its magnificent and impersonal object. It was truly an epic destiny that inspired both poet and hero.

An Ideal Background Required.

If we look closer, however, we shall see that mythical and magic elements were requisite to lend this loftiness to the argument. Had Æneas not been Venus' son, had no prophetic instinct animated him, had no Juno been planning the rise of Carthage, how could the future destinies of this expedition have been imported into it, to lift it above some piratical or desperate venture? Colonists passing in our day to America or Australia might conceivably carry with them the seeds of empires as considerable as Rome's. But they would go out thinking of their private livelihood and convenience, breaking or loosening whatever pious bonds might unite them to the past, and quite irresponsibly laying the foundations for an unknown future. A poet, to raise them to the height of their unwitting function, would have to endow them with second sight and a corresponding breadth of soul and purpose. He would need, in a word, heroic figures and supernatural machinery.

Now, what supernatural machinery and heroic figures do for an epic poet piety does for a race. It endows it, through mythical and magic symbols, with something like a vision or representation of its past and future. Religion is normally the most traditional and national of things. It embodies and localises the racial heritage. Commandments of the law, feasts and fasts, temples and the tombs associated with them, are so many foci of communal life, so many points for the dissemination of custom. The Sabbath, which a critical age might justify on hygienic grounds, is inconceivable without a religious sanction. The craving for rest and emotion expressed itself spontaneously in a practice which, as it established itself, had to be sanctioned by fables till the recurrent holiday, with all its humane and chastening influences, came to be established on supernatural authority. It was now piety to observe it and to commemorate in it the sacred duties and traditions of the race. In this function, of course, lay its true justification, but the mythical one had to be assigned, since the diffused prosaic advantages of such a practice would never avail to impose it on irrational wills. Indeed, to revert to our illustration, had Æneas foreseen in detail the whole history of Rome, would not his faith in his divine mission have been considerably dashed? The reality, precious and inestimable as on the whole it was to humanity, might well have shocked him by its cruelties, shames, and disasters. He would have wished to found only a perfect nation and a city eternal indeed. A want of rationality and measure in the human will, that has not learned to prize small betterments and finite but real goods, compels it to deceive itself about the rewards of life in order to secure them. That celestial mission, those heavenly apparitions, those incalculable treasures carried through many a storm, abused Æneas' mind in order to nerve him to his real duty. Yet his illusion was merely intellectual. The mission undertaken was truly worth carrying out. Piety thus came to bear the fruits of philanthropy in an age when the love of man was inconceivable. A dull and visionary intellect could hit on no other way of justifying a good instinct.

Philosophers who harbour illusions about the status of intellect in nature may feel that this leadership of instinct in moral life is a sort of indignity, and that to dwell on it so insistently is to prolong satire without wit. But the leadership of instinct, the conscious expression of mechanism, is not merely a necessity in the Life of Reason, it is a safeguard.

Piety Accepts Natural Conditions and Present Tasks.

Piety, in spite of its allegories, contains a much greater wisdom than a half-enlightened and pert intellect can attain. Natural beings have natural obligations, and the value of things for them is qualified by distance and by accidental material connections. Intellect would tend to gauge things impersonally by their intrinsic values, since intellect is itself a sort of disembodied and universal function; it would tend to disregard material conditions and that irrational substratum of reason without which reason would have no organs and no points of application. Piety, on the contrary, esteems things apart from their intrinsic worth, on account of their relation to the agent's person and fortune. Yet such esteem is perfectly rational, partiality in man's affections and allegiance being justified by the partial nature and local status of his life. Piety is the spirit's acknowledgment of its incarnation. So, in filial and parental affection, which is piety in an elementary form, there is a moulding of will and emotion, a check to irresponsible initiative, in obedience to the facts of animal reproduction. Every living creature has an intrinsic and ideal worth; he is the centre of actual and yet more of potential interests. But this moral value, which even the remotest observer must recognise in both parent and child, is not the ground of their specific affection for each other, which no other mortal is called to feel in their regard. This affection is based on the incidental and irrational fact that the one has this particular man for a father, and the other that particular man for a son. Yet, considering the animal basis of human life, an attachment resting on that circumstance is a necessary and rational attachment.

The Leadership of Instinct is Normal.

This physical bond should not, indeed, disturb the intellect in its proper function or warp its judgments; you should not, under guise of tenderness, become foolish and attribute to your father or child greater stature or cleverness or goodness than he actually possesses. To do so is a natural foible but no part of piety or true loyalty. It is one thing to lack a heart and another to possess eyes and a just imagination. Indeed, piety is never so beautiful and touching, never so thoroughly humane and invincible, as when it is joined to an impartial intellect, conscious of the relativity involved in existence and able to elude, through imaginative sympathy, the limits set to personal life by circumstance and private duty. As a man dies nobly when, awaiting his own extinction, he is interested to the last in what will continue to be the interests and joys of others, so he is most profoundly pious who loves unreservedly a country, friends, and associations which he knows very well to be not the most beautiful on earth, and who, being wholly content in his personal capacity with his natural conditions, does not need to begrudge other things whatever speculative admiration they may truly deserve. The ideal in this polyglot world, where reason can receive only local and temporal expression, is to understand all languages and to speak but one, so as to unite, in a manly fashion, comprehension with propriety.

Piety is in a sense pathetic because it involves subordination to physical accident and acceptance of finitude. But it is also noble and eminently fruitful because, in subsuming a life under the general laws of relativity, it meets fate with simple sincerity and labours in accordance with the conditions imposed. Since man, though capable of abstraction and impartiality, is rooted like a vegetable to one point in space and time, and exists by limitation, piety belongs to the equilibrium of his being. It resides, so to speak, at his centre of gravity, at the heart and magnetic focus of his complex endowment. It exercises there the eminently sane function of calling thought home. It saves speculative and emotional life from hurtful extravagance by keeping it traditional and social. Conventional absurdities have at least this advantage, that they may be taken conventionally and may come to be, in practice, mere symbols for their uses. Piety is more closely linked with custom than with thought. It exercises an irrational suasion, moralises by contagion, and brings an emotional peace.

Embodiment Essential to Spirit.

Patriotism is another form of piety in which its natural basis and rational function may be clearly seen. It is right to prefer our own country to all others, because we are children and citizens before we can be travellers or philosophers. Specific character is a necessary point of origin for universal relations: a pure nothing can have no radiation or scope. It is no accident for the soul to be embodied; her very essence is to express and bring to fruition the body's functions and resources. Its instincts make her ideals and its relations her world. A native country is a sort of second body, another enveloping organism to give the will definition. A specific inheritance strengthens the soul. Cosmopolitanism has doubtless its place, because a man may well cultivate in himself, and represent in his nation, affinities to other peoples, and such assimilation to them as is compatible with personal integrity and clearness of purpose. Plasticity to things foreign need not be inconsistent with happiness and utility at home. But happiness and utility are possible nowhere to a man who represents nothing and who looks out on the world without a plot of his own to stand on, either on earth or in heaven. He wanders from place to place, a voluntary exile, always querulous, always uneasy, always alone. His very criticisms express no ideal. His experience is without sweetness, without cumulative fruits, and his children, if he has them, are without morality. For reason and happiness are like other flowers—they wither when plucked.

Piety to the Gods Takes Form from Current Ideals.

The objects most commonly associated with piety are the gods. Popular philosophy, inverting the natural order of ideas, thinks piety to the gods the source of morality. But piety, when genuine, is rather an incidental expression of morality. Its sources are perfectly natural. A volitional life that reaches the level of reflection is necessarily moral in proportion to the concreteness and harmony of its instincts. The fruits which such harmonious instincts, expressed in consciousness, may eventually bear, fruits which would be the aim of virtue, are not readily imaginable, and the descrip-

tion of them has long ago been intrusted to poets and my-
thologists. Thus the love of God, for example, is said to be
the root of Christian charity, but is in reality only its symbol.
For no man not having a superabundant need and faculty of
loving real things could have given a meaning to the phrase,
"love of God," or been moved by it to any action. History
shows in unequivocal fashion that the God loved shifts his
character with the shift in his worshippers' real affections.
What the psalmist loves is the beauty of God's house and
the place where his glory dwelleth. A priestly quietude and
pride, a grateful, meditative leisure after the storms of sedi-
tion and war, some retired unity of mind after the contradictions of the world—this is what the love of God might
signify for the levites. Saint John tells us that he who says
he loves God and loves not his neighbour is a liar. Here the
love of God is an anti-worldly estimation of things and persons, a heart set on that kingdom of heaven in which the
humble and the meek should be exalted. Again, for modern
Catholicism the phrase has changed its meaning remarkably
and signifies in effect love for Christ's person, because piety
has taken a sentimental turn and centred on maintaining
imaginary personal relations with the Saviour. How should
we conceive that a single supernatural influence was actually
responsible for moral effects themselves so various, and producing, in spite of a consecutive tradition, such various notions concerning their object and supposed source?

The Religion of Humanity.

Mankind at large is also, to some minds, an object of piety.
But this religion of humanity is rather a desideratum than a
fact: humanity does not actually appear to anybody in a religious light. The *nihil homine homini utilius* remains a signal
truth, but the collective influence of men and their average
nature are far too mixed and ambiguous to fill the soul with
veneration. Piety to mankind must be three-fourths pity.
There are indeed specific human virtues, but they are those

necessary to existence, like patience and courage. Supported on these indispensable habits, mankind always carries an indefinite load of misery and vice. Life spreads rankly in every wrong and impracticable direction as well as in profitable paths, and the slow and groping struggle with its own ignorance, inertia, and folly leaves it covered in every age of history with filth and blood. It would hardly be possible to exaggerate man's wretchedness if it were not so easy to overestimate his sensibility. There is a *fond* of unhappiness in every bosom, but the depths are seldom probed; and there is no doubt that sometimes frivolity and sometimes sturdy habit helps to keep attention on the surface and to cover up the inner void. Certain moralists, without meaning to be satirical, often say that the sovereign cure for unhappiness is work. Unhappily, the work they recommend is better fitted to dull pain than to remove its cause. It occupies the faculties without rationalising the life. Before mankind could inspire even moderate satisfaction, not to speak of worship, its whole economy would have to be reformed, its reproduction regulated, its thoughts cleared up, its affections equalised and refined.

To worship mankind as it is would be to deprive it of what alone makes it akin to the divine—its aspiration. For this human dust lives; this misery and crime are dark in contrast to an imagined excellence; they are lighted up by a prospect of good. Man is not adorable, but he adores, and the object of his adoration may be discovered within him and elicited from his own soul. In this sense the religion of humanity is the only religion, all others being sparks and abstracts of the same. The indwelling ideal lends all the gods their divinity. No power, either physical or psychical, has the least moral prerogative nor any just place in religion at all unless it supports and advances the ideal native to the worshipper's soul. Without moral society between the votary and his god religion is pure idolatry; and even idolatry would be impossible but for the suspicion that somehow the brute force exorcised in prayer might help or mar some human undertaking.

Cosmic Piety.

There is, finally, a philosophic piety which has the universe for its object. This feeling, common to ancient and modern Stoics, has an obvious justification in man's dependence upon the natural world and in its service to many sides of the mind. Such justification of cosmic piety is rather obscured than supported by the euphemisms and ambiguities in which these philosophers usually indulge in their attempt to preserve the customary religious unction. For the more they personify the universe and give it the name of God the more they turn it into a devil. The universe, so far as we can observe it, is a wonderful and immense engine; its extent, its order, its beauty, its cruelty, make it alike impressive. If we dramatise its life and conceive its spirit, we are filled with wonder, terror, and amusement, so magnificent is that spirit, so prolific, inexorable, grammatical, and dull. Like all animals and plants, the cosmos has its own way of doing things, not wholly rational nor ideally best, but patient, fatal, and fruitful. Great is this organism of mud and fire, terrible this vast, painful, glorious experiment. Why should we not look on the universe with piety? Is it not our substance? Are we made of other clay? All our possibilities lie from eternity hidden in its bosom. It is the dispenser of all our joys. We may address it without superstitious terrors; it is not wicked. It follows its own habits abstractedly; it can be trusted to be true to its word. Society is not impossible between it and us, and since it is the source of all our energies, the home of all our happiness, shall we not cling to it and praise it, seeing that it vegetates so grandly and so sadly, and that it is not for us to blame it for what, doubtless, it never knew that it did? Where there is such infinite and laborious potency there is room for every hope. If we should abstain from judging a father's errors or a mother's foibles, why should we pronounce sentence on the ignorant crimes of the universe, which have passed into our own blood? The universe is the true Adam, the creation the true fall; and as we have never blamed our mythical first parent very much, in spite of the disproportionate consequences of his sin, because we felt that he was but human and that we, in his place, might have sinned too, so we may easily forgive our real ancestor, whose connatural sin we are from moment to moment committing, since it is only the necessary rashness of venturing to be without foreknowing the price or the fruits of existence.

XI

Spirituality and Its Corruptions

To Be Spiritual Is to Live in View of the Ideal.

IN honouring the sources of life, piety is retrospective. It collects, as it were, food for morality, and fortifies it with natural and historic nutriment. But a digestive and formative principle must exist to assimilate this nutriment; a direction and an ideal have to be imposed on these gathered forces. So that religion has a second and a higher side, which looks to the end toward which we move as piety looks to the conditions of progress and to the sources from which we draw our energies. This aspiring side of religion may be called Spirituality. Spirituality is nobler than piety, because what would fulfil our being and make it worth having is what alone lends value to that being's source. Nothing can be lower or more wholly instrumental than the substance and cause of all things. The gift of existence would be worthless unless existence was good and supported at least a possible happiness. A man is spiritual when he lives in the presence of the ideal, and whether he eat or drink does so for the sake of a true and ultimate good. He is spiritual when he envisages his goal so frankly that his whole material life becomes a transparent and transitive vehicle, an instrument which scarcely arrests attention but allows the spirit to use it economically and with perfect detachment and freedom.

There is no need that this ideal should be pompously or mystically described. A simple life is its own reward, and continually realises its function. Though a spiritual man may perfectly well go through intricate processes of thought and attend to very complex affairs, his single eye, fixed on a rational purpose, will simplify morally the natural chaos it looks upon and will remain free. This spiritual mastery is, of course, no slashing and forced synthesis of things into a system of philosophy which, even if it were thinkable, would leave the conceived logical machine without ideality and without responsiveness to actual interests; it is rather an inward aim and fixity in affection that knows what to take and what to leave in a world over which it diffuses something of its own peace. It threads its way through the landscape with so little temptation to distraction that it can salute every irrelevant thing, as Saint Francis did the sun and moon, with courtesy and a certain affectionate detachment.

Spirituality Natural.

Spirituality likes to say, Behold the lilies of the field! For its secret has the same simplicity as their vegetative art; only spirituality has succeeded in adding consciousness without confusing instinct. This success, unfortunately so rare in man's life as to seem paradoxical, is its whole achievement. Spirituality ought to have been a matter of course, since conscious existence has inherent value and there is no intrinsic ground why it should smother that value in alien ambitions and servitudes. But spirituality, though so natural and obvious a thing, is subject, like the lilies' beauty, to corruption. I know not what army of microbes evidently invaded from the beginning the soul's physical basis and devoured its tissues, so that sophistication and bad dreams entirely obscured her limpidity.

None the less, spirituality, or life in the ideal, must be regarded as the fundamental and native type of all life; what deviates from it is disease and incipient dissolution, and is itself what might plausibly demand explanation and evoke surprise. The spiritual man should be quite at home in a world made to be used; the firmament is spread over him like a tent for habitation, and sublunary furniture is even more obviously to be taken as a convenience. He cannot, indeed, remove mountains, but neither does he wish to do so. He comes to endow the mountains with a function, and takes them at that, as a painter might take his brushes and canvas. Their beauty, their metals, their pasturage, their defence—this is what he observes in them and celebrates in his addresses to them. The spiritual man, though not ashamed to be a beggar, is cognisant of what wealth can do and of what it cannot. His unworldliness is true knowledge of the world, not so much a gaping and busy acquaintance as a quiet comprehension and estimation which, while it cannot come without intercourse, can very well lay intercourse aside.

Primitive Consciousness May Be Spiritual.

If the essence of life be spiritual, early examples of life would seem to be rather the opposite. But man's view of primitive consciousness is humanly biassed and relies too much on partial analogies. We conceive an animal's physical life in the gross, and must then regard the momentary feelings that accompany it as very poor expressions either of its extent or conditions. These feelings are, indeed, so many ephemeral lives, containing no comprehensive view of the animal's fortunes. They accordingly fail to realise our notion of a spiritual human life which would have to be rational and to form some representation of man's total environment and interests. But it hardly follows that animal feelings are not spiritual in their nature and, on their narrow basis, perfectly ideal. The most ideal human passion is love, which is also the most absolute and animal and one of the most ephemeral. Very likely, if we could revert to an innocent and absorbed view of our early sensations, we should find that each was a little spiritual universe like Dante's, with its internal hell, purgatory and heaven. Cut off, as those experiences were, from all vistas and from sympathy with things remote, they would contain a closed circle of interests, a flying glimpse of eternity. So an infant living in his mystical limbo, without trailing in a literal sense any clouds of glory from elsewhere, might well repeat on a diminutive scale the beatific vision, insomuch as the only function of which he was conscious at all might be perfectly fulfilled by him and felt in its ideal import. Sucking and blinking are ridiculous processes, perhaps, but they may bring a thrill and satisfaction no less ideal than do the lark's inexhaustible palpitations. Narrow scope and low representative value are not defects in a consciousness having a narrow physical basis and comparatively simple conditions.

Spirit Crossed by Instrumentalities.

The spirit's foe in man has not been simplicity, but sophistication. His instincts, in becoming many, became confused, and in growing permanent, grew feeble and subject to arrest and deviation. Nature, we may say, threw the brute form back into her cauldron, to smelt its substance again before pouring it into a rational mould. The docility which instinct, in its feebleness, acquired in the new creature was to be reason's opportunity, but before the larger harmony could be established a sorry chaos was bound to reign in the mind. Every peeping impulse would drop its dark hint and hide its head in confusion, while some pedantic and unjust law would be passed in its absence and without its vote. Secondary activities, which should always be representative, would establish themselves without being really such. Means would be pursued as if they were ends, and ends, under the illusion that they were forces, would be expected to further some activity, itself without justification. So pedantry might be substituted for wisdom, tyranny for government, superstition for morals, rhetoric for art.

This sophistication is what renders the pursuit of reason so perplexing and prolonged a problem. Half-formed adjustments in the brain and in the body politic are represented in consciousness by what are called passions, prejudices, motives, animosities. None of these felt ebullitions in the least understands its own causes, effects, or relations, but is hatched, so to speak, on the wing and flutters along in the direction of its momentary preference until it lapses, it knows not why, or is crossed and overwhelmed by some contrary power. Thus the vital elements, which in their comparative isolation in the lower animals might have yielded simple little dramas, each with its obvious ideal, its achievement, and its quietus, when mixed in the barbarous human will make a boisterous medley. For they are linked enough together to feel a strain, but not knit enough to form a harmony. In this way the unity of apperception seems to light up at first nothing but disunion. The first dawn of that rational principle which involves immortality breaks upon a discovery of death. The consequence is that ideality seems to man something supernatural and almost impossible. He finds himself at his awakening so confused that he puts chaos at the origin of the world. But only order can beget a world or evoke a sensation. Chaos is something secondary, composed of conflicting organisations interfering with one another. It is compounded like a common noise out of jumbled vibrations, each of which has its period and would in itself be musical. The problem is to arrange these sounds, naturally so tuneful, into concerted music. So long as total discord endures human life remains spasmodic and irresolute; it can find no ideal and admit no total representation of nature. Only when the disordered impulses and perceptions settle down into a trained instinct, a steady, vital response and adequate preparation for the world, do clear ideas and successful purposes arise in the mind. The Life of Reason, with all the arts, then begins its career.

The forces at play in this drama are, first, the primary impulses and functions represented by elementary values; second, the thin network of signals and responses by which those functions are woven into a total organ, represented by discursive thought and all secondary mental figments, and, third, the equilibrium and total power of that new organism in action represented by the ideal. Spirituality, which might have resided in the elementary values, sensuous or passionate, before the relational process supervened, can now exist only in the ultimate activity to which these processes are instrumental. Obstacles to spirituality in human life may accordingly take the form of an arrest either at the elementary values—an entanglement in sense and passion—or at the instrumental processes—an entanglement in what in religious parlance is called "the world."

One Foe of the Spirit Is Worldliness.

Worldly minds bristle with conventional morality (though in private they may nurse a vice or two to appease wayward nature), and they are rational in everything except first principles. They consider the voluptuary a weak fool, disgraced and disreputable; and if they notice the spiritual man at all—for he is easily ignored—they regard him as a useless and visionary fellow. Civilisation has to work algebraically with symbols for known and unknown quantities which only in the end resume their concrete values, so that the journey-men and vulgar middlemen of the world know only conventional goods. They are lost in instrumentalities and are themselves only instruments in the Life of Reason. Wealth, station, fame, success of some notorious and outward sort, make their standard of happiness. Their chosen virtues are industry, good sense, probity, conventional piety, and whatever else has acknowledged utility and seemliness.

The Case For and Against Pleasure.

In its strictures on pleasure and reverie this Philistia is perfectly right. Sensuous living (and I do not mean debauchery alone, but the palpitations of any poet without art or any mystic without discipline) is not only inconsequential and shallow, but dangerous to honour and to sincere happiness. When life remains lost in sense or reverts to it entirely, humanity itself is atrophied. And humanity is tormented and spoilt when, as more often happens, a man disbelieving in reason and out of humour with his world abandons his soul to loose whimseys and passions that play a quarrelsome game there, like so many ill-bred children. Nevertheless, compared with the worldling's mental mechanism and rhetoric, the sensualist's soul is a well of wisdom. He lives naturally on an animal level and attains a kind of good. He has free and concrete pursuits, though they be momentary, and he has sincere satisfactions. He is less often corrupt than primitive, and even when corrupt he finds some justification for his captious existence. He harvests pleasures as he goes which intrinsically, as we have seen, may have the depth and ideality which nature breathes in all her oracles. His experience, for that reason, though disastrous is interesting and has some human pathos; it is easier to make a saint out of a libertine than out of a prig. True, the libertine is pursued, like the animals, by unforeseen tortures, decay, and abandonment, and he is vowed to a total death; but in these respects the worldly man has hardly an advantage. The Babels he piles up may indeed survive his person, but they are themselves vain and without issue, while his brief life has been meantime spent in slavery and his mind cramped with cant and foolish ambitions. The voluptuary is like some roving creature, browsing on nettles and living by chance;

the worldling is like a beast of burden, now ill-used and over-worked, now fatted, stalled, and richly caparisoned. Æsop might well have described their relative happiness in a fable about the wild ass and the mule.

Upshot of Worldly Wisdom.

Thus, even if the voluptuary is sometimes a poet and the worldling often an honest man, they both lack reason so entirely that reflection revolts equally against the life of both. Vanity, vanity, is their common epitaph. Now, at the soul's christening and initiation into the Life of Reason, the first vow must always be to "renounce the pomps and vanities of this wicked world." A person to whom this means nothing is one to whom, in the end, nothing has meaning. He has not conceived a highest good, no ultimate goal is within his horizon, and it has never occurred to him to ask what he is living for. With all his pompous soberness, the worldly man is fundamentally frivolous; with all his maxims and cant estimations he is radically inane. He conforms to religion without suspecting what religion means, not being in the least open to such an inquiry. He judges art like a parrot, without having ever stopped to evoke an image. He preaches about service and duty without any recognition of natural demands or any standard of betterment. His moral life is one vast anacoluthon in which the final term is left out that might have given sense to the whole, one vast ellipsis in which custom seems to bridge the chasm left between ideas. He denies the values of sense because they tempt to truancies from mechanical activity; the values of reason he necessarily ignores because they lie beyond his scope. He adheres to conventional maxims and material quantitative standards; his production is therefore, as far as he himself is concerned, an essential waste and his activity an essential tedium. If at least, like the sensualist, he enjoyed the process and ex-pressed his fancy in his life, there would be something gained; and this sort of gain, though overlooked in the worldling's maxims, all of which have a categorical tone, is really what often lends his life some propriety and spirit. Business and war and any customary task may come to form, so to speak, an organ whose natural function will be just that operation, and the most abstract and secondary activity, like that of adding figures or reading advertisements, may in this way become the one function proper to some soul. There are Nibelungen dwelling by choice underground and happy pedants in the upper air.

Facts are not wanting for these pillars of society to take solace in, if they wish to defend their philosophy. The time will come, astronomers say, when life will be extinct upon this weary planet. All the delights of sense and imagination will be over. It is these that will have turned out to be vain. But the masses of matter which the worldlings have transformed with their machinery, and carried from one place to another, will remain to bear witness of them. The collocation of atoms will never be what it would have been if their feet had less continually beaten the earth. They may have the proud happiness of knowing that, when nothing that the spirit values endures, the earth may still sometimes, because of them, cast a slightly different shadow across the moon's craters.

Two Supposed Escapes from Vanity.

There is no more critical moment in the life of a man and a nation than that in which they are first conscience-stricken and convicted of vanity. Failure, exhaustion, confusion of aims, or whatever else it be that causes a revulsion, brings them before a serious dilemma. Has the vanity of life hitherto been essential or incidental? Are we to look for a new ambition, free from all the illusions of natural impulse, or are we rather to renounce all will indiscriminately and fall back upon conformity and consummate indifference? As this question is answered in one way or the other, two different types of unworldly religion arise.

Fanaticism.

The first, which heralds a new and unimpeachable special hope, a highest duty finally recognised and driving out all lesser motives and satisfactions from the soul, refers vanity to perversity, to error, to a sort of original misunderstanding of our own nature which has led us, in pursuing our worldly interests, to pursue in truth our own destruction. The vanity of life, according to this belief, has been accidental. The taint of existence is not innate vanity but casual sin; what has misled us is not the will in general but only the false and ignorant direction of a will not recognising its only possible satisfaction. What religion in this case opposes to the world is a special law, a special hope, a life intense, ambitious, and aggressive, but excluding much which to an ingenuous will might seem excellent and tempting. Worldliness, in a word, is here met by fanaticism.

Mysticism.

The second type of unworldly religion does not propose to overwhelm the old Adam by single-minded devotion to one selected interest, nor does it refer vanity to an accidental error. On the contrary, it conceives that any special interest, any claim made by a finite and mortal creature upon an infinite world, is bound to be defeated. It is not special acts, it conceives, which are sinful, but action and will themselves that are intrinsically foolish. The cure lies in rescinding the passionate interests that torment us, not in substituting for them another artificial passion more imperious and merciless than the natural passions it comes to devour. This form of religion accordingly meets worldliness with mysticism. Holiness is not placed in conformity to a prescriptive law, in pursuit of a slightly regenerated bliss, nor in advancing a special institution and doctrine. Holiness for the mystic consists rather in universal mildness and insight; in freedom from all passion, bias, and illusion; in a disembodied wisdom which accepts the world, dominates its labyrinths, and is able to guide others through it, without pursuing, for its own part, any hope or desire.

Both Are Irrational.

If these two expedients of the conscience convicted of vanity were to be subjected to a critical judgment, they would both be convicted of vanity themselves. The case of fanaticism is not doubtful, for the choice it makes of a special law or institution or posthumous hope is purely arbitrary, and only to be justified by the satisfaction it affords to those very desires which it boasts to supplant. An oracular morality or revealed religion can hope to support its singular claims only by showing its general conformity to natural reason and its perfect beneficence in the world. Where such justification is wanting the system fanatically embraced is simply an epidemic mania, a social disease for the philosopher to study and, if possible, to cure. Every strong passion tends to dislodge the others, so that fanaticism may often involve a certain austerity, impetuosity, and intensity of life. This vigour, however, is seldom lasting; fanaticism dries its own roots and becomes, when traditionally established, a convention as arbitrary as any fashion and the nest for a new brood of mean and sinister habits. The Pharisee is a new worldling, only his little world is narrowed to a temple, a tribe, and a clerical tradition.

Mysticism, as its meditative nature comports, is never so pernicious, nor can it be brought so easily round to worldliness again. That its beneficent element is purely natural and inconsistent with a denial of will, we shall have occasion elsewhere to observe. Suffice it here to point out, that even if a moral nihilism could be carried through and all definite interests abandoned, the vanity of life would not be thereby corrected, but merely exposed. When our steps had been retraced to the very threshold of being, nothing better worth doing would have been discovered on the way. That to suffer illusion is a bad thing might ordinarily be taken for an axiom, because ordinarily we assume that true knowledge and rational volition are possible; but if this assumption is denied, the value of retracing illusions is itself impeached. When vanity is represented as universal and salvation as purely negative, every one is left free to declare that it is vain to renounce vanity and sinful to seek salvation.

This result, fantastic though it may at first sight appear, is one which mysticism actually comes to under certain circumstances. Absolute pessimism and absolute optimism are opposite sentiments attached to a doctrine identically the same. In either case no improvement is possible, and the authority of human ideals is denied. To escape, to stanch natural wounds, to redeem society and the private soul, are then mistaken and pitiable ambitions, adding to their vanity a certain touch of impiety. One who really believes that the world's work is all providentially directed and that whatever happens, no matter how calamitous or shocking, happens by divine right, has a quietistic excuse for license; to check energy by reason, and seek to limit and choose its path, seems to him a puny rebellion against omnipotence, which works through madness and crime in man no less than through cataclysms in outer nature. Every particular desire is vain and bound, perhaps, to be defeated; but the mystic, when caught in the expansive mood, accepts this defeat itself as needful. Thus a refusal to discriminate rationally or to accept human interests as the standard of right may culminate in a convulsive surrender to passion, just as, when caught in the contractile phase, the same mysticism may lead to universal abstention.

Is There a Third Course?

Must unworldliness be either fanatical or mystical? That is a question of supreme importance to the moral philosopher. On the answer to it hangs the rationality of a spiritual life; nay, the existence of spirituality itself among the types of

human activity. For the fanatic and mystic are only spiritual in appearance because they separate themselves from the
prevalent interests of the world, the one by a special persistent aggression, the other by a general passivity and unearthly calm. The fanatic is, notwithstanding, nothing but
a worldling too narrow and violent to understand the world,
while the mystic is a sensualist too rapt and voluptuous to
rationalise his sensations. Both represent arrested forms of
common-sense, partial developments of a perfectly usual
sensibility. There is no divine inspiration in having only one
passion left, nor in dreamfully accepting or renouncing all
the passions together. Spirituality, if identified with such
types, might justly be called childish. There is an innocent
and incredulous childishness, with its useless eyes wide open,
just as there is a malevolent and peevish childishness, eaten
up with some mischievous whim. The man of experience and
affairs can very quickly form an opinion on such phenomena.
He has not reason to expect superior wisdom in those quarters. On the contrary, his own customary political and humane stand-point gives him the only authoritative measure
of their merits and possible uses. "These sectaries and dream-
ers," he will say to himself, "cannot understand one another
nor the rôle they themselves play in society. It is for us to
make the best of them we can, taking such prudent measures
as are possible to enlist the forces they represent in works
of common utility."

Yes; for Experience Has Intrinsic Inalienable Values.

The philosopher's task, in these premises, is to discover
an escape from worldliness which shall offer a rational advance over it, such as fanaticism and mysticism cannot afford. Does the Life of Reason differ from that of convention?
Is there a spirituality really wiser than common sense? That
there is appears in many directions. Worldliness is arrest and
absorption in the instrumentalities of life; but instrumentalities cannot exist without ultimate purposes, and it suf-

fices to lift the eyes to those purposes and to question the
will sincerely about its essential preferences, to institute a
catalogue of rational goods, by pursuing any of which we
escape worldliness. Sense itself is one of these goods. The
sensualist at least is not worldly, and though his nature be
atrophied in all its higher part, there is not lacking, as we
have seen, a certain internal and abstract spirituality in his
experience. He is a sort of sprightly and incidental mystic,
treating his varied succession of little worlds as the mystic
does his monotonous universe. Sense, moreover, is capable of
many refinements, by which physical existence becomes its
own reward. In the disciplined play of fancy which the fine
arts afford, the mind's free action justifies itself and becomes
intrinsically delightful. Science not only exercises in itself
the intellectual powers, but assimilates nature to the mind,
so that all things may nourish it. In love and friendship the
liberal life extends also to the heart. All these interests which
justify themselves by their intrinsic fruits, make so many
rational episodes and patches in conventional life; but it
must be confessed in all candour that these are but oases in
the desert, and that as the springs of life are irrational, so its
most vehement and prevalent interests remain irrational to
the end. When the pleasures of sense and art, of knowledge
and sympathy, are stretched to the utmost, what part will
they cover and justify of our passions, our industry, our
governments, our religion?

It was a signal error in those rationalists who attributed
their ideal retrospectively to nature that they grotesquely
imagined that people were hungry so that they might enjoy
eating, or curious in order to delight in discovering the truth,
or in love the better to live in conscious harmony. Such a
view forgets that all the forces of life work originally and
fundamentally *a tergo*, that experience and reason are not
the ground of preference but its result. In order to live men
will work disproportionately and eat all manner of filth without pleasure; curiosity as often as not leads to illusion, and

argument serves to foster hatred of the truth; finally, love is notoriously a great fountain of bitterness and frequently a prelude to crime and death. When we have skimmed from life its incidental successes, when we have harvested the moments in which existence justifies itself, its profound depths remain below in their obscure commotion, depths that breed indeed a rational efflorescence, but which are far from exhausted in producing it, and continually threaten, on the contrary, to engulf it.

For These the Religious Imagination Must Supply an Ideal Standard.

The spiritual man needs, therefore, something more than a cultivated sympathy with the brighter scintillation of things. He needs to refer that scintillation to some essential light, so that in reviewing the motley aspects of experience he may not be reduced to culling superciliously the flowers that please him, but may view in them all only images and varied symbols of some eternal good. Spirituality has never flourished apart from religion, except momentarily, perhaps, in some master-mind, whose original intuitions at once became a religion to his followers. For it is religion that knows how to interpret the casual rationalities in the world and isolate their principle, setting this principle up in the face of nature as nature's standard and model. This ideal synthesis of all that is good, this consciousness that over earth floats its congenial heaven, this vision of perfection which gilds beauty and sanctifies grief, has taken form, for the most part, in such grossly material images, in a mythology so opaque and psuedo-physical, that its ideal and moral essence has been sadly obscured; nevertheless, every religion worthy of the name has put into its gods some element of real goodness, something by which they become representative of those scattered excellences and self-justifying bits of experience in which the Life of Reason consists.

That happy constitution which human life has at its best

moments—that, says Aristotle, the divine life has continually. The philosopher thus expressed with absolute clearness the principle which the poets had been clumsily trying to embody from the beginning. Burdened as traditional faiths might be with cosmological and fanciful matter, they still presented in a conspicuous and permanent image that which made all good things good, the ideal and standard of all excellence. By the help of such symbols the spiritual man could steer and steady his judgment; he could say, according to the form religion had taken in his country, that the truly good was what God commanded, or what made man akin to the divine, or what led the soul to heaven. Such expressions, though taken more or less literally by a metaphysical intellect, did not wholly forfeit their practical and moral meaning. God, for a long time, was understood to command what in fact was truly important, the divine was long the truly noble and beautiful, heaven hardly ever ceased to respond to impersonal and ideal aspirations. Under those figures, therefore, the ideals of life could confront life with clearness and authority. The spiritual man, fixing his eyes on them, could live in the presence of ultimate purposes and ideal issues. Before each immediate task, each incidental pleasure, each casual success, he could retain his sweetness and constancy, accepting what good these moments brought and laying it on the altar of what they ought to bring.

XIV

Ideal Immortality

• • • • • • • • •

Even Vicarious Immortality Intrinsically Impossible.

. . . Not only is man's original effort aimed at living for ever in his own person, but, even if he could renounce that desire, the dream of being represented perpetually by posterity is no less doomed. Reproduction, like nutrition, is a device not ultimately successful. If extinction does not defeat it, evolution will. Doubtless the fertility of whatever substance may have produced us will not be exhausted in this single effort; a potentiality that has once proved efficacious and been actualised in life, though it should sleep, will in time revive again. In some form and after no matter what intervals, nature may be expected always to possess consciousness. But beyond this planet and apart from the human race, experience is too little imaginable to be interesting. No definite plan or ideal of ours can find its realisation except in ourselves. Accordingly, a vicarious physical immortality always remains an unsatisfactory issue; what is thus to be preserved is but a counterfeit of our being, and even that counterfeit is confronted by omens of a total extinction more or less remote. A note of failure and melancholy must always dominate in the struggle against natural death.

This defeat is not really problematical, or to be eluded by reviving ill-digested hopes resting entirely on ignorance, an ignorance which these hopes will wish to make eternal. We need not wait for our total death to experience dying; we need not borrow from observation of others' demise a prophecy of our own extinction. Every moment celebrates obsequies over the virtues of its predecessor; and the possession of memory, by which we somehow survive in representation, is the most unmistakable proof that we are perishing in reality. In endowing us with memory, nature has revealed to us a truth utterly unimaginable to the unreflective creation, the truth of mortality. Everything moves in the midst of death, because it indeed *moves*; but it falls into the pit unawares and by its own action unmakes and disestablishes itself, until a wonderful visionary faculty is added, so that a ghost remains of what has perished to reveal that lapse and at the same time in a certain sense to neutralise it.

Intellectual Victory over Change.

The more we reflect, the more we live in memory and idea, the more convinced and penetrated we shall be by the experience of death; yet, without our knowing it, perhaps, this very conviction and experience will have raised us, in a way, above mortality. That was a heroic and divine oracle which, in informing us of our decay, made us partners of the god's eternity, and by giving us knowledge poured into us, to that extent, the serenity and balm of truth. As it is memory that enables us to feel that we are dying and to know that everything actual is in flux, so it is memory that opens to us an ideal immortality, unacceptable and meaningless to the old Adam, but genuine in its own way and undeniably true. It is an immortality in representation—a representation which envisages things in their truth as they have in their own day possessed themselves in reality. It is no subterfuge or superstitious effrontery, called to disguise or throw off the lessons of experience; on the contrary, it is experience itself, reflection itself, and knowledge of mortality. Memory does not reprieve or postpone the changes which it registers, nor does it itself possess a permanent duration; it is, if possible, less stable and more mobile than primary sensation. It is, in point of existence, only an internal and complex kind of sensibility. But in intent and by its significance it plunges to the depths of time; it looks still on the departed and bears witness to the truth that, though absent from this part of experience, and incapable of returning to life, they nevertheless existed once in their own right, were as living and actual as experience is today, and still help to make up, in company with all past, present, and future mortals, the filling and value of the world.

The Glory of It.

As the pathos and heroism of life consists in accepting as an opportunity the fate that makes our own death, partial or total, serviceable to others, so the glory of life consists in accepting the knowledge of natural death as an opportunity to live in the spirit. The sacrifice, the self-surrender, remains real; for, though the compensation is real, too, and at moments, perhaps, apparently overwhelming, it is always incomplete and leaves beneath an incurable sorrow. Yet life can never contradict its basis or reach satisfactions essentially excluded by its own conditions. Progress lies in moving forward from the given situation, and satisfying as well as may be the interests that exist. And if some initial demand has proved hopeless, there is the greater reason for cultivating other sources of satisfaction, possibly more abundant and lasting. Now, reflection is a vital function; memory and imagination have to the full the rhythm and force of life. But these faculties, in envisaging the past or the ideal, envisage the eternal, and the man in whose mind they predominate is to that extent detached in his affections from the world of flux, from himself, and from his personal destiny. This detachment will not make him infinitely long-lived, nor absolutely happy, but it may render him intelligent and just, and may open to him all intellectual pleasures and all human sympathies.

There is accordingly an escape from death open to man; one not found by circumventing nature, but by making use of her own expedients in circumventing her imperfections. Memory, nay, perception itself, is a first stage in this escape, which coincides with the acquisition and possession of reason. When the meaning of successive perceptions is recovered with the last of them, when a survey is made of objects whose constitutive sensations first arose independently, this synthetic moment contains an object raised above time on a pedestal of reflection, a thought indefeasibly true in its ideal deliverance, though of course fleeting in its psychic existence. Existence is essentially temporal and life foredoomed to be mortal, since its basis is a process and an opposition; it floats in the stream of time, never to return, never to be recovered or repossessed. But ever since substance became at some sensitive point intelligent and reflective, ever since time made room and pause for memory, for history, for the consciousness of time, a god, as it were, became incarnate in mortality and some vision of truth, some self-forgetful satisfaction, became a heritage that moment could transmit to moment and man to man. This heritage is humanity itself, the presence of immortal reason in creatures that perish. Apprehension, which makes man so like a god, makes him in one respect immortal; it quickens his numbered moments with a vision of what never dies, the truth of those moments and their inalienable values.

Reason Makes Man's Divinity.

To participate in this vision is to participate at once in humanity and in divinity, since all other bonds are material and perishable, but the bond between two thoughts that have grasped the same truth, of two instants that have caught the same beauty, is a spiritual and imperishable bond. It is imperishable simply because it is ideal and resident merely in import and intent. The two thoughts, the two instants, remain existentially different; were they not two they could not come from different quarters to unite in one meaning and to behold one object in distinct and conspiring acts of apprehension. Being independent in existence, they can be united by the identity of their burden, by the common worship, so to speak, of the same god. Were this ideal goal itself an existence, it would be incapable of uniting anything; for the same gulf which separated the two original minds would open between them and their common object. But being, as it is, purely ideal, it can become the meeting-ground of intelligences and render their union ideally eternal. Among the physical instruments of thought there may be rivalry and impact—the two thinkers may compete and

clash—but this is because each seeks his own physical survival and does not love the truth stripped of its accidental
associations and provincial accent. Doctors disagree in so
far as they are not truly doctors, but, as Plato would say,
seek, like sophists and wage-earners, to circumvent and defeat one another. The conflict is physical and can extend to
the subject-matter only in so far as this is tainted by individual prejudice and not wholly lifted from the sensuous to
the intellectual plane. In the ether there are no winds of
doctrine. The intellect, being the organ and source of the
divine, is divine and single; if there were many sorts of
intellect, many principles of perspective, they would fix and
create incomparable and irrelevant worlds. Reason is one in
that it gravitates toward an object, called truth, which could
not have the function it has, of being a focus for mental
activities, if it were not one in reference to the operations
which converge upon it.

This unity in truth, as in reason, is of course functional
only, not physical or existential. The beats of thought and
the thinkers are innumerable; indefinite, too, the variations
to which their endowment and habits may be subjected. But
the condition of spiritual communion or ideal relevance in
these intelligences is their possession of a method and grammar essentially identical. Language, for example, is significant in proportion to the constancy in meaning which words
and locutions preserve in a speaker's mind at various times,
or in the minds of various persons. This constancy is never
absolute. Therefore language is never wholly significant,
never exhaustively intelligible. There is always mud in the
well, if we have drawn up enough water. Yet in peaceful
rivers, though they flow, there is an appreciable degree of
translucency. So, from moment to moment, and from man
to man, there is an appreciable element of unanimity, of constancy and congruity of intent. On this abstract and perfectly
identical function science rests together with every rational
formation.

And His Immortality.

The same function is the seat of human immortality. Reason lifts a larger or smaller element in each man to the plane of ideality according as reason more or less thoroughly leavens and permeates the lump. No man is wholly immortal, as no philosophy is wholly true and no language wholly intelligible; but only in so far as intelligible is a language a language rather than a noise, only in so far as true is a philosophy more than a vent for cerebral humours, and only in so far as a man is rational and immortal is he a man and not a sensorium.

It is hard to convince people that they have such a gift as intelligence. If they perceive its animal basis they cannot conceive its ideal affinities or understand what is meant by calling it divine; if they perceive its ideality and see the immortal essences that swim into its ken, they hotly deny that it is an animal faculty, and invent ultramundane places and bodiless persons in which it is to reside; as if those celestial substances could be, in respect to thought, any less material than matter or, in respect to vision and life, any less instrumental than bodily organs. It never occurs to them that if nature has added intelligence to animal life it is because they belong together. Intelligence is a natural emanation of vitality. If eternity could exist otherwise than as a vision in time, eternity would have no meaning for men in the world, while the world, men, and time would have no vocation or status in eternity. The travail of existence would be without excuse, without issue or consummation, while the conceptions of truth and of perfection would be without application to experience, pure dreams about things preternatural and unreal, vacantly conceived, and illogically supposed to have something to do with living issues. But truth and perfection, for the very reason that they are not problematic existences but inherent ideals, cannot be banished from discourse. Experience may lose any of its data; it cannot lose, while it endures, the terms with which it operates in becoming experience. Now, truth is relevant to every opinion which looks to truth for its standard, and perfection is envisaged in every cry for relief, in every effort at betterment. Opinions, volitions, and passionate refusals fill human life. So that when the existence of truth is denied, truth is given the only status which it ever required—it is conceived.

It Is the Locus of All Truths.

Nor can any better defense be found for the denial that nature and her life have a status in eternity. This statement may not be understood, but if grasped at all it will not be questioned. By having a status in eternity is not meant being parts of an eternal existence, petrified or congealed into something real but motionless. What is meant is only that whatever exists in time, when bathed in the light of reflection, acquires an indelible character and discloses irreversible relations; every fact, in being recognised, takes its place in the universe of discourse, in that ideal sphere of truth which is the common and unchanging standard for all assertions. Language, science, art, religion, and all ambitious dreams are compacted of ideas. Life is as much a mosaic of notions as the firmament is of stars; and these ideal and transpersonal objects, bridging time, fixing standards, establishing values, constituting the natural rewards of all living, are the very furniture of eternity, the goals and playthings of that reason which is an instinct in the heart as vital and spontaneous as any other. Or rather, perhaps, reason is a supervening instinct by which all other instincts are interpreted, just as the *sensus communis* or transcendental unity of psychology is a faculty by which all perceptions are brought face to face and compared. So that immortality is not a privilege reserved for a part only of experience, but rather a relation pervading every part in varying measure. We may, in leaving the subject, mark the degrees and phases of this idealisation.

Epicurean Immortality, Through the Truth of Existence.

Animal sensation is related to eternity only by the truth that it has taken place. The fact, fleeting as it is, is registered in ideal history, and no inventory of the world's riches, no true confession of its crimes, would ever be complete that ignored that incident. This indefeasible character in experience makes a first sort of ideal immortality, one on which those rational philosophers like to dwell who have not speculation enough to feel quite certain of any other. It was a consolation to the Epicurean to remember that, however brief and uncertain might be his tenure of delight, the past was safe and the present sure. "He lives happy," says Horace, "and master over himself, who can say daily, I have lived. Tomorrow let Jove cover the sky with black clouds or flood it with sunshine; he shall not thereby render vain what lies behind, he shall not delete and make never to have existed what once the hour has brought in its flight." Such self-concentration and hugging of the facts has no power to improve them; it gives to pleasure and pain an impartial eternity, and rather tends to intrench in sensuous and selfish satisfactions a mind that has lost faith in reason and that deliberately ignores the difference in scope and dignity which exists among various pursuits. Yet the reflection is staunch and in its way heroic; it meets a vague and feeble aspiration, that looks to the infinite, with a just rebuke; it points to real satisfactions, experienced successes, and asks us to be content with the fulfilment of our own wills. If you have seen the world, if you have played your game and won it, what more would you ask for? If you have tasted the sweets of existence, you should be satisfied; if the experience has been bitter, you should be glad that it comes to an end.

Of course, as we have seen, there is a primary demand in man which death and mutation contradict flatly, so that no summons to cease can ever be obeyed with complete willingness. Even the suicide trembles and the ascetic feels the stings of the flesh. It is the part of philosophy, however, to pass over those natural repugnances and overlay them with as much countervailing rationality as can find lodgment in a particular mind. The Epicurean, having abandoned politics and religion and being afraid of any far-reaching ambition, applied philosophy honestly enough to what remained. Simple and healthy pleasures are the reward of simple and healthy pursuits; to chafe against them because they are limited is to import a foreign and disruptive element into the case; a healthy hunger has its limit, and its satisfaction reaches a natural term. Philosophy, far from alienating us from those values, should teach us to see their perfection and to maintain them in our ideal. In other words, the happy filling of a single hour is so much gained for the universe at large, and to find joy and sufficiency in the flying moment is perhaps the only means open to us for increasing the glory of eternity.

Logical Immortality, Through Objects of Thought.

Moving events, while remaining enshrined in this fashion in their permanent setting, may contain other and less external relations to the immutable. They may represent it. If the pleasures of sense are not cancelled when they cease, but continue to satisfy reason in that they once satisfied natural desires, much more will the pleasures of reflection retain their worth, when we consider that what they aspired to and reached was no momentary physical equilibrium but a permanent truth. As Archimedes, measuring the hypothenuse, was lost to events, being engaged in an event of much greater transcendence, so art and science interrupt the sense for change by engrossing attention in its issues and its laws. Old age often turns pious to look away from ruins to some world where youth endures and where what ought to have been is not overtaken by decay before it has quite come to maturity. Lost in such abstract contemplations, the mind is weaned from mortal concerns. It forgets for a few moments a world in which it has so little more to do and so much, perhaps, still to suffer. As a sensation of pure light would not be distinguishable from light itself, so a contemplation of things not implicating time in their structure becomes, so far as its own deliverance goes, a timeless existence. Unconsciousness of temporal conditions and of the very flight of time makes the thinker sink for a moment into identity with timeless objects. And so immortality, in a second ideal sense, touches the mind.

Ethical Immortality, Through Types of Excellence.

The transitive phases of consciousness, however, have themselves a reference to eternal things. They yield a generous enthusiasm and love of good which is richer in consolation than either Epicurean self-concentration or mathematical ecstasy. Events are more interesting than the terms we abstract from them, and the forward movement of the will is something more intimately real than is the catalogue of our past experiences. Now the forward movement of the will is an avenue to the eternal. What would you have? What is the goal of your endeavour? It must be some success, the establishment of some order, the expression of some experience. These points once reached, we are not left merely with the satisfaction of abstract success or the consciousness of ideal immortality. Being natural goals, these ideals are related to natural functions. Their attainment does not exhaust but merely liberates, in this instance, the function concerned, and so marks the perpetual point of reference common to that function in all its fluctuations. Every attainment of perfection in an art—as for instance in government— makes a return to perfection easier for posterity, since there remains an enlightening example, together with faculties predisposed by discipline to recover their ancient virtue. The better a man evokes and realises the ideal the more he leads the life that all others, in proportion to their worth, will seek to live after him, and the more he helps them to live in that

find an arrow; instead of a disordered room, a well-planted orchard—things which would not only have betrayed the agent's habits, but would have served and expressed his intent. Such propitious forms given by man to matter are no less instrumental in the Life of Reason than are propitious forms assumed by man's own habit or fancy. Any operation which thus humanises and rationalises objects is called art.

Art Is Plastic Instinct Conscious of Its Aim.

All art has an instinctive source and a material embodiment. If the birds in building nests felt the utility of what they do, they would be practising an art; and for the instinct to be called rational it would even suffice that their traditional purpose and method should become conscious occasionally. Thus weaving is an art, although the weaver may not be at every moment conscious of its purpose, but may be carried along, like any other workman, by the routine of his art; and language is a rational product, not because it always has a use or meaning, but because it is sometimes felt to have one. Arts are no less automatic than instincts, and usually, as Aristotle observed, less thoroughly purposive; for instincts, being transmitted by inheritance and imbedded in congenital structure, have to be economically and deeply organised. If they go far wrong they constitute a burden impossible to throw off and impossible to bear. The man harassed by inordinate instincts perishes through want, vice, disease, or madness. Arts, on the contrary, being transmitted only by imitation and teaching, hover more lightly over life. If ill-adjusted they make less havoc and cause less drain. The more superficial they are and the more detached from practical habits, the more extravagant and meaningless they can dare to become so that the higher products of life are the most often gratuitous. No instinct or institution was ever so absurd as is a large part of human poetry and philosophy, while the margin of ineptitude is much broader in religious myth than in religious ethics.

It Is Automatic.

Arts are instincts bred and reared in the open, creative habits acquired in the light of reason. Consciousness accompanies their formation; a certain uneasiness or desire and a more or less definite conception of what is wanted often precedes their full organisation. That the need should be felt before the means for satisfying it have been found has led the unreflecting to imagine that in art the need produces the discovery and the idea the work. Causes at best are lightly assigned by mortals, and this particular superstition is no worse than any other. The data—the plan and its execution—as conjoined empirically in the few interesting cases which show successful achievement, are made into a law, in oblivion of the fact that in more numerous cases such conjunction fails wholly or in part, and that even in the successful cases other natural conditions are present, and must be present, to secure the result. In a matter where custom is so ingrained and supported by a constant apperceptive illusion, there is little hope of making thought suddenly exact, or exact language not paradoxical. We must observe, however, that only by virtue of a false perspective do ideas seem to govern action, or is a felt necessity the mother of invention. In truth invention is the child of abundance, and the genius or vital premonition and groping which achieve art simultaneously achieve the ideas which that art embodies; or, rather, ideas are themselves products of an inner movement which has an automatic extension outwards; and this extension manifests the ideas. Mere craving has no lights of its own to prophesy by, no prescience of what the world may contain that would satisfy, no power of imagining what would allay its unrest. Images and satisfactions have to come of themselves; then the blind craving, as it turns into an incipient pleasure, first recognises its object. The pure will's impotence is absolute, and it would writhe for ever and consume itself in darkness if perception gave it no light and experience no premonition.

So Are the Ideas It Expresses.

Now, a man cannot draw bodily from external perception the ideas he is supposed to create or invent; and as his will or uneasiness, before he creates the satisfying ideas, is by hypothesis without them, it follows that creation or invention is automatic. The ideas come of themselves, being new and unthought-of figments, similar, no doubt, to old perceptions and compacted of familiar materials, but reproduced in a novel fashion and dropping in their sudden form from the blue. However instantly they may be welcomed, they were not already known and never could have been summoned. In the stock example, for instance, of groping for a forgotten name, we know the context in which that name should lie; we feel the environment of our local void; but what finally pops into that place, reinstated there by the surrounding tensions, is itself unforeseen, for it was just this that was forgotten. Could we have invoked the name we should not have needed to do so, having it already at our disposal. It is in fact a palpable impossibility that any idea should call itself into being, or that any act or any preference should be its own ground. The responsibility assumed for these things is not a determination to conceive them before they are conceived (which is a contradiction in terms) but an embrace and appropriation of them once they have appeared. It is thus that ebullitions in parts of our nature become touchstones for the whole; and the incidents within us seem hardly our own work till they are accepted and incorporated into the main current of our being. All invention is tentative, all art experimental, and to be sought, like salvation, with fear and trembling. There is a painful pregnancy in genius, a long incubation and waiting for the spirit, a thousand rejections and futile birthpangs, before the wonderful child appears, a gift of the gods, utterly undeserved and inexplicably perfect. Even this unaccountable success comes only in rare and fortunate instances. What is ordinarily produced is so base a hybrid, so lame and ridiculous a changeling, that we reconcile ourselves with difficulty to our offspring and blush to be represented by our fated works.

We Are Said to Control Whatever Obeys Us.

The propensity to attribute happy events to our own agency, little as we understand what we mean by it, and to attribute only untoward results to external forces, has its ground in the primitive nexus of experience. What we call ourselves is a certain cycle of vegetative processes, bringing a round of familiar impulses and ideas; this stream has a general direction, a conscious vital inertia, in harmony with which it moves. Many of the developments within it are dialectical; that is, they go forward by inner necessity, like an egg hatching within its shell, warmed but undisturbed by an environment of which they are wholly oblivious; and this sort of growth, when there is adequate consciousness of it, is felt to be both absolutely obvious and absolutely free. The emotion that accompanies it is pleasurable, but is too active and proud to call itself a pleasure; it has rather the quality of assurance and right. This part of life, however, is only its courageous core; about it play all sorts of incidental processes, allying themselves to it in more or less congruous movement. Whatever peripheral events fall in with the central impulse are accordingly lost in its energy and felt to be not so much peripheral and accidental as inwardly grounded, being, like the stages of a prosperous dialectic, spontaneously demanded and instantly justified when they come.

The sphere of the self's power is accordingly, for primitive consciousness, simply the sphere of what happens well; it is the entire unoffending and obedient part of the world. A man who has good luck at dice prides himself upon it, and believes that to have it is his destiny and desert. If his luck were absolutely constant, he would say he had the *power* to throw high; and as the event would, by hypothesis, sustain his boast, there would be no practical error in that assumption. A will that never found anything to thwart it would think itself omnipotent; and as the psychological essence of omniscience is not to suspect there is anything which you do not know, so the psychological essence of omnipotence is not to suspect that anything can happen which you do not desire. Such claims would undoubtedly be made if experience lent them the least colour; but would even the most comfortable and innocent assurances of this sort cease to be precarious? Might not any moment of eternity bring the unimagined contradiction, and shake the dreaming god?

Utility Is a Result.

Utility, like significance, is an eventual harmony in the arts and by no means their ground. All useful things have been discovered as ancient China discovered roast pig; and the casual feat has furthermore to be supported by a situation favourable to maintaining the art. The most useful act will never be repeated unless its secret remains embodied in structure. Practise and endeavour will not help an artist to remain long at his best; and many a performance is applauded which cannot be imitated. To create the requisite structure two preformed structures are needed: one in the agent, to give him skill and perseverance, and another in the material, to give it the right plasticity. Human progress would long ago have reached its goal if every man who recognised a good could at once appropriate it, and possess wisdom for ever by virtue of one moment's insight. Insight, unfortunately, is in itself perfectly useless and inconsequential; it can neither have produced its own occasion nor now insure its own recurrence. Nevertheless, being proof positive that whatever basis it needs is actual, insight is also an indication that the extant structure, if circumstances maintain it, may continue to operate with the same moral results, maintaining the vision which it has once supported.

The Useful Naturally Stable.

When men find that by chance they have started a useful change in the world, they congratulate themselves upon it and call their persistence in that practice a free activity. And the activity is indeed rational, since it subserves an end. The happy organisation which enables us to continue in that rational course is the very organisation which enabled us to initiate it. If this new process was formed under external influences, the same influences, when they operate again, will reconstitute the process each time more easily; while if it was formed quite spontaneously, its own inertia will maintain it quietly in the brain and bring it to the surface whenever circumstances permit. This is what is called learning by experience. Such lessons are far from indelible and are not always at command. Yet what has once been done may be repeated; repetition reinforces itself and becomes habit; and a clear memory of the benefit once attained by fortunate action, representing as it does the trace left by that action in the system, and its harmony with the man's usual impulses (for the action is felt to be *beneficial*), constitutes a strong presumption that the act will be repeated automatically on occasion; *i.e.*, that it has really been learned. Consciousness, which willingly attends to results only, will judge either the memory or the benefit, or both confusedly, to be the ground of this readiness to act; and only if some hitch occurs in the machinery, so that rational behaviour fails to take place, will a surprised appeal be made to material accidents, or to a guilty forgetfulness or indocility in the soul.

Intelligence Is Docility.

The idiot cannot learn from experience at all, because a new process, in his liquid brain, does not modify structure; while the fool uses what he has learned only inaptly and in frivolous fragments, because his stretches of linked experience are short and their connections insecure. But when the cerebral plasm is fresh and well disposed and when the paths are clear, attention is consecutive and learning easy; a multitude of details can be gathered into a single cycle of memory or of potential regard. Under such circumstances action is the unimpeded expression of healthy instinct in an environment squarely faced. Conduct from the first then issues in progress, and, by reinforcing its own organisation at each rehearsal, makes progress continual. For there will subsist not only a readiness to act and a great precision in action, but if any significant circumstance has varied in the conditions or in the interests at stake, this change will make itself felt; it will check the process and prevent precipitate action. Deliberation or well-founded scruple has the same source as facility—a plastic and quick organisation. To be sensitive to difficulties and dangers goes with being sensitive to opportunities.

Art Is Reason Propagating Itself.

Of all reason's embodiments art is therefore the most splendid and complete. Merely to attain categories by which inner experience may be articulated, or to feign analogies by which a universe may be conceived, would be but a visionary triumph if it remained ineffectual and went with no actual remodelling of the outer world, to render man's dwelling more appropriate and his mind better fed and more largely transmissible. Mind grows self-perpetuating only by its expression in matter. What makes progress possible is that rational action may leave traces in nature, such that nature in consequence furnishes a better basis for the Life of Reason; in other words progress is art bettering the conditions of existence. Until art arises, all achievement is internal to the brain, dies with the individual, and even in him spends itself without recovery, like music heard in a dream. Art, in establishing instruments for human life beyond the human body, and moulding outer things into sympathy with inner values, establishes a ground whence values may continually spring up; the thatch that protects from to-day's rain will last and keep out to-morrow's rain also; the sign that once expresses an idea will serve to recall it in future.

Not only does the work of art thus perpetuate its own function and produce a better experience, but the process of art also perpetuates itself, because it is teachable. Every animal learns something by living; but if his offspring inherit only what he possessed at birth, they have to learn life's lessons over again from the beginning, with at best some vague help given by their parents' example. But when the fruits of experience exist in the common environment, when new instruments, unknown to nature, are offered to each individual for his better equipment, although he must still learn for himself how to live, he may learn in a humaner school, where artificial occasions are constantly open to him for expanding his powers. It is no longer merely hidden inner processes that he must reproduce to attain his predecessors' wisdom; he may acquire much of it more expeditiously by imitating their outward habit—an imitation which, furthermore, they have some means of exacting from him. Wherever there is art there is a possibility of training. A father who calls his idle sons from the jungle to help him hold the plough not only inures them to labour but compels them to observe the earth upturned and refreshed, and to watch the germination there; their wandering thought, their incipient rebellions, will be met by the hope of harvest; and it will not be impossible for them, when their father is dead, to follow the plough of their own initiative and for their own children's sake. So great is the sustained advance in rationality made possible by art which, being embodied in matter, is teachable and transmissible by training; for in art the values secured are recognised the more easily for having been first enjoyed when other people furnished the means to them; while the maintenance of these values is facilitated by an external tradition imposing itself contagiously or by force on each new generation.

Beauty an Incident in Rational Art.

Art is action which transcending the body makes the world a more congenial stimulus to the soul. All art is therefore useful and practical, and the notable æsthetic value which some works of art possess, for reasons flowing for the most part out of their moral significance, is itself one of the satisfactions which art offers to human nature as a whole. Between sensation and abstract discourse lies a region of deployed sensibility or synthetic representation, a region where more is seen at arm's length than in any one moment could be felt at close quarters, and yet where the remote parts of experience, which discourse reaches only through symbols, are recovered and recomposed in something like their native colours and experienced relations. This region, called imagination, has pleasures more airy and luminous than those of sense, more massive and rapturous than those of intelligence. The values inherent in imagination, in instant intuition, in sense endowed with form, are called æsthetic values; they are found mainly in nature and living beings, but often also in man's artificial works, in images evoked by language, and in the realm of sound.

Inseparable from the Others.

Productions in which an æsthetic value is or is supposed to be prominent take the name of fine art; but the work of fine art so defined is almost always an abstraction from the actual object, which has many non-æsthetic functions and values. To separate the æsthetic element, abstract and dependent as it often is, is an artifice which is more misleading than helpful; for neither in the history of art nor in a rational estimate of its value can the æsthetic function of things be divorced from the practical and moral. What had to be done was, by imaginative races, done imaginatively; what had to be spoken or made, was spoken or made fitly, lovingly, beautifully. Or, to take the matter up on its psychological side, the ceaseless experimentation and ferment of ideas, in breeding what it had a propensity to breed, came sometimes on figments that gave it delightful pause; these beauties were the first knowledges and these arrests the first hints of real and useful things. The rose's grace could more easily be plucked from its petals than the beauty of art from its subject, occasion, and use. An æsthetic fragrance, indeed, all things may have, if in soliciting man's senses or reason they can awaken his imagination as well; but this middle zone is so mixed and nebulous, and its limits are so vague, that it cannot well be treated in theory otherwise than as it exists in fact—as a phase of man's sympathy with the world he moves in. If art is that element in the Life of Reason which consists in modifying its environment the better to attain its end, art may be expected to subserve all parts of the human ideal, to increase man's comfort, knowledge, and delight. And as nature, in her measure, is wont to satisfy these interests together, so art, in seeking to increase that satisfaction, will work simultaneously in every ideal direction. Nor will any of these directions be on the whole good, or tempt a well-trained will, if it leads to estrangement from all other interests. The æsthetic good will be accordingly hatched in the same nest with the others, and incapable of flying far in a different air.

X

The Criterion of Taste

Dogmatism Is Inevitable but May Be Enlightened.

DOGMATISM in matters of taste has the same status as dogmatism in other spheres. It is initially justified by sincerity, being a systematic expression of a man's preferences; but it becomes absurd when its basis in a particular disposition is ignored and it pretends to have an absolute or metaphysical scope. Reason, with the order which in every region it imposes on life, is grounded on an animal nature and has no other function than to serve the same; and it fails to exercise its office quite as much when it oversteps its bounds and forgets whom it is serving as when it neglects some part of its legitimate province and serves its master imperfectly, without considering all his interests.

Dialectic, logic, and morals lose their authority and become inept if they trespass upon the realm of physics and try to disclose existences; while physics is a mere idea in the realm of poetic meditation. So the notorious diversities which human taste exhibits do not become conflicts, and raise no moral problem, until their basis or their function has been forgotten, and each has claimed a right to assert itself exclusively. This claim is altogether absurd, and we might fail to understand how so preposterous an attitude could be assumed by anybody did we not remember that every young animal thinks himself absolute, and that dogmatism in the thinker is only the speculative side of greed and courage in the brute. The brute cannot surrender his appetites nor abdicate his primary right to dominate his environment. What experience and reason may teach him is merely how to make his self-assertion well ·balanced and successful. In the same way taste is bound to maintain its preferences but free to rationalise them. After a man has compared his feelings with the no less legitimate feelings of other creatures, he can reassert his own with more complete authority, since now he is aware of their necessary ground in his nature, and of their affinities with whatever other interests his nature enables him to recognise in others and to co-ordinate with his own.

Taste Gains in Authority as It is More and More Widely Based.

A criterion of taste is, therefore, nothing but taste itself in its more deliberate and circumspect form. Reflection re-

fines particular sentiments by bringing them into sympathy
with all rational life. There is consequently the greatest possible difference in authority between taste and taste, and
while delight in drums and eagle's feathers is perfectly genuine and has no cause to blush for itself, it cannot be compared in scope or representative value with delight in a
symphony or an epic. The very instinct that is satisfied by
beauty prefers one beauty to another; and we have only to
question and purge our æsthetic feelings in order to obtain
our criterion of taste. This criterion will be natural, personal,
autonomous; a circumstance that will give it authority over
our own judgment—which is all moral science is concerned
about—and will extend its authority over other minds also,
in so far as their constitution is similar to ours. In that
measure what is a genuine instance of reason in us, others
will recognise for a genuine expression of reason in themselves also.

Different Æsthetic Endowments May Be Compared in Quantity or Force.

Æsthetic feeling, in different people, may make up a different fraction of life and vary greatly in volume. The
more nearly insensible a man is the more incompetent he
becomes to proclaim the values which sensibility might have.
To beauty men are habitually insensible, even while they
are awake and rationally active. Tomes of æsthetic criticism
hang on a few moments of real delight and intuition. It is in
rare and scattered instants that beauty smiles even on her
adorers, who are reduced for habitual comfort to remembering her past favours. An æsthetic glow may pervade experience, but that circumstance is seldom remarked; it figures
only as an influence working subterraneously on thoughts
and judgments which in themselves take a cognitive or practical direction. Only when the æsthetic ingredient becomes
predominant do we exclaim, How beautiful! Ordinarily the

pleasures which formal perception gives remain an undistinguished part of our comfort or curiosity.

Authority of Vital over Verbal Judgments.

Taste is formed in those moments when æsthetic emotion is massive and distinct; preferences then grown conscious, judgments then put into words, will reverberate through calmer hours; they will constitute prejudices, habits of apperception, secret standards for all other beauties. A period of life in which such intuitions have been frequent may amass tastes and ideals sufficient for the rest of our days. Youth in these matters governs maturity, and while men may develop their early impressions more systematically and find confirmations of them in various quarters, they will seldom look at the world afresh or use new categories in deciphering it. Half our standards come from our first masters, and the other half from our first loves. Never being so deeply stirred again, we remain persuaded that no objects save those we then discovered can have a true sublimity. These high-water marks of æsthetic life may easily be reached under tutelage. It may be some eloquent appreciations read in a book, or some preference expressed by a gifted friend, that may have revealed unsuspected beauties in art or nature; and then, since our own perception was vicarious and obviously inferior in volume to that which our mentor possessed, we shall take his judgments for our criterion, since they were the source and exemplar of all our own. Thus the volume and intensity of some appreciations, especially when nothing of the kind has preceded, makes them authoritative over our subsequent judgments. On those warm moments hang all our cold systematic opinions; and while the latter fill our days and shape our careers it is only the former that are crucial and alive.

A race which loves beauty holds the same place in history that a season of love or enthusiasm holds in an individual life. Such a race has a pre-eminent right to pronounce upon beauty and to bequeath its judgments to duller peoples. We may accordingly listen with reverence to a Greek judgment on that subject, expecting that what might seem to us wrong about it is the expression of knowledge and passion beyond our range; it will suffice that we learn to live in the world of beauty, instead of merely studying its relics, for us to understand, for instance, that imitation is a fundamental principle in art, and that any rational judgment on the beautiful must be a moral and political judgment, enveloping chance æsthetic feelings and determining their value. What most German philosophers, on the contrary, have written about art and beauty has a minimal importance: it treats artificial problems in a grammatical spirit, seldom giving any proof of experience or imagination. What painters say about painting and poets about poetry is better than lay opinion; it may reveal, of course, some petty jealousy or some partial incapacity, because a special gift often carries with it complementary defects in apprehension; yet what is positive in such judgments is founded on knowledge and avoids the romancing into which litterateurs and sentimentalists will gladly wander. The specific values of art are technical values, more permanent and definite than the adventitious analogies on which a stray observer usually bases his views. Only a technical education can raise judgments on musical compositions above impertinent autobiography. The Japanese know the beauty of flowers, and tailors and dressmakers have the best sense for the fashions. We ask them for suggestions, and if we do not always take their advice, it is not because the fine effects they love are not genuine, but because they may not be effects which we care to produce.

Tastes Differ Also in Purity or Consistency.

This touches a second consideration, besides the volume and vivacity of feeling, which enters into good taste. What is voluminous may be inwardly confused or outwardly confusing. Excitement, though on the whole and for the moment agreeable, may verge on pain and may be, when it subsides a little, a cause of bitterness. A thing's attractions may be partly at war with its ideal function. In such a case what, in our haste, we call a beauty becomes hateful on a second view, and according to the key of our dissatisfaction we pronounce that effect meretricious, harsh, or affected. These discords appear when elaborate things are attempted without enough art and refinement; they are essentially in bad taste. Rudimentary effects, on the contrary, are pure, and though we may think them trivial when we are expecting something richer, their defect is never intrinsic; they do not plunge us, as impure excitements do, into a corrupt artificial conflict. So wild-flowers, plain chant, or a scarlet uniform are beautiful enough; their simplicity is a positive merit, while their crudity is only relative. There is a touch of sophistication and disease in not being able to fall back on such things and enjoy them thoroughly, as if a man could no longer relish a glass of water. Your true epicure will study not to lose so genuine a pleasure. Better forego some artificial stimulus, though that, too, has its charm, than become insensible to natural joys. Indeed, ability to revert to elementary beauties is a test that judgment remains sound.

Vulgarity is quite another matter. An old woman in a blonde wig, a dirty hand covered with jewels, ostentation without dignity, rhetoric without cogency, all offend by an inner contradiction. To like such things we should have to surrender our better intuitions and suffer a kind of dishonour. Yet the elements offensively combined may be excellent in isolation, so that an untrained or torpid mind will be at a loss to understand the critic's displeasure. Oftentimes barbaric art almost succeeds, by dint of splendour, in banishing the sense of confusion and absurdity; for everything, even reason, must bow to force. Yet the impression remains chaotic, and we must be either partly inattentive or partly distressed. Nothing could show better than this alternative how mechanical barbaric art is. Driven by blind impulse or tradition, the artist has worked in the dark. He has dismissed his work without having quite understood it or really justified it to his own mind. It is rather his excretion than his product. Astonished, very likely, at his own fertility, he has thought himself divinely inspired, little knowing that clear reason is the highest and truest of inspirations. Other men, observing his obscure work, have then honoured him for profundity; and so mere bulk or stress or complexity have produced a mystical wonder by which generation after generation may be enthralled. Barbaric art is half necromantic; its ascendancy rests in a certain measure on bewilderment and fraud.

To purge away these impurities nothing is needed but quickened intelligence, a keener spiritual flame. Where perception is adequate, expression is so too, and if a man will only grow sensitive to the various solicitations which anything monstrous combines, he will thereby perceive its monstrosity. Let him but enact his sensations, let him pause to make explicit the confused hints that threaten to stupefy him; he will find that he can follow out each of them only by rejecting and forgetting the others. To free his imagination in any direction he must disengage it from the contrary intent, and so he must either purify his object or leave it a mass of confused promptings. Promptings essentially demand to be carried out, and when once an idea has become articulate it is not enriched but destroyed if it is still identified with its contrary. Any complete expression of a barbarous theme will, therefore, disengage its incompatible elements and turn it into a number of rational beauties.

They Differ, Finally, in Pertinence, and in Width of Appeal.

When good taste has in this way purified and digested some turgid medley, it still has a progress to make. Ideas, like men, live in society. Not only has each a will of its own and an inherent ideal, but each finds itself conditioned for its expression by a host of other beings, on whose co-operation it depends. Good taste, besides being inwardly clear, has to be outwardly fit. A monstrous ideal devours and dissolves itself, but even a rational one does not find an immortal embodiment simply for being inwardly possible and free from contradiction. It needs a material basis, a soil and situation propitious to its growth. This basis, as it varies, makes the ideal vary which is simply its expression; and therefore no ideal can be ultimately fixed in ignorance of the conditions that may modify it. It subsists, to be sure, as an eternal possibility, independently of all further earthly revolutions. Once expressed, it has revealed the inalienable values that attach to a certain form of being, whenever that form is actualised. But its expression may have been only momentary, and that eternal ideal may have no further relevance to the living world. A criterion of taste, however, looks to a social career; it hopes to educate and to judge. In order to be an applicable and a just law, it must represent the interests over which it would preside.

There are many undiscovered ideals. There are many beauties which nothing in this world can embody or suggest. There are also many once suggested or even embodied, which find later their basis gone and evaporate into their native heaven. The saddest tragedy in the world is the destruction of what has within it no inward ground of dissolution, death in youth, and the crushing out of perfection. Imagination has its bereavements of this kind. A complete mastery of existence achieved at one moment gives no warrant that it will be sustained or achieved again at the next. The achievement may have been perfect; nature will not on that account stop to admire it. She will move on, and the meaning which was read so triumphantly in her momentary attitude will not fit her new posture. Like Polonius' cloud, she will always suggest some new ideal, because she has none of her own.

In lieu of an ideal, however, nature has a constitution, and this, which is a necessary ground for ideals, is what it concerns the ideal to reckon with. A poet, spokesman of his full soul at a given juncture, cannot consider eventualities or think of anything but the message he is sent to deliver, whether the world can then hear it or not. God, he may feel sure, understands him, and in the eternal the beauty he sees and loves immortally justifies his enthusiasm. Nevertheless, critics must view his momentary ebullition from another side. They do not come to justify the poet in his own eyes; he amply relieves them of such a function. They come only to inquire how significant the poet's expressions are for humanity at large or for whatever public he addresses. They come to register the social or representative value of the poet's soul. His inspiration may have been an odd cerebral rumbling, a perfectly irrecoverable and wasted intuition; the exquisite quality it doubtless had to his own sense is now not to the purpose. A work of art is a public possession; it is addressed to the world. By taking on a material embodiment, a spirit solicits attention and claims some kinship with the prevalent gods. Has it, critics should ask, the affinities needed for such intercourse? Is it humane, is it rational, is it representative? To its inherent incommunicable charms it must add a kind of courtesy. If it wants other approval than its own, it cannot afford to regard no other aspiration.

This scope, this representative faculty or wide appeal, is necessary to good taste. All authority is representative; force and inner consistency are gifts on which I may well congratulate another, but they give him no right to speak for me. Either æsthetic experience would have remained a chaos —which it is not altogether—or it must have tended to conciliate certain general human demands and ultimately all those interests which its operation in any way affects. The more conspicuous and permanent a work of art is, the more is such an adjustment needed. A poet or philosopher may be erratic and assure us that he is inspired; if we cannot well gainsay it, we are at least not obliged to read his works. An architect or a sculptor, however, or a public performer of any sort, that thrusts before us a spectacle justified only in his inner consciousness, makes himself a nuisance. A social standard of taste must assert itself here, or else no efficacious and cumulative art can exist at all. Good taste in such matters cannot abstract from tradition, utility, and the temper of the world. It must make itself an interpreter of humanity and think esoteric dreams less beautiful than what the public eye might conceivably admire.

Art May Grow Classic by Idealising the Familiar.

There are various affinities by which art may acquire a representative or classic quality. It may do so by giving form to objects which everybody knows, by rendering experiences that are universal and primary. The human figure, elementary passions, common types and crises of fate—these are facts which pass too constantly through apperception not to have a normal æsthetic value. The artist who can catch that effect in its fulness and simplicity accordingly does immortal work. This sort of art immediately becomes popular; it passes into language and convention so that its æsthetic charm is apparently worn down. The old images after a while hardly stimulate unless they be presented in some paradoxical way; but in that case attention will be diverted to the accidental extravagance, and the chief classic effect will be missed. It is the honourable fate or euthanasia of artistic successes that they pass from the field of professional art altogether and become a portion of human faculty. Every man learns to be to that extent an artist; approved figures and maxims pass current like the words and idioms of a mother tongue, themselves once brilliant inventions. The lustre of such successes is not really dimmed, however, when it becomes a part of man's daily light; a retrogression from that habitual style or habitual insight would at once prove, by the shock it caused, how precious those ingrained apperceptions continued to be.

Or by Reporting the Ultimate.

Universality may also be achieved, in a more heroic fash-ion, by art that expresses ultimate truths, cosmic laws, great human ideals. Virgil and Dante are classic poets in this sense, and a similar quality belongs to Greek sculpture and architecture. They may not cause enthusiasm in everybody; but in the end experience and reflection renew their charm; and their greatness, like that of high mountains, grows more obvious with distance. Such eminence is the reward of hav-ing accepted discipline and made the mind a clear anagram of much experience. There is a great difference between the depth of expression so gained and richness or realism in details. A supreme work presupposes minute study, sym-pathy with varied passions, many experiments in expression; but these preliminary things are submerged in it and are not displayed side by side with it, like the foot-notes to a learned work, so that the ignorant may know they have existed.

Some persons, themselves inattentive, imagine, for in-stance, that Greek sculpture is abstract, that it has left out all the detail and character which they cannot find on the sur-face, as they might in a modern work. In truth it contains those features, as it were, in solution and in the resultant which, when reduced to harmony, they would produce. It embodies a finished humanity which only varied exercises could have attained, for as the body is the existent ground for all possible actions, in which as actions they exist only potentially, so a perfect body, such as a sculptor might con-ceive, which ought to be ready for all excellent activities, cannot present them all in act but only the readiness for them. The features that might express them severally must be absorbed and mastered, hidden like a sword in its scab-bard, and reduced to a general dignity or grace. Though such immersed eloquence be at first overlooked and seldom ex-plicitly acknowledged, homage is nevertheless rendered to it in the most unmistakable ways. When lazy artists, backed by no great technical or moral discipline, think they, too, can produce masterpieces by summary treatment, their failure shows how pregnant and supreme a thing simplicity is. Every man, in proportion to his experience and moral distinction, returns to the simple but inexhaustible work of finished minds, and finds more and more of his own soul responsive to it.

Human nature, for all its margin of variability, has a substantial core which is invariable, as the human body has a structure which it cannot lose without perishing altogether; for as creatures grow more complex a greater number of their organs become vital and indispensable. Advanced forms will rather die than surrender a title of their character; a fact which is the physical basis for loyalty and martyrdom. Any deep interpretation of oneself, or indeed of anything, has for that reason a largely representative truth. Other men, if they look closely, will make the same discovery for themselves. Hence distinction and profundity, in spite of their rarity, are wont to be largely recognised. The best men in all ages keep classic traditions alive. These men have on their side the weight of superior intelligence, and, though they are few, they might even claim the weight of numbers, since the few of all ages, added together, may be more than the many who in any one age follow a temporary fashion. Classic work is nevertheless always national, or at least characteristic of its period, as the classic poetry of each people is that in which its language appears most pure and free. To translate it is impossible; but it is easy to find that the human nature so inimitably expressed in each masterpiece is the same that, under different circumstance, dictates a different performance. The deviations between races and men are not yet so great as is the ignorance of self, the blindness to the native ideal, which prevails in most of them. Hence a great man of a remote epoch is more intelligible than a common man of our own time.

Good Taste Demands that Art Should Be Rational, i.e.,
Harmonious with all Other Interests.

Both elementary and ultimate judgments, then, contribute
to a standard of taste; yet human life lies between these
limits, and an art which is to be truly adjusted to life should
speak also for the intermediate experience. Good taste is
indeed nothing but a name for those appreciations which the
swelling incidents of life recall and reinforce. Good taste is
that taste which is a good possession, a friend to the whole
man. It must not alienate him from anything except to ally
him to something greater and more fertile in satisfactions.
It will not suffer him to dote on things, however seductive,
which rob him of some nobler companionship. To have a
foretaste of such a loss, and to reject instinctively whatever
will cause it, is the very essence of refinement. Good taste
comes, therefore, from experience, in the best sense of that
word; it comes from having united in one's memory and
character the fruit of many diverse undertakings. Mere taste
is apt to be bad taste, since it regards nothing but a chance
feeling. Every man who pursues an art may be presumed to
have some sensibility; the question is whether he has breeding, too, and whether what he stops at is not, in the end,
vulgar and offensive. Chance feeling needs to fortify itself
with reasons and to find its level in the great world. When it
has added fitness to its sincerity, beneficence to its passion, it
will have acquired a right to live. Violence and self-justifica-
tion will not pass muster in a moral society, for vipers possess
both, and must nevertheless be stamped out. Citizenship is
conferred only on creatures with human and co-operative
instincts. A civilised imagination has to understand and to
serve the world.

The great obstacle which art finds in attempting to be
rational is its functional isolation. Sense and each of the passions suffers from a similar independence. The disarray of

human instincts lets every spontaneous motion run too far; life oscillates between constraint and unreason. Morality too often puts up with being a constraint and even imagines such a disgrace to be its essence. Art, on the contrary, as often hugs unreason for fear of losing its inspiration, and forgets that it is itself a rational principle of creation and order. Morality is thus reduced to a necessary evil and art to a vain good, all for want of harmony among human impulses. If the passions arose in season, if perception fed only on those things which action should be adjusted to, turning them, while action proceeded, into the substance of ideas—then all conduct would be voluntary and enlightened, all speculation would be practical, all perceptions beautiful, and all operations arts. The Life of Reason would then be universal.

To approach this ideal, so far as art is concerned, would involve diffusing its processes and no longer confining them to a set of dead and unproductive objects called works of art.

A Mere "Work of Art" a Baseless Artifice.

Why art, the most vital and generative of activities, should produce a set of abstract images, monuments to lost intuitions, is a curious mystery. Nature gives her products life, and they are at least equal to their sources in dignity. Why should mind, the actualisation of nature's powers, produce something so inferior to itself, reverting in its expression to material being, so that its witnesses seem so many fossils with which it strews its path? What we call museums— mausoleums, rather, in which a dead art heaps up its remains —are those the places where the Muses intended to dwell? We do not keep in show-cases the coins current in the world. A living art does not produce curiosity to be collected but spiritual necessaries to be diffused.

Artificial art, made to be exhibited, is something gratuitous and sophisticated, and the greater part of men's concern about it is affectation. There is a genuine pleasure in planning a work, in modelling and painting it; there is a pleasure in showing it to a sympathetic friend, who associates himself in this way with the artist's technical experiment and with his interpretation of some human episode; and there might be a satisfaction in seeing the work set up in some appropriate space for which it was designed, where its decorative quality might enrich the scene, and the curious passer-by might stop to decipher it. The pleasures proper to an ingenuous artist are spontaneous and human; but his works, once delivered to his patrons, are household furniture for the state. Set up to-day, they are outworn and replaced to-morrow, like trees in the parks or officers in the government. A community where art was native and flourishing would have an uninterrupted supply of such ornaments, furnished by its citizens in the same modest and cheerful spirit in which they furnish other commodities. Every craft has its dignity, and the decorative and monumental crafts certainly have their own; but such art is neither singular nor pre-eminent, and a statesman or reformer who should raise somewhat the level of thought or practice in the state would do an infinitely greater service.

Human Uses Give to Works of Art Their Highest Expression and Charm.

The joys of creating are not confined, moreover, to those who create things without practical uses. The merely æsthetic, like rhyme and fireworks, is not the only subject that can engage a playful fancy or be planned with a premonition of beautiful effects. Architecture may be useful, sculpture commemorative, poetry reflective, even music, by its expression, religious or martial. In a word, practical exigencies, in calling forth the arts, give them moral functions which it is a pleasure to see them fulfil. Works may not be æsthetic in their purpose, and yet that fact may be a ground for their being doubly delightful in execution and doubly beautiful in effect. A richer plexus of emotions is concerned in producing or contemplating something humanly necessary than something idly conceived. What is very rightly called a *sense* for fitness is a vital experience, involving æsthetic satisfactions and æsthetic shocks. The more numerous the rational harmonies are which are present to the mind, the more sensible movements will be going on there to give immediate delight; for the perception or expectation of an ulterior good is a present good also. Accordingly nothing can so well call forth or sustain attention as what has a complex structure relating it to many complex interests. A work woven out of precious threads has a deep pertinence and glory; the artist who creates it does not need to surrender his practical and moral sense in order to indulge his imagination.

The truth is that mere sensation or mere emotion is an indignity to a mature human being. When we eat, we demand a pleasant vista, flowers, or conversation, and failing these we take refuge in a newspaper. The monks, knowing that men should not feed silently like stalled oxen, appointed some one to read aloud in the refectory; and the Fathers, obeying the same civilised instinct, had contrived in their theology intelligible points of attachment for religious emotion. A refined mind finds as little happiness in love without friendship as in sensuality without love; it may succumb to both, but it accepts neither. What is true of mere sensibility is no less true of mere fancy. The Arabian Nights— futile enough in any case—would be absolutely intolerable if they contained no Oriental manners, no human passions, and no convinced epicureanism behind their miracles and their tattle. Any absolute work of art which serves no further purpose than to stimulate an emotion has about it a certain luxurious and visionary taint. We leave it with a blank mind, and a pang bubbles up from the very fountain of pleasures. Art, so long as it needs to be a dream, will never cease to prove a disappointment. Its facile cruelty, its narcotic abstraction, can never sweeten the evils we return to at home; it can liberate half the mind only by leaving the other half in abeyance. In the mere artist, too, there is always something that falls short of the gentleman and that defeats the man.

The Sad Values of Appearance.

Surely it is not the artistic impulse in itself that involves such lack of equilibrium. To impress a meaning and a rational form on matter is one of the most masterful of actions. The trouble lies in the barren and superficial character of this imposed form: fine art is a play of appearance. Appearance, for a critical philosophy, is distinguished from reality by its separation from the context of things, by its immediacy and insignificance. A play of appearance is accordingly some little closed circle in experience, some dream in which we lose ourselves by ignoring most of our interests, and from which we awake into a world in which that lost episode plays no further part and leaves no heirs. Art as mankind has hitherto practised it falls largely under this head and too much resembles an opiate or a stimulant. Life and history are not thereby rendered better in their principle, but a mere ideal is extracted out of them and presented for our delectation in some cheap material, like words or marble. The only precious materials are flesh and blood, for these alone can defend and propagate the ideal which has once informed them.

Artistic creation shows at this point a great inferiority to natural reproduction, since its product is dead. Fine art shapes inert matter and peoples the mind with impotent ghosts. What influence it has—for every event has consequences—is not pertinent to its inspiration. The art of the past is powerless even to create similar art in the present, unless similar conditions recur independently. The moments snatched for art have been generally interludes in life and its products parasites in nature, the body of them being materially functionless and the soul merely represented. To exalt fine art into a truly ideal activity we should have to knit

it more closely with other rational functions, so that to beau-
tify things might render them more useful and to represent
them most imaginatively might be to see them in their truth.
Something of the sort has been actually attained by the
noblest arts in their noblest phases. A Sophocles or a Leo-
nardo dominates his dreamful vehicle and works upon the
real world by its means. These small centres, where inter-
functional harmony is attained, ought to expand and cover
the whole field. Art, like religion, needs to be absorbed in
the Life of Reason.

What might help to bring about this consummation would
be, on the one side, more knowledge; on the other, better
taste.

They Need to Be Made Prophetic of Practical Goods.

When a mind is filled with important and true ideas and
sees the actual relations of things, it cannot relish pictures
of the world which wantonly misrepresent it. Myth and
metaphor remain beautiful so long as they are the most
adequate or graphic means available for expressing the facts,
but so soon as they cease to be needful and sincere they become false finery. The same thing happens in the plastic arts.
Unless they spring from love of their subject, and employ
imagination only to penetrate into that subject and interpret
it with a more inward sympathy and truth, they become
conventional and overgrown with mere ornament. They then
seem ridiculous to any man who can truly conceive what they
represent. So in putting antique heroes on the stage we
nowadays no longer tolerate a modern costume, because the
externals of ancient life are too well known to us; but in the
seventeenth century people demanded in such personages
intelligence and nobleness, since these were virtues which
the ancients were clothed with in their thought. A knowledge
that should be at once full and appreciative would evidently
demand fidelity in both matters. Knowledge, where it exists,
undermines satisfaction in what does violence to truth, and

bines the greater inertia will it oppose to reform, and the more self-righteously will it condemn the innocent pariah that it leaves outside.

Art has had to suffer much Pharisaical opposition of this sort. Sometimes political systems, sometimes religious zeal, have excluded it from their programme, thereby making their programme unjust and inadequate. Yet of all premature settlements the most premature is that which the fine arts are wont to establish. A harmony in appearance only, one that touches the springs of nothing and has no power to propagate itself, is so partial and momentary a good that we may justly call it an illusion. To gloat on rhythms and declamations, to live lost in imaginary passions and histrionic woes, is an unmanly life, cut off from practical dominion and from rational happiness. A lovely dream is an excellent thing in itself, but it leaves the world no less a chaos and makes it by contrast seem even darker than it did. By dwelling in its mock heaven art may inflict on men the same kind of injury that any irresponsible passion or luxurious vice might inflict. For this reason it sometimes passes for a misfortune in a family if a son insists on being a poet or an actor. Such gifts suggest too much incompetence and such honours too much disrepute. A man does not avoid real evils by having visionary pleasures, but besides exposing himself to the real evils quite unprotected, he probably adds fancied evils to them in generous measure. He becomes supersensitive, envious, hysterical; the world, which was perhaps carried away at first by his ecstasies, at the next moment merely applauds his performance, then criticises it superciliously, and very likely ends by forgetting it altogether.

Thus the fine arts are seldom an original factor in human progress. If they express moral and political greatness, and serve to enhance it, they acquire a certain dignity; but so soon as this expressive function is abandoned they grow meretricious. The artist becomes an abstracted trifler, and the public is divided into two camps: the dilettanti, who dote on the artist's affections, and the rabble, who pay him to grow coarse. Both influences degrade him and he helps to foster both. An atmosphere of dependence and charlatanry gathers about the artistic attitude and spreads with its influence. Religion, philosophy, and manners may in turn be infected with this spirit, being reduced to a voluntary hallucination or petty flattery. Romanticism, ritualism, æstheticism, symbolism are names this disease has borne at different times as it appeared in different circles or touched a different object. Needless to say that the arts themselves are the first to suffer. That beauty which should have been an inevitable smile on the face of society, an overflow of genuine happiness and power, has to be imported, stimulated artificially, and applied from without; so that art becomes a sickly ornament for an ugly existence.

Yet Prototypes of True Perfection.

Nevertheless, æsthetic harmony, so incomplete in its basis as to be fleeting and deceptive, is most complete in its form. This so partial synthesis is a synthesis indeed, and just because settlements made in fancy are altogether premature, and ignore almost everything in the world, in type they can be the most perfect settlements. The artist, being a born lover of the good, a natural breeder of perfections, clings to his insight. If the world calls his accomplishments vain, he can, with better reason, call vain the world's cumbrous instrumentalities, by which nothing clearly good is attained. Appearances, he may justly urge, are alone actual. All forces, substances, realities, and principles are inferred and potential only and in the moral scale mere instruments to bring perfect appearances about. To have grasped such an appearance, to have embodied a form in matter, is to have justified for the first time whatever may underlie appearance and to have put reality to some use. It is to have begun to live. As the standard of perfection is internal and is measured by the satisfaction felt in realising it, every artist has tasted, in his activity, what activity essentially is. He has moulded existence into the likeness of thought and lost himself in that ideal achievement which, so to speak, beckons all things into being. Even if a thousand misfortunes await him and a final disappointment, he has been happy once. He may be inclined to rest his case there and challenge practical people to justify in the same way the faith that is in them.

Pros and Cons of Detached Indulgences.

That a moment of the most perfect happiness should prove a source of unhappiness is no paradox to any one who has observed the world. A hope, a passion, a crime, is a flash of vitality. It is inwardly congruous with the will that breeds it, yet the happiness it pictures is so partial that even while it is felt it may be overshadowed by sinister forebodings. A certain unrest and insecurity may consciously harass it. With time, or by a slight widening in the field of interest, this submerged unhappiness may rise to the surface. If, as is probable, it is caused or increased by the indulgence which preceded, then the only moment in which a good was tasted, the only vista that had opened congenially before the mind, will prove a new and permanent curse. In this way love often misleads individuals, ambition cities, and religion whole races of men. That art, also, should often be an indulgence, a blind that hides reality from ill-balanced minds and ultimately increases their confusion, is by no means incompatible with art's ideal essence. On the contrary, such a result is inevitable when ideality is carried at all far upon a narrow basis. The more genuine and excellent the vision the greater havoc it makes if, being inadequate, it establishes itself authoritatively in the soul. Art, in the better sense, is a condition of happiness for a practical and labouring creature, since without art he remains a slave; but it is one more source of unhappiness for him so long as it is not squared with his necessary labours and merely interrupts them. It then alienates him from his world without being able to carry him effectually into a better one.

The Happy Imagination Is One Initially in Line with Things.

The artist is in many ways like a child. He seems happy, because his life is spontaneous, yet he is not competent to secure his own good. To be truly happy he must be well bred, reared from the cradle, as it were, under propitious influences, so that he may have learned to love what conduces to his development. In that rare case his art will expand as his understanding ripens; he will not need to repent and begin again on a lower key. The ideal artist, like the ideal philosopher, has all time and all existence for his virtual theme. Fed by the world, he can help to mould it, and his insight is a kind of wisdom, preparing him as science might for using the world well and making it more fruitful. He can then be happy, not merely in the sense of having now and then an ecstatic moment, but happy in having light and resource enough within him to cope steadily with real things and to leave upon them the vestige of his mind.

And Brought Always Closer to Them by Experience.

One effect of growing experience is to render what is unreal uninteresting. Momentous alternatives in life are so numerous and the possibilities they open up so varied that imagination finds enough employment of a historic and practical sort in trying to seize them. A child plans Towers of Babel; a mature architect, in planning, would lose all interest if he were bidden to disregard gravity and economy. The conditions of existence, after they are known and accepted, become conditions for the only pertinent beauty. In each place, for each situation, the plastic mind finds an appropriate ideal. It need not go afield to import something exotic. It need make no sacrifices to whim and to personal memories. It rather breeds out of the given problem a new and singular solution, thereby exercising greater invention than would be requisite for framing an arbitrary ideal and imposing it at all costs on every occasion.

Reason Is the Principle of Both Art and Happiness.

In other words, a happy result can be secured in art, as in life, only by intelligence. Intelligence consists in having read the heart and deciphered the promptings latent there, and then in reading the world and deciphering its law and constitution, to see how and where the heart's ideal may be embodied. Our troubles come from the colossal blunders made by our ancestors (who had worse ancestors of their own) in both these interpretations, blunders which have come down to us in our blood and in our institutions. The vices thus transmitted cloud our intelligence. We fail in practical affairs when we ignore the conditions of action and we fail in works of imagination when we concoct what is fantastic and without roots in the world.

The value of art lies in making people happy, first in practising the art and then in possessing its product. This observation might seem needless, and ought to be so; but if we compare it with what is commonly said on these subjects, we must confess that it may often be denied and more often, perhaps, may not be understood. Happiness is something men ought to pursue, although they seldom do so; they are drawn away from it at first by foolish impulses and afterwards by perverse laws. To secure happiness conduct would have to remain spontaneous while it learned not to be criminal; but the fanatical attachment of men, now to a fierce liberty, now to a false regimen, keeps them barbarous and wretched. A rational pursuit of happiness—which is one thing with progress or with the Life of Reason—would embody that natural piety which leaves to the episodes of life their inherent values, mourning death, celebrating love, sanctifying civic traditions, enjoying and correcting nature's ways. To discriminate happiness is therefore the very soul of art, which expresses experience without distorting it, as those political or metaphysical tyrannies distort it which sanctify unhappiness. A free mind, like a creative imagination, rejoices at the harmonies it can find or make between man and nature; and, where it finds none, it solves the conflict so far as it may and then notes and endures it with a shudder.

A morality organised about the human heart in an ingenuous and sincere fashion would involve every fine art and would render the world pervasively beautiful—beautiful in its artificial products and beautiful in its underlying natural terrors. The closer we keep to elementary human needs and to the natural agencies that may satisfy them, the closer we are to beauty. Industry, sport, and science, with the perennial intercourse and passions of men, swarm with incentives to expression, because they are everywhere creating new moulds of being and compelling the eye to observe those forms and to recast them ideally. Art is simply an adequate industry; it arises when industry is carried out to the satisfaction of all human demands, even of those incidental sensuous demands which we call æsthetic and which a brutal industry, in its haste, may despise or ignore.

Arts responsive in this way to all human nature would be beautiful according to reason and might remain beautiful long. Poetic beauty touches the world whenever it attains some unfeigned harmony either with sense or with reason; and the more unfeignedly human happiness was made the test of all institutions and pursuits, the more beautiful they would be, having more numerous points of fusion with the mind, and fusing with it more profoundly. To distinguish and to create beauty would then be no art relegated to a few abstracted spirits, playing with casual fancies; it would be a habit inseparable from practical efficiency. All operations, all affairs, would then be viewed in the light of ultimate interests, and in their deep relation to human good. The arts would thus recover their Homeric glory; touching human

fate as they clearly would, they would borrow something of
its grandeur and pathos, and yet the interest that worked in
them would be warm, because it would remain unmistakably
animal and sincere.

Only a Rational Society Can Have Sure and Perfect Arts.

The principle that all institutions should subserve happiness runs deeper than any cult for art and lays the foundation on which the latter might rest safely. If social structure
were rational its free expression would be so too. Many
observers, with no particular philosophy to adduce, feel that
the arts among us are somehow impotent, and they look for
a better inspiration, now to ancient models, now to the raw
phenomena of life. A dilettante may, indeed, summon inspiration whence he will; and a virtuoso will never lack some
material to keep him busy; but if what is hoped for is a
genuine, native, inevitable art, a great revolution would first
have to be worked in society. We should have to abandon
our vested illusions, our irrational religions and patriotisms
and schools of art, and to discover instead our genuine needs,
the forms of our possible happiness. To call for such self-
examination seems revolutionary only because we start from
a sophisticated system, a system resting on traditional fashions and superstitions, by which the will of the living generation is misinterpreted and betrayed. To shake off that system
would not subvert order but rather institute order for the
first time; it would be an *Instauratio Magna*, a setting things
again on their feet.

We in Christendom are so accustomed to artificial ideals
and to artificial institutions, kept up to express them, that we
hardly conceive how anomalous our situation is, sorely as we
may suffer from it. We found academies and museums, as
we found missions, to fan a flame that constantly threatens
to die out for lack of natural fuel. Our overt ideals are
parasites in the body politic, while the ideals native to the
body politic, those involved in our natural structure and situ-

ation, are either stifled by that alien incubus, leaving civic life barbarous, or else force their way up, unremarked or not justly honoured as ideals. Industry and science and social amenities, with all the congruous comforts and appurtenances of contemporary life, march on their way, as if they had nothing to say to the spirit, which remains entangled in a cobweb of dead traditions. An idle pottering of the fancy over obsolete forms—theological, dramatic, or plastic—makes that by-play to the sober business of life which men call their art or their religion; and the more functionless and gratuitous this by-play is the more those who indulge in it think they are idealists. They feel they are champions of what is most precious in the world, as a sentimental lady might fancy herself a lover of flowers when she pressed them in a book instead of planting their seeds in the garden.

Why Art Is Now Empty and Unstable.

It is clear that gratuitous and functionless habits cannot bring happiness; they do not constitute an activity at once spontaneous and beneficent, such as noble art is an instance of. Those habits may indeed give pleasure; they may bring extreme excitement, as madness notably does, though it is in the highest degree functionless and gratuitous. Nor is such by-play without consequences, some of which might conceivably be fortunate. What is functionless is so called for being worthless from some ideal point of view, and not conducing to the particular life considered. But nothing real is dissociated from the universal flux; everything—madness and all unmeaning cross-currents in being—count in the general process and discharge somewhere, not without effect, the substance they have drawn for a moment into their little vortex. So our vain arts and unnecessary religions are not without real effects and not without a certain internal vitality. When life is profoundly disorganised it may well happen that only in detached episodes, only in moments snatched for dreaming in, can men see the blue or catch a glimpse of something like the ideal. In that case their esteem for their irrelevant visions may be well grounded, and their thin art and far-fetched religion may really constitute what is best in their experience. In a pathetic way these poor enthusiasms may be justified, but only because the very conception of a rational life lies entirely beyond the horizon.

Anomalous Character of the Irrational Artist.

It is no marvel, when art is a brief truancy from rational practice, that the artist himself should be a vagrant, and at best, as it were, an infant prodigy. The wings of genius serve him only for an escapade, enabling him to skirt the perilous edge of madness and of mystical abysses. But such an erratic workman does not deserve the name of artist or master; he has burst convention only to break it, not to create a new convention more in harmony with nature. His originality, though it may astonish for a moment, will in the end be despised and will find no thoroughfare. He will meantime be wretched himself, torn from the roots of his being by that cruel, unmeaning inspiration; or, if too rapt to see his own plight, he will be all the more pitied by practical men, who cannot think it a real blessing to be lost in joys that do not strengthen the character and yield nothing for posterity.

Art, in its nobler acceptance, is an achievement, not an indulgence. It prepares the world in some sense to receive the soul, and the soul to master the world; it disentangles those threads in each that can be woven into the other. That the artist should be eccentric, homeless, dreamful may almost seem a natural law, but it is none the less a scandal. An artist's business is not really to cut fantastical capers or be licensed to play the fool. His business is simply that of every keen soul to build well when it builds, and to speak well when it speaks, giving practice everywhere the greatest possible affinity to the situation, the most delicate adjustment to every faculty it affects. The wonder of an artist's performance grows with the range of his penetration, with the instinctive sympathy that makes him, in his mortal isolation, considerate of other men's fate and a great diviner of their secret, so that his work speaks to them kindly, with a deeper assurance than they could have spoken with to themselves. And the joy of his great sanity, the power of his adequate vision, is not the less intense because he can lend it to others and has borrowed it from a faithful study of the world.

True Art Measures and Completes Happiness.

If happiness is the ultimate sanction of art, art in turn is the best instrument of happiness. In art more directly than in other activities man's self-expression is cumulative and finds an immediate reward; for it alters the material conditions of sentience so that sentience becomes at once more delightful and more significant. In industry man is still servile, preparing the materials he is to use in action. In action itself, though he is free, he exerts his influence on a living and treacherous medium and sees the issue at each moment drift farther and farther from his intent. In science he is an observer, preparing himself for action in another way, by studying its results and conditions. But in art he is at once competent and free; he is creative. He is not troubled by his materials, because he has assimilated them and may take them for granted; nor is he concerned with the chance complexion of affairs in the actual world, because he is making the world over, not merely considering how it grew or how it will consent to grow in future. Nothing, accordingly, could be more delightful than genuine art, nor more free from remorse and the sting of vanity. Art springs so completely from the heart of man that it makes everything speak to him in his own language; it reaches, nevertheless, so truly to the heart of nature that it co-operates with her, becomes a parcel of her creative material energy, and builds by her instinctive hand. If the various formative impulses

no telling what its ultimate influence will be on human practice and feeling.

Its Miscarriage in Greece.

The first period in the life of science was brilliant but ineffectual. The Greeks' energy and liberty were too soon spent, and the very exuberance of their genius made its expression chaotic. Where every mind was so fresh and every tongue so clever no scientific tradition could arise, and no laborious applications could be made to test the value of rival notions and decide between them. Men of science were mere philosophers. Each began, not where his predecessor had ended, but at the very beginning. Another circumstance that impeded the growth of science was the forensic and rhetorical turn proper to Greek intelligence. This mental habit gave a tremendous advantage in philosophy to the moralist and poet over the naturalist or mathematician. Hence what survived in Greece after the heyday of theoretic achievement was chiefly philosophies of life, and these—at the death of liberty—grew daily more personal and ascetic. Authority in scientific matters clung chiefly to Plato and Aristotle, and this not for the sake of their incomparable moral philosophy—for in ethics that decadent age preferred the Stoics and Epicureans—but just for those rhetorical expedients which in the Socratic school took the place of natural science. Worse influences in this field could hardly be imagined, since Plato's physics ends in myth and apologue, while Aristotle's ends in nomenclature and teleology.

All that remained of Greek physics, therefore, was the conception of what physics should be—a great achievement due to the earlier thinkers—and certain hints and guesses in that field. The elements of geometry had also been formulated, while the Socratic school bequeathed to posterity a well-developed group of moral sciences, rational in principle, but destined to be soon overlaid with metaphysical and reli-

gious accretions, so that the dialectical nerve and reasonableness of them were obliterated, and there survived only
miscellaneous conclusions, fragments of wisdom built topsy-
turvy into the new mythical edifice. It is the sad task reserved
for historical criticism to detach those sculptured stones from
the rough mass in which they have been embedded and to
rearrange them in their pristine order, thus rediscovering the
inner Socratic principle of moral philosophy, which is nothing but self-knowledge—a circumspect, systematic utterance
of the speaker's mind, disclosing his implicit meaning and
his ultimate preferences.

Its Timid Reappearance in Modern Times.

At its second birth science took a very different form. It
left cosmic theories to pantheistic enthusiasts like Giordano
Bruno, while in sober laborious circles it confined itself to
specific discoveries—the earth's roundness and motion about
the sun, the laws of mechanics, the development and application of algebra, the invention of the calculus, and a hundred
other steps forward in various disciplines. It was a patient
siege laid to the truth, which was approached blindly and
without a general, as by an army of ants; it was not stormed
imaginatively as by the ancient Ionians, who had reached at
once the notion of nature's dynamic unity, but had neglected
to take possession in detail of the intervening tracts, whence
resources might be drawn in order to maintain the main
position.

Nevertheless, as discoveries accumulated, they fell insensibly into a system, and philosophers like Descartes and Newton arrived at a general physics. This physics, however, was
not yet meant to cover the whole existent world, or to be the
genetic account of all things in their system. Descartes excluded from his physics the whole mental and moral world,
which became, so far as his science went, an inexplicable
addendum. Similarly Newton's mechanical principles, broad

as they were, were conceived by him merely as a parenthesis in theology. Not until the nineteenth century were the observations that had been accumulated given their full value or in fact understood; for Spinoza's system, though naturalistic in spirit, was still dialectical in form, and had no influence on science and for a long time little even on speculation.

Indeed the conception of a natural order, like the Greek cosmos, which shall include all existences—gods no less than men, if gods actually exist—is one not yet current, although it is implied in every scientific explanation and is favoured by two powerful contemporary movements which, coming from different quarters, are leading men's minds back to the same ancient and obvious naturalism. One of these movements is the philosophy of evolution, to which Darwin gave such an irresistible impetus. The other is theology itself, where it has been emancipated from authority and has set to work to square men's conscience with history and experience. This theology has generally passed into speculative idealism, which under another name recognises the universal empire of law and conceives man's life as an incident in a prodigious natural process, by which his mind and his interests are produced and devoured. This "idealism" is in truth a system of immaterial physics, like that of Pythagoras or Heraclitus. While it works with fantastic and shifting categories, which no plain naturalist would care to use, it has nothing to apply those categories to except what the naturalist or historian may already have discovered and expressed in the categories of common prose. German idealism is a translation of physical evolution into mythical language, which presents the facts now in the guise of a dialectical progression, now in that of a romantic drama. In either case the facts are the same, and just those which positive knowledge has come upon. Thus many who are not brought to naturalism by science are brought to it, quite unwillingly and unawares, by their religious speculations.

Distinction Between Science and Myth.

The gulf that yawns between such idealistic cosmogonies and a true physics may serve to make clear the divergence in principle which everywhere divides natural science from arbitrary conceptions of things. This divergence is as far as possible from lying in the merit of the two sorts of theory. Their merit, and the genius and observation required to frame them, may well be equal, or an imaginative system may have the advantage in these respects. It may even be more serviceable for a while and have greater pragmatic value, so long as knowledge is at best fragmentary, and no consecutive or total view of things is attempted by either party. Thus in social life a psychology expressed in terms of abstract faculties and personified passions may well carry a man farther than a physiological psychology would. Or, again, we may say that there was more experience and love of nature enshrined in ancient mythology than in ancient physics; the observant poet might then have fared better in the world than the pert and ignorant materialist. Nor does the difference between science and myth lie in the fact that the one is essentially less speculative than the other. They are differently speculative, it is true, since myth terminates in unverified notions that might by chance represent actual existences; while science terminates in concepts or laws, themselves not possibly existent, but verified by recurring particular facts, belonging to the same experience as those from which the theory started.

Platonic Status of Hypothesis.

The laws formulated by science—the transitive figments describing the relation between fact and fact—possess only a Platonic sort of reality. They are more real, if you will, than the facts themselves, because they are more permanent, trustworthy, and pervasive; but at the same time they are,

if you will, not real at all, because they are incompatible
with immediacy and alien to brute existence. In declaring
what is true of existences they altogether renounce existence
on their own behalf. This situation has made no end of
trouble in ill-balanced minds, not docile to the diversities
and free complexity of things, but bent on treating everything
by a single method. They have asked themselves persistently the confusing question whether the matter or the form
of things is the reality; whereas, of course, both elements
are needed, each with its incommensurable kind of being.
The material element alone is existent, while the ideal element is the sum of all those propositions which are true of
what exists materially. Anybody's *knowledge* of the truth,
being a complex and fleeting feeling, is of course but a moment of existence or material being, which whether found in
God or man is as far as possible from being that truth itself
which it may succeed in knowing.

Meaning of Verification.

The true contrast between science and myth is more nearly
touched when we say that science alone is capable of verification. Some ambiguity, however, lurks in this phrase, since
verification comes to a method only vicariously, when the
particulars it prophesies are realised in sense. To verify a
theory as if it were not a method but a divination of occult
existences would be to turn the theory into a myth and then
to discover that what the myth pictured had, by a miracle,
an actual existence also. There is accordingly a sense in
which myth admits substantiation of a kind that science
excludes. The Olympic hierarchy might conceivably exist
bodily; but gravitation and natural selection, being schemes
of relation, can never exist substantially and in their own
behoof. Nevertheless, the Olympic hierarchy, even if it happened to exist, could not be proved to do so unless it were a
part of the natural world open to sense: while gravitation and
natural selection, without being existences, can be verified

at every moment by concrete events occurring as those principles require. A hypothesis, being a discursive device, gains its utmost possible validity when its discursive value is established. It *is* not, it merely *applies*; and every situation in which it is found to apply is a proof of its truth.

The case would not be different with fables, were their basis and meaning remembered. But fables, when hypostatised, forget that they, too, were transitive symbols and boast to reveal an undiscoverable reality. A dogmatic myth is in this sorry plight: that the more evidence it can find to support it the more it abrogates its metaphysical pretensions, while the more it insists on its absolute truth the less relevance it has to experience and the less meaning. To try to support fabulous dogmas by evidence is tantamount to acknowledging that they are merely scientific hypotheses, instruments of discourse, and methods of expression. But in that case their truth would no longer be supposed to lie in the fact that somewhere beyond the range of human observation they descended bodily to the plane of flying existence, and were actually enacted there. They would have ceased to resemble the society of Olympus, which to prove itself real would need to verify itself, since only the gods and those mortals admitted to their conclave could know for a fact that that celestial gathering existed. On the contrary, a speculation that could be supported by evidence would be one that might be made good without itself descending to the plane of immediacy, but would be sufficiently verified when diffuse facts fall out as it had led us to expect. The myth in such a case would have become transparent again and relevant to experience, which could continually serve to support or to correct it. Even if somewhat overloaded and poetical, it would be in essence a scientific theory. It would no longer terminate in itself; it would point forward, leading the thinker that used it to eventual facts of experience, facts which his poetic wisdom would have prepared him to meet and to use.

Possible Validity of Myths.

If I say, for instance, that Punishment, limping in one leg, patiently follows every criminal, the myth is obvious and innocent enough. It reveals nothing, but, what is far better, it means something. I have expressed a truth of experience and pointed vaguely to the course which events may be expected to take under given circumstances. The expression, though mythical in form, is scientific in effect, because it tends to surround a given phenomenon (the crime) with objects on its own plane—other passions and sensations to follow upon it. What would be truly mythical would be to stop at the figure of speech and maintain, by way of revealed dogma, that a lame goddess of vindictive mind actually follows every wicked man, her sword poised in mid-air. Sinking into that reverie, and trembling at its painted truth, I should be passing to the undiscoverable and forgetting the hard blows actually awaiting me in the world. Fable, detaining the mind too long in the mesh of expression, would have become metaphysical dogma. I should have connected the given fact with imagined facts, which even if by chance real—for such a goddess may, for all we know, actually float in the fourth dimension—are quite supernumerary in my world, and never, by any possibility, can become parts or extensions of the experience they are thought to explain. The gods are demonstrable only as hypotheses, but as hypotheses they are not gods.

Any Dreamed-of Thing Might Be Experienced.

The same distinction is sometimes expressed by saying that science deals only with objects of possible experience. But this expression is unfortunate, because everything thinkable, no matter how mythical and supernatural or how far beyond the range of mortal senses, is an object of *possible* experience. Tritons and sea-horses might observe one another and might feel themselves live. The thoughts and decrees said to occupy the divine mind from all eternity would certainly be phenomena there; they would be experienced things. Were fables really as metaphysical and visionary as they pretend to be, were they not all the while and in essence mere symbols for natural situations, they would be nothing but reports about other alleged parts of experience. A real Triton, a real Creator, a real heaven would obviously be objects open to properly equipped senses and seats of much vivid experience. But a Triton after all has something to do with the Ægean and other earthly waters; a Creator has something to do with the origin of man and of his habitat; heaven has something to do with the motives and rewards of moral action. This relevance to given experience and its objects is what cuts those myths off from their blameless and gratuitous rôle of reporting experiences that might be going on merrily enough somewhere else in the universe. In calling them myths and denying that what they describe falls within the purview of science, we do not assert that, absolutely taken, they could not be objects of a possible experience. What we mean is rather that no matter how long we searched the sea waves, in which it is the essence of our Tritons to disport themselves, we should never find Tritons there; and that if we traced back the history of man and nature we should find them always passing by natural generation out of slightly different earlier forms and never appearing suddenly, at the fiat of a vehement Jehovah swimming about in a chaos; and finally that if we considered critically our motives and our ideals, we should find them springing from and directed upon a natural life and its functions, and not at all on disembodied and timeless ecstasy. Those myths, then, while they intrinsically refer to facts in the given world, describe those facts in incongruous terms. They are symbols, not extensions, for the experience we know.

But Science Follows the Movement of Its Subject-Matter.

A chief characteristic of science, then, is that in supplementing given facts it supplements them by adding other facts belonging to the same sphere, and eventually discoverable by tracing the given object in its own plane though its continuous transformations. Science expands speculatively, by the aid of merely instrumental hypotheses, objects given in perception until they compose a congruous, self-supporting world, all parts of which might be observed consecutively. What a scientific hypothesis interpolates among the given facts—the atomic structure of things, for instance—might come in time under the direct fire of attention, fixed more scrupulously, longer, or with better instruments upon those facts themselves. Otherwise the hypothesis that assumed that structure would be simply false, just as a hypothesis that the interior of the earth is full of molten fire would be false if on inspection nothing were found there but solid rock. Science does not merely prolong a habit of inference; it verifies and solves the inference by reaching the fact inferred.

The contrast with myth at this point is very interesting; for in myth the facts are themselves made vehicles, and knowledge is felt to terminate in an independent existence on a higher or deeper level than any immediate fact; and this circumstance is what makes myth impossible to verify and, except by laughter, to disprove. If I attributed the stars' shining to the diligence of angels who lighted their lamps at sunset, lest the upper reaches of the world should grow dangerous for travellers, and if I made my romance elaborate and ingenious enough, I might possibly find that the stars' appearance and disappearance could continue to be interpreted in that way. My myth might always suggest itself afresh and might be perennially appropriate. But it would never descend, with its charming figures, into the company of its evidences. It would never prove that what it terminated in was a fact, as in my metaphysical faith I had deputed and asserted it to be. The angels would remain notional, while my intent was to have them exist; so that the more earnestly I held to my fable the more grievously should I be deceived. For even if seraphic choirs existed in plenty on their own emotional or musical plane of being, it would not have been their hands—if they had hands—that would have lighted the stars I saw; and this, after all, was the gist and starting-point of my whole fable and its sole witness in my world. A myth might by chance be a revelation, did what it talks of have an actual existence somewhere else in the universe; but it would need to be a revelation in order to be true at all, and would then be true only in an undeserved and spurious fashion. Any representative and provable validity which it might possess would assimilate it to science and reduce it to a mere vehicle and instrument for human discourse. It would evaporate as soon as the prophecies it made were fulfilled, and it would claim no being and no worship on its own account. Science might accordingly be called a myth conscious of its essential ideality, reduced to its fighting weight and valued only for its significance.

Moral Value of Science.

A symptom of the divergence between myth and science may be found in the contrary emotions which they involve. Since in myth we interpret experience in order to interpret it, in order to delight ourselves by turning it poetically into the language and prosody of our own life, the emotion we feel when we succeed is artistic; myth has a dramatic charm. Since in science, on the contrary, we employ notional machinery, in itself perhaps indifferent enough, in order to arrive at eventual facts and to conceive the aspect which given things would actually wear from a different point of view in space or time, the emotion we feel when we succeed is that of security and intellectual dominion; science has a rational value. To see better what we now see, to see by anticipation what we should see actually under other conditions, is wonderfully to satisfy curiosity and to enlighten conduct. At the same time, scientific thinking involves no less inward excitement than dramatic fiction does. It summons before us an even larger number of objects in their fatal direction upon our interests. Were science adequate it would indeed absorb those passions which now, since they must be satisfied somehow, have to be satisfied by dramatic myths. To imagine how things might have been would be neither interesting nor possible if we knew fully how things are. All pertinent dramatic emotion, joyous or tragic, would then inhere in practical knowledge. As it is, however, science abstracts from the more musical overtones of things in order to trace the gross and basal processes within them; so that the pursuit of science seems comparatively dry and laborious, except where at moments the vista opens through to the ultimate or leads back to the immediate. Then, perhaps, we recognise that in science we are surveying all it concerns us to know, and in so doing are becoming all that it profits us to be. Mere amusement in thought as in sportive action is tedious and illiberal: it marks a temperament so imperfectly educated that it prefers idle to significant play and a flimsy to a solid idea.

Its Continuity with Common Knowledge.

The fact that science follows the subject-matter in its own movement involves a further consequence: science differs from common knowledge in scope only, not in nature. When intelligence arises, when the flux of things begins to be mitigated by representation of it and objects are at last fixed and recognisable, there is science. For even here, in the presence of a datum something virtual and potential is called up, namely, what the given thing was a moment ago, what it is growing into, or what it is contracted with in character. As

I walk round a tree, I learn that the parts still visible, those that have just disappeared and those now coming into view are continuous and belong to the same tree.

This declaration, though dialectic might find many a mare's nest in its language, is a safe and obvious enough expression of knowledge. It involves terms, however, which are in the act of becoming potential. What is just past, what is just coming, though sensibly continuous with what is present, are partially infected with nonentity. After a while human apprehension can reach them only by inference, and to count upon them is frankly to rely on theory. The other side of the tree, which common sense affirms to exist unconditionally, will have to be represented in memory or fancy; and it may never actually be observed by any mortal. Yet, if I continued my round, I should actually observe it and know it by experience; and I should find that it had the same status as the parts now seen, and was continuous with them. My assertion that it exists, while certainly theoretical and perhaps false, is accordingly scientific in type. Science, when it has no more scope than this, is indistinguishable from common sense. The two become distinct only when the facts inferred cannot be easily verified or have not yet been merged with the notion representing the given object in most men's minds.

Where science remains consciously theoretical (being as yet contrasted with ordinary apperception and current thought), it is, ideally considered, a *pis aller*, an expedient to which a mind must have recourse when it lacks power and scope to hold all experience in hand and to view the wide world in its genuine immediacy. As obliviscence is a gradual death, proper to a being not ideally master of the universal flux, but swamped within it, so science is an artificial life, in which what cannot be perceived directly (because personal limitations forbid) may be regarded abstractly, yet efficaciously, in what we think and do. With better faculties the field of possible experience could be better dominated, and fewer of its parts, being hidden from sight, would need to be mapped out symbolically on that sort of projection which we call scientific inference. The real relations between the parts of nature would then be given in intuition, from which hypothesis, after all, has borrowed its schemata.

Its Intellectual Essence.

Science is a halfway house between private sensation and universal vision. We should not forget to add, however, that the universal vision in question, if it were to be something better than private sensation or passive feeling in greater bulk, would have to be intellectual, just as science is; that is, it would have to be practical and to survey the flux from a given standpoint, in a perspective determined by special and local interests. Otherwise the whole world, when known, would merely be re-enacted in its blind immediacy without being understood or subjected to any purpose. The critics of science, when endowed with any speculative power, have always seen that what is hypothetical and abstract in scientific method is somehow servile and provisional; science being a sort of telegraphic wire through which a meagre report reaches us of things we would fain observe and live through in their full reality. This report may suffice for approximately fit action; it does not suffice for ideal knowledge of the truth nor for adequate sympathy with the reality. What commonly escapes speculative critics of science, however, is that in transcending hypothesis and reaching immediacy again we should run a great risk of abandoning knowledge and sympathy altogether; for if we *became* what we now represent so imperfectly, we should evidently no longer represent it at all. We should not, at the end of our labours, have at all enriched our own minds by adequate knowledge of what surrounds us, nor made our wills just in view of alien but well-considered interests. We should have lost our own essence and substituted for it, not something higher than indiscriminate being but only indiscriminate being in its flat, blind, and selfish infinity. The ideality, the representative faculty, would have gone out in our souls, and our perfected humanity would have brought us back to protoplasm.

In transcending science, therefore, we must not hope to transcend knowledge, nor in transcending selfishness to abolish finitude. Finitude is the indispensable condition of unselfishness as well as of selfishness, and of speculative vision no less than of hypothetical knowledge. The defect of science is that it is inadequate or abstract, that the account it gives of things is not full and sensuous enough; but its merit is that, like sense, it makes external being present to a creature that is concerned in adjusting itself to its environment, and informs that creature about things other than itself. Science, if brought to perfection, would not lose its representative or ideal essence. It would still survey and inform, but it would survey everything at once and inform the being it enlightened about all that could affect its interests. It would thus remain practical in effect and speculative in character. In losing its accidental limitations it would not lose its initial bias, its vital function. It would continue to be a rational activity, guiding and perfecting a natural being.

Perfect knowledge of things would be as far as possible from identifying the knower with them, seeing that for the most part—even when we call them human—they have no knowledge of themselves. Science, accordingly, even when imperfect, is a tremendous advance on absorption in sense and a dull immediacy. It begins to enrich the mind and gives it some inkling, at least, of that ideal dominion which each centre of experience might have if it had learned to regard all others, and the relation connecting it with them, both in thought and in action. Ideal knowledge would be an inward state corresponding to a perfect adjustment of the body to all forces affecting it. If the adjustment was perfect the inward state would regard every detail in the objects envisaged, but it would see those details in a perspective of its own, adding to sympathetic reproduction of them a consciousness of their relation to its own existence and perfection.

Unity of Science.

The fact that science expresses the character and relation of objects in their own terms has a further important consequence, which serves again to distinguish science from metaphorical thinking. If a man tries to illustrate the nature of a thing by assimilating it to something else which he happens to have in mind at the same time, it is obvious that a second man, whose mind is differently furnished, may assimilate the same object to a quite different idea: so myths are centrifugal, and the more elaborate and delicate they are the more they diverge, like well-developed languages. The rude beginnings of myth in every age and country bear a certain resemblance, because the facts interpreted are similar and the minds reading them have not yet developed their special grammar of representation. But two highly developed mythical systems—two theologies, for instance, like the Greek and the Indian—will grow every day farther and farther apart. Science, on the contrary, whatever it may start with, runs back into the same circle of facts, because it follows the lead of the subject-matter, and is attentive to its inherent transformations.

If men's fund of initial perceptions, then, is alike, their science is sure to be so; while the embroideries they make upon perception out of their own resources will differ as much as do the men themselves. Men asleep, said Heraclitus, live each in his own world, but awake they live in the same world together. To be awake is nothing but to be dreaming under control of the object; it is to be pursuing science to the comparative exclusion of mere mental vegetation and spontaneous myth. Thus if our objects are the same, our science and our waking lives will coincide; or if there is a natural diversity in our discoveries, because we occupy different points in space and time and have a varying range of experience, these diversities will nevertheless supplement one another; the discovery that each has made will be a possible discovery for the others also. So a geographer in China and one in Babylonia may at first make wholly unlike maps; but in time both will take note of the Himalayas, and the side each approaches will slope up to the very crest approached by the other. So science is self-confirming, and its most disparate branches are mutually illuminating; while in the realm of myth, until it is surveyed scientifically, there can be nothing but mutual repulsion and incapacity to understand. Languages and religions are necessarily rivals, but sciences are necessarily allies.

In Existence, Judged by Reflection, There Is a Margin of Waste.

The unity of science can reach no farther than does coherent experience; and though coherence be a condition of experience in the more pregnant sense of the word—in the sense in which the child or the fool has no experience— existence is absolutely free to bloom as it likes, and no logic can set limits or prescribe times for its irresponsible presence. A great deal may accordingly exist which cannot be known by science, or be reached from the outside at all. This fact perhaps explains why science has as yet taken so little root in human life: for even within the limits of human existence, which are tolerably narrow, there is probably no little incoherence, no little lapsing into what, from any other point of view, is inconceivable and undiscoverable. Science, for instance, can hardly reach the catastrophes and delights, often so vivid, which occur in dreams; for even if a physiological psychology should some day be able to find the causes of these phenomena, and so to predict them, it would never enter the dream-world persuasively, in a way that the dreamer could appreciate and understand, while he continued to dream. This is because that dream-world and the waking world present two disjointed landscapes, and the figures they contain belong to quite different genealogies—like the families of Zeus and of Abraham. Science is a great disciplinarian, and misses much of the sport which the absolute is free to indulge in. If there is no inner congruity and communion between two fields, science cannot survey them both; at best in tracing the structure of things presented in one of them, it may come upon some detail which may offer a basis or lodgment for the entire fabric of the other, which will thus be explained *ab extra*; as the children of Abraham might give an explanation for Zeus and his progeny, treating them as a phenomenon in the benighted minds of some of Japhet's children.

This brings the Olympian world within the purview of science, but does so with a very bad grace. For suppose the Olympian gods really existed—and there is nothing impossible in that supposition—they would not be allowed to have any science of their own; or if they did, it would threaten the children of Abraham with the same imputed unreality with which the latter boast to have extinguished Olympus. In order, then, that two regions of existence should be amenable to a science common to both and establishing a mutual rational representation between them, it is requisite that the two regions should be congruous in texture and continuous inwardly: the objects present in each must be transformations of the objects present in the other. As this condition is not always fulfilled, even within a man's personal fortunes, it is impossible that all he goes through should be mastered by science or should accrue to him ideally and become part of his funded experience. Much must be lost, left to itself, and resigned to the unprofitable flux that produced it.

Sciences Converge from Different Points of Origin.

A consequence of this incoherence in experience is that science is not absolutely single but springs up in various places at once, as a certain consistency or method becomes visible in this or that direction. These independent sciences might, conceivably, never meet at all; each might work out an entirely different aspect of things and cross the other, as it were, at a different level. This actually happens, for instance, in mathematics as compared with history or psychology, and in morals as compared with physics. Nevertheless, the fact that these various sciences are all human, and that here, for instance, we are able to mention them in one breath and to compare their natures, is proof that their spheres touch somehow, even if only peripherally. Since common knowledge, which knows of them all, is itself an incipient science, we may be sure that some continuity and some congruity obtains between their provinces. Some aspect of each must coincide with some aspect of some other, else nobody who pursued any one science would so much as suspect the existence of the rest. Great as may be the aversion of learned men to one another, and comprehensive as may be their ignorance, they are not positively compelled to live in solitary confinement, and the key of their prison cells is at least in their own pocket.

Two Chief Kinds of Science, Physics and Dialectic.

Some sciences, like chemistry and biology, or biology and anthropology, are parted only, we may presume, by accidental gaps in human knowledge; a more minute and better directed study of these fields would doubtless disclose their continuity with the fields adjoining. But there is one general division in science which cuts almost to the roots of human experience. Human understanding has used from the beginning a double method of surveying and arresting ideally the irreparable flux of being. One expedient has been to notice and identify similarities of character, recurrent types, in the phenomena that pass before it or in its own operations; the other expedient has been to note and combine in one complex object characters which occur and reappear together. The latter feat is made easy by the fact that when various senses are stimulated at once the inward instinctive reaction—which is felt by a primitive mind more powerfully than any external image—is one and not consciously divisible.

The first expedient imposes on the flux what we call ideas, which are concretions in discourse, terms employed in thought and language. The second expedient separates the same flux into what we call things, which are concretions in existence, complexes of qualities subsisting in space and time, having definable dynamic relations there and a trace-able history. Carrying out this primitive diversity in reflec-tion science has moved in two different directions. By refining concretions in discourse it has attained to mathematics, logic, and the dialectical developments of ethics; by tracing con-cretions in existence it has reached the various natural and historical sciences. Following ancient usage, I shall take the liberty of calling the whole group of sciences which elaborates ideas *dialectic*, and the whole group that describes existences *physics*.

The contrast between ideal science or dialectic and natural science or physics is as great as the understanding of a single experience could well afford; yet the two kinds of science are far from independent. They touch at their basis and they co-operate in their results. Were dialectic made clearer or physics deeper than it commonly is, these points of contact would doubtless be multiplied; but even as they stand they furnish a sufficient illustration of the principle that all science develops objects in their own category and gives the mind dominion over the flux of matter by discovering its form.

Their Mutual Implication.

That physics and dialectic touch at their basis may be shown by a double analysis. In the first place, it is clear that the science of existence, like all science, is itself discourse, and that before concretions in existence can be discovered, and groups of co-existent qualities can be recognised, these qualities themselves must be arrested by the mind, noted, and identified in their recurrences. But these terms, bandied about in scientific discourse, are so many essences and pure ideas: so that the inmost texture of natural science is logical, and the whole force of any observation made upon the outer world lies in the constancy and mutual relations of the terms it is made in. If down did not mean down and motion motion, Newton could never have taken note of the fall of his apple. Now the constancy and relation of meanings is something *meant*, it is something created by insight and intent and is altogether dialectical; so that the science of existence is a portion of the art of discourse.

On the other hand discourse, in its operation, is a part of existence. That truth or logical cogency is not itself an existence can be proved dialectically,* and is obvious to any

*For instance, in Plato's *Parmenides*, where it is shown that the ideas are not in the mind. We may gather from what is there said that the ideas cannot be identified with any embodiment of them, however perfect, since an idea means a nature common to all its possible embodiments and remains always outside of them. This is what Plato meant by saying that the ideas lay apart from phenomena and were what they were in and for themselves. They were mere forms and not, as a materialised Platonism afterward fancied, images in the mind of some psychological deity. The gods doubtless know the ideas, as Plato tells us in the same place: these are the common object of their thought and of ours; hence they are not anybody's thinking process, which of course would be in flux and phenomenal. Only by being ideal (*i.e.*, by being a goal of intellectual energy and no part of sensuous existence) can a term be common to various minds and serve to make their deliverances pertinent to one another.

That truth is no existence might also be proved as follows: Suppose that nothing existed or (if critics carp at that phrase) that a universe did not exist. It would then be true that all existences were wanting, yet this truth itself would endure; therefore truth is not an existence. An attempt might be made to reverse this argument by saying that since it would still "be" true that nothing existed, the supposition is self-contradictory, for the truth would "be" or exist in any case. Truth would thus be turned into an opinion, supposed to subsist eternally in the ether. The argument, however, is a bad sophism, because it falsifies the intent of the terms used. Somebody's opinion is not what is meant by the truth, since every opinion, however long-lived, may be false. Furthermore, the notion that it might have been true that nothing existed is a perfectly clear notion. The nature of dia-

one who sees for a moment what truth means, especially if he remembers at the same time that all existence is mutable, which it is the essence of truth not to be. But the knowledge or discovery of truth is an event in time, an incident in the flux of existence, and therefore a matter for natural science to study.

Furthermore, every term which dialectic uses is originally given embodied; in other words, it is given as an element in the actual flux, it comes by illustration. Though meaning is the object of an ideal function, and signification is inwardly appreciable only in terms of signification, yet the ideal leap is made from a material datum: that in which signification is seen is a fact. Or to state the matter somewhat differently, truth is not self-generating; if it were it would be a falsehood. Its eternity, and the infinitude of propositions it contains, remain potential and unapproachable until their incidence is found in existence. Form cannot of itself decide which of all possible forms shall be real; in their ideality, and without reference to their illustration in things, all consistent propositions would be equally valid and equally trivial. Important truth is truth about something, not truth about truth; and although a single datum might suffice to give foothold and pertinence to an infinity of truths, as one atom would posit all geometry, geometry, if there were no space, would be, if I may say so, all of the fourth dimension, and arithmetic, if there were no pulses or chasms in being, would be all algebra. Truth depends upon facts for its perspective, since facts select truths and decide which truths shall be mere possibilities and which shall be the eternal forms of actual things. The dialectical world would be a trackless desert if the existent world had no arbitrary constitution. Living dialectic comes to clarify existence; it turns

lectic is entirely corrupted when sincerity is lost. No intent can be self-contradictory, since it fixes its own object, but a man may easily contradict himself by wavering between one intent and another.

into meanings the actual forms of things by reflecting upon them, and by making them intended subjects of discourse.

Their Co-operation.

Dialectic and physics, thus united at their basis, meet again in their results. In mechanical science, which is the best part of physics, mathematics, which is the best part of dialectic, plays a predominant rôle; it furnishes the whole method of understanding wherever there is any real understanding at all. In psychology and history, too, although dialectic is soon choked by the cross-currents of nature, it furnishes the little perspicuousness which there is. We understand actions and mental developments when the purposes or ideas contained in any stage are carried out logically in the sequel; it is when conduct and growth are rational, that is, when they are dialectical, that we think we have found the true secret and significance of them. It is the evident ideal of physics, in every department, to attain such an insight into causes that the effects actually given may be thence *deduced*; and deduction is another name for dialectic. To be sure, the dialectic applicable to material processes and to human life is one in which the terms and the categories needed are still exceedingly numerous and vague: a little logic is all that can be read into the cataract of events. But the hope of science, a hope which is supported by every success it scores, is that a simpler law than has yet been discovered will be found to connect units subtler than those yet known: and that in these finer terms the universal mechanism may be exhaustively rendered. Mechanism is the ideal of physics, because it is the infusion of a maximum of mathematical necessity into the flux of real things. It is the aspiration of natural science to be as dialectical as possible, and thus, in their ideal, both branches of science are brought together.

That the ideal of dialectic is to apply to existence and

thereby to coincide with physics is in a sense no less true, although dialecticians may be little inclined to confess it. The direct purpose of deduction is to elucidate an idea, to develop an import, and nothing can be more irrelevant in this science than whether the conclusion is verified in nature or not. But the direct purpose of dialectic is not its ultimate justification. Dialectic is a human pursuit and has, at bottom, a moral function; otherwise, at bottom, it would have no value. And the moral function and ultimate justification of dialectic is to further the Life of Reason, in which human thought has the maximum practical validity, and may enjoy in consequence the richest ideal development. If dialectic takes a turn which makes it inapplicable in physics, which makes it worthless for mastering experience, it loses all its dignity: for abstract cogency has no dignity if the subject-matter into which it is introduced is trivial. In fact, were dialectic a game in which the counters were not actual data and the conclusions were not possible principles for understanding existence, it would not be a science at all. It would resemble a counterfeit paper currency, without intrinsic value and without commercial convenience. Just as a fact without implications is not a part of science, so a method without application would not be.

The free excursions of dialectic into non-natural regions may be wisely encouraged when they satisfy an interest which is at bottom healthy and may, at least indirectly, bring with it excellent fruits. As musicians are an honour to society, so are dialecticians that have a single heart and an exquisite patience. But somehow the benefit must redound to society and to practical knowledge, or these abstracted hermits will seem at first useless and at last mad. The logic of nonsense has a subtle charm only because it can so easily be turned into the logic of common sense. Empty dialectic is, as it were, the ballet of science: it runs most nearly after nothing at all.

No Science a Priori.

Both physics and dialectic are contained in common knowledge, and when carried further than men carry them in daily life, these sciences remain essentially inevitable and essentially fallible. If science deserves respect, it is not for being oracular but for being useful and delightful, as seeing is. Understanding is nothing but seeing under and seeing far. There is indeed a great mystery in knowledge, but this mystery is present in the simplest memory or presumption. The sciences have nothing to supply more fundamental than vulgar thinking or, as it were, preliminary to it. They are simply elaborations of it; they accept its presuppositions and carry on its ordinary processes. A pretence on the philosopher's part that he could get behind or below human thinking, that he could underpin, so to speak, his own childhood and the inherent conventions of daily thought, would be pure imposture. A philosopher can of course investigate the history of knowledge, he can analyse its method and point out its assumptions; but he cannot know by other authority than that which the vulgar know by, nor can his knowledge begin with other unheard-of objects or deploy itself in advance over an esoteric field. Every deeper investigation presupposes ordinary perception and uses some at least of its data. Every possible discovery *extends* human knowledge. None can base human knowledge anew on a deeper foundation or prefix an ante-experimental episode to experience. We may construct a theory as disintegrating as we please about the dialectical or empirical conditions of the experience given; we may disclose its logical stratification or physical antecedents; but every idea and principle used in such a theory must be borrowed from current knowledge as it happens to lie in the philosopher's mind.

Rôle of Criticism.

If these speculative adventures do not turn out well, the scientific man is free to turn about and become the critic and satirist of his foiled ambitions. He may exhaust scepticism and withdraw into the citadel of immediate feeling, yielding bastion after bastion to the assaults of doubt. When he is at last perfectly safe from error and reduced to speechless sensibility, he will perceive, however, that he is also washed clean of every practical belief: he would declare himself universally ignorant but for a doubt whether there be really anything to know. This metaphysical exercise is simply one of those "fallings from us, vanishings, blank misgivings of a creature moving about in worlds not realised" which may visit any child. So long as the suspension of judgment lasts, knowledge is surely not increased; but when we remember that the enemy to whom we have surrendered is but a ghost of our own evoking, we easily reoccupy the lost ground and fall back into an ordinary posture of belief and expectation. This recovered faith has no new evidences to rest on. We simply stand where we stood before we began to philosophise, only with a better knowledge of the lines we are holding and perhaps with less inclination to give them up again for no better reason than the undoubted fact that, in a speculative sense, it is always possible to renounce them.

Science, then, is the attentive consideration of common experience; it is common knowledge extended and refined. Its validity is of the same order as that of ordinary perception, memory, and understanding. Its test is found, like theirs, in actual intuition, which sometimes consists in perception and sometimes in intent. The flight of science is merely longer from perception to perception, and its deduction more accurate of meaning from meaning and purpose from purpose. It generates in the mind, for each vulgar observation, a whole brood of suggestions, hypotheses, and inferences. The sciences bestow, as is right and fitting, infinite pains upon that experience which in their absence would drift by unchallenged or misunderstood. They take note, infer, and prophesy. They compare prophecy with event; and altogether they supply—so intent are they on reality—every imaginable background and extension for the present dream.

III

Mechanism

Recurrent Forms in Nature.

A RETROSPECT over human experience, if a little extended, can hardly fail to come upon many interesting recurrences. The seasons make their round and the generations of men, like the forest leaves, repeat their career. In this its finer texture history undoubtedly repeats itself. A study of it, in registering so many recurrences, leads to a description of habit, or to natural history. To observe a recurrence is to divine a mechanism. It is to analyse a phenomenon, distinguishing its form, which alone recurs, from its existence, which is irrevocable; and that the flux of phenomena should turn out, on closer inspection, to be composed of a multitude of recurring forms, regularly interwoven, is the ideal of mechanism. The forms, taken ideally and in themselves, are what reflection first rescues from the flux and makes a science of; they constitute that world of eternal relations with which dialectic is conversant. To note here and there some passing illustration of these forms is one way of studying experience. The observer, the poet, the historian merely *define* what they see. But these incidental illustrations of form (called by Plato phenomena) may have a method in their comings and goings, and this method may in turn be definable. It will be a new sort of constant illustrated in the flux; and this we call a law. If events could be reduced to a number of constant forms moving in a constant medium according to a constant law, a maximum of constancy would be introduced into the flux, which would thereby be proved to be mechanical.

The form of events, abstracted from their material presence, becomes a general mould to which we tend to assimilate new observations. Whatever in particular instances may contravene the accredited rule, we attribute without a qualm to unknown variations in the circumstances, thus saving our faith in order at all hazards and appealing to investigation to justify the same. Only when another rule suggests itself which leaves a smaller margin unaccounted for in the phenomena do we give up our first generalisation. Not even the rudest superstition can be criticised or dislodged scientifically save by another general rule, more exact and trustworthy than the superstition. The scepticism which comes from distrust of abstraction and disgust with reckoning of any sort is not a scientific force; it is an intellectual weakness.

Generalities are indeed essential to understanding, which is apt to impose them hastily upon particulars. Confirmation is not needed to create prejudice. It suffices that a vivid impression should once have cut its way into the mind and settled there in a fertile soil; it will entwine itself at once with its chance neighbours and these adventitious relations will pass henceforth for a part of the fact. Repetition, however, is a good means of making or keeping impressions vivid and almost the only means of keeping them unchanged. Prejudices, however refractory to new evidence, evolve inwardly of themselves. The mental soil in which they lie is in a continual ferment and their very vitality will extend their scope and change their application. Generalisations, therefore, when based on a single instance, will soon forget it and shift their ground, as unchecked words shift their meaning. But when a phenomenon actually recurs the generalisations founded on it are reinforced and kept identical, and prejudices so sustained by events make man's knowledge of nature.

Their Discovery Makes the Flux Calculable.

Natural science consists of general ideas which look for verification in events, and which find it. The particular instance, once noted, is thrown aside like a squeezed orange, its significance in establishing some law having once been extracted. Science, by this flight into the general, lends immediate experience an interest and scope which its parts, taken blindly, could never possess; since if we remained sunk in the moments of existence and never abstracted their character from their presence, we should never know that they had any relation to one another. We should feel their incubus without being able to distinguish their dignities or to give them names. By analysing what we find and abstracting what recurs from its many vain incidents we can discover a sustained structure within, which enables us to foretell what we may find in future. Science thus articulates experience and reveals its skeleton.

Skeletons are not things particularly congenial to poets, unless it be for the sake of having something truly horrible to shudder at and to frighten children with: and so a certain school of philosophers exhaust their rhetoric in convincing us that the objects known to science are artificial and dead, while the living reality is infinitely rich and absolutely unutterable. This is merely an ungracious way of describing the office of thought and bearing witness to its necessity. A body is none the worse for having some bones in it, even if they are not all visible on the surface. They are certainly not the whole man, who nevertheless runs and leaps by their leverage and smooth turning in their sockets; and a surgeon's studies in dead anatomy help him excellently to set a living joint. The abstractions of science are extractions of truths. Truths cannot of themselves constitute existence with its

irrational concentration in time, place, and person, its hopeless flux, and its vital exuberance; but they can be true of
existence; they can disclose that structure by which its parts
cohere materially and become ideally inferable from one
another.

Looser Principles Tried First.

Science becomes demonstrable in proportion as it becomes
abstract. It becomes in the same measure applicable and useful, as mathematics witnesses, whenever the abstraction is
judiciously made and has seized the profounder structural
features in the phenomenon. These features are often hard
for human eyes to discern, buried as they may be in the
internal infinitesimal texture of things. Things accordingly
seem to move on the world's stage in an unaccountable fashion, and to betray magic affinities to what is separated from
them by apparent chasms. The types of relation which the
mind may observe are multifarious. Any chance conjunction,
any incidental harmony, will start a hypothesis about the
nature of the universe and be the parent image of a whole
system of philosophy. In self-indulgent minds most of these
standard images are dramatic, and the cue men follow in
unravelling experience is that offered by some success or
failure of their own. The sanguine, having once found a
pearl in a dunghill, feel a glorious assurance that the world's
true secret is that everything in the end is ordered for everybody's benefit—and that is optimism. The atrabilious, being
ill at ease with themselves, see the workings everywhere of
insidious sin, and conceive that the world is a dangerous
place of trial. A somewhat more observant intellect may
decide that what exists is a certain number of definite natures, each striving to preserve and express itself; and in
such language we still commonly read political events and
our friends' actions. At the dawn of science a Thales, observing the ways and the conditions of things somewhat
more subtly, will notice that rain, something quite adven-

titious to the fields, is what covers them with verdure, that the slime breeds life, that a liquid will freeze to stone and melt to air; and his shrewd conclusion will be that everything is water in one disguise or another. It is only after long accumulated observation that we can reach any exact law of nature; and this law we hardly think of applying to living things. These have not yet revealed the secret of their structure, and clear insight is vouchsafed us only in such regions as that of mathematical physics, where cogency in the ideal system is combined with adequacy to explain the phenomena.

Mechanism for the Most Part Hidden.

These exact sciences cover in the gross the field in which human life appears, the antecedents of this life, and its instruments. To a speculative mind, that had retained an ingenuous sense of nature's inexhaustible resources and of man's essential continuity with other natural things, there could be no ground for doubting that similar principles (could they be traced in detail) would be seen to preside over all man's action and passion. A thousand indications, drawn from introspection and from history, would be found to confirm this speculative presumption. It is not only earthquakes and floods, summer and winter, that bring human musings sharply to book. Love and ambition are unmistakable blossomings of material forces, and the more intense and poetical a man's sense is of his spiritual condition the more loudly will he proclaim his utter dependence on nature and the identity of the moving principle in him and in her.

Mankind and all its works are undeniably subject to gravity and to the law of projectiles; yet what is true of these phenomena in bulk seems to a superficial observation not to be true of them in detail, and a person may imagine that he subverts all the laws of physics whenever he wags his tongue. Only in inorganic matter is the ruling mechanism open to human inspection: here changes may be seen to be proportionate to the elements and situation in which they occur. Habit here seems perfectly steady and is called necessity, since the observer is able to deduce it unequivocally from given properties in the body and in the external bodies acting upon it. In the parts of nature which we call living and to which we impute consciousness, habit, though it be fatal enough, is not so exactly measurable and perspicuous. Physics cannot account for that minute motion and pullulation in the earth's crust of which human affairs are a portion. Human affairs have to be surveyed under categories lying closer to those employed in memory and legend. These looser categories are of every sort—grammatical, moral, magical—and there is no knowing when any of them will apply or in what measure. Between the matters covered by the exact sciences and vulgar experience there remains, accordingly, a wide and nebulous gulf. Where we cannot see the mechanism involved in what happens we have to be satisfied with an empirical description of appearances as they first fall together in our apprehension; and this want of understanding in the observer is what popular philosophy calls intelligence in the world.

Yet Presumably Pervasive.

That this gulf is apparent only, being due to inadequacy and confusion in human perception rather than to incoherence in things, is a speculative conviction altogether trustworthy. Any one who can at all catch the drift of experience —moral no less than physical—must feel that mechanism rules the whole world. There are doubleness and diversity enough in things to satiate the greatest lover of chaos; but that a cosmos nevertheless underlies the superficial play of sense and opinion is what all practical reason must assume and what all comprehended experience bears witness to. A cosmos does not mean a disorder with which somebody happens to be well pleased; it means a necessity from which every one must draw his happiness. If a principle is efficacious it is to that extent mechanical. For to be efficacious a principle must apply necessarily and proportionately; it must assure us that where the factors are the same as on a previous occasion the quotient will be the same also.

Now, in order that the flux of things should contain a repetition, elements must be identified within it; these identical elements may then find themselves in an identical situation, on which the same result may ensue which ensued before. If the elements were not constant and recognisable, or if their relations did not suffice to determine the succeeding event, no observation could be transferred with safety from the past to the future. Thus art and comprehension would be defeated together. Novelties in the world are not lacking, because the elements entering at any moment into a given combination have never before entered into a combination exactly similar. Mechanism applies to the matter and minute texture of things; but its applying there will create, at each moment, fresh ideal wholes, formal unities which mind emanates from and represents. The result will accordingly always be unprecedented in the total impression it produces, in exact proportion to the singularity of the situation in hand. Mechanical processes are not like mathematical relations, because they *happen*. What they express the form of is a flux, not a truth or an ideal necessity. The situation may therefore always be new, though produced from the preceding situation by rules which are invariable, since the preceding situation was itself novel.

Mechanism might be called the dialectic of the irrational. It is such a measure of intelligibility as is compatible with flux and with existence. Existence itself being irrational and change unintelligible, the only necessity they are susceptible of is a natural or empirical necessity, impinging at both ends upon brute matters of fact. The existential elements, their situation, number, affinities, and mutual influence all have to be begged before calculation can begin. When these surds have been accepted at their face value, inference may set to work among them; yet the inference that mechanism will continue to reign will not amount to certain knowledge until the event inferred has come to give it proof. Calculation in physics differs from pure dialectic in that the ultimate object it looks to is not ideal. Theory here must revert to the immediate flux for its sanction, whereas dialectic is a centrifugal emanation from existence and never returns to its point of origin. It remains suspended in the ether of those eternal relations which forms have, even when found embedded in matter.

Inadequacy of Consciousness.

If the total flux is continuous and naturally intelligible, why is the part felt by man so disjointed and opaque? An answer to this question may perhaps be drawn from the fact that consciousness apparently arises to express the functions only of extremely complicated organisms. The basis of thought is vastly more elaborate than its deliverance. It takes a wonderful brain and exquisite senses to produce a few stupid ideas. The mind starts, therefore, with a tremendous handicap. In order to attain adequate practical knowledge it would have to represent clearly its own conditions; for the purpose of mind is its own furtherance and perfection, and before that purpose could be fulfilled the mind's interests would have to become parallel to the body's fortunes. This means that the body's actual relations in nature would have to become the mind's favourite themes in discourse. Had this harmony been attained, the more accurately and intensely thought was exercised the more stable its status would become and the more prosperous its undertakings, since lively thought would then be a symptom of health in the body and of mechanical equilibrium with the environment.

The body's actual relations, however, on which health depends, are infinitely complex and immensely extended. They sweep the whole material universe and are intertwined most closely with all social and passionate forces, with their incalculable mechanical springs. Meantime the mind begins by being a feeble and inconsequent ghost. Its existence is intermittent and its visions unmeaning. It fails to conceive its own interests or the situations that might support or defeat those interests. If it pictures anything clearly, it is only some fantastic image which in no way represents its own complex basis. Thus the parasitical human mind, finding what clear knowledge it has laughably insufficient to interpret its destiny, takes to neglecting knowledge altogether and to hugging instead various irrational ideas. On the one hand it lapses into dreams which, while obviously irrelevant to practice, express the mind's vegetative instincts; hence art and mythology, which substitute play-worlds for the real one on correlation with which human prosperity and dignity depend. On the other hand, the mind becomes wedded to conventional objects which mark, perhaps, the turning-points of practical life and plot the curve of it in a schematic and disjointed fashion, but which are themselves entirely opaque and, as we say, material. Now as matter is commonly a name for things not understood, men materially minded are those whose ideas, while practical, are meagre and blind, so that their knowledge of nature, if not invalid, is exceedingly fragmentary. This grossness in common sense, like irrelevance in imagination, springs from the fact that the mind's representative powers are out of focus with its controlling conditions.

Its Articulation Inferior to That of Its Objects.

In other words, sense ought to correspond in articulation with the object to be represented—otherwise the object's structure, with the fate it imports, cannot be transferred into analogous ideas. Now the human senses are not at all fitted to represent an organism on the scale of the human body. They catch its idle gestures but not the inner processes which control its action. The senses are immeasurably too gross. What to them is a *minimum visible*, a just perceptible atom, is in the body's structure, very likely, a system of worlds, the inner cataclysms of which count in producing that so-called atom's behaviour and endowing it with affinities apparently miraculous. What must the seed of animals contain, for instance, to be the ground, as it notoriously is, for every physical and moral property of the offspring? Or what must the system of signals and the reproductive habit in a brain be, for it to co-ordinate instinctive movements, learn tricks, and remember? Our senses can represent at all adequately only such objects as the solar system or a work of human architecture, where the unit's inner structure and fermentation may be provisionally neglected in mastering the total. The architect may reckon in bricks and the astronomer in planets and yet foresee accurately enough the practical result. In a word, only what is extraordinarily simple is intelligible to man, while only what is extraordinarily complex can support intelligence. Consciousness is essentially incompetent to understand what most concerns it, its own vicissitudes, and sense is altogether out of scale with the objects of practical interest in life.

Science Consequently Retarded.

One consequence of this profound maladjustment is that science is hard to attain and is at first paradoxical. The change of scale required is violent and frustrates all the mind's rhetorical habits. There is a constant feeling of strain and much flying back to the mother-tongue of myth and social symbol. Every wrong hypothesis is seized upon and is tried before any one will entertain the right one. Enthusiasm for knowledge is chilled by repeated failures and a great confusion cannot but reign in philosophy. A man with an eye for characteristic features in various provinces of experience is encouraged to deal with each upon a different principle; and where these provinces touch or actually fuse, he is at a loss what method of comprehension to apply. There sets in, accordingly, a tendency to use various methods at once or a different one on each occasion, as language, custom, or presumption seems to demand. Science is reduced by philosophers to plausible discourse, and the more plausible the discourse is, by leaning on all the heterogeneous prejudices of the hour, the more does it foster the same and discourage radical investigation.

Thus even Aristotle felt that good judgment and the dramatic habit of things altogether excluded the simple physics of Democritus. Indeed, as things then stood, Democritus had no right to his simplicity, except that divine right which comes of inspiration. His was an indefensible faith in a single radical insight, which happened nevertheless to be true. To justify that insight forensically it would have been necessary to change the range of human vision, making it telescopic in one region and microscopic in another; whereby the objects so transfigured would have lost their familiar aspect and their habitual context in discourse. Without such a startling change of focus nature can never seem everywhere mechanical. Hence, even to this day, people with broad human interests are apt to discredit a mechanical philosophy. Seldom can penetration and courage in thinking hold their own against the miscellaneous habits of discourse; and nobody remembers that moral values must remain captious, and imaginative life ignoble and dark, so long as the whole basis and application of them is falsely conceived. Discoveries in science are made only by near-sighted specialists, while the influence of public sentiment and policy still works systematically against enlightenment.

And Speculation Rendered Necessary.

The maladaptation of sense to its objects has a second consequence: that speculation is in a way nobler for man than direct perception. For direct perception is wholly inadequate to render the force, the reality, the subtle relations of the object perceived, unless this object be a shell only, like a work of fine art, where nothing counts but the surface.

Since the function of perception is properly to give under-standing and dominion, direct perception is a defeat and, as it were, an insult to the mind, thus forced to busy itself about so unintelligible and dense an apparition. Æsthetic enthusiasm cares nothing about what the object inwardly is, what is its efficacious movement and real life. It revels selfishly in the harmonies of perception itself, harmonies which perhaps it attributes to the object through want of consideration. These æsthetic objects, which have no in-trinsic unity or cohesion, lapse in the most melancholy and inexplicable fashion before our eyes. Then we cry that beauty wanes, that life is brief, and that its prizes are deceptive. Our minds have fed on casual aspects of nature, like tints in sunset clouds. Imaginative fervour has poured itself out exclusively on these apparitions, which are without relevant backing in the world; and long, perhaps, before this life is over, which we called too brief, we begin to pine for another, where just those images which here played so deceptively on the surface of the flux may be turned into fixed and efficacious realities. Meantime speculation amuses us with prophecies about what such realities might be. We look for them, very likely, in the wrong place, namely, in human poetry and eloquence, or at best in dialectic; yet even when stated in these mythical terms the hidden world divined in meditation seems nobler and, as we say, more real than the objects of sense. For we hope, in those speculative visions, to reach the permanent, the efficacious, the staunch principles of experience, something to rely on in prospect and appeal to in perplexity.

Science, in its prosaic but trustworthy fashion, passes like-wise beyond the dreamlike unities and cadences which sense discloses; only, as science aims at controlling its speculation by experiment, the hidden reality it discloses is exactly like what sense perceives, though on a different scale, and not observable, perhaps, without a magic carpet of hypothesis, to carry the observer to the ends of the universe or, changing his dimensions, to introduce him into those infinitesimal abysses where nature has her workshop. In this region, were it sufficiently explored, we might find just those solid supports and faithful warnings which we were looking for with such ill success in our rhetorical speculations. The machinery disclosed would not be human; it would be machinery. But it would for that very reason serve the purpose which made us look for it instead of remaining, like the lower animals, placidly gazing on the pageants of sense, till some unaccountable pang forced us to spasmodic movement. It is doubtless better to find material engines—not necessarily inanimate, either—which may really serve to bring order, security, and progress into our lives, than to find impassioned or ideal spirits, that can do nothing for us except, at best, assure us that they are perfectly happy.

Dissatisfaction with Mechanism Partly Natural.

The reigning aversion to mechanism is partly natural and partly artificial. The natural aversion cannot be wholly overcome. Like the aversion to death, to old age, to labour, it is called forth by man's natural situation in a world which was not made for him, but in which he grew. That the efficacious structure of things should not be intentionally spectacular nor poetical, that its units should not be terms in common discourse, nor its laws quite like the logic of passion, is of course a hard lesson to learn. The learning, however—not to speak of its incidental delights—is so extraordinarily good for people that only with that instruction and the blessed renunciations it brings can clearness, dignity, or virility enter their minds. And of course, if the material basis of human strength could be discovered and better exploited, the free activity of the mind would be not arrested but enlarged. Geology adds something to the interest of landscape, and botany much to the charm of flowers; natural history increases the pleasure with which we view society and the justice with which we judge it. An instinctive sympathy, a solicitude for the perfect working of any delicate thing, as it makes the ruffian tender to a young child, is a sentiment inevitable even toward artificial organisms. Could we better perceive the fine fruits of order, the dire consequences of every specific cruelty or jar, we should grow doubly considerate toward all forms; for we exist through form, and the love of form is our whole real inspiration.

And Partly Artificial.

The artificial prejudice against mechanism is a fruit of party spirit. When a myth has become the centre or sanction for habits and institutions, these habits and institutions stand against any conception incompatible with that myth. It matters nothing that the values the myth was designed to express may remain standing without it, or may be transferred to its successor. Social and intellectual inertia is too great to tolerate so simple an evolution. It divides opinions not into false and true but into high and low, or even more frankly into those which are acceptable and comforting to its ruffled faith and those which are dangerous, alarming, and unfortunate. Imagine Socrates "viewing with alarm" the implications of an argument! This artificial prejudice is indeed modern and will not be eternal. Ancient sages, when they wished to rebuke the atheist, pointed to the very heavens which a sentimental religion would nowadays gladly prove to be unreal, lest the soul should learn something of their method. Yet the Ptolemaic spheres were no more manlike and far less rich in possibilities of life than the Copernican star-dust. The ancients thought that what was intelligible was divine. Order was what they meant by intelligence, and order productive of excellence was what they meant by reason. When they noticed that the stars moved perpetually and according to law, they seriously thought they were beholding the gods. The stars as we conceive them are not in that sense perfect. But the order which nature does not cease to manifest is still typical of all order, and is sublime. It is from these regions of embodied law that intelligibility and power combined come to make their covenant with us, as with all generations.

Biassed Judgments Inspired by Moral Inertia.

The emotions and the moral principles that are naturally allied to materialism suffer an eclipse when materialism, which is properly a primary or dogmatic philosophy, breathing courage and victory, appears as a destructive force and in the incongruous rôle of a critic. One dogmatism is not fit to criticise another; their conflict can end only in insults, sullenness, and an appeal to that physical drift and irrational selection which may ultimately consign one party to oblivion. But a philosophy does ill to boast of such borrowed triumphs. The next turn of the wheel may crush the victor, and the opinions hastily buried may rise again to pose as the fashionable and superior insights of a later day. To criticise dogmatism it is necessary to be a genuine sceptic, an honest transcendentalist, that falls back on the immediate and observes by what principles of logical architecture the ultimate, the reality discovered, has been inferred from it. Such criticism is not necessarily destructive; some construction and some belief being absolutely inevitable, if reason and life are to operate at all, criticism merely offers us the opportunity of revising and purifying our dogmas, so as to make them reasonable and congruous with practice. Materialism may thus be reinstated on transcendental grounds, and the dogma at first uttered in the flush of intelligent perception, with no scruple or self-consciousness, may be repeated after a thorough examination of heart, on the ground that it is the best possible expression of experience, the inevitable deliverance of thought. So approached, a dogmatic system will carry its critical justification with it, and the values it enshrines and secures will not be doubtful. The emotions it arouses will be those aroused by the experience it explains. Causes having been found for what is given, these causes will be proved to have just that beneficent potency and just that distressing inadequacy which the joys and failures of life show that the reality has, whatever this reality may otherwise be. The theory will add nothing except the success involved in framing it. Life being once for all what it is, no physics can render it worse or better, save as the knowledge of physics, with insight into the causes of our varied fortunes, is itself an achievement and a new resource.

Positive Emotions Proper to Materialism.

A theory is not an unemotional thing. If music can be full of passion, merely by giving form to a single sense, how much more beauty or terror may not a vision be pregnant with which brings order and method into everything that we know. Materialism has its distinct æsthetic and emotional colour, though this may be strangely affected and even reversed by contrast with systems of an incongruous hue, jostling it accidentally in a confused and amphibious mind. If you are in the habit of believing in special providences, or of expecting to continue your romantic adventures in a second life, materialism will dash your hopes most unpleasantly, and you may think for a year or two that you have nothing left to live for. But a thorough materialist, one born to the faith and not half plunged into it by an unexpected christening in cold water, will be like the superb Democritus, a laughing philosopher. His delight in a mechanism that can fall into so many marvellous and beautiful shapes, and can generate so many exciting passions, should be of the same intellectual quality as that which the visitor feels in a museum of natural history, where he views the myriad butterflies in their cases, the flamingoes and shell-fish, the mammoths and gorillas. Doubtless there were pangs in that incalculable life, but they were soon over; and how splendid meantime was the pageant, how infinitely interesting the universal interplay, and how foolish and inevitable those absolute little passions. Somewhat of that sort might be the sentiment that materialism would arouse in a vigorous mind, active, joyful, impersonal, and in respect to private illusions not without a touch of scorn.

To the genuine sufferings of living creatures the ethics that accompanies materialism has never been insensible; on the contrary, like other merciful systems, it has trembled too much at pain and tended to withdraw the will ascetically, lest the will should be defeated. Contempt for mortal sorrows is reserved for those who drive with hosannas the Juggernaut car of absolute optimism. But against evils born of pure vanity and self-deception, against the verbiage by which man persuades himself that he is the goal and acme of the universe, laughter is the proper defense. Laughter also has this subtle advantage, that it need not remain without an overtone of sympathy and brotherly understanding; as the laughter that greets Don Quixote's absurdities and misadventures does not mock the hero's intent. His ardour was admirable, but the world must be known before it can be reformed pertinently, and happiness, to be attained, must be placed in reason.

The Material World Not Dead nor Ugly.

Oblivious of Democritus, the unwilling materialists of our day have generally been awkwardly intellectual and quite incapable of laughter. If they have felt anything, they have felt melancholy. Their allegiance and affection were still fixed on those mystical sentimental worlds which they saw to be illusory. The mechanical world they believed in could not please them, in spite of its extent and fertility. Giving rhetorical vent to their spleen and prejudice, they exaggerated nature's meagreness and mathematical dryness. When their imagination was chilled they spoke of nature, most unwarrantably, as dead, and when their judgment was heated they took the next step and called it unreal. A man is not blind, however, because every part of his body is not an eye, nor every muscle in his eye a nerve sensitive to light. Why, then, is nature dead, although it swarms with living organisms, if every part is not obviously animate? And why is the sun dark and cold, if it is bright and hot only to animal sensibility? This senseless lamentation is like the sophism of those Indian preachers who, to make men abandon the illusions of self-love, dilated on the shocking contents of the human body. Take off the skin, they cried, and you will discover nothing but loathsome bleeding and quivering substances. Yet the inner organs are well enough in their place and doubtless pleasing to the microbes that inhabit them; and a man is not hideous because his cross-section would not offer the features of a beautiful countenance. So the structure of the world is not therefore barren or odious because, if you removed its natural outer aspect and effects, it would not make an interesting landscape. Beauty being an appearance and life an operation, that is surely beautiful and living which so operates and so appears as to manifest those qualities.

Nor Especially Cruel.

It is true that materialism prophesies an ultimate extinction for man and all his works. The horror which this prospect inspires in the natural man might be mitigated by reflection; but, granting the horror, is it something introduced by mechanical theories and not present in experience itself? Are human things inwardly stable? Do they belong to the eternal in any sense in which the operation of material forces can touch their immortality? The panic which seems to seize some minds at the thought of a merely natural existence is something truly hysterical; and yet one wonders why ultimate peace should seem so intolerable to people who not so many years ago found a stern religious satisfaction in consigning almost the whole human race to perpetual torture, the Creator, as Saint Augustine tells us, having in his infinite wisdom and justice devised a special kind of material fire that might avail to burn resurrected bodies for ever without consuming them. A very real truth might be read into this savage symbol, if we understood it to express the ultimate defeats and fruitless agonies that pursue human folly; and so we might find that it gave mythical expression to just that conditioned fortune and inexorable flux which a mechanical philosophy shows us the grounds of. Our own vices in another man seem particularly hideous; and so those actual evils which we take for granted when incorporated in the current system strike us afresh when we see them in a new setting. But it is not mechanical science that introduced mutability into things nor materialism that invented death.

Mechanism to Be Judged by Its Fruits.

The death of individuals, as we observe daily in nature, does not prevent the reappearance of life; and if we choose to indulge in arbitrary judgments on a subject where data fail us, we may as reasonably wish that there might be less life as that there might be more. The passion for a large and permanent population in the universe is not obviously rational; at a great distance a man must view everything, including himself, under the form of eternity, and when life is so viewed its length or its diffusion becomes a point of little importance. What matters then is quality. The reasonable and humane demand to make of the world is that such creatures as exist should not be unhappy and that life, whatever its quantity, should have a quality that may justify it in its own eyes. This just demand, made by conscience and not by an arbitrary fancy, the world described by mechanism does not fulfil altogether, for adjustments in it are tentative, and much friction must precede and follow upon any vital equilibrium attained. This imperfection, however, is actual, and no theory can overcome it except by verbal fallacies and scarcely deceptive euphemisms. What mechanism involves in this respect is exactly what we find: a tentative appearance of life in many quarters, its disappearance in some, and its reinforcement and propagation in others, where the physical equilibrium attained insures to it a natural stability and a natural prosperity.

VII

Dialectic

Dialectic Elaborates Given Forms.

THE advantage which the mechanical sciences have over history is drawn from their mathematical form. Mathematics has somewhat the same place in physics that conscience has in action; it seems to be a directive principle in natural operations where it is only a formal harmony. The formalistic school, which treats grammar in all departments as if it were the ground of import rather than a means of expressing it, takes mathematics also for an oracular deliverance, springing full-armed out of the brain, and setting up a canon which all concrete things must conform to. Thus mathematical science has become a mystery which a myth must be constructed to solve. For how can it happen, people ask, that pure intuition, retreating into its cell, can evolve there a prodigious system of relations which it carries like a measuring-rod into the world and lo! everything in experience submits to be measured by it? What pre-established harmony is this between the spinning cerebral silkworm and nature's satins and brocades?

If we but knew, so the myth runs, that experience can show no patterns but those which the prolific Mind has woven, we should not wonder at this necessary correspondence. The Mind having decreed of its own motion, while it sat alone before the creation of the world, that it would take to dreaming mathematically, it evoked out of nothing all formal necessities; and later, when it felt some solicitation to play with things, it imposed those forms upon all its toys, admitting none of any other sort into the nursery. In other words, perception perfected its grammar before perceiving any of its objects, and having imputed that grammar to the materials of sense, it was able to perceive objects for the first time and to legislate further about their relations.

The most obvious artifices of language are often the most deceptive and bring on epidemic prejudices. What is this Mind, this machine existing prior to existence? The mind that exists is only a particular department or focus of existence; its principals cannot be its own source, much less the source of anything in other beings. Mathematical principles in particular are not imposed on existence or on nature *ab extra*, but are found in and abstracted from the subject-matter and march of experience. To exist things have to wear some form, and the form they happen to wear is largely mathematical. This being the case, the mind, in shaping its barbarous prosody somewhat more closely to the nature of things, learns to note and to abstract the form that so strikingly defines them. Once abstracted and focussed in the mind, these forms, like all forms, reveal their dialectic; but that things conform to that dialectic (when they do) is not wonderful, seeing that it is the obvious form of things that the mind has singled out, not without practical shrewdness, for more intensive study.

Forms Are Abstracted from Existence by Intent.

The difference between ideal and material knowledge does not lie in the ungenerated oracular character of one of them in opposition to the other; in both the data are inexplicable and irrational, and in both investigation is tentative, observant, and subject to control by the subject-matter. The difference lies, rather, in the direction of speculation. In physics, which is at bottom historical, we study what happens; we make inventories and records of events, of phenomena, of juxtapositions. In dialectic, which is wholly intensive, we study what is; we strive to clarify and develop the essence of what we find, bringing into focus the inner harmonies and implications of forms—forms which our attention or purpose has defined initially. The intuitions from which mathematical deduction starts are highly generic notions drawn from observation. The lines and angles of geometers are ideals, and their ideal context is entirely independent of what may be their context in the world; but they are found in the world, and their ideals are suggested by very common sensations. Had they been invented, by some inexplicable parthenogenesis in thought, it would indeed have been a marvel had they found application. Philosophy has enough notions of this inapplicable sort—usually, however, not very recondite in their origin—to show that dialectic, when it seems to control existence, must have taken more than one hint from the subject world, and that in the realm of logic, too, nothing submits to be governed without representation.

Confusion Comes of Imperfect Abstraction, or Ambiguous Intent.

When dialectic is employed, as in ethics and metaphysics, upon highly complex ideas—concretions in discourse which cover large blocks of existence—the dialectician in defining and in deducing often reaches notions which cease to apply in some important respect to the object originally intended. Thus Socrates, taking "courage" for his theme, treats it dialectically and expresses the intent of the word by saying that courage must be good, and then develops the meaning of good, showing that it means the choice of the greater benefit; and finally turns about and ends by saying that courage is consequently the choice of the greater benefit and identical with wisdom. Here we have a process of thought ending in a paradox which, frankly, misrepresents the original meaning. For "courage" meant not merely something desirable but something having a certain animal and psychological aspect. The emotion and gesture of it had not been excluded from the idea. So that while the argument proves to perfection that unwise courage is a bad thing, it does not end with an affirmation really true of the original concept. The instinct which we call courage, with an eye to its psychic and bodily quality, is not always virtuous or wise. Dialectic, when it starts with confused and deep-dyed feelings, like those which ethical and metaphysical terms generally stand for, is thus in great danger of proving unsatisfactory and being or seeming sophistical.

The mathematical dialectician has no such serious dangers to face. When, having observed the sun and sundry other objects, he frames the idea of a circle and tracing out its intent shows that the circle meant cannot be squared, there is no difficulty in reverting to nature and saying that the sun's circle cannot be squared. For there is no difference in intent between the circularity noted in the sun and that which is the subject of the demonstration. The geometer has made in his first reflection so clear and violent an abstraction from the sun's actual bulk and qualities that he will never imagine himself to be speaking of anything but a concretion in discourse. The concretion in nature is never legislated about nor so much as thought of except possibly when, under warrant of sense, it is chosen to illustrate the concept investigated dialectically. It does not even occur to a man to ask if the sun's circle can be squared, for every one understands that the sun is circular only in so far as it conforms to the circle's ideal nature; which is as if Socrates and his interlocutors had clearly understood that the *virtue* of courage in an intemperate villain meant only whatever in his mood or action was rational and truly desirable, and had then said that courage, so understood, was identical with wisdom or with the truly rational and desirable rule of life.

The Fact that Mathematics Applies to Existence Is Empirical.

The applicability of mathematics is not vouched for by mathematics but by sense, and its application in some distant part of nature is not vouched for by mathematics but by inductive arguments about nature's uniformity, or by the character which the notion, "a distant part of nature," already possesses. Inapplicable mathematics, we are told, is perfectly thinkable, and systematic deductions, in themselves valid, may be made from concepts which contravene the facts of perception. We may suspect, perhaps, that even these concepts are framed by analogy out of suggestions found in sense, so that some symbolic relevance or proportion is kept, even in these dislocated speculations, to the matter of experience. It is like a new mythology; the purely fictitious idea has a certain parallelism and affinity to nature and moves in a human and familiar way. Both data and method are drawn from applicable science, elements of which even myth, whether poetic or mathematical, may illustrate by a sort of variant or fantastic reduplication.

The great glory of mathematics, like that of virtue, is to be useful while remaining free. Number and measure furnish an inexhaustible subject-matter which the mind can dominate and develop dialectically as it is the mind's inherent office to develop ideas. At the same time number and measure are the grammar of sense; and the more this inner logic is cultivated and refined the greater subtlety and sweep can be given to human perception. Astronomy on the one hand and mechanical arts on the other are fruits of mathematics by which its worth is made known even to the layman, although the born mathematician would not need the sanction of such an extraneous utility to attach him to a subject that has an inherent cogency and charm. Ideas, like other things, have pleasure in propagation, and even when allowance is made for birth-pangs and an occasional miscarriage, their native fertility will always continue to assert itself. The more ideal and frictionless the movement of thought is, the more perfect must be the physiological engine that sustains it. The momentum of that silent and secluded growth carries the mind, with a sense of pure disembodied vision, through the logical labyrinth; but the momentum is vital, for the truth itself does not move.

Its Moral Value Is Therefore Contingent.

Whether the airy phantoms thus brought into being are valued and preserved by the world is an ulterior point of policy which the pregnant mathematician does not need to consider in bringing to light the legitimate burden of his thoughts. But were mathematics incapable of application, did nature and experience, for instance, illustrate nothing but Parmenides' Being or Hegel's Logic, the dialectical cogency which mathematics would of course retain would not give this science a very high place in the Life of Reason. Mathematics would be an amusement, and though apparently innocent, like a game of patience, it might even turn out to be a wasteful and foolish exercise for the mind; because to deepen habits and cultivate pleasures irrelevant to other interests is a way of alienating ourselves from our general happiness. Distinction and a curious charm there may well be in such a pursuit, but this quality is perhaps traceable to affinities and associations with other more substantial interests, or is due to the ingenious temper it denotes, which touches that of the wit or magician. Mathematics, if it were nothing more than a pleasure, might conceivably become a vice. Those addicted to it might be indulging an atavistic taste at the expense of their humanity. It would then be in the position now occupied by mythology and mysticism. Even as it is, mathematicians share with musicians a certain partiality in their characters and mental development. Masters in one abstract subject, they may remain children in the world; exquisite manipulators of the ideal, they may be erratic and clumsy in their earthly ways. Immense as are the uses and wide the applications of mathematics, its texture is too thin and inhuman to employ the whole mind or render it harmonious. It is a science which Socrates rejected for its supposed want of utility; but perhaps he had another ground in reserve to justify his humorous prejudice. He may have felt that such a science, if admitted, would endanger his thesis about the identity of virtue and knowledge.

Quantity Submits Easily to Dialectical Treatment.

Mathematical method has been the envy of philosophers, perplexed and encumbered as they are with the whole mystery of existence, and they have attempted at times to emulate mathematical cogency. Now the lucidity and certainty found in mathematics are not inherent in its specific character as the science of number or dimension; they belong to dialectic as a whole, which is essentially elucidation. The effort to explain meanings is in most cases abortive because these meanings melt in our hands—a defeat which Hegel would fain have consecrated, together with all other evils, into necessity and law. But the merit of mathematics is that it is so much less Hegelian than life; that it holds its own while it advances, and never allows itself to misrepresent its original intent. In all it finds to say about the triangle it never comes to maintain that the triangle is really a square. The privilege of mathematics is simply to have offered the mind, for dialectical treatment, a material to which dialectical treatment could be honestly applied. This material consists in certain general aspects of sensation—its extensity, its pulsation, its distribution into related parts. The wakefulness that originally makes these abstractions is able to keep them clear, and to elaborate them infinitely without contradicting their essence.

For this reason it is always a false step in mathematical science, a step over its brink into the abyss beyond, when we try to reduce its elements to anything not essentially sensible. Intuition must continue to furnish the subject of discourse, the axioms, and the ultimate criteria and sanctions. Calculation and transmutation can never make their own counters or the medium in which they move. So that space, number, continuity, and every other elementary intuition remains at bottom opaque—opaque, that is, to mathematical science; for it is no paradox, but an obvious necessity, that the data of a logical operation should not be producible by its workings. Reason would have nothing to do if it had no irrational materials. Saint Augustine's rhetoric accordingly covered—as so often with him—a profound truth when he said of time that he knew what it was when no one asked him, but if any one asked him he did not know; which may be restated by saying that time is an intuition, an aspect of crude experience, which science may work with but which it can never arrive at.

Constancy and Progress in Intent.

When a concretion is formed in discourse and an intent is attained in consciousness, predicates accrue to the subject in a way which is perfectly empirical. Dialectic is not retrospective; it does not consist in recovering ground previously surveyed. The accretion of new predicates comes in answer to chance questions, questions raised, to be sure, about a given theme. The subject is fixed by the mind's intent and it suffices to compare any tentative assertion made about it with that intent itself to see whether the expression suggested for it is truly dialectical and thoroughly honest. Dialectic verifies by reconsideration, by equation of tentative results with fixed intentions. It does not verify, like the sciences of existence, by comparing a hypothesis with a new perception. In dialectic no new *perception* is wanted; the goal is to understand the old fact, to give it an aureole and not a progeny. It is a transubstantiation of matter, a passage from existence to eternity. In this sense dialectic is "synthetic *a priori*"; it analyses an intent which demanded further elucidation and had fixed the direction and principle of its expansion. If this intent is abandoned and a new subject is introduced surreptitiously, a fallacy is committed; yet the correct elucidation of ideas is a true progress, nor could there be any progress unless the original idea were better expressed and elicited as we proceeded; so that constancy in intent and advance in explication are the two requisites of a cogent deduction.

The question in dialectic is always what is true, what can be said, about *this*; and the demonstrative pronoun, indicating an act of selective attention, raises the object it selects to a concretion in discourse, the relations of which in the universe of discourse it then proceeds to formulate. At the same time this dialectical investigation may be full of surprises. Knowledge may be so truly enriched by it that *knowledge*, in an ideal sense, only begins when dialectic has given some articulation to being. Without dialectic an animal might follow instinct, he might have vivid emotions, expectations, and dreams, but he could hardly be said to know anything or to guide his life with conscious intent. The accretions that might come empirically into any field of vision would not be new predicates to be added to a known thing, unless the logical and functional mantle of that thing fell upon them and covered them. While the right of particulars to existence is their own, granted them by the free grace of heaven, their ability to enlarge our knowledge on any particular subject—their relevance or incidence in discourse—hangs on their fulfilling the requirements which that subject's dialectical nature imposes on all its expressions.

Intent Determines the Functional Essence of Objects.

It is on this ground, for instance, that the image of a loaf of bread is so far from being the loaf of bread itself. External resemblance is nothing; even psychological derivation or superposition is nothing; the intent, rather, which picks out what that object's function and meaning shall be, alone defines its idea; and this function involves a locus and a status which the image does not possess. Such admirable iridescence as the image might occasionally put on—in the fine arts, for instance—would not constitute any iridescence or transformation in the thing; nor would identity of aspect preserve the thing if its soul, if its utility, had disappeared. Herein lies the ground for the essential or functional distinction between primary and secondary qualities in things, a distinction which a psychological scepticism has so hastily declared to be untenable. If it was discovered, said these logicians, that space was perceived through reading muscular sensations, space, and the muscles too, were thereby proved to be unreal. This remarkable sophism passed muster in the philosophical world for want of attention to dialectic, which might so easily have shown that what a thing *means* is spatial distinction and mechanical efficacy, and that the origin of our perceptions, which are all equally bodily and dependent on material stimulation, has nothing to do with their respective claims to hypostasis. It is intent that makes objects objects; and the same intent, defining the function of things, defines the scope of those qualities which are essential to them. In the flux substances and shadows drift down together; it is reason that discerns the difference.

Also the Scope of Ideals.

Purposes need dialectical articulation as much as essences do, and without an articulate and fixed purpose, without an ideal, action would collapse into mere motion or conscious change. It is notably in this region that elucidation constitutes progress; for to understand the properties of number may be less important than empirically to count; but to see and feel the values of things in all their distinction and fulness is the ultimate fruit of efficiency; it is mastery in that art of life for which all the rest is apprenticeship. Dialectic of this sort is practised intuitively by spiritual minds; and even when it has to be carried on argumentatively it may prove very enlightening. That the excellence of courage is identical with that of wisdom still needs to be driven home; and that the excellence of poetry is identical with that of all other things probably sounds like a blind paradox. Yet did not all excellences conspire to one end and meet in one Life of Reason, how could their relative value be estimated, or any reflective sanction be found for them at all? The miscellaneous, captious fancies of the will, the menagerie of moral prejudice, still call for many a Socrates to tame them. So long as courage means a grimace of mind or body, the love of it is another grimace. But if it meant the value, recognisable by reason and diffused through all life, which that casual attitude or feeling might have, then we should be launched upon the quest for wisdom.

The want of integration in moral views is like what want of integration would be in arithmetic if we declared that it was the part of a man and a Christian to maintain that *my* two equals four or that a *green* fifteen is a hundred. These propositions might have incidental lights and shades in people's lives to make them plausible and precious; but they could not be maintained by one who had clarified his intent in naming and adding. For then the arithmetical relations would be abstracted, and their incidental associates would drop out of the account. So a man who is in pursuit of things for the good that is in them must recognise and (if reason avails) must pursue what is good in them all. Strange customs and unheard-of thoughts may then find their appropriate warrant; just as in higher mathematical calculations very wonderful and unforeseen results may be arrived at, which a man will not accept without careful reconsideration of the terms and problem before him; but if he finds the unexpected conclusion flowing from those premises, he will have enlarged his knowledge of his art and discovered a congenial good. He will have made progress in the Socratic science of knowing his own intent.

Double Status of Mathematics.

Mathematics, for all its applications in nature, is a part of ideal philosophy. It is logic applied to certain simple intuitions. These intuitions and many of their developments happen to appear in that efficacious and self-sustaining moiety of being which we call material; so that mathematics is *per accidens* the dialectical study of nature's efficacious form. Its use and application in the world rather hide its dialectical principle. Mathematics owes its public success to the happy choice of a simple and widely diffused subject-matter; it owes its inner cogency, however, to its ideality and the merely adventitious application it has to existence. Mathematics has come to seem the type of good logic because it is an illustration of logic in a sphere so highly abstract in idea and so pervasive in sense as to be at once manageable and useful.

The delights and triumphs of mathematics ought, therefore, to be a great encouragement to ideal philosophy. If in a comparatively uninteresting field attention can find so many treasures of harmony and order, what beauties might it not discover in interpreting faithfully ideas nobler than extension and number, concretions closer to man's spiritual life? But unfortunately the logic of values is subject to voluntary and involuntary confusions of so discouraging a nature that the flight of dialectic in that direction has never been long and, even when short, often disastrous. What is needed, as the example of mathematics shows, is a steadfast intent and an adventurous inquiry. It would not occur to a geometer to ask with trepidation what difference it would make to the Pythagorean proposition if the hypothenuse were said to be wise and good. Yet metaphysicians, confounding dialectic with physics and thereby corrupting both, will discuss for ever the difference it makes to substance whether you call it matter or God. Nevertheless, no decorative epithets can give substance any other attributes than those which it has; that is, other than the actual appearances that substance is needed to support. Similarly, neither mathematicians nor astronomers are exercised by the question whether π created the ring of Saturn; yet naturalists and logicians have not rejected the analogous problem whether the good did or did not create the animals.

Practical Rôle of Dialectic.

So long as in using terms there is no fixed intent, no concretion in discourse with discernible predicates, controversy will rage as conceptions waver and will reach no valid result. But when the force of intellect, once having arrested an idea amid the flux of perceptions, avails to hold and examine that idea with perseverance, not only does a flash of light immediately cross the mind, but deeper and deeper vistas are opened there into ideal truth. The principle of dialectic is intelligence itself; and as no part of man's economy is more vital than intelligence (since intelligence is what makes life aware of its destiny), so no part has a more delightful or exhilarating movement. To understand is pre-eminently to live, moving not by stimulation and external compulsion, but by inner direction and control. Dialectic is related to observation as art is to industry; it uses what the other furnishes; it is the fruition of experience. It is not an alternative to empirical pursuits but their perfection; for dialectic, like art, has no special or private subject-matter, nor any obligation to be useless. Its subject-matter is all things, and its function is to compare them in form and worth, giving the mind speculative dominion over them. It profits by the flux to fix its signification. This is precisely what mathematics does for the abstract form and multitude of sensible things; it is what dialectic might do everywhere, with the same incidental utility, if it could settle its own attitude and learn to make the passions steadfast and calm in the consciousness of their ultimate objects.

Hegel's Satire on Dialectic.

The nature of dialectic might be curiously illustrated by reference to Hegel's Logic; and though to approach the subject from Hegel's satirical angle is not, perhaps, quite honest or fair, the method has a certain spice. Hegel, who despised mathematics, saw that in other departments the instability of men's meanings defeated their desire to understand themselves. This insecurity in intent he found to be closely connected with change of situation, with the natural mutability of events and opinions in the world. Instead of showing, however, what inroads passion, oblivion, sophistry, and frivolity may make into dialectic, he bethought himself to represent all these incoherences, which are indeed significant of natural changes, as the march of dialectic itself, thus identified with the process of evolution and with natural law. The romance of an unstable and groping theology, full of warm intentions and impossible ideas he took to be typical of all experience and of all science.

In that impressionable age any effect of *chiaro-oscuro* caught in the moonlight of history could find a philosopher to exalt it into the darkly luminous secret of the world. Hegel accordingly decreed that men's habit of self-contradiction constituted their providential function, both in thought and in morals; and he devoted his Logic to showing how every idea they embraced (for he never treated an idea otherwise than as a creed), when pressed a little, turned into its opposite. This opposite after a while would fall back into something like the original illusion; whereupon a new change of insight would occur and a new thought would be accepted until, the landscape changing, attention would be attracted to a fresh aspect of the matter and conviction would wander into a new labyrinth of false steps and half-meanings. The sum total of these wanderings, when viewed from above, formed an interesting picture. A half-mystical, half-cynical reflection might take a certain pleasure in contemplating it; especially if, in the memory of Calvin and the Stoics, this situation were called the expression of Absolute Reason and Divine Will.

We may think for a moment that we have grasped the

elusive secret of this philosophy and that it is simply a Calvinism without Christianity, in which God's glory consists in the damnation of quite all his creatures. Presently, however, the scene changes again, and we recognise that Creator and creation, ideal and process, are identical, so that the glory belongs to the very multitude that suffers. But finally, as we rub our eyes, the whole revelation collapses into a platitude, and we discover that this glory and this damnation were nothing but unctuous phrases for the vulgar flux of existence.

That nothing is what we mean by it is perfectly true when we in no case know what we mean. Thus a man who is a mystic by nature may very well become one by reflection also. Not knowing what he wants nor what he is, he may believe that every shift carries him nearer to perfection. A temperamental and quasi-religious thirst for inconclusiveness and room to move on lent a certain triumphant note to Hegel's satire; he was sure it all culminated in something, and was not sure it did not culminate in himself. The system, however, as it might strike a less egotistical reader, is a long demonstration of man's ineptitude and of nature's contemptuous march over a path paved with good intentions. It is an idealism without respect for ideals; a system of dialectic in which a psychological flux (not, of course, psychological science, which would involve terms dialectically fixed and determinate) is made systematically to obliterate intended meanings.

Dialectic Expresses a Given Intent.

This spirited travesty of logic has enough historical truth in it to show that dialectic must always stand, so to speak, on its apex; for life is changeful, and the vision and interest of one moment are not understood in the next. Theological dialectic rings hollow when once faith is dead; grammar looks artificial when a language is foreign; mathematics itself seems shallow when, like Hegel, we have no love for nature's intelligible mechanism nor for the clear structure and constancy of eternal things. Ideal philosophy is a flower of the spirit and varies with the soil. If mathematics suffers so little contradiction, it is only because the primary aspects of sensation which it elaborates could not lapse from the world without an utter break in its continuity. Otherwise though mathematics might not be refuted it might well be despised, like an obsolete ontology. Its boasted necessity and universality would not help it at all if experience should change so much as to present no further mathematical aspect. Those who expect to pass at death into a non-spatial and super-temporal world, where there will be no detestable extended and unthinking substances, and nothing that need be counted, will find their hard-earned mathematics sadly superfluous there. The memory of earthly geometry and arithmetic will grow pale amid that floating incense and music, where dialectic, if it survives at all, will have to busy itself on new intuitions.

So, too, when the landscape changes in the moral world, when new passions or arts make their appearance, moral philosophy must start afresh on a new foundation and try to express the ideals involved in the new pursuits. To this extent experience lends colour to Hegel's dialectical physics; but he betrayed, like the sincere pantheist he was, the finite interests that give actual values to the world, and he wished to bestow instead a groundless adoration on the law that connected and defeated every ideal. Such a genius, in spite of incisive wit and a certain histrionic sympathy with all experience, could not be truly free; it could not throw off its professional priestcraft, its habit of ceremonious fraud on the surface, nor, at heart, its inhuman religion.

Its Empire Is Ideal and Autonomous.

The sincere dialectician, the genuine moralist, must stand upon human, Socratic ground. Though art be long, it must take a short life for its basis and an actual interest for its guide. The liberal dialectician has the gift of conversation; he does not pretend to legislate from the throne of Jehovah about the course of affairs, but asks the ingenuous heart to speak for itself, guiding and checking it only in its own interest. The result is to express a given nature and to cultivate it; so that whenever any one possessing such a nature is born into the world he may use this calculation, and more easily understand and justify his mind. Of course, if experience were no longer the same, the faculties had entirely varied, the former interpretation could no longer serve. Where nature shows a new principle of growth the mind must find a new method of expression, and move toward other goals. Ideals are not forces stealthily undermining the will; they are possible forms of being that would frankly express it. These forms are invulnerable, eternal, and free; and he who finds them divine and congenial and is able to embody them at least in part and for a season, has to that extent transfigured life, turning it from a fatal process into a liberal art.

XI

The Validity of Science

THE same despair or confusion which, when it overtakes human purposes, seeks relief in arbitrary schemes of salvation, when it overtakes human knowledge, may breed arbitrary substitutes for science. There are post-rational systems of nature as well as of duty. Most of these are myths hardly worth separating from the post-rational moralities they adorn, and have been sufficiently noticed in the last chapter; but a few aspire to be critical revisions of science, themselves scientific. It may be well, in bringing this book to a close, to review these proposed revisions. The validity of science is at stake, and with it the validity of that whole Life of Reason which science crowns, and justifies to reflection.

Various Modes of Revising Science.

There are many degrees and kinds of this critical retractation. Science may be accepted bodily, while its present results are modified by suggesting speculatively what its ultimate results might be. This is natural philosophy or legitimate metaphysics. Or science may be accepted in part, and in part subjected to control by some other alleged vehicle of knowledge. This is traditional or intuitive theology. Or science may be retracted and withdrawn altogether, on the ground that it is but methodological fiction, its facts appearances merely, and its principles tendencies to feign. This is transcendentalism; whereupon a dilemma presents itself. We may be invited to abstain from all hypostasis or hearty belief in anything, and to dwell only on the consciousness of imaginative activity in a vacuum—which is radical idealism. Or we may be assured that, science being a dream, we may awake from it into another cosmos, built upon principles quite alien to those illustrated in nature or applicable in practice—which is idealism of the mythical sort. Finally it may occur to us that the criticism of science is an integral part of science itself, and that a transcendental method of survey, which marshals all things in the order of their discovery, far from invalidating knowledge can only serve to separate it from incidental errors and to disclose the relative importance of truths. Science would then be rehabilitated by criticism. The primary movement of the intellect would not be condemned by that subsequent reflection which it makes possible, and which collates its results. Science, purged of all needless realism and seen in its relation to human life, would continue to offer the only conception of reality which is pertinent or possible to the practical mind.

We may now proceed to discuss these various attitudes in turn.

Science Its Own Best Critic.

A first and quite blameless way of criticising science is to point out that science is incomplete. That it grows fast is indeed its commonest boast; and no man of science is so pessimistic as to suppose that its growth is over. To wish to supplement science and to regard its conclusions as largely provisional is therefore more than legitimate. It is actually to share the spirit of inquiry and to feel the impulse toward investigation. When new truths come into view, old truths are thereby reinterpreted and put in a new light; so that the acquisitions of science not only admit of revision but loudly call for it, not wishing for any other authority or vindication than that which they might find in the context of universal truth.

To revise science in this spirit would be merely to extend it. No new method, no transverse philosophy, would be requisite or fitted for the task. Knowledge would be transformed by more similar knowledge, not by some verbal manipulation. Yet while waiting for experience to grow and accumulate its lessons, a man of genius, who had drunk deep of experience himself, might imagine some ultimate synthesis. He might venture to carry out the suggestions of science and anticipate the conclusions it would reach when completed. The game is certainly dangerous, especially if the prophecy is uttered with any air of authority; yet with good luck and a fine instinct, such speculation may actually open the way to discovery and may diffuse in advance that virtual knowledge of physics which is enough for moral and poetic purposes. Verification in detail is needed, not so much for its own sake as to check speculative errors; but when speculation is by chance well directed and hits upon the substantial truth, it does all that a completed science would do for mankind; since science, if ever completed, would immediately have to be summed up again and reduced to generalities. Under the circumstances of human life, ultimate truth must forego detailed verification and must remain speculative. The curse of modern philosophy is only that it has not drawn its inspiration from science; as the misfortune of science is that it has not yet saturated the mind of philosophers and recast the moral world. The Greek physicists, puerile as was their notion of natural mechanism, had a more integral view of things. They understood nature's uses and man's conditions in an honest and noble way. If no single phenomenon had been explained correctly by any philosopher from Thales to Lucretius, yet by their frank and studious contemplation of nature they would have liberated the human soul.

Obstruction by Alien Traditions.

Unfortunately the supplements to science which most philosophers supply in our day are not conceived in a scientific spirit. Instead of anticipating the physics of the future they cling to the physics of the past. They do not stimulate us by a picture, however fanciful, of what the analogies of nature and politics actually point to; they seek rather to patch and dislocate current physics with some ancient myth, once the best physics obtainable, from which they have not learned to extricate their affections.

Sometimes these survivals are intended to modify scientific conceptions but slightly, and merely to soften a little the outlines of a cosmic picture to which religion and literature are not yet accustomed. There is a school of political conservatives who, with no specific interest in metaphysics, cannot or dare not break with traditional modes of expression, with the customs of their nation, or with the clerical classes. They accordingly append to current knowledge certain sentimental postulates, alleging that what is established by tradition and what appeals to the heart must somehow correspond to something which is needful and true. But their conventional attachment to a religion which in its original essence was perhaps mystical and revolutionary, scarcely modifies, in their eyes, the sum of practical assurances or the aim of human life. As language exercises some functions which science can hardly assume (as, for instance, in poetry and communication) so theology and metaphysics, which to such men are nothing but languages, might provide for inarticulate interests, and unite us to much that lies in the dim penumbra of our workaday world. Ancient revelations and mysteries, however incredible if taken literally, might therefore be suffered to flourish undisturbed, so long as they did not clash with any clear fact or natural duty. They might continue to decorate with a mystical aureole the too prosaic kernel of known truth.

Needless Anxiety for Moral Interests.

Mythology and ritual, with the sundry divinations of poets, might in fact be kept suspended with advantage over human passion and ignorance, to furnish them with decent expression. But once indulged, divination is apt to grow arrogant and dogmatic. When its oracles have become traditional they are almost inevitably mistaken for sober truths. Hence the second kind of supplement offered to science, so that revelations with which moral life has been intertwined may find a place beside or beyond science. The effort is honest, but extraordinarily short-sighted. Whatever value those revelations may have they draw from actual experience or inevitable ideals. When the ground of that experience and those ideals is disclosed by science, nothing of any value is lost; it only remains to accustom ourselves to a new vocabulary and to shift somewhat the associations of those values which life contains or pursues. Revelations are necessarily mythical and subrational; they express natural forces and human interests in a groping way, before the advent of science. To stick in them, when something more honest and explicit is available, is inconsistent with caring for attainable welfare or understanding the situation. It is to be stubborn and negligent under the cloak of religion. These prejudices are a drag on progress, moral no less than material; and the sensitive conservatism that fears they may be indispensable is entangled in a pathetic delusion. It is conservatism in a shipwreck. It has not the insight to embrace the fertile principles of life, which are always ready to renew life after no matter what natural catastrophe. The good laggards have no courage to strip for the race. Rather than live otherwise, and live better, they prefer to nurse the memories of youth and to die with a retrospective smile upon their countenance.

Science an Imaginative and Practical Art.

Far graver than the criticism which shows science to be incomplete is that which shows it to be relative. The fact is undeniable, though the inferences made from it are often rash and gratuitous. We have seen that science is nothing but developed perception, interpreted intent, common sense rounded out and minutely articulated. It is therefore as much an instinctive product, as much a stepping forth of human courage in the dark, as is any inevitable dream or impulsive action. Like life itself, like any form of determinate existence, it is altogether autonomous and unjustifiable from the outside. It must lean on its own vitality; to sanction reason there is only reason, and to corroborate sense there is nothing but sense. Inferential thought is a venture not to be approved of, save by a thought no less venturesome and inferential. This is once for all the fate of a living being—it is the very essence of spirit—to be ever on the wing, borne by inner forces toward goals of its own imagining, confined to a passing apprehension of a represented world. Mind, which calls itself the organ of truth, is a permanent possibility of error. The encouragement and corroboration which science is alleged to receive from moment to moment may, for aught it knows, be simply a more ingenious self-deception, a form of that cumulative illusion by which madness can confirm itself, creating a whole world, with an endless series of martyrs, to bear witness to its sanity.

To insist on this situation may seem idle, since no positive doctrine can gain thereby in plausibility, and no particular line of action in reasonableness. Yet this transcendental exercise, this reversion to the immediate, may be recommended by way of a cathartic, to free the mind from ancient obstructions and make it hungrier and more agile in its rational faith. Scepticism is harmless when it is honest and universal; it clears the air and is a means of reorganising belief on its natural foundations. Belief is an inevitable accompaniment of practice and intent, both of which it will cling to all the more closely after a thorough criticism. When all beliefs are challenged together, the just and necessary ones have a chance to step forward and to re-establish themselves alone. The doubt cast on science, when it is an ingenuous and impartial doubt, will accordingly serve to show what sort of thing science is, and to establish it on a sure foundation. Science will then be seen to be tentative, genial, practical, and humane, full of ideality and pathos, like every great human undertaking.

Arrière-Pensée in Transcendentalism.

Unfortunately a searching disintegration of dogma, a conscientious reversion to the immediate, is seldom practised for its own sake. So violent a disturbance of mental habits needs some great social upheaval or some revolutionary ambition to bring it about. The transcendental philosophy might never have been put forward at all, had its authors valued it for what it can really accomplish. The effort would have seemed too great and the result too nugatory. Their criticism of knowledge was not freely undertaken, with the pure speculative motive of understanding and purifying human science. They were driven on by the malicious psychology of their predecessors, by the perplexities of a sophis-

tical scepticism, and by the imminent collapse of traditional
metaphysics. They were enticed at the same time by the
hope of finding a new basis for the religious myths associated
with that metaphysics. In consequence their transcendentalism was not a rehearsal of the Life of Reason, a retrospect
criticising and justifying the phases of human progress. It
was rather a post-rational system of theology, the dangerous
cure to a harmless disease, inducing a panic to introduce a
fable. The panic came from the assumption (a wholly gratuitous one) that a spontaneous constructive intellect cannot
be a trustworthy instrument, that appearances cannot be
the properties of reality, and that things cannot be what
science finds that they are. We were forbidden to believe in
anything we might discover or to trust in anything we could
see. The artificial vacuum thus produced in the mind ached
to be filled with something, and of course a flood of rhetorical commonplaces was at hand, which might rush in to fill it.

Its Romantic Sincerity.

The most heroic transcendentalists were but men, and
having imagined that logic obliged them to abstain from
every sort of hypostasis, they could not long remain true to
their logic. For a time, being of a buoyant disposition, they
might feel that nothing could be more exhilarating than to
swim in the void, altogether free from settled conditions, altogether the ignorant creators of each moment's vision. Such
a career evidently affords all sorts of possibilities, except
perhaps the possibility of being a career. But when a man
has strained every nerve to maintain an absolute fluidity
and a painful fidelity to the immediate, he can hardly be
blamed if he lapses at last into some flattering myth, and if
having satisfied himself that all science is fiction he proclaims
some fairy-tale to be the truth. The episodes of experience,
not being due to any conceivable machinery beneath, might
come of mere willing, or at the waving of a dialectical wand.
Yet apart from this ulterior inconsistency and backsliding

into credulity, transcendentalism would hear nothing of causes or grounds. All phenomena existed for it on one flat level. We were released from all dogma and reinstated in the primordial assurance that we were all there was, but without understanding what we were, and without any means of controlling our destiny, though cheered by the magnificent feeling that that destiny was great.

Its Constructive Impotence.

It is intelligible that a pure transcendentalism of this sort should not be either stable or popular. It may be admired for its analytic depth and its persistency in tracing all supposed existences back to the experience that vouches for them. Yet a spirit that finds its only exercise in gloating on the consciousness that it is a spirit, one that has so little skill in expression that it feels all its embodiments to be betrayals and all its symbols to be misrepresentations, is a spirit evidently impotent and confused. It is self-inhibited, and cannot fulfil its essential vocation by reaching an embodiment at once definitive and ideal, philosophical and true. We may excuse a school that has done one original task so thoroughly as transcendentalism has done its examination of the cognitive conscience, if it has failed to do something else to which it did not distinctly address itself and for which it had no aptitude—namely, to discover what is really true. But it becomes necessary to note this limitation, especially when it is virtually disallowed, and when science is systematically disparaged in favour of a method that is merely disintegrating and incapable of establishing a single positive truth.

The legitimacy of the transcendental method is so obvious that it is baffling when unfamiliar and trifling when understood. It is somewhat like the scientific discovery that man is an animal; for in spite of its pompous language and unction, transcendentalism, when not transcended, is a stopping short at the vegetative and digestive stage of consciousness, where nothing seems to be anything but a play of variations in the immediate. That is what science has risen from; it is the primordial slime. But to stop there and make life consist in hearing the mind work is illiberal and childish. Maturity lies in taking reason at its word and learning to believe and to do what it bids us. Inexperience, pedantry, and mysticism —three obstacles to wisdom—were not absent from those academic geniuses by whom transcendentalism was first brought forth. They became consequently entangled in their profundity, and never were masters of their purposes or of their tools.

Its Dependence on Common Sense.

The dethronement of empirical knowledge which these philosophers announced was occasioned by the discovery that empirical knowledge was ideal and hypothetical; that its terms, like all terms in thought, were thrown out during the fission or crystallisation of a growing experience. Science accordingly was merely a set of ideas; its subject-matter seemed to be sucked in and absorbed by the theory that presented it, so that when the history of science was written the whole substance and meaning of science was exhausted. This damaging implication, that what is ideal is imaginary and that what is inferred exists only in the fooled mind that infers it, would, if it were allowed, make short work of all philosophy. Theology would fare no better than science, and it is hard to see how transcendental idealism itself could stand, if it pretended to constitute an articulate theory of reality. All faith would be invalidated, since it would be proved to be faith only, having no real object. But then history itself is a science; and to represent a series of events or related phenomena in time would be to pretend to impossible knowledge. It would become necessary to retract and withdraw the alleged evolution of thought itself, in which science was to figure as an imaginative device and a passing episode.

History and experience would be nothing but the idea of them; and the Absolute Ego or Absolute Life also, in so far as anything could be said of it, would be simply an integral term in the discourse that described it. And this discourse, this sad residuum of reality, would remain an absolute datum without a ground, without a subject-matter, without a past, and without a future.

Its Futility.

It suffices, therefore, to take the supposed negative implication in transcendentalism a little seriously to see that it leaves nothing standing but negation and imbecility; so that we may safely conclude that such a negative implication is gratuitous, and also that in taking the transcendental method for an instrument of reconstruction its professors were radically false to it. They took the starting-point of experience, on which they had fallen back, for its ultimate deliverance, and in reverting to protoplasm they thought they were rising to God. The transcendental method is merely retrospective; its use is to recover more systematically conceptions already extant and inevitable. It invalidates nothing in science; much less does it carry with it any rival doctrine of its own. Every philosophy, even materialism, may find a transcendental justification, if experience as it develops will yield no other terms. What has reason to tremble at a demand for its credentials is surely not natural science; it is rather those mystical theologies or romantic philosophies of history which aspire to take its place. Such lucubrations, even if reputed certain, can scarcely be really credited or regarded in practice; while scientific tenets are necessarily respected, even when they are declared to be fictions. This nemesis is inevitable; for the mind must be inhabited, and the ideas with which science peoples it are simply its involuntary perceptions somewhat more clearly arranged.

Ideal Science Is Self-justified.

That the relativity of science—its being an emanation of human life—is nothing against its truth appears best, perhaps, in the case of dialectic. Dialectic is valid by virtue of an intended meaning and felt congruity in its terms; but these terms, which intent fixes, are external and independent in their ideal nature, and the congruity between them is not created by being felt but, whether incidentally felt or not, is inherent in their essence. Mathematical thinking is the closest and most intimate of mental operations, nothing external being called in to aid; yet mathematical truth is as remote as possible from being personal or psychic. It is absolutely self-justified and is necessary before it is discovered to be so. Here, then, is a conspicuous region of truth, disclosed to the human intellect by its own internal exercise, which is nevertheless altogether independent, being eternal and indefeasible, while the thought that utters it is ephemeral.

The validity of material science, not being warranted by pure insight, cannot be so quickly made out; nevertheless it cannot be denied systematically, and the misunderstood transcendentalism which belittles physics contradicts its own basis.

Physical Science Is Presupposed in Scepticism.

For how are we supposed to know that what we call facts are mere appearances and what we call objects mere creations of thought? We know this by physics. It is physiology, a part of physics, that assures us that our senses and brains are conditions of our experience. Were it not for what we know of the outer world and of our place in it, we should be incapable of attaching any meaning to subjectivity. The flux of things would then go on in their own medium, not in our minds; and no suspicion of illusion or of qualification by mind would attach to any event in nature. So it is in a dream; and it is our knowledge of physics, our reliance on the world's material coherence, that marks our awakening, and that constitutes our discovery that we exist as minds and are subject to dreaming. It is quite true that the flux, as it exists in men, is largely psychic; but only because the events it contains are effects of material causes and the images in it are flying shadows cast by solid external things. This is the meaning of psychic existence, and its differentia. Mind is an expression, weighted with emotion, of mechanical relations among bodies. Suppose the bodies all removed: at once the images formerly contrasted with those bodies would resume their inherent characteristics and mutual relation; they would become existences in their own category, large, moving, coloured, distributed to right and left; that is, save for their values, they would become material things.

It Recurs in All Understanding of Perception.

Physics is accordingly a science which, though hypothetical and only verifiable by experiment, is involved in history and psychology and therefore in any criticism of knowledge. The contradiction would be curious if a man should declare that his ideas were worthless, being due to his organs of sense, and that therefore these organs (since he had an idea of them) did not exist. Yet on this brave argument idealism chiefly rests. It asserts that bodies are mere ideas, because it is through our bodies that we perceive them. When physics has discovered the conditions under which knowledge of physics has arisen, physics is supposed to be spirited away; whereas, of course, it has only closed its circle and justified its sovereignty. Were all science retracted and reduced to symbolic calculation nothing would remain for this calculation to symbolise. The whole force of calling a theory merely a vehicle or method of thought, leading us to something different from itself, lies in having a literal knowledge of this other thing. But such literal knowledge is the first stage of science, which the other stages merely extend. So that when, under special circumstances, we really appeal to algebraic methods of expression and think in symbols, we do so in the hope of transcribing our terms, when the reckoning is over, into the language of familiar facts. Were these facts not forthcoming, the symbolic machinery would itself become the genuine reality—since it is really given—and we should have to rest in it, as in the ultimate truth. This is what happens in mythology, when the natural phenomena expressed by it are forgotten. But natural phenomena themselves are symbols of nothing, because they are primary data. They are the constitutive elements of the reality they disclose.

Science Contains All Trustworthy Knowledge.

The validity of science in general is accordingly established merely by establishing the truth of its particular propositions, in dialectic on the authority of intent and in physics on that of experiment. It is impossible to base science on a deeper foundation or to override it by a higher knowledge. What is called metaphysics, if not an anticipation of natural science, is a confusion of it with dialectic or a mixture of it with myths. If we have the faculty of being utterly sincere and of disintegrating the conventions of language and religion, we must confess that knowledge is only a claim we put forth, a part of that unfathomable compulsion by force of which we live and hold our painted world together for a moment. If we have any insight into mind, or any eye for human history, we must confess at the same time that the oracular substitutes for knowledge to which, in our perplexities, we might be tempted to fly, are pathetic popular fables, having no other sanctity than that which they borrow from the natural impulses they play upon. To live by science requires intelligence and faith, but not to live by it is folly.

It Suffices for the Life of Reason.

If science thus contains the sum total of our rational convictions and gives us the only picture of reality on which we should care to dwell, we have but to consult the sciences in detail to ascertain, as far as that is possible, what sort of a universe we live in. The result is as yet far from satisfactory. The sciences have not joined hands and made their results coherent, showing nature to be, as it doubtless is, all of one piece. The moral sciences especially are a mass of confusion. Negative, I think, must be the attitude of reason, in the present state of science, upon any hypothesis far outrunning the recorded history and the visible habitat of the human race. Yet exactly the same habits and principles that have secured our present knowledge are still active within us, and promise further discoveries. It is more desirable to clarify our knowledge within these bounds than to extend it beyond them. For while the reward of action is contemplation or, in more modern phrase, experience and consciousness, there is nothing stable or interesting to contemplate except objects relevant to action—the natural world and the mind's ideals.

Both the conditions and the standards of action lie well within the territory which science, after a fashion, already dominates. But there remain unexplored jungles and monster-breeding lairs within our nominal jurisdiction which it is the immediate task of science to clear. The darkest spots are in man himself, in his fitful, irrational disposition. Could a better system prevail in our lives a better order would establish itself in our thinking. It has not been for want of keen senses, or personal genius, or a constant order in the outer world, that mankind have fallen back repeatedly into barbarism and superstition. It has been for want of good character, good example, and good government. There is a pathetic capacity in men to live nobly, if only they would give one another the chance. The ideal of political perfection,

REASON IN SCIENCE

vague and remote as it yet seems, is certainly approachable;
for it is as definite and constant as human nature. The knowledge of all relevant truth would be involved in that ideal, and
no intellectual dissatisfaction would be felt with a system of
ideas that should express and illumine a perfect life.

THREE PHILOSOPHICAL POETS

INTRODUCTION

THE sole advantage in possessing great works of literature
lies in what they can help us to become. In themselves, as
feats performed by their authors, they would have forfeited
none of their truth or greatness if they had perished before
our day. We can neither take away nor add to their past
value or inherent dignity. It is only they, in so far as they
are appropriate food and not poison for us, that can add to
the present value and dignity of our minds. Foreign classics
have to be retranslated and reinterpreted for each generation, to render their old naturalness in a natural way, and
keep their perennial humanity living and capable of assimilation. Even native classics have to be reapprehended by every
reader. It is this continual digestion of the substance supplied by the past that alone renders the insights of the past
still potent in the present and for the future. Living criticism,
genuine appreciation, is the interest we draw from year to
year on the unrecoverable capital of human genius.

Regarded from this point of view, as substances to be
digested, the poetic remains of Lucretius, Dante, and Goethe
(though it is his *Faust* only that I shall speak of) afford
rather a varied feast. In their doctrine and genius they may
seem to be too much opposed to be at all convergent or
combinable in their wisdom. Some, who know and care for
one, perhaps, of these poets, may be disposed to doubt
whether they have anything vital to learn from the other
two. Yet it is as a pupil—I hope a discriminating pupil—

of each in turn that I mean to speak; and I venture to maintain that in what makes them great they are compatible;
that without any vagueness or doubleness in one's criterion
of taste one may admire enthusiastically the poetry of each
in turn; and that one may accept the essential philosophy, the
positive intuition, of each, without lack of definition or system in one's own thinking.

Indeed, the diversity of these three poets passes, if I may
use the Hegelian dialect, into a unity of a higher kind. Each
is typical of an age. Taken together they sum up all European philosophy. Lucretius adopts the most radical and the
most correct of those cosmological systems which the genius
of early Greece had devised. He sees the world to be one
great edifice, one great machine, all its parts reacting upon
one another, and growing out of one another in obedience to
a general pervasive process or life. His poem describes the
nature, that is, the birth and composition, of all things. It
shows how they are compounded out of elements, and how
these elements, which he thinks are atoms in perpetual motion, are being constantly redistributed, so that old things
perish and new things arise. Into this view of the world he
fits a view of human life as it ought to be led under such
conditions. His materialism is completed by an aspiration
towards freedom and quietness of spirit. Allowed to look
once upon the wonderful spectacle, which is to repeat itself
in the world for ever, we should look and admire, for to-
morrow we die; we should eat, drink, and be merry, but
moderately and with much art, lest we die miserably, and die
today.

This is one complete system of philosophy,—materialism
in natural science, humanism in ethics. Such was the gist of
all Greek philosophy before Socrates, of that philosophy
which was truly Hellenic and corresponded with the movement which produced Greek manners, Greek government,
and Greek art—a movement towards simplicity, autonomy,
and reasonableness in everything, from dress to religion.

Such is the gist also of what may be called the philosophy of the Renaissance, the reassertion of science and liberty in the modern world, by Bacon, by Spinoza, by the whole contemporary school that looks to science for its view of the facts, and to the happiness of men on earth for its ideal. The system is called naturalism; and of this Lucretius is the unrivalled poet.

Skip a thousand years and more, and a contrasting spectacle is before us. All minds, all institutions, are dominated by a religion that represents the soul as a pilgrim upon earth; the world is fallen and subject to the devil; pain and poverty are considered normal, happiness impossible here and to be hoped for only in a future life, provided the snares and pleasures of the present life have not entrapped us. Meantime a sort of Jacob's ladder stretches from the stone on which the wayfarer lays his head into the heaven he hopes for; and the angels he sees ascending and descending upon it are beautiful stories, wonderful theories, and comforting rites. Through these he partakes, even on earth, of what will be his heavenly existence. He partly understands his destiny; his own history and that of the world are transfigured before him and, without ceasing to be sad, become beautiful. The raptures of a perfect conformity with the will of God, and of union with Him, overtake him in his prayers. This is supernaturalism, a system represented in Christendom chiefly by the Catholic Church, but adopted also by the later pagans, and widespread in Asia from remote antiquity down to the present time. Little as the momentary temper of Europe and America may now incline to such a view, it is always possible for the individual, or for the race, to return to it. Its sources are in the solitude of the spirit and in the disparity, or the opposition, between what the spirit feels it is fitted to do, and what, in this world, it is condemned to waste itself upon. The unmatched poet of this supernaturalism is Dante.

Skip again some five hundred years, and there is another change of scene. The Teutonic races that had previously conquered Europe have begun to dominate and understand themselves. They have become Protestants, or protesters against the Roman world. An infinite fountain of life seems to be unlocked within their bosom. They turn successively to the Bible, to learning, to patriotism, to industry, for new objects to love and fresh worlds to conquer; but they have too much vitality, or too little maturity, to rest in any of these things. A demon drives them on; and this demon, divine and immortal in its apparent waywardness, is their inmost self. It is their insatiable will, their radical courage. Nay, though this be hard saying to the uninitiated, their will is the creator of all those objects by which it is sometimes amused, and sometimes baffled, but never tamed. Their will summons all opportunities and dangers out of nothing to feed its appetite for action; and in that ideal function lies their sole reality. Once attained, things are transcended. Like the episodes of a spent dream, they are to be smiled at and forgotten; the spirit that feigned and discarded them remains always strong and undefiled; it aches for new conquests over new fictions. This is romanticism. It is an attitude often found in English poetry, and characteristic of German philosophy. It was adopted by Emerson and ought to be sympathetic to Americans; for it expresses the self-trust of world-building youth, and mystical faith in will and action. The greatest monument to this romanticism is Goethe's *Faust*.

Can it be an accident that the most adequate and probably the most lasting exposition of these three schools of philosophy should have been made by poets? Are poets, at heart, in search of a philosophy? Or is philosophy, in the end, nothing but poetry? Let us consider the situation.

If we think of philosophy as an investigation into truth, or as reasoning upon truths supposed to be discovered, there is nothing in philosophy akin to poetry. There is nothing poetic about the works of Epicurus, or St. Thomas Aquinas, or Kant; they are leafless forests. In Lucretius and in Dante

themselves we find passages where nothing is poetical except
the metre, or some incidental ornament. In such passages the
form of poetry is thrown over the substance of prose, as
Lucretius himself confesses where he says: "As when physi-
cians would contrive to administer loathsome wormwood to
little boys they first moisten the rim of the cup round about
with sweet and golden honey, that the children's unsuspect-
ing youth may be beguiled—to the lips, but no further—
while they drink down the bitter potion, by deception not
betrayed, but rather by that stratagem made whole and restored; . . . so I have willed to set forth our doctrine before thee in sweet-sounding Pierian song, and to smear it,
as it were, with the Muses' honey."*

But poetry cannot be spread upon things like butter; it
must play upon them like light, and be the medium through
which we see them. Lucretius does himself an injustice. If
his philosophy had been wormwood to him, he could not have
said, as he does just before this passage: "Like a sharp blow
of the thyrsus, a great hope of praise vibrates through my
heart and fills my breast with tender love of the Muses,
whereby now, instinct with flowering fancy, I traverse path-
less haunts of the Pierides, by no man's foot trodden before.
It is joy to reach undefiled fountains and quaff; it is joy to
gather fresh flowers and weave a matchless crown for my
head of those bays with which never yet the Muses veiled
the brow of any man; first, in that I teach sublime truths

*Lucretius, I. 936-47:
> Veluti pueris absinthia tetra medentes
> Cum dare conantur, prius oras pocula circum
> Contingunt mellis dulci flavoque liquore,
> Ut puerorum aetas improvida ludificetur
> Labrorum tenus, interea perpotet amarum
> Absinthi laticem, deceptaque non capiatur,
> Sed potius tali pacto recreata valescat:
> Sic ego nunc . . . volui tibi suaviloquenti
> Carmine Pierio rationem exponere nostram,
> Et quasi musaeo dulci contingere melle.

and come to free the soul from the strangling knots of superstition; then, in that on so dark a theme I pour forth so clear a song, suffusing all with poetic beauty, . . . if haply by such means I might keep thy mind intent upon my verses, until thine eye fathoms the whole structure of nature, and the fixed form that makes it beautiful."†

Here, I think, we have the solution to our doubt. The reasonings and investigations of philosophy are arduous, and if poetry is to be linked with them, it can be artificially only, and with a bad grace. But the vision of philosophy is sublime. The order it reveals in the world is something beautiful, tragic, sympathetic to the mind, and just what every poet, on a small or a large scale, is always trying to catch.

In philosophy itself investigation and reasoning are only preparatory and servile parts, means to an end. They terminate in insight, or what in the noblest sense of the word may be called *theory*, θεωρία,—a steady contemplation of all things in their order and worth. Such contemplation is imaginative. No one can reach it who has not enlarged his mind and tamed his heart. A philosopher who attains it is, for the moment, a poet; and a poet who turns his practised

†Lucretius, I. 922-34, 948-50:

Acri

Percussit thyrso laudis spes magna meum cor
Et simul incussit suavem mi in pectus amorem
Musarum, quo nunc instinctus mente vigenti
Avia Pieridum peragro loca nullius ante
Trita solo: iuvat integros accedere fontes,
Atque haurire; iuvatque novos decerpere flores,
Insignemque meo capiti petere inde coronam,
Unde prius nulli velarint tempora musae.
Primum, quod magnis doceo de rebus, et artis
Religionum animum nodis exsolvere pergo:
Deinde, quod obscura de re tam lucida pango
Carmina, musaeo contingens cuncta lepore. . . .
Si tibi forte animum tali ratione tenere
Versibus in nostris possem, dum perspicis omnem
Naturam rerum, qua constet compta figura.

and passionate imagination on the order of all things, or on anything in the light of the whole, is for that moment a philosopher.

Nevertheless, even if we grant that the philosopher, in his best moments, is a poet, we may suspect that the poet has his worst moments when he tries to be a philosopher, or rather, when he succeeds in being one. Philosophy is something reasoned and heavy; poetry something winged, flashing, inspired. Take almost any longish poem, and the parts of it are better than the whole. A poet is able to put together a few words, a cadence or two, a single interesting image. He renders in that way some moment of comparatively high tension, of comparatively keen sentiment. But at the next moment the tension is relaxed, the sentiment has faded, and what succeeds is usually incongruous with what went before, or at least inferior. The thought drifts away from what it had started to be. It is lost in the sands of versification. As man is now constituted, to be brief is almost a condition of being inspired.

Shall we say, then,—and I now broach an idea by which I set some store—that poetry is essentially short-winded, that what is poetic is necessarily intermittent in the writings of poets, that only the fleeting moment, the mood, the episode, can be rapturously felt, or rapturously rendered, while life as a whole, history, character, and destiny are objects unfit for imagination to dwell on, and repellent to poetic art? I cannot think so. If it be a fact, as it often is, that we find little things pleasing and great things arid and formless, and if we are better poets in a line than in an epic, that is simply due to lack of faculty on our part, lack of imagination and memory, and above all to lack of discipline.

This might be shown, I think, by psychological analysis, if we cared to rely on something so abstract and so debatable. For in what does the short-winded poet himself excel the common unimaginative person who talks or who stares? Is it that he thinks even less? Rather, I suppose, in that he feels more; in that his moment of intuition, though fleeting, has a vision, a scope, a symbolic something about it that renders it deep and expressive. Intensity, even momentary intensity, if it can be expressed at all, comports fullness and suggestion compressed into that intense moment. Yes, everything that comes to us at all must come to us at some time or other. It is always the fleeting moment in which we live. To this fleeting moment the philosopher, as well as the poet, is actually confined. Each must enrich it with his endless vistas, vistas necessarily focussed, if they are to be disclosed at all, in the eye of the observer, here and now. What makes the difference between a moment of poetic insight and a vulgar moment is that the passions of the poetic moment have more perspective. Even the short-winded poet selects his words so that they have a magic momentum in them which carries us, we know not how, to mountain-tops of intuition. Is not the poetic quality of phrases and images due to their concentrating and liberating the confused promptings left in us by a long experience? When we feel the poetic thrill, is it not that we find sweep in the concise and depth in the clear, as we might find all the lights of the sea in the water of a jewel? And what is a philosophic thought but such an epitome?

If a short passage is poetical because it is pregnant with suggestion of a few things, which stretches our attention and makes us rapt and serious, how much more poetical ought a vision to be which was pregnant with all we care for? Focus a little experience, give some scope and depth to your feeling, and it grows imaginative; give it more scope and more depth, focus all experience within it, make it a philosopher's vision of the world, and it will grow imaginative in a superlative degree, and be supremely poetical. The difficulty, after having the experience to symbolise, lies only in having enough imagination to hold and suspend it in a thought; and further to give this thought such verbal expression that others may be able to decipher it, and to be stirred by it as by a wind of suggestion sweeping the whole forest of their memories.

the perfect beauty of soul that here and there may shine through it. Hamlet is the classic version of this imprisoned spirit; the skylark seems a symbol of what it would be in its freedom.

Poor larks! Is the proportion of dull matter in their bodies, I wonder, really less than in ours? Must they not find food and rear their young? Must they not in their measure work, watch, and tremble? Cold, hunger, and disease probably beset them more often and more bitterly than they do most of us. But we think of them selfishly, as of actors on the stage, only in the character they wear when they attract our attention. As we walk through the fields we stop to watch and to listen to them performing in the sky, and never think of their home troubles; which they, too, seem for the moment to have eluded; at least they have energy and time enough left over from those troubles for all this luxury of song. It is this glorious if temporary emancipation, this absolute defiant emphasis laid with so much sweetness on the inner life that the poet in every nice Englishman loves in the lark; it seems to reveal a brother-spirit more fortunate than oneself, almost a master and a guide.

Larks made even Shelley envious, although no man ever had less reason to envy them for their gift, either in its rapture or in its abstraction. Even the outer circumstances of Shelley's life were very favourable to inspiration and left him free to warble as much and as ardently as he chose; but perhaps he was somewhat deceived by the pathos of distance and fancied that in Nephelococcygia bad birds and wicked traditions were less tyrannous than in parliamentary England. He seems to have thought that human nature was not really made for puddings and port wine and hunting and elections, nor even for rollicking at universities and reading Greek, but only for innocent lyrical ecstacies and fiery convictions that nevertheless should somehow not render people covetous or jealous or cruelly disposed, nor constrain them to prevent any one from doing anything that any one might choose to do. Perhaps in truth the cloisters of Oxford and the streets of London are quite as propitious to the flights of which human nature is really capable as English fields are to the flights of larks; there is food in them for thought. But Shelley was impatient of human nature; he was horrified to find that society is a web of merciless ambitions and jealousies, mitigated by a quite subsidiary kindness; he forgot that human life is precarious and that its only weapon against circumstances, and against rival men, is intelligent action, intelligent war. The case is not otherwise with larks, on the fundamental earthly side of their existence; yet because their flight is bodily, because it is a festive outpouring of animal vitality, not of art or reflection, it suggests to us a total freedom of the inner man, a freedom which is impossible.

In the flight of larks, however, by a rare favour of fortune, all seems to be spontaneity, courage, and trust, even within this material sphere; nothing seems to be adjustment or observation. Their life in the air is a sort of intoxication of innocence and happiness in the blind pulses of existence. They are voices of the morning, young hearts seeking experience and not remembering it; when they seem to sob they are only catching their breath. They spring from the ground as impetuously as a rocket or the jet of a fountain, that bursts into a shower of sparks or of dewdrops; they circle as they rise, soaring through veil after veil of luminous air, or dropping from level to level. Their song is like the gurgling of little rills of water, perpetual through its delicate variations, and throbbing with a changed volume at every change in the breeze. Their rapture seems to us seraphic, not merely because it descends to us invariably from a luminous height, straining our eyes and necks—in itself a cheap sublimity—but rather because the lark sings so absolutely for the mad sake of singing. He is evidently making high holiday, spending his whole strength on something ultimate and utterly useless, a momentary entrancing pleasure which (being useless and ultimate) is very like an act of worship or of sacrifice. Sheer life in him has become pure. That is what we envy; that is what causes us, as we listen, to draw a deeper breath, and perhaps something like tears to come to our eyes. He seems so triumphantly to attain what all our labours end by missing, yet what alone would justify them: happiness, selfishness, a moment of life lived in the spirit. And we may be tempted to say to ourselves: Ah, if I could only forget, if I could cease to look before and after, if the pale cast of thought did not make a slave of me, as well as a coward!

Vital raptures such as the lark's are indeed not unknown even to man, and the suggestion of them powerfully allures the Englishman, being as he is a youth morally, still impelled to sport, still confident of carrying his whole self forward into some sort of heaven, whether in love, in politics, or in religion, without resigning to nature the things that are nature's nor hiding in God the things that are God's. Alas, a sad lesson awaits him, if he ever grows old enough to learn it. Vital raptures, unless long training or a miracle of adaptation has antecedently harmonised them with the whole orchestration of nature, necessarily come to a bad end. Dancing and singing and love and sport and religious enthusiasm are mighty ferments: happy he who vents them in their season. But if ever they are turned into duties, pumped up by force, or made the basis of anything serious, like morals or science, they become vicious. The wild breath of inspiration is gone which hurried them across the soul like a bright cloud. Inspiration, as we may read in Plato between the lines, inspiration is animal. It comes from the depths, from that hearth of Hestia, the Earth-Mother, which conservative pagans could not help venerating as divine. Only art and reason, however, are divine in a moral sense, not because they are less natural than inspiration (for the Earth-Mother with her seeds and vapours is the root of everything) but because they mount towards the ultimate heaven of order, beauty, intellectual light, and the achievement of eternal dignities. In that dimension of being even featherless bipeds can soar and sing with a good grace. But space is not their element; airmen, now that we have them, are only a new sort of sailor. They fly for the sake of danger and of high wages; it is a boyish art, with its romantic glamour soon tarnished, and only a material reward left for all its skill and hardships. The only sublimity possible to man is intellectual; when he would be sublime in any other dimension he is merely fatuous and bombastic. By intelligence, so far as he possesses it, a man sees things as they are, transcends his senses and his passions, uproots himself from his casual station in space and time, sees all things future as if they were past, and all things past as for ever present, at once condemns and forgives himself, renounces the world and loves it. Having this inner avenue open to divinity, he would be a fool to emulate the larks in their kind of ecstacy.

His wings are his intelligence; not that they bring ultimate success to his animal will, which must end in failure, but that they lift his failure itself into an atmosphere of laughter and light, where is his proper happiness. He cannot take his fine flight, like the lark, in the morning, in mad youth, in some irresponsible burst of vitality, because life is impatient to begin: that sort of thing is the fluttering of a caged bird, a rebellion against circumstances and against commonness which is a sign of spirit, but not spirit in its self-possession, not happiness nor a school of happiness. The thought which crowns life at its summit can accompany it throughout its course, and can reconcile us to its issue. Intelligence is Homeric in its pervasive light. It traces all the business of nature, eluding but not disturbing it, rendering it in fact more amiable than it is, and rescuing it from vanity.

Sense is like a lively child always at our elbow, saying, Look, look, what is that? Will is like an orator, indignantly demanding something different. History and fiction and religion are like poets, continually recomposing the facts into some tragic unity which is not in them. All these forms of mind are spiritual, and therefore materially superfluous and free; but their spirit is pious, it is attentive to its sources, and therefore seems to be care-laden and not so gloriously emancipated as the music of larks, or even of human musicians; yet thought is pure music in its essence, and only in its subject-matter retrospective and troubled about the facts. It must indeed be troubled about them, because in man spirit is not a mere truant, as it seems to be in the lark, but is a faithful chronicler of labour and wisdom. Man is hard-pressed; long truancies would be fatal to him. He is tempted to indulge in them—witness his languages and pyramids and mythologies; yet his margin of safety is comparatively narrow, and he cannot afford to spend such relatively prodigious amounts of energy in mere play as the lark does with a light heart and in the grand manner. There are words to man's music; he gives names to things; he tries to catch the rhythm of his own story, or to imagine it richer and more sublime than it is. His festivals are heavy with pathos; they mark the events on which his existence turns— harvests, funerals, redemptions, wooings, and wars. When he disregards all these tiresome things, he becomes a fop or a fanatic. There is no worthy transport for him except sane philosophy—a commentary, not a dream. His intelligence is most intense and triumphant when there is least waste in his life; for if hard thinking sometimes makes the head ache, it is because it comes hard, not because it is thinking; our fuddled brain grates and repeats itself in that it *can't* think. But if your business is in order, it requires no further pains to understand it. Intelligence is the flower of war and the flower of love. Both, in the end, are comprehension. How miraculously in our happy moments we understand, how far we jump, what masses of facts we dominate at a glance! There is no labour then, no friction or groping, no anxious jostling against what we do not know, but only joy in this intricate outspread humorous world, intoxication as ethereal as the lark's but more descriptive. If his song is raised above the world for a moment by its wantonness and idle rapture, ours is raised above it essentially by its scope. To look before and after is human; it would not be sincere nor manly in us not to take thought for the morrow and not to pine for what is not. We must start on that basis, with our human vitality (which is art) substituted for the vegetative prayerfulness of the lily, and our human scope (which is knowledge of the world) substituted for the outpourings of larks.

On this other plane we could easily be as happy as the larks, if we were as liberal. Men when they are civilised and at ease are liberal enough in their sports, and willing to *desipere in loco*, like kittens, but it is strange how barbarous and illiberal, at least in modern times, they have remained about thought. They wish to harness thought like a waterfall, or like the blind Samson, to work for them night and day, in the treadmill of their interests or of their orthodoxy. Fie upon their stupidity and upon their slavishness! They do not see that when nature, with much travail, brings something living to birth, inevitable thought is there already, and gratis, and cannot possibly be there before. The seething of the brain is indeed as pragmatic as the habit of singing and flying, which in its inception doubtless helped the larks to survive, as even the whiteness of the lily may have done through the ministry of insects which it attracted; but even material organs are bound to utility by a very loose tie. Nature does not shake off her baroque ornaments and her vices until they prove fatal, and she never thinks of the most obvious invention or pressing reform, until some complication brings her, she knows not how, to try the experiment. Nature, having no ulterior purpose, has no need of parsimony or haste or simplicity. Much less need she be niggardly of spirit, which lays no tax upon her, and consumes no energy, but laughs aloud, a marvel and a mystery to her, in her very heart. All animal functions, whether helpful or wasteful, have this fourth dimension in the realm of spirit—the joy, or the pain, or the beauty that may be found in them. Spirit loads with a lyric intensity the flying moment in which it lives. It actually paints the lily and casts a perfume on the violet; it turns into vivid presences a thousand forms which, until its flame lighted them up, were merged in the passive order and truth of things, like the charms of Lucy by the springs of Dove, before Words-worth discovered them. The smile of nature is not ponderable; and the changing harmonies of nature, out of which spirit springs, are like the conjunctions or eclipses of planets, facts obvious enough to sense in their specious simplicity, yet materially only momentary position of transit for way-farers bound each on his own errand. The songs of larks are like shooting stars that drop downwards and vanish; human intelligence is a part of the steadier music of the spheres.

XXVIII

Society and Solitude

O solitudo, sola beatitudo, Saint Bernard said; but might he not have said just as well, *O societas, sola felicitas*? Just as truly, I think; because when a man says that the only happiness is this or that, he is like a lover saying that Mary Jane is the one woman in the world. She may be truly the one woman for him, though even that is not probable; but he cannot mean to assert that she is the only woman living, nor to deny that each of the others might be the one woman for somebody. Now, when a Hegelian philosopher, contra-dicting Saint Bernard, says that society is his be-all and end-all, that he himself is nothing but an invisible point at which relations cross, and that if you removed from him his connection with Hegel, with his university, his church, his

wife, and his publishers, there would be nothing left, or at
best a name and a peg to hang a gown on, far be it from
me to revise his own analysis of his nature; society may be
the only felicity and the only reality for him. But that cannot annul the judgment of Saint Bernard. He had a great
mind and a great heart, and he knew society well; at least,
he accepted the verdict which antiquity had passed on
society, after a very long, brilliant, and hearty experience of
it; and he knew the religious life and solitude as well; and
I can't help thinking that he, too, must have been right in
his self-knowledge, and that solitude must have been the
only happiness for him.

Nevertheless, the matter is not limited to this confronting
of divers honest judgments, or confessions of moral experience. The natures expressed in these judgments have a long
history, and are on different levels; the one may be derived
from the other. Thus it is evident that the beatific solitude
of Saint Bernard was filled with a kind of society; he devoted it to communion with the Trinity, or to composing
fervent compliments to the Virgin Mary. It was only the
society to be found in inns and hovels, in castles, sacristies,
and refectories that he thought it happiness to avoid. That
the wilderness to which hermits flee must be peopled by their
fancy, could have been foreseen by any observer of human
nature. Tormenting demons or ministering angels must
needs appear, because man is rooted in society and his instincts are addressed to it; for the first nine months, or even
years, of his existence he is a parasite; and scarcely are these
parental bonds a little relaxed, when he instinctively forms
other ties, that turn him into a husband and father, and keep
him such all his days. If ever he finds happiness in solitude,
it can only be by lavishing on objects of his imagination the
attentions which his social functions require that he should
lavish on something. Without exercising these faculties
somehow his nature would be paralysed; there would be no
fuel to feed a spiritual flame. All Saint Bernard could mean,

then, is that happiness lies in this substitution of an ideal for a natural society, in converse with thoughts rather than with things. Such a substitution is normal, and a mark of moral vigour; we must not be misled into comparing it with a love of dolls or of lap dogs. Dolls are not impersonal, and lap dogs are not ideas; they are only less rebellious specimens of the genus thing; they are more portable idols. To substitute the society of ideas for that of things is simply to live in the mind; it is to survey the world of existences in its truth and beauty rather than in its personal perspectives, or with practical urgency. It is the sole path to happiness for the intellectual man, because the intellectual man cannot be satisfied with a world of perpetual change, defeat, and imperfection. It is the path trodden by ancient philosophers and modern saints or poets; not, of course, by modern writers on philosophy (except Spinoza), because these have not been philosophers in the vital sense; they have practised no spiritual discipline, suffered no change of heart, but lived on exactly like other professors, and exerted themselves to prove the existence of a God favourable to their own desires, instead of searching for the God that happens to exist. Certainly this path, in its beginnings, is arduous, and leaves the natural man somewhat spare and haggard; he seems to himself to have fasted for forty days and forty nights, and the world regards his way of living afterwards as rather ghostly and poor. But he usually congratulates himself upon it in the end; and of those who persevere some become saints and some poets and some philosophers.

Yet why, we may ask, should happiness be found exclusively in this ideal society where none intrudes? If the intellectual man cannot lay his treasures in a world of change, the natural man can perfectly well satisfy his instincts within it; and why shouldn't the two live amicably together in a house of two stories? I can see no essential reason; but historically natural society long ago proved a moral failure. It could not harmonise nor decently satisfy even the instincts on which it rests. Hence the philosophers have felt bound not only to build themselves a superstructure but to quit the ground floor—materially, if possible, by leading a monastic life, religiously in any case by not expecting to find much except weeping and wailing in this vale of tears. We may tax this despair with being premature, and call such a flight into an imaginary world a desperate expedient; at any time the attempts of the natural man to live his comic life happily may be renewed, and may succeed. Solitude peopled with ideas might still remain to employ the mind; but it would not be the only beatitude.

Yet the insecurity of natural society runs deeper, for natural society itself is an expedient and a sort of refuge of despair. It, too, in its inception, seemed a sacrifice and a constraint. The primitive soul hates order and the happiness founded on order. The barbarous soul hates justice and peace. The belly is always rebelling against the members. The belly was once all in all; it was a single cell floating deliciously in a warm liquid; it had no outer organs; it thought it didn't need them. It vegetated in peace; no noises, no alarms, no lusts, no nonsense. Ah, veritably solitude was blessedness then! But it was a spacious solitude and a precarious blessedness, resting on ignorance. The warm liquid might cool, or might dry up; it might breed all sorts of enemies; presently heaven might crack and the cell be cleft in two. Happy the hooded microbe that put forth feelers in time, and awoke to its social or unsocial environment! I am not sure that, beneath the love of ideal society, there was not in Saint Bernard a lingering love of primeval peace, of seminal slumber; that he did not yearn for the cell biological as well as for the cell monastic. Life, mere living, is a profound ideal, pregnant with the memory of a possible happiness, the happiness of protoplasm; and the advocate of moral society must not reckon without his host. He has a rebellious material in hand; his very atom is instinct with a life of its own which it may reassert, upsetting his calcu-

lations and destroying his organic systems. Only the physical failure of solitude drove the spirit at first into society,
as the moral failure of society may drive it later into solitude
again. If any one said, then, that happiness lies only in
society, his maxim would be no less sincere and solid than
Saint Bernard's, but it would not be so profound. For beneath natural society, in the heart of each of its members,
there is always an intense and jealous solitude, the sleep of
elemental life which can never be wholly broken; and above
natural society there is always another solitude—a placid
ethereal wilderness, the heaven of ideas—beckoning the
mind.

XXXVIII

The Mask of the Philosopher

AMONGST tragic masks may be counted all systems of philosophy and religion. So long as they are still plastic in the
mind of their creator, they seem to him to wear the very
lineaments of nature. He cannot distinguish the comic cast
of his own thought; yet inevitably it shows the hue and features of his race; it has its curious idiom and constitutional
grammar, its quite personal rhetoric, its ridiculous igno-
rances and incapacities, and when his work is finished and
its expression set, and other people behold it, it becomes
under his name one of the stock masks or *dramatis personae*
of the moral world. In it every wrinkle of his soul is eter-
nalised, its old dead passion persisted in, its open mouth,
always with the same *rictus*, bawling one deaf thought for
ever. Even to himself, if he could have seen his mind at a
distance, it would have appeared limited and foreign, as to
an old man the verses of his youth, or like one's own figure
seen unexpectedly in a mirror and mistaken at first for another person. His own system, as much as those of others,

would have seemed to him a mask for the truth, partial, over-emphatic, exaggerating one feature and distorting another, and above all severed from the context of nature, as a picture in a frame, where much may be shown with a wonderfully distilled beauty, yet without its substance, and without its changeful setting in the moving world. Yet this fate is in part a favour. A system, like a tell-tale glass, may reveal by a trick of reflection many a fact going on behind one's back. By it the eye of the mind travels where experience cannot penetrate; it turns into a spectacle what was never open to sight, and it disentangles things seen from the personal accidents of vision. The mask is greater than the man. In isolating what was important and pertinent in his thoughts, it rescues his spirit from the contamination of all alien dyes, and bequeaths it to posterity such as it would have wished to be.

XLIV

John Bull and His Philosophers

ENGLAND has been curiously served by her philosophers. Personally and in their first intention they have usually been sturdy Britons; but their scope has seldom been equal to their sagacity in particular matters, they have not divined the ultimate drift of their ideas, and they have often ended by adopting, a little blankly and doggedly, some foreign or fantastic system, apparently most expressive of John Bull. Nevertheless the exotic tendency in so many British philosophers, as in so many disaffected British poets, is itself a mark of British character. The crust of convention has solidified too soon, and the suppressed fires issue in little erratic streams that seem of an alien substance. In speculation as in other things the Englishman trusts his inner man; his impulse is to soliloquise even in science. At the same time his inner man dislikes to be too articulate; he is soon at a stand in direct self-expression; and as a poet may take to describing nature or Italian passions, so a philosopher may pick up some alien doctrine that comes to hand, and that seems friendly to his mind; not understanding it very well, perhaps, in his native quality, but making it a living companion in his own lucubrations, and a symbol for what remains hidden but revered in his breast. In this way the Bible or Plato may serve him to found sects upon exclusively expressing his own feelings; or remaining a plain Englishman to all practical purposes, he may become, for his greater private satisfaction, a revolutionary atheist, a spiritualist, a Catholic, or a Buddhist. In such strange allegiances something may be due to wayward learning, or to genuine plasticity of mind and power to feel as very different souls have felt in other climes; but a part is unmistakable helplessness and dire need, and a part, perhaps, affectation.

When his own resources fail, however, the most obvious easement and support for the English inner man are the classical and Anglican traditions he has been bred in, when these are not too nicely defined nor too slavishly followed. Most characteristic is John Bull the theologian, instinct with heresy and practising compromise; but the rationalistic John Bull is very like him in his alternative way of securing the same supreme object of thinking what he likes to think. In both cases he embraces his opinions much more because they are wholesome and important than because they are certain or clear. Opinions, he feels, should be summary and safe; they should express the lessons of experience.

As he conceives it at first, experience does not merely exist, it teaches. In a sporadic fashion it yields sound satisfactions, clear warnings, plain facts. It admonishes him to trust his senses, the reports of reputable travellers and naturalists, Christianity, and the British constitution, all when duly revised; and on the other hand to shun popery, scholastic quibbles, absolutism, and revolution. But evidently

experience could never teach him these things if his inner
man did not contribute its decided cravings and aversions.
His inner man detests dictation and loves opportunity; in
ideas it prefers timeliness to finality. Therefore, when his
philosophers come upon the scene they cannot appeal to him
by coercive proofs, nor by the impressive architecture of
their systems, nor by disentangling and setting clearly before
him any ultimate ideal. To win his ear they must rather
drive his current convictions home, nearer to their source in
himself; they must invite him to concentrate his empiricism.
For instance, he trusts his senses; and the philosophers can
deeply interest him if they ask him what, precisely, his senses
vouch for. Is it external things? But can he actually see
anything except colours, or touch anything except resist-
ances? Can he feel anything except his own sensations? By
appealing to his honesty, the sophists catch him in a trap,
and he changes his mind in trying to utter it. It will appear
presently, as he pursues his inquiry, that he has no knowledge of those external things and events which he had been
so sure of; they were mere empty notions, and his genuine
experience contained nothing but the pulses of his inner
life, changes in his ideas and vital temperature, which an
accurate autobiography might record. And the more scrupulously he considers these pulses of his inner life the less and
less will he find in them. He and his whole experience will
soon be reduced to a series of sensations in single file, with
nothing behind them. In reality even this is too much. Although the inertia of psychological conventions and the
romantic habit of self-consciousness have kept him from perceiving it, even to this day, yet the fact that a sensation is
occurring is not revealed by that sensation itself; no date,
place, or relation to a mind is included in its deliverance, and
no relation to anything before or beyond; so that the bare
datum of sensation is an æsthetic being, not a mental one;
an ideal term, not an event; a universal essence, not a particular fact; and immersion in sense or in absolute immediate

experience, when animal faith and intelligence are taken away from it, would remove from us every vestige of the notion that anything exists or that anything happens. But without pushing analysis so far, the empirical philosophers left John Bull, when he listened to them, singularly bereft of those comfortable impedimenta with which he had expected to travel through life—without a body, without an environment, without a ground, or any natural perfection of destiny, for his moral being. He had loved exploration, and had looked forward with the flush of confidence to the knowledge and power which his discoveries would bring him; but now he saw that all discoveries were incalculable, arbitrary, and provisional, since they were not truly discoveries, but only developments.

Here was an odd transformation. The self-educated merchants and indignant reformers who, thumping their desks dogmatically, had appealed so roundly to the evidence of their senses, little expected that their philosophy was directed to turning them in the end into inarticulate sensualists, rapt in omphalic contemplation of their states of mind. Some academic idealists, disliking this result, which cast a slur on the pre-eminence of spirituality and learning, and yet not being willing or able to give up the method by which that result had been reached, sought to push the inquiry further, and to come out of the wood on quite the other side. My sensations, they said, since I can now survey the whole series they form, must all exist together in my present apprehension; and as I cannot know them except in this single and present glance, they never can have existed out of it; so that I am not really a series of sensations, but only the idea that I am a series of sensations; in other words, I have become a single sensation instead of many. To make this clearer the same philosophers added that this single sensation or thought, which is what I really am, is also God. Experience now turned out not to be anything that goes on or happens or is endured; it is the theme of an immutable divine contemplation and divine satisfaction. I am God in so far as I think and approve; but the chequered experience which I supposed myself to be undergoing is merely imputed to myself by God and me in our thinking.

This second conclusion, like the first, has its value for some temperaments. It brings suddenly before us, as if it were an accomplished fact, the innate ideal of the intellect: to see the changing aspects of all things from above, in their true eternal relations. But this ideal, too, is utterly disparate from that practical experience and prevision which John Bull prizes so highly and thinks he possesses; indeed, the sublimity of this view lies precisely in its tendency to freeze and submerge all experience, transmuting hard facts and anxious events into painted ships upon a painted ocean, and for our stumbling and unfinished progress substituting a bound volume of travels.

What false step could bring British philosophy, in its gropings, to conclusions so un-English that even those who feel compelled to propose them do so shamefacedly, with many euphemisms and convenient confusions, or even fail altogether to understand the tremendous paradoxes they are repeating? It was a false step at which Hobbes halted, which Locke took unsuspectingly, and which sent Berkeley and Hume head over heels: the assumption that facts are known immediately. In reality none of the facts which the sturdy Briton feels that he knows—and they are the true facts of nature and of moral life—would be known to him if he were without tentative intelligence and instinctive animal faith; indeed, without these the senses would have no virtue and would inform us of nothing; and cows would not see grass nor horses hay, but only green or yellow patches, like rapt empirical philosophers. When Hobbes said that no discourse whatsoever can end in absolute knowledge of fact, he uttered a great truth, but he implied a great error, since he implied that sense—meaning the senseless sensations of idiots —could give such knowledge; whereas the absolute datum in sense is just as ideal, and just as little a fact, as the deliverance of the most theoretical discourse; and absolute knowledge—if we call such apprehension knowledge—can seize only some æsthetic or logical term, without any given date, place, or connection in experience. Empiricism in the end must substitute these ideal essences, on the ground that they are the only data, for the facts of nature—facts which animal reactions and the beliefs expressing them are requisite to discover, and which science defines by the cumulative use of reason. In making this substitution empiricism passes against its will into sensualism or idealism. Then John Bull and his philosophers part company: he sticks manfully to his confused conventional opinions, which after all give him a very tolerable knowledge of the facts; while they go digging for an absolute knowledge of fact which is impossible, in an intuitive cloudland where there are only æsthetic essences. Hence the bankruptcy of their enterprise. Immediate data are the counters of experience, but they are the money of empiricism.

XLVIII

The Progress of Philosophy

THIS war will kill the belief in progress, and it was high time. Progress is often a fact: granted a definite end to be achieved, we may sometimes observe a continuous approach towards achieving it, as for instance towards cutting off a leg neatly when it has been smashed; and such progress is to be desired in all human arts. But *belief* in progress, like belief in fate or in the number three, is a sheer superstition, a mad notion that because some idea—here the idea of continuous change for the better—has been realised somewhere, that idea was a power which realised itself there fatally, and which must be secretly realising itself everywhere else, even

where the facts contradict it. Nor is belief in progress identical with belief in Providence, or even compatible with it.
Providence would not have begun wrong in order to correct
itself; and in works which are essentially progressive, like a
story, the beginning is not worse than the end, if the artist
is competent.

What true progress is, and how it is usually qualified by
all sorts of backsliding, and by incompatible movements in
contrary directions, is well illustrated by the history of philosophy. There has been progress in it; if we start with the
first birth of intelligence and assume that the end pursued is
to understand the world, the progress has been immense.
We do not understand the world yet; but we have formed
many hypotheses about it corroborated by experience, we
are in possession of many arts which involve true knowledge,
and we have collated and criticised—especially during the
last century—a great number of speculations which though
unverified or unverifiable, reveal the problems and the possibilities in the case; so that I think a philosopher in our day
has no excuse for being so utterly deceived in various important matters as the best philosophers formerly were
through no fault of theirs, because they were misled by a
local tradition, and inevitably cut off from the traditions of
other ages and races. Nevertheless the progress of philosophy
has not been of such a sort that the latest philosophers are
the best: it is quite the other way. Philosophy in this respect
is like poetry. There is progress in that new poets arise with
new gifts, and the fund of transmitted poetry is enriched;
but Homer, the first poet amongst the Greeks, was also the
best, and so Dante in Italy, and Shakespeare in England.
When a civilisation and a language take shape they have a
wonderful vitality, and their first-fruits are some love-child,
some incomparable creature in whom the whole genius of
the young race bursts forth uncontaminated and untrammelled. What follows is more valuable in this respect or in
that; it renders fitly the partial feelings and varying fashions

of a long decadence; but nothing, so long as that language and that tradition last, can ever equal their first exuberance. Philosophy is not so tightly bound as poetry is to language and to local inspiration, but it has largely shared the same vicissitudes; and in each school of philosophy only the inventors and founders are of any consequence; the rest are hacks. Moreover, if we take each school as a whole, and compare it with the others, I think we may repeat the same observation: the first are the best. Those following have made very real improvements; they have discovered truths and methods before unknown; but instead of adding these (as they might have done) to the essential wisdom of their predecessors, they have proceeded like poets, each a newborn child in a magic world, abandoned to his fancy and his personal experience. Bent on some specific reform or wrapped up in some favourite notion, they have denied the obvious because other people had pointed it out; and the later we come down in the history of philosophy the less important philosophy becomes, and the less true in fundamental matters.

Suppose I arrange the works of the essential philosophers —leaving out secondary and transitional systems—in a bookcase of four shelves; on the top shelf (out of reach, since I can't read the language) I will place the Indians; on the next the Greek naturalists; and to remedy the unfortunate paucity of their remains, I will add here those free inquirers of the renaissance, leading to Spinoza, who after two thousand years picked up the thread of scientific speculation; and besides, all modern science: so that this shelf will run over into a whole library of what is not ordinarily called philosophy. On the third shelf I will put Platonism, including Aristotle, the Fathers, the Scholastics, and all honestly Christian theology; and on the last, modern or subjective philosophy in its entirety. I will leave lying on the table, as of doubtful destination, the works of my contemporaries. There is much life in some of them. I like their watercolour sketches of self-consciousness, their rebellious egotisms, their fervid reforms of phraseology, their peep-holes through which some very small part of things may be seen very clearly: they have lively wits, but they seem to me like children playing blind-man's buff; they are keenly excited at not knowing where they are. They are really here, in the common natural world, where there is nothing in particular to threaten or to allure them; and they have only to remove their philosophical bandages in order to perceive it.

What sort of a world this is—I will not say in itself, but in respect to us—can be perceived almost at once by any candid spirit, and the Indians readily perceived it. They saw that substance is infinite, out of scale with our sensuous images and (except in the little vortex that makes us up) out of sympathy with our endeavours; and that spirit in us nevertheless can hold its own, because salvation lies in finding joy in the truth, not in rendering fortune propitious, by some miracle, to our animal interests. The spirit is at home in the infinite, and morally independent of all the accidents of existence: nothing that nature can produce outruns its potential scope, its desire to know the truth; and its disinterestedness renders it free, free especially from any concern about its own existence. It does not deem it the part of piety to deny the fugitive, impotent, and fantastic nature of human life. It knows that the thoughts of man and his works, however great or delightful when measured by the human scale, are but the faintest shimmer on the surface of being. On the ruin of humanistic illusions (such as make up the religious philosophy of the West) it knows how to establish a tender morality and a sublime religion.

Indian wisdom, intent on the infinity and unity of substance and on the vanity of human life, neglected two inquiries which are nevertheless of the greatest interest to the spirit, so long as this vain life endures. The Indians did not study the movement and mechanism of nature: they had no science. Their poets, in a sort of spectacular physics, were content to paint vividly the images of sense, conscious of their fugitive charm, and of their monstrous and delirious diversity. They also neglected the art of rational conduct in this world; the refinements of their moral discipline were all mystical; they were determined by watching the movements of inner experience, and allowing the fancy to distinguish its objects and its stages. They thought the spirit could liberate itself by thinking, as by thinking it seemed to have entangled itself in this mesh of dreams. But how could the spirit, if it had been free originally, ever have attached its fortunes to any lump of clay? Why should it be the sport of time and change and the vicissitudes of affairs? From the point of view of the spirit (which is that of the Indians) this question is absolutely insoluble; a fact which drives them to say that this entanglement is not "real," but only an illusion of being entangled. Certainly substance is not entangled, but persists and moves according to its nature; and if what exists besides substance—its aspects and the spirit in us that notes them —is not "real" because not substantial, then the unreal has the privilege, as Democritus pointed out, of existing as well as the real, and more obviously. But this subterfuge, of denying that appearance exists, because its existence is only the seeming of its objects, was inevitable in the Indian system, and dramatically right. The spirit, left to its own fond logic, remains perfectly ignorant of its natural ancestry and cannot imagine why it finds itself caught in the vice of existence, and hanging like Prometheus on a crag of Caucasus, or like Christ on the cross. The myth of reincarnation, whilst it meets certain moral demands, leaves the problem essentially untouched. Why should spirit have fallen in the first instance, or made any beginning in sin and illusion?

It would have been better, for the moral and religious purposes of these sages, to have observed and respected the prose facts, and admitted that each little spirit falls for the first time when the body is generated which it is to dwell in. It never, in fact, existed before; it is the spirit of that body.

Its transcendental prerogatives and its impersonal aims are by no means inconsistent with that humble fact: they seem inconsistent only to those who are ignorant of the life and fertility of nature, which breeds spirit as naturally as the lark sings. Aspiration to liberate spirit from absorption in finite existence is in danger of missing its way if it is not enlightened by a true theory of existence and of spirit; for it is utterly impossible to free the spirit materially, since it is the voice of matter, but by a proper hygiene it can be freed ideally, so that it ceases to be troubled by its sluggish instrument, or conscious of it. In these matters the Indians were the sport of the wildest fancy. They mistook their early poetry for a metaphysical revelation, and their philosophy was condemned to turn in the most dreary treadmill of commentaries and homilies, without one ray of criticism, or any revision of first principles. Nevertheless, all their mythology and scholasticism did not invalidate (as they did not in the Catholic church afterwards) the initial spirit insight on which their system rested. The spirit, viewed from within, is omnipresent and timeless, and must be spoken of as falling, or coming down, or entering (as Aristotle puts it) through the house door. Spirit calls itself a stranger, because it finds the world strange; and it finds the world strange because, being the spirit of a very high-strung and perilously organised animal, it is sensitive to many influences not harmonious with its own impulses, and has to beg its daily bread. Yet it is rich in resource; and it gives itself out for a traveller and tells marvellous lies about its supposed native land, where it was a prince and an omnipotent poet. These boasts serve the spirit as a declaration of independence, and a claim to immense superiority above the world. This independence, however, is really only the independence of ignorance, that must think and act at random; and the spirit would add sanity to its spirituality if it recognised the natural, precarious, and exquisite life of which it is the spirit.

Sanity, thy name is Greece. The Greek naturalists saw

(what it needs only sanity to see) that the infinite substance of things was instinct with a perpetual motion and rhythmic order which were its life, and that the spirit of man was a spark from that universal fire. They made ə magnificent beginning in understanding what the order of nature is, and what is the relation of its substance to its spirit. They were much nearer in their outlook and their wisdom to the Indians than we are apt to imagine. The Indians meant to be naturalists too; all serious philosophers must somehow make a naturalism of their chosen elements; only the Indians were carried away by an untutored imagination. The Greeks, for their part, also meant to be discerners of substance like the Indians, and sharers in the divine life. The object which they believed in and studied was precisely the same as that which the Indians felt to be breathing deeply around and within them: it was the infinite substance and life of things; all things not as they appear but as they truly are. This is the object which animals envisaged in their perceptions from the beginning. The sciences, and all honest speculation, only substitute more refined ideas for the images of sense, to be descriptions of the same objects which the images of sense reveal. The notion that the object of sense is the very image created in sensation, or is an idea constructed afterwards by the intellect, is an aberration of confused psychologists; the intellectual construction, like the sensuous image, is and is meant to be only a symbol for the substance, whatever it may be, which confronts the living being when he eats or looks or frames a scientific hypothesis. Natural things, in their un-discovered inner texture, are the only things-in-themselves, and the object of every practical perception is the thing-in-itself, whatever its nature may happen to be.

When we enlarge our thoughts, and take in the world, as it were, at a glance, the object does not become more meta-physical than when we take common things singly. The Greeks, too, looked up into the heavens and cried, "The All is one." It was just what the Indians had said, shutting their eyes and drinking in an infinite draught of nothing; but the outward glance, the docility to fact, in the Greeks made a new thought of it, and a true one. What was now discovered was the system of nature; the spirit was naturalised in its source; it was set like a young plant in its appropriate flower-pot, where it might wax and bloom. It did grow there, but not to its primeval size. These knowing Greeks were not saints and hermits, like the venerable Indians; they were mer-chants, sniffing travellers, curiosity-hunters, who turned pebbles over and culled herbs, breeders of animals, or wan-dering soothsayers with a monkey on their shoulder; and in naturalising the spirit they stultified it. Why should knowl-edge of the world make people worldly? It ought to do the exact opposite. The Indians had, in their way, a most pro-found and mature knowledge of the world; they knew per-fectly what it could yield to the spirit, and what it was worth. But lost in their inner experience they invented for nature what structure they chose, fantastically attenuating and in-flating it as in a dream. Apparently there is not energy enough in the human intellect to look both ways at once, and to study the world scientifically whilst living in it spiritually.

The Greeks in their sanity discovered not only the natural world but the art of living well in it. Besides physics they founded ethics and politics. But here again progress was prevented by the rejection or perversion of the greater thing in the interests of the lesser. Speculatively at least some just conception of the world we live in, and of our place and des-tiny there, is more important than the choice of a definite way of life; for animals and man have, quite legitimately, each his own habits and pleasures, but they all crawl under the same heaven, and if they think of it at all, they should not blaspheme against it. The Greek naturalists had conceived nature rightly; and their sentiments and maxims, whilst very properly diverse, had all of them a certain noble frankness in the presence of the infinite world, of which they begged no favours. It was precisely these personal sentiments and

maxims, the policy in the government of cities, that interested
the Greeks most; and the Sophists and Socrates affected to
care nothing about natural science, unless it could make their
pot boil. This utilitarianism was humorous in Socrates, and
in some of the Sophists unprincipled; but the habit of treating opinions about nature as rhetorical themes, or as more
or less edifying myths, had disastrous consequences for
philosophy. It created metaphysics. Metaphysics is not merely
speculative physics, in which natural science is extended
imaginatively in congruous ways, anticipating what might
some day be discovered. This is what the naturalists had
done, and their theories were simply physical or cosmological. But after Socrates a theory constructed by reasoning, in
terms of logic, ethics, and a sort of poetic propriety, was put
in the place of physics; the economy of the human mind was
projected into the universe; and nature, in the works of the
metaphysicians, held the mirror up to man. Human nature
and the human mind, which were thus made to rule the world,
are in reality a very small incident in it; they are proper to
one animal; they are things of yesterday and perhaps not of
to-morrow. This is nothing against them in their place, as it
is nothing against the daisy that it is humble, nor against
the spray of the sea that its flight is violent and brief. The
Platonic, British, and German schools of philosophy advance
our knowledge of ourselves; what a pity that they were not
content to cultivate their own gardens, where so many moral
fruits and psychological flowers might be made to grow, but
have insisted that their domestic vegetables are the signs of
the zodiac, and that the universe was made to illustrate their
horticulture!

Taken for what they really are, these humanistic philosophies express different sides of human nature. The best
(and earliest) is the Platonic, because the side of human
nature which it expresses and fosters is the spiritual side.
Platonic metaphysics projects into the universe the moral
progress of the soul. It is like a mountain lake, in which the

aspirations and passions of a civilised mind are reflected upside down; and a certain tremor and intensity is added to them in that narrower frame, which they would hardly have in the upper air. This system renders the life of the soul more unified and more beautiful than it would other-wise be. Everything becomes magical, and a sort of perpetual miracle of grace; the forms which things wear to the human mind are deputed to be their substance; the uses of life become its protecting gods; the categories of logic and of morals become celestial spheres enclosing the earth. A monstrous dream, if you take it for a description of nature; but a suitable allegory by which to illustrate the progress of the inner life: because those stages, or something like them, are really the stages of moral progress for the soul.

The British and German philosophies belong to an analytic phase of reflection, without spiritual discipline, and their value is merely psychological. Their subject-matter is human knowledge; and the titles of many of the chief works of this school confess that this is their only theme. Not moral life, much less the natural world, but simply the articulation of knowledge occupies them; and yet, by the hocus-pocus of metaphysics, they substitute this human experience for the whole universe in which it arises. The universe is to be nothing but a flux of perceptions, or a will positing an object, or a tendency to feign that there is a world. It would ill become me, a pupil of this philosophy, to deny its profundity. These are the heart-searchings of "a creature moving about in worlds not realised." It is a wonderful thing to spin out in soliloquy, out of some unfathomed creative instinct, the various phases of one's faith and sensibility, making an inventory of one's intellectual possessions, with some notes on their presumable or reported history. I love the lore of the moral antiquary; I love rummaging in the psychological curiosity shop. The charm of modern life is ambiguous; it lies in self-consciousness. Egotism has its tender developments; there is a sort of engaging purity in its perplexities and faithful labours. The German soul has a great volume, and Hamlet is heroic even in his impotence. When in this little glow-worm which we call man there is so much going on, what must not all nature contain in its immensity? Yet all these advances in analysis and in psychological self-knowledge, far from enriching the modern philosopher and giving him fresh hints for the interpretation of the great world, have been neutralised, under the guise of scepticism, by a total intellectual cramp or by a colossal folly. This thoughtful dog has dropped the substance he held in his mouth, to snatch at the reflection of it which his own mind gave him. It is wonderful with what a light heart, with what self-satisfaction and even boasts, the youngest children of the philosophical family jettison all their heirlooms. Fichte and Nietzsche, in their fervid arrogance, could hardly outdo the mental impoverishment of Berkeley and Hume in their levity: it had really been a sight for the gods to see one of these undergraduates driving matter out of the universe, whilst the other drove out spirit.

L

Reversion to Platonism

I HEAR that Oxford is reading Plotinus—a blessed change from Hegel. The pious mind is still in the age of mythology; science has confused its own lessons, for want of a philosopher who should understand them; and what matters, so long as the age of mythology lasts, is that the myths that occupy the fancy should be wise and beautiful, and should teach men to lay up their treasures in heaven. The philosophy of Plotinus does this, and does it magnificently. Like that of Plato and of Aristotle it is little more than a rhetorical inversion or perpetual metaphor, expressing the aim of life under the figure of a cosmos which is animate and which has already attained its perfection. Considering the hurried life which we are condemned to lead, and the shifting, symbolic ideas to which we are confined, it seems hardly worth while to quarrel with such inspired fabulists, or to carp at the cosmos dress in which they present their moralities. Gentle, secluded, scholastic England does well to platonise. It has never ceased to do so. In spite of the restiveness, sometimes, of barbarian blood, in spite of Hebraic religion and Germanic philosophy, the great classical tradition has always been seated here; and England has shared, even if with a little reserve and mistrust, in the ecclesiastical, courtly, military, and artistic heritage of Europe. A genuine child of the past, who is bred to knowledge of the world, and does not plunge into it greedily like a stranger, cannot worship the world; he cannot really be a snob. Those who have profited by a long life cannot possibly identify the divine life with the human. They will not be satisfied with a philosophy that is fundamentally worldly, that cannot lift up its heart except pragmatically, because the good things are hanging from above, or because the long way round by righteousness and the ten commandments may be the shortest cut to the promised land. Their love of wisdom will not be merely provisional, nor their piety a sort of idyllic interlude, penitent but hopeful, comforting itself with the thought that the sour grapes will soon be ripe, and oh, so delicious! They will not remember the flesh-pots of Egypt with an eternal regret, and the flesh-pots of Berlin and New York will not revive their appetite.

Spirit is not an instrument but a realisation, a fruition. At every stage, and wherever it peeps out through the interstices of existence, it is a contemplation of eternal things. Eternal things are not other material things by miracle existing for ever in another world; eternal things are the essences of all things here, when we consider what they are in themselves and not what, in the world of fortune, they may bring or take away from us personally. That is why piety and prayer are spiritual, when they cease to be magic operations or efforts of a celestial diplomacy: they lead us into the eternal world. Platonism is a great window in the same direction. It is well to open it afresh. I should not say of the typical Englishman, any more than of the typical Greek, that he was spiritual; both are healthy, and the spirit in them is not so developed as to sickly o'er their native hue with the pale cast of thought, nor to surround their heads with any visible aureole of consuming fire. Yet I think that their very health saves them both from worldliness: for life would not be healthy and free, but diseased and slavish, if it were ultimately turned only towards its instruments and to the pressing need of keeping itself going; a life so employed would not be worth living, and a healthy spirit would abandon it. The normal Englishman, like the normal Greek, is addressed to spiritual things, even if distantly; so that when for any reason his spiritual life is intensified, he will create or adopt a spiritual philosophy, like that of Plotinus. His inner man is selective; he is accustomed not to accept unquestioningly the suasion of custom and not to tremble before material grandeur. He is an explorer; he has some notion of the extent and variety of nature, with enough appreciative contempt for its tropical splendours, moral and geographical; it is with a clear inward satisfaction, even if with some grumbling of the flesh, that he turns his back upon them for the sake of his sweet, separate, cool, country life at home. He loves the earth, not the world. His ideal is that people everywhere should be steady and happy, in their way, as he is in his; and if he feels some glow at the power and influence of his country, or the spread of his religion, it is not because he covets domination or a Roman grandiloquent greatness, but because he feels that when others take to his ways he will be safer in them himself, and the world more decent. He wishes to be free, free to choose his walks, his friends, his thoughts, his employments; and this freedom, although it may be employed only on commonplace and earthly things, is the very principle of spirituality, and a beginning in it.

What spirituality is when developed fully may be seen clearly in the system of Plotinus. It is a system of morals inverted and turned into a cosmology; everything in his magic universe is supposed to be created and moved by the next higher being, to which by nature it aspires; so that life everywhere is a continual prayer, and if it cannot actually shake off its fetters and take wing into a higher sphere, at least it imitates and worships the forms which beckon to it from there. All this is a true allegory; if any one takes it for natural science he must think it a very poor speculation; because if the higher thing in each instance were really the *source* of the lower, it never could have determined the time, place, number, distribution, or imperfection of its copies; and the whole drama of creation, in everything except its tendency and meaning, must be due to specific and various predispositions in matter, for which this system, in its scientific impotence, has forgotten to make room. It would be easy, however, to supply this defect. We might start, as nature actually did, at the bottom, and pass at once to the level at which the Psyche, having organised the vital functions of the human animal, begins to ask itself what it is living for. The answer is not, as an unspiritual philosophy would have it: In order to live on. The true answer is: In order to understand, in order to see the Ideas. Those Ideas which the Psyche is able and predestined to discern are such as are illustrated or suggested by its own life, or by the aspects which nature presents to it. Each Idea will be the ideal of something with which the Psyche is naturally conversant; but the good of all these psychic labours will lie precisely in clarifying and realising that ideal. To envisage and clearly to discern the Idea of what we are about is the whole art, spiritually considered; it is all the mind can or need do; and the more singly the spirit is rapt in the meaning and vision of the work, the more skilfully the hand and the tongue will perform it. And the standard and criterion of their skill is in turn precisely the same vision of the Idea: for, I ask, what makes an action or a feeling right, except that it clears away obstructions and brings us face to face with the thing we love? The whole of natural life, then, is an aspiration after the realization and vision of Ideas, and all action is for the sake of contemplation.

Plato and Aristotle had been satisfied to stop at this stage; but Plotinus carries us one step further. What is the good of seeing the Ideas? I do not ask, of course, what is its utility, because we have left that behind, but what is the nature of the excellence which various Ideas seem to have in common, like beauty, or affinity with the harmonious and perfected life of the Psyche. Plotinus says that what lends excellence to the Ideas is the One; and I cannot connect—perhaps we ought not to connect—any idea with those words. But by looking at the matter naturalistically perhaps we may discover whence the excellence of Ideas and of the vision of them actually flows. It flows from health, which is a unity of function, and it flows from love, which is an emotional unity pervading that function, and suffusing its object, when it comes before the mind, with beauty and inexpressible worth. Here, if I am not mistaken, we have the key to the whole mystery, both in Plotinus and in Plato. The One or the Good is the mythical counterpart of moral harmony in the spirit; it is the principle by which the Ideas were disentangled from the detail of experience and the flux of objects, and it is again the principle by which the Ideas themselves are consecrated, illumined, and turned into forms of Joy.

Spirituality, then, lies in regarding existence merely as a vehicle for contemplation, and contemplation merely as a vehicle for joy. Epicurus was far more spiritual than Moses. But Epicurus could free the spirit only in the presence of the simplest things; the universe terrified him, quite without reason, so that his spirituality was fumbling, timid, and sad.

For Plotinus the universe had no terrors; he liked to feel himself consumed and burning in the very heart of the sun, and poured thence in a flood of light from sphere to sphere. We, in this remote shore of time, may catch that ray and retrace it; it will lead us into good company.

SCEPTICISM AND ANIMAL FAITH

PREFACE

HERE is one more system of philosophy. If the reader is tempted to smile, I can assure him that I smile with him, and that my system—to which this volume is a critical introduction—differs widely in spirit and pretensions from what usually goes by that name. In the first place, *my system is not mine, nor new*. I am merely attempting to express for the reader the principles to which he appeals when he smiles. There are convictions in the depths of his soul, beneath all his overt parrot beliefs, on which I would build our friendship. I have a great respect for orthodoxy; not for those orthodoxies which prevail in particular schools or nations, and which vary from age to age, but for a certain shrewd orthodoxy which the sentiment and practice of laymen maintain everywhere. I think that common sense, in a rough dogged way, is technically sounder than the special schools of philosophy, each of which squints and overlooks half the facts and half the difficulties in its eagerness to find in some detail the key to the whole. I am animated by distrust of all high guesses, and by sympathy with the old prejudices and workaday opinions of mankind: they are ill expressed, but they are well grounded. What novelty my version of things may possess is meant simply to obviate occasions for sophistry by giving to everyday beliefs a more accurate and circumspect form. I do not pretend to place myself at the heart of the universe nor at its origin, nor to draw its periphery. I would lay siege to the truth only as animal exploration and fancy may do so, first from one quarter and then from another, expecting the reality to be not simpler than my experience of it, but far more extensive and complex. I stand in philosophy exactly where I stand in daily life; I should not be honest otherwise. I accept the same miscellaneous witnesses, bow to the same obvious facts, make conjectures no less instinctively, and admit the same encircling ignorance.

My system, accordingly, is *no system of the universe*. The Realms of Being of which I speak are not parts of a cosmos, nor one great cosmos together: they are only kinds or categories of things which I find conspicuously different and worth distinguishing, at least in my own thoughts. I do not know how many things in the universe at large may fall under each of these classes, nor what other Realms of Being may not exist, to which I have no approach or which I have not happened to distinguish in my personal observation of the world. Logic, like language, is partly a free construction and partly a means of symbolising and harnessing in expression the existing diversities of things; and whilst some languages, given a man's constitution and habits, may seem more beautiful and convenient to him than others, it is a foolish heat in a patriot to insist that only his native language is intelligible or right. No language or logic is right in the sense of being identical with the facts it is used to express, but each may be right by being faithful to these facts, as a translation may be faithful. My endeavour is to think straight in such terms as are offered to me, to clear my mind of cant and free it from the cramp of artificial traditions; but I do not ask any one to think in my terms if he prefers others. Let him clean better, if he can, the windows of his soul, that the variety and beauty of the prospect may spread more brightly before him.

Moreover, my system, save in the mocking literary sense of the word, is *not metaphysical*. It contains much criticism of metaphysics, and some refinements in speculation, like the doctrine of essence, which are not familiar to the public; and

I do not disclaim being metaphysical because I at all dislike dialectic or disdain immaterial things: indeed, it is of immaterial things, essence, truth, and spirit that I speak chiefly. But logic and mathematics and literary psychology (when frankly literary) are not metaphysical, although their subject-matter is immaterial, and their application to existing things is often questionable. Metaphysics, in the proper sense of the word, is dialectical physics, or an attempt to determine matters of fact by means of logical or moral or rhetorical constructions. It arises by a confusion of those Realms of Being which it is my special care to distinguish. It is neither physical speculation nor pure logic nor honest literature, but (as in the treatise of Aristotle first called by that name) a hybrid of the three, materialising ideal entities, turning harmonies into forces, and dissolving natural things into terms of discourse. Speculations about the natural world, such as those of the Ionian philosophers, are not metaphysics, but simply cosmology or natural philosophy. Now in natural philosophy I am a decided materialist—apparently the only one living; and I am well aware that idealists are fond of calling materialism, too, metaphysics, in rather an angry tone, so as to cast discredit upon it by assimilating it to their own systems. But my materialism, for all that, is not metaphysical. I do not profess to know what matter is in itself, and feel no confidence in the divination of those *esprits forts* who, leading a life of vice, thought the universe must be composed of nothing but dice and billiard balls. I wait for the men of science to tell me what matter is, in so far as they can discover it, and am not at all surprised or troubled at the abstractness and vagueness of their ultimate conceptions: how should our notions of things so remote from the scale and scope of our senses be anything but schematic? But whatever matter may be, I call it matter boldly, as I call my acquaintances Smith and Jones without knowing their secrets: whatever it may be, it must present the aspects and undergo the motions of the gross objects that fill the world:

and if belief in the existence of hidden parts and movements in nature be metaphysics, then the kitchen-maid is a metaphysician whenever she peels a potato.

My system, finally, though, of course, formed under the fire of contemporary discussions, is *no phase of any current movement*. I cannot take at all seriously the present flutter of the image-lovers against intelligence. I love images as much as they do, but images must be discounted in our waking life, when we come to business. I also appreciate the other reforms and rebellions that have made up the history of philosophy. I prize their sharp criticism of one another and their several discoveries; the trouble is that each in turn has denied or forgotten a much more important truth than it has asserted. The first philosophers, the original observers of life and nature, were the best; and I think only the Indians and the Greek naturalists, together with Spinoza, have been right on the chief issue, the relation of man and of his spirit to the universe. It is not unwillingness to be a disciple that prompts me to look beyond the modern scramble of philosophies: I should gladly learn of them all, if they had learned more of one another. Even as it is, I endeavour to retain the positive insight of each, reducing it to the scale of nature and keeping it in its place; thus I am a Platonist in logic and morals, and a transcendentalist in romantic soliloquy, when I choose to indulge in it. Nor is it necessary, in being teachable by any master, to become eclectic. All these vistas give glimpses of the same wood, and a fair and true map of it must be drawn to a single scale, by one method of projection, and in one style of calligraphy. All known truth can be rendered in any language, although the accent and poetry of each may be incommunicable; and as I am content to write in English, although it was not my mother tongue, and although in speculative matters I have not much sympathy with the English mind, so I am content to follow the European tradition in philosophy, little as I respect its rhetorical metaphysics, its humanism, and its worldliness.

There is one point, indeed, in which I am truly sorry not to be able to profit by the guidance of my contemporaries. There is now a great ferment in natural and mathematical philosophy and the times seem ripe for a new system of nature, at once ingenuous and comprehensive, such as has not appeared since the earlier days of Greece. We may soon be all believing in an honest cosmology, comparable with that of Heraclitus, Pythagoras, or Democritus. I wish such scientific systems joy, and if I were competent to follow or to forecast their procedure, I should gladly avail myself of their results, which are bound to be no less picturesque than instructive. But what exists to-day is so tentative, obscure, and confused by bad philosophy, that there is no knowing what parts may be sound and what parts merely personal and scatter-brained. If I were a mathematician I should no doubt regale myself, if not the reader, with an electric or logistic system of the universe expressed in algebraic symbols. For good or ill, I am an ignorant man, almost a poet, and I can only spread a feast of what everybody knows. Fortunately exact science and the books of the learned are not necessary to establish my essential doctrine, nor can any of them claim a higher warrant than it has in itself: for it rests on public experience. It needs, to prove it, only the stars, the seasons, the swarm of animals, the spectacle of birth and death, of cities and wars. My philosophy is justified, and has been justified in all ages and countries, by the facts before every man's eyes; and no great wit is requisite to discover it, only (what is rarer than wit) candour and courage. Learning does not liberate men from superstition when their souls are cowed or perplexed; and, without learning, clear eyes and honest reflection can discern the hang of the world, and distinguish the edge of truth from the might of imagination. In the past or in the future, my language and my borrowed knowledge would have been different, but under whatever sky I had been born, since it is the same sky, I should have had the same philosophy.

VI

Ultimate Scepticism

WHY should the mystic, in proportion as he dismisses the miscellany of experience as so much illusion, feel that he becomes one with reality and attains to absolute existence? I think that the same survival of vulgar presumptions which leads the romantic solipsist to retain his belief in his personal history and destiny, leads the mystic to retain, and fondly to embrace, the feeling of existence. His speculation is indeed inspired by the love of security: his grand objection to the natural world, and to mortal life, is that they are deceptive, that they cheat the soul that loves them, and prove to be illusions: the assumption apparently being that reality must be permanent, and that he who has hold on reality is safe for ever. In this the mystic, who so hates illusions, is the victim of an illusion himself: for the reality he has hold of is but the burden of a single moment, which in its solipsism thinks itself absolute. What is reality? As I should like to use the term, reality is being of any sort. If it means character or essence, illusions have it as much as substance, and more richly. If it means substance, then sceptical concentration upon inner experience, or ecstatic abstraction, seems to me the last place in which we should look for it. The immediate and the visionary are at the opposite pole from substance; they are on the surface or, if you like, at the top; whereas substance if it is anywhere is at the bottom. The realm of immediate illusion is as real as any other, and very attractive; many would wish it to be the only reality, and hate substance; but if substance exists (which I am not yet ready to assert) they have no reason to hate it, since it is the basis of those immediate feelings which fill them with satisfaction. Finally, if reality means existence, certainly the mystic and his meditation may exist, but not more truly than any other natural fact; and what would exist in them would be a pulse of animal being, kindling that momentary ecstasy, as animal life at certain intensities is wont to do. The theme of that meditation, its visionary object, need not exist at all; it may be incapable of existing if it is essentially timeless and dialectical. The animal mind treats its data as facts, or as signs of facts, but the animal mind is full of the rashest presumptions, positing time, change, a particular station in the midst of events yielding a particular perspective of those events, and the flux of all nature precipitating that experience at that place. None of these posited objects is a datum in which a sceptic could rest. Indeed, existence or fact, in the sense which I give to these words, cannot be a datum at all, because existence involves external relations and actual (not merely specious) flux: whereas, however complex a datum may be, with no matter what perspectives opening within it, it must be embraced in a single stroke of apperception, and nothing outside it can belong to it at all. The datum is a pure image; it is essentially illusory and unsubstantial, however thunderous its sound or keen its edge, or however normal and significant its presence may be. When the mystic asserts enthusiastically the existence of his immediate, ideal, unutterable object, Absolute Being, he is peculiarly unfortunate in his faith: it would be impossible to choose an image less relevant to the agencies that actually bring that image before him. The burden and glow of existence which he is conscious of come entirely from himself; his object is eminently empty, impotent, non-existent; but the heat and labour of his own soul suffuse that emptiness with light, and the very hum of change within him, accelerated almost beyond endurance and quite beyond discrimination, sounds that piercing note.

The last step in scepticism is now before me. It will lead me to deny existence to any datum, whatever it may be; and as the datum, by hypothesis, is the whole of what solicits my attention at any moment, I shall deny the existence of everything, and abolish that category of thought altogether. If I could not do this, I should be a tyro in scepticism. Belief in the existence of anything, including myself, is something radically incapable of proof, and resting, like all belief, on some irrational persuasion or prompting of life. Certainly, as a matter of fact, when I deny existence I exist; but doubtless many of the other facts I have been denying, because I found no evidence for them, were true also. To bring me evidence of their existence is no duty imposed on facts, nor a habit of theirs: I must employ private detectives. The point is, in this task of criticism, to discard every belief that is a belief merely; and the belief in existence, in the nature of the case, can be a belief only. The datum is an idea, a description; I may contemplate it without belief; but when I assert that such a thing exists I am hypostatising this datum, placing it in presumptive relations which are not internal to it, and worshipping it as an idol or thing. Neither its existence nor mine nor that of my belief can be given in any datum. These things are incidents involved in that order of nature which I have thrown over; they are no part of what remains before me.

Assurance of existence expresses animal watchfulness: it posits, within me and round me, hidden and imminent events. The sceptic can easily cast a doubt on the remoter objects of this belief; and nothing but a certain obduracy and want of agility prevents him from doubting present existence itself. For what could present existence mean, if the imminent events for which animal sense is watching failed altogether, failed at the very roots, so to speak, of the tree of intuition, and left nothing but its branches flowering *in vacuo*? Expectation is admittedly the most hazardous of beliefs: yet what is watchfulness but expectation? Memory is notoriously full of illusion; yet what would experience of the present be if the veracity of primary memory were denied, and if I no longer believed that anything had just happened, or that I had ever been in the state from which I suppose myself to have passed into this my present condition?

It will not do for the sceptic to take refuge in the confused notion that expectation *possesses* the future, or memory the past. As a matter of fact, expectation is like hunger; it opens its mouth, and something probably drops into it, more or less, very often, the sort of thing it expected; but sometimes a surprise comes, and sometimes nothing. Life involves expectation, but does not prevent death: and expectation is never so thoroughly stultified as when it is not undeceived, but cancelled. The open mouth does not then so much as close upon nothing. It is buried open. Nor is memory in a better case. As the whole world might collapse and cease at any moment, nullifying all expectation, so it might at any moment have sprung out of nothing: for it is thoroughly contingent, and might have begun to-day, with this degree of complexity and illusive memory, as well as long ago, with whatever energy or momentum it was first endowed with. The backward perspective of time is perhaps really an inverted expectation; but for the momentum of life forward, we might not be able to space the elements active in the present so as to assign to them a longer or a shorter history; for we should not attempt to discriminate amongst these elements such as we could still count on in the immediate future, and such as we might safely ignore: so that our conception of the past implies, perhaps, a distinction between the living and the dead. This distinction is itself practical, and looks to the future. In the absolute present all is specious; and to pure intuition the living are as ghostly as the dead, and the dead as present as the living.

In the sense of existence there is accordingly something more than the obvious character of that which is alleged to exist. What is this complement? It cannot be a feature in the datum, since the datum by definition is the whole of what is found. Nor can it be, in my sense at least of the word existence, the intrinsic constitution or specific being of this object, since existence comports external relations, variable, contingent, and not discoverable in a given being when taken alone: for there is nothing that may not lose its existence, or the existence of which might not be conceivably denied. The complement added to the datum when it is alleged to exist seems, then, to be added by *me*; it is the finding, the occurrence, the assault, the impact of that being here and now; it is the experience of it. But what can experience be, if I take away from it the whole of what is experienced? And what meaning can I give to such words as impact, assault, occurrence, or finding, when I have banished and denied my body, my past, my residual present being, and everything except the datum which I find? The sense of existence evidently belongs to the intoxication, to the *Rausch*, of existence itself; it is the strain of life within me, prior to all intuition, that in its precipitation and terror, passing as it continually must from one untenable condition to another, stretches my attention absurdly over what is not given, over the lost and the unattained, the before and after which are wrapped in darkness, and confuses my breathless apprehension of the clear presence of all I can ever truly behold.

Indeed, so much am I a creature of movement, and of the ceaseless metabolism of matter, that I should never catch even these glimpses of the light, if there were not rhythms, pauses, repetitions, and nodes in my physical progress, to absorb and reflect it here and there: as the traveller, hurried in a cloud of smoke and dust through tunnel after tunnel in the Italian Riviera, catches and loses momentary visions of blue sea and sky, which he would like to arrest, but cannot; yet if he had not been rushed and whistled along these particular tunnels, even those snatches, in the form in which they come to him, would have been denied him. So it is the rush of life that, at its open moments, floods me with intuitions, partial and confused, but still revelations; the landscape is wrapped in the smoke of my little engine, and turned into a tantalising incident of my hot journey. What appears (which is an ideal object and not an event) is thus confused with the event of its appearance; the picture is identified with the kindling or distraction of my attention falling by chance upon it; and the strain of my material existence, battling with material accidents, turns the ideal object too into a temporal fact, and makes it seem substantial. But this fugitive existence which I egotistically attach to it, as if its fate was that of my glimpses of it, is no part of its true being, as even my intuition discerns it; it is a practical dignity or potency attributed to it by the irrelevant momentum of my animal life. Animals, being by nature hounded and hungry creatures, spy out and take alarm at any datum of sense or fancy, supposing that there is something substantial there, something that will count and work in the world. The notion of a moving world is brought implicitly with them; they fetch it out of the depths of their vegetating psyche, which is a small dark cosmos, silently revolving within. By being noticed, and treated as a signal for I know not what material opportunity or danger, the given image is taken up into the business world, and puts on the garment of existence. Remove this frame, strip off all suggestion of a time when this image was not yet present, or a time when it shall be past, and the very notion of existence is removed. The datum ceases to be an appearance, in the proper and pregnant sense of this word, since it ceases to imply any substance that appears or any mind to which it appears. It is an appearance only in the sense that its nature is wholly manifest, that it is a specific being, which may be mentioned, thought of, seen, or defined, if any one has the wit to do so. But its own nature says nothing of any hidden circumstances that shall bring it to light, or any adventitious mind that shall discover it. It lies simply in its own category. If a colour, it is just this colour; if a pain, just this pain. Its appearance is not an event: its presence is not an experience; for there is no surrounding world in which it can arise, and no watchful spirit to appropriate it. The sceptic has here withdrawn into the intuition of a surface form, without roots, without origin or environment, without a seat or a locus; a little universe, an immaterial absolute theme, rejoicing merely in its own quality. This theme, being out of all adventitious relations and not in the least threatened with not being the theme it is, has not the contingency nor the fortunes proper to an existence; it is simply that which it inherently, logically, and unchangeably is.

Existence, then, not being included in any immediate datum, is a fact always open to doubt. I call it a fact notwithstanding, because in talking about the sceptic I am positing his existence. If he has any intuition, however little the theme of that intuition may have to do with any actual world, certainly I who think of his intuition, or he himself thinking of it afterwards, see that this intuition of his must have been an event, and his existence at that time a fact; but like all facts and events, this one can be known only by an affirmation which posits it, which may be suspended or reversed, and which is subject to error. Hence all this business of intuition may perfectly well be doubted by the sceptic: the existence of his own doubt (however confidently I may assert it for him) is not given to him then: all that is given is some ambiguity or contradiction in images; and if afterwards he is sure that he has doubted, the sole cogent evidence which that fact can claim lies in the psychological impossibility that, so long as he believes he has doubted, he should not believe it. But he may be wrong in harbouring this belief, and he may rescind it. For all an ultimate scepticism can see, therefore, there may be no facts at all, and perhaps nothing has ever existed.

Scepticism may thus be carried to the point of denying change and memory, and the reality of all facts. Such a sceptical dogma would certainly be false, because this dogma itself would have to be entertained, and that event would be a fact and an existence: and the sceptic in framing that dogma discourses, vacillates, and lives in the act of contrasting one assertion with another—all of which is to exist with a vengeance. Yet this false dogma that nothing exists is tenable intuitively and, while it prevails, is irrefutable. There are certain motives (to be discussed later) which render ultimate scepticism precious to a spiritual mind, as a sanctuary from grosser illusions. For the wayward sceptic, who regards it as no truer than any other view, it also has some utility: it accustoms him to discard the dogma which an introspective critic might be tempted to think self-evident, namely, that he himself lives and thinks. That he does so is true; but to establish that truth he must appeal to animal faith. If he is too proud for that, and simply stares at the datum; the last thing he will see is himself.

VII

Nothing Given Exists

SCEPTICISM is not sleep, and in casting a doubt on any belief, or proving the absurdity of any idea, the sceptic is by no means losing his sense of what is proposed. He is merely doubting or denying the *existence* of any such object. In scepticism, therefore, everything turns on the meaning of the word existence, and it will be worth while to stop a moment here to consider it further.

I have already indicated roughly how I am using the word existence, namely, to designate such being as is in flux, determined by external relations, and jostled by irrelevant events. Of course this is no definition. The term existence is only a name. In using it I am merely pointing out to the reader, as if by a gesture, what this word designates in my habits of speech, as if in saying Cæsar I pointed to my dog, lest some one should suppose I meant the Roman emperor. The Roman emperor, the dog, and the sound Cæsar are all indefinable; but they might be described more particularly, by using other indicative and indefinable names, to mark their characteristics or the events in which they figured. So the whole realm of being which I point to when I say exist-ence might be described more fully; the description of it would be physics or perhaps psychology; but the exploration of that realm, which is open only to animal faith, would not concern the sceptic.

The sceptic turns from such indefinite confusing objects to the immediate, to the datum; and perhaps for a moment he may fancy he has found true existence there; but if he is a good sceptic he will soon be undeceived. Certainly in the immediate he will find freedom from the struggle of asser-tion and counter-assertion: no report there, no hypothesis, no ghostly reduplication of the obvious, no ghostly immi-nence of the not-given. Is not the obvious, he might ask, the truly existent? Yet the obvious is only the apparent; and this in both senses of this ambiguous word. The datum is ap-parent in the sense of being self-evident and luminous; and it is apparent also in the sense of merely appearing and being unsubstantial. In this latter sense, the apparent threatens to become the non-existent. Does not the existent profess to be more than apparent: to be not so much the self-evident as that which I am seeking evidence for, in the sense of testi-mony? Is not the existent, then (which from its own point of view, or physically, is more than the apparent), cogni-tively and from my point of view less than the apparent? Does it not need witnesses to bear testimony to its being? And what can recommend those witnesses to me except their intrinsic eloquence? I shall prove no sceptic if I do not im-mediately transfer all my trust from the existence reported to the appearance reporting it, and substitute the evidence of my senses for all lawyer's evidence. I shall forget the mur-ders and embroglios talked about in the court, and gaze at the judge in his scarlet and ermine, with the pale features of an old fox under his grey wig; at the jury in their stolidity;

at the witness stammering; at the counsel, officially insolent, not thinking of what he is saying mechanically, but whispering something that really interests him in an aside, almost yawning, and looking at the clock to see if it is time for luncheon; and at the flood of hazy light falling aslant on the whole scene from the high windows. Is not the floating picture, in my waking trance, the actual reality, and the whole world of existence and business but a perpetual fable, which this trance sustains?

IX

The Discovery of Essence

SCEPTICISM is an exercise, not a life; it is a discipline fit to purify the mind of prejudice and render it all the more apt, when the time comes, to believe and to act wisely; and meantime the pure sceptic need take no offence at the multiplicity of images that crowd upon him, if he is scrupulous not to trust them and to assert nothing at their prompting. Scepticism is the chastity of the intellect, and it is shameful to surrender it too soon or to the first comer: there is nobility in preserving it coolly and proudly through a long youth, until at last, in the ripeness of instinct and discretion, it can be safely exchanged for fidelity and happiness. But the philosopher, when he is speculative only, is a sort of perpetual celibate; he is bent on not being betrayed, rather than on being annexed or inspired; and although if he is at all wise he must see that the true marriage of the mind is with nature and science and the practical arts, yet in his special theoretic vocation, it will be a boon to him to view all experience simply, in the precision and distinctness which all its parts acquire when not referred to any substance which they might present confusedly, nor to any hypothesis or action which they might suggest.

The sceptic, then, as a consequence of carrying his scepticism to the greatest lengths, finds himself in the presence of more luminous and less equivocal objects than does the working and believing mind; only these objects are without meaning, they are only what they are obviously, all surface. They show him everything thinkable with the greatest clearness and force; but he can no longer imagine that he sees in these objects anything save their instant presence and their face value. Scepticism therefore suspends all knowledge worthy of the name, all that transitive and presumptive knowledge of facts which is a form of belief; and instead it bestows intuition of ideas, contemplative, æsthetic, dialectical, arbitrary. But whereas transitive knowledge, though important if true, may always be challenged, intuition, on the contrary, which neither has nor professes to have any ulterior object or truth, runs no risks of error, because it claims no jurisdiction over anything alien or eventual.

In this lucidity and calmness of intuition there is something preternatural. Imagine a child accustomed to see clothes only on living persons and hardly distinguishing them from the magical strong bodies that agitate them, and suddenly carry this child into a costumer's shop, where he will see all sorts of garments hung in rows upon manikins, with hollow breasts all of visible wire, and little wooden nobs instead of heads: he might be seriously shocked or even frightened. How should it be possible for clothes standing up like this not to be people? Such abstractions, he might say to himself, are metaphysically impossible. Either these figures must be secretly alive and ready, when he least expects it, to begin to dance, or else they are not real at all, and he can only fancy that he sees them. Just as the spectacle of all these gaunt clothes without bodies might make the child cry, so later might the whole spectacle of nature, if ever he became a sceptic. The little word *is* has its tragedies; it marries and identifies different things with the greatest innocence; and yet no two are ever identical, and if therein lies the charm of wedding them and calling them one, therein too lies the danger. Whenever I use the word *is*, except in sheer tautology, I deeply misuse it; and when I discover my error, the world seems to fall asunder and the members of my family no longer know one another. Existence is the strong body and familiar motion which the young mind expects to find in every dummy. The oldest of us are sometimes no less recalcitrant to the spectacle of the garments of existence— which is all we ever saw of it—when the existence is taken away. Yet it is to these actual and familiar, but now disembowelled objects, that scepticism introduces us, as if to a strange world; a vast costumer's gallery of ideas where all sorts of patterns and models are on exhibition, without bodies to wear them, and where no human habits of motion distract the eye from the curious cut and precise embroideries of every article. This display, so complete in its spectacular reality, not a button nor a feather wanting or unobserved, is not the living crowd that it ought to be, but a mockery of it, like the palace of the Sleeping Beauty. To my conventional mind, clothes without bodies are no less improper than bodies without clothes; yet the conjunction of these things is but human. All nature runs about naked, and quite happy; and I am not so remote from nature as not to revert on occasion to that nakedness—which is unconsciousness—with profound relief. But ideas without things and apparel without wearers seem to me a stranger condition; I think the garments were made to fit the limbs, and should collapse without them. Yet, like the fig leaves of Eden, they are not garments essentially. They become such by accident, when one or another of them is appropriated by the providential buyer—not necessarily human—whose instinct may choose it; or else it is perfectly content to miss its chance, and to lie stacked for ever among its motley neighbours in this great store of neglected finery.

It was the fear of illusion that originally disquieted the honest mind, congenitally dogmatic, and drove it in the direction of scepticism; and it may find three ways, not equally satisfying to its honesty, in which that fear of illusion may be dispelled. One is death, in which illusion vanishes and is forgotten; but although anxiety about error, and even positive error, are thus destroyed, no solution is offered to the previous doubt: no explanation of what could have called forth that illusion or what could have dissipated it. Another way out is by correcting the error, and substituting a new belief for it: but while in animal life this is the satisfying solution, and the old habit of dogmatism may be resumed in consequence without practical inconvenience, speculatively the case is not at all advanced; because no criterion of truth is afforded except custom, comfort, and the accidental absence of doubt; and what is absent by chance may return at any time unbidden. The third way, at which I have now arrived, is to entertain the illusion without succumbing to it, accepting it openly as an illusion, and forbidding it to claim any sort of being but that which it obviously has; and then, whether it profits me or not, it will not deceive me. What will remain of this non-deceptive illusion will then be a truth, and a truth the being of which requires no explanation, since it is utterly impossible that it should have been otherwise. Of course I may still ask why the identity of this particular thing with itself should have occurred to *me*; a question which could only be answered by plunging into a realm of existence and natural history every part and principle of which would be just as contingent, just as uncalled-for, and just as inexplicable as this accident of my being; but that this particular thing, or any other which might have occurred to me instead, should be constituted as it is raises no problem; for how could *it* have been constituted otherwise? Nor is there any moral offence any longer in the contingency of my view of it, since my view of it involves no error. The error came from a wild belief about it; and the possibility of error came from a wild propensity to belief. Relieve now the pressure of that animal haste and that hungry presumption; the error is washed out of the illusion; it is no illusion now, but an idea. Just as food would cease to be food, and poison poison, if you removed the stomach and the blood that they might nourish or infect; and just as beautiful things would cease to be beautiful if you removed the wonder and the welcome of living souls, so if you eliminate your anxiety, deceit itself becomes entertainment, and every illusion but so much added acquaintance with the realm of form. For the unintelligible accident of existence will cease to appear to lurk in this manifest being, weighting and crowding it, and threatening it with being swallowed up by nondescript neighbours. It will appear dwelling in its own world, and shining by its own light, however brief may be my glimpse of it: for no date will be written on it, no frame of full or of empty time will shut it in; nothing in it will be addressed to me, nor suggestive of any spectator. It will seem an event in no world, an incident in no experience. The quality of it will have ceased to exist: it will be merely the quality which it inherently, logically, and inalienably is. It will be an ESSENCE.

Retrenchment has its rewards. When by a difficult suspension of judgment I have deprived a given image of all adventitious significance, when it is taken neither for the manifestation of a substance nor for an idea in a mind nor for an event in a world, but simply if a colour for that colour and if music for that music, and if a face for that face, then an immense cognitive certitude comes to compensate me for so much cognitive abstention. My scepticism at last has touched bottom, and my doubt has found honourable rest in the absolutely indubitable. Whatever essence I find and note, that essence and no other is established before me. I cannot be mistaken about it, since I now have no object of intent other than the object of intuition. If for some private reason I am dissatisfied, and wish to change my entertainment, nothing prevents; but the change leaves the thing I first saw possessed of all its quality, for the sake of which I perhaps disliked or disowned it. That, while one essence is before me, some one else may be talking of another, which he calls by the same name, is nothing to the purpose; and if I myself change and correct myself, choosing a new essence in place of the old, my life indeed may have shifted its visions and its interests, but the characters they had when I harboured them are theirs without change. Indeed, only because each essence is the essence defined by instant apprehension can I truly be said to have changed my mind; for I can have discarded any one of them only by substituting something different. This new essence could not be different from the former one, if each was not unchangeably itself.

There is, then, a sort of play with the non-existent, or game of thought, which intervenes in all alleged knowledge of matters of fact, and survives that knowledge, if this is ever questioned or disproved. To this mirage of the non-existent, or intuition of essence, the pure sceptic is confined; and confined is hardly the word; because though without faith and risk he can never leave that thin and bodiless plane of being, this plane in its tenuity is infinite; and there is nothing possible elsewhere that, as a shadow and a pattern, is not prefigured there. To consider an essence is, from a spiritual point of view, to enlarge acquaintance with true being; but it is not even to broach knowledge of fact; and the ideal object so defined may have no natural significance, though it has æsthetic immediacy and logical definition. The modest scope of this speculative acquaintance with essence renders it infallible, whilst the logical and æsthetic ideality of its object renders that object eternal. Thus the most radical sceptic may be consoled, without being rebuked or refuted; he may leap at one bound over the whole human tangle of beliefs and dogmatic claims, elude human incapacity and bias, and take hold of the quite sufficient assurance that any essence or ideal quality of being which he may be intuiting has just the characters he is finding in it, and has them eternally.

This is no idle assurance. After all, the only thing that can ultimately interest me in other men's experience or, apart from animal egotism, in my own, is just this character of the essences which at any time have swum into our ken; not at all the length of time through which we may have beheld them, nor the circumstances that produced that vision; unless these circumstances in turn, when considered, place before the mind the essences which it delights to entertain. Of course, the choice and the interest of essences come entirely from the bent of the animal that elicits the vision of them from his own soul and its adventures; and nothing but affinity with my animal life lends the essences I am able to discern their moral colour, so that to my mind they are beautiful, horrible, trivial, or vulgar. The good essences are such as accompany and express a good life. In them, whether good or bad, that life has its eternity. Certainly when I cease to exist and to think, I shall lose hold on this assurance; but the theme in which for a moment I found the fulfilment of my expressive impulses will remain, as it always was, a theme fit for consideration, even if no one else should consider it, and I should never consider it again.

Nor is this all. Not only is the character of each essence inalienable, and, so long as it is open to intuition, indubitable, but the realm of essences is infinite. Since any essence I happen to have hit upon is independent of me and would possess its precise character if I had never been born, or had never been led by the circumstances of my life and temperament to apprehend that particular essence, evidently all other essences, which I have not been led to think of, rejoice in the same sort of impalpable being—impalpable, yet the only sort of being that the most rugged experience can ever actually find. Thus a mind enlightened by scepticism and cured of noisy dogma, a mind discounting all reports, and free from all tormenting anxiety about its own fortunes or existence, finds in the wilderness of essence a very sweet and marvellous solitude. The ultimate reaches of doubt and renunciation open out for it, by an easy transition, into fields of endless variety and peace, as if through the gorges of death it had passed into a paradise where all things are crystallised into the image of themselves, and have lost their urgency and their venom.

XI

The Watershed of Criticism

I HAVE now reached the culminating point of my survey of evidence, and the entanglements I have left behind me and the habitable regions I am looking for lie spread out before me like opposite valleys. On the one hand I see now a sweeping reason for scepticism, over and above all particular contradictions or fancifulness of dogma. Nothing is ever present to me except some essence; so that nothing that I possess in intuition, or actually see, is ever *there*; it can never exist bodily, nor lie in that place or exert that power which belongs to the objects encountered in action. Therefore, if I regard my intuitions as knowledge of facts, all my experience is illusion, and life is a dream. At the same time I am now able to give a clearer meaning to this old adage; for life would not be a dream, and all experience would not be illusion, if I abstained from believing in them. The evidence of data is only obviousness; they give no evidence of anything else; they are not witnesses. If I am content to recognise them for pure essences, they cannot deceive me; they will be like works of literary fiction, more or less coherent, but without any claim to exist on their own account. If I hypostatise an essence into a fact, instinctively placing it in relations which are not given within it, I am putting my trust in animal faith, not in any evidence or implication of my actual experience. I turn to an assumed world about me, because I have organs for turning, just as I expect a future to reel itself out without interruption because I am wound up to go on myself. To such ulterior things no manifest essence can bear any testimony. They must justify themselves. If the ulterior fact is some intuition elsewhere, its existence, if it happens to exist, will justify that belief; but the fulfilment of my prophecy, in taking my present dream for testimony to that ulterior experience, will be found only in the realm of truth—a realm which is itself an object of belief, never, by any possibility of intuition, human or divine. So too when the supposed fact is thought of as a substance, its existence, if it is found in the realm of nature, will justify that supposition; but the realm of nature is of course only another object of belief, more remote if possible from intuition than even the realm of truth. Intuition of essence, to which positive experience and certitude are confined, is therefore always illusion, if we allow our hypostatising impulse to take it for evidence of anything else.

In adopting this conclusion of so many great philosophers, that all is illusion, I do so, however, with two qualifications. One is emotional and moral only, in that I do not mourn over this fatality, but on the contrary rather prefer speculation in the realm of essence—if it can be indulged without practical inconvenience—to alleged information about hard facts. It does not seem to me ignominious to be a poet, if nature has made one a poet unexpectedly. Unexpectedly nature lent us existence, and if she has made it a condition that we should be poets, she has not forbidden us to enjoy that art, or even to be proud of it. The other qualification is more austere: it consists in not allowing exceptions. I cannot admit that some particular essence—water, fire, being, atoms, or Brahma—is the intrinsic essence of all things, so that if I narrow my imagination to that one intuition I shall have intuited the heart and the whole of existence. Of course I do not deny that there is water and that there is being, the former in most things on earth, and the latter in everything anywhere; but these images or words of mine are not the things they designate, but only names for them. Desultory and partial propriety these names may have, but no metaphysical privilege. No more has the expedient of some modern critics who would take illusion as a whole and call it the universe; for in the first place they are probably reverting to belief in discourse, as conventionally conceived, so that their scepticism is halting; and in the second place, even if human experience could be admitted as known and vouched for, there would be an incredible arrogance in positing it as the whole of being, or as itself confined to the forms and limits which the critic assigns to it. The life of reason as I conceive it is a mere romance, and the life of nature a mere fable; such pictures have no metaphysical value, even if as sympathetic fictions they had some psychological truth.

The doctrine of essence thus renders my scepticism invincible and complete, while reconciling me with it emotionally.

If now I turn my face in the other direction and consider the prospect open to animal faith, I see that all this insecurity and inadequacy of alleged knowledge are almost irrelevant to the natural effort of the mind to describe natural things. The discouragement we may feel in science does not come from failure; it comes from a false conception of what would be success. Our worst difficulties arise from the assumption that knowledge of existences ought to be literal, whereas knowledge of existences has no need, no propensity, and no fitness to be literal. It is symbolic initially, when a sound, a smell, an indescribable feeling are signals to the animal of his dangers or chances; and it fulfils its function perfectly—I mean its moral function of enlightening us about our natural good—if it remains symbolic to the end.

Can anything be more evident than that religion, language, patriotism, love, science itself speak in symbols? Given essences unify for intuition, in entirely adventitious human terms, the diffuse processes of nature; the æsthetic image—the sound, the colour, the expanse of space, the scent, taste, and sweet or cruel pressure of bodies—wears an aspect altogether unlike the mechanisms it stands for. Sensation and thought (between which there is no essential difference) work in a conventional medium, as do literature and music. The experience of essence is direct; the expression of natural facts through that medium is indirect. But this indirection is no obstacle to expression, rather its condition; and this vehicular manifestation of things may be knowledge of them, which intuition of essence is not. The theatre, for all its artifices, depicts life in a sense more truly than history, because the medium has a kindred movement to that of real life, though an artificial setting and form; and much in the same way the human medium of knowledge can perform its pertinent synthesis and make its pertinent report all the better when it frankly abandons the plane of its object and expresses in symbols what we need to know of it. The arts of expression would be impossible if they were not extensions of normal human perception. The Greeks recognised that astronomy and history were presided over by Muses, sisters of those of tragic and comic poetry; had they been as psychological as modern reflection has become, they might have had Muses of sight, hearing, and speech. I think they honoured, if they did not express, this complementary fact also, that all the Muses, even the most playful, are witnesses to the nature of things. The arts are evidences of wisdom, and sources of it; they include science. No Muse would be a humane influence, nor worthy of honour, if she did not studiously express the truth of nature with the liberty and grace appropriate to her special genius.

Philosophers would not have overlooked the fact that

knowledge is, and ought to be, symbolical, if intuition did not exist also, giving them a taste of something which perhaps they think higher and more satisfying. Intuition, when it is placid and masterful enough to stand alone, free from anxiety or delusion about matters of fact, is a delightful exercise, like play; it employs our imaginative faculty without warping it, and lets us live without responsibility. The playful and godlike mind of philosophers has always been fascinated by intuition; philosophers—I mean the great ones—are the infant prodigies of reflection. They often take intuition of essence for their single ideal, and wish to impose it on the workaday thoughts of men; they make a playworld for themselves which it is glorious to dominate, much as other men of genius, prolonging the masterfulness of childhood, continue to play at this or at that in their politics and their religion. But knowledge of existence has an entirely different method and an entirely different ideal. It is playful too, because its terms are intuitive and its grammar or logic often very subjective. Perception, theory, hypothesis are rapid, pregnant, often humorous; they seize a fact by its skirts from some unexpected quarter, and give it a nickname which it might be surprised to hear, such as the rainbow or the Great Bear. Yet in the investigation of facts all this play of mind is merely instrumental and indicative: the intent is practical, the watchfulness earnest, the spirit humble. The mind here knows that it is at school; and even its fancies are docile. Its nicknames for things and for their odd ways of behaving are like those which country people give to flowers; they often pointedly describe how things look or what they do to us. The ideas we have of things are not fair portraits; they are political caricatures made in the human interest; but in their partial way they may be masterpieces of characterisation and insight. Above all, they are obtained by labour, by investigating what is not given, and by correcting one impression by another, drawn from the same object—a thing impossible in the intuition of essences. They therefore conduce to wisdom, and in their perpetual tentativeness have a cumulative truth.

Consider the reason why, instead of cultivating congenial intuitions, a man may be drawn to the study of nature at all. It is because things, by their impact, startle him into attention and a new thought. Such external objects interest him for what they do, not for what they are; and knowledge of them is significant, not for the essence it displays to intuition (beautiful as this may be) but for the events it expresses or foreshadows. It matters little therefore to the pertinent knowledge of nature that the substance of things should remain recondite or unintelligible, if their movement and operation can be rightly determined on the plane of human perception. It matters little if their very existence is vouched for only by animal faith and presumption, so long as this faith posits existence where existence is, and this presumption expresses a prophetic preadaptation of animal instincts to the forces of the environment. The function of perception and natural science is not to flatter the sense of omniscience in an absolute mind but to dignify animal life by harmonising it, in action and in thought, with its conditions. It matters little if the news these methods can bring us of the world is fragmentary and is expressed rhetorically; what matters is that science should be integrated with art, and that the arts should substitute the dominion of man over circumstances, as far as this is possible, for the dominion of chance. In this there is no sacrifice of truth to utility; there is rather a wise direction of curiosity upon things on the human scale, and within the range of art. Speculation beyond those limits cannot be controlled, and is irresponsible; and the symbolic terms in which it must be carried on, even at close quarters, are the best possible indications for the facts in question. All these inadequacies and imperfections are proper to perfect signs, which should be brief and sharply distinguished.

Complete scepticism is accordingly not inconsistent with animal faith; the admission that nothing given exists is not incompatible with belief in things not given. I may yield to the suasion of instinct, and practise the arts with a humble confidence, without in the least disavowing the most rigorous criticism of knowledge or hypostatising any of the data of sense or fancy. And I need not do this with a bad conscience, as Parmenides and Plato and the Indians seem to have done, when they admitted illusion or opinion as an epilogue to their tight metaphysics, on the ground that otherwise they would miss their way home. It is precisely by *not* yielding to opinion and illusion, and by *not* delegating any favourite essences to be the substance of things, that I aspire to keep my cognitive conscience pure and my practical judgement sane; because in order to find my way home I am by no means compelled to yield ignominiously to any animal illusion; what guides me there is not illusion but habit; and the intuitions which accompany habit are normal signs for the circle of objects and forces by which that habit is sustained. The images of sense and science will not delude me if instead of hypostatising them, as those philosophers did the terms of their dialectic, I regard them as graphic symbols for home and for the way there. That such external things exist, that I exist myself, and live more or less prosperously in the midst of them, is a faith not founded on reason but precipitated in action, and in that intent, which is virtual action, involved in perception. This faith, which it would be dishonest not to confess that I share, does no violence to a sceptical analysis of experience; on the contrary, it takes advantage of that analysis to interpret this volatile experience as all animals do and must, as a set of symbols for existences that cannot enter experience, and which, since they are not elements in knowledge, no analysis of knowledge can touch—they are in another realm of being.

I propose now to consider what objects animal faith requires me to posit, and in what order, without for a moment forgetting that my assurance of their existence is only instinctive, and my description of their nature only symbolic. I may know them by intent, based on bodily reaction; I know them initially as whatever confronts me, whatever it may turn out to be, just as I know the future initially as whatever is coming, without knowing what will come. That something confronts me here, now, and from a specific quarter, is in itself a momentous discovery. The aspect this thing wears, as it first attracts my attention, though it may deceive me in some particulars, can hardly fail to be, in some respects, a telling indication of its nature in its relation to me. Signs identify their objects for discourse, and show us where to look for their undiscovered qualities. Further signs, catching other aspects of the same object, may help me to lay siege to it from all sides; but signs will never lead me into the citadel, and if its inner chambers are ever opened to me, it must be through sympathetic imagination. I might, by some happy unison between my imagination and its generative principles, intuit the essence which is actually the essence of that thing. In that case (which may often occur when the object is a sympathetic mind) knowledge of existence, without ceasing to be instinctive faith, will be as complete and adequate as knowledge can possibly be. The given essence will be the essence of the object meant; but knowledge will remain a claim, since the intuition is not satisfied to observe the given essence passively as a disembodied essence, but instinctively affirms it to be the essence of an existence confronting me, and beyond the range of my possible apprehension. Therefore the most perfect knowledge of fact is perfect only pictorially, not evidentially, and remains subject to the end to the insecurity inseparable from animal faith, and from life itself.

Animal faith being a sort of expectation and open-mouthedness, is earlier than intuition; intuitions come to help it out and lend it something to posit. It is more than ready to swallow any suggestion of sense or fancy; and perhaps primitive credulity, as in a dream, makes no bones of any contradiction or incongruity in successive convictions, but yields its whole soul to every image. Faith then hangs like a pendulum at rest; but when perplexity has caused that pendulum to swing more and more madly, it may for a moment stop quivering at a point of unstable equilibrium at the top; and this vertical station may be likened to universal scepticism. It is a more wonderful and a more promising equilibrium than the other, because it cannot be maintained; but before declining from the zenith and desisting from pointing vertically at zero, the pendulum of faith may hesitate for an instant which way to fall, if at that uncomfortable height it has really lost all animal momentum and all ancient prejudice. Before giving my reasons—which are but prejudices and human—for believing in events, in substances, and in the variegated truths which they involve, it may be well to have halted for breath at the apex of scepticism, and felt all the negative privileges of that position. The mere possibility of it in its purity is full of instruction; and although I have, for my own part, dwelt upon it only ironically, by a scruple of method, and intending presently to abandon it for common sense, many a greater philosopher has sought to maintain himself acrobatically at that altitude. They have not succeeded; but an impossible dwelling-place may afford, like a mountain-top, a good point of view in clear weather from which to map the land and choose a habitation.

XIV

Essence and Intuition

To believe nothing and live immersed in intuition might be the privilege of a disembodied spirit; and if a man could share it he would not only be relieved from doubt but would, in one dimension, lose nothing in the scope of his experience, since the realm of essence, which would still be open to him, is absolutely infinite, and contains images of all the events that any existing world could enact, or that all possible worlds could enact together. Yet all this variety and richness would form a mosaic, a marble effigy of life, or chronicle of ancient wars. The pangs and horrors would be there, as well as the beauties, but each would burn ir its eternal place, balancing all the rest, and no anxious eye would glance hurriedly from one to the other, wondering what the next might be. The spirit that actually breathes in man is an animal spirit, transitive like the material endeavours which it expresses; it has a material station and accidental point of view, and a fevered preference for one alternative issue over another. It thirsts for news; and this curiosity, which it borrows of course from the insecurity and instinctive anxiety of the animal whose spirit it is, is strangely self-contradictory; because the further it ranges in the service of animal will, the more the spectacle it discloses rebukes that animal will and tends to neutralise it. It would indeed not be spirit at all if it did not essentially tend to discount its accidental point of view, and to exchange the material station to which it finds itself unaccountably attached in its birth. In so far as it is spirit, and is not called back by its animal allegiance to pleasures and ambitions which pure spirit could not share (since they imply ignorance), it accordingly tends to withdraw from preoccupation with animal life, from the bias of time and place, and from all thought of existence. In so doing, far from perishing, it seems to acquire a more intense, luminous, and placid being. Since the roots of spirit, at least in man, are in matter, this would seem to be an illusion; yet the experience is normal, and no illusion need attach to it, if once the nature of intuition is understood.

At the vanishing-point of scepticism, which is also the acme of life, intuition is absorbed in its object. For this reason, philosophers capable of intense contemplation—Aristotle, for instance, at those points where his thought becomes, as it were, internal to spirit—have generally asserted that in the end essence and the contemplation of essence are identical. Certainly the intuition of essence is oblivious of itself, and cognisant of essence only, to which it adds nothing whatever internally, either in character or in intensity; because the intensity of a thunder-clap is the chief part of its essence, and so the peculiar intolerableness of each sort of pain, or transitiveness of each sort of pleasure. If in fact when any such essence is given there had been nothing prior to this intuition, nothing beside it existentially, and nothing to follow upon it, this obliviousness to the intuition itself, as distinct from the given essence, would not be an oversight; it would be rather an absence of illusion. For it would then have been an illusion to suppose, as I should in calling the presence of that essence an intuition of it, that a soul with a history and with other adventitious qualities had come to contemplate that essence at one moment in its career. There would really be the essence only, with no relations other than those perfectly irreversible internal ones to other essences which define it in its own realm. Those very high numbers, for instance, which nobody has ever thought of specifically, have no other relations than those which they have eternally in the series of whole numbers; they have no place in any man's life. So too those many forms of torment for which nature does not provide the requisite instrument, and which even hell has neglected to exemplify; they remain essences only, of which fortunately there is no intuition. Evidently the being of such numbers or such torments is constituted by their essence only, and has not attained to existence. Yet it is this essential being alone that, if there was intuition of those numbers or those torments, would be revealed in intuition; for no external adventitious relations, such as the intuition has in the life of some soul, would be presented within it, if (as I assume) nothing but these essences was then given.

It is therefore inevitable that minds singly absorbed in

the contemplation of any essence should attribute the presence and force of that essence to its own nature, which alone
is visible, and not to their intuition, which is invisible.
Thought as it sinks into its object rises in its deliverance
out of the sphere of contingency and change, and loses itself
in that object, sublimated into an essence. This sublimation
is no loss; it is merely absence of distraction. It is the perfect fruition and fulfilment of that experience: In this manner I can understand why Aristotle could call the realm of
essence, or that part of it which he had considered, a deity,
and could declare sublimely that its inalienable being was
an eternal life. More strictly, it would have been an eternal
actualisation of cognitive life only; animal life would have
ceased, because animal life requires us to pick up and drop
the essences we consider, and to attribute temporal as well
as eternal relations to them; in other words, to regard them
not as essences but as things. But though cognitive life
begins with this attention to practical exigencies and is
kindled by them, yet its ideal is sacrificial; it aspires to
see each thing clearly and to see all things together, that is
to say, under the form of eternity, and as sheer essences
given in intuition. To cease to live temporally is intellectually
to be saved; it is ἀθανατίζειν, to fade or to brighten into
the truth, and to become eternal. It is the inmost aim and
highest achievement of cognition to cease to be knowledge
for a self, to abolish the bias and transcend the point of view
by which knowledge establishes its perspectives, so that all
things may be present equally, and the truth may be all
in all.

All this comes about, however, only subjectively, in that
vital and poetic effort of the mind to understand which
begins with a candid self-forgetfulness and ends in a passionate self-surrender. Seen from outside, as it takes place
psychologically, the matter wears an entirely different
aspect. In reality, essence and the intuition of essence can
never be identical. If all animal predicaments were resolved,

there would be no organ and no occasion for intuition; and intuition ceasing, no essences would appear. Certainly they would not be abolished by that accident in their own sphere, and each would be what it would have seemed if intuition of it had arisen; but they would all be merely logical or æsthetic themes unrehearsed, as remote as possible from life or from the intense splendour of divinity. Essence without intuition would be not merely non-existent (as it always is), but what is worse, it would be the object of no contemplation, the goal of no effort, the secret or implicit ideal of no life. It would be valueless. All that joy and sense of liberation which pure objectivity brings to the mind would be entirely absent; and essence would lose all its dignity if life lost its precarious existence.

. . . .

The first existence . . . of which a sceptic who finds himself in the presence of random essences may gather reasonable proof, is the existence of the intuition to which those essences are manifest. This is of course not the object which the animal mind first posits and believes in. The existence of things is assumed by animals in action and expectation before intuition supplies any description of what the thing is that confronts them in a certain quarter. But animals are not sceptics, and a long experience must intervene before the problem arises which I am here considering, namely, whether anything need be posited and believed in at all. And I reply that it is not inevitable, if I am willing and able to look passively on the essences that may happen to be given: but that if I consider what they are, and how they appear, I see that this appearance is an accident to them; that the principle of it is a contribution from my side, which I call intuition. The difference between essence and intuition, though men may have discovered it late, then seems to me profound and certain. They belong to two different realms of being.

XVI

Belief in the Self

EXPERIENCE, when the shocks that punctuate it are reacted upon instinctively, imposes belief in something far more recondite than mental discourse, namely, a person or self; and not merely such a transcendental ego as is requisite intrinsically for any intuition, nor such a flux of sentience as discourse itself constitutes, but a substantial being preceding *all* the vicissitudes of experience, and serving as an instrument to produce them, or a soil out of which they grow.

Shock is the great argument of common sense for the existence of material things, because common sense does not need to distinguish the order of evidence from the order of genesis. If I know already that a tile has fallen on my head, my sore head is a proof to me that the tile was real; but if I start from the pain itself in all innocence, I cannot draw any inference from it about tiles or the laws of gravity. By common sense experience is conceived as the effect which the impact of external things makes on a man when he is able to retain and remember it. As a matter of fact, of course, shocks usually have an external origin, although in dreams, madness, apparitions, and in disease generally, their cause is sometimes internal. But all question concerning the source of a shock is vain for the sceptic; he knows nothing of sources; he is asking, not whence shocks come, but to what beliefs they should lead. In the criticism of knowledge the *argumentum baculaneum* is accordingly ridiculous, and fit only for the backs of those who use it. Why, if I am a spirit beholding essences, should I not feel shocks? Why are not novelties and surprises as likely themes for my entertainment as the analysis or synthesis of some theorem or of some picture? All essences are grist for the mill of intuition, and any order or disorder, any quality of noise or violence, is equally appropriate in an experience which, for all I know or as yet believe, is absolute and groundless. And I call it experience, not because it discloses anything about the environment which produced it, but because it is composed of a series of shocks, which I survey and remember.

If, however, consenting to listen to the voice of nature, I ask myself what a shock can signify, and of what it brings me most unequivocal evidence, the least hazardous answer will be: evidence of prepossessions on my part. What shock proves, if it proves anything, is that I have a nature to which all events and all developments are not equally welcome. How could any apparition surprise or alarm me, or how could interruption of any sort overtake me, unless I was somehow running on in a certain direction, with a specific rhythm? Had I not such a positive nature, the existence of material things and their most violent impact upon one another, shattering the world to atoms, would leave me a placid observer of their movement; whereas a definite nature in me, even if disturbed only by cross-currents or by absolute accidents within my own being, would justify my sense of surprise and horror. A self, then, not a material world, is the first object which I should posit if I wish the experience of shock to enlarge my dogmas in the strict order of evidence.

But what sort of a self? In one sense, the existence of intuition is tantamount to that of a self, though of a merely formal and transparent one, pure spirit. A self somewhat more concrete is involved in discourse, when intuition has been deployed into a successive survey of constant ideal objects, since here the self not only sees, but adds an adventitious order to the themes it rehearses, traversing them in various directions, with varying completeness, and suspending or picking up the consideration of them at will; so that the self involved in discourse is a thinking mind. Now that I am consenting to build further dogmas on the sentiment of shock, and to treat it, not as an essence groundlessly revealed to me, but as signifying something pertinent to the alarm or surprise with which it fills me, I must thicken and substantialise the self I believe in, recognising in it a nature that accepts or rejects events, a nature having a movement of its own, far deeper, more continuous and more biassed than a discoursing mind: the self posited by the sense of shock is a living psyche.

XVIII

Knowledge Is Faith Mediated by Symbols

IN the claims of memory I have a typical instance of what is called knowledge. In remembering I believe that I am taking cognisance not of a given essence but of a remote existence, so that, being myself here and now, I can consider and describe something going on at another place and time. This leap, which renders knowledge essentially faith, may come to seem paradoxical or impossible like the leap of physical being from place to place or from form to form which is called motion or change, and which some philosophers deny, as they deny knowledge. Is there such a leap in knowing? Am I really here and now when I apprehend some remote thing? Certainly, if by myself I understand the psyche within my body, which directs my outer organs, reacts on external things, and shapes the history and character of the individual animal that bears my name. In this sense I am a physical being in the midst of nature, and my knowledge is a name for the effects which surrounding things have upon me, in so far as I am quickened by them, and readjusted to them. I am certainly confined at each moment to a limited space and time, but may be quickened by the influence of things at any distance, and may be readjusting myself to them. For the naturalist there is accordingly no paradox in the leap of knowledge other than the general marvel of material interaction and animal life.

If by myself, however, I meant pure spirit, or the light of attention by which essences appear and intuitions are rendered actual, it would not be true that I am confined or even situated in a particular place and time, nor that in considering things remote from my body, my thoughts are taking any unnatural leap. The marvel, from the point of view of spirit, is rather that it should need to be planted at all in the sensorium of some living animal, and that, being rooted there, it should take that accidental station for its point of view in surveying all nature, and should dignify one momentary phase of that animal life with the titles of the Here and the Now. It is only spirit, be it observed, that can do this. In themselves all the points of space-time are equally central and palpitating, and every phase of every psyche is a focus for actual readjustments to the whole universe. How then can the spirit, which would seem to be the principle of universality and justice, take up its station in each of these atoms and fight its battles for it, and prostitute its own light in the service of that desperate blindness? Can reason do nothing better than supply the eloquence of prejudice? Such are the puzzles which spirit might find, I will not say in the leap of knowledge, but in the fatality which links the spirit to a material organ so that, in order to reach other things, it is obliged to leap; or rather can never reach other things, because it is tethered to its starting-point, except by its intent in leaping, and cannot even discover the stepping-stone on which it stands because its whole life is the act of leaping away from it. There is no reason, therefore, in so far as knowledge is an apanage of spirit, why knowledge should not bathe all time and all existence in an equal light, and see everything as it is, with an equal sympathy and im-mediacy. The problem for the spirit is how it could ever come to pick out one body or another for its cynosure and for its instrument, as if it could not see save through such a little eye-glass, and in such a violent perspective. This problem, I think, has a ready answer, but it is not one that spirit could ever find of itself, without a long and docile apprenticeship in the school of animal faith. This answer is that spirit, with knowledge and all its other prerogatives, is intrinsically and altogether a function of animal life; so that if it were not lodged in some body and expressive of its rhythms and relations, spirit would not exist at all. But this solution, even when spirit is humble enough to accept it, always seems to it a little disappointing and satirical.

Spirit, therefore, has no need to leap in order to know, because in its range as spirit it is omnipresent and omnimodal. Events which are past or future in relation to the phase of the psyche which spirit expresses in a particular instance, or events which are remote from that psyche in space, are not for that reason remote from spirit, or out of its cognitive range: they are merely hidden, or placed in a particular perspective for the moment, like the features of a landscape by the hedges and turns of a road. Just as all essences are equally near to spirit, and equally fit and easy to contemplate, if only a psyche with an affinity to those essences happens to arise; so all existing things, past, future, or infinitely distant, are equally within the range of knowledge, if only a psyche happens to be directed upon them; and to choose terms, however poor or fantastic, in which to describe them. In choosing these terms the psyche creates spirit, for they are essences given in intuition; and in directing her action or endeavour, backward or forward, upon those remote events, she creates intent in the spirit, so that the given essences become descriptions of the things with which the psyche is then busied.

But how, I may ask, can intent distinguish its hidden object, so that an image, distorted or faithful, may be truly or falsely projected *there*, or used to describe *it*? How does the spirit divine that there is such an object, or where it lies?

And how can it appeal to a thing which is hidden, the object of mere intent, as to a touchstone or standard for its various descriptions of that object, and say to them, as they suggest themselves in turn: You are too vague, You are absurd, You are better, You are absolutely right?

I answer that it does so by animal presumption, positing whatsoever object instinct is materially predisposed to cope with, as in hunger, love, fighting, or the expectation of a future. But before developing this reply, let me make one observation. Since intuition of essence is not knowledge, knowledge can never lie in an overt comparison of one datum with another datum given at the same time; even in pure dialectic, the comparison is with a datum *believed* to have been given formerly. If both terms were simply given they would compose a complex essence, without the least signification. Only when one of the terms is indicated by intent, without being given exhaustively, can the other term serve to define the first more fully, or be linked with it in an assertion which is not mere tautology. An object of faith—and knowledge is one species of faith—can never, even in the most direct perception, come within the circle of intuition. Intuition of things is a contradiction in terms. If philosophers wish to abstain from faith, and reduce themselves to intuition of the obvious, they are free to do so, but they will thereby renounce all knowledge, and live on passive illusions. No fact, not even the fact that these illusions exist, would ever be, or would ever have been, anything but the false idea that they had existed. There would be nothing but the realm of essence, without any intuition of any part of it, nor of the whole: so that we should be driven back to a nihilism which only silence and death could express consistently; since the least actual assertion of it, by existing, would contradict it.

Even such acquaintance with the realm of essence as constitutes some science or recognisable art—like mathematics or music—lies in intending and positing great stretches of essence not now given, so that the essences now given acquire significance and become pregnant, to my vital feeling, with a thousand things which they do not present actually, but which I know where to look for eventually, and how to await. Suppose a moment ago I heard a clap of thunder, loud and prolonged, but that the physical shock has subsided and I am conscious of repose and silence. I may find some difficulty, although the thing was so recent, in *rehearsing* even now the exact volume, tone, and rumblings of that sound; yet I *know* the theme perfectly, in the sense that when it thunders again, I can say with assurance whether the second crash was longer, louder, or differently modulated. In such a case I have no longer an intuition of the first thunderclap, but a memory of it which is knowledge; and I can define on occasion, up to a certain point and not without some error, the essence given in that particular past intuition. Thus even pure essences can become objects of intent and of tentative knowledge when they are not present in intuition but are approached and posited indirectly, as the essences given on another particular occasion or signified by some particular word. The word or the occasion are natural facts, and my knowledge is focussed upon them in the first instance by ordinary perception or conception of nature: and the essence I hope to recover is elicited gradually, imaginatively, perhaps incorrectly, at the suggestion of those assumed facts, according to my quickness of wit, or my familiarity with the conventions of that art or science. In this way it becomes possible and necessary to learn about essences as if they were things, not initially by a spontaneous and complete intuition, but by coaxing the mind until possibly, at the end, it beholds them clearly. This is the sort of intuition which is mediated by language and by works of fine art; also by logic and mathematics, as they are learned from teachers and out of books. It is not happy intuition of some casual datum: it is laborious recovery, up to a certain point, of the *sort* of essence somebody else may have intuited. Whereas intuition, which reveals an essence directly, is not knowledge, because it has no ulterior object, the designation of some essence by some sign does convey knowledge, to an intelligent pupil, of what that essence was. Obviously such divination of essences present elsewhere, so that they become present here also, in so far as it is knowledge, is trebly faith. Faith first in the document, as a genuine natural fact and not a vapid fancy of my own; for instance, belief that there is a book called the Bible, really handed down from the ancient Jews and the early Christians, and that I have not merely dreamt of such a book. Faith then in the significance of that document, that it means some essence which it is not; in this instance, belief that the sacred writers were not merely speaking with tongues but were signifying some intelligible points in history and philosophy. Faith finally in my success in interpreting that document correctly, so that the essences it suggests to me now are the very essences it expressed originally: in other words, the belief that when I read the Bible I understand it as it was meant, and not fantastically.

I revert now to the question how it is possible to posit an object which is not a datum, and how without knowing positively what this object is I can make it the criterion of truth in my ideas. How can I test the accuracy of descriptions by referring them to a subject-matter which is not only out of view now but which probably has never been more than an object of intent, an event which even while it was occurring was described by me only in terms native to my fancy? If I know a man only by reputation, how should I judge if the reputation is deserved? If I know things only by representations, are not the representations the only things I know?

This challenge is fundamental, and so long as the assumptions which it makes are not challenged in turn, it drives critics of knowledge inexorably to scepticism of a dogmatic sort, I mean to the assertion that the very notion of knowl-

edge is absurd. One assumption is that knowledge should be
intuition: but I have already come to the conclusion that
intuition is not knowledge. So long as a knowledge is demanded that shall be intuition, the issue can only be laughter
or despair; for if I attain intuition, I have only a phantom
object, and if I spurn that and turn to the facts, I have
renounced intuition. This assumption alone suffices, therefore, to disprove the possibility of knowledge. But in case
the force of this disproof escaped us, another assumption
is at hand to despatch the business, namely, the assumption
that in a true description—if we grant knowledge by description—the terms should be identical with the constituents of the object, so that the idea should *look like* the thing
that it knows. This assumption is derived from the other,
or is a timid form of it: for it is supposed that I know by
intuiting my idea, and that unless that idea resembled the
object I wish to know, I could not even by courtesy be said
to have discovered the latter. But the intuition of an idea,
let me repeat, is not knowledge; and if a thing resembling
that idea happened to exist, my intuition would still not be
knowledge of it, but contemplation of the idea only.

Plato and many other philosophers, being in love with
intuition (for which alone they were perhaps designed by
nature), have identified science with certitude, and consequently entirely condemned what I call knowledge (which
is a form of animal faith) or relegated it to an inferior position, as something merely necessary for life. I myself have
no passionate attachment to existence, and value this world
for the intuitions it can suggest, rather than for the wilderness of facts that compose it. To turn away from it may
be the deepest wisdom in the end. What better than to blow
out the candle, and to bed! But at noon this pleasure is
premature. I can always hold it in reserve, and perhaps
nihilism is a system—the simplest of all—on which we shall
all agree in the end. But I seem to see very clearly now that
in doing so we should all be missing the truth: not indeed by

any false assertion, such as may separate us from the truth now, but by dumb ignorance—a dumb ignorance which, when proposed as a solution to actual doubts, is the most radical of errors, since it ignores and virtually denies the pressure of those doubts, and their living presence. Accordingly, so long as I remain awake and the light burning, that total dogmatic scepticism is evidently an impossible attitude. It requires me to deny what I assert, not to mean what I mean, and (in the sense in which seeing is believing) not to believe what I see. If I wish, therefore, to formulate in any way my actual claim to knowledge—a claim which life, and in particular memory, imposes upon me—I must revise the premises of this nihilism. For I have been led to it not by any accidental error, but by the logic of the assumption that knowledge should be intuition of fact. It is this presumption that must be revoked.

Knowledge is no such thing. It is not intramental nor internal to experience. Not only does it not require me to compare two given terms and to find them similar or identical, but it positively excludes any intuitive possession of its object. Intuition subsists beneath knowledge, as vegetative life subsists beneath animal life, and within it. Intuition may also supervene upon knowledge, when all I have learned of the universe, and all my concern for it, turn to a playful or a hypnotising phantom; and any poet or philosopher, like any flower, is free to prefer intuition to knowledge. But in preferring intuition he prefers ignorance. Knowledge is knowledge because it has compulsory objects that pre-exist. It is incidental to the predicaments and labour of life: also to its masterful explorations and satirical moods. It is reflected from events as light is reflected from bodies. It expresses in discourse the modified habits of an active being, plastic to experience, and capable of readjusting its organic attitude to other things on the same material plane of being with itself. The place and the pertinent functions of these several things are indicated by the very attitude of the animal who notices them; this attitude, physical and practical, determines the object of intent, which discourse is about.

When the proverbial child cries for the moon, is the object of his desire doubtful? He points at it unmistakably; yet the psychologists (not to speak of the child himself) would have some difficulty in recovering exactly the sensations and images, the gathering demands and fumbling efforts, that traverse the child's mind while he points. Fortunately all this fluid sentience, even if it could be described, is irrelevant to the question; for the child's sensuous experience is not his object. If it were, he would have attained it. What his object is, his fixed gaze and outstretched arm declare unequivocally. His elders may say that he doesn't know what he wants, which is probably true of them also: that is, he has only a ridiculously false and inconstant idea of what the moon may be in itself. But his attention is arrested in a particular direction, his appetition flows the same way; and if he may be said to know anything, he knows there is something there which he would like to reach, which he would like to know better. He is a little philosopher; and his knowledge, if less diversified and congealed, is exactly like science.

The attitude of his body in pointing to the moon, and his tears, fill full his little mind, which not only reverberates to this physical passion, but probably observes it: and this felt attitude *identifies the object* of his desire and knowledge *in the physical world*. It determines what particular thing, in the same space and time with the child's body, was the object of that particular passion. If the object which the body is after is identified, that which the soul is after is identified too: no one, I suppose, would carry dualism so far as to assert that when the mouth waters at the sight of one particular plum, the soul may be yearning for quite another.

The same bodily attitude of the child *identifies the object in the discourse of an observer*. In perceiving what his senses are excited by, and which way his endeavour is turned, I can see that the object of his desire is the moon, which I too am looking at. That I am looking at the same moon as he can be proved by a little triangulation: our glances converge upon it. If the child has reached the inquisitive age and asks "What is that?" I understand what he means by "that" and am able to reply sapiently "That is the moon," only because our respective bodies, in one common space, are discoverably turned towards one material object, which is stimulating them simultaneously. Knowledge of discourse in other people, or of myself at other times, is what I call literary psychology. It is, or may be, in its texture, the most literal and adequate sort of knowledge of which a mind is capable. If I am a lover of children, and a good psycho-analyst, I may feel for a moment exactly as the child feels in looking at the moon: and I may know that I know his feeling, and very likely he too will know that I know it, and we shall become fast friends. But this rare adequacy of knowledge, attained by dramatic sympathy, goes out to an object which in its existence is known very indirectly: because poets and religious visionaries feel this sort of sympathy with all sorts of imaginary persons, of whose existence and thoughts they have only intuition, not knowledge. If I ask for evidence that such an object exists, and is not an *alter ego* of my private invention, I must appeal to my faith in nature, and to my conventional assumption that this child and I are animals of the same species, in the same habitat, looking at the same moon, and likely to have the same feelings: and finally the psychology of the tribe and the crowd may enable me half to understand how we know that we have the same feelings at once, when we actually share them.

The attitude of the child's body also *identifies the object for him, in his own subsequent discourse*. He is not likely to forget a moon that he cried for. When in stretching his hand towards it he found he could not touch it, he learned that this bright good was not within his grasp, and he made a beginning in the experience of life. He also made a beginning in science, since he then added the absolutely true predicate "out of reach" to the rather questionable predicates "bright" and "good" (and perhaps "edible") with which his first glimpse had supplied him. That active and mysterious thing, co-ordinate with himself, since it lay in the same world with his body, and affected it—the thing that attracted his hand, was evidently the very thing that eluded it. His failure would have had no meaning and would have taught him nothing—that is, would not have corrected his instinctive reactions—if the object he saw and the object he failed to reach had not been identical; and certainly that object was not brightness nor goodness nor excitements in his brain or psyche, for these are not things he could ever have attempted or expected to touch. It is only things on the scale of the human senses and in the field of those instinctive reactions which sensation calls forth, that can be the primary objects of human knowledge: no other things can be discriminated at first by an animal mind, or can interest it, or can be meant and believed in by it. It is these instinctive reactions that select the objects of attention, designate their locus, and impose faith in their existence. But these reactions may be modified by experience, and the description the mind gives of the objects reacted upon can be revised, or the objects themselves discarded, and others discerned instead. Thus the child's instinct to touch the moon was as spontaneous and as confident at first as his instinct to look at it; and the object of both efforts was the same, because the same external agency aroused them, and with them the very heterogeneous sensations of light and of disappointment. These various terms of sense or of discourse, by which the child described the object under whose attractions and rebuffs he was living, were merely symbols to him, like words. An animal naturally has as many signs for an object as he has sensations or emotions in its presence. These signs are miscellaneous essences—sights, sounds, smells, contacts, tears, provocations—and they are alternative or supplementary to one another, like words in different languages. The most diverse senses, such as smell and sight, if summoned to the same point in the environment, and guiding a single action, will report upon a single object. Even when one sense brings all the news I have, its reports will change from moment to moment with the distance, variation, or suspension of the connection between the object and my body: and this without any relevant change in the object itself. Nay, often the very transformation of the sensation bears witness that the object is unchanged; as music and laughter, overheard as I pass a tavern, are felt and known to continue unabated, and to be no merriment of mine, just because they fade from my ears as I move away.

The object of knowledge being that designated in this way by my bodily attitude, the æsthetic qualities I attribute to it will depend on the particular sense it happens to affect at the moment, or on the sweep and nature of the reaction which it then calls forth on my part. This diversity in signs and descriptions for a single thing is a normal diversity. Diversity, when it is not contradiction, irritates only unreasonably dogmatic people; they are offended with nature for having a rich vocabulary, and sometimes speaking a language, or employing a syntax, which they never heard at home. It is an innocent prejudice, and it yields easily in a generous mind to pleasure at the wealth of alternatives which animal life affords. Even such contradictions as may arise in the description of things, and may truly demand a solution, reside in the implication of the terms, not in their sensuous or rhetorical diversity: they become contradictory only when they assign to the object contrary movements or contrary effects, not when they merely exhibit its various appearances. Looking at the moon, one man may call it simply a light in the sky; another, prone to dreaming awake, may call it a virgin goddess; a more observant person, remembering that this luminary is given to waxing and waning, may call it the crescent; and a fourth, a full-fledged astronomer, may say (taking the æsthetic essence before him merely for a sign) that it is an extinct and opaque spheroidal satellite of the earth, reflecting the light of the sun from a part of its surface. All these descriptions envisage the same object—otherwise no relevance, conflict, or progress could obtain among them. What that object is in its complete constitution and history will never be known by man; but that this object exists in a known space and time and has traceable physical relations with all other physical objects is a fact posited from the beginning; it was posited by the child when he pointed, and by me when I saw him point. If it did not so exist and (as sometimes happens) he and I were suffering from a hallucination, in thinking we were pointing at the moon we should be discoverably pointing at vacancy: exploration would eventually satisfy us of that fact, and any bystander would vouch for it. But if in pointing at it we were pointing to it, its identity would be fixed without more ado; disputes and discoveries concerning it would be pertinent and soluble, no matter what diversity there might be in the ideal essences —light, crescent, goddess, or satellite—which we used as rival descriptions of it while we pointed.

I find that the discrimination of essence brings a wonderful clearness into this subject. All data and descriptions— light, crescent, goddess, or satellite—are equally essences, terms of human discourse, inexistent in themselves. What exists in any instance, besides the moon and our various reactions upon it, is some intuition, expressing those reactions, evoking that essence, and lending it a specious actuality. The terms of astronomy are essences no less human and visionary than those of mythology; but they are the fruit of a better focussed, more chastened, and more prolonged attention turned upon what actually occurs; that is, they are kept closer to animal faith, and freer from pictorial elements and the infusion of reverie. In myth, on the contrary, intuition wanders idly and uncontrolled; it makes epicycles, as it were, upon the reflex arc of perception; the moonbeams bewitch some sleeping Endymion, and he dreams of a swift huntress in heaven. Myth is nevertheless a relevant fancy, and genuinely expressive; only instead of being guided by a perpetual fresh study of the object posited by animal faith and encountered in action, it runs into marginal comments, personal associations, and rhetorical asides; so that even if based originally on perception, it is built upon principles internal to human discourse, as are grammar, rhyme, music, and morals. It may be admirable as an expression of these principles, and yet be egregiously false if asserted of the object, without discounting the human medium in which it has taken form. Diana is an exquisite symbol for the moon, and for one sort of human loveliness; but she must not be credited with any existence over and above that of the moon, and of sundry short-skirted Dorian maidens. She is not other than they: she is an image of them, the best part of their essence distilled in a poet's mind. So with the description of the moon given by astronomers, which is not less fascinating; this, too, is no added object, but only a new image for the moon known even to the child and me. The space, matter, gravitation, time, and laws of motion conceived by astronomers are essences only, and mere symbols for the use of animal faith, when very enlightened: I mean in so far as they are alleged to constitute knowledge of a world which I must bow to and encounter in action; for if astronomy is content to be a mathematical exercise without any truth, an object of pure intuition, its terms and its laws will, of course, be ultimate realities, apart from what happens to exist: realities in the realm of essence. In the description of the natural world, however, they are mere symbols, mediating animal faith. Science at any moment may recast or correct its conceptions (as it is doing now), giving them a different colour; and the nerve of truth in them will be laid bare and made taut in proportion as the sensuous and rhetorical vesture of these notions is stripped off, and the dynamic relations of events, as found and posited by material exploration, are nakedly recorded.

Knowledge accordingly is belief: belief in a world of events, and especially of those parts of it which are near the self, tempting or threatening it. This belief is native to animals, and precedes all deliberate use of intuitions as signs or descriptions of things, as I turn my head to see who is there, before I see who it is. Furthermore, knowledge is true belief. It is such an enlightening of the self by intuitions arising there, that what the self imagines and asserts of the collateral thing, with which it wrestles in action, is actually true of that thing. Truth in such presumptions or conceptions does not imply adequacy, nor a pictorial identity between the essence in intuition and the constitution of the object. Discourse is a language, not a mirror. The images in sense are parts of discourse, not parts of nature: they are the babble of our innocent organs under the stimulus of things; but these spontaneous images, like the sounds of the voice, may acquire the function of names; they may become signs, if discourse is intelligent and can recapitulate its phases, for the things sought or encountered in the world. The truth which discourse can achieve is truth in its own terms, appropriate description: it is no incorporation or reproduction of the object in the mind. The mind notices and intends; it cannot incorporate or reproduce anything not an intention or an intuition. Its objects are no part of itself even when they are essences, much less when they are things. It thinks the essences, with that sort of immediate and self-forgetful attention which I have been calling intuition; and if it is animated, as it usually is, by some ulterior interest or pursuit, it takes the essences before it for messages, signs, or emanations sent forth to it from those objects of animal faith; and they become its evidences and its description for those objects. Therefore any degree of inadequacy and originality is tolerable in discourse, or even requisite, when the constitution of the objects which the animal encounters is out of scale with his organs, or quite heterogeneous from his possible images. A sensation or a theory, no matter how arbitrary its terms (and all language is perfectly arbitrary), will be true of the object, if it expresses some true relation in which that object stands to the self, so that these terms are not misleading as signs, however poetical they may be as sounds or as pictures.

Finally, knowledge is true belief grounded in experience, I mean, controlled by outer facts. It is not true by accident; it is not shot into the air on the chance that there may be something it may hit. It arises by a movement of the self sympathetic or responsive to surrounding beings, so that these beings become its intended objects, and at the same time an appropriate correspondence tends to be established between these objects and the beliefs generated under their influence.

In regard to the original articles of the animal creed—that there is a world, that there is a future, that things sought can be found, and things seen can be eaten—no guarantee can possibly be offered. I am sure these dogmas are often false; and perhaps the event will some day falsify them all, and they will lapse altogether. But while life lasts, in one form or another this faith must endure. It is the initial expression of animal vitality in the sphere of mind, the first announcement that anything is going on. It is involved in any pang of hunger, of fear, or of love. It launches the adventure of knowledge. The object of this tentative knowledge is things in general, whatsoever may be at work (as I am) to disturb me or awake my attention. The effort of knowledge is to discover what sort of world this disturbing world happens to be. Progress in knowledge lies open in various directions, now in the scope of its survey, now in its accuracy, now in its depth of local penetration. The ideal of knowledge is to become natural science: if it trespasses beyond that, it relapses into intuition, and ceases to be knowledge.

XIX

Belief in Substance

* * * * * * * *

THE instinct and ability to posit objects, and the occasion
for doing so, are incidents in the development of animal life.
Positing is a symptom of sensibility in an organism to the
presence of other substances in its environment. The sceptic,
like the sick man, is intent on the symptom; and positing is
his name for felt plasticity in his animal responses. It is not
a bad name, because plasticity, though it may seem a passive
thing, is really a spontaneous quality. If the substance of
the ego were not alive, it would not leap to meet its opportunities, it would not develop new organs to serve its old
necessities, and it would not kindle itself to intuition of
essences, nor concern itself to regard those essences as appearances of the substances with which it was wrestling. The
whole life of imagination and knowledge comes from within,
from the restlessness, eagerness, curiosity, and terror of the
animal bent on hunting, feeding, and breeding; and the
throb of being which he experiences at any moment is not
proper to the datum in his mind's eye—a purely fantastic
essence—but to himself. It is out of his organism or its
central part, the psyche, that this datum has been bred. The
living substance within him being bent, in the first instance,
on pursuing or avoiding some agency in its environment, it
projects whatever (in consequence of its reactions) reaches
its consciousness into the locus whence it feels the stimulus
to come, and it thus frames its description or knowledge of
objects. In this way the ego really and sagaciously posits the
non-ego: not absolutely, as Fichte imagined, nor by a gratuitous fiat, but on occasion and for the best of reasons, when
the non-ego in its might shakes the ego out of its primitive
somnolence.

Belief in substance is accordingly identical with the claim to knowledge, and so fundamental that no evidence can be adduced for it which does not pre-suppose it. In recognising any appearance as a witness to substance and in admitting (or even in rejecting) the validity of such testimony, I have already made a substance of the appearance; and if I admit other phenomena as well, I have placed that substance in a world of substances having a substantial unity. It is not to external pressure, through evidence or argument, that faith in substance is due. If the sceptic cannot find it in himself, he will never find it. I for one will honour him in his sincerity and in his solitude. But I will not honour him, nor think him a philosopher, if he is a sceptic only histrionically, in the wretched controversies of the schools, and believes in substance again when off the stage. I am not concerned about make-believe philosophies, but about my actual beliefs. It is only out of his own mouth, or rather out of his own heart, that I should care to convince the sceptic. Scepticism, if it could be sincere, would be the best of philosophies. But I suspect that other sceptics, as well as I, always believe in substance, and that their denial of it is sheer sophistry and the weaving of verbal arguments in which their most familiar and massive convictions are ignored.

It might seem ignominious to believe something on compulsion, because I can't help believing it; when reason awakes in a man it asks for reasons for everything. Yet this demand is unreasonable: there cannot be a reason for everything. It is mere automatic habit in the philosopher to make this demand, as it is in the common man not to make it. When once I have admitted the facts of nature, and taken for granted the character of animal life, and the incarnation of spirit in this animal life, then indeed many excellent reasons for the belief in substance will appear; and not only reasons for using the category of substance, and positing substance of some vague ambient sort, but reasons for believing in a substance rather elaborately defined and scientifically describable in many of its habits and properties. But I am not yet ready for that. Lest that investigation, when undertaken, should ignore its foundations or be impatient of its limits, I must insist here that trust in knowledge, and belief in anything to know, are merely instinctive and, in a manner, pathological. If philosophy were something prior to convention rather than (as it is) only convention made consistent and deliberate, philosophy ought to reject belief in substance and in knowledge, and to entrench itself in the sheer confession and analysis of this belief, as of all others, without assenting to any of them. But I have found that criticism has no first principle, that analysis involves belief in discourse, and that belief in discourse involves belief in substance; so that any pretensions which criticism might set up to being more profound than common sense would be false pretensions. Criticism is only an exercise of reflective fancy, on the plane of literary psychology, an after-image of that faith in nature which it denies; and in dwelling on criticism as if it were more than a subjective perspective or play of logical optics, I should be renouncing all serious philosophy. Philosophy is nothing if not honest; and the critical attitude, when it refuses to rest at some point upon vulgar faith, inhibits all belief, denies all claims to knowledge, and becomes dishonest; because it itself claims to know.

Does the process of experience, now that I trust my memory to report it truly, or does the existence of the self, now that I admit its substantial, dynamic, and obscure life underlying discourse, require me to posit any other substances? Certainly it does. Experience, for animal faith, begins by reporting what is not experience; and the life of the self, if I accept its endeavours as significant, implies an equally substantial, dynamic, ill-reported world around it, in whose movements it is implicated. In conveying this feeling, as in all else, experience *might* be pure illusion; but if I reject this initial and fundamental suasion of my cognitive life, it will be hard to find anything better to put in its place. I am unwilling to do myself so much useless violence as to deny the validity of primary memory, and assert that I have never, in fact, had any experience at all; and I should be doing myself even greater violence if I denied the validity of perception, and asserted that a thunder-clap, for instance, was only a musical chord, with no formidable event of any sort going on behind the sound. To be startled is to be aware that something sudden and mysterious has occurred not far from me in space. The thunder-clap is felt to be an event in the self and in the not-self, even before its nature as a sound—its æsthetic quality for the self—is recognised at all; I first know I am shaken horribly, and then note how loud and rumbling is the voice of the god that shakes me. That first feeling of something violent and resistless happening in the world at large is accompanied by a hardly less primitive sense of something gently seething within me, a smouldering life which that alien energy blows upon and causes to start into flame.

If this be not the inmost texture of experience, I do not know what experience is. To me experience has not a string of sensations for its objects; what it brings me is not at all a picture-gallery of clear images, with nothing before, behind, or between them. What such a ridiculous psychology (made apparently by studying the dictionary and not by studying the mind) calls hypotheses, intellectual fictions, or tendencies to feign, is the solid body of experience, on which what it calls sensations or ideas hang like flimsy garments or trinkets, or play like a shifting light and shade. Experience brings belief in substance (as alertness) *before* it brings intuition of essences; it is appetition *before* it is description. Of course sensation would precede idea, if by sensation we understood contact with matter, and by idea pure reverie about ideal things; but if idea means expectation, or consciousness having intent, and if sensation means æsthetic contemplation of data without belief, then idea precedes sensation: because an animal is aware that something is happening long before he can say to himself what that something is, or what it looks like. The ultimate datum to which a sceptic may retreat, when he suspends all life and opinion, some essence, pure and non-existent and out of all relation to minds, bodies, or events—surely that is not the stuff out of which experience is woven: it is but the pattern or picture, the æsthetic image, which the tapestry may ultimately offer to the gazing eye, incurious of origins, and contemptuous of substance. The radical stuff of experience is much rather breathlessness, or pulsation, or as Locke said (correcting himself) a certain uneasiness; a lingering thrill, the resonance of that much-struck bell which I call my body, the continual assault of some masked enemy, masked perhaps in beauty, or of some strange sympathetic influence, like the cries and motions of other creatures; and also the hastening and rising of some impulse in me in response. Experience, at its very inception, is a revelation of *things*; and these things, before they are otherwise distinguished, are distinguishable into a here and a there, a now and a then, nature and myself in the midst of nature.

It is a mere prejudice of literary psychology, which uses the grammar of adult discourse, like a mythology, in which to render primitive experience—it is a mere prejudice to suppose that experience has only such categories as colour, sound, touch, and smell. These essences are distinguished eventually because the senses that present them can be separated at will, the element each happens to furnish being thus flashed on or cut off, like an electric light; but far more primitive in animal experience are such dichotomies as good and bad, near and far, coming and going, fast and slow, just now and very soon. The first thing experience reports is the existence of something, merely as existence, the weight, strain, danger, and lapse of being. If any one should tell me that this is an abstraction, I should reply that it would seem an abstraction to a parrot, who used human words without having human experience, but it is no abstraction to a man, whose language utters imperfectly, and by a superadded articulation, the life within him. Aristotle, who so often seems merely grammatical, was not merely grammatical when he chose substance to be the first of his categories. He was far more profoundly psychological in this than the British and German psychologists who discard the notion of substance because it is not the datum of any separate sense. None of the separate data of sense, which are only essences, would figure at all in an experience, or would become terms in knowledge, if a prior interest and faith did not apprehend them. Animal watchfulness, lying in wait for the signals of the special senses, lends them their significance, sets them in their places, and retains them, as descriptions of things, and as symbols in its own ulterior discourse.

This animal watchfulness carries the category of substance with it, asserts existence most vehemently, and in apprehension seizes and throws on the dark screen of substance every essence it may descry. To grope, to blink, to dodge a blow, or to return it, is to have very radical and specific experiences, but probably without one assignable image of the outer senses. Yet a nameless essence, the sense of a moving existence, is there most intensely present; and a man would be a shameless, because an insincere, sceptic, who should maintain that this experience exists *in vacuo*, and does not express, as it feels it does, the operation of a missile flying, and the reaction of a body threatened or hit: motions in substance anterior to the experience, and rich in properties and powers which no experience will ever fathom.

Belief in substance, taken transcendentally, as a critic of knowledge must take it, is the most irrational, animal, and primitive of beliefs: it is the voice of hunger. But when, as I must, I have yielded to this presumption, and proceeded to explore the world, I shall find in its constitution the most beautiful justification for my initial faith, and the proof of its secret rationality. This corroboration will not have any logical force, since it will be only pragmatic, based or beg ging the question, and perhaps only a bribe offered by fortune to confirm my illusions. The force of the corrobation will be merely moral, showing me how appropriate and harmonious with the nature of things such a blind belief was on my part. How else should the truth have been revealed to me at all? Truth and blindness, in such a case, are correlatives, since I am a sensitive creature surrounded by a universe utterly out of scale with myself: I must, therefore, address it questioningly but trustfully, and it must reply to me in my own terms, in symbols and parables, that only gradually enlarge my childish perceptions. It is as if Substance said to Knowledge: My child, there is a great world for thee to conquer, but it is a vast, an ancient, and a recalcitrant world. It yields wonderful treasures to courage, when courage is guided by art and respects the limits set to it by nature. I should not have been so cruel as to give thee birth, if there had been nothing for thee to master; but having first prepared the field, I set in thy heart the love of adventure.

XXIV

Literary Psychology

SCIENTIFIC psychology is a part of physics, or the study of nature; it is the record of how animals act. Literary psychology is the art of imagining how they feel and think. Yet this art and that science are practised together, because one characteristic habit of man, namely speech, yields the chief terms in which he can express his thoughts and feelings. Still it is not the words, any more than the action and attitude which accompany them, that are his *understanding* of the words, or his *sense* of his attitude and action. These can evidently be apprehended only dramatically, by imitative sympathy; so that literary psychology, however far scientific

psychology may push it back, always remains in possession
of the moral field.

When nature was still regarded as a single animal, this
confusion extended to science as a whole, and tinctured the
observation of nature with some suggestion of how a being
that so acts must be minded, and what thoughts and sentiments must animate it. Such myths cannot be true; not because nature or its parts may not be animate in fact, but
because there is no vital analogy between the cosmos and
the human organism; so that if nature is animate as a whole,
or in her minute or gigantic cycles, animation there is sure
not to resemble human discourse, which is all we can attribute to her. Myth and natural theology are accordingly
fabulous essentially and irremediably. If literary psychology is to interpret the universe at large, it can be only very
cautiously, after I have explored nature scientifically as far
as I can, and am able to specify the degree of analogy and the
process of concretion that connect my particular life with
the universal flux.

Myth is now extinct (which is a pity) and theology discredited; but the same confusion subsists in the quarters
where it is not fashionable to doubt. History, for instance,
is partly a science, since it contains archæological and anti-
quarian lore and a study of documents; but it is also, in most
historians, an essay in dramatic art, since it pretends to rehearse the ideas and feelings of dead men. These would not
be recoverable even if the historian limited himself to quoting their recorded words, as he would if he was conscientious;
because even these words are hard to interpret afterwards,
so as to recover the living sentiment they expressed. At least
authentic phrases, like authentic relics, have an odour of
antiquity about them which helps us to feel transported out
of ourselves, even if we are transported in fact only into a
more romantic and visionary stratum of our own being.
Classic historians, however, are not content with quoting
recorded words: they compose speeches for their characters,

under the avowed inspiration of Clio; or less honestly, in modern times, they explain how their heroes felt, or what influences were at work in the spirit of the age, or what dialectic drove public opinion from one sentiment to another. All this is shameless fiction; and the value of it, when it has a value, lies exclusively in the eloquence, wisdom, or incidental information found in the historian. Such history can with advantage be written in verse, or put upon the stage; its virtue is not at all to be true, but to be well invented.

Philosophy fell into the same snare when in modern times it ceased to be the art of thinking and tried to become that impossible thing, the science of thought. Thought can be found only by being enacted. I may therefore guide my thoughts according to some prudent rule, and appeal as often as I like to experience for a new starting-point or a controlling perception in my thinking; but I cannot by any possibility make experience or mental discourse at large the object of investigation: it is invisible, it is past, it is nowhere. I can only surmise what it might have been, and rehearse it imaginatively in my own fancy. It is an object of literary psychology. The whole of British and German philosophy is only literature. In its deepest reaches it simply appeals to what a man says to himself when he surveys his adventures, re-pictures his perspectives, analyses his curious ideas, guesses at their origin, and imagines the varied experience which he would like to possess, cumulative and dramatically unified. The universe is a novel of which the ego is the hero; and the sweep of the fiction (when the ego is learned and omnivorous) does not contradict its poetic essence. The composition is perhaps pedantic, or jejune, or overloaded; but on the other hand it is sometimes most honest and appealing, like the autobiography of a saint; and taken as the confessions of a romantic scepticism trying to shake itself loose from the harness of convention and of words, it may have a great dramatic interest and profundity. But not one term, not one conclusion in it has the least scientific value, and it is only when this philosophy is good literature that it is good for anything.

The literary character of such accounts of experience would perhaps have been more frankly avowed if the interest guiding them had been truly psychological, like that of pure dramatic poetry or fiction. What kept philosophers at this task—often quite unsuited to their powers—was anxiety about the validity of knowledge in physics or in theology. They thought that by imagining how their ideas might have grown up they could confirm themselves in their faith or in their scepticism. Practising literary psychology with this motive, they did not practise it freely or sympathetically; they missed, in particular, the decided dominance of the passions over the fancy, and the nebulous and volatile nature of fancy itself. For this reason the poets and novelists are often better psychologists than the philosophers. But the most pertinent effect of this appeal of science to a romantic psychology was the *hypostasis of an imagined experience*, as if experience could go on in a void without any material organs or occasions, and as if its entire course could be known by miracle, as the experiences of the characters in a novel are known to the author.

Criticism of knowledge is thus based on the amazing assumption that a man can have an experience which is past, or which was never his own. Although criticism can have no first principle, I have endeavoured in this book to show how, if genuinely and impartially sceptical, it may retreat to the actual datum and find there some obvious essence, necessarily without any given place, date, or inherence in any mind. But from such a datum it would not be easy to pass to belief in anything; and if the leap was finally taken, it would be confessedly at the instance of animal faith, and in the direction of vulgar and materialistic convictions. Modern critics of knowledge have had more romantic prepossessions. Often they were not really critics, saying *It seems*, but rebels saying *I find*, *I know*, or empiricists saying *Every-*

body finds, Everybody knows. Their alleged criticism of science is pure literary psychology, gossip, and story-telling. They are miraculously informed that there are many minds, and that these all have a conventional experience. What this experience contains, they think is easily stated. You have but to ask a friend, or make an experiment, or imagine how you would feel in another man's place. So confident is this social convention, that the natural world in which these experiences are reported to occur, and the assumed existence of which renders them imaginable, may be theoretically resolved into a picture contained in them. Thus the ground is removed which sustained all this literary psychology and suggested the existence of minds and thei. known experience at all; yet the groundless belief in these minds, and in copious knowledge of their fortunes, is retained as obvious; and this novelesque universe is called the region of facts, or of immediate experience, or of radical empiricism. Literary psychology thus becomes a metaphysics for novelists. It supplies one of the many thinkable systems of the universe, though a fantastic one; and I shall return to it, under the name of psychologism, when considering the realm of matter. Here I am concerned only with the evidence that such masses of experience exist or are open to my inspection.

No inspection is competent to discover anything but an essence; what social intuition touches is therefore always a dramatic illusion of life in others or in myself, never the actual experience that may have unfolded itself elsewhere as a matter of fact. Yet this dramatic illusion, like any given essence, may be a true symbol for the material events upon which the psyche is then directed; in this case, the life of other people, or my own past life, as scientific psychology might describe it. A good literary psychologist, who can read people's minds intuitively, is likely to anticipate their conduct correctly. His psychological imagination is not a link in this practical sagacity but a symptom of it, a poetic by-product of fineness in instinct and in perception. Slight indications in the attitude or temper of the persons observed, much more than their words, will suggest to the sympathetic instinct of the observer what those persons are in the habit of doing, or are inclined to do; and the stock idea assigned to them, or the stock passion attributed to them, will be but a sign in the observer's discourse for that true observation. I watch a pair of lovers; and it requires no preternatural insight for me to see whether the love is genuine, whether it is mutual, whether it is waxing or waning, irritable or confident, sensual or friendly. I may make it the nucleus of a little novel in my own mind; and it will be a question of my private fancy and literary gift whether I can evolve language and turns of sentiment capable of expressing all the latent dispositions which the behaviour of those lovers, unconscious of my observation, suggested to me. Have I read their minds? Have I divined their fate? It is not probable; and yet it is infinitely probable that minds and fates were really evolving there, not generically far removed from those which I have imagined.

The only facts observable by the psychologist are physical facts, and the only events that can test the accuracy of his theories are material events; he is therefore in those respects simply a scientific psychologist, even if his studies are casual and desultory. Whence, then, his literary atmosphere? For there is not only the medium of words which intervenes in any science, but the ulterior sympathetic echo of feelings truly felt and thoughts truly rehearsed and intended. I reply that whereas scientific psychology is addressed to the bodies and the material events composing the animate world, literary psychology restores the essences intervening in the perception of those material events, and re-echoes the intuitions aroused in those bodies. This visionary stratum is the true immediate as well as the imagined ultimate. Even in the simplest perceptions on which scientific psychology, or any natural science, can be based, there is an essence present which only poetry can describe or sympathy conceive.

Schoolroom experiments in optics, for instance, are initially a play of intuitions, and exciting in that capacity; I see, and am confident and pleased that others see with me, this colour of an after-image, this straight stick bent at the surface of the water, the spokes of this wheel vanishing as it turns. For science, these given essences are only stepping-stones to the conditions under which they arise, and their proper æsthetic nature, which is trivial in itself, is forgotten in the curious knowledge I may acquire concerning light and perspective and refraction and the structure of the eye. Yet in that vast, vibrating, merciless realm of matter I am, as it were, a stranger on his travels. The adventure is exhilarating, and may be profitable, but it is endless and, in a sense, disappointing; it takes me far from home. I may seem to myself to have gained the whole world and lost my own soul. Of course I am still at liberty to revert in a lyrical moment to the immediate, to the intuitions of my childish senses; yet for an intelligent being such a reversion is a sort of *gran rifiuto* in the life of mind, a collapse into lotus-eating and dreaming. It is here that the Muses come to the rescue, with their dramatic and epic poetry, their constructive music, and their literary psychology. Knowledge of nature and experience of life are presupposed; but as at first, in the beginnings of science, intuition was but a sign for material facts to be discovered, so now all material facts are but a pedestal for images of other intuitions. The poet feels the rush of emotion on the other side of the deployed events; he wraps them in an atmosphere of immediacy, luminous or thunderous; and his spirit, that piped so thin a treble in its solitude, begins to sing in chorus. Literary psychology pierces to the light, to the shimmer of passion and fancy, behind the body of nature, like Dante issuing from the bowels of the earth at the antipodes, and again seeing the stars.

Such a poetic interpretation of natural things has a double dignity not found in sensuous intuitions antecedent to any knowledge of the world. It has the dignity of virtual truth,

because there are really intuitions in men and animals, varying with their fortunes, often much grander and sweeter
than any that could come to me. The literary psychologist
is like some antiquary rummaging in an old curiosity shop,
who should find the score of some ancient composition, in its
rude notation, and should sit down at a wheezy clavichord
and spell out the melody, wondering at the depth of soul in
that archaic art, so long buried, and now so feebly revealed.
This curious music, he will say to himself, was mighty and
glorious in its day; this moonlight was once noon. There is
no illusion in this belief in life long past or far distant; on
the contrary, the sentimentalist errs by defect of imagination, not by excess of it, and his pale watercolours do no
justice to the rugged facts. The other merit that dignifies
intuitions mediated by knowledge of things is that they release capabilities in one's own soul which one's personal
fortunes may have left undeveloped. This makes the mainspring of fiction, and its popular charm. The illusion of
projecting one's own thoughts into remote or imaginary
characters is only half an illusion: these thoughts were never
there, but they were always here, or knocking at the gate;
and there is an indirect victory in reaching and positing elsewhere, in an explicit form, the life which accident denied me,
and thereby enjoying it *sub rosa* in spite of fate. And there
are many experiences which are only tolerable in this dreamlike form, when their consequences are negligible and their
vehemence is relieved by the distance at which they appear,
and by the show they make. Thus both the truth and the
illusion of literary psychology are blessings: the truth by
revealing the minds of others, and the illusions by expanding
one's own mind.

These imaginative blessings, however, are sometimes despised, and philosophers, when they suspect that they have
no evidence for their psychological facts, or become aware of
their literary flavour, sometimes turn away from this conventional miscellany of experience, and ask what is the

substantial texture of experience beneath. Suppose I strain my introspection in the hope of discovering it; the picture (for such a method can never yield anything but pictures) may be transformed in two ways, to which two schools of recent literary psychology are respectively wedded. One transformation turns experience, intensely gaped at, into a mere strain, a mere sense of duration or tension; the other transformation unravels experience into an endless labyrinth of dreams. In the one case, experience loses its articulation to the extent of becoming a dumb feeling; and it is hard to see how, if one dumb undifferentiated feeling is the only reality, the illusion of many events and the intuition of many pictures could be grafted upon it. In the other case experience increases its articulation to the extent of becoming a chaos; and the sensitive psychology that dips into these subterranean dreams needs, and easily invents, guiding principles by which to classify them. Especially it reverts to sexual and other animal instincts, thus grafting literary psychology (which in this field is called psycho-analysis) again on natural substance and the life of animals, as scientific psychology may report it.

This natural setting restores literary psychology to its normal status; it is no longer a chimerical metaphysics, but an imaginative version, like a historical novel, of the animation that nature, in some particular regions, may actually have possessed. The fineness and complexity of mental discourse within us may well be greater than we can easily remember or describe; and there is piety as well as ingenuity in rescuing some part of it from oblivion. But here, as elsewhere, myth is at work. We make a romance of our incoherence, and compose new unities in the effort to disentangle those we are accustomed to, and find their elements. Discourse is not a chemical compound; its past formations are not embedded in its present one. It is a life with much iteration in it, much recapitulation, as well as much hopeless loss and forgetfulness. As the loom shifts, or gets out of order, the woof is recomposed or destroyed. It is a living, a perpetual creation; and the very fatality that forces me, in conceiving my own past or future, or the animation of nature at large, to imagine that object afresh, with my present vital resources and on the scale and in the style of my present discourse—this very fatality, I say, reveals to me the nature of discourse everywhere, that it is poetry. But it is poetry about facts, or means to be; and I need not fear to be too eloquent in expressing my forgotten sentiments, or the unknown sentiments of others. Very likely those sentiments, when living, were more eloquent than I am now.

XXV

The Implied Being of Truth

THE experience which perhaps makes even the empiricist awake to the being of truth, and brings it home to any energetic man, is the experience of other people lying. When I am falsely accused, or when I am represented as thinking what I do not think, I rebel against that contradiction to my evident self-knowledge; and as the other man asserts that the liar is myself, and a third person might very well entertain that hypothesis and decide against me, I learn that a report may fly in the face of the facts. There is, I then see clearly, a comprehensive standard description for every fact, which those who report it as it happened repeat in part, whereas on the contrary liars contradict it in some particular. And a little further reflection may convince me that even the liar must recognise the fact to some extent, else it would not be *that* fact that he was misrepresenting; and also that honest memory and belief, even when most unimpeachable, are not exhaustive and not themselves the standard for belief or for memory, since they are now clearer and now vaguer,

and subject to error and correction. That standard comprehensive description of any fact, which neither I nor any man
can ever wholly repeat, is the truth about it.

The being of truth thus seems to be first clearly posited in
disputation; and a consequence of this accident (for it is
an accident from the point of view of the truth itself under
what circumstances men most easily acknowledge its authority)—a consequence is that truth is often felt to be
somehow inseparable from rival opinions; so that people say
that if there was no mind and consequently no error there
could be no truth. They mean, I suppose, that nothing can
be correct or incorrect except some proposition or judgement
regarding some specific fact; and that the same constitution
of the fact which renders one description correct, renders
any contradictory description erroneous. "Truth" is often
used in this abstract sense for correctness, or the quality
which all correct judgements have in common; and another
word, perhaps "fact" or "reality," would then have to be
used for that standard comprehensive description of the object to which correct judgements conform. But a fact is not
a description of itself; and as to the word "reality," if it
is understood to mean existence, it too cannot designate a
description, which is an essence only. Facts are transitory,
and any part of existence to which a definite judgement is
addressed is transitory too; and when they have lapsed, it is
only their essence that subsists and that, being partially recovered and assigned to them in a retrospective judgement,
can render this judgement true. Opinions are true or false by
repeating or contradicting some part of the truth about the
facts which they envisage; and this truth about the facts is
the standard comprehensive description of them—something
in the realm of essence, but more than the essence of any
fact present within the limits of time and space which that
fact occupies; for a comprehensive description includes also
all the radiations of that fact—I mean, all that perspective
of the world of facts and of the realm of essence which is

obtained by taking this fact as a centre and viewing everything else only in relation with it. The truth about any fact is therefore infinitely extended, although it grows thinner, so to speak, as you travel from it to further and further facts, or to less and less relevant ideas. It is the splash any fact makes, or the penumbra it spreads, by dropping through the realm of essence. Evidently no opinion can embrace it all, or identify itself with it; nor can it be identified with the facts to which it relates, since they are in flux, and it is eternal.

The word truth ought, I think, to be reserved for what everybody spontaneously means by it: the standard comprehensive description of any fact in all its relations. Truth is not an opinion, even an ideally true one; because besides the limitation in scope which human opinions, at least, can never escape, even the most complete and accurate opinion would give precedence to some terms, and have a direction of survey; and this direction might be changed or reversed without lapsing into error; so that the truth is the field which various true opinions traverse in various directions, and no opinion itself. An even more impressive difference between truth and any true discourse is that discourse is an event; it has a date not that of its subject-matter, even if the subject-matter be existential and roughly contemporary; and in human beings it is conversant almost entirely with the past only, whereas truth is dateless and absolutely identical whether the opinions which seek to reproduce it arise before or after the event which the truth describes.

The eternity of truth is inherent in it: all truths—not a few grand ones—are equally eternal. I am sorry that the word eternal should necessarily have an unction which prejudices dry minds against it, and leads fools to use it without understanding. This unction is not rhetorical, because the nature of truth is really sublime, and its name ought to mark its sublimity. Truth is one of the realities covered in the eclectic religion of our fathers by the idea of God. Awe very

properly hangs about it, since it is the immovable standard
and silent witness of all our memories and assertions; and
the past and the future, which in our anxious life are so differently interesting and so differently dark, are one seamless
garment for the truth, shining like the sun. It is not necessary
to offer any evidence for this eternity of truth, because truth
is not an existence that asks to be believed in, and that may
be denied. It is an essence involved in positing any fact, in
remembering, expecting, or asserting anything; and while no
truth need be acknowledged if no existence is believed in,
and none would obtain if there was no existence in fact, yet
on the hypothesis that anything exists, truth has appeared,
since this existence must have one character rather than another, so that only one description of it in terms of essence
will be complete; and this complete description, covering all
its relations, will be the truth about it. No one who understands what is meant by this eternal being of truth can possibly deny it; so that no argument is required to support it,
but only enough intensity of attention to express what we
already believe.

XXVI

Discernment of Spirit

* * * * *

By spirit I understand the light of discrimination that marks
in that pure Being differences of essence, of time, of place,
of value; a living light ready to fall upon things, as they
are spread out in their weight and motion and variety, ready
to be lighted up. Spirit is a fountain of clearness, decidedly
wind-blown and spasmodic, and possessing at each moment
the natural and historical actuality of an event, not the im-

puted or specious actuality of a datum. Spirit, in a word, is no phenomenon, not sharing the æsthetic sort of reality proper to essences when given, nor that other sort proper to dynamic and material things; its peculiar sort of reality is to be intelligence in act. Spirit, or the intuitions in which it is realised, accordingly forms a new realm of being, silently implicated in the apparition of essences and in the felt pressure of nature, but requiring the existence of nature to create it, and to call up those essences before it. By spirit essences are transposed into appearances and things into objects of belief; and (as if to compensate them for that derogation from their native status) they are raised to a strange actuality in thought—a moral actuality which in their logical being or their material flux they had never aspired to have: like those rustics and servants at an inn whom a travelling poet may take note of and afterwards, to their astonishment, may put upon the stage with applause.

It is implied in these words, when taken as they are meant, that spirit is not a reality that can be observed; it does not figure among the *dramatis personae* of the play it witnesses. As the author, nature, and the actors, things, do not emerge from the prompter's box, or remove their makeup so as to exhibit themselves to me in their unvarnished persons, but are satisfied that I should know them only as artists (and I for my part am perfectly willing to stop there in my acquaintance with them); so the spirit in me which their art serves is content not to be put on the stage; that would be far from being a greater honour, or expressing a truer reality, than that which belongs to it as spectator, virtually addressed and consulted and required in everything that the theatre contrives. Spirit can never be observed as an essence is observed, nor encountered as a thing is encountered. It must be enacted; and the essence of it (for of course it has an essence) can be described only circumstantially, and suggested pregnantly. It is actualised in actualising something else, an image or a feeling or an intent or a belief; and it can be discovered only by implication in all discourse, when discourse itself has been posited. The witnesses to the existence of spirit are therefore the same as those to the existence of discourse; but when once discourse is admitted, the existence of spirit in it becomes self-evident; because discourse is a perusal of essence, or its recurring presence to spirit.

Now in discourse there is more than passive intuition; there is intent. This element also implies spirit, and in spirit as man possesses it intent or intelligence is almost always the dominant element. For this reason I shall find it impossible, when I come to consider the realm of spirit, to identify spirit with simple awareness, or with consciousness in the abstract sense of this abused word. Pure awareness or consciousness suffices to exemplify spirit; and there may be cold spirits somewhere that have merely that function; but it is not the only function that only spirits could perform; and the human spirit, having intent, expectation, belief, and eagerness, runs much thicker than that. Spirit is a category, not an individual being: and just as the realm of essence contains an infinite number of essences, each different from the rest, and each nothing but an essence, so the realm of spirit may contain any number of forms of spirit, each nothing but a spiritual fact. Spirit is a fruition, and there are naturally as many qualities of fruition as there are fruits to ripen. Spirit is accordingly qualified by the types of life it actualises, and is individuated by the occasions on which it actualises them. Each occasion generates an intuition numerically distinct, and brings to light an essence qualitatively different.

XXVII

Comparison with Other Criticisms of Knowledge

A SINKING society, with its chaos of miscellaneous opinions, touches the bottom of scepticism in this sense, that it leaves no opinion unchallenged. But as a complete suspense of judgement is physically impossible in a living animal, every sceptic of the decadence has to accept some opinion or other. Which opinions he accepts will depend on his personal character or his casual associations. His philosophy therefore deserts him at the threshold of life, just when it might cease to be a verbal accomplishment; in other words, he is at intervals a sophist, but at no time a philosopher. Nevertheless, among the Greek sceptics there were noble minds. They turned their scepticism into an expression of personal dignity and an argument for detachment. In such scepticism every one who practises philosophy must imitate them; for why should I pledge myself absolutely to what in fact is not certain? Physics and theology, to which most philosophies are confined, are dubious in their first principles: which is not to say that nothing in them is credible. If we assert that one thing is more probable than another, as did the sceptics of the Academy, we have adopted a definite belief, we profess to have some hold on the nature of things at large, a law seems to us to rule events, and the lust of scepticism in us is chastened. This belief in nature, with a little experience and good sense to fill in the picture, is almost enough by way of belief. Nor can a man honestly believe less. An active mind never really loses the conviction that it is scenting the way of the world.

Living when human faith is again in a state of dissolution, I have imitated the Greek sceptics in calling doubtful everything that, in spite of common sense, any one can possibly doubt. But since life and even discussion forces me to break away from a complete scepticism, I have determined not to do so surreptitiously nor at random, ignominiously taking cover now behind one prejudice and now behind another. Instead, I have frankly taken nature by the hand, accepting as a rule in my farthest speculations the animal faith I live by from day to day. There are many opinions which, though questionable, are inevitable to a thought attentive to appearance, and honestly expressive of action. These natural opinions are not miscellaneous, such as those which the Sophists embraced in disputation. They are super-posed in a biological order, the stratification of the life of reason. In rising out of passive intuition, I pass, by a vital constitutional necessity, to belief in discourse, in experience, in substance, in truth, and in spirit. All these objects may conceivably be illusory. Belief in them, however, is not grounded on a prior probability, but all judgements of prob-ability are grounded on them. They express a rational in-stinct or instinctive reason, the waxing faith of an animal living in a world which he can observe and sometimes remodel.

This natural faith opens to me various Realms of Being, having very different kinds of reality in themselves and a different status in respect to my knowledge of them. I hope soon to invite the friendly reader to accompany me in a fur-ther excursion through those tempting fields.

DIALOGUES IN LIMBO

III

Normal Madness

Democritus. You reappear in season, inquisitive Pilgrim, and today you must take a seat beside me. These young men are compelling my hoary philosophy to disclose the cause of all the follies that they perpetrated when alive. They still wear, as you see, their youthful and lusty aspect; for when we enter these gates Minos and Rhadamanthus restore to each of us the semblance of that age at which his spirit on earth had been most vivid and masterful and least bent by tyrant circumstance out of its natural straightness. Therefore Alcibiades and Dionysius and Aristippus walk here in the flower of their youth, and I sit crowned with all the snows and wisdom of extreme old age; because their souls, though essentially noble, grew daily more distracted in the press of the world and more polluted, but mine by understanding the world grew daily purer and stronger. They are still ready for every folly, though luckily they lack the means; and the chronicle of vanity remains full of interest for them, because they are confident of shining in it. Yet the person whom this subject most nearly touches is you, since you are still living, and life is at once the quintessence and the sum of madness. Here our spirits can be mad only vicariously and at the second remove, as the verses in which Sophocles expresses the ravings of Ajax are themselves sanely composed, and a calm image of horror. But your thoughts, in the confusion and welter of existence, are still rebellious to metre; you cannot yet rehearse your allotted part, as we do here, with the pause and pomp of a posthumous self-knowledge. My discourse on madness, therefore, will not only celebrate your actions, but may open your eyes; and I assign to you on this occasion the place of honour, as nearest of kin to the goddess Mania, who today presides over our games.

There is little philosophy not contained in the distinction between things as they exist in nature, and things as they appear to opinion; yet both the substance and its appearance often bear the same name, to the confusion of discourse. So it is with the word madness, which sometimes designates a habit of action, sometimes an illusion of the mind, and sometimes only the opprobrium which a censorious bystander may wish to cast upon either.

Moralists and ignorant philosophers like Socrates—of whom women and young men often think so highly—do not distinguish nature from convention, and because madness is inconvenient to society they call it contrary to nature. But nothing can be contrary to nature; and that a man should shriek or see wild visions or talk to the air, or to a guardian genius at his elbow, or should kill his children and himself, when the thing actually occurs, is not contrary to nature, but only to the habit of the majority. The diseases which destroy a man are no less natural than the instincts which preserve him. Nature has no difficulty in doing what she does, however wonderful or horrible it may seem to a fancy furnished only with a few loose images and incapable of tracing the currents of substance; and she has no hostility to what she leaves undone and no longing to do it. You will find her in a thousand ways unmaking what she makes, trying again where failure is certain, and neglecting the fine feats which she once easily accomplished, as if she had forgotten their secret. How simple it was once to be a Greek and ingenuously human; yet nature suffered that honest humanity to exist only for a few doubtful years. It peeped once into being, like a weed amid the crevices of those Ægean mountains, and all the revolving æons will not bring it back. Nature is not love-sick; she will move on; and if to the eye of passion her works seem full of conflict, vanity, and horror, these are not horrors, vanities, or conflicts to her. She is no less willing that we should be mad than that we should be sane. The fly that prefers sweetness to a long life may drown in honey; nor ís an agony of sweetness forbidden by nature to those inclined to sing or to love.

Moral terms are caresses or insults and describe nothing; but they have a meaning to the heart, and are not forbidden. You may, therefore, without scientific error, praise madness or deride it. Your own disposition and habit will dictate these judgements. A weak and delicate animal like man could have arisen only in an equable climate, in which at all seasons he might hunt and play, and run naked or gaily clad according to his pleasure: he therefore at first regards the Hyperborean regions, where summer and winter are sharply contrasted, as cruel and uninhabitable; yet if by accident or necessity he becomes hardened to those changes, he begins to think his native forests pestiferous and fit only for snakes and monkeys. So it is also with the climates of the mind. Every nation thinks its own madness normal and requisite; more passion and more fancy it calls folly, less it calls imbecility. Of course, according to nature, to possess no fancy and no passion is not to possess too little, and a stone is no imbecile; while to have limitless passion and fancy is not to have too much, and a drone among bees or a poet among men is not a fool for being all raptures. In the moralist aspiration is free to look either way. If some gymnosophist sincerely declares that to move or to breathe or to think is vanity, and that to become insensible is the highest good, in that it abolishes illusion and all other evils, to him I object nothing; if starkness is his treasure, let him preserve it. If on the other hand Orpheus or Pythagoras or Plato, having a noble contempt for the body, aspire to soar in a perpetual ecstasy, and if with their eyes fixed on heaven they welcome any accidental fall from a throne or from a housetop as a precious liberation of their spirits, fluttering to be free, again I oppose nothing to their satisfaction: let them hug Icarian madness to their bosoms, as being the acme of bliss and glory.

What, Aristippus and Dionysius, are you so soon asleep? I confidently expected you at this point to applaud my oration. But sleep on, if you prefer dreams to an understanding of dreams.

Perhaps you others, whose wits are awake, may ask me how, if in nature there be nothing but atoms in motion, madness comes to exist at all. I will not reply that motion and division are themselves insanity, although wise men have said so; for if division and motion are the deepest nature of things, insanity would be rather the vain wish to impose upon them unity and rest. For by sanity I understand assurance and peace in being what one is, and in becoming what one must become; so that the void and the atoms, unruffled and ever ready, are eminently sane. Not so, however, those closed systems which the atoms often form by their cyclical motion: these systems are automatic; they complete and repeat themselves by an inward virtue whenever circumstances permit; yet even when circumstances do not permit, they madly endeavour to do so. This mad endeavour, when only partially defeated, may restore and propagate itself with but slight variations, and it is then called life. Of life madness is an inseparable and sometimes a predominant part: every living body is mad in so far as it is inwardly disposed to permanence when things about it are unstable, or is inwardly disposed to change when, the circumstances being stable, there is no occasion for changing. That which is virtue in season is madness out of season, as when an old man makes love; and Prometheus or Alexander attempting incredible feats is a miracle of sanity, if he attempts them at the right moment.

So much for madness in action, inevitable whenever the impulses of bodies run counter to opportunity. But life, both in its virtue and in its folly, is also expressed in fancy, creating the world of appearance. In the eye of nature all appearance is vain and a mere dream, since it adds something to substance which substance is not; and it is no less idle to think what is true than to think what is false. If ever appearance should become ashamed of being so gratuitous and like an old gossip should seek to excuse its garrulity by alleging its truth, neither the void nor the atoms would heed that excuse or accept it. Are they, forsooth, insecure that they should call upon that sleepy witness to give testimony to their being? Their being is indomitable substance and motion and action, and to add thought, impalpable and ghostly, is to add madness. Indeed fancy, as if aware of its vanity, makes holiday as long as it can; its joy is in fiction, and it would soon fade and grow weary if it had to tell the truth. The heroes in the *Iliad*, instead of doing a man's work in silence, like honest atoms, love to recite their past exploits and to threaten fresh deeds of blood: had they respected reality they would have been content to act, but they must prate and promise, because they live by imagination. If their boasts are lies, as is probable, they are all the more elated. These fools might almost have perceived their own idiocy, if they had merely described their true actions, saying, "I am standing on two legs; I am hurling a spear, I am running away, I am lying flat and dead on the ground." The truth, my friends, is not eloquent, except unspoken; its vast shadow lends eloquence to our sparks of thought as they die into it. After all there was some sense in that nonsense of Socrates about the sun and moon being governed by reason, for they go their rounds soberly, without talking or thinking.

That the intoxication of life is the first cause of appearance you have all observed and experienced when you have danced in a chorus, or performed your military exercises, stamping on the ground in unison and striking your swords together; ordered motion being naturally fertile in sound, in flashing light, and in gladness. Such appearances, in the safe and liberal life of a god, would not be deceptive, since a god need not be concerned about his own existence, which is secure, or that of other things, which is indifferent, and he is not tempted to assert falsely, as men do, that sound and splendour and gladness are the substance of those things or of himself. In him the intoxication of life in creating appearance would not create illusion, but only an innocent and divine joy. Accordingly, when the voice of a god traverses the air, the burden of it is neither true nor false; only the priest or the people, anxiously interpreting that oracle according to their fears and necessities, render false or true by their presumption such scraps of it as they may hear. The god, however, was not mindful of them but was singing to himself his own song. This divine simplicity of nature is ill understood by mortals, who address everything to their mean uses and vain advantage; whereby in the struggle to lengthen their days a little they fill them with distraction.

This is a third and most virulent form of madness, in which the dreams of the vegetative soul are turned into animal error and animal fury. For animals cannot wait for the slow ministrations of earth and air, but as you see in birds and kittens and young children, must be in a fidget to move; prying in all directions and touching and gobbling everything within reach. This is their only entertainment, for they have lost all finer inner sensibility, and their feelings and fancies arise only when their whole soul is addressed to external things of which they are necessarily ignorant—for what can a simpleton know of the streams of atoms actually coursing about him? His mind is furnished only with feelings and images generated within, but being distracted by the urgency of his lusts and fears, he takes those images and feelings for pleasant lures or fantastic and stalking enemies. Thus whereas locomotion by itself would be unconscious and fancy by itself would be innocent and free from error, fancy married with locomotion, as it must be in the strife of animals, begets false opinion and wraps the naked atoms in a veil of dreams.

Such is the origin of opinion; and as the chief endeavour of the animal body is to defend and propagate itself at all costs, so the chief and most lasting illusion of the mind is the illusion of its own importance. What madness to assert that one collocation of atoms or one conjunction of feelings is right or is better, and another is wrong or is worse! Yet this baseless opinion every living organism emits in its madness, contradicting the equal madness of all its rivals. They say the stars laugh at us for this, but what is their own case? The sun and the planets may seem to gaping observation to lead a sane life, having found paths of safety; yet to the sharp eye of science the ambush is visible into which they glide. If they think themselves immortal gods, and feast and laugh together as they revolve complacently, they are mad, because a sudden surprise awaits them, and the common doom. Had they been wise, the philosophers who know themselves mortal, they should have consented and made ready to die, seeing that they are not pure atoms or the pure void, and that in forming them nature was not in earnest but playing. They would have done well to laugh, if they had laughed at themselves; for those who will not laugh with nature in her mockery and playfulness turn her sport first into delusion and then into anguish.

Such being the nature and causes of madness, is there no remedy for it? In answering this question I broach the second and kindlier part of my discourse, when having described the disease I bring hope of health and prescribe the cure. A radical cure, though it exists, I will not propose to you, for you are young and inquisitive and not ready to renounce all life and all knowledge. Only some great and heroic sage can begin by disowning madness altogether and felling the tree of opinion at the root; nor would he, by leaping into total salvation, attain to any understanding of his former distress. In abolishing illusion he would have forgotten its existence and virtually denied it; so that for the blatant errors of his lusty years he would have substituted one great mute and perpetual error: the total ignorance which besets the atoms regarding the patterns and the dreams which in fact they generate. Suddenly to renounce all madness is accordingly to miss the truth about madness, together with the whole comic rout of this world, which is marvellously fertile in comedy.

My physic accordingly will be more gentle; I will not prescribe instant death as the only medicine. Wisdom is an evanescent madness, when the dream still continues but no longer deceives. In all illusions there is some truth, since being products of nature they all have some relation to nature, and a prudent mind by lifting their masks may discover their true occasions. Doubtless the number and swiftness of the atoms, even in a little space, must always elude human discernment; but the more foolish images of sense may be disallowed in favour of others more faithful to the true rhythms and divisions of nature. Thus to the innocent eye the six stout spokes of a chariot-wheel revolving rapidly are merged and blurred in one whirling disc; but the philosopher, though no less subject than other men to this illusion, on seeing the disc will remember the spokes, and in all his fevers and griefs will be mindful of the atoms; his forced illusions will not deceive him altogether, since he knows their cause, and it is in his power, if the worst befall, by a draught of atoms artfully mingled, to dispel all his griefs and fevers for ever. Meantime, in the interests of human life, without inquiring into its ultimate vanity, a conventional distinction may be drawn between madness and sanity. Belief in the imaginary and desire for the impossible will justly be called madness; but those habits and ideas will be conventionally called sane which are sanctioned by tradition and which, when followed, do not lead directly to the destruction of oneself or of one's country. Such conventional sanity is a normal madness like that of images in sense, love in youth, and religion among nations.

Two protecting deities, indeed, like two sober friends supporting a drunkard, flank human folly and keep it within bounds. One of these deities is Punishment, and the other Agreement. The very mad man chokes, starves, runs into the sea, or having committed some fearful rape or murder is sentenced to death by the magistrates. Even if harmless, he is tied with a chain, and dies like a dog in his kennel. Punishment thus daily removes the maddest from the midst of mankind. The remnant, though their thoughts be in their homely way still dull or fantastic, then plod on in relative safety, while the unhappy souls whom Punishment has over-taken rest from their troubles. For no sooner has the system of atoms forming an animal body lost its equilibrium and been dispersed in death, than no pain or fancy or haggard hope subsists in that system any longer, and the peace of indifference and justice returns to the world; and if here or in the memory of men some echo of that life reverberates, it rings without anguish, the note once sounded repeating itself perpetually, pure and undisturbed. This is the good work which Punishment does daily, healing and harmonis-ing the worst of follies.

Yet before dying in the arms of Punishment madness may be mitigated and tamed by Agreement, like a young colt broken in and trained to gallop in harness. The automatism of life, which is necessarily spontaneous and blind, may by adjustment with its occasions become a principle of health and genius, the parent of noble actions and beautiful works. Fancy, too, in creating images which have no originals in nature—since in nature there is nothing but atoms and the void—may by union with the times and order of natural events become the mother of names, pleasant and familiar, by which those events are called in the language of sense. Thus the most diverse imaginations in various species of animals may be rendered compatible with sagacity and with a prosperous life. Migratory fowl do not record their voyages in books, like human geographers, yet they have appointed dreams and secret sensations which warn them of the season for flight, and they are well informed about Egypt without consulting Herodotus. If omens were observed scientifically and not superstitiously interpreted, augury might be a true art of substitution, like language. There are many false tales told both by Greeks and barbarians which at times are useful to the state, because by an artful disposition of signs and sounds they dispose the inner parts of men favourably for breasting labour or war. Thus the most deepdyed illusion, if it be interwoven with good habits, may flourish in long amity with things, naming and saluting them, as we do the stars, or the gods, without understanding their nature.

Such amity can the god Agreement establish even between aliens, but between brothers he weaves a subtler and a sweeter bond. For when kindred bodies have the same habitat and the same arts they also have the same illusions; and their common madness gives to each a perfect knowledge of the other's mind. Whereas the images in the eye or the thoughts of the heart can agree but loosely and, as it were, politically with material things, they may agree exactly with the images in another eye, and the thoughts of another heart. This free unanimity was called friendship by the Greeks, who alone of all nations have understood the nature of friendship. Barbarians of course may fight faithfully in bands, and may live in tribes and in cities, hugging their wives and children to their bosom; but such instinctive love, which all animals manifest, is not friendship. It moves in the realm of nature, and concerns only action and fate, whereas friendship is agreement in madness, when the same free thoughts and the same fraternal joys visit two kindred spirits. It was not for fighting loyally side by side that the Spartan phalanx or the Theban band were incomparable in the annals of war, but for fighting side by side for the sake of the beautiful, and in order that the liberal madness of their friendship might not end, unless it ended in death. All the glories of Greece are the fruits of this friendship and belong to the realm of madness tempered by Agreement; for out of the very fountain of madness Apollo and the Muses drew that intoxication which they taught to flow in the paths of health and of harmony. The Greeks in the intervals between their wars, instead of sinking into luxury and sloth, or into a vain industry, instituted games, in which peace was made keen and glorious by a beautiful image of war. Actual war is a conflict of matter with matter, as blind as it is inevitable; but the images which it breeds survive in peace, as we survive in these removed spaces after the battle of existence. So even the wisest when alive play with images and interests, and the glitter of many rival opinions hides the deep harmony with nature by which these opinions live. There is sweetness and quaint reason in these frail thoughts of our after-life, as in the wisdom of children. What could be madder than a ghost? Yet by the harmony which each of us has long since attained with himself, and by the freedom and peace which we gladly grant to one another, we immortalise the life of friendship and share it with the gods.

Let such, then, be my discourse upon madness. Philosophers are unjust to the madness of the vulgar, and the vulgar to that of madmen and philosophers, not seeing how plausible a substitute it is for their own, because everybody thinks himself sane; wherein precisely shines his blinding illusion. I have wished in a manner to remove the mystery and the odium from this universal predicament of mortals, and to show it to be no anomaly. Madness is natural and, like all things natural, it loves itself, and often, by its innocence or by its signification, it lives in harmony with the rest of nature; otherwise, by the action it comports, it finds its quietus in punishment and death.

Alcibiades. Your discourse, indomitable Sage, has filled us with wonder, and left us without the wish to speak. The

Stranger, if he had dared, should have broken this silence rather than I, for you tell us that madness comes of being alive, and very likely he thinks that such an opinion comes of being dead.

Democritus. Very likely, but let him speak for himself.

The Stranger. I should not hesitate to do so if I had anything to object to so persuasive a discourse, but words on my part are superfluous, since I recognise the truth of every part of it. To show you, however, that the living are not always unwilling to confess their plight, I will repeat an old story of the sort which we compose for children. It seems curiously to confirm all that the noble Democritus has taught us.

Once upon a time, so the story runs, the whole world was a garden in which a tender fair-haired child, whose name was Autologos, played and babbled alone. There was, indeed, an old woman who tended the garden, a goddess in disguise; but she lived in a cave and came out only at night when the child was asleep, for like the bat and the astronomer she could see better in the dark. She had a sharp pruning-hook on a very long pole, with which she silently pruned every tree and shrub in the garden, even the highest branches, cutting off the dead twigs and shaking down the yellow leaves in showers; and often, muttering surly words to herself which were not intelligible, she would cut off some flower or some bud as well, so that when the child awoke he missed them and could not imagine what had become of them. Now the child in his play gave names to everything that he liked or disliked; and the rose he called Beauty, and the jasmin Pleasure, and the hyacinth Sweetness, and the violet Sadness, and the thistle Pain, and the olive Merit, and the laurel Triumph, and the vine Inspiration. He was highly pleased with all these names, and they made those flowers and plants so much more interesting to him that he thought those names were their souls. But one day, having pricked himself with the thorns of a rose, he changed her name to Love; and this caused him to wonder why he had given those particular names to everything rather than quite different names; and the child began to feel older. As he sat brooding on this question, for he had stopped playing, a man in a black gown came into the garden who was a botanist, and said: "It matters little what names you give to flowers because they already have scientific names which indicate their true genera and species; the rose is only a rose, and is neither Beauty nor Love; and so with all the other flowers. They are flowers and plants merely, and they have no souls." Hearing this the child began to cry, very much to the botanist's annoyance, for being a busy man he disliked emotion. "After all," he added, "those names of yours will do no harm, and you may go on using them if you please; for they are prettier than those which truly describe the flowers, and much shorter; and if the word soul is particularly precious to you, you may even say that plants and flowers have souls: only, if you wish to be a man and not always a child, you must understand that the soul of each flower is only a name for its way of life, indicating how it spreads its petals in the morning and perhaps closes them at night, as you do your eyes. You must never suppose, because the flower has a soul, that this soul does anything but what you find the flower actually doing." But the child was not comforted, and when the wind had dried his tears, he answered: "If I cannot give beautiful names to the plants and flowers which shall be really their souls, and if I cannot tell myself true tales about them, I will not play in the garden any more. You may have it all to yourself and botanise in it, but I hate you." And the child went to sleep that night quite flushed and angry. Then, as silently as the creeping moonlight, the old woman came out of her cave and went directly to the place where the child was sleeping, and with a great stroke of her pruning-knife cut off his head; and she took him into her cave and buried him under the leaves which had fallen on that same night, which were many. When the botanist returned in the morning and found the child gone he was much perplexed. "To whom," said he to himself, "shall I now teach botany? There is nobody now to care for flowers, for I am only a professor, and if I can't teach anybody the right names of flowers, of what use are flowers to me?" This thought oppressed the poor man so much that he entirely collapsed, and as he was rather wizened to begin with, he was soon reduced to a few stiff tendons and bones, like the ribs of a dry leaf; and even these shreds soon crumbled, and he evaporated altogether. Only his black gown remained to delight the rag-picker. But the goddess in guise of that old woman went on pruning the garden, and it seemed to make no difference in her habits that the child and the botanist were dead.

I think we may surmise that the true name of this goddess must have been Dikè, the same that the wise Democritus was calling Punishment; and the botanist's name must have been Nomos, whom he was calling Agreement; and of course the child Autologos was that innocent illusion which was the theme of his whole discourse.

Aristippus. If this be the nature of madness, I propose that we immediately raise an altar to that deity, and worship him hereafter as the only beneficent god; and in order to avoid the protests of the vulgar, who think madness an evil, we will disguise our deity under the name of Autologos, borrowed from the Stranger's tale; and we will not identify him with the Furies or Harpies, but with Pan, Apollo, Orpheus, and Dionysus.

Dionysius. Agreed: and since my name is derived from that of Dionysus, who must have been my ancestor, I proclaim myself high priest of the new temple.

Democritus. You pay my speech a great tribute. I have celebrated the mad god so fitly that I have filled his votaries with a new frenzy of worship.

Alcibiades. Aristippus and Dionysius are enemies of science, and you, Democritus, are a believer in it. Being no judge in the matter, I will not pronounce between you, but I can conceive that a man who has spent his whole long life distilling herbs and grinding stones into powder should believe that he knows something of their substance. Nevertheless, intense study, too, is hypnotic, and might not the lucid theory of nature which you think partly awakens you out of the dream of life, be but a dream within a dream and the deepest of your illusions? My whole career seems a myth to me now in memory; yet when I interpret it in terms of your philosophy and imagine instead nothing but clouds of atoms drifting through a black sky, I seem to be descending into an even deeper cavern of reverie. Suppose I was dreaming of a chariot race, hearing the shouting crowds, blushing to be myself the victor, and reining in my quivering steeds to receive the crown, and suppose that suddenly my dream was transformed, and Olympia and the sunshine and myself and my horses and my joy and the praises of the Athenians turned to atoms fatally combined—I am afraid that, like the child in the Stranger's tale, I should burst into tears at that change of dreams.

Democritus. Do you think I should blame you? Is the sublimity of truth impatient of error? I know well the shock that comes to innocence on discovering that the beautiful is unsubstantial. The soul, too, has her virginity and must bleed a little before bearing fruit. You misconceive my philosophy if you suppose that I deny the beautiful or would madly forbid it to appear. Has not my whole discourse been an apology for illusion and a proof of its necessity? When I discover that the substance of the beautiful is a certain rhythm and harmony in motion, as the atoms dance in circles through the void (and what else should the substance of the beautiful be if it has a substance at all?) far from destroying the beautiful in the realm of appearance my discovery raises its presence there to a double dignity; for its witchery, being a magic birth, is witchery indeed; and in it its parent nature, whose joy it is, proves her fertility. I deny nothing. Your Olympian victory and your trembling steeds, spattered with foam, and your strong lithe hand detaining them before the altar of Apollo, while you receive the crown—how should science delete these verses from the book of experience or prove that they were never sung? But where is their music now? What was it when passing? A waking dream. Yes, and grief also is a dream, which if it leaves a trace leaves not one of its own quality, but a transmuted and serene image of sorrow in this realm of memory and truth. As the grief of Priam in Homer and the grief of Achilles, springing from the dreadful madness of love and pride in their two bosoms, united in the divine ecstasy of the poet, so all the joys and griefs of illusion unite and become a strange ecstasy in a sane mind. What would you ask of philosophy? To feed you on sweets and lull you in your errors in the hope that death may overtake you before you understand anything? Ah, wisdom is sharper than death and only the brave can love her. When in the thick of passion the veil suddenly falls, it leaves us bereft of all we thought ours, smitten and consecrated to an unearthly revelation, walking dead among the living, not knowing what we seem to know, not loving what we seem to love, but already translated into an invisible paradise where none of these things are, but one only companion, smiling and silent, who by day and night stands beside us and shakes his head gently, bidding us say Nay, nay, to all our madness. Did you think, because I would not spare you, that I never felt the cold steel? Has not my own heart been pierced? Shed your tears, my son, shed your tears. The young man who has not wept is a savage, and the old man who will not laugh is a fool.

the saint it remains profoundly indifferent to the occasion that may have kindled its flame, be this occasion religious faith or sensuous vision, be it passion, study, or practical dominion over the world. All is grist for the mill, if only there be force of intellect actually to grind that experimental substance and reduce it to some pure essence on which contemplation can feed. But moralities and religions, if they merely extend or exaggerate the pressure of circumstance on the soul, are as dreadful an incubus on the spirit as ever was the animal search for food, love, or safety; indeed, they are but a monstrous and terrifying shadow of these radical compulsions cast needlessly on the screen of heaven.

I ask myself sometimes, is not morality a worse enemy of spirit than immorality? Is it not more hopelessly deceptive and entangling? Those romantic poets, for instance, whose lives were often so irregular—were they not evidently far more spiritual than the good people whom they shocked? Shelley, Leopardi, Alfred de Musset were essentially children of the spirit: they were condemned to flutter on broken wings only for lack of measure and discipline; they were spiritual waifs, untaught to see the relativity and absurdity of their proud passions. The perfect spirit must be a patient hearer, a sober pupil, not an occasional automatic skylark. Yet when spirituality, as in Wordsworth, has to struggle instead against a black coat and a white choker, it seems to be more sadly and decisively stifled, buried alive under a mountain of human alarms and a heavy tombstone of sanctimony. The world, he sighed, is too much with us; but the hills and even the mock Tritons blowing their wreathed horns were not able to banish the world from his conscientious concern. Nothing is able to banish the world except contempt for the world, and this was not in him. It would even have been contrary to his Protestant religion—that so unspiritual determination to wash the world white and clean, adopt it, and set it up for a respectable person. The world is not respectable; it is mortal, tormented, confused, deluded for ever; but

THE REALM OF ESSENCE

PREFACE TO REALMS OF BEING

THE world is old, and can have changed but little since man arose in it, else man himself would have perished. Why, then, should he still live without a sure and sufficient philosophy? The equivalent of such a philosophy is probably hereditary in sundry animals not much older than man. They have had time to take the measure of life, and have settled down to a routine of preferences and habits which keeps their heads, as a race, above water; and they are presumably visited at appropriate seasons by magic images, which are symbols to them for the world or for the cycles of their destiny. Among groups of men an equilibrium of this moral sort has been sometimes approached—in India, in China, under the Moslem or the Catholic regimens; and if socialist or other panaceas now exercise such a strange influence over men's hearts, it is perhaps because they are impatient of being so long the sport of divers ignorant dogmas and chance adventures, and aspire to live in a stable harmony with nature.

In fact, beneath these various complete systems which have professed but failed to be universal, there is actually a dumb human philosophy, incomplete but solid, prevalent among all civilised peoples. They all practise agriculture, commerce, and mechanical arts, with artificial instruments lately very much complicated; and they necessarily possess, with these arts, a modicum of sanity, morality, and science requisite for carrying them on, and tested by success in doing so. Is not this human competence philosophy enough? Is it not at least the nucleus of all sound philosophy? In spite of the superficial confusion reigning in the world, is not the universal wisdom of the future actually gathering about this human competence in engineering, in chemistry, in medicine, in war?

The Realm of Matter.

It might seem so, since the sort of knowledge involved in the arts, though it may not go very far, is compulsory so far as it goes, and being sanctioned by success, it ought to be permanent and progressive. There is indeed a circle of material events called nature, to which all minds belonging to the same society are responsive in common. Not to be responsive to these facts is simply to be stupid and backward in the arts; those who explore and master their environment cannot help learning what it is. In this direction competence involves enlightenment. Among minds forming a moral society, and able to compare their several opinions, this enlightenment in the expert is coercive over the layman also, because the same facts confront them both. Did not the same facts confront them, communication would be impossible between them, or if communication was reputed to exist by magic there would be no possible conflict or progress among their opinions, because they would not refer to the same events. Even if each declared himself competent and prosperous in his own world, he would know nothing of the world of his neighbours. Their several minds would simply be variously or similarly brilliant, like jewels, signifying nothing to one another.

If any mind hopes to address another (or even itself) persuasively, as I now wish to address the reader and my own thoughts, it must assume a single system of events to which both minds are responsive, and which includes their respective bodies and actions. Assuming such a common world, it is easy to see how animals may acquire knowledge of it and may communicate it. Material events will arouse in them intuitions conformable to their several stations, faculties, and passions; and their active nature (since they are animals, not plants) will compel them to regard many of the essences so given in intuition as signs for the environment in which they move, modifying this environment and affected by it. This assumption justifies itself at every turn in practice, and establishes in the habits of all men, in proportion to their competence, an appropriate adjustment to the *Realm of Matter*, and in their imagination a suitable picture of the same.

The Realm of Essence.

Nevertheless, since the station, faculties, and passions of all men are not identical, these pictures will not be similar. Different observers may be addressed to different regions of nature, or sensitive to different elements in the same region; thus dwellers in distinct planets must evidently have distinct geographies, and the same battle in the clouds will be known to the deaf only as lightning and to the blind only as thunder, each responding to a different constituent of the total event, and not simultaneously. So an eclipse—itself but one aspect of a constellation of events in the heavens—may be known in various entirely different terms; by calculation before it occurs, by sense when it is occurring, by memory immediately afterwards, and by reports to posterity. All these indications are entirely inadequate to the facts they reveal in the realm of matter, and qualitatively unlike those facts; they are a set of variegated symbols by which sensitive animals can designate them. Of course, the existence and use of such languages is an added fact in nature—a fact so important and close to the egotism of the animals themselves as perhaps to obscure all else in their eyes. Their instinct, indeed, keeps their attention stretched upon the material world that actually surrounds them; but sometimes sensation and language, instead of being passed over like the ticking of the telegraph, may become objects in themselves, in all their absolute musical insignificance; and then animals become idealists. The terms in which they describe things, unlike the things they meant to describe, are purely specious, arbitrary, and ideal; whether visual, tactile, auditory, or conceptual these terms are essentially *words*. They possess intrinsically, in their own ontological plane, only logical or æsthetic being; and this contains no indication whatever of the material act of speaking, touching, or looking which causes them to appear. All possible terms in mental discourse are essences existing nowhere; visionary equally, whether the faculty that discovers them be sense or thought or the most fantastic fancy.

Such diversity in animal experience taken in itself exhibits sundry qualities or forms of being, a part of the infinite multitude of distinguishable ideal terms which (whether ever revealed to anybody or not) I call the *Realm of Essence*. Pure intuition, in its poetic ecstasy, would simply drink in such of these essences as happened to present themselves; but for a wakeful animal they are signals. They report to his spirit, in very summary and uncertain images, the material events which surround him and which concern his welfare. They may accordingly become terms in knowledge if interpreted judiciously, and if interpreted injudiciously they may become illusions.

All Mental Discourse Is More or Less Significant Poetry.

The dumb philosophy of the human animal, by which he rears his family and practises the arts and finds his way home, might take definite shape and establish a healthy routine in all his dealings with matter (which includes society), and yet his imaginative experience might retain all its specious originality. The control which the environment exercises over the structure and conduct of animals is decidedly loose. They can live dragging a long chain of idle tricks, diseases, and obsolete organs; and even this loose control fails almost entirely in the case of alternative senses or languages, one of which may serve as well as another. Many species survive together, many rival endowments and customs and religions. And the same control fails altogether in regard to the immaterial essences which those senses or languages call up before the mind's eye. Adaptation is physical, and it is only the material operation in sensation or speech that can possibly be implicated in the clockwork of nature. The choice of those visionary essences which meantime visit the mind, though regular, is free; they are the transcript of life into discourse, the rhetorical and emotional rendering of existence, which when deepened and purified, becomes poetry or music. There can be no reason why differences in these spheres, even among men of the same race, should not be perpetual. It would be mere sluggishness and egotism to regret it. Such differences are not merely added like a vain luxury to a sane recognition, in other conscious terms, of the facts of nature. The "sane" response to nature is by action only and by an economy which nature can accept and weave into her own material economy; but as to the terms of sense and discourse, they are all from the very beginning equally arbitrary, poetical, and (if you choose) mad; yet all equally symptomatic. They vary initially and intangibly from mind to mind, even in expressing the same routine of nature. The imagination which eventually runs to fine art or religion is the same faculty which, under a more direct control of external events, yields vulgar perception. The promptings and the control exercised by matter are continuous in both cases; the dream requires a material dreamer as much as the waking sensation, and the latter is a transcript of his bodily condition just as directly as the dream. Poetic, creative, original fancy is not a secondary form of sensibility, but its first and only form. The same manual restlessness and knack which makes man a manufacturer of toys makes him, when by chance his toys prove useful, a manufacturer of implements. Fine art is thus older than servile labour, and the poetic quality of experience is more fundamental than its scientific value. Existence may revert at any moment to play, or may run down in idleness; but it is impossible that any work or discovery should ever come about without the accompaniment of pure contemplation, if there is consciousness at all; so that the inherent freedom of the spirit can never be stamped out, so long as spirit endures.

The Realm of Spirit.

Nor is it safe to imagine that inspired people, because they dream awake in their philosophy, must come to grief in the real world. The great religious and political systems which I mentioned above have had brilliant careers. Their adepts have been far from making worse soldiers than sceptics make, or worse workmen than materialists; nor have they committed suicide or been locked up in the madhouse more often than exact philosophers. Nature drives with a loose rein, and vitality of any sort, even if expressed in fancy, can blunder through many a predicament in which reason would despair. And if the mythical systems decline at last, it is not so much by virtue of the maladjustments underlying their speculative errors—for their myths as a whole are wisely contrived—as because imagination in its freedom abandons these errors for others simply because the prevalent mood of mankind has changed, and it begins dreaming in a different key. Spirit bloweth where it listeth, and continually undoes its own work. This world of free expression, this drift of sensations, passions, and ideas, perpetually kindled and fading in the light of consciousness, I call the *Realm of Spirit*. It is only for the sake of this free life that material competence and knowledge of fact are worth attaining. Facts for a living creature are only instruments; his play-life is his true life. On his working days, when he is attentive to matter, he is only his own servant, preparing the feast. He becomes his own master in his holidays and in his sportive passions. Among these must be counted literature and philosophy, and so much of love, religion, and patriotism as is not an effort to survive materially. In such enthusiasms there is much asseveration; but what they attest is really not the character of the external facts concerned, but only the spiritual uses to which the spirit turns them.

The Range of Reasonable Curiosity.

A philosopher cannot wish to be deceived. His philosophy is a declaration of policy in the presence of the facts; and therefore his first care must be to ascertain and heartily to acknowledge all such facts as are relevant to his action or sentiment—not less, and not necessarily more. The pursuit of truth is a form of courage, and a philosopher may well love truth for its own sake, in that he is disposed to confront destiny, whatever it may be, with zest when possible, with resignation when necessary, and not seldom with amusement. The facts to which it is prudent and noble in him to bare his bosom are the morally relevant facts, such as touch his fortunes or his heart, or such as he can alter by his efforts; nor can he really discover other facts. Intuition, or absolute apprehension without media or doubt, is proper to spirit perusing essences; it is impossible to animals confronting facts. Animals know things by exploration, reaction, and prophetic fancy; they therefore can know only such parts and depths of nature as they explore materially and respond to vitally. The brave impulse to search may, indeed, become eager and may wish to recognise no limits; and there may be spirits so utterly practical and serious that the pursuit of material facts absorbs them altogether, to the exclusion of all play of mind. Yet such hectic exactitude is an expression of fear, and automatic rather than rational. Curiosity in an animal always has limits which it is foolish to transgress, because beyond them theory insensibly lapses into verbal myths, and if still taken for true knowledge defeats the honest curiosity that inspired it. What renders knowledge true is fidelity to the object; but in the conduct and fancy of an animal this fidelity can be only rough, summary, dramatic; too much refinement renders it subjective, as does too much haste. This is true of mathematical refinements no less than of verbal pedantries. The realm of matter can never be disclosed either to hypothesis or to sensation in its presumable inmost structure and ultimate extent: the garment of appearance must always fit it loosely and drape it in alien folds, because appearance is essentially an adaptation of facts to the scale and faculty of the observer.

There are also moral limits to seriousness and utter literalness in thought. The tragic compulsion to honour the facts is imposed on man by the destiny of his body, to which that of his mind is attached. But his destiny is not the only theme possible to his thought, nor the most congenial. The best part of this destiny is that he may often forget it; and existence would not be worth preserving if it had to be spent exclusively in anxiety about existence.

Relativity of Knowledge.

It follows from all this that knowledge of facts merely because they are facts cannot be the ultimate object of a philosopher, although he must wish to know the whole unvarnished truth about relevant matters. A liberal mind must live on its own terms, and think in them; it is not inferior to what surrounds it; fact-worship on its part would accordingly be a fault in taste and in morals. What is the function of philosophy? To disclose the absolute truth? But is it credible that the absolute truth should descend into the thoughts of a mortal creature, equipped with a few special senses and with a biassed intellect, a man lost amidst millions of his fellows and a prey to the epidemic delusions of the race? Possession of the absolute truth is not merely by accident beyond the range of particular minds; it is incompatible with being alive, because it excludes any particular station, organ, interest, or date of survey: the absolute truth is undiscoverable just because it is not a perspective. Perspectives are essential to animal apprehension; an observer, himself a part of the world he observes, must have a particular station in it; he cannot be equally near to everything, nor internal to anything but himself; of the rest he can only take views, abstracted according to his sensibility and foreshortened according to his interests. Those animals which I was supposing endowed with an adequate philosophy surely do not possess the absolute truth. They read nature in their private idioms. Their imagination, like the human, is doubtless incapable of coping with all things at once, or even with the whole of anything natural. Mind was not created for the sake of discovering the absolute truth. The absolute truth has its own intangible reality, and scorns to be known. The function of mind is rather to increase the wealth of the universe in the spiritual dimension, by adding appearance to substance and passion to necessity, and by creating all those private perspectives, and those emotions of wonder, adventure, curiosity, and laughter which omniscience would exclude. If omniscience were alone respectable, creation would have been a mistake. The single duty of all creatures would then be to repair that creative error, by abolishing their several senses and desires and becoming indistinguishable from one another and from nothing at all; and if all creation could attain to this sort of salvation, the absolute substance, in whose honour all else had been abandoned, would become unconscious. The time will doubtless come for each of us, if not for the universe at large, to cease from care; but our passage through life will have added a marvellous episode to the tale of things; and our distinction and glory, as well as our sorrow, will have lain in being something in particular, and in knowing what it is.

Thus if there is a sense in which all special and separable existence is illusion, there is another sense in which illusion is itself a special and separable existence; and if this be condemned for not being absolute substance and for excluding knowledge of the absolute truth, it may also be prized for these very reasons. Sensation is true enough. All experience yields some acquaintance with the realm of essence, and some perspective of the material world; and this would always be a true perspective (since things seen at that angle and with that organ really look like that) if the appearance were not stretched to cover more than it covers in reality. Of such true perspectives the simplest and most violently foreshortened may be as good as the most complicated, the most poetical or pictorial as good as the most scientific, not only æsthetically but even cognitively, because it may report the things concerned on that human scale on which we need to measure them, and in this relation may report them correctly. Nor is the error which such very partial knowledge may breed, when inflated by precipitate judgements and vanity, altogether unavoidable. The variety of senses in man, the precarious rule of his instincts, and the range of his memory and fancy, give rise in him eventually to some sense of error and even of humour. He is almost able to pierce the illusions of his animal dogmatism, to surrender the claim to inspiration, and in one sense to transcend the relativity of his knowledge and the flightiness of his passions by acknowledging them with a good grace.

The Realm of Truth.

This relativity does not imply that there is no absolute truth. On the contrary, if there were no absolute truth, all-inclusive and eternal, the desultory views taken from time to time by individuals would themselves be absolute. They would be irrelevant to one another, and incomparable in point of truth, each being without any object but the essence which appeared in it. If views can be more or less correct, and perhaps complementary to one another, it is because they refer to the same system of nature, the complete description of which, covering the whole past and the whole future, would be the absolute truth. This absolute truth is no living view, no actual judgement, but merely that segment of the

realm of essence which happens to be illustrated in existence.
The question whether a given essence belongs to this segment
or not—that is, whether a suggested idea is or is not true—
has a tragic importance for an animal intent on discovering
and describing what exists, or has existed, or is destined to
exist in his world. He seldom has leisure to dwell on essences
apart from their presumable truth; even their beauty and
dialectical pattern seem to him rather trivial, unless they are
significant of facts in the realm of matter, controlling human
destiny. I therefore give a special name to this tragic segment of the realm of essence and call it the *Realm of Truth*.

Human Values of Knowledge.

The knowledge of relevant truth, while it has this fundamental moral importance, is far from being our only concern
in the life of reason. It comes in only incidentally, in so far
as a staunch and comprehensive knowledge of things makes
a man master of things, and independent of them in a great
measure. The business of a philosopher is rather to be a
good shepherd of his thoughts. The share of attention and
weight which he gives to physical speculation or to history
or to psychology will express his race and disposition, or the
spirit of his times; everyone is free to decide how far material arts and sciences are worth pursuing, and with what
free creations they shall be surrounded. Young and ardent
minds, and races without accumulated possessions, tend to
poetry and metaphysics; they neglect or falsify the truth in
the heat of their imaginative passion. Old men, and old
nations, incline to mix their wine with larger dilutions of
reality; and they prefer history, biography, politics, and humorous fictions; because in all these, while the facts are
neither conceived nor tested scientifically, the savour of
earth and of experience remains dominant.

By the philosopher, however, both the homeliest brew and
the most meticulous science are only relished as food for the
spirit. Even if defeated in the pursuit of truth, the spirit

may be victorious in self-expression and self-knowledge; and if a philosopher could be nothing else, he might still be a moralist and a poet. He will do well to endow his vision of things with all the force, colour, and scope of which his soul is capable. Then if he misses the truth of nature, as in many things is probable, he will at least have achieved a work of imagination. In such a case the universe, without being mapped as a whole in the fancy, will be enriched at one point, by the happy life enacted there, in one human focus of art and vision. The purer and more distinct the spirit which a philosopher can bring to light in his thoughts, the greater the intellectual achievement; and the greater the moral achievement also, if the policy to set forth is actually carried out in his whole life and conversation.

Legitimate Variety in Speculation.

As for me, in stretching my canvas and taking up my palette and brush, I am not vexed that masters should have painted before me in styles which I have no powers and no occasion to imitate; nor do I expect future generations to be satisfied with always repainting my pictures. Agreement is sweet, being a form of friendship; it is also a stimulus to insight, and helpful, as contradiction is not; and I certainly hope to find agreement in some quarters. Yet I am not much concerned about the number of those who may be my friends in the spirit, nor do I care about their chronological distribution, being as much pleased to discover one intellectual kinsman in the past as to imagine two in the future. That in the world at large alien natures should prevail, innumerable and perhaps infinitely various, does not disturb me. On the contrary, I hope fate may manifest to them such objects as they need and can love; and although my sympathy with them cannot be so vivid as with men of my own mind, and in some cases may pass into antipathy, I do not conceive that they are wrong or inferior for being different from me, or from one another. If God and nature can put up with them, why should I raise an objection? But let them take care; for if they have sinned against the facts (as I suspect is often the case) and are kicking against the pricks of matter, they must expect to be brought to confusion on the day of doom, or earlier. Not only will their career be brief and troubled, which is the lot of all flesh, but their faith will be stultified by events, which is a needless and eternal ignominy for the spirit. But if somehow, in their chosen terms, they have balanced their accounts with nature, they are to be heartily congratulated on their moral diversity. It is pleasant to think that the fertility of spirit is inexhaustible, if matter only gives it a chance, and that the worst and most successful fanaticism cannot turn the moral world permanently into a desert.

The pity of it is only that contrary souls should often fight for the same bodies, natural or political, as if space and matter in the universe were inadequate (as on earth indeed they are) for every essence in its own time to see the sun. But existence is precipitate and blind; it cannot bide its time; and the seeds of form are often so wantonly and thickly scattered that they strangle one another, call one another weeds and tares, and can live only in the distracted effort to keep others from living. Seldom does any soul live through a single and lovely summer in its native garden, suffered and content to bloom. Philosophers and nations cannot be happy unless separate; then they may be single-minded at home and tolerant abroad. If they have a spirit in them which is worth cultivating (which is not always the case) they need to entrench it in some consecrated citadel, where it may come to perfect expression. Human beings allowed to run loose are vowed to perdition, since they are too individual to agree and too gregarious to stand alone. Hence the rareness of any polity founded on wisdom, like that of which ancient Greece affords some glimpses, and the equal rareness of a pure and complete philosophy, such as that of Dante or of Spinoza, conceived in some moment of wonderful unanimity or of fortunate isolation.

The Temper of This System.

My own philosophy, I venture to think, is well knit in the same sense, in spite of perhaps seeming eclectic and of leaving so many doors open both in physics and in morals. My eclecticism is not helplessness before sundry influences; it is detachment and firmness in taking each thing simply for what it is. Openness, too, is a form of architecture. The doctrine that all moralities equally are but expressions of animal life is a tremendous dogma, at once blessing and purging all mortal passions; and the conviction that there can be no knowledge save animal faith positing external facts, and that this natural science is but a human symbol for those facts, also has an immense finality: the renunciation and the assurance in it are both radical and both invincible.

In confessing that I have merely touched the hem of nature's garment, I feel that virtue from her has passed into me, and made me whole. There is no more bewitching moment in childhood than when the boy, to whom someone is slyly propounding some absurdity, suddenly looks up and smiles. The brat has understood. A thin deception was being practised on him, in the hope that he might not be deceived, but by deriding it might prove he had attained to a man's stature and a man's wit. It was but banter prompted by love. So with this thin deception practised upon me by nature. The great Sphinx in posing her riddle and looking so threatening and mysterious is secretly hoping that I may laugh. She is not a riddle but a fact; the words she whispers are not oracles but prattle. Why take her residual silence, which is inevitable, for a challenge or a menace? She does not know how to speak more plainly. Her secret is as great a secret to herself as to me. If I perceive it, and laugh, instantly she draws in her claws. A tremor runs through her enigmatical body; and if she were not of stone she would embrace her boyish discoverer, and yield herself to him altogether. It is so simple to exist, to be what one is for no reason, to engulf all questions and answers in the rush of being that sustains them. Henceforth nature and spirit can play together like mother and child, each marvellously pleasant to the other, yet deeply unintelligible; for as she created him she knew not how, merely by smiling in her dreams, so in awaking and smiling back he somehow understands her; at least he is all the understanding she has of herself.

II

The Being Proper to Essences

Each Essence Is by Being Identical and Individual.

THE principle of essence, we have seen, is identity: the being of each essence is entirely exhausted by its definition; I do not mean its definition in words, but the character which distinguishes it from any other essence. Every essence is perfectly individual. There can be no question in the realm of essence of mistaken identity, vagueness, shiftiness, or self-contradiction. These doubts arise in respect to natural existences or the meanings or purposes of living minds: but in every doubt or equivocation both alternatives are genuine essences; and in groping and making up my mind I merely hesitate between essences, not knowing on which to arrest my attention. There is no possibility of flux or ambiguity within any of the alternatives which might be chosen at each step.

Also Universal.

This inalienable individuality of each essence renders it a universal; for being perfectly self-contained and real only by virtue of its intrinsic character, it contains no reference to any setting in space or time, and stands in no adventitious relations to anything. Therefore without forfeiting its absolute identity it may be repeated or reviewed any number of times. Such embodiments or views of it, like the copies of a book or the acts of reading of it, will be facts or events in nature (which is a net of external relations); but the copies would not be copies of the same book, nor the readings readings of it, unless (and in so far as) the same essence reappeared in them all. Physical obstacles to exact repetitions or reproductions do not affect the essential universality of every essence, even if by chance it occurs only once, or never occurs at all; because, in virtue of its perfect identity and individuality, it cannot fall out of the catalogue of essences, where it fills its particular place. If I try to delete it, I reinstate it, since in deleting *that* I have recognised and defined it anew, bearing witness to its possessing the whole being which it can claim as an essence. There accordingly it stands, waiting to be embodied or noticed, if nature or attention ever choose to halt at that point or to traverse it. Every essence in its own realm is just as central, just as normal, and just as complete as any other: it is therefore always just as open to exemplification or to thought, without the addition or subtraction of one iota of its being. Time and space may claim and repeat it as often or as seldom as they will: that is their own affair. The flux is free to have such plasticity as it has, and to miss all that it misses; and it is free to be as monotonous as it likes, if it finds it easier to fall again and again into the same form, rather than to run away into perpetual and unreturning novelties. The realm of essence is the scale of measurement, the continuum of variation, on which these repetitions or these novelties may be plotted and compared. Re-embodiments or re-surveys of an essence (if they occur) bind the parts of the flux together ideally, and render it amenable to description. The essential universality of these forms makes any fact, in so far as it exhibits them, distinct and knowable: the universal and the individual being so far from contrary that they are identical. I am not myself unless I re-enact now the essence of myself, which I may re-enact at all times and places.

Essences Are Infinite in Number.

Since essences are universals not needing to figure in any particular place or time, but fit to figure in any, it is not possible to investigate the realm of essence by empirical exploration. You cannot go in search of that which is nowhere. Some essences will appear or occur to you, since whatever intuition life may awaken in you must light up some essence or other; but what further essences, if any, there may be is not discoverable by simply waiting for them to turn up. Nature is indeed very rich in forms, compared with the inertia and monotony of experience in home-keeping animals, revolving in their private circle of habits and ideas; but nature too is built on a single plan—all nuclei and planets, all life and death—and as much a slave of routine as any of her creatures. The unexemplified is not exemplified there, the unthought of is not thought of: not because in itself it resists being created or described, but because nature and thought happen not to bloom in any way but that in which they have taken to blooming. In part, indeed, this restriction may be due to local prejudice and ignorance in the observer, who draws the periphery of nature with his compass. Another man, a different animal, a spirit native to another world may even now be greeting the essences which it has not entered into my heart to conceive. Evidently my limitations cannot forbid them to rejoice in their different experience; nor can the limitations of any actual experience forbid the essences it leaves out to be just those which are absent. An essence is an inert theme, something which cannot bring itself forward, but must be chosen, if chosen, by some external agent; and evidently the choice made by this agent, contingent as it is and wholly arbitrary, cannot render unavailable the other inert themes which other agents, or itself in a different moment of its flux, might choose instead. The very contingency of existence, the very blindness of life, throws the doors wide open towards the infinity of being. Even if some philosopher or some god thought himself omniscient, surprises might be in store for him, and thoughts new to his thought; nay, even supposing that his whole experience and the entire history of his world lay synthesised before him under the form of eternity, and that he was not a victim of sheer egotism in asserting that nothing more could ever exist, still the wanton idiosyncrasy of that total fact, the enormity of that accident, could not be blustered away. Existence is irrational for a deeper and more intrinsic reason than because one part of it may not be deducible from another: any part, and all its parts together, are irrational in merely existing, and in being otherwise than as essences are, that is, identical with themselves and endowed with that formal being which it is impossible that anything, whatever it be, should not possess. Not that essence can resist or resent this irrational selection which existence makes of its riches: on the contrary, essence is a sort of invitation to the dance; it tempts nature with openings in every direction; and in so doing it manifests its own inexhaustible variety. Its very being is to set no limits to the forms of being. The multitude of essences is absolutely infinite.

*But Non-existent; They Form an Indelible Background to
All Transitory Facts.*

This assertion has an audacious sound, and I should not venture upon it, had it not a counterpart or corollary which takes away all its venom, namely, that essences do not *exist*. If I were in pursuit of substance (as I shall be in the Second Book) I should distrust any description of it not purely tentative, empirical, and scrupulously modest: but the bold definition which Spinoza gives of what he calls substance, that it is Being absolutely infinite, seems to me a perfect and self-justifying definition of the realm of essence: because in conceiving and defining such an object we prove it to possess the only being which we mean to ascribe to it. Denying it to be infinite, or denying that any supposed element in it existed, we should be designating these missing elements and that absent infinity: whereby we should be instituting them ideally, and recognising them to be essences. The realm of essence is comparable to an infinite Koran—or the Logos that was in the beginning—written in invisible but indelible ink, prophesying all that Being could ever be or contain: and the flux of existence is the magical re-agent, travelling over it in a thin stream, like a reader's eye, and bringing here one snatch of it and there another to the light for a passing moment. Each reader may be satisfied with his own verse, and think it the whole of Scripture: but the mere assertion of this limit, or suspicion that other readers might find other texts, is enough to show that the non-existent cannot be limited, since the limits of the existent might always be changed. To deny the being of essence, because it may happen to be unrealised, is self-contradictory: for if it is not realised, it must have a quality, distinguishing it from realised forms. Unrealised forms may not interest a sluggish mind: an arithmetician who was happy in the thought of whole numbers, might deprecate all mention of vulgar fractions or repeating decimals, and might swear to die without them, lest his safe and honest arithmetic should be complicated with unrealities. But unrealities of that sort nevertheless envelop his realities on every side; and it is his arrest at his realities that, if you like, is unreal; there is no reason in it, and no permanence; whereas the unrealities are unchangeable, inevitable, and always standing behind the door. Even if the whole realm of essence (as Spinoza assumed) were realised somewhere at some time in the life of nature, essence would remain a different and a non-existent realm: because the realisation of each part could be only local and temporary, and for all the rest of time and in all the worlds that excluded it, each fact would fade into the corresponding essence, and would remain certain and inevitable as an essence only, and as a fact merely presumptive.

Existence and Truth Borrow Their Individuality from Essence.

Essence so understood much more truly *is* than any substance or any experience or any event: for a substance, event, or experience may change its form or may exist only by changing it, so that all sorts of things that are proper to it in one phase will be absent from it in another. It will not be a unit at all, save by external delimitation. Perhaps some abstract constancy in quantity, energy, or continuity may be discovered to run through it, but this constant element will never be the actual experience, event, or substance in its living totality at any moment. Or perhaps all the phases of such an existence may be viewed together and synthesised into one historical picture; but this picture would again not be the existent substance, experience, or event unrolling itself in act. It would be only a description of that portion of the flux seen under the form of eternity; in other words, it would be an essence and not an existence. Essence is just that character which any existence wears in so far as it remains identical with itself and so long as it does so; the very character which it throws overboard by changing, and loses altogether when it becomes something else. To be able to become something else, to suffer change and yet endure, is the privilege of existence, be it in a substance, an event, or an experience; whereas essences can be exchanged, but not changed. Existence at every step casts off one essence and picks up another: we call it the same existence when we are able to trace its continuity in change, by virtue of its locus and proportions; but often we are constrained to give up the count, and to speak of a new event, a new thing, or a new experience. The essences or forms traversed in mutation render this mutation possible and describable: without their eternal distinctness no part of the flux could differ in any respect from any other part, and the whole would collapse into a lump without order or quality. So much more profound is the eternal being of the essences traversed in change than that of the matter or attention or discourse which plays with those essences at touch and go.

Notion of the Realm of Essence.

Nothing, then, more truly *is* than character. Without this wedding garment no guest is admitted to the feast of existence: whereas the unbidden essences do not require that invitation (with which very low characters are sometimes honoured) in order to preserve their proud identity out in the cold. There those few privileged revellers will soon have to rejoin them, not a whit fatter for their brief surfeit of being. After things lose their existence, as before they attain it, although it is true of them that they have existed or will exist, they have no internal being except their essences, quite as if they had never broached Existence at all: yet the identity of each essence with itself and difference from every other essence suffices to distinguish and define them all in eternity, where they form the Realm of Essence. True and false assertions may be made about any one of them, such, for instance, as that it does not exist; or that it includes or excludes some other essence, or is included or excluded by it.

Its Eternity Is the Counterpart of Its Non-existence.

Here is a further character inseparable from essence: all essences are eternal. No hyperbole or rhetorical afflatus is contained in this assertion, as if some prophet pronounced some law or some city to be everlasting. That any existing thing should be everlasting, though not impossible, is incongruous with the contingency of existence. God or matter, if they are everlasting, are so by a sort of iterated contingency and perpetual reproduction; for it is in the nature of existence to be here and perhaps not there, now and perhaps not then; it must be explored to discover how far it may stretch; it must wait and see how long it shall last. The assumption that it lasts or stretches for ever can be made only impetuously, by animal enthusiasm, when the feeling of readiness and omnipotence makes some living creature defy all threats of disaster. Yet so long as we live in time, the ghost of the murdered past will always fill the present with a profound uneasiness. If the eternity of essence were conceived after that fashion, it would indeed be a rash boast; no essence has an essential lien on existence anywhere, much less everywhere and always. Its eternity has nothing to do with such mortal hazards. It is merely the self-identity proper to each of the forms which existence may put on or off, illustrate somewhere or perhaps illustrate always, or very likely never illustrate at all.

IV

Pure Being

Confusions about Pure Being.

Of all essences the most lauded and the most despised, the most intently studied in some quarters and the most misunderstood in others, is pure Being. It has been identified with nothing, with matter, and with God; and even among those who regard it in its logical purity, it is sometimes said to be the richest and most comprehensive of essences and sometimes the poorest and most abstract.

No essence, as we have seen, is abstract essentially, since it defines itself and might appear alone to an intellect strung to that key: and in the case of pure Being we have high testimony (which there is no reason to distrust) assuring us that, in fact, it appears alone to the human intellect in its ultimate reaches; and even when not realised separately in intuition, it can be discerned both analytically and intuitively in every essence whatsoever. Pure Being supplies, as it were, the logical or æsthetic matter which all essences have in common, and which reduces them to comparable modes on one plane of reality. Pure Being is thus found in all essences somewhat as light is in all colours or life in all feeling and thought; and philosophers like Parmenides and Spinoza (not to speak here of the Indians) assure us that we always have an adequate intuition of this pure Being, usually buried under vain illusions, but when unearthed and isolated seen to be very mighty in itself and easily recognisable. Nevertheless such assurances may mean little to other mortals. Language at these depths of attentiveness is perforce the language of solitaries. When repeated it may not carry with it the intuition which it was first meant to record. The very logicians who distinguish this essence, because they call it Being, may conclude that nothing else can *be*—a most perplexing inference and, in view of the many meanings of the word *is*, a most misleading one; while other logicians, because pure Being is different from all other essences, may hastily identify it with nothing, by a strange equivocation between nothing and nothing else.

The Sense of Existence Is Not the Intuition of Pure Being.

Confusion in this matter comes chiefly from the equivocation between being and existence. Initially this equivocation is normal, innocent, and even expedient, like any substitution of names for things: it is only when defended theoretically that it becomes perverse. Intelligence begins with it: animals are surrounded by things that affect their condition and prompt their reactions, so that their attention is necessarily intent upon existing things; yet the intellectual transcript of their condition, in that agony of attention, is only some intuited essence, some sensuous or logical term which, being their sole description for the object before them, they take to be that object itself in its whole existing nature. So individual forms of being stand in discourse for particular things. But sometimes, rather than some specific thing, a certain equilibrium of influences absorbs attention: a noon pause comes in our labour; and more special sensations being fused and blurred, we endure dull strain and duration without diversity—a vast, strange feeling. We return, then, as it were, to the sleep preceding life, to the peace of the womb: there is vitality without urgency, pressure without light, potential movement without object or express direction. Such, we may fancy, might be the inner sense of matter: perhaps some forms of animal or vegetable life never yield any other experience.

Profound Contrast Between the Sense of Existence and the Intuition of Pure Being.

A vague world is posited as existing; for in expectation and intent, as in memory and the sense of movement, there is a tacit assumption of things removed, threatening, eventual, as yet unknown. There is accordingly nothing pure in this sense of existence, simple or vague as its deliverance may seem; for this vagueness and simplicity are uneasy. The peace of the womb is precarious; it is but a muffled and initial phase of distraction, confusion, hope, and fear. Care fills its heart, as it does our dreams; and we might identify it with the Universal Will of German transcendentalism, vaguely pregnant with worlds and worlds. But slumber is not contemplation, and the buzz of matter is not the beatific vision. The pleasure, if pleasure be found in it, is that of original sin: the father of lies is whispering in that paradise. The intuition of pure Being looks in the opposite direction. In order to reach it, attention would need to abandon all concern for transitions, events, ulterior or external facts, and to concentrate all its light on the positive intrinsic nature of the present datum; nor would that suffice, but from this special essence it would need to pass to the inner essence of all those alien half-known things, all those absent times, and eventual passions, which animal faith may posit, or fancy may conceive; since pure Being resides in them all equally, no less than in the here and now. The force of insight would thus have to vanquish all will and transcend all animal limitations, cancelling every fear, preference, or private perspective which a station now and here would involve. In other words, in order to reach the intuition of pure Being, it is requisite to rise altogether above the sense of existence.

Flux Eludes Intuition.

The reason for this lies in the very nature of existence, which is flux and, as Plato would say, non-being. The more truly existence is felt, therefore, the less possible it is to concentrate attention on anything, and to say, Existence is this. He is closest to existence, and most at its heart, who lives on the wing, intent always on the not-given; and even when the present fact is atrociously absorbing, as in pain, the sense of existence remains empty essentially and indescribable, by the very force and distraction of its presence. If we are asked to describe it, we are reduced to naming the circumstances or using some metaphor; and if in the midst of it we pause to consider the internal character of that which we feel, raising it thereby for the first time to distinct intuition, the distraction, the belief, the assurance of existence which filled us before have *ipso facto* disappeared: some image, some word, some finely shaded sensible essence alone is left. In other words, the proper nature of existence is distraction itself, transition at least virtual; so that it cannot be synthesised in intuition without being sublimated into a picture of itself, and washed clean of its contradiction and urgency. The relations which were external from the station of each of the parts as it arose separately, now become internal to the system of the whole; and the intuition in which this whole is synthesised drops the flux of existence in order to retain only its form and the truth about it.

The One Is Primitive, the Other Ultimate.

If, then, being and existence seem in common parlance almost interchangeable terms, it is only so long as their respective objects are merely named or designated from the outside: when they are conceived positively and at close quarters they turn out to be exact opposites. Existence exists by virtue of oppositions in the place, time, and exclusive characters of particulars: being has being by virtue of its universal identity. This is true of the being of each individual essence; and it is true pre-eminently of pure Being. Its identity is omnipresent and internal everywhere; it equalises those centres of existence which in their single blindness become nests for external relations; it makes all times simultaneous; and by excluding change renders existence, from its point of view, inconceivable. Moreover, in reducing all things and all external relations to their internal being, that is, to their essences, it transports them into a realm of being which is necessarily infinite, in which their presence, therefore, is no temporary accident, as is their existence in the world: so that the existent becomes continuous with the non-existent, and neither more nor less real than any other eternal essence

Every Essence Is Pure, by Its Freedom from Adventitious Relations.

This contrast between being and existence is indicated by calling being pure. "Pure" is an epithet proper to all essences. Objects become pure when intuition permeates them and rests in them without the intervention of any ulterior intent or cross-lights, as we speak of pure mathematics or pure pleasure. Purity of this sort is no thinness of form, but the perfection of it. It admits any amount of detail, if it is all overt and clear, on the plane of actuality, and not latent. In this acceptation of the word "pure," pure Being is no purer than any other essence, but all are pure in so far as they are considered in their proper character, freed from the irrelevancies that may encumber them when they figure for a moment in some material world or in some labouring mind.

Pure Being Is So, by Its Freedom from Internal Diversity.

It would therefore be useless and redundant habitually to speak of "pure Being" if nothing were meant save that Being is an essence. What is indicated is that pure Being is related to other essences very much as any essence is related to its existing manifestations; for whereas any special essence, such as colour or sound, sky-blue or B-flat, is exclusive and definable by contrast, pure Being is present in them all, somewhat as space is in all geometrical figures, at once permeating and transcending each of them; for this essence, if not fertile casually as facts are fertile, is in its own way infinitely pregnant. The nature of pure Being anywhere implies the whole realm of essence, since being could not possess its full extension if any sort of being were forbidden to be.

Easy but Fatal Confusion of Pure Being with Substance.

That pure Being, in the sphere of essence, should have this simple, intense, and pervasive sort of reality, provokes afresh in the minds of dialecticians that tendency to identify essence with existence which is native to the animal mind. For in the natural world too there seems to be an omnipresent, simple, intensely real something which dwells in particular things, is transmitted from one to another, and compels them to arise in their infinite variety and endless succession. This omnipresent something is called substance. Might not then pure Being, which lies in all essences and therefore also in all existing things, be the substance of these things, and the universal internal cause of their existence? This is a suggestion which has worked powerfully in the thoughts of those metaphysicians, like the Eleatics, whose physics has been dominated by dialectic. Nor is the suggestion altogether false. That something exists, that there is a world, is very true;

also that whatever else this world may be, is substantial—
that is, exists in itself independently of all report or opinion.
The hypostasis of being into substance is therefore no error,
but a first awakening of curiosity and belief, which in so far
as it posits the existence of something errs only by its extreme inadequacy. It honestly sets about using the category
of substance, but without any notion of what, in detail, this
substance is. This inadequacy itself is inevitable: how should
animals in the womb, or just out of it, conceive truly that
constitution of the world which is not disentangled even to-
day by science or philosophy? Positive error only appears
when this natural inadequacy of our ideas is denied, and
when mere being is deputed to reveal the whole substance and
complete reality of things. The belief in substance, which
should have been the beginning of art and science, then suddenly makes an end of them; for if there were truly nothing
in nature or in experience except mere being, all events and
appearances would be sheer illusions, since in reality they
would be all identical.

Examples of Parmenides and Spinoza.

I shall return to this subject in considering the properties
requisite in any substance fit to subtend appearances and
the life of nature; such a substance must be unequally distributed and in motion; its proper name is matter. Here I
will only notice in passing how the notion of pure Being is
likely to be contaminated in the effort to identify it with
substance. Pure Being—as is indicated by calling it infinite
and eternal, if we ponder these epithets—is utterly absolved
from all subservience to contingent facts and to the momentary casual forms of human experience; it is the most immaterial, untameable, inexhaustible of essences. Yet Parmenides—no tyro in dialectic—denied that it was infinite, because it had to give body to an existing spherical cosmos;
and indeed, apart from ancient astronomy, existence always
involves a certain concentration and contrast with what is

not, and thereby excludes infinity. Again, we find Spinoza asserting that the entire nature of being—which he actually calls substance—must be manifested in existence, and that all these manifestations must be parallel to the forms of the material world, of which indeed those other manifestations can be only complementary aspects, by chance unknown to us. Here is the cosmic frog prodigiously swollen in rivalry with the ontological ox; but the ox, lest that ambition should seem too absurd, is accommodated to the frog nature, and pure Being is thought of as a sort of matter or force resident in natural things and lending them their existence, while at the same time enriching them with an infinite number of attributes which they hide from view.

Substance Is Thereby Deprived of Its Natural Function, Nature Is Abolished, and Pure Being Is Obscured.

On the one hand, then, if pure Being is substance, existence must be illusion; and on the other hand pure Being must be, not the infinite essence which it is, but a hard kernel for existence. Hence the see-saw in the views of those metaphysicians who hypostatise pure Being; sometimes their substance annuls all particulars, and sometimes it supports them. Pure Being excludes particular determinations within its own bosom, but it does not annul them in the world, because it is not on the plane of existence at all: it is by no means a matter within particulars which lends them existence. Substance, on the other hand, is such a matter; and by its movements and redistribution it gives rise in turn to every fact and relation in the natural world. Were pure Being an existing substance, nothing else could exist or arise, not even the occasional intuition of pure Being. All that exists exists by being other than pure Being, under circumstances which themselves are particular and contingent; and if substance were not contingent, unequally distributed, and in motion, it would evidently not be the ground of any event or of any actual appearance.

Thus the hypostasis of pure Being, after being fatal to the reality of all facts, is fatal to respect for pure Being itself; because, considered as a substance, it would be useless, unknowable, and nowhere to be found. Pure Being, although a supreme degree of detachment and concentration be requisite to conceive it adequately, is, like any other essence, perfectly open to intuition; its sublimity is not obscurity; and it is excluded from "knowledge" only in the sense in which any immediate object, being an object of intuition, need not and should not be posited as a removed existence, by the transitive and precarious sort of knowledge by which facts may be known. But pure Being hypostatised into substance is a metaphysical spectre: matter congealed, arrested, emptied, and deprived of its cosmic fertility.

. . . .

Privation Is a Relative Non-entity, but Absolute Non-entity Is an Impossible Term.

Pure Being, like any other essence, is individual and distinguished by exclusions, for it excludes those limitations which render all other essences specific; somewhat as light, which fills up and dynamically constitutes all colours, nevertheless excludes each particular tint. This is far from being a reason for calling pure Being a non-entity: the exclusion of all exclusions renders it infinite, not vacant. Vacancy and nothingness are terms applicable to existence, to which external relations are indispensable, and which at any moment may lapse, so that the place thereof knows it no more; they are meaningless in respect to essences each of which, including pure Being, is grounded in itself, and like a jewel or a star, shines all the brighter in isolation. Non-entity figures, indeed, in the realm of essence, because it is eternally impossible that anything there should be anything else; there are therefore always many things which anything is not. This non-entity is purely relative; an absolute non-entity would be self-contradictory, a false suggestion of discourse like the round square or the son of the barren woman. You cannot make a void of the realm of essence, as you so easily might of existence, by waving a magic wand. Its indestructibility is not an accident, a stubborn matter of fact, like that of matter or of God. If you flatter yourself to abolish the realm of essence, you actually refer to it and reinstate it; if you deny it, you affirm it. The only negation of it which, in one sense, might be staunch, would be utter oblivion; but oblivion is subjective. It destroys nothing save the feeling or thought by which something was formerly recognised.

Pure Being Is Infinitely Positive.

All essences, therefore, partake of non-being, and pure Being does so in an eminent degree, since it excludes the special forms of being proper to all the others. Bread partakes of non-being by not being meat; but food, or pure succulence, partakes of it doubly, by not being either bread or meat specifically; yet it is the positive being in both, in so far as they can sustain life. This pure essence of food is something positive, present in both but limited to neither. Pure Being, like all essences, rejects alien attributes by virtue of its positive character. When an infinite amount of entity has been denied of it, an infinite amount remains, compelling those denials. For the relative non-entity of all essences comes to them in so far as they exclude one another's characters, whereas the positive character of each is its share of being; and pure Being, far from falling outside, is the absolute being in each. It is also the totality of all, when they are regarded not in their distinction (in which they form the realm of essence) but in their continuity and in their common latency within the essence of pure Being itself; because we may say (though such language is figurative and inadequate) that pure Being contains all essences within itself virtually or eminently, since, though it cannot be any of them, it requires each of them to be what it is. The essence of food (for we are not talking of accidental facts) requires and includes all sub-

stances that could be turned into flesh and blood. The very
non-exclusiveness or intensive infinity of pure Being opens
the way for all essences equally, and, since each is something, cannot suffer any of them not to be. It denies each
because it remembers all.

It Is Not an Existence or a Power; Therefore Not the God of Theism or of Pantheism.

In some sense, evidently, pure Being is the supreme being:
may it, then, be identified with God? I think that a religion
is possible which should have pure Being for its object, and
that it might even become a popular cult; Brahmanism, as
the initiated explain it, seems actually to be such a religion.
In theory it is entirely directed to identification with Brahma,
that is, to eluding all finitude and existence; and the Mo-
hammedans have a somewhat similar discipline, in so far as
they abstain from all petitions, and cultivate absolute conformity to the will of Allah. But human religion inevitably
has another side. Prudence and piety require a wise man to
study the ways of nature, to cleave to good and to eschew
evil. Among Greeks and Romans, Jews and Christians, the
object of worship is fundamentally a fostering power; God is
a dominant force in nature, creating, thundering, issuing commandments sanctioned by rewards and punishments, and in
his inner being conceived to be a spirit, thinking, willing,
loving, offended, and propitiated. A piety of this sort tends
towards natural religion; its superstitions, if it remains superstitious, are superstitions about fortune; forces and events
are its sole objects of reverence, and pure Being is nothing
to it. The very earnestness of the fact-seeker compels him to
reduce all myths as far as possible to literal science. Salvation
he will identify with prosperity, eternity with survival, God
with nature, or with some flattering purpose seeming to preside over human destinies. Divine commandments, or the will
of God, will become in his lips merely an archaic phrase for
the discoverable conditions of human well-being; divine om-

niscience will become the truth of things, and divine love their friendliness and beauty.

Yet in Natural Piety Spirituality Intervenes.

This makes a perfect religion for the irreligious; it means death to the spirit; but the spirit is not so easily killed. Action, like physical life, is free to perfect itself, if it can, in its own plane, adjusting itself absolutely to its conditions and carrying out all its impulses in harmony; this executive success, far from abolishing consciousness, will clarify it and make it musical. As the flux of matter, however self-contained and self-forgetful, cannot avoid casting an eternal shadow of its every phase upon the page of truth, so physical life cannot, by becoming very economical, avoid kindling all the more brightly the light of spirit: natural existence has these spiritual extensions, whether it will or no. And in respect to the realization of pure Being, ultimate and supremely difficult as it is to achieve ascetically, instinctively it lies curiously near to the simple heart. Wherever there is peace—not the peace of death, but that which comes of liberation from constraint or distraction—there is a beginning of spirituality. Consciousness is nothing but intuition thwarted or achieved. Even distraction, until it disrupts consciousness, is tossed between intuitions; it can therefore turn into contemplation at any favourable moment, by the mere suspension of animal will, anxiety, and care. Certainly the dark peace of the womb is far removed from the peace of the mountain-top, all clear articulation and self-consuming vision; yet animal consciousness, when perfect, is not unspiritual. It may rest on nothing more recondite than a warm heart or a sound digestion, or the overwhelming magic of some absolute lure: yet in its contemplative simplicity, in its disregard of all ambushed alternatives and material threats, it brings a foretaste of superhuman sympathies, which discipline might one day render disillusioned and habitual. When the object is pure, the spirit intent upon it is pure also.

Contemplation of Pure Being Is the Last Phase of Spiritual Progress.

Hence that strange solace which so many millions find in their religious devotions; under some disguise of fable or image, pure Being is their sanctuary from the world and their liberation from themselves. Natural religion itself, when reflected upon, drives them in this direction. Force and fact are reverenced by the humanist because in them he finds the sources of his happiness; but as he watches and studies them his reverence changes its hue; it becomes disinterested, sacrificial, liberating. Contemplation, even of destiny, neutralises the will. The exuberance of nature, the disproportion between her wantonness and the clean interests of man, must give the humanist pause; he will find the world cruel, and he may react on its cruelty by asking himself what thoughtless pledge he has given to it, that he should be subject to these vain torments. His piety will still forbid him to rebel against fate; rebellion would be a fresh form of vanity. There is no reason why man, or the transitory world in which he finds himself living, should have any prerogative amongst the realms of being. Traditional religion, for all its motherly coddling of human conceit, is not without a door towards the infinite. Theology must somehow reconcile the special mercies and graces coming to men from God, with the immutability and eternity attributed to him. Nor is this an idle theoretical question; for of what ultimate use would the graces and mercies be, if they did not lead men to share that immutability and eternity? In order to keep well and live long hygiene is better than religion. If the fear of power— that is, of matter—was the beginning of wisdom for the natural man, the possession of power cannot be the end of wisdom for the spirit; and the spirit will not permanently worship in God a life inferior to that which it enjoys in itself. Power is a relation between existences; but where did existence and power come from, and how long will they last? There can be no safety in existence even for the gods. Safety in a living world means only forgetfulness of danger, because perhaps, on the scale and in the habitat of that particular being, danger may not be imminent. True safety, spiritual peace, profound reconciliation with fate, lie in another dimension: they spring from a new and superhuman direction of the affections. Piecemeal, amid the accidents of existence, ultimate good is attained whenever the senses and the heart are suddenly flooded by the intuition of those essences to which they were secretly addressed: synthetically, for perfect recollection, it is realised by the contemplative intellect absorbed in pure Being.

The Perfect Realisation of It Is Incompatible with Continued Existence.

This absorption, the union or ecstasy of which mystics speak, has always been the goal of religious discipline in India, and wherever else the spiritual life has been seriously cultivated. This union is sacrificial, like that of the insect in its bridal flight. In it the spirit loses its self-consciousness, the sense of its own or any other separable existence: and it loses this existence actually, because it cannot attain that ecstasy without dropping all connection with its body—that is, without dying. The body may subsist afterwards automatically, or perhaps generate new sensations and dreams; but these will not belong to the liberated spirit, which will have fled for good, fled out of existence altogether. It would seem, then, to unspiritual apprehension, that the end of spiritual life is an end indeed: it is annihilation. This is the plain truth of the matter, when spirit is regarded from the outside, psychologically and historically. Intuitions are placed and dated in the natural world by their occasions and their organs: an actual intuition of pure Being—something absolutely infinite—is evidently irrelevant to any place or time, and disproportionate to any natural organ. We may safely say, therefore, that it cannot exist. Yet if we transfer our point of view to that of the spirit itself, and energise with it and by it, we shall see that intellectually and morally the spirit is fulfilled by the being of its object, not by its own existence. The soul, says Aristotle, is everything that it knows: but then, we may add with equal truth, the soul is no longer itself, nor a soul at all. There lies the selfless nature of intellect, that existence is indifferent and imperceptible to it, either in other things or in itself: so that in losing its existence—if it has died victorious—it has lost what was no part of its prize, and in attaining its prize it has saved itself entire. Certainly a song that ends full in the quieting of all its impulses and the synthesis of all its notes comes to an end just as truly as if it had broken down in the middle; both the soul saved and the soul lost cease living in time; yet what a strange blindness there would be in giving to both the same evil name, and making no difference between dying defeated and being perfected in death! If in the act of union with pure Being the spirit drops the separate existence which it had before, it drops only what it wished to drop; its separation consisted in not having yet attained perfect intuition, which must be without a natural center or personal perspectives. On attaining that intuition the spirit abolishes itself by passing into that which it wished to find. Whether saved or lost, liberated or dissolved, the soul ceases to exist equally; but this fact does not touch the interests of the spirit seeking liberation, whose office, even from the beginning, was worship, not thrift or self-assertion.

It is only when we have thoroughly renounced self-assertion and thrift that we can begin to understand the spiritual view, which otherwise might seem to contradict what the psychologist knows about spirit. But there is no real contradiction: there is only a transference of exclusive attention from one plane of reality to another. Wherever spirit exists, it exists at some particular place and time, by the operation of its natural organs; but wherever it thinks, it regards only some essence, eternal and non-existent, a more or less ample manifestation of pure Being. It is perfectly possible for anyone who will consider the realms of being together, to honour each in its place and to disregard the scorn which those who have eyes for one only must needs pour upon the others.

It Implies No Precepts or Scale of Values, and Does Not Command the Worship Which It May Receive.

If, then, contemplation of pure Being ever becomes the last secret of a religious life, it does so only when religion is transformed into a purely intellectual and sacrificial discipline. Positively religious or moral feelings then drop into their very small, very human places. Where otherwise would be the transforming force, the sublimity and sure finality, of this insight? No fond eulogistic words such as "high," "deep," "living," "spiritual," "true," patter any longer about it; they have lost their afflatus and their contraries have lost their sting. It is not because the sage finds more in pure Being than pure Being itself that he aspires to union with it, but exactly because he does not find more. The fervent estimation in which he held it before he possessed it would render possession of it impossible if it continued afterwards. Like every other object, pure Being appears under the form of the good only to those who are moving towards it, or are carried away from it against their will. Both creation and contemplation are vital processes which lend a relative value to their chosen ends; and when in a religious life the end happens to be union with pure Being, this union becomes as precious and as legitimate as any other natural end could be to any spirit, but in no way more legitimate or more precious. Pure Being itself is neither ruffled nor flattered by these opposite currents in the flux of existence. Its authority—if we figuratively assign authority to it—cannot be invoked by either party, but both parties, like everything actual or conceivable, have its connivance and silent toleration. The artist and the moralist may shudder at pure and infinite Being, and may diversify and limit it in their own spheres to their hearts' content; but understanding also has licence to be; it, too, is free to choose a good and perhaps to realise it; and it may weave again all those diversities and contrasts into the seamless but many-coloured garment which wraps Brahma in his slumber. There no praise or dispraise can intrude; all this flutter of spirits escapes from it unheeded and returns to it uncalled.

The Estimation in Which Pure Being Is Held Is Optional and Relative to Some Finite Nature.

Here, before leaving this subject, I beg the reader to allow me a personal confession, lest he should misunderstand the temper in which I approach these speculations. Every pursuit has a certain warmth about it and sees its object in a golden light which, from that point of view, is a part of the thing discerned; and he who sees it can hardly avoid using disparaging terms in regard to those who miss that revelation or are indifferent to it. So any artist in regard to his art, or any patriot in regard to his country. For the same reason the intellectual or spiritual life, especially when cultivated in unison with some long-established religious tradition, sets up its precise standards and prizes them absolutely: whatsoever satisfies other ambitions seems to it either a stepping-stone in its own path or else sheer vanity and illusion. Nevertheless it would be senseless to demand insight of a stone; in the spiritual life there is nothing obligatory. Those who have spirit in them will live in the spirit, or will suffer horribly in the flesh; but this very insight into pure Being and into the realm of essence shows that both are absolutely infinite, the one implicitly, the other explicitly; they therefore release the mind from any exclusive allegiance to this or that good. It is only by the most groundless and unstable of accidents that any such good has been set up, or any such world as that to which this good is relevant; and only to the merest blindness does *this* world or *this* good seem absolute or exclusive. Now it would be stupid in a blind man, because he was blind, to deny the greatness of a painter who was admittedly supreme in his art, or the sanctity of a saint, or

in ideas, political or theological, which often renders them ominous, secretly absurd, and as it were hypocritical, having at heart implications which on the surface they disown?

The very notion of pregnancy gives, I think, a hint of the answer. Pregnancy belongs to matter, not to essence. The difference between what follows logically and what follows actually cannot be due to the conflict of two different orders of existence, one logical and the other natural. An existing logical order would be something metaphysical, a monster half essence and half force. The difference must be due rather to two levels of natural organisation, one cosmic and inanimate, the other animate and proper to the innate involution of the psyche in man, which opens to his imagination and reason paths other than those actually traced by outer nature even in his own action or explicit discourse.

In the realm of essence, if ever we shake ourselves loose from our animal distractions and presumptions, everything that appears at all, appears patently; but in reasoning there is initially a hidden affinity or tendency in the terms, which does not become patent until the conclusion is reached. Then indeed the implication of those terms in this conclusion becomes clear, because they now simply define a new essence to which they are intrinsic. This new essence I know by intuition: no dialectic is involved in seeing or defining it to be thus. When the number *two* is given in intuition, the number *one*, repeated, is involved in it: this repetition of *one* is the very essence in view. But when the number *one* is given first, it is an accident whether I begin to count, and whether I go on living until I reach the notion of *two*. Therefore it is possible for me to define or deduce the number *one* by analysis when I have the number *two*, but not possible to define *two* when I have only *one*. On the other hand, it is quite possible, by living, to climb to the notion of *two* from that of *one*, but impossible to climb to *one* from *two*, because *one* is then already in my possession and under my foot.

The Pre-eminence of the Number "One" Not Essential.

I may observe in passing (confirming what I have said above about pure Being) that dialecticians who find in *one* the root of all numbers, or in the One the fountain of the universe, seem to be at heart less lovers of essence than of substance; they are not intent on form, but are searching for ultimate elements in the depths of time or of evolution, for something materially radical and indestructible in this existing world. High numbers do not satisfy them, and seem to them secondary, as they seem unreal or even humorous to idle human fancy: yet in the realm of essence all numbers are equally primitive and equally in the foreground. The parity and eternity of all essences has hardly dawned on the minds of philosophers—at least not in the West.

Transition, Repetition, and Comparison Are External to Essences.

Dialectic evidently involves transition; it is progressive; but any actual transition transcends the realm of essence (where every term traversed must always retain its intrinsic character) and proves that an existential and moving factor is at work, namely, attention and whatever may be the basis or organ of attention and of its movement. In a word, a psyche is involved, which herself involves (as we shall see) an existing material world. But dialectic contains more than transition, since this transition is often assumed to be a reversion; in reasoning, intent continually harks back to the object of a previous intuition and compares it with that of the present one. This feat is materially impossible; but it suffices if we perform it presumptively, by assuming that our successive objects are identical and that we should find them to be so if it were possible for us to observe them simultaneously. To transition, then, reasoning professes to add repetition and the assurance of repetition; so that besides a series of intuitions we must admit a power in thought which is not intuition but intent, since its object is something not given, but posited at a distance and identified in character only, not in position, with the given term. Intent is a sort of projection through faith, positing a relation of which only one term is given, the terminus or point of origin here, together with a gesture, word, or sense of direction indicating what and where the other term ought to be. This assumption—logically entirely in the air—is necessary to establish any instance of cogency, contradiction, or fallacy in reasoning; for the obvious disparity of two terms given simultaneously (whence comes all the emotional and essential assurance that the square is not round) does not prove any contradiction in discourse, until we assume that these very essences were present to some mind professing to identify them; and this assumption is very likely to be false, and is always hazardous. It is the great source of futility in argument. The first postulates of dialectic, therefore, the constant meaning of terms and the principle of contradiction, are rooted in animal faith. The light of intuition cannot avail to establish that use of them which alone renders them potent in discourse, or applicable to any subject of ulterior interest. The obvious is obvious, but terminates in itself; that which we say *must* be so, need not be so unless our habits of inference are independently justified by the course of nature.

Biological Nature of the Generic or General.

Now that part of nature which is the organ of mind, the psyche, is a relatively closed system of movements, and hereditary; the living seed, as it matures, puts forth predeterminate organs and imposes specific actions and feelings on the young creature: he must eat, fall in love, build a nest, resent interference or injury. But this predetermination is not exact, only generic; the seed develops as it can, under fire of the environment; the psyche in each individual grows into a somewhat different system of organs and habits, and these vary with time, not merely according to the predetermined sequence of phases in the race, but according to the fortunes of the individual. This partial predetermination of life—which in man is especially imperfect, and dependent on the chances of education and experience—is the source of the generic; the general, absent from the realm of essence, is omnipresent in impulse and action. Every living creature aims at and needs something generic, not anything in particular: *some* food, *some* shelter, *some* mate, *some* offspring, *some* country, *some* religion. The impetuous soul, half-baked and addressed only to the generic, pounces on what it happens to find; it receives it into the stomach, or into the mind, and digests it if it can; but there remains almost always a distinct disparity between hereditary capacities and demands, in their potent vagueness, and the satisfaction provided for them. *Not this, not all this, not merely this*, says the psyche at every turn; and her sustenance leaves her half disgusted and half hungry. Experience at the same time clarifies the instincts which it disappoints; and it is in terms of actual perceptions, expurgated or transformed, that secret ideals can first come to expression.

The Generic Prejudices of the Psyche Are Hardened and Made Specific by Habit.

Dialectic is fledged in this nest, and obeys the same conjoined forces of innate impulse and casual experience. Each thought, in its existence, is due equally to the predisposition of the psyche and to the course of nature outside; but the *presumptions* inherent in the thought, or accompanying and flowing out of it, are determined by the psyche alone, by the momentum and direction of her life at that moment. Hence the whole moral conflict and tragedy between reason and fact, desire and event, the ideal and the actual, nature according to philosophers and nature according to nature. In pure reasoning this conflict takes the form of opposing relevance, consistency, and implication to wandering thoughts or chance perceptions; but the force of logic, as we have amply seen, does not reside in the essences actually inspected, which have no transitive relations, but expresses the habit and range of the psyche in the thinking animal. A mind not buffeted by change, in a world in which rain and shine were not alternate, would never think of any complements to a present object; it might even passionately deny their essential reality, and might call China impossible, life in the water unthinkable, and any mortality but the familiar one self-destructive. In minds, as in insects, the vehemence of littleness is remarkable. Man, although born plastic and immature, soon borrows fixed prejudices from casual experience; he is teachable, and achieves littleness, or has it thrust upon him by custom and dogma. Acquaintance with facts—and with how many facts is any man acquainted?—narrows his generic native demands into specific requirements; he must now have only *this* food, *this* shelter, *this* mate, *these* children, *this* country, *this* religion. In the same way the mind, when indoctrinated, will suffer only *this* physics, and only *this* logic. Nevertheless, any given world or any given flow of imagination is an accident; its very character would be inexpressible were it not surrounded in the realm of essence with an infinitude of variations any one of which, had it been realised instead, would have been equally accidental. Even the true sage, who passes through the school of experience and learning only to recover his spiritual freedom, cannot range impartially over the realm of essence; the paths he traces in that labyrinth are imposed on him by accident, because a psyche is at work within him obeying special instincts and biassed by a special experience. Even in him the transitions of dialectic and the course of contemplation are not determined by the structure of the realm of essence, since the realm of essence, by definition, is the home of all possible structures.

Dialectic, then, while ostensibly following ideal implications absolved from any allegiance to facts or to actual instances of reasoning, secretly expresses a material life, and this in two stages. The psyche is predetermined at birth to certain generic conceptions and transitions; and these are rendered precise and irrevocable by habits formed under the pressure of circumstances.

Moral Function of Dialectic.

Everything in dialectic hangs upon strength of soul; it is an effort to carry over intuition from one moment to another, to be true to oneself, and to wander into no vision not congruous with one's first insight, and complementary to it, so that at the end the mind may believe that it has gathered in and preserved all its riches, and unearthed the secret of all its objects. This is something which no living mind does or can do; and in so far as the ambition to do it is successful, the success is balanced by a great illusion, almost inevitable to the complete logician; the unity which his discourse has achieved he imposes on the realm of essence and on the existing world as if it drew their circumference and repeated their intrinsic order. This illusion does not destroy the dialectical coherence of the system which occasions it; but the philosopher probably aspires to describe the truth; and in that he fails, in proportion to the vehemence with which he posits his system, with its dialectical structure, in lieu of essence in its infinity and nature in her unknown depths. Dialectic is the conscience of discourse and has the same function as morality elsewhere, namely, to endow the soul with integrity and to perfect it into a monument to its own radical impulse. But as virtue is a wider thing than morality, because it includes natural gifts and genial sympathies, or even heroic sacrifices, so wisdom is a wider thing than logic. To coherence in thought it adds docility to facts, and humility even of intellect, so that the integrity of its system becomes a human virtue, like the perfect use of a single language, without being an insult to the nature of things or a learned madness.

A Priori Logic Expresses Physiological Pre-formations.

Being *a priori*, that is, being the assertion in the face of things of a pre-formation in the soul, dialectic is fundamentally romantic; but its romanticism may become austere and ascetic, in so far as it desists from professing to drag the world with it in its speculative flight. How far the *a priori* rules in a mind is a biological accident; we may imagine some insect or some angel, created full-fledged, in whom it should rule exclusively; and we might perhaps find fanatics in whom it rules exclusively in speculative matters, once they have been thoroughly indoctrinated. For we must not suppose that anything is *a priori* in origin; every instinct and organ has its history, just as every custom has; but once the organ is formed, it imposes *a priori* certain responses on the body and certain ideas on the mind. The *a priori* is such only in function. So when an intuition has become dominant, and has established its settled affinities in a well-organised mind, the further march of mundane experience becomes useless to the logician, or even distracting. As young poets on a slender experience sometimes reach the greatest heights and the greatest depths, finding nothing to intercept the impetuous flight of their spirits, so the dialectician who most resolutely hedges in his thought in one lane of logic may go farthest in that direction, and most unerringly. He unveils some integral pattern, perhaps never copied by things, in the realm of essence; the integrity of his pure intent and undivided attention have enabled him to unveil it. He has laid on himself the difficult task of being consistent, of being loyal, not to the realm of essence, which cannot be betrayed, but to his own commitments; he is determined to find and clarify the meaning of his spoken thoughts. Dangers lie to right and left of his path: he may slip into a change in his premises or into forgetfulness of his goal. Fulfilment is moral, even in logic. The mind bears burdens no less than the body, from which indeed the mind borrows them; and the pregnancy and implication of ideas are signs of that vital bias.

*Intuitions Have a Natural Context with Which the Essences
Revealed Are Associated in Discourse.*

Intuitions are themselves incidental to animal life; in revealing the purest essence, like a colour or a number, they
remain rooted in the soil, and render every image symbolic
of the conditions under which it arises. Thus colour brings
with it extension, form, position, and an aerial emotional
redolence drawn from the vital influence of light and room
upon the psyche; number suggests a certain particularity in
its units, as if it were a mere aggregate, yet this particularity
is proper only to the moments or parts of existence and is
absent from the constitutents of number in its purity; for in
a number the logical units numbered are merely fractions of
that number, not particulars in themselves. Yet these physical roots of intuition are far from jeopardising the essential
purity of the flower to which they lend these human affinities.
Horticulture simply becomes more varied and expression
richer. Intuition lyrically marks the chief crises in material
life, when some organ composes and accelerates its movement, turning it into a musical note. Dialectic is merely a
change of scope in this organic synthesis by which a new
essence is substituted for the one first given, that is, for the
theme and terms of the analysis or deduction; a change by
which the original essence, in disappearing, is identified with
a part of the new one, or with a whole of which the new one
is a part. The transitions are discursive, their necessity is
merely psychical; but they lead to intuitions in which essences appear having intrinsically a logical complexity corresponding more or less perfectly to the stages of discourse
which preceded; this correspondence, so far as it goes, makes
the validity of dialectic a validity which cannot be intrinsic
to the essence reached in the conclusion, since it is the validity of a process, of a series of substitutions and identifications.

The Progression of Discourse Is a Natural Flux, Controlled Physically.

Essences are related to dialectic somewhat as things are related to experience. A stick or stone, dead in itself, may exercise a living influence on the imagination. If I strike it, or if it falls upon me, or if I take shelter beside it, I encounter a reality unfathomable in its complexity and pre-established in its station; but in my romantic experience it has become an enemy or a friend. So the terms of discourse, taken in themselves, are passive and complete, implying no development; but I had arrived at them by the quick exercise of my senses or by a concretion of elements in my thought; there is a history and a momentum in my apprehension of them, and it is by no means indifferent to me, as it is to them, how they shall be superseded or transformed. Most sequels open in the realm of essence (and these sequels are infinite), or even most sequels likely in a dream, would prove irrelevant to the interest dominating waking discourse, which is not these pure appearances but some problem in the material or moral world.

Discourse is not contemplation; dialectic is more laboriously intertwined with the accidents of existence than is intuition. It is selective, responsible, perilous; like everything in flux it moves forward by a kind of treachery to its parent world, and subtly pretends to fulfil that which it is destroying. The continuity is physical, not logical. The navigators who in the age of discovery followed in one another's traces or sought to outdo one another's exploits, had a common background and a common field; otherwise their new worlds, however marvellous, would have added nothing to the old world, and would not have discovered one another; America, China, and India would have retained their ancient self-sufficiency; while Castile and Aragon, England and Holland, would have grown no richer and no wiser. So with every problem, however ethereal. A problem is a natural predicament, a living perplexity, limiting the relevance of the solution

sought and creating its value. Discourse would not be cumulative, it would set and solve no problems, if it did not share
and express the adventures of a psyche in a material world;
for the controlling force in reasoning is not reason, but instinct and circumstance, opening up some path for the mind,
and pledging it to some limited issue.

The End of Discourse, Intuition, Is Itself a Function of Animal Life.

Dialectic, like investigation, is a path to an end; it is instrumental. When successful and finished, it yields to intuition, for which the facts and relations discovered become
an ordered system, a single complex essence. Then the predicament and the problem lose their malignity; they survive
only in the interest or beauty which, in dying, they bequeath
to the new object spread before the mind. Contemplation becomes disinterested, but remains pleasant; for it is not the
contemplation of *any* essences at random, but of those precisely to which a vital affinity drew the current of my blood,
the hidden essences to which my nature was directed, partly
from birth, partly by ingrained habit and arts learned by
experience. It is the consecutive sanity and moral integrity
of a mind that hold it down to dialectical consistency. There
are goals in animal thought, as in animal action and passion,
of which thought, in its material basis, is indeed an integral
part. These goals are set by the nature of the organs at work,
a nature in its turn more or less adapted to its external opportunities; so that the goals of a healthy intellect—for
instance, geographical knowledge—like those of hunger or
love, are not unattainable, except by misadventure. When a
geometer analyses the triangle or a lawyer points out the implications of an alleged fact, he is appealing to a fund of principles domesticated in the minds of his hearers, principles
which he may call axioms or simply common sense. His
dialectic will be cogent if it leads in the end to an intuition
in which all the details gathered during the argument may

find their places: that is, although the successive intuitions and the essences they revealed will have disappeared, the stimulus and momentum which created them will proceed synthetically to a fresh intuition, as it were their joint heir, combining them without loss or friction. This total intuition will perfect the operation of its organ, raising rational life at that point to its natural entelechy. The many bypaths of fancy or logic either not traced or explicitly excluded will be called false or irrelevant; and so they will be in this final system to which they are logically repugnant; but they cannot be false or irrelevant in themselves, nor in such other systems as they might help to build up. These other systems are rejected, not by logic but by the structure of the psyche and of her environment. Thus Euclid clarifies the intuition of space which the Egyptian builders, and earlier perhaps their arboreal ancestors, had gathered in the prosperous course of their sports; Euclid brings to light the real implications of such building and such swinging. His science guides those early arts to their ultimate self-knowledge. That those first terms of animal observation and this ultimate geometry are alike well chosen is a truth of physics and morals; their application perfect in the fields from which they were drawn; they give the true rationale of human building and swinging. But the realm of essence cannot suffer violence, and the constructions favoured by man or by nature do not prevent the same elements from entering, if occasion arises, into other designs.

Absolute Evidence Is Intuitive and Internal to Essence.

The purely logical cogency of a system lies accordingly in the internal relations of that system when completed. The included elements have no intrinsic obligation to belong to such a system; but if they fall within the intuition of a living mind, which if well knit can have only one such ulterior system for its natural goal, they should be, and probably will be, addressed by that mind to that system. Were the elements left detached, or combined into other wholes, the dialectic proper to that mind would be lost in the sands of a vain experience, and its congenial system would never take shape. If, for instance, any other man had undertaken to compose this book, it is certain that at every cross-road in the argument he would have taken a turn somewhat different from mine, without necessarily doing more violence to the elements combined. Our systems might have been equally coherent, if in each case the elements became parts of a single essence, clearly intuited; but each system would have been a monument to a different spirit and a different life.

Validity in a System Can Be Only Symbolic and Moral.

The value of two such logical systems for the description of nature would be a second and distinct question. The more cogent system might easily be the more extravagant or childish one, if the elements combined were few or fantastic, or the harmony sought merely poetical. On each animal species, on each man and nation, nature imposes a special way of thinking, and they would be foolish to quarrel with their endowment; they will not attain truth, or anything else, by eluding it. Their thought will issue in a coherent system if their original intuitions were sharp, the synthesis of them broad, and the interpretation honest. Then all random trains of thought inconsistent with that system will be instinctively discarded; and through many a council and controversy, as in the formation of Christian dogma, heresies will be excluded as they suggest themselves, and the scattered original revelations will be interpreted in such a sense that the spirit which originally received them may honour them together. Every science and language and religion is big with unsuspected harmonies; it is for the genuine poet or philosopher to feel and to express them. Only an orthodoxy can possibly be right, as against the bevy of its heresies, which represent wayward exclusions, or a fundamental disloyalty. But no orthodoxy is right as against another orthodoxy, if this expresses an equal sensitiveness to the facts within its purview and an equal intellectual power. All values are moral, and consistency is but a form of honour and courage. It marks singleness of purpose, and the pressure of the total reality upon an earnest mind, capable of recollection. The spirit of system, though it so often renders the mind fanatical and obdurately blind to some facts, is essentially an effort to give all facts their due, not to forget things once discovered and understood, and not to leave illusions and vices comfortably unchallenged. Certainly the total reality will elude any human system; but that is no reason why human nature, which is itself a system, should not exist and assert itself; and it cannot exist congenially without intellectual clearness or without translating its natural economy into a system of ideas. In the realm of essence no such system can have any pre-eminence over any other; each is the pattern of only one possible world; but it may be the full revelation which the existing world brings to one particular creature, and it may render valid, for his description of things, those dialectic bonds which are internal to it.

XI

Comparison with Some Kindred Doctrines

. . . . . .

NATURAL facts are objects of intent only; and then the propriety of the names, images, categories, or other essences which we use in conceiving them becomes problematical.

The Realm of Essence Is the Infinite Background of Everything.

On the other hand, essences problematical as descriptions of facts are manifest as ideas. The more hypotheses we try, and the more alternatives we consider, whether we attain absolute truth or a sufficient symbolic truth, or no truth at all, we are still entertained by ideas which are innocent if we do not abuse them, and perhaps beautiful and significant if they express our own playful or creative impulses. Nor is this entertainment with essence a trivial bond with reality. Facts, however momentous, are transient and local, and truths, however eternal, are relative to these transient and local facts; but every essence, whether it ever have or not the adventitious dignity of a truth, is in its own right a something —a verse or a letter in that infinite Koran sealed from all eternity in the bosom of Allah, of which the trembling angel of life may read to us a few Surahs. That it should be these and not those is the tragic mystery of our fate, and of all existence; that others also should some day be manifested in other worlds or to other spirits, would be a further decree of fate; but that all should lie for ever in the realm of essence is a luminous necessity raised far above any accident of destiny or decree of power. It could not be otherwise. If you deny that realm, you acknowledge it. If you forget it, you consent that it should silently laugh at you in your sleep.

this amphibious character of existence is far from being a reason for not distinguishing those realms. On the contrary, besides the inherent differences in them which nothing can ever obliterate, there is an added reason why the naturalist should discriminate them. He is not merely living, like the animals, but professing to describe the world; and the sense of existence would remain a merely emotional burden, and life a blind career, unless he began by discriminating the essences which it discloses, in their heterogeneity, hierarchy, and succession.

If, then, in turning to the study of existence I had avoided the word matter, there would have been a sort of treason in the subterfuge. I do not mean treason so much to matter itself, because the intrinsic essence of matter being unknown, it may be figured almost indifferently by any image of sense or thought, as by "the gods" or "the devil," provided that expectation and action are not misled by that symbol. I mean rather treason to spirit, to truth, to essence, to those trembling immaterial lights and that infinite immutable background which, unless sharply contrasted with the matter which they surround, may be transposed in confused apprehension to the plane of matter, and saddled with material functions. Have not both truth and spirit, not to speak of essence, been represented in our day as things physical, temporal, instrumental, and practical? Ontologically, this attitude is absurd, and a mere failure in discernment; but taken apostolically—for it is zealously espoused—it expresses a genuine and perfectly legitimate allegiance: that respect for matter only, which characterises the psyche when absorbed in action and in circumstances. Life marks a mechanical complication, maintained in a world where it did not always exist; and the psyche, in her fundamental impulse, is perfectly content that all her ardent labour should end in a vain redistribution of matter, or should never end. It would seem idle from her point of view, and rather mad, that any spirit should ever disengage itself from that process and should come to find in it some satisfying essence, so that in discerning and possessing this essence it might transcend that remorseless flux and might look away from it to an eternal world. In the reversion of philosophy (which in spite of itself is a form of spirit) to exclusive sympathy with the flux of matter, there is accordingly a too domestic virtue or exaggerated piety, like that of a fair daughter devoting her whole existence to nursing her old mother. Free spirit lets the dead bury their dead, and takes no thought for the morrow; and it redeems the labouring world by bringing joy into it.

Theoretical scruples about the reality of matter are of two sorts: they may be sceptical and empirical, based on the fact that matter is no immediate datum of intuition; or they may be scientific and logical, based on the suspicion that some particular idea of matter may be unfit or inadequate to express its true nature. These two kinds of objection are mutually contradictory; for the one condemns matter for not being a human sensation, and the other condemns matter for being only a human idea. The first objection involves a retreat to the subjective sphere; and however legitimate such a retreat may be in romantic soliloquy, it is in principle destructive of all science or even belief. The postulate of substance—the assumption that there are things and events prior to the discovery of them and independent of this discovery —underlies all natural knowledge. The refinements which may supervene on this conviction ought never to shake it, and do not do so when they are fruitful. Therefore the first sort of obection against matter—that it is a thing-in-itself antecedent to human experience—may be dismissed at once as vain and sophistical; for it rescinds that animal faith, or that common sense, which is the beginning of art and of science and their perpetual presupposition.

There remains the second difficulty: the suspicion, or the clear perception, that some special description of matter— say that of Democritus or that of Descartes—is inadequate or mistaken. But of course all human notions of matter, even if not positively fabulous, must be wholly inadequate; otherwise the natural philosopher would be claiming a plenitude of miraculous illumination such as no prophet ever thought to possess. Human ideas of matter are initially as various as human contacts with it, and as human sensations in its presence. These ideas are sensuous and pictorial from the beginning. They are then variously sifted and refined according to people's progress in the arts of comparison and calculation. In popular speech the word matter continues to suggest the popular aspects of natural things; in scientific speech, at each stage of it, the word comes to denote such aspects of those same things as have become calculable at that stage. Thus to a stonecutter extension and impenetrability may well seem the essence of matter; the builder, intent on the strains and dangers of position, will add degrees of cohesion and weight to his definition. At this stage metaphysicians and moralists will look down on matter as something gross and dead, and will imagine that motion and organisation must be imposed on matter from without: not seeing that this external force, if it governed and moved matter, would be the soul of matter, and much nearer to its proper essence than the æsthetic aspects which its aggregates may wear to the human eye. Yet what could be more obviously material than thunder and lightning, sunshine and rain, from which the father of the gods borrowed his poetic substance? Weight and figure are not more characteristic of matter than are explosiveness, swiftness, fertility, and radiation. Planters and breeders of animals, or poets watching the passing generations of mankind, will feel that the heart and mystery of matter lie in the seeds of things, *semina rerum*, and in the customary cycles of their transformation. It is by its motion and energy, by its fidelity to measure and law, that matter has become the substance of our world, and the principle of life and of death in it. The earliest sages, no less than the latest moderns, identified matter with fire, æther, or fluids, rather than with stocks and stones; the latter are but temporary concretions, and always in the act of growing or crumbling. Even those who, partly for dialectical reasons, reduced matter to impenetrable atoms, attributed all its fertility to the play of collisions which swept perpetually through the void and drove those dead atoms into constellations and vortices and organisms. This endless propulsion and these fated complications were no less material, and far more terrible, than any monumental heap into which matter might sometimes be gathered, and which to a gaping mind might seem more substantial. If any poet ever felt the life of nature in its truth, irrepressible, many-sided, here flaming up savagely, there helplessly dying down, that poet was Lucretius, whose materialism was unqualified.

Finally, in our own times, when physics speculates chiefly on bodies so remote or minute as to be known only through variations in light, matter seems to evaporate into these visible variations, as if light had no source, or as if man had no contact with nature except through the eye. But the seat of these perceptions is not the heavens or the æther, but the human organism; and even if the human organism were composed of these or of other such perceptions, the conditions for the existence of these elements and their relation to the heavens, the æther, and one another, would constitute a material world. A psychological nature might thus be ascribed to matter, in its unapproachable internal essence but that hypothesis, or rather myth, would materialise a late human idea, removed by the whole diameter of evolution and mundane time from the primeval matter which was its object; an object which cannot be found in the landscape of intuition, but must be posited in action, from the outside, in its dynamic and truly material capacity. Criticism, I think, would induce us to stop with this functional definition of matter, which represents our actual approach to it. We should then attach the landscape of intuition to matter only at the summit of evolution, when the psyche becomes a poet, and learns to transcribe her material passions and experiences into terms of essence.

All these partialities in the conception of matter are honest and inevitable. Each view, in stretching its special language as far as possible, may serve to disclose some side of the true order of nature. But this order is that of actual generation and existential flux, something that happens and is not conceived; so that no sensuous or graphic or mathematical transcript of it should be so pressed as to be substituted for it. Nor is it reasonable for those familiar with one side of nature to deride those who, seeing some different side, unsuspectingly identify it with the substance before them. They are wrong; but the critic would be wrong also if he did not tolerate their error, and even prize it for its measure of subjective truth.

The realm of matter, then, from the point of view of our discovery of it, is the field of action: it is essentially dynamic and not pictorial. Moreover, our action is interpolated in a world already in existence. Our existence and purposes are things of yesterday; they were evidently drawn from that very world on which they react. From the point of view of origins, therefore, the realm of matter is the matrix and the source of everything: it is nature, the sphere of genesis, the universal mother. The truth cannot dictate to us the esteem in which we shall hold it: that is not a question of fact but of preference. Yet natural philosophy may disclose the source of our preferences and their implications, so that it may lead us to reconsider them, or to express them differently. So if, with this conception of the realm of matter before us, we turn back to the moral prejudices against matter, we shall be amazed at their levity. A spiritual mind might well look over the head of nature to a First Cause, and beyond the vicissitudes of life to a supreme good: therein there would be a genuine aversion from the realm of matter, and absorption in essences which, at best, existence can illustrate or suggest for a moment to the mind, as it does beauty or the laws of number. But, though not prized for itself, the realm of matter would remain standing; otherwise those divine essences would never have been illustrated or suggested at all. If in clinging to the immaterial we denied the material, it would not be merely ashes or dust that we should be despising, but all natural existence in its abysmal past and in its indefinite fertility; and it would be not some philosopher's sorry notion of matter that we should be denying, but the reality of our animal being, the fact that we are creatures of time, rooted in a moving universe in which our days are numbered. And rather than blaspheme in this way against our own nature and origin, we might well say with the Irish poet.*

> Who is that goddess to whom men should pray,
> But her from whom their hearts have turned away,
> Out of whose virgin being they were born,
> Whose mother-nature they have named with scorn,
> Calling her holy substance common clay. . . .
>
> Ah, when I think this earth on which I tread
> Hath borne these blossoms of the lovely dead,
> And makes the living heart I love to beat,
> I look with sudden awe beneath my feet—

and here the poet adds the questionable line:

> As you with erring reverence overhead.

If I look overhead, I see the cosmic spaces, the sun or the stars: all this is as much a part of nature, and a source of life, as the nether earth. Or if by "overhead" we understand the spiritual sphere, why should it not be looked upon with as much respect as that realm of matter which, for a free spirit, can be only a means and an instrument? But I think I understand what the poet means, and the justness of his sen-

---

*"A. E." (George Russell) in *The Virgin Mother*.

timent. *Reverence* is something due to antiquity, to power, to the roots and the moral supports of existence; it is therefore due really to the realm of matter only, and there is a profound error and self-deception in attributing those genetic functions, or directing that piety, to ideal objects. Towards these appropriate feeling is not reverence so much as love, enthusiasm, contemplative rapture, mystic union: feelings which it would be as silly to address to matter as to address a dutiful reverence to essences or to attribute power to them. In reality, the realm of matter contains more than half of that which from the dawn of life has been the object of human religion: it contains "the gods," or the veritable influences represented by their names and conciliated by the worship of them. Hell and heaven, for any honest and serious religion, are parts of nature; if ever they cease to be so regarded, they are immediately replaced, as among liberal Protestants, by the goods and evils of this world. The residue of human religion is something private, generous, and not obligatory: it rises from the earth in incense and music, never to return; it forms a spiritual life, akin to poetic love, to happiness, to philosophy. In contrast with it, the tremendous sanctions and fixed duties of established religion, being instinct with prudence and great hopes, belong to the sober economy of life; and they all regard, if people's eyes were only unsealed, this despised realm of matter.

I

The Scope of Natural Philosophy

Contrast Between Ideal and Natural Science.

THE measure of confidence with which I have spoken of essence forsakes me when I approach existence. Logic, grammar, and poetry are free; no alien fact, no vociferation, can prevent intuition from beholding what it actually beholds.

The public censor has indeed some rights over the persons in whom intuition arises, and may condemn their habit of mind if he thinks that it comports idleness or the disruption of happy national conventions; but, in this instance, fortune having relegated me, like the gods of Epicurus, to the interstices of the worlds, I may escape that censure or disregard it. Who knows? Perhaps some kindred spirit may tell me that I have chosen the better part. In any case, I deny nothing and prejudge nothing concerning the intuitions of others; if I cultivate my own with a certain ardour, it is only as any man cultivate his language and tastes, if his mind is at all liberal; and I am confident no god or man will be justly angry with me for browsing so innocently in my own pasture. But when the active impulse of curiosity and dogmatism asserts itself in its turn, as it must in the most contemplative mind, and I ask myself what dark objects or forces have created or are threatening my contemplation, then indeed I am at a loss: and as in positing such natural agencies at all I assume that they are objects obligatory to every other mind with which I can communicate, I bind myself to make my opinions conformable with their reports, and my reports agreeable to their experience. Of course the belief that I can communicate with other minds, and that the reports reaching me signify an experience of theirs over and above my own, is a part of this extraordinary compulsory assumption which I make in living; the assumption that I am surrounded by a natural world, peopled by creatures in whom intuition is as rife as in myself: and as all my concern in perception and action turns on what those external things may do, so half my interest in my own thoughts turns on what other people may be thinking.

Assumption of an Existing World.

It is not the task of natural philosophy to justify this assumption, which indeed can never be justified. Its task, after making that assumption, is to carry it out consistently and honestly, so as to arrive, if possible, at a conception of nature by which the faith involved in action may be enlightened and guided. Such a description of nature, if it were ever completed in outline, would come round full circle, and in its account of animals it would report how they came to have intuitions (among them this natural philosophy) and to use them in the description of the world which actually surrounded them. The whole field of action and of facts would then be embraced in a single view, summary and symbolic, but comprehensive.

Inevitable Attempt to Describe It.

The dream of the natural philosopher would be to describe the world from its beginning (if it had a beginning), tracing all its transformations; and he would like to do this analytically, not pictorially—that is, not in the sensuous language of some local observer composing a private perspective, but in terms of the ultimate elements (if there are ultimate elements) concerned in the actual evolution of things. Out of those elements he would conceive each observer and his perspective arising, and of course varying from moment to moment. Even if the natural philosopher were an idealist, and admitted only observing spirits and their perspectives, he would endeavour to trace the evolution of these intuitions, which would be his atoms, in their universal order and march, by no means contenting himself with one intuition and one perspective; for, if he did so, his idealism (like that of some philosophies of history) would not be a system of physics or of logic, but a literary entertainment, the lyrical echo of many verbal reports in a romantic imagination. This echo might be interesting in itself: but it would remain only an incident in that natural world which indeed it presupposed, but which it deliberately ignored. So that when the idealist became a man again in the world of action, and began to live (as he must) by animal faith, his philosophy would entirely forsake him; yet it is in the service of this animal faith that philosophy exists, when it is science and wisdom. Indeed, a theoretical refusal to trust natural philosophy cannot absolve the most sceptical of us from framing one, and from living by it. I *must* conceive a surrounding world, even if in reflection I say to myself at every step: Illusion, Illusion. It then becomes almost as interesting to know what sort of illusions must accompany me through life, as it would be to imagine what sort of world I really live in. Indeed, if all spurious substitutes for natural philosophy were discarded (spurious because irrelevant to the animal faith which alone posits existence) those two positions might coincide, since the picture of the natural world framed by common sense and science, while framed with the greatest care, would be admittedly only a picture; and belief in the existence of that world, though assumed without wobbling, would be admittedly but an article of inevitable faith.

Positive Religions Involve Cosmologies.

Non-scientific beliefs about existence, whether inspired by religious feeling, reasoning, or fancy, are alternatives to the current natural philosophy, or extensions of it. Nobody would believe in his ideas if he had not an initial propensity to believe in things, as if his ideas described them. Dogmatic religions are assertions about the nature of the universe; what is called supernatural is only ultra-mundane, an extension of this world on its own plane, and a recognition of forces ruling over it not reckoned with in vulgar commerce. The assertions made by such religious faith, if not superstitious errors, are ultimate truths of natural philosophy, which intuition or revelation has supplied in advance of experiment: but if the assertions are true at all, experiment might one day confirm them. Thus Christian orthodoxy maintains that men will carry their memories and their bodies with them into hell or heaven. Theology is the natural philosophy of that larger world which religion posits as truly existing: it therefore has precise implications in politics and science.

The absence of such implications and commitments, far from showing that religion has become spiritual, proves it a sham; it is no longer a manly hypothesis, honestly made about the world confronted in action. No doubt there is an inner fountain of religious feeling which a person accepting his theology on hearsay might wholly lack; but it was religious instinct of some kind that originally prompted those hypotheses about the hidden nature of things, and if this instinct is lacking those hypotheses will soon be discarded. On the other hand, religious feeling may not always require ultra-mundane extensions of the natural world; it may find a sufficient object and sanction in the course of earthly history and domestic life, as was the case, at bottom, with Jewish and Protestant righteousness: the politics and science dictated by religious faith will then coincide with those recommended by worldly wisdom. Religious feeling may take still other forms; for instance, it may smile mystically at action and belief altogether, retreating into the invisible sanctuary of the spirit, or floating incredulously amid mere music and dreams. But mysticism, whether austere or voluptuous, since it regards the absolute, ceases to regard existence which, by definition, is relative, since it consists in having external relations. Positive and virile minds may find indulgence in such mysticism irreligious, because their earnestness is directed upon alleged facts, in this world or in another: facts essentially relevant to action and policy, and open to natural philosophy.

Idolatrous Character of Metaphysics.

Much restraint, and some disillusion, may enable a man to entertain ideas without believing them to describe any matter of fact: such ideas will be avowedly mere terms of grammar, logic, or fancy, to be discarded, or at least discounted, on broaching a serious natural philosophy. They may still be indispensable as a medium, as some language is indispensable to science; but they will be optional and interchangeable, as the scientific part of a book of science (which is never the whole of it) is perfectly translatable from one language into another. This is not to say that the medium of intuition, even in natural philosophy, is indifferent in itself; nothing is dearer to a man or a nation than congenial modes of expression; I would rather be silent than use some people's language; I would rather die than think as some people think. But it is the quality of life that is concerned here, not the truth of ideas. To attempt to impose such modes of intuition or expression, as if they were obligatory tenets, is metaphysics: a projection of the constants or the creations of thought into the realm of matter. The authority of intuition would be entire if it kept to the definition of essences, and of their essential relations; but when zeal intervenes, and we profess to find our favourite dialectic in things, we are betrayed into disrespect for nature, and are inflating our egotism into cosmic proportions. At best the metaphysician has given a useful hint to the naturalist: he has supplied categories which may be convenient or even indispensable for expressing the ways of nature in human discourse. The palmary instance of this is mathematics, which, long after having ceased to be empirical and become dialectical, still continues to serve for construction and even for prophecy in the material sphere: yet the symbols employed grow more abstruse and tenuous as they grow more exact, so that people are little tempted to substitute the notation for the thing denoted; and they thus escape metaphysics.

When the experience interpreted is spiritual or passionate, the categories used are, as in religion and poetry, clearly mythological: yet they are not without a real, though indirect, object in the realm of matter. This object is the psyche, with all those profound currents in her life which create the passions, and create the spirit which expresses the passions, yet which in expressing them is so entangled that it often comes to regard them as its enemies. Those psychic currents, being dynamic, are material; but they are hidden from the eye of spirit, which alone is spiritual, by layer upon layer of vague sensation, rhetoric, and imagery.

Nature Is the Nexus of All Substances and Forces.

Belief, in its very soul, is belief about nature; it is animal faith. To entangle belief in anything non-natural, or avowedly tangential to action, would be to cheat at the game. Honest speculative belief is always speculative physics. But its terms are inevitably the essences present to intuition; and the very faith which, in the presence of these essences, posits existing things, drags something of the given apparition into the presumed substance of the thing revealed: the theophany humanises the god. In correcting this illusion, and in discarding one mythical or metaphysical image after another, science must still retain some symbol for the overpowering reality of the world. This reality is not that symbol itself, nor a collection of such symbols: if we cling to these we shall never quit the realm of essence. Nor am I sure that the most learned symbols are the least deceptive; if any human ideas must be idolised, I should almost prefer those of the senses and of the poets. Yet it would be ignominious for a philosopher voluntarily to succumb to illusion at all, when the artificiality and relativity of all human views, especially of learned and beautiful systems, is so patent to reflection. Yet views we must have, none the worse, surely, if they are beautiful and learned; so that the natural philosopher is driven to a deeper question, to which I mean to devote this book: How much, when cleared as far as possible of idolatry, can sense or science reveal concerning the dark engine of nature? In what measure do they truly enlighten animal faith?

How Far Is Science Knowledge?

In broaching this question I am not concerned with repeating, correcting, or forecasting the description which men of science may give of the world. I accept gladly any picture of nature honestly drawn by them, as I accept gladly any picture drawn by my own senses. Different circumstances or different faculties would certainly have produced different pictures. From Genesis to Thales, to Ptolemy, to Copernicus, to Newton and to Einstein the landscape has pleasantly varied; and it may yet open other vistas. These variations and prospects show the plasticity of human thought, for it is not the facts that have much varied, nor the material station of man, nor his senses and destiny. The incubus of existence remains exactly the same. Is it merely imagination that has become more laboured but no less fantastic? Or has the path of destiny been really cleared and the forces that control destiny been better understood? Within what limits does any description of nature, picturesque or scientific, retain its relevance to animal faith and its validity as knowledge of fact, and at what point does it become pure speculation and metaphor? That is the only question which I shall endeavour to answer.

My survey of the realm of matter will accordingly be merely transcendental, and made from the point of view of a sceptic and a moralist criticising the claims of experience and science to be true knowledge.

The Transcendental Method Applied to Animal Faith.

By transcendental reflection I understand reversion, in the presence of any object or affirmation, to the immediate experience which discloses that object or prompts that affirmation. Transcendental reflection is a challenge to all dogmatism, a demand for radical evidence. It therefore tends to disallow substance and, when it is thorough, even to disallow existence. Nothing is ultimately left except the passing appearance or the appearance of something passing. How, then, if transcendental reflection disallows substance, can it lead me to distinguish the properties of substance?

In *Scepticism and Animal Faith* I have considered the transcendental motives which oblige me to believe in substance. The belief must always remain an assumption, but one without which an active and intelligent creature cannot honestly act or think. Transcendentalism has two phases or movements—the sceptical one retreating to the immediate, and the assertive one by which objects of belief are defined and marshalled, of such a character and in such an order as intelligent action demands. The enterprise of life is precarious, and to the sceptic it must seem an adventure in the dark, without origins or environment or results. Yet this flying life, by its forward energy, breeds from within certain postulates of sanity, certain conceptions of the conditions which might surround it and lend it a meaning, so that its own continuance and fortunes may be conceived systematically and affirmed with confidence. Thus the faith that posits and describes a world is just as transcendental as the criticism which reduces that world to an appearance or a fiction. If so many transcendental philosophers stop at the negative pole, this arrest is not a sign of profundity in them, but of weakness. It is by boldly believing what transcendental necessity prompts any hunting animal to believe, that I separate myself from that arrested idealism, and proceed to inquire what existences, what substances, and what motions are involved in the chase.

Action Posits a Field Existing Substantially for Science to Describe.

In the chase, for those who follow it, the intensity of experience is not like the intensity (limitless if you will) of contemplating pure Being—immutable, equable, and complete. The hunter and the hunted believe in something ambushed and imminent: present images are little to them but signs for coming events. Things are getting thick, agents are coming together, or disappearing: they are killing and dying. The assurance of this sort of being is assurance of existence, and the belief in this sort of agent is belief in substance. If this belief and assurance are not illusions (which the acting animal cannot admit them to be), several properties must belong to substances and to the world they compose. These properties I may distinguish in reflection and call by philosophical names, somewhat as follows.

I I

Indispensable Properties of Substance

A World in Which Action Is to Occur Must Be External, Spatial, and Temporal, Possessing Variety and Unity.

1. SINCE substance is posited, and not given in intuition, as essences may be given, *substance is external to the thought which posits it.*

2. Since it is posited in action, or in readiness for action, the substance posited is external not merely to the positing thought (as a different thought would be) but is external to the physical agent which is the organ of that action, as well as of that thought. In other words, *Substance has parts and constitutes a physical space.* Conversely, the substantial agent in action and thought is external to the surrounding portions of substance with which it can interact. *All the parts of substance are external to one another.*

3. Since substance is engaged in action, and action involves change, *substance is in flux and constitutes a physical time.* Changes are perpetually occurring in the relations of its parts, if not also in their intrinsic characters.

4. Since the agents in action and reaction are distinct in position and variable in character, and since they induce changes in one another, *substance is unequally distributed.* It diversifies the field of action, or physical time and space.

5. Since there is no occasion for positing any substance save as an agent in the field of action, all recognisable substance must lie in the same field in which the organism of

the observer occupies a relative center. Therefore, wherever it works and solicits recognition, *substance composes a relative cosmos*.

The First Property, Externality to Thought, Belongs to All Existence.

A mutual externality, or *Auseinandersein*—an alternation of centres such as moment and moment, thing and thing, place and place, person and person—is characteristic of existence. Each centre is equally actual and equally central, yet each is dependent on its neighbours for its position and on its predecessors for its genesis. The existential interval from one centre to another is bridged naturally by generation or motion—by a transition actually taking place from one moment, place, or character to another, in such a manner that the former moment, place, or character is abandoned and lost. The same interval may still be bridged cognitively by faith or intent, cognition being a substitute for a transition which cannot be executed materially, because the remote term of it is past or not next in the order of genesis or transformation. But this interval can never be bridged by synthesis in intuition. Synthesis in intuition destroys the existential status of the terms which it unites, since it excludes any alternation or derivation between them. It unites at best the essences of some natural things into an ideal picture. On the other hand the conjunction of existences in nature must always remain successive, external, and unsynthesised. Nature shows no absolute limits and no privileged partitions; whereas the richest intuition, the most divine omniscience, is imprisoned in the essence which it beholds. It cannot break through into existence unless it loses itself and submits to transition; and the foretaste or aftertaste of such transition, present in feeling, must posit something eventual, something absent from intuition, if even the sense or idea of existence is to arise at all. Then the mind engaged in action may begin to live by faith in the outlying

conditions of life, and by an instinctive tension towards obscure events.

Memory, When Cognitive, a Relation Between Separate Natural Facts.

It might seem that memory eludes this necessity, and
actually encloses some parts of the past in the present, and
brings the movement of events bodily within the circle of
intuition. But this is an illusion founded on the fact that
memory contains both imagery and knowledge: the imagery
is all present, but that of which it gives knowledge, when
memory is true, is past and gone. Even if, by a rare favour,
the original aspect of the past experience should be reproduced exactly, it will not be the past event, nor even the
present one, that will be given in intuition, but the dateless
essence common to both.

The cognitive value of this apparition will hang on the
ulterior fact that such an apparition, or the event which it
reports, occurred before, at a point of time which was its
own centre, and not a marginal feature in the present perspective. Memory, then, in so far as it is, or even claims to
be, knowledge, is faith in the absent, and bridges external
relations by intent only, not by synthesis in intuition.

Existing Thoughts Are Separate Events Lodged Each in Its Place in Nature.

A mutual externality is also requisite among the instances
of spirit, that is, among thoughts that are to be regarded as
existences and events. This at first sight might seem contrary to the apparent self-existence and self-evidence of conscious being, and to the transcendental status of spirit,
which, because it is a logical counterpart to any datum,
might be alleged to be an omnipresent fact, existing absolutely. But this, although it may pass for criticism, is the
sophistry of reflection, which can readily take its verbal
terms for existences or substances, and ignore the natural

springs of feeling and of reflection itself. An instance of spirit, a pure feeling or intuition, if it had no date or place in nature, would not be an event or existence at all, but only another name, and a mythical name, for the essence conceived to be present there. The life of thought, in its conscious intensity, lies in the synthesis which it is perpetually making among its changing materials. These acts of synthesis, these glances and insights, are historical facts; they arise and are distinguishable on the level of experience from their material conditions; but they are not substances. Their substance is their organ in its movement and in its changing tensions: it is the psyche. The case is like that of a collision between two vehicles, or checkmate in a game of chess. The collision is a new fact, on the plane of human affairs, as is the checkmate which ends the game; so, too, are the chagrin or the severe pain which these events may occasion. But the pain or the chagrin could no more arise, or come into existence, without the living persons who endure them—persons moving in the realm of matter—than the checkmate could occur without the match, or the collision without the vehicles. If a feeling or thought is to be actual, and not a metaphorical name for some eternal essence, it must therefore arise out of material events, and in the midst of them: it must stand in external relations.

Thus the first indispensable condition for the being of substance is indispensable also to any form of existence, mental or historical as well as physical. Existence, like substance, is essentially diffuse and many-centred. One fact can be reached cognitively from another fact only by faith, and materially only by transition; and the cognitive or the initial fact itself can exist only by virtue of its position or action in a natural system extending beyond it.

Existence Being Contingent Is Essentially Unstable.

It follows that substance is in flux, virtual, if not actual. External relations are such as are due to the position, not to the inherent character, of the terms. They are, therefore, always variable, and existence, although it may endure by accident for any length of time, is inherently mortal and transitory, being adventitious to the essences which figure in it. When Hamlet says, *To be or not to be*, he is pondering the alternative between existence and non-existence, and feeling the contingency of both. The question is not whether he shall be or not be Hamlet: death might cause him to forget his essence, but could not abolish it or transform it into another essence. In the realm of essence all these essences are eternally present and no alternative arises: which is perhaps the ultimate truth conveyed by the doctrine of eternal salvation or punishment. But the accidents of death, or dreams, or oblivion continually confront this life, and existence is an optional form of being. Shall this beloved or detested essence presently lose it? And on what other essence shall it fall next? To this pressing question the realm of essence supplies no answer, and the contemplative mind is hopelessly puzzled by it. *Solvitur ambulando*: the event, the propulsive currents of substance merging and rushing into new forms, will precipitate a solution without ever considering alternatives; and it is perhaps because they never stop to think before they act, that they are able to act at all.

The Substance Which Determines Events Is Itself in Motion.

Something not essence, then, actualises and limits the manifestation of every essence that figures in nature or appears before the mind. To this dark principle of existence we give the name of substance; so that substance, by definition, is the soil, the medium, and the creative force which secretly determines any option like that of Hamlet. Every such option is momentary and local; for although substance is external to essence and to thought, and its parts are external to one another, yet substance is internal to the things which it forms by occupying those contrasted places and assuming these various qualities. It is *their* substance, the principle of their existence, the ground of all the spontaneous changes which they undergo. It is indefinitely, perhaps infinitely, deep and inhuman; but whatever else its intrinsic essence may be, it is certainly complex, local, and temporal. Its secret flux involves at least as many contrasts and variations as the course of nature shows on the surface. Otherwise the ultimate core of existence would not exist, and the causes of variation would not vary. But how shall that which puts on this specious essence here and not there be in the same inner condition in both places? Or how shall that which explodes now have been equally active before? Substance, if it is to fulfil the function in virtue of which it is recognised and posited, must accordingly be for ever changing its own inner condition. It must be in flux.

Permanence Need Not Be Attributed to Substance Otherwise than as Implied in Flux.

Undoubtedly the word substance suggests permanence rather than change, because the substances best known to man (like the milk and the wet sand of the young architect) evidently pass from place to place and from form to form while retaining their continuity and quantity. Such permanence is not contrary to flux, but a condition of flux. The degree of permanence which substance may have in any particular process, and the name which should be given to this permanent factor, are questions for scientific discussion. They may not, and need not, receive any ultimate answer. But that *some* permanence, not the casual persistence of this or that image, is interwoven with the flux of things, follows from the reality of this flux itself. If change were total at any point, there transformation and existence would come to an end. The next, completely new, fact would not be next; it would be the centre, or the beginning, of a separate world. In other words, events, if they are to be successive or contiguous, must be pervaded by a common medium, in which they may assume relations external to their respective essences; for the internal or logical relations between these essences will never establish any succession or continuity among them, nor transport them at all into the sphere of existence. The critics of empiricism who have insisted that a series of sensations is not the sensation of a series, might well have added that the sensation of a series is no more than an isolated term on its own account, unless there is a background common to those terms and to this synthetic idea —a background in relation to which they may respectively take such places as shall render them contiguous or successive, although there is nothing within any of them to indicate such a position. This background, for human perception, is the field of vision symbolising the field of action; in this specious field the position of objects is distinguished before the objects are clearly specified or posited; but this unity of perspective, relative to the momentary station and thought of the observer, cannot embrace the existential flux itself, in which the events reported and the observer, with his thought, are incidental features. For the continuity and successiveness of this existing series, synthesis in apprehension is useless: it merely creates one more item—a living thought— to be ranged among its neighbours in the flux of existence. That which is requisite is the *natural derivation* of one phase in this flux from another, or a *natural tension* between them, determining their respective characters and positions. Such derivation and such tension, essential to action, involve a substance within or between events. There may be very much more in substance than that; but this is enough to disclose the existence of a substance, and to begin the human description of it by its functions.

Permanence, therefore, need not be set down separately among the radical properties attributed to substance: it is sufficiently expressed in the possibility of change, of continuity, of succession, and of the inclusion of actual events in a natural series, which shall not be a mere perspective in imagination.

Action Presupposes a Diversified Field.

Action and animal faith look in some specific direction; the butt of action, which is what I call substance, must be particular, local, and circumscribed. It must be capable of varying its position or its condition; for otherwise I could neither affect it by my action, nor await and observe its operation. In battle, in the chase, or in labour, attention is turned to a particular quarter, to something substantial there: it would defeat all action and art if all quarters were alike, and if I couldn't face a fact without turning my back on exactly the same fact in the rear; and the price of bread would be indifferent, if one substance being everywhere present I could find the same substance in the air. Action evidently would be objectless in an infinite vacuum or a homogeneous plenum; and even the notion or possibility of action would vanish if I, the agent, had not distinguishable parts, so that at least I might swim forward rather than backward in that dense vacuity.

The Substance of Things Is Physical: Metaphysical Substance Is Only a Grammatical Term.

A field of action must, then, be diversified substantially, not pictorially only; that which is at work in it here must not be equally at work in it there; the opportunities which it opens to me now must not be the same which it opened and will open always. Any conception of substance which represents it as undivided and homogeneous is accordingly not a conception of nature or of existence: and if such an object is ever called substance, it must be in a metaphysical sense which I do not attach to the word. One test of such evasions into the realm of essence is ability, or ambition, to give a precise definition of what substance is. *Materia prima* may be defined—Plotinus has an admirable exposition of it, like the Athanasian creed—because it is avowedly something incapable of existence, and at best one of those ideal terms which serve to translate nature into the language of thought. *Materia prima* is a grammatical essence, comparable to the transcendental ego, the "I think," which according to Kant must accompany all experience. The discrimination of such essences distinguishes one logic from another, and leaves everything in nature, except human language, just as it was. The existing substance of things, on the contrary, is that which renders them dynamic; it is wherever dynamic things are, not where they are not; it determines their aspects and powers; and we may learn, since it exists in us also, to play with it and to let it play on us, in specific ways. But it would be frivolous to attempt to define it, as if a set of words, or of blinking ideas, could penetrate to the heart of existence and determine how, from all eternity, it must have been put together. What we may discover of it is not its essence but its place, its motion, its aspects, its effects. Were it an essence given in intuition, a visionary presence to sense or to language, it would forfeit those very functions which compel us to posit it, and which attest its formidable reality. Chief of these functions is a perpetual and determinate revolution in the heavens, and fertility and decay upon earth. In this flux there is a relative permanence and continuity; but substance is not for that reason less agitated than the familiar face of nature, or nearer to the impassibility of an eternal essence. Far otherwise. Investigation rather shows that this substance (which may be traced experimentally in many of its shifts) is in a continual silent ferment, by which gross visible objects are always being undermined and transformed: so much so that science often loses its way amid those subtle currents of the elements, and stops breathless at some too human image.

In Physics Parmenides Must Give Way to Democritus.

There are certain celebrated doctrines which, in their forms of expression, are excluded at once from natural philosophy by these considerations. I may not say, for instance, with Parmenides that Being is and Not-Being is not, if what I am seeking to describe is the substance of nature. If for dialectical reasons, which are not directly relevant to physics, I wished to regard pure Being as the essence of matter, I should be compelled to distribute this pure Being unequally in a void: a result which would contradict my premise that Not-Being is not, since this void would not only exist but would be the only true theatre of existence, because it would be the only seat of change. The pure Being or matter distributed in it, by hypothesis, is impassible and everywhere identical. Nature and life would therefore be due to the redistribution in the bosom of Not-Being of a pure Being in itself immutable. We should thus be led to the system of Democritus: a possible and even a model system of physics, although, in its expression, too Eleatic, and borrowing from that dialectical school a false air of necessity.

The Vedanta Must Give Way to the Samkhya System.

Similarly, at the threshold of natural philosophy, the Vedanta system must yield to the Samkhya: and this the Indians seem to have admitted by regarding the two systems as orthodox and compatible. It might be well if in the West we could take a hint from this comprehensiveness. The unity and simplicity of pure Being is not incompatible with the infinite variety of essences implied in it; and many things are true in the realm of essence which, if taken to describe existence, would be unmeaning or contrary to fact. It would suffice to distinguish the two spheres more carefully, for the legitimacy of systems, verbally most unlike, to become equal: although certainly those which were drawn from insight into essence would be more profound and unshakable than those drawn from observation of nature, since nature might as well have offered quite a different spectacle. On the other hand, it is the order and ground of this spectacle that interests the natural philosopher; and to him that more inward and more sublime intuition of essential Being is a waste of time, or a rhetorical danger.

And Spinoza Must Give Way to Aristotle.

One more illustration: the language of Spinoza about substance ought to yield, in physics, to that of Aristotle, in spite of the fact that a follower of Descartes could not help being more enlightened in mechanical matters than a follower of Socrates. Nevertheless it was Aristotle who gave the name of substance to compound natural things actually existing, and Spinoza who bestowed it on an ambiguous metaphysical object, now pure Being, now the universe in its infinity—in either case an ideal unity and an essence incapable of realisation all at once, if at all, in any natural locus. No discrimination of infinite Being into infinitely numerous attributes would ever generate existence, since all would remain eternal; and no enumeration of the possible modes of each attribute would turn them into particular things or into living minds, since each mode would imply all the others, and all would be equally rooted everywhere. In Aristotle, on the contrary, the name of substance is given where the office of substance is performed, and where one fact here asserts itself against another fact there; so that substance is the principle of individuation and exclusion, the condition of existence, succession, and rivalry amongst natural things. Even if these things, as conceived by Aristotle, have too much of an animate unity, and are mysteriously fixed in their genera and species, and redolent of moral suggestions, all this is but the initial dramatic rendering of their human uses, and the poetry of good prose. It does not prevent a more disinterested analysis, a microscopic and telescopic science, from disclosing in time the deeper mechanisms and analogies of nature, and its finer substance: just as the static zoology and the political psychology of Aristotle do not prevent us from peeping into the seething elementary passions beneath those classical masks. Things have not ceased to wear the sensuous and moral forms which interested the Greeks; but we may discover how those shells were generated, and what currents of universal substance have cast them up.

The Field of Action Must Have a Dynamic Unity.

Finally, the practical intellect, in positing substance, imposes on it a certain relevance to the agent, who is to be in dynamic relations with it. The objects which art and sanity compel me to recognise as substantial, must affect me together, even if in very different ways. They must all impinge, directly or indirectly, on my action now; and it is by this test that I distinguish fact from fiction and true memory from fancy. Facts are dynamically connected with that which I now posit as substantial, and objects of fancy are not so connected. The field of animal faith spreads out from a living centre; observation cannot abandon its base, but from this vital station it may extend its perspectives over everything to which it can assign existence. Among these accredited things there may be other centres of observation, actual or eventual; but if the original organ and station, and these other stations and organs accredited by it, were not parts of one and the same substantial world, no means would remain of identifying the objects observed from one centre with those observed from another. I can acknowledge the existence of other moral centres in the world which I posit, but only if these centres are agencies, earthly or celestial, at work in my field of action, and dynamically connected with my own existence. All credible animation, of ascertainable character, must animate substances found in the same world with myself, and collateral with my own substance.

This System Is Relative and Need Not Cover All Reality.

Perhaps this argument has some analogy to Spinoza's proof of the unity of substance. He tells us that substance is one, because if there were two or more substances they could bear no relation to one another. In other words, there can be but one universe, since anything outside, by being outside, would be related to it and collateral, and so after all would form a part of it. Yet if one universe, or one substance, can exist absolutely, and out of all relation to anything else, why should not any number of them exist, each centred in itself? The necessity of lying in external relations in order to exist, far from proving that only one system of facts is possible, proves that any closed circle of facts, in interplay with one another and with nothing else, will form a complete universe. Each part of this system will exist by virtue of its active position there, and may be discovered by any members of it who are sufficiently intelligent and adventurous; but from no part of that universe will anything beyond that universe be discoverable. Does this fact preclude the being of a different system, a separate universe, possessing the same sort of inward life and reality? I cannot think so. Transcendental necessities are relative to particular centres of experience; they have no jurisdiction beyond. Those other universes, to us, would be undiscoverable; but ours, too, would be undiscoverable to them; and yet we exist here without their leave. Might they not exist without ours?

If There Are Many Worlds Their Mutual Relations Are Not Physical, But Are the Eternal Relations of Their Essences in the Realm of Truth.

What logic enables us to assert, therefore, is not that there is only one universe, but that each universe must be one, by virtue of a domestic economy determining the relative position and character of the events which compose it. Anything beyond this dynamic field is beyond the field of posited existence and possible knowledge. If there are other centres and active substances moving in other spheres, the relation of these disconnected spheres is not a physical relation: no journey and no transformation can bridge it: it lies in the realm of truth. Each of these worlds will exemplify its chosen essence; and the internal and unchangeable relations between these essences will be the only relations between those worlds. One will not exist before the other, nor will they be simultaneous; nor will either lie in any direction from the other, or at any distance. No force or influence will pass between them of any traceable physical or historical kind. If omniscience should see any harmony, contrast, or mutual fulfilment between their natures, that spiritual bond would be of the sort which links essences together by a logical necessity, and which a contemplative spirit may stop to disentangle and admire if it can and will.

Indeed, we may go further and say even of a single universe taken as a whole that its status is that of a truth rather than of an existence. Each part of it will exist, and if animate may truly feel its internal tension and life, and may truly assert the existence of the other parts also; yet the whole system—perhaps endless in its time and space—never exists at once or in any assignable quarter. Its existence is only posited from within its limits: externally its only status is that of a truth. Its essence was not condemned to be a closet-tragedy; living actors have been found to play it and a shifting stage to exhibit for a moment those convincing scenes. This essence has therefore the eternal dignity of a truth: it is the complete description of an event. Yet this event, taken as a whole, being unapproachable from outside, dateless, and nowhere, is in a sense a supernatural event. Those scenes are undiscoverable, save to those who play them, and that tumult is an ancient secret in the bosom of truth.

The First Object of Animal Faith Is Nature as a Whole.

Indeed, good sense might suffice to convince anyone that no arguments or definitions can prevent things from being as numerous and as separate as they may chance to be. There is an infinite diversity of essences: what shall dissuade the fatality of existence, which must be groundless, from composing such changeful systems as it likes, on planes of being utterly incommensurable and incommunicable? The most a man can say for himself, or for any other element from which exploration may start, is that whatever is to enter his field of action must belong to the same dynamic system with himself. In experience and art, as in the nebular hypothesis, this dynamic oneness of the world is primitive. It is not put together by conjoining elements found existing separately, but is the locus in which they are found; for if they were not found there, they would be essences only and not facts. In mature human perception the essences given are doubtless distinct and the objects which they suggest are clearly discriminated: here is the dog, there the sun, the past nowhere, and the night coming. But beneath all this definition of images and attitudes of expectancy, there is always a voluminous feeble sensibility in the vegetative soul. Even this sensibility posits existence; the contemplation of pure Being might supervene only after all alarms, gropings, and beliefs had been suspended—something it takes all the discipline of Indian sages to begin to do. The vegetative soul enjoys an easier and more Christian blessedness: it sees not, yet it believes. But believes in what? In whatever it may be that envelopes it; in what we, in our human language, call space, earth, sunlight, and motion; in the throbbing possibility of putting forth something which we call leaves, for which that patient soul has no name and no image. The unknown total environment is what every intellect posits at birth; whatever may be attempted in action or discovered in nature will be a fresh feature in that field

Everything relevant to mortal anxiety lies within that immensity, be it an object of earthly fear or pursuit of religious hope. Animal faith and material destiny move in a relative cosmos.

III

Presumable Properties of Substance

THE properties which, willy-nilly, we assign to substance by trusting it and by presuming to act upon it, are relative and functional properties. Has substance no other properties, positive and native to it, which we may discover by observation or experience?

Besides Its Necessary Functions, Substance Manifests Many Positive Properties.

That substance has many native and positive characters is certain: in its diffusion it lends existence to certain eternal essences, and enables them to figure in a flux of events. At each point, then, substance must exemplify some essence, of which, then and there, it creates an instance; but it does so by setting that essence in a frame of external relations; so that substance is always more and other than the essence which it exemplifies at any point. It is also more than the set of external relations, or the natural medium, into which these exchangeable essences fall; for this framework, apart from the exchange of alternative essences which diversify it and individuate its parts, would itself be a mere essence, like geometrical space or time, eternal and unsubstantial. This is not to say that, besides the essences which it exemplifies at each point, and the manner in which it connects and exchanges them, substance need have any *other* essence of its own. Its residual being, or not-being, is antithetical to essence altogether, and irrational. We may enjoy it, we may enact it, but we cannot conceive it; not because our intellect by accident is inadequate, but because existence, which substance makes continuous, is intrinsically a surd, a flux, and a contradiction.

The question for the natural philosopher is therefore reduced to this: Which, if any, of the essences revealed in human experience or observation may we assign to substance and regard as belonging to its essence?

All Exemplified Essences Are in Some Respect Qualities of Substance.

This question might be answered easily and rather gloriously in a single word, All! Every character, every relation, every event which occurs anywhere qualifies substance and is a property of it. We should thus come at once upon a perfectly correct, if perfectly useless, definition of substance: the essence of substance would be that of the universe, or so much of the realm of essence as is ever exemplified in existence, when, where, and in the manner in which it is exemplified. This definition, I say, would be correct, because the essences which substance takes on in detail are certainly forms of substance at those points; while those essences which it takes on in its larger sweeps (or, as I shall call them, its tropes) are forms of substance on that scale and in those cycles. In this way a man is a substance, because his human and his personal essence have become forms of substance in him; and the universe is the sum of all substance, the form of which is called the truth. Even those instances of essence which are not forms of substance in this passive manner, are manifestations of substance by way of active expression or epigenesis; though not embodied in substance they are evoked from it and compose the realm of spirit, which is a natural manifestation of substance in man, but not a true description of it. The freest intuition is free only outwards, in that, like music, it need not look towards substance or towards truth; but, like music, the freest intuition is closely bound to substance by its genesis, and rooted there altogether; so that all the essences appearing in contemplation belong to the essence of substance, as all the subtlest developments of music or dialectic belong to the essence of man.

But None Is a Substance in Itself.

Nevertheless the proposed definition of substance would be useless: it would merely say that all that exists exists, without indicating what is its tenure of existence or the mode of its attachment to substance; and this is the question which arises in action and which gives the category of substance its meaning. Indeed, if from the truth that all phenomena are manifestations of substance, in some direction and at some remove, we passed to the idea that all phenomena are equally substantial, we should have fallen into a positive error; and the word substance itself would have become superfluous; which is the reason why modern philosophers have dropped it. Not that in dropping the word they have abandoned the category: something somewhere must exist in itself and be substantial; but this self-existence would be made to migrate from the heart of things to their surface, or to the total picture which they make in the mind's eye, or to this mind's eye itself, assumed though perhaps not mentioned. Any of these dislocations of substance would render it irrelevant to action. Action cannot accept phenomena simply as phenomena, but must trace the substantial thread on which they are strung together; for it is quite false that any phenomenon taken in itself is substantial; it is a mere essence, save for its backing in nature, which, although it always exists, is often very recondite, and definable by essences very different from that which it wears on the surface.

The Dog and the Bone.

The dog in the fable, who dropped the substance for the shadow, might have found substance even in that shadow, namely, water and light reflected from the water; and if he had been a natural philosopher, he might have traced that ray back to the very bone which he had held in his mouth, and had let slip for the sake of its deceptive image. This complication in the manifestations of substance misled his action, because he was not interested in manifestations at all, but only in a substance which he might assimilate blindly and turn into the hidden substance of himself: and *this* substance was not to be found where he sought it. There is a natural hierarchy in the manifestations of substance; and while no appearance is a mere appearance, but all are in some way appearances of substance, yet some of the essences exhibited to human intuition fit the dynamic movement of nature tightly and consecutively, and can be true guides to action, whereas others are poised delicately there, like a mood or a dream, not long to be traced or trusted; for the flux of substance has other forms beneath to which it proves more faithful. While we halt and disport ourselves at the human level, substance slips on in its merely material career, and that poem is ended. The study of substance is the pursuit of these deepest and most pervasive of its properties, and of the manner in which the rarer properties and the supervening unities are generated in that context. It is the study of physics.

Pharaoh's Dream.

In dreams substance mocks the pursuer; he wastes the emotions of action in a direction in which substance is absent, and action therefore impossible; but in another direction, namely, in himself, substance is always at hand, and he may ironically trace his dream back to it on waking. Pharaoh's dream was all about substance, yet much interpretation was needed before his fat and lean kine could disclose their relevance to the world of action. They had such relevance initially in his royal preoccupation with animals and with the fat of the land; but this backward reference of ideas to their seat and their origin is seldom conveyed by the deliv-

erance of the ideas themselves; when it is, they become reflection or memory. In the forward impulse of perception or
policy, ideas have, or are taken to have, a forward reference
to substance as well: appetition turns them into prophecies.
Fortunately Pharaoh had at his elbow a prophetic materialist, to whom ideas were signs, and who readily conceived
what genuine substances might be signified by them; and
the event having justified his prudent guess, the statesman
needed to go no further in his interpretation of ideas: the
people's stomach and the king's treasury were ultimate substances for him. Had Joseph been a more curious philosopher, even a treasury or a stomach might have seemed to
him but covering ideas, standing for undeciphered operations of nature; and he might have begun to speculate about
earth and water, the sun and the miracle of seeds; but even
if his science had advanced as far as the science of to-day, it
would not have reached anything but some more abstract
term, or more refined covering idea. He had found substance, as substance may be found, in the thick of action, in
those harvests and granaries; there he had touched the hand
of the Lord.

Narcissus.

There is another fable which renders the matter more
subtly, and dwells more on its ideal side. Narcissus was not
deceived like the dog; he knew that the fair image was but
a reflection of himself; but in his love of form he was seized
with a sort of desperate enthusiasm, and coveted that celestial object with an earthly passion; so that his fate was
worse than the dog's, and in plunging after the shadow he
lost not only that fancied substance, but his true substance
and life as well. Not that self-love need always be suicidal.
Had Narcissus been content to enjoy his own substance
blindly, in its coursing life through his members, he might
have possessed himself mightily and long, being all action,
all ignorance, all irresponsibility; he might have reverted

from the Narcissus of fable to the Narcissus of Freud. But the poets have made him a symbol for a higher fate, for the great deviation of attention from substance to essence. This deviation, as we see in him, has two stages, one confused and mad, at which he stopped, and another sublime and musical, to which he might have proceeded. For Narcissus is the forerunner of Apollo, or Apollo in embryo; he explains the mystery of Apollo having been born so free and so deeply inspired; for high things must have deep and hidden foundations. The foundation of intuition, and of all the free arts, lies in the substance of the self, with its long vegetable and animal evolution; until one day, in the person of Narcissus, attention is arrested on the form which the self lends to all nature, or wears in its own eyes. If at first this intuition is not pure, and Narcissus wildly pursues essence as if it were substance, he becomes Dionysus, inspired but drunk: if on the contrary his intuition liberates the form of substance from its flux, and sees it in its wholeness and in its unsubstantiality, then Narcissus becomes Apollo, inspired but sane.

However Unprecedented Their Form, All Things Are Traceable by Their Substance.

These parables have a common moral. Ideas, or the forms which things wear in human experience, are unsubstantial in themselves, cheating every action or hope that may be directed upon them in their literal immediate being, or given essence; but they may all be traced, either by interpretation outwards or by reversion inwards to their origin in the self, until they lead us to substance; that is, to something that can be the butt of action, and in which the effects of action may be fertile and prolonged. Experience and the arts of life thus seem to justify the presumption that all things are natural, even the most ideal, and that nothing, even in a dream, appears by chance, but that all is symptomatic, significant, and grounded in substance.

Which on Its Own Plane Is a Continuous Process.

And as all things unsubstantial may be traced to substance, so all the movements of substance may be traced to one another. It is sheer ignorance to stare at anything as if it were inexplicable and self-created, a mere intruder in the world. The universe itself no doubt is groundless and a perpetual miracle; but it is a tame wonder, and terribly self-imitative; and everything in it bears its hall-mark and stamp of origin, if we only are clever enough to turn it inside out, and inspect its fabric. The habits of nature are marvellous, but they are habits; and the flux of substance fills quite innocently and automatically the intervals which its own lapse may create. This assumption is not justifiable by induction, because no experience covers any great part of nature, nor that part thoroughly; but it is nevertheless the anchor of rational life. All prudence, all art, all calculation rely upon it, and prosper —in so far as they prosper—by that confidence.

Some Things Are Traceable Because Roughly Persistent.

The simplest sort of continuity is persistence, or sustained identity: and this is often found or assumed in the field of action. Leaving my hat and umbrella in the cloak room, I expect, on my departure, to find the same objects. I conceive them to have endured unchanged in the interval. And when I take fresh possession of them, and carry them into quite another place, I conceive that, save for a little wear and tear, they still remain identical. And I assume a similar battered identity in my own person. If things lapsed in nature as they lapse in immediate experience, objects that disappeared at any point would be annihilated, and some new thing, perhaps like them but not the same, would presently be created somewhere else. This magical world may be acceptable to a laughing child, or a desperate sceptic, but it will never do for a sportsman. If the scent is lost for a moment, he must assume that the fox is still in existence, or he could not pursue the chase. To wait and wonder whether another fox might not be created anywhere else at any other time would not be hunting; nor would it be labour, nor art, nor science; it would be treating objects not as substances but as apparitions. That which appears, if it is posited as a thing to be chased, must exist continuously even when it does not appear. The object at each instant must occupy some particular position in the field of action, a place determinable by exploration; and belief and action may be directed upon it when invisible with entire confidence that its path is traceable and calculable.

Persistence in Substance Need Not Be Everlasting or Universal.

That substances persist through motion is a veritable postulate of practical reason: not a mock postulate known to be false (as Kant's postulates were apparently meant to be) but one believed to be true, and constantly revived by events. If it were not true, action, and even the thought of action, would be farcical, and would in fact never have arisen. Yet this postulate, as action implies and verifies it, does not extend further than action itself. The huntsman need not assume that his fox will live for ever. Possibly its haunting image, surviving the chase, may of old have suggested to him his totems and animal gods; but in the chase itself only a brief persistence, limited to this particular fox, is posited or proved. Soon this substance is expected to disappear; true, it may feed the hunter or his dogs; yet no theory of a total and absolute indestructibility of substance, through all its transformations, need be broached in practice. The persistence which the human mind tends to attribute to things, especially when they are loved or feared, is less that of their substance than of their ghosts. It is a confused intermixture of essences with facts, of casual circumstances with profound reverberations in memory. Experience, even in those of us who think ourselves enlightened, is full of increments and losses which seem to us absolute, as if they were souls, strengths, or illuminations coming from other spheres. The field of action remains to that extent an animated chaos in which at best certain magic rhymes may be detected, which superstition raises into laws. Were it not for sane instinct, custom, and the steadying machinery of the arts, we should all be little better than poets. It is but a thin thread of calculable continuity that runs through immediate experience: the postulate of permanence is applicable and reasonable only in the field of action posited outside, and only in so far as exact arts and sciences may be able to dominate it.

It Might Exist Discretely at Separate Moments.

Might not substance, then, be as intermittent and spasmodic as experience itself? Might it not be a fire whose very nature was to lapse: not merely to lapse inwardly and devour its own flames, but occasionally to lapse from existence altogether, like the setting sun of Heraclitus? A different sun, he observed, was created in the morning; and perhaps not all the intervals or pauses between existences would be so regular, nor the existences so much alike. Some sun might be the last; it would not follow that it had not existed. So all existence might be occasional, and destined some day to fail altogether. A playful philosopher, now that science has again become playful, might conceive that all things are totally destroyed at each instant, and fresh things created—I was going to say "in their place," but I should rather say in fresh places, since times and spaces in such a system would also have no unity and no continuity. Yet these momentary worlds would still be substantial, in the transcendental sense; they would not be merely phenomenal, if they were independent, while they lasted, of the notice taken of them by any mind. Perhaps a moralist or a poet might call them unsubstantial, because transitory; but in that sense existence itself would be unsubstantial, and all our categories would become confused. Let us reconcile ourselves once for all to transitive existence: the eternal is ours if we truly honour it, but in another sphere; and meantime let us inquire what forms of iteration and of persistence appear in the flux of existence, which is substantial because it flows, and at each moment assaults and betrays our charmed conceptions.

But in Fact Nature Is Full of Inheritance, Potentiality, and Latent Phases.

It was well known to the ancients, and is confirmed daily, that when things die they leave heirs: the flies that seem to vanish every winter return every summer. And this pertinacity in substance is not always intermittent; a phase of latency, silent but deeply real, often connects the phases of activity. Sleep and night are not nothing: in them substance most certainly endures, and even gathers strength, or unfolds its hidden coils. Then the spirit, in withdrawing into slumber, seems to return into the womb, into a security and naturalness much deeper than its distracted life. It knows that while it sleeps all things wait, last, and ripen; they all breathe inwardly with that same peace which returns to it only in the night. Those heavenly bodies, which when gaped at seemed but twinkling specks, are in reality sleeping giants; they roll with an enormous momentum at prodigious distances, and keep the world in equilibrium. The rocks are rooted in their buried foundations, the bed of the sea stretches beneath it, and holds it; the earth broods over its ominous substance, like a fiery orange with a rind of stone. It is this universal pause and readiness in things, guarding us unwatched, that chiefly supports our sanity and courage. This constancy gives us security; the eyes may close in peace, while the child's dreaming hand, half closing, prepares to grasp a sword.

Substance Is Quantitative and Its Changes Proportionate and Measurable.

The ancients also observed how regularly some objects may be transformed into others, as water into ice or vapour; and that there is a certain equivalence through these phases in their quantity or energy. The seasons return, their fruits varying with the weather; the generations repeat themselves, but mixing their breed; and there is always a potentiality of reversion to a former constellation of properties, prevented only by cross-currents of change. Even where evolution is not cyclical, but creates new forms, it is proportionate and still conservative; anything does not succeed anywhere to anything else. Nothing new arises except out of seeds differently watered, measurably, locally, conditionally. A limited potentiality, an inherited substance, links all the transformations of things together. They pass their matter on to one another; their matter is the principle of their equivalence and continuity. When objects are mutually convertible, they are substantial: were they disembodied essences it would be neither necessary nor intelligible that one should yield to the other in any order, or with any proportion in quantity or quality. But when substantial things perish, we know very well that their elements are simply dispersed, and go to swell the substance of other parts of nature. A long and victorious husbandry has enabled us to trace these migrations of substance; so much so that it has become a plausible hypothesis, countenanced by many an art and many an experiment, that substance is constant in quantity, and never created or destroyed. Only a certain number of loaves can be baked from a barrel of flour; and it would be a miracle if twelve loaves could satisfy the hunger of 5000 people. Famine and war, commerce and prosperity are evident phases in this natural economy: friction and crowding of substance here, scarcity there, and everywhere a limited, special, temporary opportunity for existence.

Substance Need Not Endure After the Manner of Feelings or Image in Sense.

It is to be observed, however, that this quantitative limitation in things is, for human experience and science, rather a matter of averages and of proportion between desultory facts than any traceable persistence in particular substances; genesis is roughly subject to calculation and responsive to custom, but its inner texture eludes observation. Nor is this to be wondered at, or set down as an argument against substance altogether: because, if we remember how and why substance is posited in the beginning, we shall not expect it to exhibit the sort of permanence which belongs to specious objects. Specious objects are mere essences; in themselves they are eternal and always recoverable in their absolute identity, except for physical difficulties in reproducing the same attitude in the psyche. Substance, on the contrary, is internally in flux. So that the presumption of identity with which we revert to an essence, or to a term in discourse, is likely to be ill grounded if we transfer it to a thing, the substance of which is always changing its form. Moreover, the very notion of persistence, like all notions, is a specious essence: it is cumulative and emotional and given in that dumb feeling of duration of which a certain specious philosophy has made so much. It is not to be expected that substance should realise internally this specious quality, which may express in human intuition one aspect of its movement. The feeling of blank duration itself covers a slumbering life in the psyche, roughly sustained and rhythmical, like breathing, but by no means changeless or simple. Obvious persistence is a comment made superficially on a physical flux not clearly discerned; whereas the persistence of substance is something integral to that flux itself, rendering its changes changes, and its phases successive or contiguous.

Pictorial Character of Geometrical Atoms.

If the elements of substance resembled persistent images in sense, or were indestructible cubes, spheres, or pyramids, these Egyptian solids would hardly possess the sort of permanence impressing the traveller who stops to admire the Pyramid of Cheops. This pyramid was once built, yet it defies time paradoxically. The stars have the same sublimity, for they ought to burn out or fall from heaven and yet (in our limited experience) they do not: so that an existence seems to us to have put on the eternity of an essence, and by this marvel our own steps and breath and vapid thoughts are rebuked and arrested. But atoms having immutable geometrical forms and no inner substance save pure Being, would be eternal by definition, and not suitable elements of existence at all. They would have no scale for time within them, no sensitiveness to motion or change of relations. Their inner nature would be irrelevant to that flux of existence which it was designed to render intelligible. It would be only their changing arrangement in the void that would determine the field of action. And since the void has pure Being in it no less than an atom (both having geometrical extension for their essence) it is not easy to see how the limits or the position of an atom could themselves be determined. A crumbling pyramid is more substantial than an eternal one.

If Substance Takes Geometrical Forms, It Still Supports and Survives Them.

Indeed if those Egyptian solids were existing bodies and not merely geometrical essences, their indestructibility, supposing them indestructible, would be a contingent and merely historical fact. It is evident that a spherical, cubical, or pyramidal body *might* at any time fall to pieces; it is an atom provisionally, by courtesy, by virtue of its function in a given mechanism; in its existence and substance, which are centred equally in every part, it is thoroughly divisible. Yet, in admitting this undeniable possibility, or rather this natural presumption, that Egyptian atoms should some day crumble, we still posit and imply persistence in the world; for the principle of existence in those fragments would be the same as in the atoms when they were whole, and the same medium of space and time, or whatever else it may be, and the same fatality of motion and of order would permeate that dust

and govern its destinies. It was evidently these deeper properties of substance that kept those atoms whole, if perhaps
during some cycle of natural existence they remained indestructible; and among those deeper properties we must count
the void in which those atoms could move and the mysterious
cohesion and fertility of some of their aggregates, by which
nature is diversified and made alive.

*Yet Substance Is Atomic inasmuch as Existence Is Discrete;
and All Enveloping Unities Are Only Truths about It.*

The atomic theory is, nevertheless, in one sense, inherent
in physics, and alone possible; because the very nature of
existence is to be dispersed in centres, dislocated, corpuscular,
granular; the parts must be particulars externally related.
Any demand for a unity not a unity of arrangement, derivation, or conjunction turns its back on existence. Indeed these
very unities of arrangement, when substance realises them,
are not contained in the substance at any point, or at any
moment; they are not seated, for instance, in any intuition
which may define them or in any perception which may posit
them in the world. They belong, if they are realised, to the
realm of truth. It is simply true that the parts of substance
have assumed that arrangement; and this truth is not proved
by the mere intuition of such a unity, which might be specious only, but must be made the goal of a laborious investigation and a practical faith. The seen unities are not false;
they are manifestations of substance like the intuitions which
we have when we read poetry; but they express our reaction
to a manifold object and our gross relation to it, rather than
the diffuse substance of that object itself. The unities and
arrangements embodied in substance are not separable from
it or from its flux; and like substance and its flux these can
be known only functionally.

Illusion of Scientific Gnosticism.

For this reason an atomism which professes to *define* its
atoms trespasses against the modesty of our genuine contacts

with things. The atomism of Democritus, with the Cartesian notion of substance and the Newtonian notion of space, time, and matter, are all too graphic and mathematical; they betray their Eleatic and Pythagorean origin; they share a poetic or mythological gnosticism which thinks to decipher the heart of nature in terms of human intuition. These terms may be admirably chosen and the best possible; but their value is not exhaustive and must always remain symbolical. The persistence of substance can hardly be intrinsically similar to the stubbornness of some ghostly image that will not down.

Intuitive Knowledge or Divination Is Proper Only to Moral Subjects.

Great philosophers, having been men of universal mind, have instinctively set the same standard of accuracy and truth for all their investigations. As there is a possibility of literal or intuitive knowledge in some fields, they have desired such knowledge everywhere; but in physics, and in regard to the intrinsic properties of substance, such knowledge is impossible. Intuition lies at the opposite end of the gamut of nature; its simplest object covers an immense complexity, a voluminous heritage, in the animal soul. Where literal knowledge is possible—apart from contemplation of essence, which is complex feeling rather than knowledge— is in literary psychology. Here we often conceive our object exactly as it was or may be: because it is no more improbable than two brothers should feel and think alike than that two similar leaves should sprout on the same tree. Therefore poetry is, in one sense, truer than science, and more satisfactory to a seasoned and exacting mind. Poetry reveals one sort of truth completely, because reality in that quarter is no more defined or tangible than poetry itself; and it clarifies human experience of other things also, earthly and divine, without falsifying these things more than experience falsifies them already. Science, on the contrary, the deeper it goes, gets thinner and thinner and cheats us altogether, unless we discount its symbols.

We may leave it then for literary psychologists and intuitive metaphysicians to record their experience in ways appealing to men of their own mind; and we may leave it for mathematicians to construct possible worlds. The practical naturalist is concerned only with such properties of substance as are implied, measured, and elicited in his arts and in his explorations. The study of nature is the most picturesque of studies, and full of joy for the innocent mind; but in natural science all is familiarity and nothing comprehension, save as there is a humorous or devout comprehension in foresight and trust.

I may now add to the indispensable properties of substance others which substance seems to possess, and which, since they too are assumed in practice, may be assumed in natural philosophy.

6. *Substance, in diversifying the field of nature, sometimes takes the form of animals in whom there are feelings, images, and thoughts. These mental facts are immaterial.* They offer no butt for action and exercise no physical influence on one another.

Action, when Rational, Presupposes that the Transformations of Substance Are Continuous, Quantitatively Constant, and Regular in Method; and that the Spirit, Without Being a Part of That Material World, Is the Consciousness Proper to One of the Agents There.

7. The same *mental facts are manifestations of substance*; in their occurrence they are parts of a total natural event which, on its substantial side, belongs to the plane of action. They are therefore significant and relevant to action as signs, being created and controlled by the flux of substance beneath.

8. Beneath the intermittence of phenomena, *the phases or modes through which sub-substance flows are continuous.*

9. As far as action and calculation can extend, *the quantity of substance remains equivalent throughout.*

10. *Each phase or mode of substance, although not contained in its antecedents, is predetermined by them in its place and quality, and proportionate to them in extent and intensity.* An event will be repeated if ever the constellation of events which bred it should recur. This regularity in the genesis of modes or phases of substance is constantly verified in action on a small scale. To expect it in substance is the soul of science and art; but to expect it in phenomena is superstition.

Summary.

When, then, in perception, action, memory, or hope experience is treated as significant, a substance is posited which must be external to thought, with its parts external to one another and each a focus of existence; a substance which passes through various phases is unequally distributed in the field of action, and forms a relative cosmos surrounding each agent. Action on these assumptions makes it further appear that this substance is the source of phenomena unsubstantial in themselves but significant of the phases of substance which produce them; that these phases are continuous and measurable; and that each transformation, though spontaneous in itself, is repeated whenever the same conditions recur. Now a substance possessing these functions and these characteristics has a familiar name: it is called matter. Matter is the medium of calculable art. But I have found from the beginning that the impulse to act, and the confidence that the opposite partner in action has specific and measurable resources, are the primary expressions of animal faith; also that animal faith is the only principle by which belief in existence of any kind can be justified or suggested to the spirit. It follows that the only object posited by animal faith is matter; and that all those images which in human experience may be names or signs for objects of belief are, in their ultimate signification, so many names or signs for matter. Their perpetual variety indicates the phases through which the flux of matter is passing in the self, or those which the self is positing in the field of action to which it is responsive. Apart from this material signification, those feelings and perceptions are simply intuitions of essences, essences to which no existence in nature can be assigned. The field of action is accordingly the realm of matter; and I will henceforth call it by that name.

SOME TURNS OF THOUGHT
IN MODERN PHILOSOPHY

IV

A Long Way Round to Nirvana

THAT the end of life is death may be called a truism, since the various kinds of immortality that might perhaps supervene would none of them abolish death, but at best would weave life and death together into the texture of a more comprehensive destiny. The end of one life might be the beginning of another, if the Creator had composed his great work like a dramatic poet, assigning successive lines to different characters. Death would then be merely the cue at the end of each speech, summoning the next personage to break in and keep the ball rolling. Or perhaps, as some suppose, all the characters are assumed in turn by a single supernatural Spirit, who amid his endless improvisations is imagining himself living for the moment in this particular solar and social system. Death in such a universal monologue would be but a change of scene or of metre, while in the scramble of a real comedy it would be a change of actors. In either case every voice would be silenced sooner or later, and death would end each particular life, in spite of all possible sequels.

The relapse of created things into nothing is no violent fatality, but something naturally quite smooth and proper. This has been set forth recently, in a novel way, by a philosopher from whom we hardly expected such a lesson, namely

Professor Sigmund Freud. He has now broadened his conception of sexual craving or *libido* into a general principle of attraction or concretion in matter, like the Eros of the ancient poets Hesiod and Empedocles. The windows of that stuffy clinic have been thrown open; that smell of acrid disinfectants, those hysterical shrieks, have escaped into the cold night. The troubles of the sick soul, we are given to understand, as well as their cure, after all flow from the stars.

I am glad that Freud has resisted the tendency to represent this principle of Love as the only principle in nature. Unity somehow exercises an evil spell over metaphysicians. It is admitted that in real life it is not well for One to be alone, and I think pure unity is no less barren and graceless in metaphysics. You must have plurality to start with, or trinity, or at least duality, if you wish to get anywhere, even if you wish to get effectively into the bosom of the One, abandoning your separate existence. Freud, like Empedocles, has prudently introduced a prior principle for Love to play with; not Strife, however (which is only an incident in Love), but Inertia, or the tendency towards peace and death. Let us suppose that matter was originally dead, and perfectly content to be so, and that it still relapses, when it can, into its old equilibrium. But the homogeneous (as Spencer would say) when it is finite is unstable: and matter, presumably not being co-extensive with space, necessarily forms aggregates which have an inside and an outside. The parts of such bodies are accordingly differently exposed to external influences and differently related to one another. This inequality, even in what seems most quiescent, is big with changes, destined to produce in time a wonderful complexity. It is the source of all uneasiness, of life, and of love.

"Let us imagine [writes Freud]* an undifferentiated

*The following quotations are drawn from *Beyond the Pleasure Principle*, by Sigmund Freud; authorised translation by C. J. M. Hubback. The International Psycho-Analytic Press, 1922, pp. 29-48. The italics are in the original.

vesicle of sensitive substance: then its surface, exposed as it is to the outer world, is by its very position differentiated, and serves as an organ for receiving stimuli. . . . This morsel of living substances floats about in an outer world which is charged with the most potent energies, and it would be destroyed . . . if it were not furnished with protection against stimulation. [On the other hand] the sensitive cortical layer has no protective barrier against excitations emanating from within. . . . The most prolific sources of such excitations are the so-called instincts of the organism. . . . The child never gets tired of demanding the repetition of a game . . . he wants always to hear the same story instead of a new one, insists inexorably on exact repetition, and corrects each deviation which the narrator lets slip by mistake. . . . According to this, *an instinct would be a tendency in living organic matter impelling it towards reinstatement of an earlier condition*, one which it had abandoned under the influence of external disturbing forces—a kind of organic elasticity, or, to put it another way, the manifestation of inertia in organic life.

"If, then, all organic instincts are conservative, historically acquired, and directed towards regression, towards reinstatement of something earlier, we are obliged to place all the results of organic development to the credit of external, disturbing, and distracting influences. The rudimentary creature would from its very beginning not have wanted to change, would, if circumstances had remained the same, have always merely repeated the same course of existence. . . . It would be counter to the conservative nature of instinct if the goal of life were a state never hitherto reached. It must be rather an ancient starting point, which the living being left long ago, and to which it harks back again by all the circuitous paths of development. . . . *The goal of all life is death.* . . .

"Through a long period of time the living substance may have . . . had death within easy reach . . . until decisive external influences altered in such a way as to compel [it] to ever greater deviations from the original path of life, and to ever more complicated and circuitous routes to the attainment of the goal of death. These circuitous ways to death, faithfully retained by the conservative instincts, would be neither more nor less than the phenomena of life as we know it."

Freud puts forth these interesting suggestions with much modesty, admitting that they are vague and uncertain and (what it is even more important to notice) mythical in their terms; but it seems to me that, for all that, they are an admirable counterblast to prevalent follies. When we hear that there is, animating the whole universe, an *élan vital,* or general impulse toward some unknown but single ideal, the terms used are no less uncertain, mythical, and vague, but the suggestion conveyed is false—false, I mean, to the organic source of life and aspiration, to the simple naturalness of nature: whereas the suggestion conveyed by Freud's speculations is true. In what sense can myths and metaphors be true or false? In the sense that, in terms drawn from moral predicaments or from literary psychology, they may report the general movement and the pertinent issue of material facts, and may inspire us with a wise sentiment in their presence. In this sense I should say that Greek mythology was true and Calvinist theology was false. The chief terms employed in psycho-analysis have always been metaphorical: "unconscious wishes," "the pleasure-principle," "the Œdipus complex," "Narcissism," "the censor"; nevertheless, interesting and profound vistas may be opened up, in such terms, into the tangle of events in a man's life, and a fresh start may be made with fewer encumbrances and less morbid inhibition. "The shortcomings of our description," Freud says, "would probably disappear if for psychological terms we could substitute physiological or chemical ones. These too only constitute a metaphorical language, but one familiar to us for a much longer time, and perhaps also simpler." All human discourse is metaphorical, in that our perceptions and thoughts are adventitious signs for their objects, as names are, and by no means copies of what is going on materially in the depths of nature; but just as the sportsman's eye, which yields but a summary graphic image, can trace the flight of a bird through the air quite well enough to shoot it and bring it down, so the myths of a wise philosopher about the origin of life or of dreams, though expressed symbolically, may reveal the pertinent movement of nature to us, and may kindle in us just sentiments and true expectations in respect to our fate—for his own soul is the bird this sportsman is shooting.

Now I think these new myths of Freud's about life, like his old ones about dreams, are calculated to enlighten and to chasten us enormously about ourselves. The human spirit, when it awakes, finds itself in trouble; it is burdened, for no reason it can assign, with all sorts of anxieties about food, pressures, pricks, noises, and pains. It is born, as another wise myth has it, in original sin. And the passions and ambitions of life, as they come on, only complicate this burden and make it heavier, without rendering it less incessant or gratuitous. Whence this fatality, and whither does it lead? It comes from heredity, and it leads to propagation. When we ask how heredity could be started or transmitted, our ignorance of nature and of past time reduces us to silence or to wild conjectures. Something—let us call it matter—must always have existed, and some of its parts, under pressure of the others, must have got tied up into knots, like the mainspring of a watch, in such a violent and unhappy manner that when the pressure is relaxed they fly open as fast as they can, and unravel themselves with a vast sense of relief. Hence the longing to satisfy latent passions, with the fugitive pleasure in doing so. But the external agencies that originally wound up that mainspring never cease to operate; every fresh stimulus gives it another turn, until it snaps, or grows flaccid, or is unhinged. Moreover, from time to time, when circumstances change, these external agencies may encrust that primary organ with minor organs attached to it. Every impression, every adventure, leaves a trace or rather a seed behind it. It produces a further complication in the structure of the body, a fresh charge, which tends to repeat the impressed motion in season and out of season. Hence that perpetual docility or ductility in living substance which enables it to learn tricks, to remember facts, and (when the seeds of past experiences marry and cross the brain) to imagine new experiences, pleasing or horrible. Every act initiates a new habit and may implant a new instinct. We see people even late in life carried away by political or religious contagions or developing strange vices; there would be no peace in old age, but rather a greater and greater obsession by all sorts of cares, were it not that time, in exposing us to many adventitious influences, weakens or discharges our primitive passions; we are less greedy, less lusty, less hopeful, less generous. But these weakened primitive impulses are naturally by far the strongest and most deeply rooted in the organism: so that although an old man may be converted or may take up some hobby, there is usually something thin in his elderly zeal, compared with the heartiness of youth; nor is it edifying to see a soul in which the plainer human passions are extinct becoming a hotbed of chance delusions.

In any case each fresh habit taking root in the organism forms a little mainspring or instinct of its own, like a parasite; so that an elaborate mechanism is gradually developed, where each lever and spring holds the other down, and all hold the mainspring down together, allowing it to unwind itself only very gradually, and meantime keeping the whole clock ticking and revolving, and causing the smooth outer face which it turns to the world, so clean and innocent, to mark the time of day amiably for the passer-by. But there is a terribly complicated labour going on beneath, propelled with difficulty, and balanced precariously, with much secret friction and failure. No wonder that the engine often gets visibly out of order, or stops short: the marvel is that it ever manages to go at all. Nor is it satisfied with simply revolving and, when at last dismounted, starting afresh in the person of some seed it has dropped, a portion of its substance with all its concentrated instincts wound up tightly within it, and eager to repeat the ancestral experiment; all this growth is not merely material and vain. Each clock in revolving strikes the hour, even the quarters, and often with lovely chimes. These chimes we call perceptions, feelings, purposes, and dreams; and it is because we are taken up entirely with this mental music, and perhaps think that it sounds of itself and needs no music-box to make it, that we find such difficulty in conceiving the nature of our own clocks and are compelled to describe them only musically, that is, in myths. But the ineptitude of our æsthetic minds to unravel the nature of mechanism does not deprive these minds of their own clearness and euphony. Besides sounding their various musical notes, they have the cognitive function of indicating the hour and catching the echoes of distant events or of maturing inward dispositions. This information and emotion, added to incidental pleasures in satisfying our various passions, make up the life of an incarnate spirit. They reconcile it to the external fatality that has wound up the organism, and is breaking it down; and they rescue this organism and all its works from the indignity of being a vain complication and a waste of motion.

That the end of life should be death may sound sad: yet what other end can anything have? The end of an evening party is to go to bed; but its use is to gather congenial people together, that they may pass the time pleasantly. An invitation to the dance is not rendered ironical because the dance cannot last for ever; the youngest of us and the most vigorously wound up, after a few hours, has had enough of sinuous stepping and prancing. The transitoriness of things is essential to their physical being, and not at all sad in itself;

it becomes sad by virtue of a sentimental illusion, which makes us imagine that they wish to endure, and that their end is always untimely; but in a healthy nature it is not so. What is truly sad is to have some impulse frustrated in the midst of its career, and robbed of its chosen object; and what is painful is to have an organ lacerated or destroyed when it is still vigorous, and not ready for its natural sleep and dissolution. We must not confuse the itch which our unsatisfied instincts continue to cause with the pleasure of satisfying and dismissing each of them in turn. Could they all be satisfied harmoniously we should be satisfied once for all and completely. Then doing and dying would coincide throughout and be a perfect pleasure.

This same insight is contained in another wise myth which has inspired morality and religion in India from time immemorial: I mean the doctrine of Karma. We are born, it says, with a heritage, a character imposed, and a long task assigned, all due to the ignorance which in our past lives has led us into all sorts of commitments. These obligations we must pay off, relieving the pure spirit within us from its accumulated burdens, from debts and assets both equally oppressive. We cannot disentangle ourselves by mere frivolity, nor by suicide: frivolity would only involve us more deeply in the toils of fate, and suicide would but truncate our misery and leave us for ever a confessed failure. When life is understood to be a process of redemption, its various phases are taken up in turn without haste and without undue attachment; their coming and going have all the keenness of pleasure, the holiness of sacrifice, and the beauty of art. The point is to have expressed and discharged all that was latent in us; and to this perfect relief various temperaments and various traditions assign different names, calling it having one's day, or doing one's duty, or realising one's ideal, or saving one's soul. The task in any case is definite and imposed on us by nature, whether we recognise it or not; therefore we can make true moral progress or fall into real errors. Wisdom and genius lie in discerning this prescribed task and in doing it readily, cleanly, and without distraction. Folly on the contrary imagines that any scent is worth following, that we have an infinite nature, or no nature in particular, that life begins without obligations and can do business without capital, and that the will is vacuously free, instead of being a specific burden and a tight hereditary knot to be unravelled. Some philosophers without self-knowledge think that the variations and further entanglements which the future may bring are the manifestation of spirit; but they are, as Freud has indicated, imposed on living beings by external pressure, and take shape in the realm of matter. It is only after the organs of spirit are formed mechanically that spirit can exist, and can distinguish the better from the worse in the fate of those organs, and therefore in its own fate. Spirit has nothing to do with infinite existence. Infinite existence is something physical and ambiguous; there is no scale in it and no centre. The depths of the human heart are finite, and they are dark only to ignorance. Deep and dark as a soul may be when you look down into it from outside, it is something perfectly natural; and the same understanding that can unearth our suppressed young passions, and dispel our stubborn bad habits, can show us where our true good lies. Nature has marked out the path for us beforehand; there are snares in it, but also primroses, and it leads to peace.

spiritual life after stating it in the hardest, sharpest, most cruel terms. Let us nerve ourselves to-day to imitate his example, not by simply accepting his solution, which for some of us would be easy, but by exercising his courage in the face of a somewhat different world, in which it may be even more difficult for us than it was for him to find a sure foothold and a sublime companionship.

There is a brave and humorous saying of Luther's, which applies to Spinoza better, perhaps, than to Luther himself. When asked where, if driven out of the Church, he would stand, he replied: "Under the sky." The sky of Luther was terribly clouded: there was a vast deal of myth tumbling and thundering about in it: and even in the clear sky of Spinoza there was perhaps something specious, as there is in the blue vault itself. The sun, he tells us, seemed to be about two hundred feet away: and if his science at once corrected this optical illusion, it never undermined his conviction that all reality was within easy reach of his thought. Nature was dominated, he assumed, by unquestionable scientific and dialectical principles; so that while the forces of nature might often put our bodily existence in jeopardy, they always formed a decidedly friendly and faithful object for the mind. There was no essential mystery. The human soul from her humble station might salute the eternal and the infinite with complete composure and with a certain vicarious pride. Every man had a true and adequate idea of God: and this saying, technically justified as it may be by Spinoza's definitions of terms, cannot help surprising us: it reveals such a virgin sense of familiarity with the absolute. There could not but be joy in the sweep of an intelligence that seemed so completely victorious, and no misgivings could trouble a view of the world that explained everything.

To-day, however, we can hardly feel such assurance: we should be taking shelter in a human edifice which the next earthquake might shake down. Nor is it a question really of times or temperaments: anyone anywhere, if he does not wish to construct a plausible system, but to challenge his own assumptions and come to spiritual self-knowledge, must begin by abstention from all easy faith, lest he should be madly filling the universe with images of his own reason and his own hopes. I will therefore ask you to-day, provisionally, for an hour, and without prejudice to your ulterior reasonable convictions, to imagine the truth to be as unfavourable as possible to your desires and as contrary as possible to your natural presumptions; so that the spirit in each of us may be drawn away from its accidental home and subjected to an utter denudation and supreme trial. Yes, although the dead cannot change their minds, I would respectfully beg the shade of Spinoza himself to suspend for a moment that strict rationalism, that jealous, hard-reasoning, confident piety which he shared with the Calvinists and Jansenists of his day, and to imagine—I do not say to admit—that nature may be but imperfectly formed in the bosom of chaos, and that reason in us may be imperfectly adapted to the understanding of nature. Then, having hazarded no favourite postulates and invoked no cosmic forces pledged to support our aspirations, we may all quietly observe what we find; and whatever harmonies may then appear to subsist between our spirits and the nature of things will be free gifts to us and, so far as they go, unchallengeable possessions. We shall at last be standing unpledged and naked, under the open sky.

In what I am about to say, therefore, I do not mean to prejudge any cosmological questions, such as that of free will or necessity, theism or pantheism. I am concerned only with the sincere confessions of a mind that has surrendered every doubtful claim and every questionable assurance. Of such assurances or claims there is one which is radical and comprehensive: I mean, the claim to existence and to directing the course of events. We say conventionally that the future is uncertain: but if we withdrew honestly into ourselves and examined our actual moral resources, we should feel that what is insecure is not merely the course of particular events but the vital presumption that there is a future coming at all, and a future pleasantly continuing our habitual experience. We rely in this, as we must, on the analogies of experience, or rather on the clockwork of instinct and presumption in our bodies; but existence is a miracle, and, morally considered, a free gift from moment to moment. That it will always be analogous to itself is the very question we are begging. Evidently all interconnections and sequences of events, and in particular any consequences which we may expect to flow from our actions, are really entirely beyond our spiritual control. When our will commands and seems, we know not how, to be obeyed by our bodies and by the world, we are like Joshua seeing the sun stand still at his bidding; when we command and nothing happens, we are like King Canute surprised that the rising tide should not obey him: and when we say we have executed a great work and re-directed the course of history, we are like Chanticleer attributing the sunrise to his crowing.

What is the result? That at once, by a mere act of self-examination and frankness, the spirit has come upon one of the most important and radical of religious perceptions. It has perceived that though it is living, it is powerless to live; that though it may die, it is powerless to die; and that altogether, at every instant and in every particular, it is in the hands of some alien and inscrutable power.

Of this felt power I profess to know nothing further. To me, as yet, it is merely the counterpart of my impotence. I should not venture, for instance, to call this power almighty, since I have no means of knowing how much it can do; but I should not hesitate, if I may coin a word, to call it *omnificent*: it is to me, by definition, the doer of everything that is done. I am not asserting the physical validity of this sense of agency or cause: I am merely feeling the force, the friendliness, the hostility, the unfathomableness of the world. I am expressing an impression; and it may be long before my sense of omnipresent power can be erected, with many qualifications, into a theological theory of the omnipotence of God. But the moral presence of power comes upon a man in the night, in the desert, when he finds himself, as the Arabs say, alone with Allah. It reappears in every acute predicament, in extremities, in the birth of a child, or in the face of death. And as for the unity of this power, that is not involved in its sundry manifestations, but rather in my own solitude; in the unity of this suffering spirit overtaken by all those accidents. My destiny is single, tragically single, no matter how multifarious may be the causes of my destiny. As I stand amazed, I am not called upon to say whether, if I could penetrate into the inner workings of things, I should discover omnificent power to be simple or compound, continuous or spasmodic, intentional or blind. I stand before it simply receptive, somewhat as, in Rome, I might stand before the great fountain of Trevi. There I see jets and cascades flowing in separate streams and in divers directions. I am not sure that a single Pontifex Maximus designed it all, and led all those musical waters into just those channels. Some streams may have dried up or been diverted since the creation; some rills may have been added to-day by fresh rains from heaven; behind one of those artificial rocks some little demon, of his own free will, may even now be playing havoc with the conduits; and who knows how many details, in my image, may not have been misplaced or multiplied by optical tricks of my own? Yet here, for the spirit, is one total marvellous impression, one thunderous force, confronting me with this theatrical but admirable spectacle.

Yet this it not all. Power comes down upon me clothed in a thousand phenomena; and these manifestations of power open to me a new spiritual resource. In submitting to power, I learn its ways; from being passive my spirit becomes active; it begins to enjoy one of its essential prerogatives. For like a child the spirit is attracted to all facts by the mere assault of their irrational presence and variety. It watches all that happens or is done with a certain happy excitement, even at the most fearful calamities. Although the essence of spirit may be merely to think, yet some intensity and progression are essential to this thinking; thinking is a way of living, and the most vital way. Therefore all the operations of universal power, when they afford themes for perception, afford also occasions for intellectual delight. Here will and intellect, as Spinoza tells us, coincide: for omnificent power flows in part through our persons; the spirit itself is a spark of that fire, or rather the light of that flame: it cannot have an opposite principle of motion. With health a certain euphoria, a certain alacrity and sense of mastery are induced in the spirit; and a natural effect of perspective, the pathos of nearness, turns our little spark for us into a central sun. The world moves round us, and we move gladly with the world. What if the march of things be destined to overwhelm us? It cannot destroy the joy we had in its greatness and in its victory. There may even be some relief in passing from the troubled thought of ourselves to the thought of something more rich in life, yet in its own sphere and progression, untroubled: and it may be easier for me to understand the motion of the heavens and to rejoice in it than to understand or rejoice in my own motions. My own eclipse, my own vices, my own sorrows, may become a subject to me for exact calculation and a pleasing wonder. The philosophical eye may compose a cosmic harmony out of these necessary conflicts, and an infinite life out of these desirable deaths.

Does it not begin to appear that the solitude of a naked spirit may be rather well peopled? In proportion as we renounce our animal claims and commitments, do we not breathe a fresher and more salubrious air? May not the renunciation of everything disinfect everything and return everything to us in its impartial reality, at the same time disinfecting our wills also, and rendering us capable of charity? This charity will extend, of course, to the lives and desires of others, which we recognise to be no less inevitable than our own; and it will extend also to their ideas, and by a curious and blessed consequence, to the relativity and misery of our own minds. Yet this intellectual charity, since it is inspired by respect for the infinite, will by no means accept all views passively and romantically, as if they were equal and not subject to correction; but doing better justice to the holy aspiration which animates them in common, it will rise from them all, and with them all, to the conception of eternal truth.

Here we touch the crown of Spinoza's philosophy, that intellectual love of God in which the spirit was to be ultimately reconciled with universal power and universal truth. This love brings to consciousness a harmony intrinsic to existence: not an alleged harmony such as may be posited in religions or philosophies resting on faith, but a harmony which, as far as it goes, is actual and patent. In the realm of matter, this harmony is measured by the degree of adjustment, conformity, and co-operation which the part may have attained in the whole; in a word, it is measured by *health*. In the realm of truth, the same natural harmony extends as far as do capacity and pleasure in understanding the truth: so that besides health we may possess *knowledge*. And this is no passive union, no dead peace; the spirit rejoices in it; for the spirit, being, according to Spinoza, an essential concomitant of all existence, shares the movement, the *actuosa essentia* of the universe; so that we necessarily *love* health and knowledge, and *love* the things in which health and knowledge are found. In so far as omnificent power endows us with health, we necessarily love that power whose total movement makes for our own perfection; and in so far as we are able to understand the truth, we necessarily love the themes of an intense and unclouded vision, in which our imaginative faculty reaches its perfect function.

Of this religion of health and understanding Spinoza is a sublime prophet. By overcoming all human weaknesses, even when they seem kindly or noble, and by honouring power and truth, even if they should slay him, he entered the sanctuary of an unruffled superhuman wisdom, and declared himself supremely happy, not because the world as he conceived it was flattering to his heart, but because the gravity of his heart disdained all flatteries, and with a sacrificial prophetic boldness uncovered and relished his destiny, however tragic his destiny might be. And presently peace descended; this keen scientific air seemed alone fit to breathe, and only this high tragedy worthy of a heroic and manly breast. Indeed the truth is a great cathartic and wonderfully relieves the vital distress of existence. We stand as on a mountain-top, and the spectacle, so out of scale with all our petty troubles, silences and overpowers the heart, expanding it for a moment into boundless sympathy with the universe.

Nevertheless, the moral problem is not solved. It is not solved for mankind at large, which remains no less distracted than it was before. Nor is it solved even for the single spirit. There is a radical and necessary recalcitrancy in the finite soul in the face of all this cosmic pomp and all this cosmic pressure: a recalcitrancy to which Spinoza was less sensitive than some other masters of the spiritual life, perhaps because he was more positivistic by temperament and less specifically religious. At any rate many a holy man has known more suffering than Spinoza found in the long work of salvation, more uncertainty, and also, in the end, a more lyrical and warmer happiness. For in the first place, as I said in the beginning, a really naked spirit cannot assume that the world is thoroughly intelligible. There may be surds, there may be hard facts, there may be dark abysses before which intelligence must be silent, for fear of going mad. And in the second place, even if to the intellect all things should prove perspicuous, the intellect is not the whole of human nature, nor even the whole of pure spirit in man. Reason may be the *differentia* of man; it is surely not his essence. His essence, at best, is animality qualified by reason. And from this animality the highest flights of reason are by no means separable. The very life of spirit springs from animal predicaments: it moves by imposing on events a perspective and a moral urgency proper to some particular creature or some particular interest.

Good, as Spinoza would tell us, is an epithet which we assign to whatsoever increases our perfection. Such a doctrine might seem egotistical, but is simply biological; and on its moral side, the maxim is a greater charter of liberty and justice than ever politician framed. For it follows that every good pursued is genuinely good, and the perfection of every creature equally perfection. Every good therefore is a good forever to a really clarified, just, and disinterested spirit; such a spirit cannot rest in the satisfaction of any special faculty, such as intelligence, nor of any special art, such as philosophy. That the intellect might be perfectly happy in contemplating the truth of the universe, does not render the universe good to every other faculty; good to the heart, good to the flesh, good to the eye, good to the conscience or the sense of justice. Of all systems an optimistic system is the most oppressive. Would it not be a bitter mockery if, in the words of Bradley, this were the best of possible worlds, and everything in it a necessary evil? The universal good by which the spirit, in its rapt moments, feels overwhelmed, if it is not to be a mystical illusion, cannot fall short of being the sum of all those perfections, infinitely various, to which all living things severally aspire. A glint or symbol of this universal good may be found in any moment of perfect happiness visiting any breast: but it is impossible unreservedly to love or worship anything, be it the universe or any part of it, unless we find in the end that this thing is completely good: I mean, unless it is perfect after its kind and a friend to itself, and unless at the same time it is beneficent universally, and a friend to everything else. Pure spirit would be lame, and evidently biassed by some biological accident, if it did not love every good loved anywhere by anybody. These varied perfections are rivals and enemies in the press of the world, where there seems not to be matter or time enough for everything: but to impartial spirit no good can render another good odious. Physically, one good may exclude another: nature and natural morality must choose between them, or be dissolved into chaos: but in eternity the most opposite goods are not enemies; rather little brothers and sisters, as all odd creatures were to Saint Francis. And that all these various perfections are not actually attainable is a material accident, painful but not confusing to a free spirit. Their contrariety increases sorrow, but does not diminish love; the very pain is a fresh homage to the beauty missed, and a proof of loyalty; so that the more the spirit suffers the more clearly, when it unravels its suffering, it understands what it loves. Every perfection then shines, washed and clear, separate and uncontaminated: yet all compatible, each in its place, and harmonious. To love things spiritually, that is to say, intelligently and disinterestedly, means to love the love in them, to worship the good which they pursue, and to see them all prophetically in their possible beauty. To love things as they are would be a mockery of things: a truer lover must love them as they would wish to be. For nothing is quite happy as it is, and the first act of true sympathy must be to move with the object of love towards its happiness.

Universal good, then, the whole of that to which all things aspire, is something merely potential; and if we wish to make a religion of love, after the manner of Socrates, we must take universal good, not universal power, for the object of our religion. This religion would need to be more imaginative, more poetical, than that of Spinoza, and the word God, if we still used it, would have to mean for us not the universe, but the good of the universe. There would not be a universe worshipped, but a universe praying; and the flame of the whole fire, the whole seminal and generative movement of nature, would be the love of God. This love would be erotic; it would be really love and not something wingless called by that name. It would bring celestial glimpses not to be retained, but culminating in moments of unspeakable rapture, in a union with all good, in which the soul would vanish as an object because, as an organ, it had found its perfect employment.

For there is a mystery here, the mystery of seeming to attain emotionally the logically unattainable. Universal good is something dispersed, various, contrary to itself in its opposite embodiments; nevertheless, to the mystic, it seems a single living object, the One Beloved, a good to be embraced all at once, finally and for ever, leaving not the least shred of anything good outside. Yet I think this mystery may be easily solved. Spirit is essentially synthetic; and just as all the known and unknown forces of nature make, in relation to experience and destiny, one single omnificent power; and just as all facts and all the relations between facts compose for the historical and prophetic mind one unalterable realm of truth; so exactly, for the lover, all objects of love form a single ineffable good. He may say that he sees all beauties in a single face, that all beauties else are nothing to him; yet perhaps in this hyperbole he may be doing his secret heart an injustice. Beauty here may be silently teaching him to discern beauty everywhere, because in all instances of love only the sheer love counts in his eyes: and in the very absoluteness of his love he may feel an infinite promise. His ecstasy, which passes for a fulfilment, remains a sort of agony: and though itself visionary, it may, by its influence, free his heart from trivial or accidental attachments and lead it instead to a universal charity. Beggars in Catholic and Moslem countries used to beg an alms, sometimes, for the love of God. It was a potent appeal; because God, according to the Socratic tradition, was the good to which all creation moved; so that anyone who loved deeply, and loved God, could not fail, by a necessary inclusion, to love the good which all creatures lived by pursuing, no matter how repulsive these creatures might be to natural human feeling.

Thus the absolute love of anything involves the love of universal good; and the love of universal good involves the love of every creature.

Such, in brief, seems to me the prospect open to a mind that examines its moral condition without any preconceptions. Perhaps an empirical critic, strictly reducing all objects to the functions which they have in experience, might see in my meagre inventory all the elements of religion. Mankind, he might say, in thinking of God or the gods have always meant the power in events: as when people say: *God willing*. Sometimes they have also meant the truth, as when people say: *God knows*. And perhaps a few mystics may have meant the good, or the supreme object of love, union with whom they felt would be perfect happiness. I should then have merely changed the language of traditional religion a little, translated its myths into their pragmatic equivalents, and reduced religion to its true essence. But no: I make no such professions: they would be plainly sophistical. The functions which objects have in experience no doubt open to us different avenues to those objects: but the objects themselves, if they exist, are not mere names for those functions. They are objects of faith: and the religion of mankind, like their science, has always been founded on faith. Now there is no faith invoked in the examination of conscience which I have made before you this evening: and therefore, properly speaking, what I come to is not religion. Nor is it exactly philosophy, since I offer no hypotheses about the nature of the universe or about the nature of knowledge. Yet to be quite sincere, I think that in this examination of conscience there is a sort of secret or private philosophy perhaps more philosophical than the other: and while I set up no gods, not even Spinoza's infinite *Deus sive Natura*, I do consider on what subjects and to what end we might consult those gods, if we found that they existed: and surely the aspiration that would prompt us, in that case, to worship the gods, would be our truest heart-bond and our ultimate religion.

If then any of us who are so minded should ever hear the summons of a liturgical religion calling to us: *Sursum corda, Lift up your hearts*, we might sincerely answer, *Habemus ad*

Dominum, Our hearts by nature are addressed to the Lord.
For we recognise universal power, and respect it, since on it
we depend for our existence and fortunes. We look also with
unfeigned and watchful allegiance towards universal truth, in
which all the works of power are eternally defined and recorded; since in so far as we are able to discover it, the truth
raises all things for us into the light, into the language of
spirit. And finally, when power takes on the form of life, and
begins to circle about and pursue some type of perfection,
spirit in us necessarily loves these perfections, since spirit is
aspiration become conscious, and they are the goals of life:
and in so far as any of these goals of life can be defined or
attained anywhere, even if only in prophetic fancy, they become glory, or become beauty, and spirit in us necessarily
worships them: not the troubled glories and brief perfections
of this world only, but rather that desired perfection, that
eternal beauty, which lies sealed in the heart of each living
thing.

FOREWORD TO "LEOPARDI"*

THERE is only one thing that the purely English reader may miss [in this portrait of Leopardi], because without familiarity with the Italian language and sympathy with the classic temperament it is incommunicable: I mean the poignant accent, the divine elevation of this poet. The student, the writer, the sufferer, the wanderer was only Conte Giacomo Leopardi, but the poet was Orpheus himself. Long passages are fit to repeat in lieu of prayers through all the watches of the night. How shall I express their quality? Suppose you were held up in some minor Italian town where by chance an itinerant company was to perform *Il Trovatore*. Suppose that having nothing better to do you strolled into the theatre, resigned in advance to a meagre stage-setting, a harsh orchestra, a prima donna past her prime, a rhetorical little tenor saving his breath for the gymnastic prodigy of his final high note. But suppose also that, having found things in general much as you expected, suddenly you heard, coming from behind the wings, an unexampled heavenly voice, a voice pure as moonlight, rich as sorrow, firm as truth, singing *Solo in terra*. Alone on earth that voice might indeed seem, and far from earth it would carry you; and no matter how commonplace the singer might look, or even ridiculous, when he stepped before the footlights, if ever that sheer music sounded again, there would be something not himself that sang and something not yourself that listened.

I speak of voice and of music, but that is only a metaphor. What works the miracle in Leopardi is far from being mere sound or diction or the enigmatic suggestion of strange words.

*From *Leopardi,* by Iris Origo.

His versification is remarkable only when a divine afflatus blows through it, which is not always. This afflatus is intellectual, this music is a flood of thoughts. We are transported out of ourselves ascetically, by the vision of truth. Leopardi lived in a romantic tower, a dismal, desolate ruin; but through the bars of his prison he beheld the same classic earth and Olympian sky that had been visible to Homer, Pindar, and Sophocles. The world is always classical, the truth of human destiny is always clear, if only immersion in our animal cares does not prevent us from seeing it. Lifting the eyes would be so easy, yet it is seldom done; and when a rapt poet compels us to do so, we are arrested, we are rebuked, we are delivered.

The misfortunes of Leopardi were doubtless fortunate for his genius. Every classic poet has his romantic accent, corresponding with the scope of his intuition and the degree of harmony or conflict that the vision of the truth creates in his heart. In Leopardi this vision was saturated with anguish; narrowed by it, no doubt, but not distorted. The white heat of his anguish burned all anguish away, and cleared the air. Beneath the glorious monotony of the stars he saw the universal mutation of earthly things, and their vanity, yet also, almost everywhere, the beginning if not the fullness of beauty; and this intuition, at once rapturous and sad, liberated him from the illusions of the past and from those of the future.

THE LAST PURITAN

A Memoir in the Form of a Novel

EPILOGUE

[MARIO, *a character in the novel, and the author are conversing about the book*:]

"Shall I tear the book up, or will it do as a fable?"

"As a fable you may publish it. It's all your invention; but perhaps there's a better philosophy in it than in your other books."

"How so?"

"Because now you're not arguing or proving or criticising anything, but painting a picture. The trouble with you philosophers is that you misunderstand your vocation. You ought to be poets, but you insist on laying down the law for the universe, physical and moral, and are vexed with one another because your inspirations are not identical."

"Are you accusing me of dogmatism? Do I demand that everybody should agree with me?"

"Less loudly, I admit, than most philosophers. Yet when you profess to be describing a fact, you can't help antagonising those who take a different view of it, or are blind altogether to that sort of object. In this novel, on the contrary, the argument is dramatised, the views become human persuasions, and the presentation is all the truer for not professing to be true. You have said it somewhere yourself, though I may misquote the words: After life is over and the world has gone up in smoke, what realities might the spirit in us still call its own without illusion save the form of those very illusions which have made up our story?"